CW01646601

ARCHAIC ERETRIA

This book presents for the first time a history of Eretria during the Archaic Era, the city's most notable period of political importance.

Keith Walker examines all the major elements of the city's success. One of the key factors explored is Eretria's role as a pioneer coloniser in both the Levant and the West – its early Aegean 'island empire' anticipates that of Athens by more than a century, and Eretrian shipping and trade was similarly widespread.

We are shown how the strength of the navy conferred thalassocratic status on the city between 506 and 490 BC, and that the importance of its rowers (Eretria means 'the rowing city') probably explains the appearance of its democratic constitution. Walker dates this to the last decade of the sixth century; given the presence of Athenian political exiles there, this may well have provided a model for the later reforms of Kleisthenes in Athens.

Eretria's major, indeed dominant, role in the events of central Greece in the last half of the sixth century, and in the events of the Ionian Revolt to 490, is clearly demonstrated, and the tyranny of Diagoras (*c.* 538–509), perhaps the golden age of the city, is fully examined.

Full documentation of literary, epigraphic and archaeological sources (most of which have previously been inaccessible to an English-speaking audience) is provided, creating a fascinating history and a valuable resource for the Greek historian.

Keith Walker is a Research Associate in the Department of Classics, History and Religion at the University of New England, Armidale, Australia.

ARCHAIC ERETRIA

A political and social history from the earliest times to 490 BC

Keith G. Walker

Routledge
Taylor & Francis Group
LONDON AND NEW YORK

First published 2004
by Routledge
2 Park Square, Milton Park, Abingdon, Oxfordshire OX14 4RN

Simultaneously published in the USA and Canada
by Routledge
711 Third Avenue, New York, NY 10017

Routledge is an imprint of the Taylor & Francis Group

First issued in paperback 2012

© 2004 Keith G. Walker

Typeset in Garamond by Prepress Projects Ltd, Perth, Scotland

All rights reserved. No part of this book may be reprinted or reproduced or utilised in any form or by any electronic, mechanical, or other means, now known or hereafter invented, including photocopying and recording, or in any information storage or retrieval system, without permission in writing from the publishers.

British Library Cataloguing in Publication Data
A catalogue record for this book is available from the British Library

Library of Congress Cataloging in Publication Data
A catalog record for this title has been requested

ISBN 978-0-415-51853-6

This work is dedicated with gratitude and love
to Geoff Cooke *amico socioque carissimo*;
without your patience, help and
encouragement it could never have been
completed

CONTENTS

List of illustrations ix
Preface xii
Documentation and conventions xiv
Acknowledgements xvi

1 The geography of Euboia and the Eretrias 1

2 Prehistory, mythology and cult: the earliest inhabitants of Euboia from the late Neolithic Age to the end of the Mycenaean Age 26

3 Old Eretria (Lefkandi) during the Dark Ages and early Iron Age (*c.* 1050 to *c.* 750) 73

4 Eretria from *c.* 825 to *c.* 650 90

5 Eretria: its history in the wider Greek world during the seventh and early sixth centuries 141

6 Eretria: emergent 'great power' of the mid-sixth century 183

7 The tyranny of Diagoras (*c.* 538–509) 207

8 The Eretrian democracy (*c.* 509–490) 236

9 Eretria in the 490s 270

10 Epilogue 288

Appendix 1: Chronological tables and notes 290
Appendix 2: Minoan notes 293
Appendix 3: The Kypselidai, Theognis and the low chronology 295
Appendix 4: The source of Strabo's description of the Amarynthos stele (10, 1, 10, c. 448) 298
Appendix 5: Corinth in central Greece (519–506) 301
Index locorum 321
General index 331
Index of authors 347

LIST OF ILLUSTRATIONS

Maps

1 Euboia 1
2 The Eretrias 2
3 The site of Lefkandi 74
4 Site location plan of Archaic Eretria 97

Figures

1.1 The Euripos narrows and the old swing bridge at Khalkis 3
1.2 Hot springs erupting at the site of the ancient spa on the coast at Aidepsos 3
1.3 The ancient pass between Khalkis and Kerinthos 4
1.4 Cape Artemision and the Straits of Oreoi 5
1.5 The Throne of Hera at the summit of Mt Dirphys 5
1.6 Barley and vegetable crops on the Lelantine Plain near Myktas 6
1.7 The Kerinthos Plain near Mantoudhi 7
1.8 The dry bed of the River Lelas at Vasilikon in summer 8
1.9 View of Khalkis and the Euripos from the mainland 9
1.10 View of Karystos and its harbour from the Venetian castro on the slopes of Mt Okhe 10
1.11 The bed of the Boudoros in spring; levée banks protect against flash-flooding 11
1.12 Flowering *Cercis siliquastrum* (Judas tree) against a background of fir and pine forests, central Euboia 12
1.13 Forests of fir (*Abies alba* and *A. cephalonica*) 13
1.14 Eretrian tetradachm *c.* 550–11 BC, with gorgoneion and bull's/cow's head, in the British Museum 13
1.15 Mt Olympos from the site of the gymnasion at Eretria 16
1.16 Rugged mountain and valley near Avlonari in the Eretrias 17

1.17 The Eretrian (Amarynthian) Plain from the southern slopes of the acropolis of Eretria 17
1.18 The 'acropolis' of Dystos from the drained lake bed 18
1.19 The stone quarry on the north-east slope of the Eretrian acropolis 18
1.20 (a) The kalos inscription high on the cut face of the acropolis quarry: (Δ?)ΑΜΑΝΔΡΟΣ ΚΑΛΟΣ (sixth century); (b) detail of the kalos inscription with the visible letters emphasised 19
2.1 The Xeropolis headland, Lefkandi, the site of the prehistoric settlement, from the west bay 47
2.2 The headland of Palaioekklisies, thought to be the site of prehistoric Amarynthos 50
3.1 Animal-style LH IIIC pyxis from Lefkandi, Eretria Museum 75
3.2 The 'Ship Vase' (globular pyxis) 850–25 BC from Lefkandi, Eretria Museum 78
3.3 Line drawing of the ship vase 78
3.4 The *Centaur of Lefkandi*, Eretria Museum 79
3.5 The MPG 'Archer Hydria' from Lefkandi, Eretria Museum 82
3.6 View from Xeropolis Hill over the east bay, towards the acropolis of Eretria and Mt Olympos 86
4.1 The Eretrian Plain – orchards and cropland on shallow limestone soils 95
4.2 The ashlar Hellenistic north-west acropolis wall tower 99
4.3 The acropolis from near the West Gate 99
4.4 View over Eretria from the acropolis hill showing the harbour, the city delta plain, etc. 100
4.5 The bridge at the West Gate 102
4.6 Fine-fitting archaic polygonal masonry at the West Gate 103
4.7 The channel of the western stream and the ashlar masonry of the western section of the enceint wall, which served also as a retaining wall 104
4.8 Polygonal masonry of the acropolis wall 105
4.9 The author at the site of the temenos of Apollo Daphnephoros 106
4.10 The *temenos* site 106
4.11 The small Thesmophoreion on the slopes of the acropolis 108
4.12 Bronze burial cauldrons from the heroön site, Eretria Museum 110
4.13 Geometric burial amphora from the south-west cemetery, Eretria Museum 111
4.14 Burial amphoras from the south-west cemetery 112
6.1 The Laws of Eretria (*IG* XII 9, 1273/4) 193
6.2 The Laws of Eretria (*IG* XII 9, 1273/4) 194
7.1 View of mountainous country between Khalkis and Kerinthos 215

7.2 Κήρινθόν τ' ἔφαλον (Hom. Il. 2, 258) 216
7.3 The grave-marker of Khairion (*IG* XII 9, 296): (ΧΑΙΡΙŌΝ Ι ΑΘĒΝΑΙΟΣ Ι ΕΥΠΑΤΡΙΔŌΝ Ι ΕΝΘΑΔΕ ΚΕΙ Ι ΤΑ[Ι]). From Kourouniotis 1899, 144, no. 10. 220
7.4 Grave stele of Pleistias the Lakedaimonian (*IG* XII 9, 286): ΠΛΕΙΣΤΙΑΣ Ι ΣΠΑΡΤΑ ΜΕΝ ΠΑΤΡΙΣ ΕΣΤΙΝ, ΕΝ ΕΥΡΥΧ Ι ΟΡΟΙΣ Ι ΑΘΑΝΑΙΣ ΕΘΡΑΦΘΕ, ΘΑΝΑΤΟ Ι ΔΕ ΕΝΘΑΔΕ ΜΟΙΡ' ΕΧΙ[Χ]Ε. From the Eretria Museum. 228
8.1 *IG* XII 9, 241: inscribed face, Eretria Museum 242
8.2 *IG* XII 9, 241: (a) line 37 showing the positions of the names (1) ΜΕΣΟΧΩΡΟΥ and (2) ΛΑΡΑΣΙΟΥ (or, I suggest, ΠΑΡΑΛΙΟΥ); (b) close-up photograph of (1); (c) line 77, as it presently appears on the stone, where the second district name (2) [or (3)] occurs 244
8.3 The Horos Phratrikos, Eretria Museum 247
8.4 The proxeny decree for Aristoteles Kheiloniou (*IG* XII Suppl. 549), Eretria Museum 250
8.5 *IG* XII Suppl. 549 251
8.6 The base with the dedication of the Eretrian bull monument at Olympia 260
8.7 The dedicatory inscription: ΦΙΛĒΣΙΟΣ ΕΠΟΙΕ Ι ΕΡΕΤΡΙĒΣ ΤŌΙ ΔΙ. 261
8.8 The surviving horn and ear of the bronze bull 261

Tables

4.1 Text with notes of the papyrus fragment of an early Elegaic poem 139
8.1 Comparative readings of *IG* XII 9, Suppl. 549 241
8.2 The known and hypothetical names of the tripartite territorial divisions of the Corinthia, the Eretrias and Attica 249
8.3 Comparison of the formulae of Attic proxeny decrees and the Eretrian decree *IG* XII 9, Suppl. 549 253
8.4 The readings of Peek and Wallace of *IG* XII, Suppl. 549 267
A1.1 From the Neolithic Age to the sub-Mycenaean period 290
A1.2 From the sub-Mycenaean period to the sub-Geometric period 290
A1.3 Euboian colonisation in the West 291
A1.4 Some significant dates in Eretrian history 291

PREFACE

> For the historian of early Greece, one of the most pressing tasks is the study in depth of specific [geographical] areas.
>
> J. N. Coldstream 1977, 19

It is now sixty-one years since the only study in English of the history of Eretria was written. It was never published, and access to it has been practically impossible for students of Euboian history.[1] Since then there have been a few monograph studies of other Euboian cities in English, but only one has appeared in published form.[2] There have, of course, been a small number of journal articles on special topics dealing with Euboia but those who wish to pursue Euboian studies must turn to the more plentiful material in French and German, though even in these languages it is almost exclusively to be found in the journal literature. The Swiss scholar Denis Knoepfler has been the author of a massive amount of work on Eretria, especially its epigraphy and related topics. No researcher on Eretria can possibly ignore his contribution.

The neglect of Euboia is hard to justify in view of the increasing body of evidence indicating that the Euboian cities played a significant role in the history of Greece, especially during the Archaic period. Their part in the so-called Second Colonial Movement to Italy and Sicily has long been acknowledged, but the results of the excavations at Lefkandi and at Eretria itself have demonstrated that Euboia had a flourishing civilisation that goes back to the tenth century and even earlier.

The principal objective of this study is to exploit the considerable body of evidence embedded in the literary record, along with the results of archaeological investigations at and around Eretria, to argue that the city played a quasi-hegemonial role in the affairs of central Greece and the Aegean during the last half of the sixth century and probably even earlier, while also attempting a reconstruction of its constitutional and monumental antiquities. I shall suggest that some elements of the Kleisthenic democracy came to Athens via Eretria and that at least three successive regimes in Eretria [the pre-540s oligarchy; the tyranny of Diagoras (*c.* 538 to *c.* 510) and the democracy (509–490)] directly and indirectly intervened in Athenian internal affairs to effect changes in the government there. A second objective is to bring before English-speaking scholars and other interested people the large volume of material on Euboian-related matters that has appeared in other languages, French, German, Italian and modern Greek, over the last half-century.

The ancient literary evidence for Euboia is widely scattered among writers other than Herodotos and Thucydides, although these two, especially the former, do provide us with information. The seventh- and sixth-century poets, as well as Plato, Aristotle and Plutarch, the symposiac compiler Athenaios, the geographers, especially Strabo, and lexicographers are also important sources of evidence. Their details are often, in turn, derived from the works of earlier historians such as Ephoros of Kyme, Hellanikos and others whose works are largely lost. Perhaps our greatest losses have been: (1) the Περί 'Ερετρίας of Lysanias of Mallos – Plutarch preserves the content of a vital passage from this work which gives us an inkling of how differently the history of Greece in the late sixth and early fifth centuries might have appeared to us had it survived *in toto*; and (2) works of Arkhemakhos of Khalkis, Proxenos and some by Aristotle himself, whose series of *Constitutions* survive only in fragments, except for that of the Athenians. He is known to have written *Constitutions* for Khalkis, Corinth, Kerkyra and Keos, all of which would have been of direct interest to us, and, although there appears to be no specific ancient reference to it, there was undoubtedly also one for Eretria.

Originally I had intended to include chapters on dialect, demes, the arts and architecture, coinage and (especially) cult. The limitations of length imposed on this book have unfortunately precluded them, though all these topics do emerge from time to time.

Notes

1 W. P. Wallace, *The History of Eretria to 198 BC*, unpubl. PhD thesis, Johns Hopkins University, Baltimore, MD, 1936a. This work is, apparently, not held in the library of the university, and I have only had access to it thanks to the generosity of his son, Dr Malcolm Wallace, who told me that he plans to deposit a copy in the Library of the American School of Classical Studies at Athens.

2 D. W. Bradeen, *A History of Chalkis to 338 BC*, unpubl. PhD thesis, University of Pennsylvania, Philadelphia, PA, 1947a; T. W. Jacobsen, *Prehistoric Euboia*, unpubl. PhD thesis, University of Pennsylvania, Philadelphia, PA, 1964; R. G. Vedder, *Ancient Euboea, Studies in the History of a Greek Island from the Earliest Times to 404 BC*, unpubl. PhD thesis, University of Arizona, Tucson, AZ, 1978. The exception to this sad record is S. C. Bakhuizen's study, *Chalcis-in-Euboea: Iron and Chalcidians Abroad*, Chalcidian Studies No. 3, Leiden, 1976.

DOCUMENTATION AND CONVENTIONS

The general bibliography lists all works referred to in the book, along with a few that may be of interest to readers, with full publication details. Throughout, works are fully described (although without the publishing house) in the footnote of the first reference. Thereafter they are referred to by author, year of publication and page(s) thus: Knoepfler 1985b, 50–2.

All dates are BC unless specifically indicated as AD (BC is omitted everywhere except in quotations, article titles, etc.). The abbreviations for the archaeological periods are standard and are related to those in the chronological tables in Appendix 1, which also outline the chronological framework adopted in this study. Abbreviations of journal titles generally follow the system used in *L'année philologique*; the few exceptions are straightforward (e.g. *TAPA* rather than *TAPhA*). Other abbreviations used throughout the footnotes are: *AR* (the annual Archaeological Reports of the *Journal of Hellenic Studies*, London); *ATL* (B. D Meritt *et al.*, *The Athenian Tribute Lists*, Princeton, NJ, vols I: 1939; II: 1949; III: 1950); *CAH* (the *Cambridge Ancient History*); *FGH* (C. and T. Müller, *Fragmenta Historicorum Graecorum*, Berlin, vols I: 1841; II: 1848;. III: 1849; IV: 1851); *FGrH*; (F. Jacoby, *Die Fragmente der Griechischen Historiker*, Leiden, 1954–69); *IG* (the volumes of *Inscriptiones Graecae*); *LGPN* (P. Fraser and E. Matthews, *A Lexicon of Greek Personal Names* I: *The Aegean Islands, Cyprus, Cyrenaica*, Oxford, 1987); *LSJ* (the Greek *Lexicon* of Liddell–Scott–Jones); *OCD* (*Oxford Classical Dictionary*); *PASCl.St.* (Papers of the American School of Classical Studies at Athens); *RE* (Pauly–Wissowa–Kroll, *Real-Encyclopädie der klassischen Altertumswissenschaft*); *Roscher* (W. H. Roscher, *Ausfurliches Lexikon der Griechischen und Romischen Mythologie*, Leipzig, 1886–90); *SEG* (*Supplementum Epigraphicum Graecum*).

The rendering of Greek is a sore point. I have succumbed to arguments against my preference to transliterate *all* names literally, e.g. Thoukydides, Arkhilokhos, Strabon or Aristoteles, and have compromised by making well-known names conform to common usage, thus Thucydides, Strabo or Aristotle, but with less frequently noticed authors I transliterate, thus Arkhemakhos, Polyainos or Stephanos Byzantios. With the exception of Thucydides, I use 'k' everywhere to render 'κ' and 'kh' for 'χ', thus Bakkhylides. The masculine ending '-us' is never used for Greek names. Similarly, too, with place names: Corinth, Athens, Thessaly, Attica, but Khalkis, Rhaikelos, Epeiros. Adjectival forms from place names are given their normal English termination: Eretrian, Thessalian. Ethnics used as personal names are transliterated: Thessalos, Eretrieus. Greek institutional and other technical terms are given in their Greek form literally rendered (and, where appropriate, rhotacised): thus *arkhon* (pl. *arkhontes*), *epimenieuon* (pl. *epimenieuontes*) but also *epimenieuoures* (fem. gen. sing.), *boule*, *Hippobotai*. *Demos* presents a problem; it will be used to refer to three separate (but related) ideas: the People, the assembly and the political/territorial division of the deme. Hence *Demos* (People), *demos* (assembly) and deme (territory). If Anglo-Latin forms, such as Euboea, Chalcis, ecclesia, archon, etc., occur, it presupposes quotation from a secondary source. I have not appended a glossary of Greek terms as I have given an English equivalent or explanation in parentheses after their first appearance.

Abbreviations of Greek literary names in endnotes, however, follow the standard forms of the Liddell–Scott–Jones *Lexicon* or the *Oxford Classical Dictionary,* whatever the form of the name used throughout the book, thus Callim. is Kallimakhos. In the quotation of Greek texts, I have generally employed traditional Greek orthography, except that in quoting archaic inscriptions I have usually followed the usage of the editor of the text available to me. Translations, unless acknowledged, are all mine, although I here take the opportunity to acknowledge the assistance of readings of various other translators. Where I disagree strongly with a particular rendering, I make this clear in an appropriate footnote.

The appendices supply additional thoughts on a number of related topics. They are not exhaustive in any case but amplify/qualify the point they illustrate in the main body of the text. Had I the luxury of more words, most would have been incorporated into the main body of the book.

All photographs are my own, as are the drawings and maps.

ACKNOWLEDGEMENTS

It is a pleasant duty to record my thanks and appreciation to people who have assisted me in the course of researching this book. Professor Michael Osborne, presently Vice-Chancellor of Latrobe University in Melbourne, must bear responsibility for turning my attention to Eretria in the first place, for it was he who directed and supervised my first incursions into Eretrian epigraphy. My PhD research supervisor, Dr Greg Stanton of the University of New England, kept me to my main task for over eight years and readily spent time helping me with problems and reading chaotic drafts. This was no easy task; a propensity for wandering down minor research byways is still my besetting sin. Following the successful completion of my thesis, the Head of Classics at New England, Dr Greg Horsley, 'harassed' me for several years until I finally gave up and began work recasting the thesis in book form. In this endeavour, he was more than ably assisted by my friends Dr Victor Minichiello, Dean of the Faculty of Health, Education and Professional Studies at the University of New England, and Dr Gae Callender of Macquarie University, Sydney. Without their efforts, this book would never have been written.

Of the many others who encouraged me, special mention must be made of the late Dr Peter Connor of the University of Melbourne, whose untimely death on 8 December 1996 has been such a great loss to classical scholarship. He was my first supervisor at the beginning of this whole project. I recall with much pleasure his stimulating lectures on archaic Greek sculpture and on the colonisation of the western Mediterranean. We discussed at great length the iconography of the temple of Apollo Daphnephoros at Eretria. Unfortunately, due to constraints of length imposed on this book, I have not been able to include the results of those discussions, though I hasten to add that he would not have agreed with all my conclusions. Others I would like to thank are Dr Victor Parker, many of whose comments on my thesis are incorporated within this work, Professor Raphael Sealey of the University of California at Berkeley, and Professor Bob Milns of the University of Brisbane, who examined the thesis and made valuable comments; all three encouraged me to work towards this publication. It was Professor Denis Knoepfler of the University of Neufchâtel, with whom I corresponded from time to time during my thesis research, who (unwittingly) encouraged me to explore Archaic Eretria; his great contributions to *eretriaka* have already been acknowledged. Dr Alan Treloar, Honorary Fellow of the Department of Classics and Ancient History at the University of New England, generously helped me with linguistic problems, and the Department of Classics, History and Religion has supported my work, awarding me an Honorary Research Associateship.

Then there are the many scholars, too numerous to mention every one individually, whose work I have consulted and whose ideas I have absorbed during my research. I hope that my debt to them is clear from the detailed and frequent references to their work in the chapter notes. Foremost among them, however, are the excavators of the Greek Archaeological Service and of the Swiss School of Archaeology at Athens who have been labouring patiently over the last forty years resurrecting the ancient city of Eretria. Without their work, this antipodean contribution to Eretrian studies would have been impossible. The kindness of Dr Stephan Schmit and the museum staff at Eretria in helping me find the stone with *IG* XII 9, 241 in the museum storerooms at Eretria is much appreciated; Dr Schmidt went well beyond the call of duty in helping me to carry the heavy stone outside, where it was possible to photograph it. Mme Peppa-Delmouzou, former Director of the Epigraphical Museum at Athens, and her staff facilitated my examination of several inscriptions held there. Dr Malcolm Wallace of the University of Toronto has helped by providing a copy of his father's pioneering thesis on Eretria and by discussing problems with me during a pleasant afternoon in Athens. Dr Hans Goette of the Deutsches Archäologisches Institut Athen was an enjoyable and informative companion on our excursion to the site of Ancient Kerinthos. The Australian Archaeological Institute at Athens helped me financially to travel to Eretria during 1993 and 1995 to examine particularly several inscriptions at Eretria and Athens. I extend to the Institute, its director Professor Alexander Cambitoglou, its former and current deputy directors Dr Kenneth Sheedy and Dr Stavros Paspalas, and its administrative officer Jan Casson-Medhurst (who has arranged museum passes, appointments with Greek administrators and permission to photograph inscriptions, etc. over many years) my sincere thanks. My travelling in Euboia since 1965, when I disembarked at Karystos en route to Andros and never rejoined the ship, has led to an enduring love affair with the island and its people.

Over the last year, I have had the good fortune to have had the benefit of the help of the technical and editorial staff of Routledge and, in particular, Richard Stoneman's assistance and advice with the preparation of the manuscript of this book for publication. I especially wish to thank him for his patience; at least it did not take thirteen years to get to you! Also my gratitude goes to Gillian Whytock, production editor, and the team at Prepress Projects – her patience, cheerfulness and concern are much appreciated – and to Anne Wilson, graphic artist, who took my rough drawings and maps and re-created them in their present form.

1

THE GEOGRAPHY OF EUBOIA AND THE ERETRIAS[1]

Euboia

The island of Euboia (Map 1) extends for some 220 km parallel to the coastline of Boiotia and Attica on the Greek mainland opposite,[2] to which it is presently linked by a swing bridge across the narrowest part of the Euboian Channel, which is known as the Euripos, as well as by a suspension bridge, constructed in the 1980s, farther to the south. The Euripos was first bridged in 411/10, and the structure was subsequently repaired or renewed several times.[3] The Greeks believed that the island (Figure 1.1) had once upon a time been

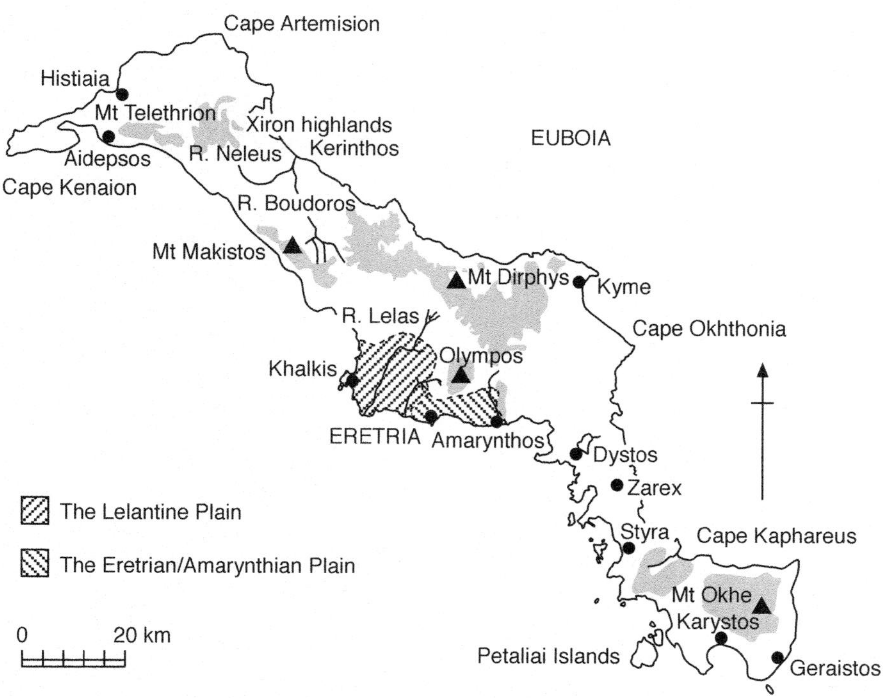

Map 1 Euboia.

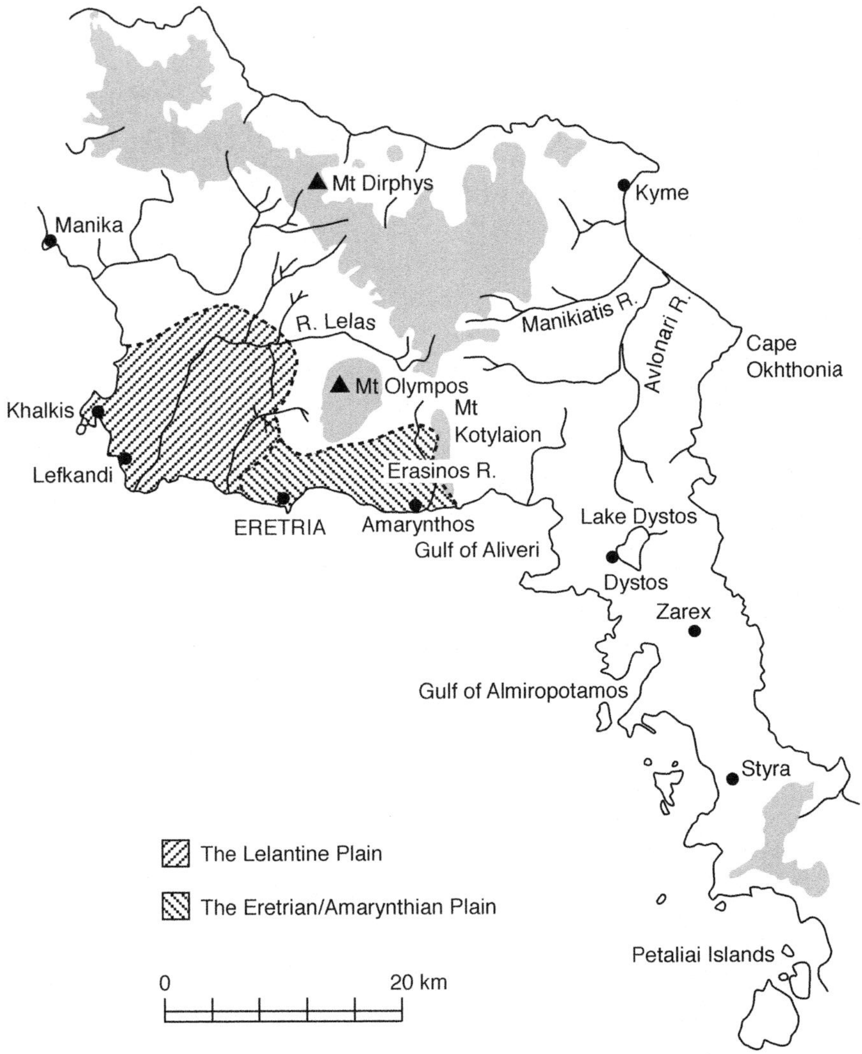

Map 2 The Eretrias.

violently torn away from the mainland as a result of earthquakes, and these are indeed still of frequent occurrence. The presence on the island of a number of thermal springs that both in ancient times and today attract tourists to try 'the cure', are a legacy of its seismic history (Figure 1.2).[4] Its area is 3,770 km^2, a large island by Mediterranean standards.[5] It varies between about 60 km at its widest to 3.2 km at its narrowest point. But it was its length that most impressed the ancients, and so it was sometimes called Makris ('Long' Island). Over its history it was given some seven different names, although only Euboia, Makris/Makra and Abantis/Abantias (and perhaps Ellopia) are likely

Figure 1.1 The Euripos narrows and the old swing bridge at Khalkis.

ever to have applied to the whole island. Apart from Euboia, Abantis was the most commonly used, especially by poets. Although Homer refers to the island as Euboia, he calls the inhabitants Abantes. The Canadian Euboian specialist W. Wallace believes that the variety of names reflects the political separateness of the island's regions and the difficulties of intercommunication. The name Abantis persisted, perhaps, because the area was traditionally associated in later times with the warlike Homeric Abantes.[6]

Figure 1.2 Hot springs erupting at the site of the ancient spa on the coast at Aidepsos.

Mountains

As is the case with most of Greece, Euboia is very mountainous with only a few small plains, which in historical times were controlled by four principal *poleis*, Histiaia, Khalkis, Eretria, which between them held the largest and most fertile plains on the island, and Karystos. Although the latter is generally considered one of the principal city-states, its cultivable land was quite restricted. On the other hand, Kerinthos, which similarly had only a smallish plain, was never of great significance politically, was never regarded as a *polis* and was dependent on its larger and more powerful neighbours during most periods of its history. By the sixth century, it was certainly a dependency of Khalkis.[7] The extensive tracts of rugged terrain separating the towns on the island were undoubtedly a significant reason why there was no real movement towards unity on the island until late in the fourth century (Figure 1.3).

In the far north-east[8] is the large mountain known in ancient times as Telethrion, which Strabo[9] unambiguously locates in the Histiaiotis and which rises to an altitude of 970 m. It is an offshoot of the Knemis Range in Epiknemidian Lokris on the mainland opposite. A series of ranges thrust themselves out from Telethrion. One to the west ends as Mt Likhas on the Kenaion Peninsula, another to the north forms the promontory of Artemision (Figure 1.4), while a third, today called Kandeli (1,209 m), extends south-eastward. In ancient times, it was known as Makistos.[10] Other spurs and ridges extend

Figure 1.3 The ancient pass between Khalkis and Kerinthos.

Figure 1.4 Cape Artemision and the Straits of Oreoi.

out from it in a wide arc to the east and then curve around the north coast to link with Mt Dirphys (1,962 m), the highest point on the island (Figure 1.5), across the eastern and southern flanks of which were the marches between the territory of Khalkis and the Eretrias (Map 2). This chain then continues southward, although at a lower altitude, by way of the narrow neck of territory on which are located the considerable towns of Zarex and Styra (demes of Eretria

Figure 1.5 The Throne of Hera at the summit of Mt Dirphys.

by the fourth century), finally to connect with the most southerly of the great mountains of Euboia, Mt Okhe (1,398 m) in the Karystia. In the middle of the large amphitheatre formed by Dirphys and a range of moderately high ridges, presently called Servouni (in ancient times, Kotylaion)[11] and which terminates on the coast near the important town of Amarynthos, there rose another high mountain, Olympos, in the Eretrias proper (1,172 m). Close to the east coast of the Eretrias and somewhat isolated rises Mt Okhthonia (771 m).

Plains and lowlands

There are only four significant plains on the island and, clearly, they are of the greatest importance as factors influencing its history. The most famous was the Lelantine Plain, an area of fertile grazing and agricultural land that lies between Eretria and Khalkis. On it, between these cities, lies the very important prehistoric settlement at Lefkandi, which has yielded finds of a richness that is almost unique for the so-called Greek Dark Age of the eleventh to the ninth centuries, testament to the prosperity provided by the plain as well as overseas trading. Its destruction led to the rise of Eretria. It is no accident that the best-known 'event' in the early history of Euboia, the so-called Lelantine War, takes its name from this plain for control of which it was fought. It is a part of the semicircle of lowlands and coastal plains enclosed by the peaks and ridges of Makistos, Dirphys and Kotylaion. Cut off to some extent from its most easterly sector, known as the Plain of Eretria (or Amarynthos) south-east of Eretria, by the mass of Mt Olympos, it was (and is still) a very fertile region, ploughed for the barley for which in later centuries Eretria was renowned (Figure 1.6). Its soil is deep and thick, as Theophrastos observed.[12] Nineteenth-century travellers wax eloquent on its fruitfulness:

Figure 1.6 Barley and vegetable crops on the Lelantine Plain near Myktas.

> Our course lay through the famous Lelantine Plain which, in spite of the rain, was seen to be a paradise. Such vines and fig trees and, further on, such grain fields! I had not seen the like in Greece. It is no wonder that it was a bone of contention almost before the dawn of history.[13]

It was on the pasturage of the upland fringes, on the slopes of the surrounding foothills, and on an extensive area of irregular terrain north of Khalkis called the Diakria that were located the horse-rearing lands of the *Hippobotai*, as the Khalkidian aristocrats were called. Two other areas of relatively flat land are in the north and north-east of the island, one around the town of Histiaia and the other the Plain of Mantoudhi near Kerinthos (Figure 1.7). They are separated by ridges of hill land, presently called Korakolithos and Xeronoros, and were famous in antiquity for the viticulture carried out on the surrounding hill slopes.[14] Karystos in the far south of the island had its own modest plain that supported its smallish population. But Kyme on the Aegean coast north of Eretria, which must in most periods have been insignificant almost to the point of being non-existent, had no coastal plain and the inhabitants had to rely on narrow strips of flat land along the river valleys for cultivable terrain.[15] The fourth, which lies within the Eretrias, is a fertile intermontane valley plateau, stretching from the head of the Gulf of Aliveri northwards via Lepoura and Avlonari to the modern town of Kipi.

Rivers and streams

As might be expected from the description of the island so far, Euboia is not a land of notable rivers. The largest is the Boudoros, which waters the Plain of Mantoudhi around Kerinthos. It is fed from two smaller streams, the Kereus (from the north) and the Neleus, which were reputed to change the colour

Figure 1.7 The Kerinthos Plain near Mantoudhi.

of the fleeces of animals that drank from their waters black or white respectively.[16] The Lelantine Plain is traversed by the River Lelas. Dry in summer, in winter it can become torrential and sometimes constituted a barrier to communication between Eretria and Khalkis (Figure 1.8).[17] Two small rivers, the Erasinos (today called the Sarandapotamos), not far from Amarynthos, and the Imbrasos (Parthenios), which flowed east of Kotylaion, water the Eretrian Plain.[18] The names are significant for Eretrian cult. The much larger Avlonari River flows into the Gulf of Kimi at Mourteri and the Manikiatis to the north empties into the same gulf at Paralia.

Coasts and harbours

All the protected harbours of the island face the Euboian Gulf. Neither Kerinthos nor Kyme has good shelter for shipping in time of storm and the Aegean coast is still notorious for tempestuous weather; even the Gulf can be violent.[19] Consequently, no town of any importance arose on the Aegean side of Euboia. The promontories of Cape Kaphareus and the Leuke Akte in the south and Artemision in the north are well known for their storms and were avoided as far as possible by ancient mariners. So indeed they should have been, as the story of Nauplios' revenge shows. It was from Kaphareus that he exacted vengeance for the stoning of his son Palamedes at Troy by luring the returning Greeks to destruction on its rocks.[20] The Aegean coast 'is rocky, irregular, precipitous, destitute of harbours; therefore it must always be avoided', says the *Mediterranean Pilot* of 1831.[21] Thus, control of the Euboian Gulf and of the Euripos in particular was of prime importance politically in all periods of

Figure 1.8 The dry bed of the River Lelas at Vasilikon in summer.

Greek history. Khalkis was later, due to its potentially controlling position on the Euripos (Figure 1.9), regarded as one of the so-called Fetters of Greece,[22] and the Euboian Gulf was always one of the most important trade routes on the Greek coasts. Picard reminds us that it was the route for the expedition of the Greeks to Troy (via Aulis).[23]

Just where the treacherous stretch of coast known in ancient times as the Hollows of Euboia should be located is still controversial. Famous for their wild storms from as early as the times of the poet Arkhilokhos, I would locate them on either side of the island, from roughly Cape Okhthonia on the Aegean coast to the Petalioi (anciently, Petaliai) Islands[24] in the south Euboian Gulf, where the coasts curve inward on both sides of the island. The majority of ancient writers connect them to Kaphareus; thereafter opinions diverge.[25]

Khalkis had two excellent harbours. This city was, along with Eretria, an early coloniser in the West, and from these facts, and from its position on the Euripos,[26] most historians have, somewhat uncritically, assumed that it was an important naval power in the Archaic period; this view will be challenged in this study but not for the first time.[27] I believe that the most important maritime power on the island in most periods of its history, up until the fifth century and perhaps even later, was, in fact, Eretria. It had a good harbour, which was improved over the centuries with protective moles and harbour works.[28] A full description of the site of Eretria is given in Chapter 4. It became the refuge for inhabitants from the prehistoric Lefkandi settlement when it was destroyed *c.* 825, probably as a result of a war with neighbouring Khalkis.[29] The Lefkandiot refugees had already been engaged in seaborne commerce. Their town had two anchorages but both were inferior to the harbour at Eretria.[30]

Figure 1.9 View of Khalkis and the Euripos from the mainland.

South-east of Eretria, Karystos lies on a wide and beautiful bay (Figure 1.10), which offered good moorings for large fleets at several times throughout its history, and in view of the paucity of arable land near the city, the inhabitants no doubt early on took to the sea. We have echoes of an early conflict with Miletos in Asia Minor,[31] which, if true, would presuppose the involvement of ships, though not necessarily Karystian. However, Karystos was never later reckoned to be a naval power of any great importance.

Climate

Euboia shares the general climatic regime prevalent over most of the southern and central eastern coastal region of Greece, having the general characteristics of Attica and neighbouring Andros. Summers are hot and dry, with occasional downpours that turn seasonal streams into torrents that used to cause temporary breaks in communication between settlements (Figure 1.11). Winters are mild on the protected gulf side of the island , but the Aegean coast is subject to very cold winter winds from the north and shipping along that coast virtually ceases because of the fear of storms that, even in summer, can suddenly rage in from the open sea. Overall however, the island provides a healthy climate for its people, although Eretria has, from time to time, constituted a notable exception. Near the city to the east lay the Ptekhai swamp, which, until the twentieth century, was lethally malarial in summer. It was this fact indeed that led to

Figure 1.10 View of Karystos and its harbour from the Venetian castro on the slopes of Mt Okhe.

Figure 1.11 The bed of the Boudoros in spring; levée banks protect against flash flooding.

the gradual abandonment of the site in late antiquity, when ancient drainage works were allowed to deteriorate and the marshlands expanded.[32] One of the early archaeologists who worked at Eretria, the American J. Pickard, has described the elaborate plans by Othon, first king of modern Greece, to build a large metropolis with a naval base and school on the site in 1825 (using the excellent harbour), which were thwarted by the malarial climate arising from this swamp that had given the city its unhealthy reputation in antiquity.[33]

Vegetation

In ancient times, the island was largely covered by forests, and even today there are remnants of these woodlands on the higher or more inaccessible areas (Figures 1.12 and 1.13), especially on Mt Telethrion. As Strabo noted: 'Telethrion is [also] called Drymos' (woodland).[34] The two major species of fir (*Abies alba* and *A. cephalonica*) unfortunately produced timber of very poor quality according to Pliny,[35] quite unsuited to the needs of ship building, and so prime-quality timber must have been imported from Thrace and Macedonia via the Eretrian and Khalkidian colonies that were established in that region at an early date. Other species were larch (*Larix decidua*), Mediterranean plane (*Platanus orientalis*), hellebore (*Helleborus* sp.), laurel (*Prunus laurocerasus*), and heather (*Calluna vulgaris*). The sweet chestnut (*Castanea sativa*) was common and supplemented the diet of the inhabitants. Theophrastos and Pliny[36] also record a number of medicinal plants that grew wild on the mountainsides of Euboia.

Figure 1.12 Flowering *Cercis siliquastrum* (Judas tree) against a background of fir and pine forests, central Euboia.

Pastoralism, agricultural production and other primary industries

The commonly used name of the island, Euboia (eu-boia means well-cattled),[37] reflects its earliest principal industry. Pastoralism in Greece was more widespread in early Archaic antiquity than it was in the Classical and later periods.[38] Histiaia, Eretria and Karystos all, at one period or another, used the cow as a symbol on their coinage (Figure 1.14). Moreover, the names of the dominant social groups in Khalkis, the *Hippobotai* (horse rearers), and in Eretria, the *Hippeis* (cavalrymen) indicate the importance, at least in the early Archaic period, of horse rearing. It was to Euboia that the Athenians transferred their herds during the Peloponnesian War because of its good grazing lands. Euboia was exporting sheep to Hellenistic Egypt in the reign of Ptolemy II Philadelphus (283–45) and animal pelts and wool were items of trade with Mycenaean Thebes in prehistoric times.[39] Other animals attested as being raised and herded in Euboia are goats and pigs: Euboians still wore pigskins in Pausanias' time (second century AD). The Khalkidians raised cocks for fighting and the hunting dogs of Eretria were famous and much sought after.[40]

Figure 1.13 Forests of fir (*Abies alba* and *A. cephalonica*).

Although of lesser social significance than livestock herding in the Archaic period, agricultural activity was varied and as the population of the island grew, it became increasingly important.[41] It was especially diverse on the Lelantine Plain, where barley and wheat were planted along with fruit and vegetable crops and vines. Eretria was in later times famous for a kind of cabbage, said to be the very best![42] Viticulture was important especially on

Figure 1.14 Eretrian tetradachm *c.* 550–11 BC, with gorgoneion and bull's/cow's head, in the British Museum.

the northern plains. The production here was favoured with a mention by The Poet himself,[43] while Theognis later writes: 'I once came to the vine-clad plain of Euboia', perhaps that around the city of Kerinthos where he himself certainly took part in a battle (Chapter 7, pp. 212–17), although elsewhere he talks of 'the good vine-lands of Lelanton' as having been laid waste.[44] It was, in fact, Eretria rather than Khalkis that stressed the vine and its product. One of the principal temples in the city was that of Dionysos,[45] and Hiller von Gaertringen observes: 'Only Eretria amongst the Euboian *poleis* produces such *Oinos*-names and these days one will pass through estates and vineyards from Eretria town to Vathy (Amarynthos).'[46] That is, the Eretrian vinelands are east of the city, not on the western (Lelantine) side. On the Eretrian Plain, vines were most probably interspersed with olives, as is the case today. In addition, of course, the ubiquitous olive was grown on marginal land in the foothills of the mountains and olive oil formed a major export. Other fruits grown on the island in ancient times and which are even today still major crops there are apples, pears and figs. Chestnuts were known as 'the Euboian' nut. They were called *karya*; Karystos presumably had an industry producing them.[47] Lastly, the production of honey was of some importance in Euboia.[48]

Fishing was important for coastal communities, for the seas of Euboia were particularly rich. We have testimony for both Eretrians and Khalkidians being engaged seriously in fishing and there are several references to much-sought-after fish species from Euboia in that gastronomic encyclopaedia the *Deipnosophistai* of Athenaios.[49] Oysters were also harvested from Euboian waters; those of Khalkis were especially praised.[50] The gathering and processing of murex shells for their purple dye was a major secondary industry, especially for the Eretrians and Styraians[51] It is likely that the Khalkidians were also engaged in this activity. The product was probably exported to Corinth for use in the cloth industry there, although the notice in Philostratos implies (and S. Schmid has shown for Roman times[52]), that there was a local cloth-dyeing industry at Eretria itself. Themelis has found murex shells in Geometric strata in Eretria-*polis*.[53] There is evidence of direct Corinthian political interest in Euboia in the sixth century, as we shall see in Chapter 6. We would expect a cloth-making industry in most ancient Greek towns, but the discovery of an elaborately woven 'shroud' that was still preserved in the Hero Tomb (1000–950) at Lefkandi confirms this.[54]

Minerals

The name Khalkis is frequently derived by scholars ancient and modern from *khalkos* (copper) but there are other possible interpretations, recognised even among the ancient lexicographers, despite their fondness for simplistic etymologising, and there are modern scholars who in fact deny a connection to any known Greek word. Bakhuizen regards all ancient references to Khalkidian copper as aetiological; he is probably right.[55] There are indeed few, if any, signs of local copper sources near Khalkis.[56] There is, however, physical evidence of other metallic ores, particularly iron,[57] in its territory and there is a persistent tradition linking the city with the development of the 'Khalkidian (steel) sword'. But the iron deposits are not within particularly easy reach of workshops in Khalkis itself, judging from Bakhuizen's own maps. Moreover, iron ore (even purified metal) is not easily transported in large quantities overland, especially across mountainous areas. Nevertheless, he believed that Khalkis was a centre of iron manufacture based on exploitation of local ores and that production was not restricted to finished items such as swords. He acknowledges the paucity of evidence, literary or archaeological, for iron mining at Khalkis in ancient times and he, rightly, dismisses the story of Strabo's miraculous 'double' (copper/iron) mine.[58] But Aidepsos in the north was a centre of copper and iron mining and it was noted for sword manufacture.[59] In the Karystia, at least in later times, the famous green cippolino marble, as well as asbestos, was mined from open cuts on the slopes of Mt Okhe above the modern town called Marmari.[60]

To conclude, Euboia was considered by Herodotos to be 'blessed by fortune',[61] thanks to the variety of its resources, while Isokrates later wrote that: Euboia 'was fitted for command of the sea and surpassed all the other islands as far as her general resources are concerned'.[62]

The Eretrias

By the Hellenistic Age, the Eretrias (Map 2) was a large *polis*-territory by Greek standards. Wallace thinks that it covered *c.* 500 square miles (approximately 1,300 km^2) but admits that 'the extent of Eretrian territory cannot be accurately estimated because of the uncertainty over her western and northern boundaries – the exact line between her territory and that of Karystos is also uncertain.'[63] This estimate would make the Eretrias half the size of Attica, which, along with Laconia, is a giant among Greek states. For comparison, the Corinthia was only about 350 square miles (approximately 910 km^2), while the Sikyonia was only 180 (approximately 468 km^2).[64] In the Archaic Age, however, the territory controlled by Eretria was smaller, perhaps by about a third, than it later became following its annexation of the south-easternmost districts based on Dystos and Styra *c.* 411/10.[65]

Before the ninth century, the western boundary of 'Eretrian' territory was probably west of the River Lelas, which crosses the Lelantine Plain, over which there was much warfare during Archaic times. Strabo mentions a place that was called Old Eretria in his time (64/3 BC to *c.* 21 AD). I subscribe to the theory that the settlement at Lefkandi/Xeropolis was 'Old' Eretria, which however is not at all the same thing as saying that it was Strabo's Old Eretria. Following the destruction of this town (*c.* 825)[66] and the withdrawal of the greater part of its population to the site of the historical *polis* of Eretria, this border would have moved considerably further to the east, removing the narrow coastal plain linking the Lelantine and Eretrian plains from Eretrian control. It is reasonable to suppose with Wallace that the boundary between Khalkidian lands and the Eretrias stretched roughly north from near Malakonda on the Euboian Gulf, via the valley between Olympos and Arabi Tsouka, on past the town of Theologos to the Aegean coast at the Ormos Metohiou. Kyme in the north was in Eretrian control probably even as early as the sixth century.[67] To the east, the town of Amarynthos certainly lay within Eretrian territory, which extended further east, to include the plain around the present day town of Aliveri east of the Kotylaion Range and on as far as the low hills between Aliveri and Dystos.

I have described the original Eretrias as resembling a huge semi-circular amphitheatre, with a mountain – Olympos – at centre-stage (Figure 1.15). The foothills of Mount Dirphys and the Servouni Range form the auditorium, while the two plains west and east are the orchestra. These surrounding mountains, however, are rough and stony limestone ridges that quickly absorb rainfall and are rather unsuitable for agriculture (Figure 1.16), although one today finds farmlets in some valley floors. The slopes themselves can support small herds of sheep and goats and even some cattle on the uplands. On marginal land, where plain meets hills and on the Eretrian/Amarynthian Plain, olives and fruit, such as figs and vines, were grown (Figure 1.17).[68] The plain itself is, however, reasonably fertile. Barley was grown here in antiquity and may have been the chief crop, for Leukalphitos (rich in pearl barley) was an epithet bestowed on Eretria by the comic poet Sopater in the third century.[69]

Figure 1.15 Mt Olympos from the site of the *gymnasion* at Eretria.

Figure 1.16 Rugged mountain and valley near Avlonari in the Eretrias

Figure 1.17 The Eretrian (Amarynthian) Plain from the southern slopes of the acropolis of Eretria; Mt Olympos is on the left, the Kotylaion Range in the far background.

Today, what was in antiquity a very large swamp with a high citadel hill in the middle, the site of the ancient deme-town of Dystos (Figure 1.18),[70] has been drained and is very fertile crop and vine land. However, we should remember that generally, the Eretrias was less favoured by nature for agriculture than was the territory of neighbouring Khalkis, especially after the loss of the area of the

Figure 1.18 The 'acropolis' (the town itself lay on this hill) of Dystos from the drained lake bed.

Figure 1.19 The stone quarry on the north-east slope of the Eretrian acropolis. The arrow indicates the position of the *kalos* inscription (Figure 1.20).

Lelantine Plain east of the River Lelas. The socio-political consequences of the poorer soils and the lower productivity of the Eretrian Plain will be dealt with in some detail in Chapter 4.

The Eretrias seems generally not to have possessed mineral deposits of mineable quality, though today a type of marble called 'Eretrian Red' (*sic*) is advertised internationally on the Internet. However the Eretrians quarried for building stone on the north-east slope of the acropolis, where a sixth-century

(a)

(b)

Figure 1.20 (a) The *kalos* inscription high on the cut face of the acropolis quarry: (Δ?)ΑΜΑΝΔΡΟΣ ΚΑΛΟΣ (sixth century); (b) detail of the *kalos* inscription with the visible letters emphasised.

kalos-inscription visible high on the quarry wall indicates (roughly) the ancient traffic level (Figures 1.19 and 1.20).[71]

Given the relative paucity of natural resources, it is not surprising that the ancient Eretrians soon turned to trade and secondary industries, based on imported raw materials, for a livelihood. The existence in Eretria of a cloth-dyeing industry based on the harvesting of murex shellfish for their famous purple colour has already been mentioned. To this may be added the working of gold (and possibly silver) based on imported raw material from Eretrian *emporia* established early on in Italy.[72] Metalworking was an 'Eretrian' craft even before the move to the new site of the city, for the British excavators of Lefkandi have found evidence of bronze working there.[73] Wood is a perishable material and so we have no surviving evidence, but woodworking must have been a significant craft in the town. Eretria was at all periods a centre for the production of pottery; in later periods, output of reasonable quality degenerated into mediocre.[74] The level of quality seems to indicate that the ware was churned out for utilitarian purposes in the local area settlements or that it was bought in bulk by exporters of Eretrian olive oil. Wine, however, was exported in skins rather than ceramic ware as the air could be squeezed out before sealing.

Thus, the Eretrias provided its citizens with adequate, though not spectacular, agricultural land and good fishing grounds but few other outstanding natural resources, obliging them to turn early to trade and small-scale industry as alternatives to the traditional reliance of the Euboian *poleis* on pastoralism and agriculture. The loss of the fertile farming and pastoral lands of the eastern Lelantine Plain was a blow to the old landed classes, but in the end it would prove to be something of a benefit to the population as a whole.

Notes

1 I use the name 'Eretriás' for the territory of Eretria since this was what the Eretrians themselves certainly called it by the fourth century in the law against tyranny, *c.* 340: καὶ ἐὰν] ἀποκλεισθεῖ ὁ δῆμος τῶν τειχέων, καταλ[αμβάνειν χωρίον τι τῆ]ς Ἐρετριάδος ὅτι ἂν δοκεῖ σύνφορον εἶνα[ι κ.τ.λ.: *SEG* 31, 1981, item 184; D. Knoepfler, 'Loi d'Érétrie contre la tyrannie et oligarchie' (Pt 1), *BCH* 125, 2001b, 195–238. Others, e.g. Hekataios (sixth/fifth century) ap. Paus. 4, 2, 3 called it the 'Eretriké'. Earlier descriptive studies and travellers' accounts of Euboia that provide information concerning the geography, geology, botany, etc. include those of J. Girard, 'Mémoire sur l'île d'Eubée' in *Archives des missions scientifiques* II, 1851, Paris, 635–728 (translated by G. Fousaras, 'Η ῾Ιστορία τῆς ᾿Αρχαίας Εὐβοίας τοῦ Jules Girard', *AEM* 11, 1964, 5–135); A. Baumeister, *Topographische Skizze der Insel Euboia*, Lubeck, 1864; K. Bursian, *Quæstionum Euboïcarum capita selecta*, Leipzig, 1856; idem, *Geographie von Griechenland* II, Pt 3: (die Inselwelt), Leipzig, 1871; J. Pickard, 'A topographical survey of Eretria', *PASCl.St.* 6, 1890–7, 371–89; Al. Rangavé, 'Mémoire sur la partie méridionale de l'île d'Eubée' in *Mémoires presentés à l'Académie des Inscriptions* ser. 1, vol. III, 1853; R. Richardson, 'Eretria; a historical sketch', *AJA* 7, 1891, 236–46; (reprinted in *PASCl.St.* 6, 1890–7, 59–69). Especially useful is A. Philippson, *Die Griechischen Landschaften. Ein Landeskunde* I 1, (Herausgegeben unter Mitwirkung von H. Lehmann), Frankfurt am Main, 1950/59, 549–739. For a recent description

with photographs of contemporary Euboia: M. Aryiriadou, *Εὔβοια ὅπως τὴν εἶδα καὶ τὴ φωτογράφησα*, Athens, 1981; for accounts of life in modern Euboia and Euboians abroad: J. du Boulay, *Portrait of a Greek Mountain Village*, Oxford: Limni Evvias, 1974/79; S. Wheeler, *An Island Apart*, London, 1992; N. Tsigros, *Vyriotes in Australia*, Norwood, 1989, 18–44 (but one ought not take too seriously the brief 'history' of 'Argoura', equated here by him with Virra, south-east of Eretria; for Argoura, cf. D. Knoepfler, 'Argoura: un toponym dans la "Midienne" de Démosthène', *BCH* 105, 1981, 289–329; C. Bérard, 'Argoura, fût-elle la «capitale» des futurs Érétriens?', *MH* 41, 1985a, 268–75; L. Tritle, 'Eretria, Argoura and the Road to Tamynai. The Athenians in Euboia, 348 BC' *Klio* 74, 1992, 131–65. While writing this study, I have used the detailed physical map of Euboia published by the 'Εθνικὴ Στατιστικὴ 'Υπερεσία, (National Statistics Service of Greece), *Νόμος Εὐβοίας; 1:200,000*, 1961/72, supplemented by observations made during driving visits in Euboia together with detailed local maps in various journal articles and descriptive books. A useful guidebook for modern Greek readers is that by A. Kalemis, *Η Αποκάλυψη των φυσικών και Ιστορικών Θησαυρών της Ευβοιας*, Athens, 2000.

2 Between lat. 37°56′ and 39°02′ and long. 23°53′ and 24°51′. Str. 10, 1, 2 C444 and Plin. *HN* 4, 63 give its length as 1200 *stadia*. Skylax 58 and Agathemeros 5, 25 [K. Muller (ed.), *Geographi Graeci Minores* II, Hildesheim, 1965, 486] both overstate it at 1350 and 1700 *stadia* respectively. 1 *stadion* = 1.82 m.

3 The channel is 2 *plethra* (*c.* 70 m) wide. For the Euripos and its famous reversals of current: H.-J. Gehrke 'Zur Rekonstruktion antiker Seerouten: Das Beispiel des Golfs von Euboia', *Klio* 74, 1992, 98–117. F. Geyer, *Topographie und Geschichte der Insel Euboïa im Altertum, I: Bis zum Peloponnischen Kriege*, Berlin, 1903 lists the ancient sources (I have used the modern Greek translation by A. Zambalos: 'Τοποραφία καὶ 'Ιστορία τοῦ Νήσου Εὐβοίας μέχρι τὸν Πελοποννησιακὸν πόλεμον' in *AEM* 9, 1962, 18–124; page references are henceforth to this edition) 29–30.

4 For earthquakes: Th. 3, 89, 2; D.S. 12, 59, 2; Str. 1, 3, 16 C58; 10, 1, 9 C 447; Ion ap. Str. 1, 3, 19–20 C60; Arist. *Mete.* 2, 8; Sen. *QN* 4, 17, 25; for the Lelantine springs: Plin. *HN* 4, 64. The Roman dictator Sulla was just one of many who came to Aidepsos for medical reasons: Plut. *Sull.* 26. Geyer 1903, 101 believed that the fact that the thermal springs at Aidepsos were dedicated to Herakles indicates a very early date for their use. The Eretrian deme-name Χυτ (= Χύτροι?) may indicate the presence of warm springs: cf. D. Knoepfler, 'Le territoire d'Érétrie at l'organisation politique de la cité (démoi, chōroi, phylai)' in M. Hansen (ed.), *Acts of the Copenhagen Polis Centre* IV, Copenhagen, 1997, 362 and nn. 83–4. R. Jebb, *Sophocles. 'Trachiniae'*, Cambridge, 1908, 98, nn. to ll. 633–9. There are today several notable springs in the Eretrias although none are listed as warm in P. Rhodhakis and K. Triandafillidis, *Σύγχρονη Γεωγραφία 'Ατλας τῆς 'Ελλάδος* II, Athens, (no date: *c.* 1965), 531.

5 It is the sixth largest, after Sicily, Sardinia, Cyprus, Corsica and Crete.

6 **Abantis/Abantias**: Str. 10, 1, 3 C445; D.P. *Orbis descr.* 520; Eust. *ad Hom. Il. pert.* 536–41; Hes. fr. 3; St. Byz. s.v. 'Αβαντίς; Call. *Hymn.* 4, 20; schol. ad loc.; Menaikhmos ap. Plin. *HN* 4, 64; Prisc. *Perieg.* 544 (*Geog. gr. min.* II 195); Nikephoros 512–54 (*Geog. gr. min.* II 462, ll. 12–13); Suid. s.v. 'Αβαντίς; **Makris**: Str. 10, 1, 2 C444: διὰ δὲ τὴν στενότητα καὶ τὸ λεχθὲν μῆκος ὑπὸ τῶν παλαιῶν Μάκρις ὀνομάσθη; Agathemeros 5, 25 (*Geog. gr. min.* II 486). Str. 10, 1, 3 C445; Plin. *HN* 4, 64; D.P. *Orbis descr.* 520; Call. *Hymn* 3, 188; 4, 20 and schol. ad loc.; Scymn. 568; Eust. *ad Dion. Perieg.* 517; 520; Prisc. 514; schol. ad Ar. *Nu.* 212; Hom. *Il.* 2, 535 and schol. ad loc.; A.R. 2, 392 and schol. ad loc.; 4, 1175; Agathemeros, 5, 25; *E.M.* 389, 2 s.v.; **Ellopia**: Str. 10, 1, 3 C445; Euphorion, *P. Oxy.* 2528; **Okhe**: Str. 10, 1, 3 C445); **Khalkis**: Kallidemos ap. Plin. *HN* 4, 64; **Khalkodontis**: Plin. *HN* 4, 64; **Asopis**: Plin. *HN* 4, 64; Scymn. 569; and, of course, **Euboia**. For the mythology of the nymph Euboia: Eust. *ad Hom. Il. pert.* 2 535; cf. Str. 10, 1, 3 C445; Plin. *HN* 4, 64; Skymn. 567–78; Hsch. s.v. Τιτανίδα. W. Wallace, *The History of Eretria to 198 BC*, unpubl. PhD thesis, Baltimore, MD, 1936a, 3–4. Abantis was also the

name of an area in Epeiros (Albania), later associated with Eretrian colonisation (Paus. 5, 22, 4), as well as the name of one of the *phylai* (tribes) of Khalkis.

7 Ch. 7, pp. 214–17. Geyer, 1903, 96; 107, however, believed that it was under Histiaian domination.

8 Euboia lies along a north-west to south-east axis. If we imagine Eretria as the central point for our purposes, Histiaia and Khalkis are 'north-west', Kyme 'north-east'; Amarynthos and Karystos 'south-east' (i.e. of Eretria). Generally I refer to the Aegean coast as 'north', and the Euboian Gulf coast as 'south'.

9 10, 1, 3 C445. He is to be preferred to St. Byz. s.v. Τελέθριον, who places it near Oikhalia in the Eretrias and actually claims Strabo as his source! Cf. the mistaken comments of A. Meineke, *Stephan von Byzanz: Ethnika* (*Stephani Byzantii Ethnicorum quae supersunt, ex recensione Augusti Meinekii*), 2nd edn, Graz, 1958, 612 in his notes.

10 Its precise location and identity have been disputed: cf. J. Quincey, 'The Beacon-sites in the *Agamemnon*', *JHS* 83, 1963, 125–6 (weakened by his ignorance of Μηκιστίς as a *phyle*-name at Eretria) has Dirphys as Makistos; W. Calder, 'The geography of the Beacon passage in the 'Agamemnon'', *CR* 36, 1922, 157 likewise refers the name to the 'highest' mountain (Dirphys). A. Beattie, 'Aeschylus "Agamemnon" 281–316', *CR* ns 4, 1954, 78, makes Dirphys and Olympos one and so by implication equates Makistos with Olympos within the Eretrias. Cf. J. Denniston and D. Page, *Agamemnon*, Oxford, 1957, 94–5.

11 The highest point is 775 m. Knoepfler, 1997, 368 and n. 129, has questioned this identification which, however, other recent commentators (H.-J. Gehrke, 'Eretria und sein Territorium', *Boreas* 11, 1988, 29–30; Tritle 1992, 135) accept, even though sometimes with reservations.

12 Thphr. *HP* 8, 8, 5. Call. *Hymn.* 4, 289. Eust. *in Hom. Il. pert.* 2, 537; Ath. *Deipn.* 4, 160a–b also note its fertility.

13 R. Richardson, 'A journey from Athens to Eretria', *Vacation Days in Greece*, London, 1903, 114; cf. also Geyer, 1903, 33.

14 Hom. *Il.* 2, 537; Plin. *HN* 14, 76. In Ath. *Deipn.* 1, 30: Euboian wine is favourably compared with Corinthian.

15 There is controversy over its very existence as a town in antiquity: see below Ch. 5, p. 143. I continue to believe in its existence but I do note Knoepfler's, 1997, 358 and n. 47; 360–1 and n. 70, recent doubts.

16 Str. 10, 1, 14 C449 (Kereus > white; Neleus > black); Antigonos of Karystos, *Mirab.* 78 (O. Keller, *Rerum naturalium scriptores Graeci minores*, Leipzig, 1877) reverses the order.

17 Richardson, 1903, 114–16, amusingly describes an occasion in the late nineteenth century, when he had to cross the stream in flood to reach Eretria. On the name: Plin. *HN* 4, 64; Knoepfler 1981, 308; Bérard 1985a, 268–75, Tritle 1992, 140–1.

18 The Erasinos: Str. 8, 6, 8 C371; *RE* s.v.: 'wahrscheinlich das jetzt Bach von Vathya genannt' (Philippson). The Imbrasos (Parthenios): schol. Pi. *Ol.* 6, 149; Geyer 1903, 29 and n. 1; Baumeister 1864, 17 and n. 45.

19 Richardson 1903, 111–14.

20 Apollod. 6, 7–11; schol. ad Lyc. 386; 1093; Hyg. 116; schol. ad Stat. *Achill.* 1, 93; Serv. *ad Aen.* 9, 260; E. *Helen* 766–7; 1126–31. Cf. *RE* s.v. Nauplios, and T. Gantz, *Early Greek Myth. A Guide to Literary and Artistic Sources,* Baltimore MD, 1996, vol. II, 695–7.

21 Quoted in A. Zimmern, *The Greek Commonwealth*, Oxford, 1915, 30.

22 An expression attributed to Philip V of Macedonia: Plb. 18, 11, 5; Liv. 32, 37, 4.

23 O. Picard, *Chalcis et la Confédération eubéenne (IV-I siècle)*, Paris, 1979, 212–18. See also Gehrke 1992, 98–117. For Prasiai on the Euboian Gulf coast of Attica as the principal port for the export of grain in the first half of the sixth century: A. French, 'The party of Peisistratos', *G&R* 6 1959, 46–57. See below, Ch. 6, pp. 185–7.

24 On the Petaliai Islands: see below, Chs 4, pp. 122–3 and nn. 237–9; and 6, p. 225–6.

25 Geyer 1903, 25–6: his discussion includes a list of ancient writers who mention them. Cf. C. M. Bowra, 'Signs of storm: Archilochus fr. 56', *CR* 54, 1940, 127–9; F. Sandbach,

'ΑΚΡΑ ΓΥΡΕΩΝ once more', *CR* 56, 1942, 63–5. Str. 10, 1, 5 C446; the Epitomator of Strabo appears to correct his own author from Ptol. *Geog.* 3, 15, 25; they are the only ancients to place the 'Hollows' on the Aegean coast; all others put them on the gulf side of the island. See W. Smith, *Dictionary of Greek and Roman Geography*, London, 1856, I, 641–2 s.v. *Coela*.

26 For a useful map: S. Bakhuizen, 'The two citadels of Chalcis on Euboea', *AAA* 5, I, 1972, 134–46, Figs 1 and 2. Idem, *Chalcis-in-Euboea: Iron and Chalcidians Abroad*, Leiden, 1976 (with a contribution by R. Kreulin, geologist), 5–6.

27 N. Kondoleon, 'Οἱ Ἀειναῦται τῆς Ἐρετρίας', *AE* 1963 [1965], 1–45: a novel, but seriously flawed, essay.

28 The relationship of the geology, geography, etc. of the site of Eretria to the later development of the city is dealt with by E. Kambouroglou, *Ερέτρια· παλαιογεωγραϊκή και γεωμορφολογική εξέλιξη κατά το Ολόκαινο. Σχέση φυσικου περιβάλλοντος και αρχαίων οικισμών*, Athens, 1989, and C. Krause, 'Structure et developpement urbanistique d'Érétrie archaïque', *Gli Eubei in Occidente. Atti del diciottesimo Convegno di Studi sulla Magna Grecia, Taranto, 8–12 ottobre, 1978*, Taranto, 1979, 37–52 and idem. 'Zur Städtebaulichen Entwicklung Eretrias', *AK* 25, 1982b, 137–44. Kambouroglou's study covers the area roughly from Malakonda, west of Eretria to east of Magoula, and inland to include Mt Olympos.

29 This theory is widely though not universally accepted: see Chs 2, pp. 46–7; 3, pp. 84–7; 4, pp. 91–6 and p. 113. For the date: M. Popham, L. Sackett and P. Themelis, *Lefkandi I: the Iron Age*, London, 1980: their introduction n. 4, and section 14, Pt IVb, 367.

30 For a full description of this important site: ibid. section 1, Pt I, 1–3; pll. 2–4 and of the harbour: Tritle 1992, 17, 139.

31 Konon *FGrH* 26F1, 44.

32 The identification of this marsh with the deme Ptekhai has been challenged by Gehrke, 1988, 30–2 and 1992, 107 n. 52, who identifies it with the lake at Dystos and by Knoepfler, 1997, 380–2, who would have it on the plateau of Velousia-Lepoura. Wherever it really was, we are fortunate to have preserved a decree (*IG* XII 9, 191) of the Eretrian *Demos* dated to the period 322–309 ratifying an agreement with the entrepreneur Khairephanes to drain it and turn it into productive farming land. See M. Holleaux, 'Note sur un décret d'Érétrie', *REG* 10, 1897, 189 n. 1.

33 D.L. 2, 133 and Ath. *Deipn.* 2, 46c–d, who appears self-contradictory, but quotes Euenor on the poor quality of Eretrian water. Pickard 1890–7, 375.

34 Str. 10, 1, 4 C445–6. Cf. Thphr. *HP* 9, 20, 5.

35 Plin. *HN* 16, 197. This contradicts Thphr. 5, 1, 5–8.

36 Thphr. *HP* 4, 5, 2; 9, 15, 4; 9, 15, 8; Plin. *HN* 25, 94. On the flora of Euboia: A. Huxley and W. Taylor, *Flowers of Greece and the Aegean*, London, 1977; G. Sfikas, *Self-Propagating Trees and Shrubs of Greece*, Athens, 1978.

37 Dr V. Parker, in a private note to me, considers that the folk-etymology of the name is hardly secure; we may note however that Str. 10, 1, 3 C445 indicates that the island was in fact 'well-cowed'.

38 On this coin, B. Head, *Historia Numorum. A Manual of Greek Numismatics*, Oxford, 1887, rev. 1911, 361 remarks that 'The Gorgoneion and Bull's head may be symbols of the worship of Artemis Amarynthia (*the Refulgent*), a Moon-goddess whose sanctuary near Eretria remained, down to a late date, a kind of Amphictyonic centre for all central and southern Euboea.'

39 Ath. *Deipn.* 5, 201c. On Mycenaean trade, see Ch 2, pp. 49–51; on PG trade, Ch. 3, pp. 77–81 and p. 85 (see Appendix 1: Chronological tables, for periods and abbreviations).

40 On Euboian rural industries generally: N. Settas, "Η Ἀγροτικὴ Ἀνάπτυξις τῆς Εὐβοίας', *AEM* 10, 1963, 142–217. On sheep: Paus. 8, 1, 5; Ath. *Deipn.* 5, 201c (the procession of Ptolemy II). On fowl: Varr. *RR* 8, 2, 4; Plin. *HN* 10, 48. On Eretrian dogs: Pollux 5, 37; 40; Ael. *NA* 7, 40; 17, 8; Makarios 4, 5; On pigs: Paus. 8, 1, 5.

41 The political consequences are dealt with in Ch. 4, pp. 96, 116–18.
42 Ath. *Deipn.* 9, 369–70.
43 *Il.* 2, 537.
44 Theognis 784; 892.
45 P. Auberson, 'Le temple de Dionysos', *Eretria; Fouilles et Recherches* V, Berne, 1976, 59–67, pl. 5.
46 *IG* XII Suppl., Test. et Not. 203, 94–102: 'Sola Eretria inter urbes Euboeae talia (Oinos-) nomina exhibit, quod qui vicos atque vineas hodierna ab Eretria urbe usque ad vicum Bathy (Amarynthos) peragraverit' and he further notes: 'Alia series nominum Eretriensium incipit ab οἰνο-, cf. Οἰνοχαρης, Οἴναργος "funkelnd wie Wein" aut "funkelnd von Wein" secundum Bechtel.' F. Bechtel, *Die historischen Personennamen des Griechischen bis zur Kaiserzeit*, Hildesheim, 1917/1964, 64, offers other examples: Οἴνων, Οἰνόθεος, Οἰνανθίσκος.'
47 For figs, see Ath. *Deipn.* 3, 75e; chestnuts, Ath. *Deipn.* 2, 54b; 54d [they were called both κάρυα (Karystos?) and λόπιμα]; apples and pears, Hermippos ap. Ath. *Deipn.* 1, 27–8. Athens imported pears and apples from Euboia: Ar. *Ach.* 878–9; *Pax* 1000–01.
48 Arist. *Aud.* 20 (831b); Plin. *HN* 11, 42.
49 Ath. *Deipn.* 4, 135e (Lopades = mezedhes: Geyer 1903, 34); 7, 284b; 7, 295c; 7, 330b. See also Paus. 5, 13, 3; Philostr. *VA* 1, 24; Arist. *HA* 4, 6. For the abundance of fish, see Ath. *Deipn.* 7, 295c; 302a; 304d. Ael. *NA* 2, 8; Plin. *HN* 32, 18.
50 Ath. *Deipn.* 4, 132c.
51 Arist. *HA* 5, 15; Ath. *Deipn.* 3, 88f; For Eretrian involvement: Philostr. *VA* 1, 24: '[the grave-stones show] that the various individuals had lived in Euboia and engaged either in seafaring trade or in that of purple either as sailors or dyers.' Apollonios has been reading old Eretrian epitaphs at Kissia in Mesopotamia where, apparently, the Eretrian captives of the Persians in 490 ended up following the capture of the city. S. Schmid, 'Decline or prosperity at Roman Eretria? Industry, purple dye works, public buildings and gravestones', *JRA* 12, 1999, 273–93. For Styreans: Ath. *Deipn.* 4, 132c.
52 Schmid 1999, 278, with his preliminary reports cited 275, n. 15.
53 *PAAE* 1977, 30.
54 Described more fully in Ch. 3, pp. 81–3.
55 Hsch. s.v. χάλκη makes this a synonym of πορφύρα. Bakhuizen 1976, 63–4, denies any link with χαλκός; he believes that the root χαλκ- is pre-Greek (58–64).
56 Or indeed on Euboia except for Aidepsos in the north. See n. 59 below.
57 Ibid., Pt II, *passim*.
58 Bakhiuzen 1976, 48–57 (despite Str. 10, 1, 9 C447). For another explanation of the association of central Euboia with bronze work, see Ch. 5, p. 160.
59 Ibid. In Pt II, he shows, convincingly, that any metallurgy carried on in Khalkis was related to the production of iron, not copper, and discusses the sources, local and foreign, of the raw materials. For Aidepsos: St. Byz. s.v. Αἴδηψος.
60 For marble, see Str. 9, 5, 16 C437; 10, 1, 6 C446; Plin. *HN* 36, 48; 49; D.Chr. *Disc.* 79, 2. For asbestos, see Plut. *de def. or.* 43 (*Mor.* 434a); Str. 10, 1, 6 C446.
61 Hdt. 5, 31, 3.
62 Isoc. *Paneg.* 108.
63 W. Wallace, 'The Demes of Eretria', *Hesperia* 16, 1947, 146. His reservations concerning its boundaries are shared by Knoepfler 1997, 353–4.
64 F. Adcock, 'The growth of the Greek city state', *CAH* III, 1965, XXVI, 698. His comparative figures are interesting although his remarks about the Euboian *poleis* are misleading: he divides the island among eight *poleis,* whereas there were, effectively, only four. See Wallace 1947, 146.
65 The date of the Eretrian annexation of these two areas will be of great importance when the socio-political territorial divisions of the Eretrias at the end of the sixth century are discussed in Ch. 8. The generally accepted period for the conquest of Styra has been the

end of the Lamian War (i.e. *c.* 324/3) but D. Knoepfler, 'La Date de l'Annexation de Styra par Érétrie', *BCH* 95, 1971, 242–4, argues convincingly for the end of the fifth century, following the Eretrian revolt against Athens in 411/10.

66 Popham *et al.*, 1980b, 367–9. See my own notes, Ch. 2, pp. 46–7.

67 For Kyme, see above n. 15.

68 This is still the case: Rodhakis and Triandafillidis II, *c.* 1965, 544–6.

69 Ath. *Deipn.* 4, 160 a–b. *LSJ* s.v. λευκάλφιτος, 1041.

70 T. Wiegand, 'Dystos', *MDAI(A)* 24, 1899, 458–67: the remains of fifth century houses (almost unique in Greece) are visible. The site has still not been fully excavated.

71 P. Friedemann, 'De la «carrière» au sanctuaire: investigations archéologiques sur l'acropole d'Érétrie', *AK* 37, 1994, 93–4.

72 P. Themelis, 'An eighth century goldsmith's workshop at Eretria', in R. Hågg (ed.), *The Greek Renaissance in the Eighth Century*, Stockholm, 1983, 157–65. For Eretrian industry, see Chs 4, p. 91 and 5, pp. 146–7. On the importation of gold for workshops and colonisation to supply raw materials lacking locally, see Ch. 5, pp. 146–7.

73 Popham *et al.* 1980b, 7; 359.

74 J. Boardman, 'Pottery from Eretria', BSA 47, 1952, 1–48; idem. 'Early Euboean pottery and history', BSA 52, 1957, 1–29. For pottery as trade containers, see Ch. 5, n. 239.

2

PREHISTORY, MYTHOLOGY AND CULT

The earliest inhabitants of Euboia from the late Neolithic Age to the end of the Mycenaean Age

PART 1: THE MYTHOLOGICAL AND QUASI-MYTHOLOGICAL INHABITANTS

The origins and history of the Euboians, as of all ancient Greek peoples, must be sought in myths and traditions going back into the mists of prehistory as well as in the reports of archaeologists, scientists, epigraphists, linguists and sociologists, since classical writers preserve only vague and disjointed details (often of dubious value) scattered throughout their works, seldom forming a coherent account with a Euboian focus. The island was largely neglected by the scholars of the nineteenth century, that great age of encyclopaedic collection and collation of ancient historical and mythological data, because, until the last half of the twentieth century, Euboia had been merely peripheral to the main concerns of classical historians, which were Athenian and, to a lesser extent, Spartan history and culture. When they did notice Euboia, it was generally because some particular detail had relevance to their central interest in the great cities of the Classical Age. Indeed, this neglect has persisted, especially in the English-speaking scholarly community, until the present. So we must search hard for the information that we require to attempt any kind of reconstruction of the prehistory (or even, for that matter, the later history) of the peoples of Euboia. Work by archaeologists and epigraphists in Euboia itself during the last century has added much to that knowledge of the earliest times, which is provided by the sparse literary record. Several sites have yielded artefacts and pottery (though few architectural remains), attesting to Bronze Age and even earlier settlements, especially in the Eretrias itself, going back to the late Neolithic Age. It is there, in fact, that the Greek archaeologist A. Sampson has undertaken the most thorough investigation of any Neolithic site on the island, that at the Skoteini cave near Tharrounia, some 15 km inland from Amarynthos. The current, ongoing excavation of Eretria itself by Swiss and Greek archaeologists began in the early 1960s, building on the pioneering work done at the end of the nineteenth century by the American School at Athens. Although work done at Eretria during the intervening period, in the first half of the twentieth century, was sporadic at best, the excavations since

1964 have given us a very good idea of the development of the city and the epigraphical corpus is probably now second only to that of Athens.[1]

Toponyms in both Euboia and other parts of Greece throw fitful light on the movements of prehistoric peoples who migrated via Euboia. Inscriptions of the Classical and later periods from the Eretrias give us more than fifty deme names, some of which suggest more ancient ethnic and religious associations. Names survive in the literary record of several ethnic groups who passed through the island, leaving settlers behind them who established their own place names and cults in the areas that they occupied. Some of these groups, such as the Dryopes and the Abantes, were historical peoples who lived in Euboia at various periods of its history, although others, such as the Kouretes, are mythical.[2] The terms Pelasgoi and Leleges, sometimes used to designate migrating groups, are so vague and confused in the tradition that we can at most say that they may indicate pre-Hellenic populations.

We need to try to establish from where and in what sequence these early peoples reached and settled in Euboia and the Eretrias itself.

The Kouretes and associated beings

According to the literary tradition, the Kouretes are the earliest people who lived in Euboia. Some ancients believed that they were the *autochthonous* (sprung from the soil itself; aboriginal) inhabitants of the island, others that they were from Aitolia on the west coast of mainland Greece or from Crete. Strabo summarises the thoroughly confused tradition: 'As for the Kouretes, some include them among the Akarnanes, some among the Aitolians; others maintain that the tribe originated in Crete, while still others say it was in Euboia.'[3] In one part of his book *The Geographika,* he has them migrating westward from Khalkis, where they had begun their characteristic practice of shaving the front of their scalps (later called the 'Abantic' hairstyle from its association with the historical Abantes): 'Arkhemakhos the Euboian says that the Kouretes lived in Khalkis, fighting continuously for control of the Lelantine Plain . . . and they [later] migrated to Aitolia', driving out the inhabitants whom the Kouretes then 'called Akarnanians because they did not shave their hair'.[4] Elsewhere, he implies that they came from the west coast to Euboia. Whichever direction the traffic moved, toponymic and cult associations between the peoples who settled in Euboia and those in the northern and western regions of Greece, Epeiros, Akarnania, Aitolia and Elis are very numerous.

Both Strabo and Epaphroditos (ap. St. Byz.) preserve a tradition that the Kouretes came to Khalkis from Crete, where they had been mythical priests and worshippers of Zeus, who was born there on Mt Dikte. This Cretan tradition also credits them with introducing the use of copper (*khalkos*) to Khalkis and hence its name: 'The Kouretes, who came [to Euboia] with Zeus and whom he left there as guardians of the temple of [his mother] Rhea, were the first to clad themselves in bronze there, from which fact the Khalkidians got their name.'[5] In mythology, Zeus, as a *kouros* (boy-child), was entrusted to the care of the Kouretes by Rhea, to be protected from his cannibalistic father Kronos and thus they became the first *kourotrophoi* (child nurturers). Nevertheless, western Greece was also a notable area of Zeus worship; one need remember only the two great sanctuaries of the god at Epeirote Dodona in the north and Olympia in the Peloponnese.[6]

It is usually with Zeus and Artemis that the Kouretes in their kourotrophic guise are associated. Indeed, in a *hymnos kletikos* (hymn sung to bid a god come to a ritual place) from an inscription found at Palaiokastro in eastern Crete, Zeus is repeatedly called *Megiste Koure* (Greatest Youth) and the Kouretes are alluded to in it. They are the *Dioskouroi* (Zeus-boys).[7] Bowra stresses the ritualistic nature of the refrain of the hymn and its place in the yearly cycle of seasonal death and rebirth and the Kouretes as bringers of the arts of settled community life.[8] The god celebrated was an *Eniautos Kouros*, a fertility deity dying and being reborn each year and ever young.[9] A dedication to such a god, simply called Megistos, has been found on the acropolis of Eretria.[10] Both Mekistis, one of the Eretrian tribal names and the Euboian toponym (Mt) Makistos may ultimately, via intermediate eponymous heroes, derive from this epithet.[11]

The worship of Zeus was also important in south-eastern Euboia, at Tamynai, Dismaros and Styra, later deme centres in the area of the Eretrias bordering on the Karystia, as well as at Karystos itself. These place names, together with others in the region such as Grynkhai, Dystos and Zarex, are pre-Hellenic, and several of their eponymous heroes are mythologically related. Examples are Geraistos, eponym of the cape and town south-east of Karystos, who was a son of Zeus, and Zarex, whose eponymous hero was the son of Karystos. [12] Zeus was worshipped as Tamynaios at Tamynai,[13] as Olbios at Dismaros (near Styra) and as Soter at Karystos.[14] The antiquity of these cults may be supposed from the fact that all these places were settled by one of the earliest invading peoples, the Dryopes (who are discussed later in this chapter), and that the south-east of the Eretrias and the Karystia in particular escaped total cultural modification by the later Ionian invaders, so retaining their essentially Dryopian character for Thucydides and Herodotos to note in the fifth century. The former tells us that: 'Those who were subjects and tributaries of Athens were the Eretrians, Khalkidians, Styreans and Karystians from Euboia, . . . And of these . . . almost all were Ionians, except the Karystians [who are Dryopes].' Herodotos observes that: 'the Khalkidians provided twenty [ships] at Artemision and the Eretrians seven; they are Ionians. . . . the Styreans . . . are Dryopes' and elsewhere: 'not the least part of them [i.e. the Ionians of Asia Minor] are Abantes from Euboia, who are not even Ionian in name.'[15]

At Eretria itself, cult practices incorporated into civic ceremonies involving the graduation of young men from the ephebate into full citizen dignity, which took place in conjunction with the Artemiria, the great festival of the ancient goddess Artemis Amarysia,[16] had marked Kouretic characteristics. They are reminiscent of the rites of the *Eniautos Kouros* of Crete, in which, to save the *kouros*-god, the Kouretes clashed their swords on their shields while leaping and dancing around the child. This was later believed to have been the origin of the Pyrrhic, a dance in arms often performed during initiation rituals for males and at public festivals in historic times and which was a major feature of the Artemiria. As rearers and guardians of the child god Zeus, they were called *kourotrophoi* and *phylakes* (guardians). Kourouniotis wonders whether a *horos* (or dedication?) to *Kourotrophoi* (pl.) from Eretria may indicate worship of the Kouretes, who he says are 'quintessentially the Kourotrophoi of Zeus'.[17] This kourotrophic role provided one of two ancient aetiological explanations of their name.

Another explanation was derived from the Greek word *koura* (hair cropping). The Kouretes were associated specifically with this hairstyle in Euboia, Aitolia and other centres of sub-Mycenaean culture – Athens, Crete and Cyprus – and we have representations on pottery of the hairstyle from the last. The famously warlike – but mythical – Euboian Kouretes reputedly were the first to shave the front of their head so that enemies could not grasp their hair and pull the heads forward, thus unbalancing them and exposing their necks to the sword. However another – historical – Euboian people, the Abantes, likewise followed this custom. As the legend of Abantic prowess in battle spread, the hairstyle took their name, the so-called *Comae Abanticae* becoming a particular symbol of the Euboian warrior, a badge of courage, if you will.[18] It was also called the *Theseïs* from Theseus who, according to a specifically Athenian tradition, introduced the hairstyle to Delphi as an element of the rituals ending adolescence and from whom the Abantes adopted it because of their practice of fighting close to their enemies. Elephenor, the Abantic *hegemon* of Euboia in Homer's *Iliad* was a near contemporary of Theseus, for Pausanias says that Theseus sent his children to Elephenor for safety and Plutarch adds that they accompanied Elephenor to Troy before returning to claim their inheritance after the death of Menestheus.[19] Despite this no doubt later Athenian claim, it is likely that the military aspects of mythical Kouretic practice are to be related to and derived from customs of the later, historical Euboian Abantes.

In summary, the Kouretes were perceived, in the words of an *Orphic Hymn*, as 'both nurturers and killers'.[20]

They were associated with several other early, some pre-Hellenic, mythological groups: the dancing Korybantes[21] of Asia Minor, the Kabeiroi of Samothrake and Boiotia,[22] and the Telkhines of Rhodes. They were also later confused with the Cretan Idaioi Daktyloi,[23] divine or semi-divine beings responsible for the arts of civilisation and crafts, especially the discovery of forging iron in fire, so that it is not unexpected to find this last group worshipped in central Euboia, as the area has long been traditionally associated with metalworking and mining. A hymn dedicated to them[24] found at the temple of Apollo Daphnephoros at Eretria, although much damaged, mentions two of the three original Daktyloi, Kelmis ('Smelter') and Damnameneus

('Hammer'): the missing name is Akmon (Anvil). It reveals a divine genealogy incorporating an otherwise quite unknown figure, Eurytheos, who must be a specifically Eretrian culture hero and who brought the various life-skills (healing, planting, metalworking, etc.) to the Eretrias, in a similar way to the pan-Hellenic Prometheus.[25] He is associated in the hymn with the Daktyloi and Olympian Apollo as well as, significantly, with the Phrygian Great Mother.[26] Archaeological evidence of metalworking has come to light within the *temenos* of Apollo at Eretria.[27]

The Great Mother goddess in her pre-Olympian phase is often referred to as *Potnia Theron kai Phyton* (Mistress of Wild Animals and Plants, or simply Mistress). She was originally patron and protector of the ancient totem clans and later of the *polis* itself. Some later Eretrian deme and *phyle* names reveal their original animal, plant or natural feature totem: Boudion (ox), Khoireai (pig – a symbol of fertility?), Minthous (the mint plant), Aig. (goat), Karkinousioi (crab), Oropos [the Asopos (rhotacised) river], Khytroi (springs) and the plant hero Narkissos. Several of these are clearly very ancient forms. Sometimes they became epithets of Artemis and other deities and *daimones* (e.g. Boudaia, Asopos, Minthe, and Narkissos).[28] Nilsson has argued that the prehistoric *Potnia* represented a plurality of female divinities from the very beginning and that in her various guises she is a syncretistic equivalent of Artemis, Hekate, Rhea, Demeter, etc. Since Artemis Amarysia was such a very important deity at Eretria – he calls her 'The High-Goddess of Euboia',[29] we should therefore identify the eastern Mother Goddess of the late hymn with the much more ancient Artemis Amarysia who had been long venerated in the Eretrias. The Daktyloi (the Kouretes who are not mentioned as such in the hymn) have become her attendants. Kourotrophic males had always been associated with the ancient *Potniai,* and Kouretic ritual was a major feature of the Artemis cult at Eretria (as it was elsewhere: Pausanias explicitly links her with Kouretic rituals in Messenia and Aitolian Kalydon; both had mythological associations with Eretria).[30] Indeed, it is precisely this close association with the important Eretrian state cult of Artemis Amarysia that justifies giving so much attention to the Kouretes.

However, the Daktyloi/Kouretes, being culture-*daimones* closely involved with metallurgy and crafts as well as with cultivation, rather than hunting and gathering, are unlikely to have been creations of Neolithic hunter–gatherers. First, the Kouretes are specifically credited with giving husbandry to man. The commentator Servius notes that 'the Kouretes are said to have been the first cultivators of Crete.'[31] Second, the culture myths of the Kouretes with their warrior 'Abantic' hairstyle and craft associations are likely to belong to a time when a patriarchically organised and Greek-speaking people, the Abantes, arrived in central Euboia, bringing with them the sky gods presided over by the Olympian supreme god Zeus, as opposed to the older religion of the *Potnia* of the wild animals. With her annually dying, chthonic subordinate, the *Kouros*-type Zeus, her cult was possibly associated with a matriarchal social system, which seems to have lasted longer in the south-east Eretrias and the Karystia than on the Lelantine Plain, whence Olympian Apollo was brought by refugees to Eretria at the end of the ninth century.[32] The story of the birth and survival of Zeus, thanks to his Kouretes, is far older and belongs to the earlier religion which, however, always remained popular, and the Mother Goddess, as Amarysia, together with her shadowy consort, ultimately re-established herself at Eretria as the principal popular deity of the *polis*, as is clear from the number of later dedications to her and the importance of her festival, even in Roman times.

In the Dryopian Eretrias and Karystia, Zeus Kouros may have been called Amarynthos, the eponym of the principal cult site of Amarysia. Certainly, in later times both Eretrians and Karystians shared the festival at Amarynthos. Another possibility was that he was called Aristaios, for this deity was particularly venerated in Dryopian settlements elsewhere in Greece and a representation of him has been found at Eretria. Aristaios was associated with hunting and was famous for discovering and teaching men how to make olive oil and cheese and to gather honey. He was also a weather deity as well as a healer and prophet.[33] According to the poet Bakkhylides (of the neighbouring Dryopian island of Keos, once ruled by Eretria), Aristaios was a son of Karystos and so brother of Zarex.[34] He was also the father of the nymph Makris, an ancient eponymous heroine of the island.[35] Whatever the Euboian *Kouros* may have been called, his shrine, which has been thought to have been within the sanctuary of Amarysia at Amarynthos, may have been an oracle of the dead. An *omphalos* (similar to that at Delphi) has been found at Amarynthos. Menedemos the Eretrian philosopher/statesman (who appears in *IG* XII 9, 246A, 66) was demesman of Aigale near Amarynthos. His family were the Theopropidai, whom Knoepfler's interpretation of *IG* XII 9, 213 leads him to believe was a religious corporation (similar to the Kerukes and Eumolpidai at Eleusis) with special privileges concerning consultation of the oracle, which he believes was at the Amarysion at Amarynthos.[36] Boardman[37] mentions a snake being worshipped there, which he interprets as symbolic of the soul of a dead man,[38] but it is more likely that it represents a chthonic snake deity such as that known elsewhere as Zeus Ktesios.[39] On the other hand, chthonic Artemis was identified with Hekate, a goddess who was closely associated with Zeus and oracles of the dead: 'Zeus having mated with Demeter, he sired Hekate . . . who is now called Artemis and Phylake.'[40]

The cult of Artemis Amarysia

It is convenient at this point to consider in more detail the important cult of Amarysia, the later descendant at Eretria of the prehistoric kourotrophic *Potnia*,[41] and her great annual festival, known as the Artemiria. We have already seen that practices that seem to be derived from Kouretic mythological tradition are a major feature of the rites. The principal cult centre in later times was at Amarynthos, which Strabo tells us was 'some seven stades from Eretria',[42] although in Chapter 4[43] I present evidence, rather slight it must be said, for a *hekatompedon* temple and large *temenos* in Eretria itself and dated to the eighth/seventh centuries, which may have been her early *intra-muros* shrine. Initiation rituals for new citizens were a major ceremony during the festival, which was celebrated in Anthesterion (March), when the earth begins to emerge from its winter sleep.[44] Some idea of the scope of the festival can be obtained from the great decree (*IG* XII 9, 189) of *c.* 340 setting out rules for the contests involved. Various musical (instrumental and rhapsodic) and heraldic declamation contests and doubtless, too, athletic events – though these are not mentioned in the inscription – together with elaborate and precisely defined sacrifices took place over five days.[45] The nature of the sacrifices is interesting for it reveals the complex nature of the goddess. The decree specified both 'selected' sheep and bulls. Most Olympian gods were offered cattle and oxen; sheep as sacrifices were rare but certainly the sacrificial beasts could not be defective in any way.[46] However, Eretrian Artemis specifically required the sacrifice of maimed or defective sheep. Were these the selected beasts required?

The picture emerges from several literary references to Amarysia and related Artemis cults such as that of Kolainis,[47] as well as those established along the Attic coast of the South Euboian Gulf, especially that at Aulis, since here, as at Amarynthos, Artemis accepted every kind of animal sacrifice: 'It is said that a favourable wind did not blow for the Greeks at Aulis' – while on their way to Troy – 'and when a favourable wind did spring up, each of them sacrificed to Artemis whatever victim he happened to have, female and male alike. From this time on, the rule at Aulis is that all victims are suitable.'[48] Several commentators take Kolainis as identical to Amarysia, including the Scholiast on Aristophanes' *Birds*,[49] who says: 'Euphronios relates that at Amarynthos [Artemis is] Kolainis and they sacrifice to her there a docked ram on behalf of Agamemnon', while Aelian says that: 'The Eretrians sacrifice docked rams to Artemis at Amarynthos.'[50] The perplexed comments of Pausanias:

> The wooden image at Myrrhinous [in Attica] is of Kolainis. The Athmoneis worship Artemis Amarysia. On enquiry, I discovered that the guides knew nothing about these goddesses, so I conjecture as follows: Amarynthos is a town in Euboia, the inhabitants of which worship Amarysia, while the festival of Amarysia which the Athenians celebrate is no less splendid than the Euboian. The name of the goddess came, I think, from there and the Kolainis in Myrrhinous is called after Kolainos [an ancient Attic king][51]

together with information from the playwright Metagenes,[52] and the *Diegesis* to Callimachus' *Iambos* 10 and fragment 200b,[53] add further details, so that we can generate a quite vivid picture of the sacrificial ritual associated with the goddess, one that reveals a darker and more primitive cult than was usual for

Olympian deities. Thus, even as late as Pausanias or Aelian in Roman times, Artemis Amarysia was still basically a chthonic deity although no doubt in later times overlaid with 'more civilised' Olympian characteristics. We can think of her as Artemis-Hekate, and therefore, as a goddess who was both chthonian and Olympian, it was entirely proper for her to receive offerings appropriate to both her aspects.

In the inscription we have evidence that there were indeed two sacrifices: two specially selected sheep to begin the festival to chthonic Artemis and her partner Amarynthos and later a sacrifice of the bulls to Artemis Olympia.[54] However, bulls or oxen are unusual as offerings to Artemis but perhaps not to Hekate, for Artemis was associated with this animal among others.[55] In the Classical Age, goats were usually the appropriate victims for Artemis. We may, however, remember that Artemis was worshipped with the by-name Tauropolos at Aulis, an epithet that is variously interpreted.[56] It has some early association with human sacrifice. Artemis and human sacrifice is a combination not by any means unknown in Greek authors;[57] the sacrifice of Iphigeneia at Aulis comes easily to mind but there are other documented examples.[58] Iphigeneia herself was identified with Artemis at Brauron. Hughes, in his study of human sacrifice in ancient Greece, argues that there may be archaeological evidence for the practice in Euboia from Manika, Lefkandi and Aulonari (in the Eretrias),[59] not to mention the Attic sanctuaries along the Euboian Gulf at Aulis, Brauron and Halai: Euripides[60] has Athene say to Orestes:

> Taking the image and your sister, go.
> When you come to the god-built towers of Athens,
> there is a place in Attica, near its furthest limits,
> opposite the high ridges of the Karystia,
> a sacred place, which my people call Halai;
> build there a temple and set up the image,
>
> Men shall praise her in song as Artemis Tauropolos.
> And establish this law: when the people celebrate,
> as penalty for your slaughter, a sword be held
> to a man's throat, and spill his blood
> for the sake of purification and in honour of the goddess.

It is always men's blood that flows on the altars of these goddesses. Hughes[61] remarks that the lines would not make much sense to Euripides' Athenian audience if there was no connection at all with a contemporary ritual that 'involved the (non-fatal) cutting of a male's neck with a sword',[62] a relic of prehistoric matriarchy perhaps. It is thus by no means unlikely that the Artemis cult at Amarynthos originally involved such rites.

On a lighter note, the decree lets us see what the festival would have been like in the Classical period. People came from Karystos as a matter of course but in later times from other parts of Euboia and beyond, as is testified both epigraphically and in the literary record: 'At exactly that very moment (i.e. 192) there was taking place at Eretria the annual festival in honour of Artemis Amarynthis in the celebration of which participated not only the inhabitants of this city but also those of Karystos.'[63] *IG* XII 9, 189 informs us that before the festival proper, there was the inspection and selection process that we have discussed together with the reimbursement of costs by the temple supervisors to the providers of the sacrificial animals sent by the *khoroi*. Throughout the period of the festival there was a general fair, perhaps a *panegyris* (carnival), with people selling things – no doubt food, trinkets and votives – in the *temenos*, which was exempt from state or temple taxes. In the *agora,* the demarchs assembled the procession of all those who wished to sacrifice: first, the public officials with state offerings, followed by the private citizens. They were charged with ensuring that everything proceeded as befitted the great occasion. Unruly behaviour was not to be tolerated. Then everyone, including all the contestants in the music competitions, proceeded to the temple in a splendid concourse that included a military contingent comprised of chariots, cavalry and hoplites. Strabo records that:

> The stele, which they set up in the temple of Amarynthian Artemis, is witness to the power that the Eretrians once wielded; on it is written that three thousand hoplites, six hundred *hippeis*, and sixty chariots took part in the procession.[64]

Following the procession began contests and ceremonies that lasted over the next four days. Our decree is concerned only for the regulation of the music events but we may be sure that there were athletic contests as well. Perhaps the preoccupation of those who formulated the decree with musical matters was because the music competitions were added to the festival only at this time (*c.* 340).

But the political centrepiece of the great occasion was a performance of the Pyrrhic dance[65] in armour, by young men about eighteen years old in their final year of the *ephebeia* and so about to enter upon full citizenship and military service. The surviving Eretrian ephebic lists, especially *IG* XII 9, 240, 244 and 555, show that at the time that they were inscribed, there was a tendency to put brothers and cousins through the ephebate together, a practice that would tend to reinforce kinship ties.[66] Evidence from the lists suggests that the age for entering the ephebate, sixteen years, was a lower limit and that a boy could be enrolled later if it so convenienced the family groups.[67] It is therefore clear that these rituals and ceremonies were designed to reinforce the power of the social groups involved, in practice the upper classes. The Pyrrhic dance was characteristically a feature of festivals for deities of war. There are several other references to Pyrrhic dancing in the *corpus* of Eretrian inscriptions, as well as in one from Histiaia, in which the war goddess Artemis Proseoa had the additional by-names Parthenos Agrotera (virgin huntress),[68] epithets of the Artemis who was worshipped at Athens alongside Enyalios, the god of bloody war,[69] and who was likewise associated with the Pyrrhic. As at the Artemiria, the Athenian *epheboi* in arms marched in procession to the temple of the war goddess Artemis Agrotera at Agrai, where the *polemarkhos* sacrificed during the Thargelia festival.[70] In a similar fashion, the Salii (leapers) danced for the war god Mars Gravidus in Rome, as did the Kouretes for Zeus *Kouros*. All these were also vegetation and procreation deities,[71] and the same is clearly true of the Eretrian Artemis Amarysia, while the military nature of the Artemiria, as we learn of it from both the literary sources and the inscriptions, has been often commented on: 'The Amarynthia are celebrations in honour of Artemis the warrior.'[72] The importance of the ceremony of the Pyrrhic for citizen status becomes apparent from an important Hellenistic inscription from Eretria[73] in which the term *pyrrhikistai* (Pyrrikh dancers) is used to denote, in a formal and legal context, the group of incoming new citizens, i.e. the youths in the final year of the *ephebeia*. They, along with the existing body of citizens, swear to uphold the agreement recorded in the inscription between the Eretrian state and the entrepreneur/developer Khairephanes to drain the Ptekhai swamp. The unusual term is thus used here as an Eretrian equivalent for the more usual *epheboi*. The archaic Cretan hymn likewise stresses the importance of young/new citizens in the annual dance ritual: it exhorts Zeus' Kouretes to 'leap for the young/new (*neous*) citizens'.[74]

From the Archaic to the Roman period, the Artemiria was an occasion for aristocratic display.[75] The *Hippeis* who took part in the great procession were the Eretrian 'nobility',[76] roughly the equivalent of the Attic class of the *pentekosiomedimnoi*, while the presence of chariots, well and truly obsolete militarily when the stele recording the display was inscribed (since the text referred to hoplites) indicates very conspicuous upper-class exhibitionism. There is an interesting LH IIIC pottery fragment from nearby Lefkandi showing part of a man riding in a horse-pulled chariot or cart of light construction,[77] which may be a ceremonial vehicle. If so, the driver's social descendants at Eretria were still maintaining the archaic practice of riding in chariots in the great procession in honour of Artemis Amarysia in the sixth century. Horse-drawn chariots were always a sign of great wealth and high social standing in Greece from the Bronze to the Classical Age. We may recall Kimon's and Philip II's Olympic chariot exploits.

On a less military but no less aristocratic level, a poem by the Hellenistic poet Theodoridas for a youth entering adulthood clearly indicates the 'noble' values that dominated the festival for most of its history:

> To the Amarynthian nymphs Kharixenos dedicated his shorn locks,
> Along with his beautiful cicada-shaped hair-pin,
> All purified with holy water, together with an ox.
> The boy shines like a star, like a foal having shed his coat of down.[78]

The symbolism of the hairpin and the comparison with a young horse is totally Hippobotic/Eupatrid. This young *kalos k'agathos* may be the man named in a roughly contemporary dedication on a statue base from Khalkis whose father Dexitelos was *hegemon* of that city and so clearly among the upper classes of the period.[79] Given the pan-Euboian fame of the festival by Roman times, he may have come from his own city to make his dedication at Amarynthos to the great goddess of the Euboians *par excellence*. A similar practice took place at Athens and in other Ionian communities at the festival of the Apatouria, the third day of which was called *Koureotis*: 'A day of the month Pyanepsion on which they sacrifice to Artemis the hair shorn from the heads of boys', according to Hesykhios.[80]

To return to the Kouretes, we may note finally that the prominence of the Pyrrhic and of other Kouretic rituals in Euboia has led to speculation that they may even have been brought by Minoan colonists at Khalkis who fought for control of the Lelantine Plain.[81] This theory is underpinned by Strabo: 'Some call . . . the Kouretes "Kretes" and say that the Kretes were the first people to wear bronze armour in Euboia and for this reason they were also called Khalkidians', and he cites Arkhemakhos of Euboia: 'the Kouretes inhabited Khalkis and continually warred for control of the Lelantine Plain.' Epaphroditos, as we saw earlier in this chapter, said much the same thing.[82] Indeed, in Euboia most tradition bases the Kouretes originally at Khalkis.

However, are the Kouretes simply mythic legendary warriors or do they in fact represent a race of people who inhabited Euboia or part of it in a distant prehistoric age? Geyer, for example, believes that they were entirely mythical. Jacobsen characterises them as 'semi-mythical' but accepts that they may have been a race of Anatolian origin on the island in the early Bronze Age,[83] who once occupied the whole of Euboia before the first Greek speakers arrived and they are identified with LN–EH I invaders from Asia Minor by Faraklas (see below, p. 39 and n. 106). The traditions, as they are revealed to us through the mythology and cult rituals, are clearly made up of conflicting elements, some, such as the association with hunter–gathering *kouros*-daimones, such as Aristaios, and their kourotrophic functions, belonging to a pre-agricultural, possibly matriarchal society and so pre-Greek. On the other hand, the strong association of the Kouretes with farming and crafts as well as their militaristic character belongs to a later age. It is useless now to try to identify them with any group of people in particular although we shall see that their warlike aspect was shared (appropriated?) by the Abantes.

The pre-Hellenes in Euboia spoke a language (or languages), the only surviving traces of which are a number of toponyms and a few other names ending in *-ssos* and *-nthos*,[84] and perhaps those ending in *-ai* and *-stos*, together with a few with the medial *-op(s)-*. The first group has long been regarded as pre-Hellenic. The *-ai, -stos, -op(s)-* group may in fact represent a second, pre-Greek, and perhaps even pre-Indo-European, language.[85] Toponyms of these types are found throughout Euboia, and specifically Eretrian examples include Amarynthos, Minthous, Dystos, Pherai, Grynkhai (a name so strange that later Greeks were totally uncertain as to how it should be spelt or even pronounced, to judge from the variations found in the lexical works and inscriptions from outside Eretria), Ptekhai, Tamynai and Oropos.[86] Narkissos the plant hero is intimately linked to Eretria. A *heroön* dedicated to Narkissos the Eretrian with the by-name Sigelos, which people had to pass by in silence, was located in adjacent Boiotia close to (if not part of) the sanctuary of Amphiaraos, as Strabo noted: 'Near Oropos is a place called Graia and also the temple of Amphiaraos and the monument of Narkissos the Eretrian who is known as the Silent One.'[87] He was also remembered as the son of Amarynthos: 'The narcissus flower, as Akousilaos suggests, is named after Narkissos, son of Amarynthos, who was an Eretrian from the island of Euboia, slain by Epops (Pomponius Sabinus adds: 'his lover').'[88] 'From his blood were procreated the flowers that bore his name.'[89] The slaying of Narkissos, son of Amarynthos by Epops (Ellops, eponym of the Ellopians?) may be symbolic of the supplanting of the earlier *-nthos/-ssos* people by the *-op(s)-/-ai/-stos* people, identified in the next section with the Dryopians and Ellopians.

However, when did these pre-Greek peoples inhabit Euboia? Jacobsen has observed that the geographical distribution of these toponyms throughout Euboia corresponds well with the distribution of LN and EH settlements on the island. Vermeule likewise favours EH (I/II), a period of widespread uniformity of culture: she believes that the *-nthos/-ssos* language could only 'have spread so widely . . . in a time of diffuse contact, of international *koine*.'[90] Perhaps it was the subsequent *op(s)-/-ai/-stos-* people who were still in occupation when the first Greek speakers arrived (according to this view in EH III/beginning of MH), bringing widespread disruption in Euboia as elsewhere in Greece.[91]

However, dating 'the coming of the Greeks' as early as *c.* 2000–1900 (the beginning of the MH) has now been seriously challenged. R. Drews supplies non-specialists with an overview of the scholarship concerning the controversy in his 1989 survey,[92] discussing the question using both the traditional philological and the linguistic evidence and supplementing it with that provided by recent excavations. The new evidence points rather to *c.* 1600 (the beginning of LH I), and pottery from Euboian Lefkandi plays a significant role in the argument for the later date. Rutter, in two articles discussing pottery from Lerna in the Argolis,[93] argues that the style known as Gray-burnished ware, found there in EH III levels and which also occurs in the northern Peloponnese (Elis) and at Lefkandi,[94] is the direct ancestor of the later Gray Minyan ceramic, in other words, there is no indication of cultural discontinuity (invasion by outsiders) and that Gray Minyan is therefore not an alien fabric. Thus, invasion of the first Greeks at the earlier time is very unlikely. Drews observes that: 'Rutter goes so far as to say that the EH III Gray-burnished ware "is universally recognised to be the ancestor of MH Gray Minyan".' That is not literally the case . . . but there is no doubt that the old view is on the way out',[95] and the emergence of Gray Minyan cannot be the signal of the arrival of the Greeks. On the other hand, the appearance of the horse-drawn chariot in Greece *c.* 1600, and its subsequent prominence in Mycenaean (LH) society, and an increasing cosmopolitanism of grave goods from this time are likely indicators of an invasion of newcomers. Moreover, the people buried in the shaft graves at Mycenae are physically bigger than their MH predecessors; perhaps they were of a different racial type.[96] Rutter believes that the EH Gray-burnished ware that he discusses originated in eastern Greece and later spread to the West. He points out that the technology of the fast wheel came to the Peloponnese during EH III but that it had been used already in Euboia during EH II and was taken, by separate routes, to Olympia and the Argolis.[97] This notion runs counter to most of the literary sources,[98] and it is not the general opinion among scholars. I think that it is not impossible that there were in fact several population movements in different directions and at different periods passing between the western coastal regions of Greece and Euboia. The confused traditions concerning the movements of population groups such as the Kouretes and the Abantes that are recorded by later writers may be a result of just such a complex situation. The mythological connections of the Kouretes with both Euboia and Aitolia have already been noted; we shall also find that groups from Elis may have moved into the Eretrias and there are links that appear in the mythology, suggesting that Dryopians moved to the Argolis in the Peloponnese from Euboia.

PART 2: THE 'HISTORICAL' INHABITANTS – PRE-HELLENIC TO LATE-BRONZE-AGE (MYCENAEAN) EUBOIA

The pre-Greek peoples

Euboia and the Eretrias themselves were certainly inhabited in prehistoric times. The Skoteini cave and its associated settlement near Tharrounia show more or less continuous occupation from at least LN to Roman times and there are indications that it may even go back to middle Palaeolithic times. The Tharrounia people apparently practised a nomadic way of life. They made a simple pottery and Sampson believes that they may have been able to use the climate in the cave to store perishable products such as cheese.[99] Themelis has reported the discovery of a Neolithic axe on the site of Eretria itself,[100] while other LN and EH finds from within the Eretrias have been noted at various places; the indications point to a considerable population in the area. The site of Eretria was thus occupied from at least LN onwards and, perhaps extensively, in EH. In fact, there is evidence of EH constructions of brick, and even a potter's kiln,[101] indicating a settled society at this time. However, it is unlikely that the settlement will ever be shown to have been on the same scale as at the EH settlements of Lefkandi before 800 or at Manika north of Khalkis.

The Pelasgoi and Leleges

General ancient opinion was that these were the earliest inhabitants of the Aegean basin, the autochthonous people, self-generated from the soil. Herodotos[102] records Pelasgic settlements in the Thracian Khalkidike and in Asia Minor that spoke a non-Hellenic language, and for him the name covers all the aboriginal peoples in the Greek world.[103] They are found in Crete, Epeiros, Thessaly and Boiotia, as well as Euboia. Homer's hero Achilles venerates 'Pelasgian Zeus' and his priests the Selloi of Dodona.[104] The Leleges are more closely identified with Asia Minor, though some believed that they had inhabited western and central Greece. Herodotos calls them Kares (Carians) and makes them the rowers of King Minos' navy.[105] For us today, there is not much distinction to be made.

The supposed passage of the Pelasgoi and/or Leleges from Asia Minor to Boiotia has been traced archaeologically by N. Faraklas across the Aegean and in central Euboia,[106] where Cycladic influences and artefacts have been found at several LN–EH sites, that at Manika [EH I and (especially) II], which eventually covered 40 ha during EH II, being the most comprehensively excavated.[107] It has been argued that there are signs at Manika that even at this early period there was a 'bourgeois' class, whose demands for an 'aura artistique' associated with practical objects as well as in their offerings to the gods 'implies the presence there of talented artists and not just unsophisticated artisans'.[108] Faraklas identifies the Kouretes with the Pelasgoi (and/or Leleges)[109] and suggests the presence of Cycladic objects as confirmation of their route of approach.[110] However, an alternative explanation is to have them migrating from a Thessalian homeland, setting out from the Malian Gulf, travelling via Euboia to the Cyclades, and thence to the areas around the Argolic Gulf and Asia Minor.

The Dryopians, the Ellopians and Perrhaibians

The Dryopians

The Dryopians originated in the Sperkheios valley in Thessaly. Dr Parker points to a town in the south of Thessaly called Dryopā (Dryopē) and notes that:

> This suffix -ā is in historical times no longer productive; all place names formed by suffixion of -ā are old (Krētā from Krēs/Krētes, Libyā from Libyes) and cannot have been invented in later times. The toponym means that Dryopians once dwelt in this region; all our sources say they migrated thence.[111]

They also inhabited parts of Epeiros.[112] The ancients considered them autochthonous and so very ancient. Settlements that were originally Dryopian are often characterised by names ending in *-stos*, *-op(s)-* and *-ai*. A people called Dolopes are said to have inhabited Skyros, which lies only about 40 km off the coast of the Eretrias. This *-ops*-named people are related to the Dryopians of southern Euboia; they too came originally from Epeiros.[113] Later tradition has the Dryopians driven out of Thessaly by Herakles (representing the Dorians). They then migrated to Euboia, the Argolis and elsewhere. The Dryopians are associated with both Hermione and Asine in Argolis and Asine in Messenia.[114] Wallace locates the Eretrian deme *ex As.*, which I supplement *ex As(ine)*, in District I, on the border with Dryopian Karystia, although Knoepfler identifies it with the 'Old City' [As(typalaia)] and places it on the acropolis at Eretria.[115] Pausanias however discusses Asine in the Argolis (the people of which were proud of their Dryopian origins) in the context of a battle waged by Herakles and somehow linked to the Styraians of Euboia (who took no part in the battle as they lived at some distance from the city). If the battle were the sack of Oikhalia, the relationship of the people of Asine and Styra is understandable, for there was an Oikhalia in the Eretrias.[116] Schumacher implies that the Dryopian settlements in the Argolis were settled from Euboia. He may well be right.[117] Themelis notes the penetration of Euboia by new tribes during the proto-Helladic period [*c.* 2500, beginning in the LN (=Troy IV)] and which, he believes, set out from Asia Minor.[118] Jacobsen, for whom the Kouretes were the pre-Greeks (the *-nthos* people),[119] has the Dryopians arrive at the end of the Mycenaean period, which would certainly make them Greek speakers. In Euboia in historical times they were noted, as we have already seen, by Herodotos and Thucydides who identified them with the later inhabitants of the south-eastern region only, and this is largely confirmed by the distribution of the *-stos* [and, possibly, *-op(s)-*] toponyms.[120]

As their original homelands were Thessaly and Epeiros, they may have invaded via Cape Kenaion and gradually spread over the whole island until they reached Karystos in the far south, their most notable settlement in later times. However, as they have left little or nothing in Euboia of their passing that can be distinguished in the archaeological record,[121] and since there are few surviving toponyms that can definitely be said to be Dryopian outside the Karystia and the south-eastern Eretrias,[122] if this was their route, they must have been driven further and further southwards by later invaders who eventually eliminated almost all traces of them north of the Eretrias.[123] An alternative explanation, which would explain the absence of material and toponymic traces, is that they set out from Thessaly by sea and bypassed the northern part of the island, and that some put in at Karystos and the Eretrias while others continued further south and east, settling in parts of the Argolis and elsewhere. Dr Parker observed to me that: 'Carystus was settled by a people surveying the site by sea',[124] noting how cut off the site is from access to the rest of the island and noting Phokaia in Asia Minor as a parallel case of a city that could only have been selected by people surveying it from the sea.

An early name for Eretria was Melaneïs. The eponymous hero was Melaneus, concerning whom Antoninus Liberalis says that he was a son of Dryops and king of the Dryopians.[125] He was the father of Eurytos, king of Dryopian Oikhalia in the Eretrias and, possibly, of Eretrieus, the eponymous hero of the later city,[126] and indeed Liberalis calls the daughter of Eurytos Dryope.[127] Oikhalia was located in the same general region as those places that have already been seen to have attested Dryopian associations and its name survived into historical times as a deme of the classical Eretrias.[128] The Dryopians had another king called Phylakos, who may be the eponym of Phylake, possibly one of the five districts (*khoroi*) of the Eretrias mentioned in the fourth century Eretrian inscription (*IG* XII 9, 189), in which was set out the organisational procedure for the Artemiria festival and which was, along with another called Metaxy in the document, responsible for its staging. However the toponymic attribution of these names has been recently challenged by Knoepfler who prefers to see both as by-names of Artemis, reading the dative forms as 'for' rather than ablatively as 'by' Phylake and Metaxy.[129]

The process of attrition against the Dryopians may have begun quite soon after their arrival, with the subsequent invasion of the Ellopians, and been completed by the Abantes.[130] Perhaps a consequence was the sack of Oikhalia and the killing of its king Eurytos by Herakles (during LH IIIA). This episode became the subject of an epic poem, *The Destruction of Oikhalia*, variously ascribed to Homer, Kreophylos or Linos[131] and would explain its absence from the Homeric catalogue of Euboian cities under the later Abantic leader, Elephenor.[132] The association of Herakles with its destruction may in fact suggest the later Abantes as the perpetrators, for Herakles is said to be one of the Daktyloi, associated with the Kouretes and thus with the Abantes.

The Ellopians and Perrhaibians

The Ellopians and Perrhaibians would have entered the island via Cape Kenaion, for they are exclusively identified with the northern parts of Euboia, meagre though the evidence is. They were probably dialectically and ethnically related to the Dryopes and followed them, since they are traditionally identified with the same original homelands.[133] Their principal towns were Histiaia and Kerinthos; the latter was indeed once called Ellopia.[134] Whether they spread further to the south and east it is impossible to say with certainty, although there was an Eretrian deme called Histiaieis. Wallace, however, did not believe that the Ellopians came so far south (or even to Khalkis), although he cannot explain why there was a deme Histiaieis in the Eretrias.[135] Geyer, however, thought that it was they who had overrun Oikhalia. However, Dryopians may have held Histiaia earlier; if so, they could have brought the name themselves.

Perhaps the Ellopians did come this far but were driven back. The Dryopians in the Karystia were apparently able to hold off even the later Ionians. Although Dystos, Styra and Zarex are Dryopian names, Thucydides, as we have seen, regarded them as Ionian cities, since he specifically names the Styreans as Ionians, whereas the Karystians are not. However Herodotos is not so sure,[136] and Pausanias[137] notes that the later Styreans 'disdain the name of Dryopians'. However, if Styra, which is further south than both Dystos and Zarex was later 'ionianised', then the latter must have been also. Both Wallace and Knoepfler locate the deme Histiaieis in the vicinity of Zarex,[138] and, indeed, it cannot have been too far away since both are epigraphically attested in District II.[139] Where any defensive line was drawn, again we do not know. The 'historical' likelihood is that if there had been any Ellopian attack, it was foiled by a defence either of the narrow neck of land at Styra, which is less than 6 km wide, or that at Zarex (8 km wide) at the head of the Gulf of Almiropotamos. The Athenian general Phokion similarly exploited this line in the fourth century.[140] Perhaps the invaders remained there for enough time before finally retreating to leave the toponym behind them.

Along with the Ellopians in northern Euboia, are mentioned the Perrhaibians.[141] Geyer equates them with the Ellopians and says that they extended their rule as far as Khalkis. Evidence concerning them is very slight. However, they are nowhere associated with the Eretrias.

There are six reasons for placing the Dryopians, Ellopians and Perrhaibians before the Abantes in the chronological sequence of Euboian peoples:

1 The ancients themselves thought that the Dryopians were Pelasgoi, i.e. autochthonous, but the Abantes are never so described.
2 Of all the peoples of Euboia, they alone are never associated with the Kouretic/Abantic hairstyle. This, I believe, came to Euboia with the later elements of Kouretic mythology, the Olympian religion and patriarchal social system of the first Greek speakers in Euboia, whom I identify below with the Abantes.[142]
3 Amarynthos/Aristaios, the shadowy *kouros*-consort of the ancient goddess Amarysia at Amarynthos, is associated with the Dryopian south (and nearby Keos and elsewhere) but never with northern Euboia.
4 Both the *-nthos/-ssos* (almost universally acknowledged to be pre-Greek) and *-stos* (widely thought to be Dryopian)[143] toponyms were certainly already in use at Amarynthos and Karystos when the Mycenaean Linear B sealings from Thebes were inscribed, since both names occur in them. I will discuss these sealings during my treatment of the economic relationship between Abantic Euboia and the Mycenaean palace at Thebes.
5 The story of Epops/Ellops killing Narkissos, the son of Amarynthos,[144] and the attribution of Ellops as the founder of Kerinthos, suggests that the *-ops* people followed the *-nthos* group.
6 That Dryopians, Ellopians and Perrhaibians preceded the Abantes is strongly suggested by the fact that, in Homer, the whole island, including Dryopian Karystos, was united under the hegemony of the Abantes and also that the latter must have subsequently conquered and inhabited (or at least gained control of) northern Euboia since it was from there,

> specifically from Histiaia, that Abantes are said to have set out to colonise Chios and the neighbouring coast of Asia Minor: 'Carians too came to the island [Chios] in the reign of Oinopion and Abantes from Euboia. Oinopion and his sons were succeeded by Amphiklos, who because of an oracle from Delphi, came from Histiaia in Euboia.'[145] However, Bury thought that Kyme, the Aegean port of Eretria in later times, was the starting point.[146] This expedition occurred during the early stages of the Greek colonisation of Asia Minor, before the coming of the Ionians who, in Chios as in Euboia, followed Aeolic speakers, who should be identified with the Abantes.[147] There is no literary evidence of Dryopians in Ionia.[148] Archaeology confirms the dating from the literary sources, placing the coming of the Ionians to Asia in the eleventh century,[149] following the fall of the Mycenaean kingdoms. In Chios there are LH IIIC pottery finds from Emborio showing affinities with Lefkandi, and it is very likely that Euboian Abantes occupied this settlement in LH IIIC.[150] If a Euboian-style pendent semicircle *skyphos* found at Emborio[151] were taken there by migrating Abantes, it would suggest a late-tenth-/early-ninth-century date,[152] although it could as easily be a later import.

If the Dryopians, Ellopians and Perrhaibians were the pre-Greek inhabitants of Euboia, then they were probably the people who inhabited the Skoteini cave in the Eretrias from LN to EH and certainly predate the Kouretic/Abantic martial tradition.[153]

From the early Bronze Age to the Mycenaean period

The Abantes

I believe that the first group of Greek-speaking invaders[154] were the Abantes, who gave the name Abantis to the island, long used, especially by poets.[155] They are the ruling people in Homer's *Iliad*:[156]

> Men of Euboia, then, the Abantes
> breathing fury, who held Khalkis, Eiretria,
> and Histiaia of the laden vines and
> Kerinthos-on-the-sea, the crag of Dion,
> those of Karystos, those of Styra – all
> had as leader Elephenor Khalkodontiades,
> companion of Ares, chief of the greathearted Abantes.
> And with him there followed the swift Abantes,
> with hair flowing long at the back, ravenous
> spearmen, with outstretched ash-wood spears
> to pierce the breast-corselets of their enemies.
> And with him there followed forty black ships.

The characteristic feature of their appearance, shared with the Kouretes, is their long, back-flowing hair, which became the visible symbol of all subsequent warriors of Euboia down to the Archaic period. In Homer, the whole island, from Karystos in the south to Histiaia in the north, is united under the hegemony of the Abantes. Homer does not call their leader, Elephenor, *basileus* (king) or *wanax* (high king) but rather *hegemon* and *arkhos* (leader), although Plutarch later called his father Khalkodon[157] *basileus*: 'Amphiktyon came to the city of the Thebans and finding them tributaries of the Khalkidians, freed them from the tribute by killing Khalkodon, king of the Euboians.'[158] But, since Elephenor and Khalkodon ruled a territory that included several important regions, as Homer makes clear that they did, the Euboia of the Mycenaean and sub-Mycenaean periods was a state of a type later known as an *ethnos*, presided over by the *hegemones* of Lefkandi. Normally, a leader of such a state would have been called *basileus*, or even *wanax*. In later times, the Thessalians, who like other *ethne* preserved ancient customs had such a 'national' war leader called *tagos,* whose office, like that of the Macedonian monarchs, was both hereditary and semi-elective. The status of the Khalkodontid rulers may have been similar.

It is difficult to generalise about this form of political organisation. The inhabitants of *ethne* shared a common cult centre but rarely a clearly defined political one. They have been variously described as 'tribal' or 'cantonal' states. Similarly, there is disagreement concerning how they were ruled. Ehrenberg[159] says categorically: 'no traces of kingship can be pointed out in these states' (he excludes the Macedonians and the Molossoi). But Aristotle clearly says that 'initially the *poleis* were ruled by *basileis* and even now the *ethne* [are so ruled].'[160] However Homer calls the leader of the Euboian Abantes *hegemon*. I prefer Homer to Aristotle, or any other later writer, and call our hero-ruler *hegemon* especially for the period when Lefkandi, his likely 'capital',[161] was subordinate to the Theban *wanax*. However, his status probably changed after the fall of Thebes to that of a *wanax* of an independent Euboian entity. The *ethnos* was a political form later particularly characteristic of north-west and central Greece, precisely the areas through which the ancestors of the Euboians passed. Ehrenberg says that they were remote from the great Mycenaean monarchies, but there were in fact *ethne* in Elis and Arkadia, close to Pylos in Messenia and Mycenae in the Argolis.[162] Moreover, these Peloponnesian *ethne,* as well as the north-western *ethne*, the Aitolians, the Akarnanians and the Molossoi, all had strong mythological associations with Euboia.

However, the term *ethnos* does suggest a tribal origin and presumably harks back to the prehistoric wandering, and final settling down in hamlets, of the early peoples. In later times, they remained rather loose arrangements of individual *komai* (villages), which, for reasons probably mostly to do with self-preservation, agreed to acknowledge the overlordship of a powerful leader of a larger *kome*.[163] Sometimes villages would coalesce to form still larger units, as did the Spartan *obai*. There is evidence that many large cities of the Classical

Age, such as Athens, Sparta and Corinth, evolved in this way. Eretria itself was originally inhabited by people living in hamlets scattered over the area of the later city. This early situation was to some extent frozen in the classical geopolitical organisation of the Eretrias, in which many of the ancient *komai* seem to have become the *demoi*, one of which even had the name Komaieis. Earlier, those that were big enough in themselves, or were able to amalgamate, and that possessed a stronghold, were sometimes able to exert control over surrounding areas and build up a local feudal overlordship. Such were possibly larger *demoi* such as Amarynthos, Styra, Zarex, Dystos, etc. Styra was still independent in the fifth century, and probably Zarex and Dystos as well. But Lefkandi, with its citadel and harbour and especially with its location in the middle of the richest agricultural and pastoral land on the island, seems early on to have assumed the principal hegemonial position.

Mele thinks that 'It does not seem doubtful, therefore, that the tradition concerning the Abantes represents a pan-Euboian ethnic unity and, at the same time it indicates, up to the first mention in Homer and Hesiod, the hegemony of Khalkis in this unity.'[164] We will shortly see that there are good reasons for doubting the primacy of Khalkis. He strongly supports the concept of Abantic unity in Euboia, but he assumes an Iron Age setting for this unit and incorporates within it the island of Skyros, which he believes was a 'colony of Khalkis' (founded by Abantes en route to Chios?). As is the case with the Kouretes, all our sources say only that the main territory of the Abantes in Euboia was on the Lelantine Plain itself, whence they extended their control over the whole island. They came from Phokis and Boiotia, seizing the coastal lands directly opposite.[165] The Euripos has in all ages been a relatively easy point of entry. Strabo[166] cites 'Aristotle', claiming that 'Abantes issued forth from Abai in Phokis and they proceeded to colonise Euboia and name the [existing] inhabitants Abantes' after themselves; he is supported in this opinion by Arrian.[167] Geyer,[168] too, thought that they were 'Archaeo-aeolians', originally from southern Thessaly and Phokis. In later times, the dialect of Phokis had Aeolic features.[169] Plutarch reports that the Ionians, 'Aiklos and Kothos, sons of Xouthos, came to Euboia to live at a time when Aeolians occupied the greater part of the island',[170] and it is clear from the context that he thought this Aeolian occupation was before the arrival of the brothers, who are said to have founded Eretria and Khalkis respectively. As sons of Xouthos, they were descendants of Erekhtheus of Athens by his daughter Kreousa and so 'brothers' of Ion, son of Kreousa and the god Apollo, who gave his name to the Ionians.[171] Ion in this tradition is said to be the father of Ellops. However, Xouthos, who represents an earlier generation, was son of Hellen and brother of Aiolos and Doros, eponymous heroes of the Hellenes, Aeolians and Dorians; in other words, they all precede Aiklos and Kothos. Strabo thought their names to be barbarian.[172] His mention of them occurs during his discussion of a Boiotian tribe, the Hyantes, within a general context of pre-Hellenic migrations of Epeirotes and Thessalians. Abai, for Strabo the putative homeland of the Abantes, was adjacent to their main settlement, Hyampolis. Later writers moreover never consider the Abantes to be Ionians.[173] We have noted that Aeolian speakers preceded Ionians in Chios, and that these were Abantes from Euboia. Thus, all our evidence suggests that the Abantes were Aeolic speakers.

But Abantia/Amantia, a district in Epeiros,[174] might also claim to be the original homeland of the Abantes given the many links between Euboia and Epeiros, particularly in view of Fossey's[175] assertion that the archaeological evidence indicates that Boiotian Abai was uninhabited until Geometric times. Another tradition makes them descendants of the Argive Abas, son of Lynkeus and Hyperm(n)estra, and there are still other genealogies in our sources, the most interesting, perhaps, being that Abas was the son of a certain Khalkon; was this an ancestor, or alternative form of Khalkodon? There is thus as much confusion of traditions concerning the origins of the Abantes as there is concerning all the early peoples of Euboia.[176]

The Eretrias in the Mycenaean Age (LH II/IIIC)

It was the Abantes who ruled Euboia during the Mycenaean Age, so it is appropriate that at this point I summarise what we can tease out of the evidence, archaeological and literary, concerning this period in Euboia, generally, and the Eretrias, in particular. Because the history of the settlement at Lefkandi (Figure 2.1) will figure importantly in the remainder of this chapter and in Chapters 3 and 4, two points of clarification need to be made at once, for I will argue that it was the 'capital' of the Abantic state. The ancient settlement lies on a promontory, today called Xeropolis (parched city), which juts out from the Lelantine Plain near the modern village of Lefkandi, between Khalkis and Eretria. The name 'Lefkandi' has been generally used in the literature to refer to the area where both settlement and cemeteries lay, whereas 'Xeropolis' is used of the settlement, exclusive of the cemeteries, on the headland. The geographer Strabo states that there had been an Old Eretria before the city of his day and that he had seen the ruins: 'they still point out the foundations. The place is called Old Eretria and the city of the present day was re-established.'[177] There appears nothing in the text to compel us to assume that this was on the same site. There has been much scholarly controversy as to the actual location of this 'Old' Eretria, with suggestions ranging from the Eretrian acropolis itself, or Amarynthos and Oikhalia east of Eretria, to Lefkandi to the west. Although there has been a shift recently from earlier 'certainty', I suspect that it is true that, often with reservations, many still hold the view, as I do myself, that Lefkandi is Old Eretria. Henceforth 'Eretria' unqualified signifies the settlement on the classical site, i.e. 'New' Eretria, while 'Lefkandi' always means de facto Old (i.e. pre-ninth century) Eretria. This is not to say that the abandoned settlement at Lefkandi was in fact what Strabo saw (or thought he saw), for his distances make that unlikely, but merely that, in the ninth century, a

Figure 2.1 The Xeropolis headland, Lefkandi, the site of the prehistoric settlement, from the west bay.

substantial body of refugees from Lefkandi migrated to the site of the later *polis* of Eretria and expanded the already existing small settlement there.

Lefkandi was certainly the most important town in Euboia, indeed one of the most significant in all Greece, from MH[178] to the sub-Mycenaean and early Iron Age. The inhabited area was 'approximately as extensive as the Citadel of Mycenae, and more than twice that of the Acropolis at Athens'.[179] It suffered the cycle of disasters and prosperity experienced by the island as a whole, but it differs from most other places in Greece following the collapse of Mycenaean civilisation, because it actually experienced something of a revival. On the other hand, there is little evidence of a sizeable settlement on the site of later Eretria before the ninth century, except perhaps during the EH, and there are only a few signs of a Helladic settlement at Khalkis,[180] although how extensive it may have been we still cannot say, because the modern city covers most of the evidence for all earlier periods, and it is unlikely that there will ever be systematic excavation. It is, however, safe to say that Lefkandi was the most important settlement on the island during this period.

The site of Lefkandi was occupied as early as the LN period,[181] well before the arrival of the Abantes, and the earliest evidence of settlement buildings comes from EH levels. The first (EH I/II) settlement was large, and made up of substantial buildings. The 'native EH pottery', which seems to have had Anatolian characteristics,[182] was succeeded by what the archaeologists describe as an 'alien' fabric 'unrelated' to the earlier EH ware.[183] We may keep in mind that J. Rutter argues that there was an invasion (technological, if not also military) of the Argolid from central Greece and Euboia.[184] I have already discussed[185] this later, 'alien' pottery, the so-called EH Gray-burnished ware. This new fabric is, in turn, the natural ancestor of the subsequent MH Gray Minyan ware, related to contemporary pottery on the mainland and so a sign of contact with other parts of Greece.[186]

During the MH, the settlement spread over the whole of the 'intensively occupied' Xeropolis hill. By the time of the Mycenaean acme (LH II/IIIA), the pottery had changed again, showing that Lefkandi was 'in touch with the main trend of Mycenaean developments, probably through connections with the nearby important centre of Thebes though it would be premature, with the small quantity of material yet recovered, to define how early or close this relationship might have been'.[187] Although there have as yet been no direct links to Lefkandi that can be detected in the Linear B dossier from Thebes, for we do not even know what the name of the settlement was in ancient times,[188] there are tablets that mention both Amarynthos and Karystos. Even as early as his 1964 thesis, Jacobsen was talking of extensive Euboian trade interchange with Thebes, especially via Khalkis, noting Amarynthos as a find site, although neither Lefkandi (where excavation only began in 1964) nor the evidence of the Theban LH IIIB sealings (the 'Of' group was found in 1964, the 'Wu' group in 1982) had yet been brought to light.[189] We must, if we accept the new, later, dating of the arrival of Greek speakers in Greece, assume that *c.* 1600 there was a change of inhabitants or, rather, their rulers. The new Mycenaean pottery of Lefkandi, similar to that at other Boiotian Mycenean sites, perhaps indicates an invasion by Theban Mycenaeans.

The excavators likewise could not know of the evidence of contacts between Euboia and Thebes that would later be provided by the Theban Linear B sealings. These prove that both the Eretrias and the Karystia were trading with, and probably dependent on, both economically and politically, the Mycenaean palace-kingdom at Thebes. It is thus quite improbable that Lefkandi was not also trading with Thebes. The great age of the palaces was LH II/IIIA and there are many sites in central Euboia that report surface finds from this period. But, unfortunately, no Mycenaean site on Euboia has yet been fully excavated. Lefkandi was certainly occupied during the Mycenean period, but in fact the findings from the excavations (for early levels these were from trial soundings only) are too few for firm conclusions. Desborough, also writing in 1964, observed that:

> So far as the Mycenaean period is concerned, one need do little more than refer to two accounts: the work of Papavasileiou . . . and the article by Mrs Hankey recording in full the excavations of Papavasileiou at the site of Trypa-Vromousa near Chalkis. This site is the only one both excavated and published.

Since then, there has been little systematic excavation on Bronze Age sites, except at Lefkandi. One of the few exceptions is the trial/rescue operation undertaken at Palaioekklisies Amarynthou in 1977 by L. Parlama.[190]

The civilisation that we call Mycenaean arose during LH I/II (1550–1400) and by the end of LH II it had embraced most of mainland Greece and was trading overseas, both in the East and the West. During LH II the Euripos was a major north/south trade artery between the Argolis and Thessaly, and undoubtedly Lefkandi played an important role as a transit point between this sea route and the overland way to central Boiotia and Thebes. Both Hammond and Jacobsen[191] believe that at least the central part of Euboia (including Khalkis and the Lelantine Plain) was under the control of the Theban *wanax*. In the meantime, any influence of Crete in central and northern Aegean trade had died out after LM II (ended *c.* 1380),[192] but there may have previously been a period when Euboia, and many other Aegean islands, were part of a Minoan thalassocracy.[193] The copper ingots from Cyprus (dated *c.* 1550) in the National Museum at Athens, found in the sea off modern Kimi, represent part of a flourishing Minoan/Mycenaean trade system.

In 1964, the 'Of' series of LH IIIB Linear B clay sealings were uncovered on the Kadmeia in Thebes and it included one with the toponym *a-ma-ru-to-de* (Amarunthon-de), Amarynthos, with the allative prepositional ending *de* (to).[194] Every tablet in the series is characterised by the ideogram 'LANA' (wool).[195] Chadwick initially wondered whether this was the 'well-known Amarynthos', or a hitherto unknown location in Boiotia. Why? He had in fact already noted that a small number of Mycenaean finds had been reported from Palaiokhora/Palaioekklisies (Figure 2.2),[196] now shown to be the site of the Artemision at Amarynthos by Knoepfler,[197] and concluded that control from Thebes reached to the south coast of Euboia and that the Artemision there was recipient of the consignment of wool listed in the document. This by itself would not be sufficient evidence to postulate Theban control over the Eretrias, but, in 1982, a further cache, the 'Wu' series, was discovered,[198] including two more seals[199] that confirm and extend Chadwick's theory. Wu 58 (γ) once more has *a-ma-ru-to* (Amarynthos) while Wu 55 (β) has *ka-ru-to* (Karystos) as the places from which the sealed consignments had been sent.[200] The contents are unknown, although the ideogram 'SUS' on both documents may indicate consignments of pelts.[201] However, the 'pig' ideogram may suggest a relationship with the nearby Eretrian deme Khoireai; the area was possibly famous for wild boar and other game animals and later writers mention pig products in relation to Euboia.[202] The latter consignments bring to mind the Euboian pigskin cloaks that Pausanias noted. We have contemporary archaeological evidence for Euboian trade with the much more distant Egypt (eighteenth dynasty) and the Levantine interior.[203] The toponym *ka-ru-to* (a *hapax* in the Linear B corpus) clearly indicates that Theban commercial intercourse extended to Karystos, in the very south-east of Euboia.[204] Thus, in the thirteenth century[205] trading activity was taking place between south-central Euboia and Thebes.

But Chadwick also reports on another two sealings,[206] which have a place

Figure 2.2 The headland of Palaioekklisies, thought to be the site of prehistoric Amarynthos.

name, *a-ki-a*$_2$*-ri-ja* (Of 25.1), also spelt *a*$_3$*-ki-a*$_2$*-ri-ja-de* with allative *-de* (Of 35.2), and says that this must represent */Aigihaliān-de/*, that 'both [forms] must be derivatives of *aigialos* (beach), and the form does little to assist the etymology, except that the use of *-a*$_3$*-* confirms that the second part of the compound begins *hal-*, suggesting that it is from ἅλς. No such place name seems to be recorded in Boeotia or Euboea . . . One would naturally assume that "the coast" to a Theban would be the east coast facing Euboea.'[207] I have been asked by Dr Parker: 'Why not on the Gulf of Corinth? Any town on a sea-beach can be named "sea-beach."' [208] However, I agree with Chadwick to the extent that the coastal site would most likely have been that on the Euboian Gulf rather than on the Corinthian. I have already mentioned more than once the importance of the Euboian Gulf as a very ancient and major trade route and its significance will yet again be referred to in a later Eretrian–Athenian context. It leads out to the east and south, and while certainly Mycenaean trade with the West did take place, commerce with the East was much more important. Besides, there is the evidence of the other Euboian toponyms. Nevertheless, it was not, in my opinion, on the Boiotian, but on the Euboian, coast.

Chadwick is apparently unaware of the Eretrian deme Aigale, probably that called Aigilea by Herodotos, as one of the locations, along with Temenos and Khoireai with which it is contextually linked and which are all attested epigraphically as demes of Eretria,[209] where the Persians disembarked prior to attacking Eretria in 490, and which was therefore on the coast of the Eretrias.[210] Its mention with Khoireai reminds us of the contents sign of the consignments, while Temenos suggests a link with the Eretrian sanctuary par excellence, that of Artemis Amarysia at Amarynthos.[211] Wallace[212] locates both Khoireai and Temenos on the plain east of Mt Kotylaion, while both Gehrke and Knoepfler[213] place them further west and closer to Eretria, on the Eretrian–Amarynthian plain near Magoula *c.* 4 km east of Eretria, the find-place of a tombstone for a man from the deme Tem (*IG* XII 9, 772).

Why then, since we already have two toponyms (Amarynthos; Karystos) unambiguously belonging to central and south-eastern Euboia, coastal moreover, should we not identify *Aigihalian-de* with Aigale/Aigilea? Taken all together, they imply significant contact between Thebes and the south-east of Euboia, which involved, on the evidence of the seals, doubtful though the precise interpretation of the designatory ideograms may be, trade in livestock, animal skins and fleeces that were then returned as woven fabric along with, presumably, other manufactured goods.

This trading activity, combined with the literary evidence of Abantic occupation of the Lelantine Plain and the possible later counter-occupation of Thebes by Euboian Abantes (see p. 53), along with the discovery at Lefkandi and the above-mentioned sites of Mycenaean pottery, with affinities to that produced at Thebes, all lead me to the conclusion that Lefkandi was conquered by Mycenaeans from Thebes. This conquest occurred in mid-LH IIIB if we accept, as we should, the dating of the seals by Chadwick. The territory they ruled from there extended over both the Eretrias and the Karystia, or at least the coastal plains bordering the south Euboian Gulf.[214] I believe that Lefkandi became the 'capital' of the Mycenaean 'province' on Euboia and of the native Abantic polity that succeeded it in LH IIIC2,[215] because of not only its undoubted size and wealth, but also the repeated assertion that the Lelantine was the base of both the Abantes and the Kouretic peoples. Also in favour of viewing Lefkandi as the Mycenaean/Abantic capital is the close proximity of historical Khalkis (and Eretria), something that would explain the literary confusion, since not much would have been visible on the site of Lefkandi by Strabo's or Plutarch's times.

Jacobsen held that Thebes fell in LH IIIA and that its fall is reflected both in the decline in the number of finds at Khalkis and in the absence of Thebes itself in the Homeric *Catalogue of the Achaians*.[216] But, on his own admission,[217] the state of excavation of Mycenaean sites in Euboia when he wrote was very haphazard, and any attempt to set a firm dating from the then available archaeological data was risky. Moreover, Oikhalia in the Eretrias was still flourishing at the beginning of LH IIIA but destroyed afterwards ('by Herakles'). If the Trojan War is to be assigned to LH IIIB, then presumably its destruction occurred before then, thus explaining its absence from the Homeric *Catalogue* and the involvement of Herakles in the story. This is Jacobsen's view. However, the Trojan War is rather to be dated *c.* 1200, i.e. the end of IIIB.[218] Thus, I will for the present hold to the dating of the Linear B nodules as a more reliable guide to the likely period of the Mycenaean trade 'empire' in south-eastern Euboia, and that this ended with the fall of Thebes *c.* 1200, which moreover is approximately when the destruction of Iolkos took place.[219] Thus, Theban/Mycenaean rule in Euboia must be placed between *c*. 1325 and 1200 (mid-LH IIIA to near the end of LH IIIC).

Who then were these Mycenaean Lefkandiots? Were they foreign overlords ruling a population conquered earlier in the thirteenth century? Jacobsen's maps (12a/12b: Mycenaean habitation/burial sites in Euboia), and his descriptions of the sites where Mycenaean remains have been found,[220] show quite clearly a strong concentration in central Euboia, a few in the south, and almost nothing north of Politika. He lists nine habitation sites for the Eretrias alone (out of only twenty-three for all Euboia, including Lefkandi) and eight tombs (of a total of twelve) of the LH,[221] making it clearly the most thickly settled by 'Mycenaeans' on the island by far. The regional capital of a local *basileus*, subordinate to the *hegemon-wanax* at Lefkandi, was probably at Palaioekklisies (ancient Amarynthos),[222] a site where remains (including architectural) dating from LN to Byzantine have been found and which show 'that the hill was the most important prehistoric settlement of the Eretrian plain.'[223] Certainly, it was a major settlement before the eighth century: 'The excavation . . . revealed walls of EH buildings and part of a strong wall, probably a circuit wall. The pottery found is dated mainly to EH II and III periods.'[224] We may also assume that such *basileis* resided at other places such as Karystos and Khalkis, as well as at Histiaia and Kerinthos in the north, since they are all mentioned in Homer's Abantic Euboian catalogue, although Amarynthos is not. That the Eretrias and Karystia must have been part of the area of Mycenaean overlordship in Euboia is clear from the three toponyms that appear in the Theban seals.

If we combine the archaeological data with the description in the *Iliad* of the status of Elephenor Khalkodontiades as *hegemon* of all Euboia and the evidence of Theban trade contacts, we are left with the impression that a group, possibly of relatively limited numbers, had entered Euboia across the narrows (there is a second narrows, nearer Lefkandi, that is a less hazardous crossing than the Euripos) and established themselves firmly at Lefkandi. They subsequently extended their hegemony over lesser rulers and peoples in the more remote areas to the north and south and were strong enough to be able to demand levies to go to Ilion. Thus, we may compare them to the Norman overlords in England in the two centuries following the conquest of 1066. In fact, trade links between Euboia and Troy had already existed from the EH: 'The Trojans sent their typical tall jugs and the famous *depas* westward too – the jugs to Euboia, the *depas* to Syros and Orchomenos, although one cannot be sure how late in the millennium this happened.'[225] Pottery with Trojan (Troy II/III) affinities was found in the remains of the earliest settlement at Lefkandi.[226] Euboians certainly already knew about Ilion, and later the epic of Homer would have found an appreciative audience.

In the context of Theban/Mycenaean rule in Euboia, we may consider the significance of the name Elephenor. If Mastrocinque[227] is right that the

Abantic hairstyle implies that the warriors so distinguished must have fought bare-headed, then they were probably not typical Mycenaean warrior chiefs, for the helmet, especially of the type fashioned from boar tusks, seems to have been one of the distinguishing pieces of armour worn by Mycenaean heroes. But, there may indeed be a link between this type of helmet and the status of the Abantic rulers of Euboia. Elephenor's name is derived from *elephas,* which in Homer only ever means ivory.[228] Perhaps what distinguished the leaders/rulers of the Abantic/Euboian contingent in the Trojan War was their typical Mycenaean boar's tusk helmet. That is, it was the distinguishing 'badge' of the Mycenaean nobles, just as the hairstyle was that of their Abantic subjects. If so, the Homeric Abantic chiefs of Euboia, remembered by later traditions, were a Mycenaean ruling class, originally from Thebes,[229] who invaded *c.* 1380, settling first on the Lelantine Plain and in the Eretrias, and thereafter proceeding to bring the rest of the island and its peoples under their hegemony, including the long-established indigenous local population within whose name they were later subsumed but upon whom they subsequently conferred their aura of glory.

That the Abantic ruler was called *hegemon* in the *Iliad* and not *wanax* was probably because of his subordinate status to the Theban *wanax*. But a passage from Plutarch, already referred to for Khalkodon, father of Elephenor, as *basileus* of the Euboians, says that Thebes was at some time actually ruled from Khalkis and that: 'Amphiktyon came to the city of the Thebans and finding them tributaries of the Khalkidians, freed them from the tribute by killing Khalkodon, king of the Euboians.' [230] Pausanias tells more or less the same story, that Khalkodon was killed by Amphytrion in a battle between Thebans and Euboians.[231] Amphytrion is wrongly called Amphiktyon by Plutarch. But even if we were to take this story at face value, it is hard to imagine such a rapid transformation in the fortunes of the Khalkodontid rulers from a catastrophic loss of sovereignty over Thebes, and the death of Khalkodon in the process, to the hegemonial status of his son, who raises and leads the whole of the Euboian levies to Troy! On the other hand, Homer tells of the *wanax* Mekisteus going to Thebes after the fall of Oedipus and defeating all the Kadmeiones.[232] He was the son of Talaos whose wife Lysimakhe was a daughter of Abas, eponym of the Abantes, and was the eponym of the epigraphically attested Eretrian tribe Mekistis. These stories may, however, preserve a faint memory of a short period, during which Lefkandi was a residual outpost of Mycenaean power following the fall of the palace at Thebes and perhaps a takeover, albeit brief, of the fallen city.[233] Indeed, as we shall see in the next chapter, Lefkandi experienced a notable revival of prosperity immediately after the disaster that overwhelmed Thebes, although there were no similar revivals at other mainland sites.

The fame of the Abantes persisted into later times as a consequence of the comparative magnitude of the civilisation represented by the Mycenaean elite on the island and by the Mycenaeans generally in Greece, and the universal popularity of the Homeric poems that celebrate them. When their rule collapsed in Euboia following the fall of Thebes, indicated by evidence of destruction at Lefkandi,[234] the memory of these powerful Mycenaean overlords would have long remained in the Euboian popular and epic imagination. In many places throughout Greece, including some not very far from Euboia (Orkhomenos and Thebes in Boiotia; Menidi in Attica), hero-shrines and associated cults were established at large and impressive 'royal' Mycenaean tombs. Through these, reverence for the representatives of the past glorious age was immortalised, and a similar process was probably responsible for the perpetuation of the glory of the Abantes.[235] Henceforth, the shaven forehead and long, back-flowing locks,[236] the distinctive warrior symbol of the local Abantic inhabitants who now resumed control in central Euboia, free of their Theban overlords but inheriting their glory, was attributed by later poets to most of the inhabitants of the island who came before and after them, rather as the name Pelasgoi was applied for the same reasons to other peoples, as described by Ephoros: 'They chose a military life and influencing many peoples to the same lifestyle, they conferred their name to all and thus acquired much glory.'[237]

The Ionians

Since the Abantes were not Ionic speakers, as Herodotos and Thucydides explicitly say, there must have been at least one more population influx, because the island in classical times was regarded as completely Ionian north of the Karystia.[238] The Ionian invasion would have occurred in the late eleventh or tenth centuries.[239] I have already suggested that this may be represented in the tradition by the arrival of the brothers of Ion, Kothos and Aiklos, the legendary founders of Khalkis and Eretria respectively. One variant makes them founders, en route to Euboia, of Eleutherai on the Attic–Boiotian border,[240] while both Strabo and Plutarch[241] have them coming directly to Euboia from Athens itself. There were persistent claims throughout antiquity of early Athenian/Ionian colonisation of Euboia (at Eretria, Khalkis and Histiaia in particular), which are usually explained as propaganda invented to bolster Athenian claims to control of the island after its conquest in 446 by Perikles. This is very likely, but for any propaganda to be credible, there must have been some element of accepted truth behind the claims, so that there may well have been a prior tradition of Ionian penetration of Euboia from Attica, which was taken up and exploited by the Athenians. There were Attic demes 'of the Histiaians', and according to Strabo, 'of the Eretrians': 'Some say that Histiaia was colonised by Athenians from the [Attic] deme of the Histiaians, as Eretria was from that of the Eretrians.'[242] It was from these two places that Aiklos and Kothos were believed to have set out. While the deme Histiaieis is attested epigraphically, there is no such confirmation of that 'of the Eretrians'.[243] There was, however, a major shrine to the goddess Artemis Amarysia in the Attic deme Athmonon, still today called Marousi,[244] from her epithet, whose cult came at an early time from Eretrian Amarynthos to Attica according to Strabo, so he was perhaps thinking of Athmonon as the Eretrian deme. If this tradition means anything, it is a vague remembrance of an incursion of Ionians from the borderlands between Attica and Boiotia centred on Eleutherai, which entered Euboia near Khalkis and spread from there: one band of invaders, under Kothos, occupied Khalkis, while the other, under Aiklos, moved into the Eretrias.

Since 1954/5 and the work of Porzig and Risch,[245] modern linguistic opinion has moved away somewhat from the nineteenth-century view that the various Greek dialects were brought by successive waves of invaders. The latter scholar argued that, in the LH, there were only two dialects and that Ionic, for example, developed when the dialect of the area south of central Greece was influenced by speakers from the north, and that in similar fashion, Aeolic arose in eastern Thessaly from the reverse interaction, from south to north.[246] Thus, according to him, all later dialects emerged from the original two, which themselves had evolved from an original proto-Greek. Drews has set out the consequences of these new linguistic ideas for the older 'wave' theory.[247] Nevertheless, it seems to me that for the kind of interaction between 'north' and 'south' dialects required by these scholars, a considerable intermingling of a kind that would follow the invasion of territory, already occupied by speakers of an alternative speech type, would be necessary, so that we do not have to completely abandon the idea of people moving, often across considerable distances, into new homelands. By the historical period, all Euboia north of the Karystia was speaking a purely Ionian dialect[248] – or rather, not quite all. There is one more hint of a prehistoric influx of people into Euboia.

Migrants from Triphylia and Elis

Strabo, in fact, presents both the alternative traditions (Athenian and Eleian) of the founding of Eretria: 'Some say that Eretria was colonised from Makistos in Triphylia [on the border between Elis and Messenia] by Eretrieus, but others say from the Eretria at Athens, which is now a market centre.'[249] This Eleian connection is exclusively Eretrian and is not associated with any other place in Euboia. Much cult and mythology, associated particularly with the Eretrias, has close links with these western Peloponnesian regions.[250] Töpffer has suggested a confluence of migrating tribes from the west in the area of Boiotia around the River Asopos but he includes people from Thessaly and the Argolis as well. He dates this to *c.* 1400.[251]

The supporting evidence for an Eleian origin of at least some of the Eretrians is that first, there was, in historical times, a tribe at Eretria called Mekistis,[252] whose eponym was a hero called Mekisteus-stos (Doric: Makisteus-stos), for whom the literary tradition provides a number of candidates, including the sacker of Oikhalia, Herakles himself.[253] But Themelis believes that in the tribal name 'Mekistis',[254] along with the 'Abantis' *phyle* in Khalkis, we have the survival of pre-*polis* ethnic divisions, i.e. those who came from Makistos in Triphylia and Abai in Phokis.[255]

Second, the dialect spoken in Eretria in historic times is characterised by rhotacism, the substitution of rho for intervocalic sigma,[256] and even, possibly, of final sigma in speech, though not apparently in writing, since it does not, strictly speaking, occur in any inscription. Plato, however: 'While we say sklerotes, the Eretrians say skleroter' and Strabo: 'they often used the letter *rho* not only at the end of words but medially [and so] they were mocked in comedies' both noted it,[257] while in a few cases it occurs between consonant and vowel.[258] Eretria shares rhotacism with both Elis (though in Eleian it was, without exception, final, and never medial) and the area around Oropos, located on the coast of Boiotia and Attica opposite Eretria itself and which was originally a colony of Eretria.[259] Oropos is also linked to Elis, through the myth of Eunostos, referred to by Plutarch.[260] The father of this haughty youth from Tanagra near Oropos was named Elieus, whom D. Roller thinks was 'possibly connected with the nearby town of Eleon'[261] on the banks of the River Asopos. However, the name may equally well be associated with immigrants from Elis. The dialect may have gone at an early time from Euboia to the West, as is perhaps implied by Rutter.[262] It used to be thought that rhotacism was late in coming to both Eretria and Elis,[263] but it is certainly attested inscriptionally at Eretria for the sixth century, indeed in the very decree mentioning the tribe Mekistis, dated by most commentators to the early fifth, but for which I shall argue later a late-sixth-century date on both epigraphical and political grounds,[264] in the agonistic epigram of the mid-sixth[265] and in an inscription from the deme Zarex of the late sixth century.[266] This, with later examples from Styra and Tamynai,[267] suggests that it was already present in the speech of sixth-century Eretrians and that the practice was not just a city affectation but continued as a feature of the dialect even of some south-eastern demes of the Eretrias. It was apparently a source of amusement and mockery for outsiders, as we have seen, for the Eretrians apparently used it excessively in their speech. Strabo blamed the Elean connection.[268] This may explain its grudgingly inconsistent use in public inscriptions after the great age of Eretria in the late sixth/early fifth centuries, that is, a form of cultural cringe by people trying, in the face of political decline, to write in the Attic manner.[269]

If it was not the Eleans who brought in the idiosyncracy, it is impossible to say with which other known group of people it did come. Perhaps the Eleians were an isolated band somehow forced out of their western homeland, who wandered eastward pausing at Oropos and who may then have crossed the Gulf and settled in Lefkandi. If so, the speech practice spread from there to both Khalkis and Eretria, following the destruction of the settlement, for Knoepfler suggests that it may have been a feature of the dialect in the territory of Khalkis, though he admits that the evidence on which to base this belief is rather slight. We should take note of his comments concerning Eretrian linguistic habits among the population living on the formerly Eretrian side of the Lelantine Plain. Though rhotacism was generally perceived as a peculiarly Eretrian phenomenon, Suidas notes under the entry *khalkidizein* (to play/imitate the Khalkidian) that: 'as regards rhotacism, they, along with the Eretrians seem to have used *rho* excessively, inserting it instead of *sigma*.'[270] That it survived more persistently in the speech of the later Eretrians may be because many more Lefkandiot refugees ended up in Eretria, while those who chose to live under Khalkidian rule were most probably landowners who stayed on their Lelantine lands. Indeed rhotacism is so slightly attested inscriptionally for later Khalkis that it may have been the dialect practice of only a limited area, the eastern (Lefkandiot) part of the Lelantine Plain. Alternatively, the inscriptions Knoepfler cites may have been set up by people from Eretria living in Khalkis. There is some, very slight, external support for Khalkidian rhotacism: a name dated *c.* 475–50 from Rhegion, a Khalkidian colony, rhotacised Thrarus from Thrasus.[271]

Notes

1 Excavation reports for sites in Euboia of all periods may be found in the annual *Archaeological Reports* (*AR*), a supplement of the *Journal of Hellenic Studies* (*JHS*) and the *Chronique des fouilles*, published in the *Bulletin de Correspondance Héllenique* (*BCH*), together with those in the *Arkhaiologikon Deltion* (*AD*), the *Arkhaiologike Ephemeris* (*AE*), the *Praktika tes en Athenais Arkhaiologikes* (*H*)*etaireias* (*PAAE*). The reader may consult also T. Jacobsen, *Prehistoric Euboea*, PhD thesis, University of Pensylvania, Philadelphia, 1964 (with maps etc.); L. Sackett *et al.*, 'Prehistoric Euboea: contributions towards a survey', *BSA* 61, 1966, 33–112; D. Leekley and N. Efstratiou, *Archaeological Excavations in Central and Northern Greece*, Park Ridge, NJ, 1980, 57–73 (Euboia); R. Hope-Simpson, *Mycenaean Greece*, Park Ridge, NJ, 1981, 51–7; 82–4; map B, (42); and A. Sampson, 'Euboea: prehistoric sites and settlements in Euboea', *AEM* 23, 1980, all of which provide summaries of excavation sites over the whole island, showing when each was inhabited and the nature of the archaeological evidence up to the time of publication. Specifically for Eretria there are the various papers and reports published since 1964 in *Antike Kunst* (*AK*). For the late-nineteenth-century excavations, the American reports may be found in the *American Journal of Archaeology* (*AJA*) [some issued separately in *Papers of the American School of Classical Studies at Athens* (*PASCl.St.*) 1890–97]; for Tharrounia, A. Sampson, Σκοτεινή Θαρρουνίων. Το σπήλαιο, ο οικισμός και το νεκροταφείο, Athens, 1993 (with English and French summaries); for Kyme, idem, Εὐβοϊκὴ Κύμη, Athens, 1981a (English summary); for the Neolithic and proto-Helladic in Euboia, idem, Ἡ Νεολιθικὴ καὶ ἡ Πρωτοελλαδικὴ I στὴν Εὔβοια, 1981; for the early and middle Bronze Age settlement at Kaloyerovrisi (on the borders of the Eretrias and the territory of Khalkis), idem, Καλογεροβρύση. Ἕνας οἰκισμὸς τῆς Πρώιμης καὶ Μέσης Χαλκοκρατίας στὰ Φύλλα τῆς Εὐβοίας, Athens, 1993 (English summary); for the proto-Helladic site at Manika in the territory of Khalkis, the volumes of idem Μάνικα· μιὰ Πρωτοελλαδικὴ πόλη στὴ Χαλκίδα, Athens, 1985 et seq. (English summaries).

2 Hdt. 1, 56–7. Geyer 1903, 37; cf. Jacobsen, 1964.

3 Str. 10, 3, 1 C462; see also 10, 3, 19 C472; 10, 3. 3 C464; 10, 3, 6 C465. Cf. S. Bommelje, 'Aeolis in Aetolia: Th. III, 102.5 and the origins of the Aetolian "Ethnos"', *Historia* 37, 1988, 300; bibliography in his n. 9.

4 Str. 10, 3, 6 C465. For an extensive treatment of the Kouretes and Kouretic rituals: H. Jeanmaire, *Couroi et Courètes: essai sur l'education spartiate et sur les rites d'adolescence dans l'antiquité hellénique*, Lille/New York, 1938/1975.

5 Epaphroditos ap. St. Byz. s.v. Αἴδηψος. Str. 10, 3, 19 C472 repeats this tradition. For an explanation of the association of central Euboia and Khalkis with bronze working, see Chapter 5, pp. 160–1.

6 For the many Epeirote toponymic links with Euboia: N. Hammond, 'Prehistoric Epirus and the Dorian invasion', *BSA* 32, 1931/32, 131–79: For the literary evidence for pre-Dorians: 147–55; Ellopians: 140; the Homeric Perrhaiboi and Enienes of Dodona: 148–9. (Hom. *Il.* 2, 749–50). There was an Eretrian deme ἐξ 'Ενι.; but see Knoepfler 1997, 356 and nn. 34–5. Wallace 1947, 138 tentatively suggests that ἐξ 'Ενι. lay between Dystos and Styra. N. Hammond, *Epirus. The Geography, the Ancient Remains, the History and the Topography of Epirus and Adjacent Areas*, Oxford, 1967, 386: 'It is beyond doubt that some of these legends originated at a date much earlier than the classical period.' There was possibly also an Eretrian deme called Akheron (though doubted by Wallace 1947, 144–5 and Knoepfler 1997, 355–6 and n. 31). A Lelante was wife of Mynikhos, king of the Molossoi. For Io/Euboia and Ionian Sea: Hes. fr. 47. For Dodona: Plin. *HN* 4, 53; R. Beaumont, 'Greek influences in the Adriatic', *JHS* 56, 1936, 169–70; 198–9; 204, etc. D. Evangelidis, Οἱ 'Αρχαῖοι Κάτοικοι τῆς 'Ηπείρου και ἄλλα Μελετήματα, Ioannina, 1962, 18–9; 77, identifies the Kouretes with the priests of Dodonaian Zeus, the Selloi. Plin. *HN* 4, 2 lists an Epeirote tribe called Hellopes (Ellopes).

7 Διὸς κοῦροι. For the text, translation and commentary: J. Harrison, *Themis. A Study of the Social Origins of Greek Religion*, London, 1963, 6–12; and J. Powell and E. Barber, *New Chapters in Greek Literature. Recent Discoveries in Greek Poetry and Prose of the Fourth and Following Centuries*, New York, 1974, 50–4 (translation and commentary). M. West, 'The Diktaean Hymn to the Kouros', *JHS* 85, 1965, 149–59.

8 C. M. Bowra, 'A Cretan Hymn', in M. Kelly (ed.), *For Service to Classical Studies. Essays in honour of Francis Letters*, Melbourne, 1966, 31–46.

9 'Ενιαυτὸς κοῦρος.

10 *IG* XII 9, 263 (from a shrine of the *phyle* Mekistis?).

11 *IG* XII Suppl. 549: Μηκισ⟨σ⟩τ[ιδ] | ος φυλῆς. Apart from Zeus himself, the eponymous Mekisteus might be: (1) son of Talaos and Lysimakhe (daughter of Abas, eponym of Abai in Phokis, whence the Abantes), brother of Adrastos, one of the Seven at Thebes; (2) (unlikely) a son of Lykaion; (3) Herakles, who had this by-name in Elis (schol. Tzetzes ad Lyc. *Alex.* 651; Str. 8, 3, 21 C348) – he was, according to some ancients, the first and greatest of the Daktyloi/Kouretes (Harrison 1963, 370–2); or (4) an otherwise unknown Eretrian figure.

12 *Roscher* s.v. Karystos (with refs). R. Schumacher, 'Three related sanctuaries of Poseidon: Geraistos, Kalaureia and Tainaron', in Marinatos, N. and Hågg, R. (eds), *Greek Sanctuaries. New Approaches*, London, 1993, 63.

13 For Zeus Tamynaios: St. Byz. Τάμυνα· πόλις 'Ερετρίας . . . οὕτω γὰρ ὁ Ζεὺς ἐν αὐτῇ τιμᾶται with Meineke's commentary. There was also (later?) a cult of Apollo at Tamynai (*IG* XII 9, 90–95a). For Dryopians and the worship of Apollo: Paus. 4, 34, 10; Str. 10, 1, 6 C446. For Apollo and Zeus elsewhere in the south-east of the Eretrias: *IG* XII 9, 53; 54; 58; 59 (Styra); and W. Forrest, 'The First Sacred War', *BCH* 80, 1956, 46. For locations: Wallace 1947, 138 and Fig. 1, 131; Knoepfler 1997, 368 and n. 141; 402 map.

14 Wallace 1947, 131; 136–7; Knoepfler 1997, 378, n. 214; *AR* 1978/9, 9 (but see A. Wilhelm's doubts concerning Zeus Soter at Karystos: 'Εὐβοϊκά', *AE* 1912, 236–9). Zeus and Dryopians are associated in many places even in the Peloponnese: St. Byz. s.v. Νεμέα says that Nemea was Dryopian and refers to Nemean Zeus. Nemea was not far from other Dryopian settlements in the Argolis (see p. 40). So, was Zeus a Dryopian god par excellence?

15 Th. 7, 57, 4. Hdt. 1, 146; 8, 46. On Dryopians in Euboia, see below, pp. 39–41.

16 Amarynthia is an alternative (non-Eretrian) name for Amarysia, derived from the location of her great temple at Amarynthos, or from its eponymous hero; it is the name used by Strabo and Livy (see below, n. 63).

17 Str. 10, 3, 19 C472. K. Kourouniotis, ''Επιγραφαὶ Χαλκίδος και 'Ερετρίας', *AE* 1899, 143. *IG* XII 9, 269: ἱερὸν Κουροτρόφων. Perhaps it is to Apollo, Artemis (as Eileithyia) and Leto. See generally on *kourotrophoi*: J. Harrison, 'The Kouretes and Zeus Kouros: a study in pre-historic sociology', *BSA* 15, 1908/9, 308–38; T. Hadzisteliou-Price, *Kourotrophos: Cults and Representations of the Greek Nursing Deities*, Leiden, 1978: Pt I, Ch. 5 (*Kourotrophoi*-types); Pt II, Chs 12–3 (Boiotia; Euboia); Pt IV, Ch. 20 (cult).

18 As a symbol of bravery: Eust. *ad Hom. Il. pertin.* 282, 8–10 (on l. 542). As the 'Euboian/Abantic' style: ibid. 282, 9; A. Mastrocinque, 'La 'Kourá' degli Eubei e la Guerra lelantea', *Athenaeum* 58, 1980, 460–2; S. Marinatos, 'Kleidung Haar und Barttracht', *Arch.Hom.* I B, 1967, 15; see the diagrams of a Cypriot Geometric clay tripod and a painted vase from Mouliana, Crete in ibid. 16. A. Brelich, *Guerre, Agone e Culti nella Grecia arcaica*, Bonn, 1961, 9–10; associated with the Abantes (and even the Ellopians: Nonn. *D.* 13, 166). Cf. the isolated mention of the Abantic hairstyle as effeminate in Dion Chrysostom 2, 12.

19 Plut. *Thes.* 5; 35; Hom. *Il.* 2, 536–49; Paus. 1, 17, 6. A. Mele, 'I caratteri della società eretriese arcaica', *Cahiers du Centre Jean Bérard*, II, Naples, 1975, 19–20. Theseus is also said to have sought refuge on Skyros, traditionally a colony of Khalkis: Ps.-Skymn. 184. Was it founded by the Abantes en route to Ilion?

20 τροφέες τε καὶ αὖτ' ὀλετῆρες (38, 14).

21 Mythical priests of Kybele/Rhea in Phrygia, whose rituals included frenzied dancing to drums and cymbals and associated with Hekate (*RE* s.v.), a goddess closely akin and related to Eretrian Amarysia. They were identified with the Sali in Rome (D.H. *Ant.Rom.* 1, 61; 2, 70–1; Eust. *ad Hom. Il. pert.* 1204; Serv. *in Verg. Aen.* 8, 285.

22 On the Kabeiroi: P. Rodhakis, Τὰ Καβείρια Μυστήρια, Athens, 1997.

23 The *locus classicus* is Str. 7 fr. 50 (51), where Kabeiroi, Korybantes, Kouretes and Idaioi Daktyloi are all identified. For Herakles, as first of the Daktyloi/Kouretes, see above n. 11; the Kouretes as sons of the Daktyloi: *D.S.* 5, 65, 1. See also Harrison 1963, 26–7; 62; 107; 370–6; Jacobsen 1964, 14 ; *RE* s.v. Kureten.

24 *IG* XII 9, 259; *IG* XII Suppl., p. 184.

25 Ll. 18–22. On culture heroes generally: Harrison 1908/9, 27.

26 For the Idaioi Daktyloi as servants of the Phrygian Magna Mater (Adrasteia): schol. *AR* 1, 1126. On the Magna Mater: E. James, *The Cult of the Mother Goddess*, London, 1959, Chs V–VI; C. Kerényi, *The Gods of the Greeks*, New York, 1960, 84–5. For Rhea as Artemis (etc.): P. Streep, *Sanctuaries of the Goddess*, Boston, 1994. The identification with the Phrygian goddess is a result of Asian influences coming in during the the fourth century to which the inscription belongs.

27 See Ch. 3, pp. 85–6 and Ch. 4, pp. 91, 95, 104–5, 107.

28 Note also the *phyle* name Narkittis (the narcissus flower). D. Knoepfler, 'Le héros Narkittos et le système tribal d'Erétrie' in M. Bats and B. d'Agostino, *EUBOICA. L'Eubea e la presenza euboica in Calcida e in Occidente*, Naples 1998, 105–8. Knoepfler (1997, 376–7 and nn.) sees Artemis in the role of *polis* guardian when he attributes to her the epithets Phylake and Metaxy (she who guards the city and she who stands between the factions). See below, nn. 87–9, on Narkissos and the flower.

29 'Die Hauptgöttin von Euböa': M. Nilsson, *Griechische Feste von religiöser Bedeutung, mit Außchluss der attischen*, Leipzig, 1906/1957, 238.

30 Paus. 4, 32, 9.

31 Serv. *in Verg. Aen.*, 3, 131: 'Curetes primi cultores Cretæ esse dicuntur.'

32 Ch. 4, pp. 107–9, 113.

33 For Dryopian Amarynthos/Aristaios: *LIMC* II 603–7 (especially the list of sources); *RE* s.v. Keos. I. Psyllas, 'Ιστορία τῆς Νήσου Κέας, ἀπὸ τῶν 'Αρχαιοτάτων Χρόνων μέχρι τῶν καθ' ὑμᾶς, Athens(?), 1920/1992, 13–21. Zeus had the epithet 'Amarios' (from ἀμαρύς, 'boundless': *LSJ* s.v.).

34 Schol. *AR* 2, 527; he was also associated with Kyrene in Libya (see Ch. 5, pp. 151–2, for Euboians in Africa).

35 *AR* 4, 1131.

36 K. Kourouniotis, ''Εκ τοῦ ἱεροῦ τῆς 'Αμαρυσίας'Αρτέμιδος', *AE* 1900, coll. 19–21, Fig. 1. C. Vial (a summary of the presentation of D. Knoepfler's thesis), 'La cité de Ménédème', *Revue Historique*, 108[272], 1984, 241–5.

37 Boardman 1957, 27 and pl. C12; also Knoepfler 1988, 242.

38 See Harrison 1963, 268–75.

39 For Ktesios (protector of house and property) as a snake: M. Nilsson, 'Schlagenstele des Zeus Ktesios', *AM* 33, 1908, 279; Harrison 1963, 297 (illustration).

40 Schol. Theocr. 2, 12: τῇ Δήμητρι μιχθεῖς ὁ Ζεὺς τεκνοῖ 'Εκάτη. . .καὶ νῦν ῎Αρτεμις καλεῖται και Φυλακή and schol. E. *Med.* 397: ὅταν μὲν ᾖ τριῶν ἡμερῶν, Σελήνη ὀνομάζεται, ὅταν δὲ ἕξ, ῎Αρτεμις, ὅταν δὲ δεκαπέντε 'Εκάτη (when she was Selene for three days, Artemis for six and Hekate for fifteen). See *RE* s.v. Hekate: with Zeus (2772); and oracles of the dead (2781).

41 Artemis was very much a *kourotrophos*, often identified with Eileithyia, not least in Eretria: *IG* XII 9, 258; *IG* XII Suppl. 559; 572 and 560 cf. D. Knoepfler, 'Dédicaces érétriennes à Ilithyie', *AK* 33, 1990b, 115–27; P. Themelis, ''Ερετριακά', *AE* 1969a, 149, mentions a Mycenaean O-type figurine from Eretria identified as a θείαν τροφὸν of a type beginning in LH II.

42 Str. 10, 1, 10 C448. Modern Amarynthos is in fact about 10.5 km from Eretria and D. Knoepfler, 'Sur les traces de l' Artemision d' Amarynthos pres de l' Eretrie', *CRAI* 1988, 420–1, has vindicated Strabo by a simple correction of the ancient alphabetic notation from Ζ´ (7) to Ξ´ (60) Attic stades of 177.7 m.

43 See pp. 107–9.

44 The Artemisia. The Athenian Χύτραι (Khytrai – 'Pots') festival, was similarly a chthonic festival: R. Hamilton *Choes and Anthesteria. Athenian Iconography and Ritual*, Ann Arbor, MI, 1992. For the vocabulary of such rites: E. Borthwick, 'P.Oxy. 2738: Athena and the Pyrrhic Dance', *Hermes* 98, 1970, 318–31.

45 Are these the five days of the festival taken collectively, i.e. a single sacrifice of two sheep on the day before the five days of the festival, or does it mean that there was a sacrifice of two sheep on each of the five days of the festival (Greg Stanton)? Or was there a sacrifice of two sheep on each of five days prior to the festival?

46 Arist. fr. 101 (Rose).

47 This is undobtedly the correct form; the single alternative is by Theognostos the Grammarian in J. Cramer, *Anecdota Graeca, e codd. manuscriptis bibliothecarum Oxoniensium*, Amsterdam, 1963, 66, ll. 30–1 who offers Κολαινία.

48 Paus. 9, 19, 7 as was the case at Amarynthos: see below, n. 49.

49 Schol. Arist. *Av.* 873: Εὐφρόνιος δέ φησιν ὅτι ἐν 'Αμαρύνθῳ ἡ Κολαινὶς διὰ τὸν 'Αγαμέμνονα θῦσαι αὐτῇ ἐκεὶ κριὸν κόλον.

50 Ael. *NA* 12, 34. This seems to confirm Euphronios' reference to a κριὸν κόλον

51 Pausanias 1, 31, 5.

52 Kock, *CAF* I, 705: τίς ἡ Κολαινὶς ῎Αρτεμις;
ἱερεὺς γὰρ ὢν τετύχηκα τῆς Κολαινίδος.

So also schol. Arist. *Av.* 873. However Kock: 'scribendum videtur τί σοι, *quid ad te pertinet?*' instead of τίς ἡ in line 1.

53 Callim. fr. 200b Pfeiffer: τὴν ὠγαμέμνων, ὡς ὁ μῦθος, εἵσατο,
τῇ καὶ λίπουρα καὶ μονῶπα θύεται.

which C. Trypanis, *Callimachus. Aetia, Iambi, Hecale and other Fragments*, (Loeb) Cambridge, MA, 1975, 141, translates as follows: 'whose effigy (of Artemis Kolainis), as the story goes, Agamemnon dedicated, and to whom even tail-less and one-eyed animals are sacrificed.

Dieg. Iamb. 10: 'The poet also commends Artemis of Eretria because she rejects nothing that is sacrificed to her.' (translated by Trypanis). In his commentary on this fragment and the *Diegesis* he says: '. . . he (Callimachus) spoke about the cult of Artemis

Kolainis, worshipped at Amarynthos in Euboia, near Eretria.' The cult of the latter goddess seems also to have been popular in Attica, and various efforts have been made to explain the derivation of the name Kolainis. Kallimakhos appears to have favoured the suggestion that the origin of the name was due to the sacrifice of a mutilated ram (κριὸς κόλος) by Agamemnon on his way to Troy. See also ibid. 139, n. 101.

54 There in fact exists a dedicatory inscription to Artemis Olympia: *IG* XII 9, 260: Χρυσαλλὶς Σημίον Ἀρτέμιδι Ὀλυμπίαι with the note, 'Cognomen Olympiae W(ilhelm, *EA* 1892, 141, 9) iure rettulit ad montem qui planitiem Eretriensium claudit.' But it might, however, be intended to distinguish one aspect from the other of Artemis.

55 Porph. *de Abst.* 3, 17 and 4, 16.

56 *LSJ* s.v., p. 1761.

57 D. Hughes, *Human Sacrifice in Ancient Greece*, London, 1991, index s.v. Artemis.

58 Hughes 1991, 11; 81; 89–90; 116–7; 119; 121–2 etc.; see L. Farnell, *Cults of the Greek States* II, Oxford, 1896, 452–5.

59 Hughes 1991, 46–7 (Lefkandi); 194–6 (Manika and Aulonari).

60 *IT* 1448–53 and 1458–61.

61 Hughes 1991, 81.

62 R. Graves, *The Greek Myths*, London, 1962, 116 i, j (p. 483).

63 Inscription from Karystos: *REG* 1932, 217 (amended by D. Knoepfler in: 'Karystos et les Artemisia d' Amarynthos', *BCH* 96, 1972, 282–301, with commentary). Liv. 35, 38, 3: 'Sacrum anniversarium eo forte tempore Eretriae Amarynthidis Dianae erat, quod non popularium modo sed Carystiorum etiam coetu celebratur.' See Knoepfler 1988, 382–421. For participation of worshippers from beyond Eretria and Karystos in later times: *IG* XII 9, 234, 25–33.

64 Str. 10, 1, 10 C448. See Appendix 4 for a discussion of Strabo's source for his description of the stele.

65 For the dance in so far as its character can be reconstructed: W. Downes, 'The Offensive Weapon in the Pyrrhic', *CR* 18, 1904, 101–6. For the Pyrrhic at the Artemiria: D. Stavropoulos, ''Ερετρικὰ Μελετήατα', *AE* 1895, 156.

66 F. Cairns, '*IG* XII Suppl. 555, Reinmuth no. 15 and the demes and tribes of Eretria', *ZPE* 64, 1986, 153–4.

67 C. Bérard, 'L'Hérôon à la Porte de l'Ouest', *Eretria; Fouilles et Recherches*, III, Berne, 1970, 53.

68 *IG* XII 9, 191A 58; 236, 46; 237, 23. Histiaia: *IG* XII 9, 1190, 1 as well as the herm inscription described by F. Cairns, 'A herm from Histiaia with an agonistic epigram of the fifth century BC', *Phoenix* 37, 1983, 16–37 (especially 34–5); its lexicon includes words associated with Kouretic dancing in other sources. Cairns believes that the dedication was to Artemis Proseoa of Artemision. Also *SEG* 33 (1983), item 716. See an agonistic epigram (*c.* 550/30 BC) from Eretria, also involving dancing: A. Altherr-Charon and F. Lasserre, 'Heracles à Érétrie, une nouvelle inscription agonistique', *Études de Lettres,* Lausanne, IV 4, 1981, 25–35; W. Luppe, 'Zum neuen agonistischen Epigramm aus Eretria', *ZPE* 49, 1982, 22, who criticises the metre of their supplements, rejects their attribution of the dedication to Herakles and attributes it to Zeus. Luppe thinks that the victory was at the Olympic games. But the edd. prr. point to the existence of Herakleia at Eretria (*IG* XII 9, 272). schol. Pi. *Ol.* 1, 11 refers to a Basileia festival of Zeus Basileios at Khalkis. I. Ringwood, 'Local festivals of Euboea chiefly from inscriptional evidence', *AJA* 33, 1929, 386, n. 1.

69 *RE* s.v. Artemis, 1349. Enyalios was an epithet for Ares in the *Iliad* but in later times was seen as a separate war god, son of Ares and Enyo, goddess of bloody war who delights in the destruction of towns.

70 Pollux 8, 91. *CIA* II, 467. It was here that Miltiades sacrificed 300 goats to Artemis in gratitude for the victory of Marathon on 6 Thargelion (Artemis' sacred day).

71 Bowra 1966, 41. Gravidus 'heavy', hence pregnant; gravido 'I impregnate': e.g. '[ipsa terra] gravidata seminibus omnia pariat et fundat ex sese': Cic. *ND* 2, 33, 83. For Artemis as Proseoa, Parthenos, Agrotera: Farnell *Cults* II 1896, s.v. and esp. 562–3, nn. 26f and 26g. The Athenian Thargelia was a festival in which first fruits were offered to Apollo and Artemis as deities of vegetation and fertility: H. Parke, *Festivals of the Athenians*, London, 1986, 147.

72 F. Bornman, *Hymnus in Dianam*, Firenze, 1968, 90: 'le Amarinzie sono feste in onore di Artemide guerriera.'

73 *IG* XII 9, 191A, 58 (fourth century).

74 Bowra 1966, 41. θόρε κὲς *ν[έος* πολείτας (l. 35).

75 Aristocratic display at festivals: W. Donlan, 'The aristocratic ideal in Ancient Greece' in idem, *The Aristocratic Ideal in Ancient Greece and Other Papers*, Wauconda, IL, 1999, 99–105.

76 It will become apparent later why I place the word in inverted commas. The natures and roles of the Eretrian socio-political classes are discussed below, Chs 3–4 and 7, *passim*.

77 H. Catling, 'A Mycenaean puzzle from Lefkandi in Euboea', *AJA* 72, 1968, 41–9.

78 Theodoridas (third century), *Anth. gr.* 6, 156.

79 *IG* XII 9, 900 (father as *hegemon*) and 945 (statue base), both early second century.

80 Hsch. s.v. Κουρεῶτις.

81 L. Curchin, 'Minoans at Chalcis?', *Quaderni di Storia* 9, 1979, 271–8.

82 Str. 10, 3, 19 C472; Arkhemakhos ap. Str. 10, 3, 6 C465; Epaphroditos ap. St. Byz. The latter is M. Mettius Epaphroditus (first century AD), like Plutarch a native of Khaironeia who wrote commentaries on Homer, Hesiod and Kallimakhos and is cited elsewhere by Stephanos.

83 Jacobsen 1964, 14; 180.

84 Plus a few natural features, plants etc.; see E. Vermeule, *Greece in the Bronze Age*, Chicago, 1972, 37; 60–4.

85 Evangelides, 1960, 12, believed (Epeirot) names with medial -οπ- (e.g. Ellopia, Dryopes, Dolopes and Oropos) to be pre-Hellenic; see also Miller, *RE* s.v. Dryopes: 'sie an unter den führen barbarischen Einwohnern Griechenlands, doch sind sie nach der Endung -οψ ohne Zweifel Griechen.'

86 In addition, Euboian from outside the Eretrias: Karystos, Kerinthos, Ellopia.

87 Str. 9, 2, 10 C404. That the monument of Narkissos had to be passed in silence (like the tomb of the Erinyes at Kolonos: S. *OC* 128–33) is probably due to the association of the Erinyes (and Persephone) with the narcissus flower: see Probus *ad Verg. Ecl.* 2, 48: 'procreati a pictore Narcissi floribus Erinyas, primas esse coronatas aiunt' (see below, n. 89). Eust. *ad Hom. Od. pert.* 24, 465 says that *sigelos* is the proper name of the narcissus. See A. Charbonnet, 'Amphiaraos à Érétrie', *MH* 41, 1984, 49–53.

88 Eius amatore.

89 Translation of the emended *scholion* by Akousilaos (ap. Probus, *ad Verg. 'Eclog.'* 2, 48): 'Narcissus flos, ut Akousilaos refert, a Narcisso Amaranthi, qui fuit Erechtheis, ex insula Euboea, interemptus ab Epope. Ex cruore eius flores, qui nomen eius acceperunt, procreati' (where 'Amaranthos' is wrongly written for Amarynthos and 'Erekhtheis' for Eretrieis). Eitrem *RE*, associating this variant with the Boiotian Narkissos story, makes the slaying the result of a lover's quarrel: 'wahrscheinlich von einem verschmähten Liebhaber getötet wird.' Narkissos was, in this tradition, seen as the son of Amarynthos, a king of the area: *E.M.* 77, 42: Ἀμάρυνθος· Πόλις Εὐβοίας. Ὠνόμασται δὲ ἀπὸ Ἀμαρύνθου βασιλέως. Narkissos was closely linked to Artemis cult: *RE* s.v. Ellops/Ellopieis. Epops has been associated with Eretria: D. Knoepfler, '"ΟΦΡΥΟΕΣΣΑ ΠΟΛΙΣ; note sur l' acropole d' Érétrie', *AK* 12, 1969, 83–7. Epops was a hero who had rites according to the calendar of sacrifices from the Attic deme Erkhia as also did Zeus Epopetes: see G. Daux, 'La grande Démarchie', *BCH* 87, 1963, 603–34; M. Jamieson, 'Notes on the sacrificial calendar from Erchia', *BCH* 89, 1965, 154–72; S. Dow, 'The Greater Demarkhia of

Erkhia', *BCH* 89, 1965, 180–213. Parke 1977, 175–81 and pl. 65. Epops' sacrifice took place on 5 Boedromion and consisted of a holocaust of pigs; the date falls during the Genesia at Athens, a festival of the dead.

90 Vermeule 1972, 60–4.

91 Loc. cit.

92 R. Drews, *The Coming of the Greeks. Indo-European Conquests in the Aegean and the Near East*, Princeton, NJ, 1989.

93 J. Rutter, 'A group of distinctive pattern-decorated early Helladic III pottery from Lerna and its implications', *Hesperia* 51, 1982, 459–88; idem 'Fine Gray-burnished pottery of the early Helladic III period: The ancestry of Gray Minyan', *Hesperia* 52, 1983, 327–55.

94 Rutter 1983, 339; 344–9.

95 Drews 1989, 42.

96 O. Dickinson, 'The shaft graves and Mycenaean origins', *BICS* 19, 1972–3, 146; Drews 1989, 158.

97 Rutter 1983, 347–8.

98 However, see Str. 10, 3, 6 C465.

99 A. Sampson, 'Late Neolithic remains at Tharrounia, Euboea: a model for the seasonal use of settlements and caves', *BSA* 87, 1992, 61–101; idem, 1993.

100 P. Themelis, *PAAE* (*Praktika*) 1983, 134.

101 In the excavation zone G/10: S. Müller, 'Des Néolithiques aux Mycéniens', *Dossiers d'archéologie*, 94, 1985, 2–16 (with English summary, 86); Krause 1982b, 138, map 1; Themelis 1969a, 172–6 for EH in Eretria.

102 Hdt. 1, 57.

103 Str. 5, 2, 4 C221. For the ancient literary evidence and traditions: J. Myres, 'A history of the Pelasgian Theory', *JHS* 27, 1907, 170–225; J. Munro, 'Pelasgians and Ionians', *JHS* 54, 1934, 109–28.

104 Hom. *Il.* 16, 233.

105 Hdt. 1, 171; Str. 7, 7, 1–2 C321. Rodhakis, 1997, 12–13, assigns a more important role to these people.

106 N. Faraklas, 'Περὶ τῆς κατοικήσεως τῶν Λελέγων ἐν Βοιωτίᾳ', *AAA* 2, 1969, 96–7.

107 Idem; For Manika, see the excavation reports of Sampson 1985 onwards (also n. 1 above); Leekley and Efstratiou 1980 68; Jacobsen 1964, 71–3; 160–4; *passim* (Manika); D. Theokhares, ''Εκ τῆς προϊστορίας τῆς Εὐβοίας καὶ τῆς Σκύρου', *AEM* 6, 1959, 279–328.

108 E. Sapouna-Sakellaraki, 'Nouvelles figurines cycladiques et petite glyptique du Bronze Ancien d'Eubée', *AK* 34, 1991, 3–12.

109 Faraklas 1969, 3–4 and n. 11. For criticism of the Pelasgic Theory: Myres 1907, 170–225.

110 Sapouna-Sakellaraki 1991, 10 ad fin.

111 From a personal note to me discussing the origins and migration patterns of the Dryopians.

112 Str. 9, 5, 10 C434 (calls Mt Tymphrestos in Thessaly Dryopian, but locates it in Epeiros); Hdt. 1, 56; 8, 31. schol. ad Luc. 3, 179–80: 'Dryopes, gens Epiri'; Str. 5, 2, 4 C221; Plin. *HN* 4, 2; Dion. Calliphr. 30 (in *Geogr.gr.min.* II). J. Croon, *The Herdsman of the Dead. Studies of some Cults, Myths and Legends of the Ancient Greek Colonization Area*, Utrecht, 1952, 51–2.

113 Evangelides 1962, 10; 16. For the Dolopians in Skyros: *D.S.* 11, 60, 2; Th. 1, 98, 2. Jacobsen 1964, 20, n. 53 for the ancient references.

114 Str. 7, 7, 1 C321; 8, 6, 13 C373; Paus. 4, 8, 3; 4, 18, 3. *RE* s.v. Dryopes 1748–50. Schumacher, 1993, 62–87, notes the common worship of Poseidon (as Geraistios) at both Karystos and Hermione.

115 For ἐξ 'Ασ. I suggest ἐξ 'Ασίνης; see Knoepfler 1997, 363: 'Ασ[τυπάλαια], and Wallace 1947, 131.

116 Paus. 4, 34, 9–11.
117 *D.S.* 4, 37, 1–2; Hdt. 8, 73; Str. 8, 6, 13 C373; Schumacher 1993, 63.
118 1969a, 175–6.
119 1964, 240.
120 See above, nn. 84–6; 113.
121 For completeness: in the Karystia and as far north as Eretrian Styra there are enigmatic structures known as 'Dragon Houses', generally regarded as Hellenistic or later. With one isolated exception, they are found only here and in Karia. By an interesting argument, J. Carpenter and D. Boyd, 'Dragon Houses: Euboia, Attika, Karia', *AJA* 81, 1977, 211–5, postulate that Pelasgoi/Leleges/Dryopians, brought in from Caria as slave labourers in Hellenistic/Roman times for the marble quarries, reintroduced a Dryopian architectural type to the Dryopian Karystia!
122 Hdt. 1, 146; Th. 7, 57, 4 and 4, 61, 2. Styra was thus originally Dryopian, but no longer so considered itself later, as Paus. 4, 34, 11 makes clear.
123 Is Ellopia an exception? It was an alternative name for Kerinthos; Ellops was its eponymous hero. Has the older name here reasserted itself?
124 This is preferred by Dr Parker (personal note).
125 Ant. Lib. 4.
126 Knoepfler, 1997, 387, has Melaneus as son of Eurytos, though I can find neither any source for this nor for making Eretrieus anything other than the son of the Titan Phaethon (St. Byz. s.v. Ἐρέτρια = Eust. *ad Hom. Il. pert.* 279, 29–32) or the leader of a colony to Euboia from Triphyllian Makistos (Str. 10, 1, 10 C447). The later Ionian inhabitants of Eretria may have found it desirable to develop new foundation myths, which said that their city had been founded by Eretrieus, son of the Titan Phaethon. See P. Grimal, *The Dictionary of Classical Mythology*, Oxford, 1996, s.vv. Eurytus; Melaneus; *Roscher*, *Lexicon*, s.v. Μελανεύς (3). For the mythology of Oikhalia: C. Talamo, 'Il Mito di Melaneo: Oichalia e la Protostoria eretriese' in *Contributions à l' Étude de la Colonisation et la Société eubéennes. Cahiers du Centre Jean Bérard*, No. 2, Naples, 1975, 27–36 and Appendix 2 for Minoan links.
127 Ant. Lib. 32.
128 Wallace 1947, 140, nn. 72–4: it may have been located north/west of Avlonari (in District V). J. Konstantinou and J. Travlos, reported by P. Amandry in 'Chronique des Fouilles en 1942', *BCH* 1942/43, 327, situate it on the east slope of Palaiokastritsa hill west of Avlonari (giving no reasons for the identification). Oikhalia and Nedon were close together in the Eretrias. Ziebarth (*IG* XII 9, p. 165); Geyer 1903. Both toponyms also occur together in Thessaly/Trakhis in the general area of the original homeland of the Dryopians: Thessaly (Str. 8, 3, 6 C339; 8, 3, 25 C350; Paus. 4, 2, 3), Trakhis (Str. 8, 3, 6 C339; 10, 1, 10 C448) and Messenia. Pausanias (4, 2, 3) regarded the Messenian tradition as more authentic than the Euboian: 'The story told by the Euboians agrees with the statements of Kreophylos in his *Herakleia*; and Hekataios of Miletos averred that Oikhalia is in Skios, a part of the territory of Eretria. Nevertheless I think that on the whole the version of the Messenians is more likely than theirs.' Knoepfler, 1997, 386–7, sensibly emends Hekataios' statement: Ἑκαταῖος δὲ ὁ Μιλήσιος ἐν Σκίῳ μοίρᾳ τῆς Ἐρετρικῆς ἔγραψεν εἶναι Οἰχλίαν as follows: ἐν <τῇ πρὸς> Σκύαρῳ (vel Σκῦρον) μοίρᾳ τῆς Ἐρετρικῆς [in the part of the Eretrias close to (or facing) Skyros]. Hekataios' *floruit* means that Oikhalia (located by both Wallace and Knoepfler in District V) was already Eretrian in the sixth century. Talamo, 1975, 27–36, implies that Oikhalia was 'Old Eretria'. See St. Byz. s.v. Σκιάς. On Kreophylos: Suid. s.v. Κρεώφυλος.
129 Contra Gehrke, 1988, 21, who thinks that they are time indicators, I believe that Μεταζύ and Φυλακή are either district names, or perhaps, with Knoepfler 1997, 375–7, epithets of Artemis Amarysia. For discussion of these names and of the Eretrian districts χῶροι (*khoroi*) generally: Ch. 8, pp. 240–3.
130 Jacobsen 1964, 225–6 (by Abantes); Geyer 1903, 90 (by Ellopians).

131 The Οἰχαλίας ἅλωσις. For Euboian Oikhalia as the location: schol. S. *Tr.* 354. See above, p. 40 and n. 116; p. 41 and n. 128 for Kreophylos. St. Byz. makes the legendary minstrel a native of Oikhalia (s.v.) although he is alone in this assertion: see app. crit. by Meinecke, 488; *D.L.* 1, 4 makes him a Theban killed in Euboia by Apollo; Herakleides (ap. Plut. *de mus.* 1132a) a Euboian.

132 See below, pp. 41, 51–2, 55.

133 There were places called Ellopia in Epeiros, Boiotia and Thessaly: *RE* s.v. Hellopia.

134 Eust. *ad Hom. Il. pertin.* 280, 29–30: Ἡ δὲ Κήρινθος ἐκλήθη ποτέ, φασί, καὶ Ἐλλοπία ὑπο Ἔλλοπος, υἱοῦ Τιθονοῦ.

135 Wallace 1947, 138. There was also a homonymous deme in Attica: St. Byz. s.v. Ἱστίαια and Ἑστίαια

136 See above, n. 122.

137 Paus. 4, 34, 11.

138 Wallace 1947, 131 (map of demes). Note Gehrke's (1988, 20, n. 4) worries about any attempts 'to locate demes with precision'. This is not my intention here.

139 *IG* XII 9, 241 ll. 25; 36. and therefore secure. This district also contains Styra, Zarex and Dystos.

140 Plut. *Phoc.* 13, 4.

141 Str. 9, 5, 12 C434; 9, 5, 17 C437; 9, 5, 22 C442; Plin. *HN* 4, 2. They inhabited Thesprotia in Epeiros: Evangelides 1962, 17, 45, 47, 61, 77.

142 But see M. Sakellariou, *La migration grecque en Ionie*, Athens, 1958: 'De tout façon (the Abantes) doivent avoir été d'origine non-hellénique.'

143 Jacobsen, 1964, 20–2, nn. 54–7, who advises caution.

144 See above, p. 37, nn. 87–9. Akousilaos ap. Probus *ad Verg. 'Eclog.'* 2, 48.

145 Ion of Chios ap. Paus. 7, 4, 9; Hdt. 1, 146. St. Byz. s.v. Βολισσός refers to this place as an Aiolian city in Khios; see Str. 14, 1, 4 C634. Thus Kyme in Asia Minor may have derived its name and original settlers from Kyme in Euboia.

146 J. Bury, *History of Greece*, London, 1955, 65.

147 C. J. Emlyn-Jones, *The Ionians and Hellenism. A Study of the Cultural Achievements of Early Greek Inhabitants of Asia Minor*, London, 1980, 15.

148 Sakellariou 1958, 298. But see above n. 121.

149 Ibid. 14; G. Huxley, *The Early Ionians*, London, 1966, 23 (*c.* 1100); J. Cook, *The Greeks in Ionia and the East*, London, 1962, 23 (1000 or slightly earlier). Sakellariou, 1958, 287–8, is more cautious: we do not know when Abantes arrived in Khios, or whether they arrived before or after the Ionians.

150 M. Hood, 'Mycenaeans in Chios', in J. Boardman and C. Vaphopoulou-Richardson (eds), *CHIOS: a Conference at the Homereion in Chios, 1984*, Oxford, 1986, 179–80; note also the statement by Hood quoted by Desborough in *CAH*[3] II, Pt 2b, Cambridge, 1980, 663 ad fin.

151 V. Desborough, *Protogeometric Pottery*, Oxford, 1952, 180–94; Boardman 1957, 9.

152 Kearsley 1989, 133; probably Type 2: 137.

153 See above, p. 26 and n. 1.

154 See above, pp. 37, 42.

155 Throughout the following discussion, I should point out Dr Parker's caveat to me: 'They [the Abantes] – like the Couretes – are a tribe which disappeared early. Their presence on Euboia is well enough attested through "Homer" who mentions them for one reason in particular: "Homer" – the Catalogue of Ships is no different from the rest of the two epics in this respect; questions of authorship and date on this point *mal à propos* – always endeavours to describe the circumstances of his imagined Heroic Age. He avoids references to contemporary events and situations where he is aware that they are indeed contemporary. When he is not, they naturally creep in willy-nilly. Since "Homer" does know that the migrations of Ionians to Euboea is post-Heroic, he presents a pre-Ionic tribe as ruling over the island. Thus owing to the mention in the

Catalogue of the Ships the Abantes are far more reliably attested as present on Euboea than the Couretes. But many tribes may have dwelt on the island both simultaneously and in succession in those "centuries of darkness".' This, however, does not account for Homer's choice of the Abantes from the many tribes who may have dwelt on the island both simultaneously and/or in succession in those 'centuries of darkness'. It also ignores evidence that the Abantes were associated with a number of cultural changes, which may suggest Mycenaean influence: metalworking, the Olympian pantheon (and others that Dr Parker would dismiss, e.g. patriarchy), as well as the memory of a saga cited (pp. 53–4) concerning the fall of (Mycenaean) Thebes. See also p. 30 and pp. 53–4 above, where I suggest an identification of the Kouretes and Abantes).

156 Hom. *Il.* 2, 536–45. On this section, see G. Kirk, *The Iliad: A Commentary* I: Books 1–4, Cambridge, 1985, 202–5. H. Lorimer, 'The hoplite phalanx with special reference to Archilochus and Tyrtaeus', *BSA* 42, 1947, 114, esp. 121: she holds the passage to be a later interpolation (contra Kirk 205), reflecting the adoption of hoplite tactics. Mele 1975, 19: Elephenor was not a hoplite.

157 The name has obvious echoes of Khalkis and its supposed bronze-making traditions: A. Mele, 'I Ciclopi, Calcodonte e la metallurgia calcidese', *Cahiers du Centre Jean Bérard* VI, Naples, 1981, 9–33.

158 *Amat. narr.* (*Mor.*774c). Is this just another case of a later writer confusing the archaic *basileus*, or district chief, with its later Hellenistic/Roman meaning of 'king'? The archaic Amphidamas of Khalkis and the Emperor Hadrian, to whom the document called Περὶ 'Ομήρου καὶ 'Ησιόδου καὶ τοῦ γένους καὶ ἀγῶνος αὐτῶν is dedicated, are both described as *basileus* in almost sequential passages: H. Evelyn-White, *Hesiod, the Homeric Hymns and Homerica* (Loeb), Cambridge, MA, 1926, 566–97. The same story is found in Dion Chrysostom 2, 12 delivered before Trajan in AD 104. They possibly derive from a single Hellenistic original. Dion alludes to anti-Euboian bias in Homer, attributed to his defeat by Hesiod in the Euboian contest. Later scholiasts considered Elephenor a true king: Porphyrios ap. Eust. *ad Hom. Il. pert.* 281, 40–2. R. Drews, *Basileus. The Evidence of Kingship in Geometric Greece*, New Haven, CT, 1983, 94–5, discusses Eretria and Khalkis but makes no mention of Khalkodon or his son. Sophokles represents Elephenor [in a fragment of his lost Σκύριοι; D. Page (ed./tr.), *Select Papyri III: Literary Papyri; Poetry*, Cambridge, MA, 1970, 20–1] as the friend of Achilles' son Triptolemos, who sought refuge with him in the 'glens of Euboia'.

159 V. Ehrenberg, *The Greek State*, Oxford, 1960, 25.

160 *Pol.* 1252b and his discussion of monarchy at 1285a–b.

161 Ehrenberg 1960, 24–5. See also Drews 1983, 43; 73–4; 96; 130.

162 See below, pp. 54–7.

163 Gehrke 1988, 15–42: Parthenion (30), Boudiothen (34). Gehrke sometimes rejects a proposed location on the grounds that a mere strong point is insufficient for a deme-centre. G. Papavasileiou, 'Εὐβοϊκά [2]: Τοπονυμίαι ἀρχῖαι καὶ νῦν ἔτι σῳζομέναι', *AE* 1905, 27. But many were apparently so small that nothing now remains that can be assigned to them, not unexpected if the original units were just small groups of farm dwellings.

164 Mele 1975, 16–7. G. Huxley, 'Mycenaean decline and the Homeric "Catalogue of Ships" ', *BICS* 3, 1956, 26–7, regards the Homeric catalogues in the *Iliad* as reliable guides to political realities at the end of LM IIIC. An epigram from Khalkis [*IG* XII 9, 954, 12; W. Peek, *Griechische Vers-Inschriften; Grab-Epigramme*, Chicago, 1988, no. 755 l. 9, dated to the time of Philon, founder of the so-called Fourth Academy (159–80)] refers to the soil/land of Khalkis as βῶλος (or κόνις) 'Ελεφηνορίς (sod/dust of Elephenor), so the association of the Abantic leader's name with Khalkis was still strong enough then to be used as an epithet.

165 Geyer 1903, 36. Whether we can take the fact that Homer places the cities of Khalkis and Eretria first as evidence of this, as Geyer does, seems doubtful to me, but the fact

that in later times Khalkis still preserved the name in its tribe Abantis is better evidence, along with the Kouretic connection. The archaeological record likewise favours this interpretation. The area was also vital for trade with Boiotia, and control of the rich Lelantine Plain must have been a major attraction for any invader.

166 Str. 10, 1, 3 C445. He is probably the local historian, Aristoteles of Khalkis (fourth century) and not the philosopher. For Abai: V. Yorke, 'Excavations at Abae and Hyampolis in Phocis', *JHS* 16, 1896, 291–312 (has little reference to the pre-Classical period); J. M. Fossey, *The Ancient Topography of Eastern Phokis*, Amsterdam, 1986, 78–81; 95 (confirms that there is nothing on the site earlier than Geometric/Archaic); *RE* s.v.

167 Arr. ap. Eust. *ad DP* 520.

168 1903, 36, citing Busolt, Meyer, Töpffer (*RE* s.v. Abantes) and Wilamowitz (*Philol. Untersuch*. I, 204).

169 C. Buck, *The Greek Dialects*, Chicago, 1928/1965, 156 (Item 229).

170 Plut. *Quaest.Graec.* 22.

171 Ion, son of Xouthos and Kreusa: Plut. *Quaest.Graec.* 22; Apollod. 1, 7, 3. Aiklos and Kothos were sons of Xouthos; Ellops, the son of Ion: Str. 7, 7, 1 C321; 10, 1, 3 C445; 10, 1, 8 C446; Vell. Paterc. 1, 4; Scym. 575; Alkman fr. 66. St. Byz. s.v. Ἐλευθερίς. K. Schefold and D. Knoepfler, 'Forschungen in Eretria, 1974/1975', *AK* 19, 1976, 56–7; *SEG* 32, 1982, item 855, reports a *horos* from a *temenos* of Kothos, *oikistes* of Khalkis, at Eretria. R. Buck, *A History of Boeotia*, Edmonton, 1979, 79: 'Eleutheris was the foundation (or birthplace) of Kothos and Aiklos, who are commonly held to be the founders of Eretria, Cerinthus and sometimes Chalcis', citing Str. 10. 1, 8 C446, but overlooking Plutarch for Kothos at Khalkis. J. Toepffer, *Attische Genealogie*, Berlin, 1889, 164, stresses the importance of the mythological connections of the north-east coastal region of Attica with Euboia and Boiotia. Buck (1979, 78–81) describes the ancient links between these localities in more detail. See also L. Farnell, 'An unrecorded Attic colony in Euboea?', *CR* 20, 1906, 28.

172 Str. 7, 7, 1 C321.

173 Hdt. 1, 146; Paus. 7, 2, 3; 7, 4, 9.

174 Perhaps Amant- is a barbarised form of Abant-. For Abantis in Thesprotia: *RE* s.v. Amantia; Abantis. Paus. 5, 22, 4 uses 'b' not 'm'. Cf. J. Wilkes, *The Illyrians*, Oxford, 1995, 96; map 3; A. Plassart, 'Inscriptiones de Delphes: la liste des théorodoques', *BCH* 45, 1921, 22–3: has *theorodokoi* from Abantia.

175 Fossey 1986, 95.

176 Son of Lynkeus: Paus. 2, 16, 2; 10, 35, 1; schol. ad Pi. *Pyth.* 8, 73; Apollod. 2, 2, 1; of Khalkon: schol. ad *Il.* 2, 536; of Melampos: Apollod. 1, 9, 13; Schol. ad *AR* 1, 143; of Alkon (Attic hero): Eust. *ad Hom. Il. pertin.* 232; of Poseidon/Arethousa: Hyginos 157; grandson of Metion son of Kekrops; Aristokrates ap. St. Byz. s.v. Ἀβαντίς. The mother of Abas (and of Amphiaraos) appears to be Hypermnestra: Paus. 2, 21, 2; Apollod. 2, 1, 5; 2, 2, 1. O. Seyffert, *A Dictionary of Classical Antiquities; Mythology, Religion, Literature and Art*, London, 1891, s.vv. Catreus; Nauplius; Palamedes. A. Room, *Room's Classical Dictionary. The Origins of the Names of Characters in Classical Mythology*, London, 1983 s.v. Hypermestra/Hypermnestra.

177 Str. 10, 1, 10 C448. I render ἐπέκτισται as 'was re-established': *LSJ* s.v ἐπικτίζω.

178 For a survey of the material culture of MH, during which the settlement at Lefkandi developed extensively: R. Buck, 'The Middle Helladic Period', *Phoenix* 20, 1966, 193–209; for sub-Mycenaean to Geometric Lefkandi: Ch. 3, pp. 74–87.

179 L. Sackett and M. Popham, 'Lefkandi: a Euboean town of the Bronze Age and early Iron Age (2100–700 BC)', *Archaeology* 25, 1972, 11. The archaeological history of post-Mycenean Lefkandi is discussed more fully in Ch. 3.

180 V. Hankey, 'Late Helladic tombs at Chalcis', *BSA* 47, 1952, 49–95 (twenty tombs); Jacobsen, 1964, 208–10, bases his account exclusively on Hankey's work and, for reasons already alluded to, the situation at Khalkis is not greatly different now. Cf. P. Auberson,

'Chalcis, Lefkandí, Érétrie au VIII siècle', *Contribution à l'étude de la société et de la colonisation eubéennes: Cahiers du Centre Jean Bérard* II, Naples, 1975, 9–14.

181 Popham *et al.* 1980b, 6.
182 Rutter 1983, 339; 344–7; Popham *et al.* 1980b, 6.
183 Popham *et al.* 1980b, 6.
184 Rutter 1983, 347–8.
185 See above, pp. 37–8.
186 Sackett and Popham, 1972, 6.
187 Ibid. 7 for both citations.
188 For the early history: Popham *et al.* 1980b, 1–8; see their suggestions for an identification of site in their Appendix B: The Ancient Name of the Site, 423–7.
189 Generally see V. Aravantinou, 'The Mycenaean inscribed sealings from Thebes. Preliminary notes', *Tractata Mycenæa*, 1987a, *Tractata Mycenaea* 1987, 13–27.
190 Jacobsen 1964, 208–10; Popham *et al.* 1980b, 6; R. Desborough, *The Last Mycenaeans and their Successors*, Oxford, 1964, 222; L. Parlama, 'Μικρὴ ἀνασκαφικὴ ἔρευνα στὸν προϊστορικὸ λόφο τῆς 'Αμαρύνθου (Εὔβοια)', *AAA* 12, 2, 1979; E. Sapouna-Sakellaraki, 'Un dépôt de temple et le sanctuaire d'Artémis en Eubée', *Kernos* 5, 1992, 235–63 (map and plates); G. Papavasileiou, *Περὶ τῶν ἐν Εὐβοίᾳ ἀρχαίων τάφων*, Athens, 1910.
191 N. Hammond, *A History of Greece to 322 BC*, Oxford, 1959, 44, is quite categoric. Jacobsen 1964, 233; 246.
192 W. Biers, *The Archaeology of Greece; an Introduction*, Ithaca, NY, 1980, 24.
193 Curchin 1978, 271–8; Appendix 2.
194 T. Spyropoulosa and J. Chadwick, 'The Thebes Tablets II', *Supplementos a Minos* 4, 1975: TH Of 25.2, 94–5; 98; 104: drawing, text, commentary; Aravantinos, 1987a, 19–20; idem, 'Mycenaean place-names from Thebes: the new evidence', in J. Killen, J. Melena and J.-P. Olivier (eds), *Studies in Mycenaean and Classical Greek presented to John Chadwick* (= *Minos* 20–2), 1987b, 33–40.
195 Spyropoulos and Chadwick 1975, 86–7.
196 Ibid. 94–5; Hope-Simpson 1981, 55–6 (B70); Sackett *et al.* 1966, 64–6, no. 62.
197 Knoepfler 1988, 382–421.
198 Aravantinos 1987a, 13
199 Wu 58 (γ), and Wu 55 (β).
200 Aravantinos 1987a, 19–20.
201 Aravantinos 1987b, 37; Ventris and Chadwick 1973, 50; 131.
202 For the location of this deme: Wallace 1947, 131, Fig. 1 (map); and Knoepfler 1997, 402 (map). Paus. 8, 1, 5 (ὑῶν MS); Athen. 2, 54b acorns for pig feed. See Ch. 1, p. 12 and n. 40.
203 Jacobsen 1964, 237, n. 78 for details.
204 Aravantinos 1987b, 36–8. The consignment had the same ideographic designation as Wu 58 (γ)
205 Idem 1987b, 40.
206 Of 25.1; Of 35.2: Chadwick, in Spyropoulos and Chadwick 1975; Aravantinos, eodem, 35.
207 Chadwick, in Spyropoulos and Chadwick 1975, 95.
208 Private note.
209 Αἰγαλ[ῆθεν] Hdt. 6, 101, 1: Αἰγίλια, Τέμενος (see below, n. 211), Χοίρεαι (see above, n. 202). See Polyain. 1, 9. The abbreviations used in Eretrian inscriptions are: Αἰγα., Αἰγ. and Αἰγαλ. Gehrke 1988, 25 [Aig(ale)]; Knoepfler 1997, 369 n. 142 (Aigale or Aigalea). It appears in an Attic inscription: *IG* I^2 376, 9; *SEG* 10, 1949, 304 as [ἐν 'Ερε]τρίαι Αἰγαλ[εθεν] (emendment by Knoepfler: Αἰγαλ[ησι]). A. Raubitschek, 'The Athenian property on Euboia', *Hesperia* 12, 1943, n. 67, rejects the identification with the 'Styrean island' (Hdt. 6, 107, 4), as does Wallace 1947, 133. For the full form, we are dependent

on the now lost *IG* XII 9, 243: P. Girard, 'Inscriptions d'Eubée', *BCH* 1878, 278. Wallace, 133, n. 43, omits mention of l. 3: Θεοφάνης Πουλυχάρου Αἰγαλι-. [Is the 'I' the left hand *hasta* of eta (H)?] It is possible that [Αἰ]γα and Αἰ[γα] should be restored in ll. 7 and 8 respectively of *IG* II^2, 230b: for the text: Wallace, 145. *LSJ* s.v., 34: Αἰγᾶθεν; Doric for Αἰγῆθεν from Αἰγαί: schol. ad Pi. *Nem.* 5, 37: 'island off Euboea'; but Aigai was near Rovies (Orobiai), north of Khalkis. There were many other places called Αἰγιαλός (St. Byz. s.v.). There is, however, a reference to a place αἰγια[λο]ῖο in a fragment of Euphorion in a Euboian 'heroic' context (*Pap. Oxyrh.* 2528, l. 2); cf. Lobel's comment linking it with Oikhalia, Kerinthos and the Ellopians. B. van Groningen, *Euphorion*, Amsterdam, 1977, 210–1, with commentary. It is probably the location referred to by Herodotos as Ἀἰγίλεα; if so, it was on the coast (with Τέμενος and Χοίρεαι): Wallace, 130–3 (map: 131); Gehrke, 25–6; Knoepfler 1997, 379 and nn. 220–1 (map: 402). Sackett *et al.*, 1966, 63 with n. 83; and Knoepfler 1988, 382–421 and map 4. Knoepfler's thesis opinion (reported by Cl. Vial in *Rev.Hist.* 108^{272}, 1984, 241–5) is that Menedemos the philosopher (who appears in *IG* XII 9, 246A, 66) was demesman of Aigale whose family was associated with the Amarysion at adjacent Amarynthos. See above, p. 31, nn. 36–9 and references.

210 On the location of these demes: the maps and commentaries in Wallace 1947 and Knoepfler 1997.

211 According to Stavropoulos, 1895, 153 n. 11, Temenos was at the Amarysion, as the sanctuary κατ'ἐξοχήν of the Eretrians, but against this we also have the certain deme name 'Amarynthos'. Gehrke, 1988, 26, locates Temenos at Aghia Paraskevi, just outside the walls of classical Eretria. Themelis, 1969a, 167–8, puts the Amarysion at this site: contra Gehrke, 26, n. 61. Hdt., 6, 101, makes it clear, however, that Temenos lay on the coast and was near Αἰγ., i.e in Wallace's District IV; see Knoepfler 1988, 396, map 4 and 1997, 402 (map), where this deme is in his District I. Both Knoepfler and Sapouna-Sakellaraki (1992) locate the great sanctuary at Ayia Kiriaki on the east bank of the river Sarandapotamos (the Erasinos?); Knoepfler's map suggests that it was not in a deme Temenos but in Amarynthos. However, since only two restored deme names in one inscription for Temenos (*IG* XII 9, 191 B10: Τ[εμ] and C44: Τε[μ]) are known, they give no certain evidence in themselves for a deme name Temenos, but they do reinforce the reference in Herodotos.

212 1947, 130–3.

213 Gehrke 1988, 25–6, n. 58; Knoepfler 1988 and 1997 (see maps).

214 Popham, in Sackett *et al.* 1966, 104, though he does not think they are 'such as to indicate a dominating Theban influence over the island.'

215 F. Schachermeyr, *Die griechische Rückerinnerung im Lichte neuer Forschungen*, Vienna, 1983, 250–4; 302; 318.

216 Jacobsen 1964, 236; 238: Thebes' successor, Hypothebai was 'a miserable hamlet'; this does not seem to be what Homer (*Il.* 2, 505) is saying when he writes: 'Hypothebai, the well-built citadel'! Huxley, 1956, 22, refers to its inhabitants as 'miserable survivors'; his n. 42 indicates that the originator of this vision of abject poverty was Keramopoulos [*EA* 1909, 106 (non vidi)], presumably based upon archaeological *dedomena* given there. Huxley argues that the Homeric catalogues indeed reflect political reality in the LH IIIC (conclusions 25–7); so also does Jacobsen, 216–7 and n. 23.

217 Jacobsen 1964, 10, n. 52.

218 For Oikhalia: see above, p. 41 and nn. 126–8; 131. Jacobsen 1964, 225–6. F. Stubbings, 'The recession of Mycenaean civilization', *CAH*^{3} II 2a, 1980, Ch. 27, section II (The Trojan War), esp. 350; R. Drews, *The End of the Bronze Age. Changes in Warfare and the Catastrophe of ca.1200* BC, Princeton, NJ, 1993.

219 N. Hammond, 'The literary tradition for the migrations', *CAH*^{3} II, 2b, 1980, Ch. 36b, 701.

220 Jacobsen 1964, 12a: 205, 12b: 207; site descriptions: his Ch. IV, 208–40.

221 Ibid. 203–7, including 2 maps.
222 Knoepfler 1988, 382–421; Sapouna-Sakellaraki 1992, 235–63.
223 Parlama 1979, 3–14 (with summary in English).
224 Ibid. 14 (quotation from the English summary).
225 Vermeule 1972, 64; C. Blegen, *Troy and the Trojans*, London, 1963, 89; for Trojan trade with the Cyclades, 174: Troy II. *Depas*: this is a Homeric term for a two-handled cup (mis)applied to a peculiar Trojan shape (early Bronze Age) and used in Linear B as the sign for a large jar (Vermeule).
226 Sackett and Popham 1972, 11: from Troy II and succeeding levels.
227 1980.
228 Ἐλέφας (*LSJ* s.v.). Hom. *Il.* 5, 583; Hes. *Aspis*. 141.
229 For a Boiotian origin for the Abantes: Busolt 1893, 289; Meyer 1937, 191–2; Wilamowitz, *Philol. Untersuch.* I, 204; Buck 1979, 79.
230 Plut. *Amat. narr.* (*Mor.* 774c).
231 9, 19, 3.
232 Hom. *Il.* 23, 678–80. M. Nilsson, *The Mycenaean Origin of Greek Mythology*, Berkeley, CA, 1932/1972, 108.
233 A parallel may be the Pontic rump of the Byzantine Empire after 1453.
234 V. Desborough, *The Greek Dark Ages*, London, 1972, 24, citing destruction at Lefkandi.
235 J. Coldstream, 'Hero cults in the Age of Homer', *JHS* 96, 1976, 8–17; J. Whitley, 'Early states and hero cults; a reappraisal', *JHS* 108, 1988, 73–182, esp. 175 (Cl. Bérard and Euboia). A. Snodgrass, *Archaic Greece: The Age of Experiment*, Los Angeles, CA, 1980, 38–40, proposes a sociological explanation as an alternative.
236 Hom. *Il.* 2, 542.
237 Ap. Str. 5, 2, 4 C221.
238 Hdt. 1, 146; 8, 46; Th. 4, 61; 7, 57, 4. There was possibly an audible speech/dialect distinction, making the Karystians appear different from other Euboians for educated Athenians such as Thucydides. For Styreans: see above, p. 28 and n. 15.
239 Drews 1989, 37–41.
240 St. Byz. s.v. Ἐλευθερίς (*sic*).
241 Str. 10, 1, 8 C445; Plut. *Quaest. Graec.* 22.
242 Str. 10, 1, 3 C445; see Str. 10, 1, 10 C448.
243 In *RE* s.v Eretria (3), Wachsmuth observes that his (or any other) theories concerning its location are entirely speculative: 'Ein Marketplatz in Athen. Strabon X 447 (*sic*; it is 448) erwähnt, daß einige erzählten, das euboeische E. sei gegründet ἀπὸ τῆς Ἀθήνησιν Ἐρετρίας, ἣ νῦν ἐστιν ἀγορά.
244 Amarousion. Ch. 5, p. 143 and n. 15 for notes on the 'Old Athenian' dialect and its preservation of the phoneme /u/ ('ou') for the ancient υ (/y/ = German 'ü').
245 W. Porzig, 'Sprachgeographische Untersuchungen zu den griechischen Dialekten', *IF* 61, 1954, 147–69; E. Risch, 'Die Gleiderung der griechischen Dialekte in neuer Sichte', *MH* 12, 1955, 61–75.
246 See J. Chadwick, 'The Greek dialects and Greek pre-history', *G&R*, n.s. 3, 1956, 38–50.
247 Drews 1989, 37–41.
248 That is West Ionic or Euboian: C. Buck 1928/65, 143 (items 186–8).
249 Str. 10, 1, 10 C448. See also Eust. *ad Hom. Il. pert.* 279, 44–5 and St. Byz. s.v. Ἐρέτρια. For Makistos in Elis: G. Papandreou, *Ἡ Ἠλεία διὰ Μέσου τῶν Αἰώνων*, Athens, 1924/90, 57–8; Ch. 7 *passim*.
250 *RE* s.v.: Minthe in Elis: there was an Eretrian deme Minthountothen.
251 *RE* s.v. Abantes.
252 *IG* XII Suppl. 549. Mekistodoros occurs as a personal name at Eretria: the Doric Mākistos of Elis = Mēkistos in the Ionic of Euboia: Δροπίδης Μηκισοδόρου Δια. (*IG* XII 9, 245A 82). There was also a deme Mekistos at Histiaia: see *IG* XII 9, 1189, 31, which Geyer (1903) thinks was on the slopes of Mt Makistos in its territory. On the deme name: F.

Cairns, 'A duplicate copy of IG XII9, 1189 (Histiaia)', *ZPE* 54, 1984c, 135 (text ll. 31–2). There was a River Makestos, a tributary of the Rhyndakos in Phrygia: schol. ad *AR* 1, 1165d links this area with Euboia – see the relationship between Kouretes and the Phrygian Magna Mater (see above, pp. 29–30, nn. 21; 26.

253 See above, pp. 29–30 and nn. 10–11. *RE*; Roscher, s.v. Mekisteus.

254 Μακισ(σ)τίδι φυλη *sic*. In fact *IG* XII Suppl. 549, 4–5 has the Ionic and genitive forms Μεκισστίδος φυλῆς.

255 Themelis 1969a, 161. But he is mistaken in supposing three Eretrian tribes; Knoepfler shows, based on inscriptional evidence, that Eretria had 6–10 tribes: D. Knoepfler, 'Les Cinq-cents à Érétrie', *REG* 98, 1985a, 246, n. 12; idem 1997, 390–400; Schefold and Knoepfler, 1976, 57 (also eidem in *AD* 30, 1975/83: Khronika, 169). See Ch. 8, pp. 241–4. Themelis' (161) remark that Mākistis must 'ὁπωσδήποτε' (without fail, anyway) has comprised the aristocratic *gene* of the ancient colonists, as well as the great landowners of the Hippobotic class, is pure supposition.

256 Examples of intervocalic rhotacism are found in the Eretrian inscriptions; e.g.: σίτησις > σίτηρις, Λυσάνιας > Λυράνιας, ἐπιμενιεύουσες > ἐπιμενιεύουρες (*IG* XII Suppl. 549). Further examples: *IG* XII 9, p. 224: Rhotacismi Eretriensium exempla.

257 Rhotacism of final sigma: τ[οὺ]ρ ἀδελφε[ὸς αὐτõ] (*IG* XII Suppl. 549, ll. 13–4); ὅπως ἂν > ὅπωρ ἂν (*IG* XII 9, 189, l. 1) The last is, perhaps, not strictly rhotacism of final sigma, but cf. Str. 10, 1, 10 C448 and Pl. *Crat.* 434c. Thus, while they may not have written it, their speech may have voiced a final ρ. It has been argued that the ancient commentators are of no use, that Strabo is justifying his contention that settlers came to Eretria from Elis, while Plato is not attempting to define the Eretrian dialect, but merely giving an example of a particular dialectical variation from Attic. The argument is that knowing that the Eretrians often said 'r' where Athenians said 's', he may have given an inapposite example (i.e. of rhotacism but in the wrong position). So indeed he may, but are both Strabo and Plato wrong? The first example above (τ[οὺ]ρ) is precisely of the kind emphasised by Buck 1928/65, 56 (60a): 'In the earlier inscriptions ρ is relatively most frequent in the forms of the article.' Perhaps if we had more inscriptions from the early period (sixth century) the question would not arise. *IG* XII Suppl. 549 is, as a matter of fact, the earliest lengthy public inscription from Eretria that is generally dated to the early fifth century but which I argue below (Ch. 8, pp. 248, 251–3) should belong to the late sixth.

258 *IG* XII 9, 56 l. 281: Styra: Μίσγος > Μίργος. There is only one other case in the lead tablets from Styra. However, although Styra was originally a Dryopian town (and rhotacism seems to have occurred in Thessalian: H. Smyth, *Greek Grammar*, Cambridge, MA, 1920/1959, 33, item 132), these two men were perhaps Eretrians. Phrynikhos 88 specifically attributes the practice to Eretrians; W. Rutherford, *The New Phrynichus, Being a Revised Text of The 'Ecloga' of the Grammarian Phrynichus*, London, 1881, 195.

259 U. v. Wilamowitz-Möllendorf, 'Oropos und der Graer', *Kleine Schriften* IV, Amsterdam, 1971, 9–10; D. Knoepfler, 'Oropos: colonie d'Érétrie', *Dossiers d'archéologie* 94, 1985b, 50. See above, n. 85: Evangelides' opinion was that Oropos was Dryopian. Oropos is probably a rhotacised form of Asopos.

260 Plut. *Quaest.Graec.* 40.

261 D. Roller, 'Graia and Eunostos', in J. Fossey and H. Giroux (eds), *Proceedings of the Third International Conference on Boiotian Antiquities, Montreal (31/10–4/11, 1979)*, Amsterdam, 1985, 154; idem, *Tanagran Studies I: Sources and Documents on Tanagra in Boiotia*, Amsterdam, 1989; *RE* s.v. 'Eleion'. Zeus at Thebes had the by-name Elieus (Hsch. s.v.). There was a tribe, the *Eunostidai,* at Naples from Εὔνοστος: Ch. 5, n. 12.

262 Rutter 1982 and 1983 (see above, n. 93). There is evidence of ceramic affiliation with Elis as early as 1600, when the first Greek speakers arrived (Drews 1989). If this dialect feature was exchanged then, it was certainly very ancient indeed and may explain the divergences in usage; the direction implied is from Euboia to Elis. I think it rather unlikely however. For Oropos in Wallace's District III (Knoepfler's IV): Ch. V, pp. 155–6.

263 On Eretrian rhotacism: Buck 1928/65, 56–7; Eleian: 56: only final at Elis, a fact used as an argument by both Wallace and Parker for rejecting the connection with Eretria. Rhotacism occurred at Elis at least as early as the sixth century. For Elis; W. Dittenberger and K. Purgold, *Die Inschriften von Olympia*, Berlin, 1896, 11; Buck, 261, no. 63; Wallace 1936a, 14–5. For Eretria: W. Wallace, 'An Eretrian proxeny decree of the early fifth century', *Hesperia* 5, 1936b, 279, nn. 1; 3. L. Jeffery, *The Local Scripts of Archaic Greece – a Study of the Origin of the Greek Alphabet and its Development from the Eighth to the Fifth Centuries* BC, Oxford, 1961 (rev. A. Johnston, 1990), 86; 88; M. Wallace, 'Early Greek proxenoi', *Phoenix* 24, 1970, 207: first quarter of the fifth century. H. Smyth, *The Greek Dialects: Ionic*, Oxford, 1894, (very dated) 331: mid-fifth century. Wallace, 1936b, notes that this inscription pushes the date back some fifty years.

264 *IG* XII Suppl. 549. More likely it belongs to the late sixth century. The political implications of the details of this decree for the Eretrian democracy are discussed in Ch. 8, pp. 251–5.

265 See above, n. 68.

266 *IG* XII 9, 75. Knoepfler, reported by O. Masson, 'Noms grecs des femmes formés sur des participes (Type *Θάλλουσα*)', *Tyche* 2, 1987, 108, n. 12, believes that the word πρέσβος should be read πρέρβος, following his examination of the stone. *SEG* 37, 1987, item 737 gives a sixth century date.

267 Styra: *IG* XII 9, 56 and 213 (fifth century); Tamynai: *IG* XII 9, 90 (fourth).

268 Str. 10, 1, 10 C448. Eust. *ad Hom. Il. pert.* 239, 34 calls such speakers βαρβαρόφωνοι. Also Suidas s.v. χαλκιδίζειν; see Hsch. s.v. Ἐρετριέων ῥῶ; Diogenian. 4, 59.

269 In *IG* XII 9, 189 (*c.* 340) intervocalic rhotacism occurs only five times out of a possible twenty-five, and all examples are in the first fourteen (of a total of forty) lines; was the provincialism subsequently 'corrected'?

270 Knoepfler, 1981, 317–8 and nn., cites three funerary *stelai* (*IG* XII 9, 1050; 1105; *IG* XII Suppl. 681) from Khalkis. See eodem 1997, n. 280, where he is more positive. All are Hellenistic and rhotacism occurs only in patronyms. It is possible that they were either *pierres errantes,* as Ziebarth thought, or that they were for people who had moved from Eretria. But, by the Hellenistic period there must have been some (probably considerable) population exchange between the two cities. Knoepfler cites Suid. 782 ll. 25–6 (Adler): Χαλκιδίζειν.

271 Θράρυος (gen.): Jeffery 1961/90, 244; 248; R. Arena, 'Di alcuni tratti dialettali delle colonie euboiche d'occidente', *Acme* 40/1, 1988, 17–19.

3

OLD ERETRIA (LEFKANDI) DURING THE DARK AGES AND EARLY IRON AGE (*c.* 1050 TO *c.* 750)

'The eleventh century was a century of great changes and profound social upheavals within the Helladic world.'[1] The collapse of the Mycenaean world, very likely the result of natural disasters that precipitated internal social disorders and predatory invasions, resulted in the destruction and abandonment of many old settlements and the dispersion of their populations. Social and political disintegration led to a 'temporary economic and cultural recess'[2] over much of Hellas, although this was not uniform across the country or as complete in some regions as is sometimes imagined, for while Thebes and Iolkos experienced destruction, nearby Lefkandi seems to have escaped relatively unscathed and to have actually experienced something of a cultural flowering.[3] At least some of its inhabitants were able to re-establish a degree of settled life and material wealth accumulation that in our – admittedly meagre – archaeological records appears impressive and at a level of sophistication that makes Euboia not entirely unexpected as the place where the 'Greek Renaissance of the eighth century' would begin.[4] Unlike at many other places,

> the subsequent LH IIIC occupants undertook around 1200 an ambitious scheme of rebuilding in the course of which most of the earlier settlement was levelled away. This reconstruction naturally resulted in the destruction of much of the evidence for earlier [MH to LH IIIC] habitation. An increase in population is however certain and the amount of new building suggests a wholesale take-over, whether or not it was peacefully achieved.[5]

Major tribal invasions of Euboia came to an end with the arrival of the Ionians in the tenth century, although there may have been some minor population movements during the so-called Dark Ages (*c.* 1125–900),[6] such as the possible influx of migrants from Elis via Oropos referred to in Chapter 2.[7] By the end of the twelfth century, during LH III[2] when conditions had again settled down and some stability returned, there had emerged a quite different cultural pattern throughout the Greek world from that which prevailed in the Mycenaean period and which is now called sub-Mycenaean.

Despite the lack of excavation of prehistoric sites in Euboia, it is reasonable to suggest that, with the exceptions of the Lefkandi settlement and that at Amarynthos east of Eretria, no other Mycenaean settlement in south-eastern Euboia was much more than an unfortified *kome*.[8] The paucity of excavation at Amarynthos is regrettable because, during the EH, the town seems to have had a circuit wall, testifying to an early permanent settlement of some status there. However, Mycenaean Euboia had no site as important as Thebes, and so there was little scope for monumental catastrophe.

Late Mycenaean and sub-Mycenaean Lefkandi

A short time after the collapse of Thebes, the Abantic population of Lefkandi, whom I have differentiated from their Mycenaean overlords, the Khalkodontid rulers, resumed control of their homeland and may even have, for a short period, ruled Thebes itself.[9] The excavators of Lefkandi believed that newcomers brought in the sub-Mycenaean culture, a conclusion that they base not only on pottery styles but also on changes in burial customs about this time. But these 'newcomers' may have been, and in fact probably were, indigenous landowners resuming ruling status, and in fact the excavators allow that: 'It is not certain whether these people were all newcomers or, in part, survivors.'[10] Moreover, Lefkandi was a likely refuge for those fleeing the destruction of the great Bronze Age palace-centres on the nearby mainland,[11] for the excavators speculate that the settlement on Xeropolis defied the general trend of destruction and that the clearing and reconstruction at this time was due to the need to improve and expand the settlement rather than to clear away debris, but they

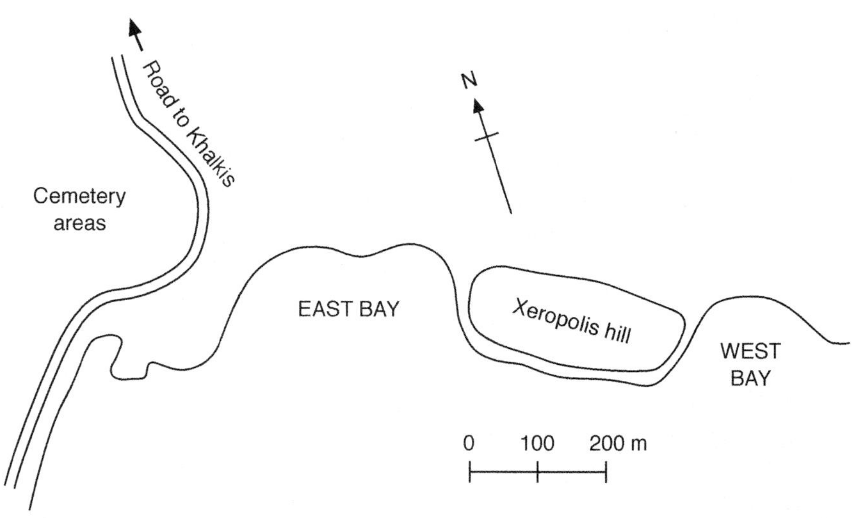

Map 3 The site of Lefkandi.

admit that the evidence is still inconclusive. Subsequently for some 100–150 years, 'when much of Greece was depopulated, Lefkandi was an active centre'[12] throughout LH IIIC.

This period may be divided into two sub-phases separated by a destruction interval:

1 LH IIIC[1]: during this period ceramic output decorated in a distinctive pictorial style was from local workshops distinctive from, but having similarities to, that of Attica and Mycenae itself (the so-called Mycenaean *koine* style). Desborough thinks that Lefkandi experienced troubles in the early LH IIIC, though his words leave it open whether he means a short or long time after the end of LH IIIB: 'the style of Lefkandi which emerged after a destruction subsequent to the end of LH IIIB'[13] is 'curiously fantastic', quite distinctive, indeed unique, with animal and even human representations (Figure 3.1).[14] There is some slight evidence of overseas trade: for example, what the excavators believe is a vase of foreign (Italian?) origin.[15] However Rutter has argued[16] that such manifestly non-Mycenaean and 'foreign' pieces possibly indicate the permanent arrival of invaders.
2 Destruction of the LH IIIC[1] settlement: the excavators think that the perpetrators were other 'Mycenaeans', for the pottery continues in the pictorial style.[17] There is evidence of violence that suggests a siege. In one of the destruction intervals, the inhabitants were reduced to interring their dead under the floors of houses in simple, poorly equipped graves, consisting of a pit into which the body was placed and covered with *pithos* fragments: one skeleton shows clear signs of severe battle wounds,

Figure 3.1 Animal-style LH IIIC *pyxis* from Lefkandi, Eretria Museum.

possibly received defending the settlement. Some buildings in the town were definitely now destroyed. I believe that this is when the Mycenaean overlords lost control of Lefkandi to its native Abantic inhabitants.[18]

3 The destruction was followed *c.* 1150 by a new phase of reconstruction (LH IIIC^{2}). Potters now began producing the style known as sub-Mycenaean, with a more simple decoration of wavy lines. This, as its name implies, represents a continuity with its predecessor though the product is generally of inferior quality and it deteriorated even more towards the end of the sub-Mycenaean period. Its decoration became progressively more 'closed' and fussy.[19] The style overlaps with LH IIIC^{1} in some other areas, including Attica, finally dying out in modified form *c.* 1050, or perhaps slightly later.[20]

For any reconstruction of conditions of life at Lefkandi during the sub-Mycenaean period (LH IIIC^{2}), we have only evidence from tombs, whereas the reverse is true for the earlier Mycenaean periods, the finds for which come from the settlement on Xeropolis itself.[21] The sub-Mycenaean community was large for the times, say the excavators. However, they base their opinion mainly on the number of burials,[22] for we do not know where the actual sub-Mycenaean town was, since excavation of the settlement area has so far been only by means of trial trenches.[23] The people buried in the cemeteries must obviously have lived somewhere nearby.[24] That it was on the promontory of Xeropolis, where the Mycenaean town had existed, cannot be ruled out. Only complete excavation of the citadel will answer the question of whether it was on the same site or whether the Abantes moved it elsewhere, but still close enough to continue using the Lefkandi cemeteries. A likely possibility in my opinion is that, when the Mycenaean overlords were driven out, many of the local landholders who would have assumed the reins of authority continued for some time to live on their properties, with the result that the town was, in fact, small enough at this time to have escaped detection by the excavators' trial trenches.

The Mycenaean–sub-Mycenaean period at Lefkandi ends with a whimper rather than a bang: 'It appears that there was a final period of gradual degeneration ending in abandonment' of the settlement, which occurred between *c.* 1100 and 1025.[25] It was a time, Desborough thinks, that marks a turning point in the Greek Dark Ages[26] and is synchronous with 'the creation of the protogeometric style of pottery in Athens'.[27] PG in Euboia, as in Attica, began *c.* 1050 and lasted until *c.* 900, when it merged with Euboian sub-PG I/II (roughly contemporary with Attic EG I/II),[28] which in turn ended *c.* 825.[29]

Protogeometric Lefkandi

The local PG ceramic phase opens with 'a burst of initiative at, or soon after, the transition from Sub-Mycenaean',[30] but progressively creativity slows and becomes very conservative. The development of Geometric pottery is particularly well illustrated from Lefkandi, where the sequences are well ordered and practically uninterrupted[31] from the re-establishment of the settlement after the short but significant break in occupation.[32] Desborough in his 1952 study, *Protogeometric Pottery*, could devote only a half page of a total of some 330 to Euboia: 'The material from this island is even more disappointing than that from Boeotia; nothing has been published whatever . . .', [33] so the excavation of Lefkandi has greatly contributed to our understanding of the ceramic of this period, as have discoveries in the last half-century at Al Mina, and other sites in the Levant, and in the west at Cumae and Pithekoussai, where Lefkandiots traded and where Euboian pottery is common. The PG sequences, like the sub-Mycenaean, are derived mainly from grave finds. The burials in all the cemeteries cover the whole period from LH IIIC^2 to EPG.[34] Up to the middle of the eleventh century, the practice at Lefkandi was to cremate the dead on pyres near the burial site, interring only the grave offerings in the tombs themselves. Significantly, however, *c.* 1025–1000, there was a change in the typical mode of interment to urn burials, similar to contemporary Attic and Boiotian custom[35] but hitherto unknown at Lefkandi. These sometimes included weapons and both imported and imitated Attic pottery.[36] This change may indicate the first arrivals of Ionians from Attica, symbolised in the literary tradition by the expedition led by Kothos and Aiklos. Xeropolis is at this time (re?)occupied.[37]

But as well as Attic products and cultural influences, there are imports from Cyprus and imitations of Egyptian and perhaps Cretan pottery,[38] evidence of trading over a wide area of the eastern Mediterranean. Finger-rings, fibulae, dress-pins, etc. of bronze, as well as some faience beads, have been recovered from the tombs, as well as hair ornaments and ear-rings of gold in quantities attesting to a degree of wealth hitherto thought unlikely for this Dark Age period and which affirm the importance and affluence of Lefkandi in the contemporary Greek world. There is every possibility that the carriers of these exotic finds were Lefkandiots themselves. After all, Homer relates that Abantes went to Troy in forty ships, while the Homeric 'Hymn to Apollo' proclaims that: 'You [Apollo] landed on Kenaion in Euboia, famous for its ships. [You stood] on the Lelantine Plain, but you were not pleased to establish a temple there and wooded groves.'[39] From Lefkandi itself we have pictorial representations on vases of two ships, one an armed merchantman, or perhaps a warship, on a *pyxis* dated 850–25 (Figures 3.2 and 3.3).[40] It has two spears in the stern, perhaps the *naumakhon xyston*, a weapon designed for sea fighting mentioned in the *Iliad*.[41] It is 'amongst the earliest, if not the earliest, post-Bronze Age representation of a ship to be found in Mainland Greece'.[42] Its accompanying tomb deposit contained gold ornaments and faience beads, suggesting that it may have been the pyre of a merchant or his wife. The second fragment, dated *c.* 825, shows only the front of a ship.[43]

There is archaeological evidence for what must have become, towards the end of the life of the settlement, an increasingly important group of traders

Figure 3.2 The 'Ship Vase' (globular *pyxis*) 850–25 from Lefkandi, Eretria Museum.

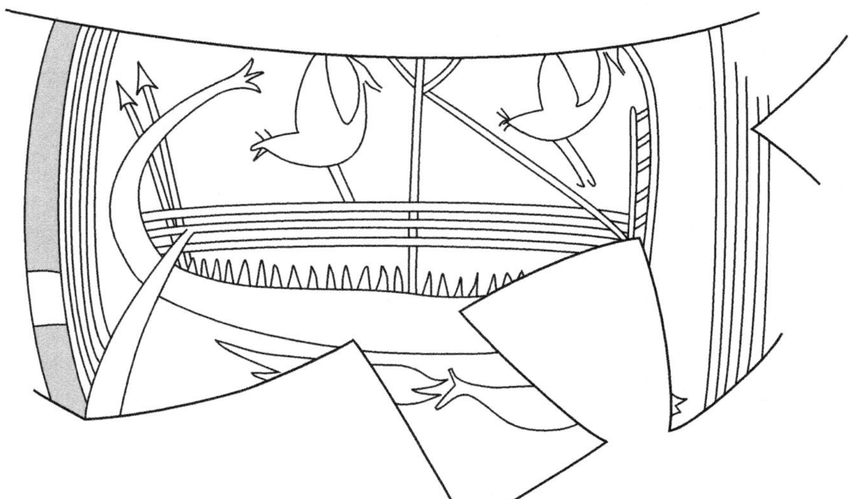

Figure 3.3 Line drawing of the ship vase (Figure 3.2).

and craftsmen in the town. Their economic and thus political importance should not be underestimated. Though perhaps some landowners were also merchants, it is doubtful whether more than an isolated adventurous few actually did sail. If landowners were involved in trade, they were probably at this stage guarantors of the sailors. Since monetary capital did not exist at this early period, the backing would have been in the form of sureties, a guaranteed market or assistance with distribution of the cargoes. Of the craftsmen, the main evidence is for metal workers and potters. Their raw materials, products and by-products are relatively indestructible and have been found in the remains of their foundries and workshops. 'Evidently by now (the tenth century) the Lefkandiots were expert metalsmiths',[44] producing a very characteristic fibula[45] and bronze tripods, for the casting of which there is evidence in the form of casting moulds and slag. Gold funerary offerings are again found, at first only a small number, but the excavators regard their presence as significant.[46] In the late tenth century, the artistic conservatism of the earlier Dark Age pottery styles is thrown off and 'new ideas flood in and are eagerly absorbed'.[47] A new local pottery type and decoration was invented, which remained characteristic of Euboian ceramic output for over 200 years, the pendent-semicircle *skyphos*.[48] Lefkandi also produced fine modelling in the round, exemplified by the famous *Centaur of Lefkandi* (Figure 3.4).[49] Other craftsmen working in perishable materials, (especially wood and cloth) must also have been present in

Figure 3.4 The *Centaur of Lefkandi*, Eretria Museum.

the settlement. Products of timber, from houses to wooden implements, were required in all settlements. The remains of the ruler buried in the PG building at Toumba were wrapped in a fine woollen cloth, some of which was still preserved for the archaeologists. It is of particular interest, for it is very rare for fabrics to be preserved for so long in the climate of Greece. We need not doubt the existence of cloth production using local woollen fibre, along with dyeing; production of the murex shell in Euboia was later a noteworthy industry from Khalkis to Karystos.[50] All these industries would require assistant workers and suppliers, so that in a smallish place such as Lefkandi the artisans were a not inconsiderable part of the population. Their innovation, combined with the appearance of wealth in the community, shows that at least the upper classes enjoyed enough prosperity and confidence in the ninth century to patronise them. The foreign trade implied in these finds, the direct import of both novel goods and raw materials for local workshops, such as gold and other metals, needed a local product or service to exchange for them. If some Lefkandiots were maritime carriers on a scale that was large for the times, as the evidence suggests, this service itself might have paid for the imports.[51] But there is no reason to suppose that many of the items of natural production for which Euboia was later famous, and for the trade in some of which we have noted the evidence of the Mycenaean dockets from Thebes, were not in demand during this period. Thus, the evidence suggests that in the ninth century Euboia was a trading island and that Lefkandi was still the centre of commercial activity, as it had been in the previous Mycenaean period.

However, the Lefkandiots also lived beside the fertile Lelantine Plain, so there must also have been an important section of the community involved in the agricultural and pastoral industries. This we would expect, given the fame of the island as 'well-cattled' and the tradition of Hippobotic aristocracy there. Traditionally landowners, as the main wealth producers, had a preponderant, if not exclusive, political control over early Greek states. The excavators think that the commercial/manufacturing innovations that appear from the beginning of the tenth century were brought in by outward-looking newcomers,[52] who supplied the needs of the aristocratic families whose wealth was based on the possession of the productive Lelantine Plain. They would initially have been welcome additions to the community and as the taste of the magnates was whetted for the new luxuries, they became ever more indispensable to them. Equally, the wealth of the commercial operators and artisans would have grown. The potential for socio-political conflict is apparent enough. In any community, men energetic and ambitious enough to acquire economic power will inevitably want some say in the political decision making of their community, particularly where it affects their private activities: tax imposts, regulations of all sorts on trade and manufacture, decisions on war and peace. Would the traditional power holders give part of it up? It is not very likely. Nevertheless, should anything occur to weaken them or cause a diminution of the available land and/or its productive capacity, a potentially revolutionary situation would be created, involving landowners and landless. Socio-political problems might emerge should the population outstrip the food-producing capacity of the land, or if prolonged drought were to cause food shortages, and there is indeed evidence that there was a major drought at the end of this very period.[53] Such natural events sometimes caused significant population shifts in ancient Greece.[54] But, while there was prosperity and enough wealth to satisfy both the landed and the commercial interests, there would be little scope for ambitious or discontented individuals (or, less likely, the poor) to cause friction.[55] Such conflicting interests must have played a role in the so-called 'rise of the *polis*-state'.[56]

There has been a significant architectural discovery at Lefkandi, which has relevance to an understanding of its political position, the so-called 'Hero Tomb'. Its discoverers more cautiously refer to it in their publication simply as 'The Protogeometric Building at Toumba'.[57] A large apsidal building, it is dated *c.* 1000–950, a period of which we know very little architecturally. The date is established by the absence of the well-known later Euboian pottery type, the *skyphoi* with pendent-semicircle decoration,[58] in the tomb itself and in the subsequent filling. This decorative *schema* was introduced at about the time that the Ionians entered Euboia[59] so that the occupants of the *heroön* were Abantes, possibly among the last of the Abantic rulers. There is debate over precisely what the building actually represents but there is, I think, conclusive enough evidence for a heroic burial, involving two individuals, a man and a woman, generally styled 'royals'. It contains other burial shafts with skeletons of at least three, probably four, horses.[60] The woman was inhumed; her skeleton was adorned with gold jewellery, and beside her head was a knife with an ivory handle. Some have suspected ritual murder in this scene. The cremated male was buried at the centre of the building in a decorated bronze amphora covered by the remnants of a decorated cloth mentioned already and closed over with a bronze bowl. Alongside were an iron sword, a spearhead and a whetstone; clearly, the weapons were not merely ceremonial accoutrements. Lefkandiot warriors also used bows and arrows (Figure 3.5). Here are all the trappings of burial ceremonies in the grand manner of a Homeric hero such as Patroklos.[61] Powell[62] has argued that the Homeric epics were set down in writing in Euboia for its Hippobotic lords. If he is right, they reflect, in so far as they are based on the lifestyle of any actual communities, the aristocratic values and lifestyle in Euboia during the early Iron Age.[63] At any rate, the Euboian aristocrats must have been able to identify readily with the attitudes expressed in the poems. Patroklos' funeral, with its similar ritual slaughter of humans and horses, costly offerings and the heaping up of a barrow over the pyre, suggests that this burial, or another like it on Euboia, could indeed have been a model for Homer. The building existed for only a short time. Subsequently it was deliberately filled in and covered over with a mound.[64] The excavators do not know why. They suggest that it may have been due to a feeling of desecration when part of the building collapsed, revealing earlier

Figure 3.5 The MPG 'Archer *Hydria*' from Lefkandi, Eretria Museum.

tombs beneath.[65] Perhaps it was the consequence of social upheaval,[66] or the building may have been destroyed by the invading Ionians more or less immediately after their arrival/conquest, before the pendent-semicircle decorative motif had taken hold among the potters of Lefkandi. The covering-over of the building may then have been a symbolic gesture on the part of the new rulers, stamping their authority on the town and its people.

The structure is so impressive and the interment so 'heroic' that we must ask what sort of society erected it and what was the status of the town, the hero-ruler of which this warrior was. It did not stand in isolation but was surrounded by other, less grandiose burials, but which nevertheless contained grave goods that give evidence of the wealth of their occupants in life. The poor, of course, in this as in many other ages, had no permanent burial markers.[67] A number contained, as did the great tomb, weapons of war buried as personal treasures of their owners. While weapons per se do not necessarily indicate a military role for the possessors, the fact that swords appear relatively frequently would seem to me to indicate soldiering as a major preoccupation of these men, as the sword in particular is not a hunting tool. I have already mentioned the late-Mycenaean fragment with the chariot-riding man.[68] I therefore suggest that in this building and cemetery one of the last *wanaktes* of Lefkandi was buried among his nobles, the *Hippobotai*, men of substance and their families, as their grave furnishings attest. Postulating an exclusive upper-class cemetery would explain the rather small number of burials per period in it, vis-à-vis the apparent extent of the settlement on the citadel, a paradox touched on briefly by the excavators and by Desborough, for we may be dealing here with burial grounds that contained only the graves and pyres of the king's peers.[69]

Homer has the Abantic *hegemon*, Elephenor Khalkodontiades, leading levies from all over Euboia against Troy. Hesiod describes heroic funeral games for the later *basileus*, Amphidamas of Khalkis. Later poets and commentators always imply a wealthy and exclusive landed, horse-rearing aristocracy as the dominant class in early Euboia. Some of them, such as Arkhilokhos and Theognis, were contemporary with events they describe. Strabo, on the other hand, quotes from an early stele preserved in the temple of Amarysia at Amarynthos describing the ceremonial gathering of the horse- and chariot-riding nobility of Eretria. Aristotle uses the governments of the *Hippobotai* of Khalkis and the *Hippeis* of Eretria as paradigms of those early states in which this class was dominant. The ruling class at Lefkandi will have shared these pursuits. Moreover, Lefkandi in the period from the eleventh to the mid-ninth centuries was foremost among the towns, not only of Euboia but also of all Greece. As yet, 'New' Eretria was hardly more than an insignificant village, whereas PG Khalkis to this day lies concealed beneath the modern city, if indeed it ever existed. There is no real hint that either could have equalled, much less eclipsed, Lefkandi in wealth or size. Thus, we should see the ruler of Lefkandi and his nobles as pre-eminent in wealth and power among the petty rulers of the individual *komai* such as Oikhalia and its mythical leader Eurytos. The Lefkandiot princes were military rulers. Their manner of burial with their weapons, surrounded by their nobles, as well as the hints in the literary tradition of chivalric codes of military conduct characteristic of Euboians at several points in their history, suggest that they were feudal rulers. Their town had the agricultural and commercial capacity to support their status and pretensions and the horse-rearing landowners were, at least until almost the end, the undisputed ruling class.

During the period of the Dark Ages corresponding to Euboian sub-PG I, II and III in the ceramic sequences (*c.* 900 to *c.* 750), the Euboian *ethnos*-state based on Lefkandi must have broken down, because by the latter date the Euboians, who were the first to send out colonies to Italy and Sicily, did so by *poleis* and not as Euboians. There are signs of possible trouble. In their pottery the Lefkandiots lose their innovative flair and return to conservatism and a restrictiveness of shapes and decorative motifs.[70] The pendent-semicircle *skyphos* becomes the dominant popular form almost to the exclusion of other styles. Indeed, at Lefkandi and in Euboia as a whole, the Geometric style does not develop fully until the Attic MG period,[71] earlier decorative styles lingering on longer than in nearby areas, and the same observation applies to other crafts such as metalworking.[72] Though burial customs remain unchanged and some still have military equipment as grave offerings, imports from Attica become fewer and remain rare until *c.* 825. Nevertheless, finds from the cemeteries do not otherwise indicate recession or a falling-off of overseas trade generally. Imports (and imitations of them) from Thessaly, Egypt, Cyprus, Macedonia and Phoenicia continue, and indeed increase.[73] Moreover, the offerings are luxurious: gold rings, necklaces, faience, glass, bronze bowls, etc. indicate a still considerable material prosperity. The evidence from imports of flourishing trade is reinforced by finds of Euboian goods abroad, particularly in Cyprus and Crete before 825. After this date, Attic imports resume and indeed become for a while preponderant among the grave goods in Lefkandi cemeteries.[74] One local(?) ceramic product at least defies this conservatism, the *Centaur of Lefkandi*, which Desborough has described as 'one of the masterpieces of the Dark Ages.' It is 'a figure of great dignity: the modelling of the head is especially remarkable but, knowing as little as we do, dare we say that it is in advance of its time?'[75] The mythical home of the Centaurs was Thessaly, and numerous Thessalian imports are found in the grave deposits of this period. Several early tribal groups had arrived in Euboia from or through Thessaly and so the mythology of the Centaurs was no doubt imported into the island from there at an early date. The Centaur Nessos was associated with the events surrounding the capture of Oikhalia by Herakles.[76] We therefore cannot exclude the possibility that the statuette itself was an import from Thessaly. However, local or not, the mythology was not unknown already to the people of central Euboia.

At this point, the excavators are perplexed; contrasting with these material indications of prosperity there is the decline in local artistic initiative, perhaps evidence of a crisis of confidence similar to that which seems to have earlier afflicted Greece prior to the collapse of the Mycenaean civilisation. Moreover, there is evidence of fire destruction, not necessarily of the whole settlement, although this is not clear. Was there a slow deterioration of harmony within the community? Was there a perceived threat from outside? Was the town in fact wholly destroyed? Shortly after 825, the cemeteries ceased to be used. It is very likely that there was a disaster, and the excavators think that a severe dislocation of the population occurred.[77] They stress, however, the ambiguous nature of the evidence so far and the need for further excavation, especially of the settlement area on Xeropolis hill. The abandonment of the cemeteries 'indicates that the families that used them had either been wiped out or moved elsewhere'.[78] Did the potentially revolutionary situation suggested above[79] now come to pass? Alternatively, was the social structure overturned as a result of invasive warfare for the control of the Lelantine Plain, as Calligas thinks?[80] There is no help from archaeology towards a solution to what happened at Lefkandi shortly after 825. What is strange is that this time it is the burial ground that has never been located, although we know that the settlement continued for a while to be inhabited.

When the settlement was destroyed, 'Lefkandian' exports did not stop and, in fact, they increased.[81] How can that be? The excavators' language is ambiguous. They note the large quantity of central Euboian pottery found at Al Mina and Tell es Sûkâs in Syria, as well as on Cyprus. They rightly use the term 'Euboian', but in the context they are implying 'Lefkandian'. It is possible that Lefkandiots were still involved in the Eastern trade, but that the production of the 'Euboian' goods was being undertaken elsewhere, perhaps by Lefkandiots now living in a new town. There is no evidence for this trade from Lefkandi itself, since the known cemeteries were abandoned and the town is still incompletely excavated; it all came from overseas, from both the East and the West. Chemical/crystal analyses tell us only that the clay conforms to the general type for the Lelantine area.[82] There are thus three possible sites of origin for this Euboian pottery found abroad: Lefkandi itself, Eretria and Khalkis. The excavators think that Lefkandi was still playing a major role, but we cannot rule out Eretria or, though less likely, Khalkis as sources for the Euboian products sold in the markets of the Levant, Italy and Sicily. That the export of central Euboian pottery to the East continued and even expanded for a while, coupled with the planting of the first commercial Greek colony in the west at Pithekoussai in the next century and the apparent removal of artisans and their industries to other locations, suggests that the abandonment of the cemeteries of Lefkandi and partial or total destruction of the town[83] represents a defeat for the landowning ruling class that had buried its dead in the shadow of the *heroön*. As a consequence, burial probably now took place on the landowners' private estates rather than in any common cemetery. However, was defeat the result of civil war or foreign invasion? If the latter, from where did the destroyers come? Not from what would now become Eretria, since that had been up to then a very minor settlement. Amarynthos? Hardly likely, for why then allow the population to resettle itself even closer to home and pose a continuing threat? Khalkis is the only possibility from within Euboia. It might thus be tempting to suggest internal dissension, with the traders and artisans attempting to assert control, and the excavators indeed think it possible.[84] Perhaps the *Hippobotai* of Lefkandi actually called in their Khalkidian peers to suppress the revolt and they then took advantage of the situation to seize control. The commercial/artisan part of the population may then have migrated to the site of Eretria,[85] which presents some commercial advantages over the old town, notably its potentially better harbour and a site that would allow for expansion within easily defensible walls. Landowners, however, would naturally be reluctant to leave their ancestral lands and may well have retired to them after a defeat, acquiescing in Khalkidian rule, burying their dead on their estates. No doubt, a few with enemies in the new order went to Eretria, but if settled from Lefkandi it was probably, from the first, a town with predominantly commercial interests. And, if their defeat involved the Khalkidians, that would explain the failure of Lefkandi to revive as it had always done in the past, for the latter would not have allowed a serious political or economic challenger to continue to exist so close to their territory.

Figure 3.6 View from Xeropolis Hill over the east bay, towards the acropolis of Eretria and Mt Olympos.

Overpopulation as an explanation for the move to Eretria would seem unlikely, as the Lefkandi cemeteries do not indicate any increase in burial rates leading up to the catastrophe. However, the number of burials may be a misleading indicator of population changes in this case, because the cemeteries appear to have been the preserve of only a small elite class of *basileis*. If the landowners retreated to their estates, it is unlikely that any later collective burial ground will ever be discovered. If this scenario is near the truth, then the Euboian ware found in the East in increasing quantities was probably Eretrian. At Khalkis on the other hand, its non-commercial, Hippobotic class was reinforced by the addition to its territory of the Lelantine lands of Lefkandi. The site remained sparsely occupied after 825, but it is unlikely that the town played any further significant economic or political role.[86] Its very existence came to an end in 'no more than a generation and perhaps less'.[87] The residual population may have been an outpost left behind by the retreating refugees. The settlement moved to the east bay facing Eretria (Figure 3.6), thus perhaps indicating its allegiance between 825 and 700.[88] It perhaps survived long enough to have been involved in the founding of Pithekoussai (before 750). Sending out the colony may have solved the problem of Lefkandian refugees who remained behind in Khalkidian territory. Eretria, too, would have had an interest in the venture, as its dominant group was now made up primarily of traders and artisans with a need for raw materials. The newcomers may now have taken the opportunity to remove any members of the indigenous population that still remained hostile. So, if the settling of Pithekoussai were a joint venture, both sides profited.

Lefkandi lasted long enough to have received the alphabetic script that was adopted about this time.[89] 'Then, around 700 BC, Xeropolis was [again] sacked and virtually abandoned thereafter.'[90] The British archaeologists believe that the town was destroyed in the war between Khalkis and Eretria that some scholars have called the Lelantine War. By the sixth century, 'Xeropolis was already well on the way to earning its present name of the deserted city.'[91]

Notes

1 P. Calligas, 'Hero-cult in early Iron Age Greece', in R. Hågg, N. Marinatos and G. Nordquist (eds), *Early Greek Cult Practice*, Proceedings of the Fifth International Symposium at the Swedish Institute at Athens, 26–29 June, 1986, Stockholm, 1988, 229. For the end of Mycenaean civilisation on Euboia: V. Desborough, 'The end of Mycenaean civilization and the Dark Ages: the archaeological background', CAH II, 2[a], 1980, Ch. XXXVIa, 666.

2 Calligas 1988, 229–30.

3 Popham *et al.* 1980b, 7.

4 The phrase is taken from title of the Second International Symposium held at the Swedish Institute in Athens, 1–5 June, 1981.

5 Popham *et al.* 1980b, 7.

6 Desborough 1972, 11.

7 Ch. 2, pp. 55–7.

8 Parlama 1979, 3–14; Sapouna-Sakellaraki 1992, 235–63 (map and plates); see also Ch. 2, pp. 48–9 and n. 190; pp. 51–2 and nn. 222–4.

9 Ch. 2, pp. 52–4.

10 Popham *et al.* 1980b, 7.

11 Dr Doniert Evely's notes for a lecture given at the University of New England, Armidale, Australia, 17 August, 1994.

12 L. Sackett and M. Popham 1972, 13; see photo/plan.

13 Desborough 1972, 32.

14 Ibid. 32. Catling 1968, 41–9 and pl. 21, Fig. 1).

15 M. Popham and L. Sackett, *Excavations at Lefkandi, Euboea, 1964–1966*, London, 1968, 18; Fig. 34; M. Popham and E. Milburn, 'The late Helladic IIIC pottery of Xeropolis (Lefkandi), a summary', *BSA* 66, 1971, 338, n. 8; Popham *et al.* 1980b, 7; Sackett and Popham 1972, 14.

16 J. Rutter, 'Ceramic evidence for northern intruders in southern Greece at the beginning of the late Helladic IIIC Period', *AJA* 79, 1975, 17–32.

17 Sackett and Popham 1972, 14.

18 J. Musgrave and M. Popham, 'The late Helladic IIIC intramural burials at Lefkandi, Euboea', *BSA* 86, 1991, 273–96. See above, Ch. 2, pp. 53–4.

19 Biers 1980, 83: in the 'closed' style the 'whole surface is covered with a close-fitting net of conventional designs'.'The 'open' style leaves more of the vessel untouched by paint.

20 Desborough, 1964, 17–8, equates sub-Mycenaean with LH IIIC[2] and scarcely uses the term. But in idem, 1972, 32, he implies that it followed LH IIIC: 'and this (a description of LH IIIB to IIIC ware) was more or less the situation when Sub-Mycenaean pottery made its appearance.' See Biers 1985, 100–4.

21 Popham *et al.* 1980b, 355.

22 Ibid. 356.

23 Ibid. 4–5, 7–8. Only one small area has been fully excavated.

24 Ibid. 356.

25 Sackett and Popham 1972, 14.

26 Desborough 1972, 79.

27 Idem 133.

28 J. Coldstream, *Geometric Greece*, London, 1977, 385.
29 Popham *et al.* 1980b, 8; 367–8.
30 Ibid. 356.
31 Desborough 1972, 188.
32 Popham *et al.* 1980b, 7; Sackett and Popham 1972, 14–5. Cf. Desborough 1972, 189: 'reoccupied after a possibly long interval.' Evely (see above, n. 15): depopulated *c.* 1100; by *c.* 1000 recovered and 'the veritable centre of the Greek world' (my notes from the lecture).
33 Ibid. 199.
34 Desborough 1972, 68; Popham *et al.* 1980, 7–8.
35 Popham *et al.* 1980b, 358.
36 Ibid. 200–2: (Tomb T 14, Toumba cemetery); 361–2 and 358 (Attic imports).
37 Ibid. 358.
38 M. Popham, E. Touloupa and L. Sackett, 'The Hero of Lefkandi', *Antiquity* 56, 1982, 171, diag. 3.
39 Hom. *Il.* 2, 545; [Hom.] ad *AP* 219–21. The Pythian part of the Hymn is no later than the seventh century: H. Evelyn-White, *Hesiod, the Homeric Hymns and Homerica (Loeb)*, Cambridge, MA, intro. xxxvii.
40 M. Popham, 'An early Euboean ship', *OJA* 6 1987, 353–9: dated fairly certainly 950/825 from Attic MG I pottery found in association with it (tomb 61) and by comparison with other locally produced pots dated by associated Attic MG I pottery; Popham *et al.* 1980b, 7. To the Euboian examples may be added the 'shipwreck vase', *c.* 720 from the Euboian settlement at Pithekoussai: see S. Brunnsåker, 'The Pithecusan shipwreck', *Opusc.Romana* 4, 1962, 165–242.
41 The ναύμαχον ξυστόν Hom. *Il.* 15, 388–9; 15, 677.
42 Popham, 1987, 355–6, discusses the type of ship in relation to other representations on ceramic.
43 Popham *et al.* 1980b, 267; 274 [918]; 284 [11].
44 Popham *et al.* 1980b, 359.
45 Ibid. 239; 264.
46 Ibid. 359.
47 Ibid. 358–9.
48 Ibid. 359.
49 See below, p. 84 (and photo of the Centaur).
50 Ch. 1, p. 14, nn. 51–3; pp. 17, 20
51 Euboians in the Levant: J. Boardman, *The Greeks Overseas; their Early Colonies and Trade*, London, 1980, 40–1; 42: 'It seems likely then that it was the Euboeans who led the Greeks to Al Mina . . . The evidence for the Euboeans' role in the east is wholly archaeological.'
52 Popham *et al.* 1980b, 360.
53 R Carpenter, *Discontinuity in Greek Civilization*, Cambridge, 1966; and J. Camp, 'A drought in the late eighth century BC', *Hesperia* 48, 1979, 397–411. On drought: see Ch. 4, p. 93 and n. 30.
54 J. Cook, 'The Palai-names', *Historia* 4, 1955, 41; and N. Demand, *Urban Relocation in Archaic and Classical Greece. Flight and Consolidation*, Bristol, 1990, especially Ch. 2, 13 for some reasons for people to shift their urban centre to another site.
55 On the potential for social revolution in the early Greek towns: I. Morris, *Burial and Ancient Society: The Rise of the Greek City-state*, Cambridge, 1987, 202–10.
56 Chs 4, pp. 91–3, and especially 5, pp. 156–62.
57 M. Popham *et al.*, *Lefkandi II: The Proto-geometric Building at Toumba*, London (Part 1: *The Pottery*, by R. Catling and I. Lemos, 1990; and Part 2: *The Excavation, Architecture and Finds*, by J. Coulton and H. Catling, 1993). However Calligas had earlier (1988, 230–2) disagreed with this designation, preferring to see it as a 'patriarchal' oikos.
58 R. Kearsley, 'The pendent semi-circle Skyphos', *BICS* Suppl. 44, 1989.

59 Ch. 2, pp. 45–6, 54–5.
60 Popham *et al.* 1982, 171–4. For the horse-drawn chariot from Lefkandi: Catling 1968.
61 Hom. *Il.*, 23, 127 ad. fin.
62 B. Powell, *Homer and the Origin of the Greek Alphabet*, Cambridge, 1991; idem, 'Did Homer sing at Lefkandi?', *Electronic Antiquity* 1, ii, 1993, from the website: gopher: //babel.its.utas.edu.au/00/Publications/Electronic%20Antiquity%20.../Powell-Home (8 pp.); idem, 'Homer and writing', in I. Morris and B. Powell (eds), *A New Companion to Homer*, Leiden, 1997, 3–32.
63 Kirk 1980a, 205.
64 Evely lecture (see above, n. 11); Popham *et al.* 1982, 174.
65 Ibid. 174.
66 Evely; Morris 1987, 202–10.
67 Morris 1987, 97–109.
68 Ch. 2, p. 35.
69 See the later *heroön* at Eretria: see below Ch. 4, pp.109–10 (and photo).
70 Popham *et al.* 1980b, 362.
71 Idem; Coldstream 1977, 385.
72 Popham *et al.* 1980b, 362.
73 Ibid. 362–3.
74 Ibid. 363.
75 Desborough 1972, 199; photo pl. 46; 200.
76 S. Trakh., *passim*.
77 Popham *et al.* 1980b, 364.
78 Ibid. 365.
79 See above, pp. 77–82.
80 Calligas, 1988, 232, thinks that the abandonment was the result of invasion.
81 Popham *et al.* 1980b, 367.
82 For the problems of differentiating clays used in Euboian pottery found at Al Mina (and so determining place of manufacture): M. Popham, H. Hatcher and A. Pollard, 'Al-Mina and Euboea', *BSA* 75, 1980, 151–60; J. Boardman and F. Schweitzer, 'Clay analyses of Archaic Greek pottery', *BSA* 68, 1973, 273–8 (Euboian pottery types). Euboian finds at Tell Sûkâs: P. Riis, *Sûkâs I. The North-East Sanctuary and the First Settling of Greeks in Syria and Palestine*, Publications of the Carlsberg Expedition to Phoenicia 1, Copenhagen, 1970, 126; 150–2, Fig. 51 (pendent semicircle skyphoi). Kearsley 1989, esp. Ch. 8, 133: Lefkandiot origin; generally: 155; 165, map of shipping routes. A. Pollar and H. Hatcher, 'Euboean exports to Al Mina', *BSA* 78, 1983, 281–90 (the archaeological conclusions are by Popham).
83 Leekley and Efstratiou 1980, 66; Sackett and Popham 1972; Popham *et al.* 1980b, 363: burials ceased *c.* 825 (p. 364); at least one building in the settlement destroyed by fire (p. 365).
84 Popham *et al.* 1980b, 366.
85 On the contrary Popham *et al.*, 1980b, 366, suggest that the artisans (metalworkers) generally went to Khalkis ('copper city'?) and the traders to Eretria.
86 Ibid. 368.
87 Ibid. 367.
88 Ibid. 368. J. Coulton, 'Euboean Phylla and Greek barracks', in D. Evely, I. Lemos and S. Sherratt (eds), *Minotaur and Centaur. Studies in the Archaeology of Crete and Euboea presented to Mervyn Popham*, Oxford, 1996, 163–4, is less positive.
89 Popham *et al.* 1980b, 89–93.
90 Ibid. 368.
91 Idem.

4

ERETRIA FROM *c.* 825 TO *c.* 650

PART 1: THE ARCHAEOLOGICAL HISTORY, THE SITE OF THE CITY AND ITS EARLY CONSTITUTIONAL EVOLUTION

The history of New Eretria[1] begins with the first exodus from Lefkandi, *c.* 825,[2] and the 'foundation' of what Schefold has called the 'first colony of Old Eretria'.[3] This statement should not be taken as indicating that I believe that the site of the city was at that time a *terra nullius*, for we have seen that there is archaeological evidence from the ancient city area, as well as the acropolis[4] and other nearby locations, of occupation from the LN and EH to the Geometric period. Indeed, there are signs of LN settlement on the site of the city itself.[5] Although in 1974 Themelis had observed that 'Up to now, by reason of the small dimensions of the trial trench, the [then recently discovered] EG *amphoriskos* has not been linked to any architectural remains of the same period', and adds that 'we hope that the continuation of the investigation will uncover also buildings of the ninth century BC and perhaps even earlier, which would bridge the gap which exists today in Eretrian studies, between the Mycenaean and LG periods', by 1982 he felt able to say that the discovery of the vessel 'further strengthens our opinion that Eretria has been located on the same site even from prehistoric (Protohelladic) times'. Then, in:

> the lowest natural sandy/pebbly layer was found also a fragment from the shoulder of a *prokhous* (ritual washing jug) decorated with concentric semicircles which may be compared with examples from the LPG–sub-PG I cemeteries at Lefkandi. The appearance of early pottery of the ninth century BC in the lowest layer of the natural overfill along with LG sherds shows that there also existed on the ancient red earth bed-soil remains (buildings or tombs) of the LPG period, which were removed and deposited in the fill during the LG period. With such PG remains belongs the EG *amphoriskos* from area Δ, together with a number of PG vessels which were found in a deep trench in layers of red earth north of the temple of Apollo.[6]

We may thus live in hope that time will reveal more of the earliest settlement on the site.

At about the same time as the final abandonment of Lefkandi (*c.* 700),[7] there was a catastrophe at the new settlement at Eretria as well: there are repeated references in Themelis' excavation reports to fire destruction in the late-eighth-/early-seventh-century levels. 'Remains of unbaked bricks from the upper structure, which were found wedged in the stones of the foundations, were reddish-colour from the action of fire, a fact that could mean that the apsidal building was destroyed by a conflagration.'[8] Themelis believed that: 'with the [archaeological] data presently at our disposal, we can maintain that [Eretria] was occupied without interruption from the second half of the ninth to the late-eighth/early-seventh centuries, when, for unknown reasons, it was abandoned.'[9] The reason for this is, however, suggested by the discovery of the existence of a fortification wall that was constructed between 710 and 675,[10] which clearly indicates that the inhabitants feared attack. At any rate, the Eretrians built their fortification and it apparently failed.[11] Eretria was deserted by its inhabitants, including the now well-known goldsmith, who fled, leaving behind his cache of precious metal and incomplete jewellery.[12] Themelis believed in 1974 that the abandonment of *c.* 700 was not confined just to the immediate area of his excavations but that the whole city area remained largely unoccupied until the fourth century![13] It was for this reason that Themelis was unwilling to identify Lefkandi as the so-called 'Old' Eretria.[14] Nevertheless, the absence of archaeological data is not as complete as is suggested by Themelis' 1974 statement, which started the theory of total abandonment. Not only the fact of the continued existence of the temple of Apollo through several phases of rebuilding but also scattered finds throughout the city area during subsequent excavations deter any acceptance of a total and prolonged abandonment of the whole site.[15] Moreover, the idea defies both probability and the literary-historical record, which point to the importance of Eretria during the Archaic period. Mazarakis-Ainian has suggested that there might have been only a brief abandonment of Eretria at this time due to a 'counter-attack' by the Khalkidians.[16] His choice of words thus implies that the final destruction of Lefkandi was the consequence of an original Eretrian attack. If such an attack occurred, it represents an attempt by the refugees to recover the lost Lelantine area east of the River Lelas. By 1983 Themelis had changed his opinion: 'it is a fact nevertheless that it [the first settlement at Eretria] was rebuilt and re-inhabited immediately after the first catastrophe.'[17] But whether the (final) destruction of Lefkandi was significantly before that of Eretria in *c.* 700, or whether the two disasters occurred more or less simultaneously, is unknown. Whatever the precise truth, we may be sure that Eretria was soon reoccupied and continued to develop throughout the seventh and subsequent centuries. It can thus still be argued that:

1 *c.* 825: there was an attack on Lefkandi/Xeropolis causing the greater part

of the population to flee to Eretria and establish the ninth-/eighth-century settlement on an already partially occupied site.

2 Between *c.* 825 and *c.* 700: a much reduced settlement continued to exist at the Lefkandi/Xeropolis site, its east bay location facing Eretria perhaps indicating allegiance to the new settlement at Eretria.[18] 'We may wonder whether [Lefkandi] was not by this time occupied mainly by remnants of that element of its population which had largely moved to Eretria, so retaining a protective presence nearer the plain, part of which it continued to cultivate.'[19]

3 *c.* 700: there was a final and decisive attack on Lefkandi, followed by/synchronous with one on Eretria, leading to its brief temporary abandonment.

There are explanations that would account for the present relative dearth of archaeological material at Eretria for the period between then and the fifth century. First, we must remember that the Persians extensively destroyed the city in 490, followed shortly afterwards by extensive clearing and rebuilding. Furthermore, there is evidence of several previous phases of demolition and clearing of the Geometric and earlier settlement areas for redevelopment,[20] as well as of the clearing and reuse of cemeteries.[21] Second, as Morris points out, there is, due to the close similarity of pottery styles, with the persistence of particular shapes and motifs over long periods in Euboia, considerable difficulty in establishing precise dates for deposits based on ceramic finds, and there has been a too-ready assumption by researchers that most, if not all, of certain types must necessarily be early; this may not be so. The explanation therefore may be, and indeed is likely to be, partly the result of failures of retrieval and recognition of the archaeological material: 'There may be serious errors in interpretation of the settlement pottery.'[22] That Eretria was a total casualty of the Lelantine War and was largely deserted for over two centuries is hard to believe, but that Khalkis, where there is likewise an absence of a material record, was also stretches credulity to its limits.[23]

It has naturally been tempting to see these early destructions at Lefkandi and Eretria as outcomes of the Lelantine War, particularly since most scholars have viewed this conflict as a single war and many would date it to the eighth century.[24] The nature of the war is discussed in Chapter 5, where I make clear my belief that it was not a single war/battle but rather a centuries-long struggle by Eretria and Khalkis, since at least Mycenaean times, for control of the Lelantine Plain and that it does not belong to one restricted period.[25] Themelis thinks that the *c.* 700 destruction of Eretria 'should be related to the last and crucial phase of the Lelantine War, which resulted in the definitive defeat of Eretria by Khalkis'.[26] I naturally do not agree. He later modifies this view:

> Finally, it appears likely that the decline and abandonment of the LG settlement of Eretria at the beginning of the seventh century should not be

> attributed solely to the Lelantine War as we earlier suggested but to crop failure which accompanied a period of drought.[27]

Nowhere else in his reports however does he mention a 'period of decline'.

Camp had already argued for a prolonged drought at the end of the eighth–early seventh centuries for Attica.[28] Themelis rightly points out that both it and Euboia constitute a single climatic entity, and so if Camp's theory holds for Attica, it does also for Euboia. Contemporary drought is suggested by the increase in offerings made at the sanctuary of Zeus Ombrios on Mt Hymettos in Attica.[29] Themelis, moreover, reports geological evidence for drought at this time at Eretria itself, describing deposition layers (containing ceramic sherds of the late eighth/early seventh centuries) with hard upper crusts:

> The creation of these thin successive layers beginning at a depth of 10 cm and reaching approximately 1.10/1.12 m must be due to natural causes . . . They are perhaps the product of a period of drought during which rainwater stagnated in places, while the material which the water brought down (soil, pebbles, sand, clay) settled out and formed the thin successive layers whose upper surface hardened and took on the appearance of a crust.[30]

Drought would have been a powerful force impelling the two cities that coveted the fertile Lelantine Plain to war. Moreover at this same time Zagora, the Eretrian *emporion* on Andros (ninth–eighth centuries), was deserted systematically and without violence.[31] Water seems to have been a problem at Zagora even in its heyday,[32] and Andros is also in fact a part of our climatic entity. However, the Australian excavators do not mention drought as a possible contributory cause of the abandonment:

> The reason for this move is not certain at present. It may have been caused by an earthquake which damaged their houses and reduced the quantity of water in the nearby springs or they might have decided to abandon their settlement not because of an act of God but rather because of a general improvement of conditions in the Aegean.[33]

Earthquakes also destroyed Smyrna at this time.[34] If one occurred on such a scale that it could have seriously damaged both Zagora on Andros and Smyrna on the Asia Minor coast, then it could have destroyed Eretria (and Lefkandi) also. Such a cataclysm is most unlikely, however, for there is no hint of it at all in the surviving literary tradition. This in no way precludes any or all three (drought/earthquake/war) from being responsible. However, the literary references to persistent warfare between Eretria and Khalkis makes this, along with drought, the likely direct causes.

There are various traditions concerning the original name of Eretria, one or more of which may go back to the LN/EH settlement on the site. Melaneïs, Arotria and Eretria are mentioned.[35] Melaneïs refers to blackness or darkness, perhaps to the general complexion colour of the pre-Hellenic inhabitants compared with that of later (northern) immigrants.[36] The eponymous hero, father of Eurytos, king of Dryopian Oikhalia, who was killed by Dorian Herakles, was called Melaneus. However, if the name referred to soils, it would be appropriate enough for Eretria or the Eretrian Plain generally, where they are of the red-earth type.[37] Perhaps it reflects a dark and forested location to which the new settlers came from Lefkandi on the open Lelantine Plain.[38] We may note, too, that the goddess Hekate, closely associated with Zeus and who had oracles of the dead, is given epithets with the eponymic element 'Mel-'[39]. I have identified her already with the chthonic Artemis, principal early deity of the area.[40] The pairing of Arotria/Eretria is interesting for the phonetic similarity. They may be meant to indicate the primary occupational interests of the inhabitants. Arotria is derived from the stem *arot-* (denoting tillage; husbandry), whereas Eretria is usually derived from *eretto* (to row).[41] Arotria is, however, not especially suitable as a name for the area of the new city. The Eretrian Plain is fertile enough as agricultural lands in Greece go. However, Arotria, interpreted as 'the ploughing city', would have been much more appropriate to Lefkandi, the site of which commanded the fabulously fertile soils of the Lelantine Plain. Greeks at all times were amused by word games and Greek interest in descriptive toponymy goes back to, and probably beyond, Homer's time. The apparent punning on the two names might appear at first sight a later piece of sophisticated wordplay, but it would not at all have been out of character for settlers arriving at the site of their new home from Lefkandi to have invented a punning name for it, highlighting the new social and economic realities.[42] Finally, it may simply be a later literary conceit. In any case, the 'ploughing city' became the 'rowing city'. Arotria is not listed among possible names for the site of Lefkandi by the authors of *Lefkandi I;*[43] perhaps it should!

In the previous chapter, I suggested that the abandonment of Lefkandi might have followed the defeat of the traditional landowning aristocracy in the wake of a Khalkidian invasion. This conforms with the view of the excavators, though they are cautious in expressing this opinion.[44] Military defeat of the traditional power holders would provide the best hope for another group to seize control. Demand thinks such an explanation 'anachronistic'. However, desire for political power is never anachronistic, and we have noted evidence of two distinct socio-economic groups in Lefkandi that would have had quite different political attitudes and objectives.[45] We are, after all, not so far from the time of the earliest tyrants, and no one thinks their seizure of power, backed by dissatisfied elements, to be anachronistic. Socio-economic forces during the eighth/seventh centuries, which ultimately led to the rise of Pheidon, the Kypselidai and others, may have operated in central Euboia even earlier. That the area was the earliest to send out colonies suggests that political/economic strains were becoming apparent by then. In the new environment at Eretria, the political balance must have been severely altered. While any landowners compelled to flee would naturally have lost their land, and probably their livestock, and therefore the basis of their wealth to the invaders, artisans would have been able to take most of their wealth-producing means with them: their tools of trade and even some of their raw materials and wares. There was certainly metalworking in gold and copper within the early Geometric settlement of Eretria.[46] It is likely that these skills were brought in from elsewhere, for the products suggest both Lefkandiot and Cypriot models[47]. Sailors too would have taken their ships and trade goods. There can be no doubt where economic, and therefore political, power lay in the new city: in the hands of the artisan and commercial classes. This is not to say that there must necessarily have been an immediate 'revolution'. If there were a large enough number of emigré landowners they would have had some chance of maintaining control for a while, since they would still have been armed and had a virtual monopoly of military skills. Although defeated and dislodged from their ancestral estates, they may have been able to successfully usurp possession of the farmlands on the Eretrian Plain and with them their wealth-producing capacity. Although not the equal of the Lelantine Plain for crops, it nevertheless makes good grazing land, and olives, vines and fruit are grown there today (Figure 4.1). Nevertheless, such a scenario requires us to postulate that a substantial number of armed landowners migrated, and this is not likely. Anyhow, time and economic strength were on the side of the artisan and commercial classes. Their skills were in immediate demand both in the new community and beyond, so that they would

Figure 4.1 The Eretrian Plain – orchards and cropland on shallow limestone soils.

relatively quickly have begun to generate new wealth. We need not doubt that trade was not only flourishing but also socially and politically important. Its development was one way of providing a living for the new settlement. But it may not have been enough.

Even the agriculturally wealthier Khalkidian territory, now substantially expanded by the conquest of the Lelantine Plain west of the River Lelas, was apparently becoming overpopulated, and it should have, but never has I believe, been noted that Eretria, with far less food-producing potential, must have been overstrained even sooner, especially with the arrival of the new settlers. Population pressure and consequent 'land hunger' are often adduced as the main reasons for early colonisation, and the Euboians were the first to colonise in the West. Pithekoussai, the earliest, and its offshoot Kyme (Cumae), were founded in the period 775–50 by Eretrian, Khalkidian and, presumably, Kymaian settlers, indicating a land/population problem in Euboia generally, perhaps exacerbated by drought. However, Pithekoussai and, to a lesser degree, Kyme were founded for commercial reasons, although land hunger may also have played a role, for though the town of Pithekoussai was from the first clearly a manufacturing and trading place, the island is, as Snodgrass and Ridgeway both point out, quite fertile and agriculturally productive; the hinterland at Kyme is even more so.[48] Therefore, it is possible that Eretrians settled mainly in the towns, whereas the Khalkidians gravitated to the surrounding farmland. Both settlements soon reveal evidence of internal discord,[49] no doubt reflecting the situation back home and the different interests of the constituent population groups. However, colonies never, in the final analysis, accounted for the removal of many people, perhaps only the most vocal dissidents. So the population/land impasse could not thereby have been solved and hence the two states resumed their ongoing struggle for control of the Lelantine Plain (*c.* 700).

The poorer productivity of the Eretrian lands was never in any case going to make its holders especially rich. Land at Eretria conferred status but not necessarily great wealth. If the aristocratic Lefkandiot *Hippeis* were to maintain their traditional wealth differential at Eretria, they would have to acquire income from other sources. It would not have been long before some of them anticipated Alkaios' brother Antimenidas or the Athenian aristocrat Solon and invested in trading ventures. Thus would have begun the merging of the upper classes into a broader grouping, oligarchic rather than truly aristocratic, whose power was based primarily on its liquid assets. The Eretrian *emporion* that was established on Andros possibly as early as 800,[50] shortly after the arrival at Eretria of the first refugees, appears to have been devoted solely to commercial activities. It has been suggested that not only was the settlement itself Eretrian, but that: 'the whole island [Andros] had passed over into Eretrian control.'[51] Some of the pottery found there has close affinities with slightly earlier types typical of Lefkandi[52] and the 'most common imported fabric is Euboean',[53] indeed Eretrian.[54] The excavators also mention some ceramic characteristic of Tenos,[55]

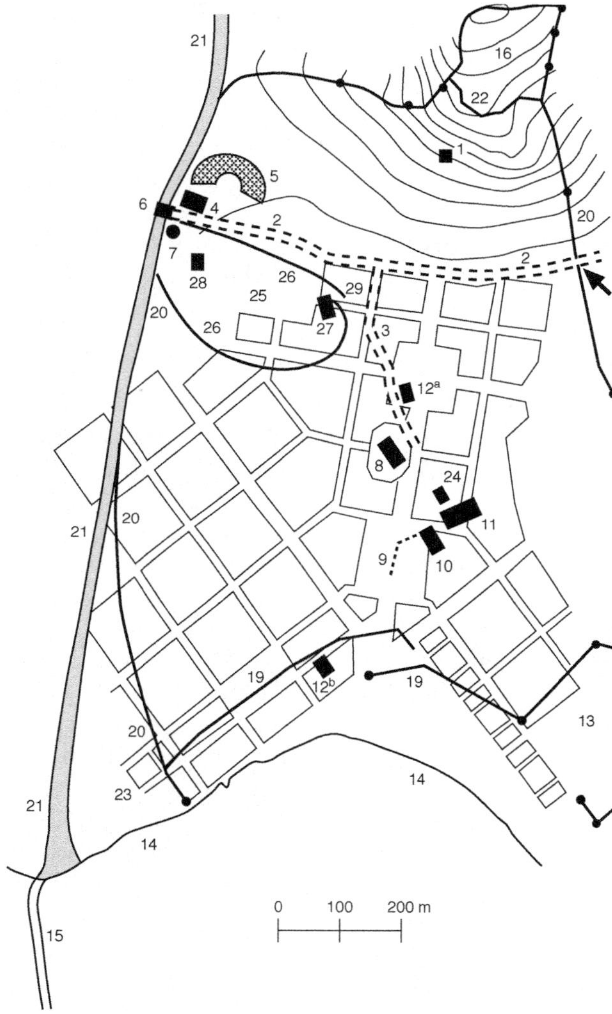

1 Thesmophoreion
2–2 W–E main road
3 N–S road
4 Temple of Dionysos
5 Hellenistic theatre
6 West Gate complex and monumental bridge
7 Heroön
8 Temple and temenos of Apollo Daphnephoros and associated structures
9 Boundary line of the Archaic agora
10 Eastern stoa
11 MH habitations
12[a,b] Geometric habitations
13 Ancient harbour area
14–14 Modern coastline
15 Western mole
16 Acropolis
17–17 Eastern swampy area (Ptekhai)
18 Hypothetical eastern gate
19 Hellenistic diateichisma and sea wall
20–20 Line of the enceinte
21 Western stream
22 Archaic diateichisma of the acropolis
23 Archaic south-west cemetery
24 Sixth-century fountain house
25 Probable LG (*c.* 725–690 BC) fortified settlement area
26 Probable line of fortifications
27 Geometric buildings, including the temenos with the hekatompedon (Themelis)
28 Temple of Aphrodite-Astarte
29 Possible gate in LG fortifications

Map 4 Site location plan of Archaic Eretria.

reminding us of Strabo's assertion that Eretria once ruled an island empire including Andros and Tenos as well as Keos and other islands.[56] Lefkandi/Old Eretria had long been playing an important trading role in the wider Aegean and Levantine area. The destructions at both Lefkandi and Eretria, and the abandonment of Zagora *c.* 700, are almost certainly to be related to the fact that, about this time, all Euboian trade with Al Mina in North Syria ceased.[57]

We must now consider what the newcomers found on and around the site that they chose for their new city by way of physical and human resources and what political, social and cultural baggage they brought with them.

PART 2: THE NATURE OF THE SITE OF ERETRIA AND ITS SUBSEQUENT MODIFICATION

The city developed on a roughly triangular area of alluvial deposition, at the southern foot of its acropolis hill, which extends some 800 m to the coast and is about 1000 m wide. This plain was formed by repeated flooding by a torrent that issued from the valley between the acropolis and the neighbouring rise to its north-west, on which can presently be seen an impressive Macedonian tomb. The stream passes the western side of the acropolis and then, in very early times before the coming of the refugees from Lefkandi in the ninth century, it bifurcated, one branch flowing east and skirting the southern flank of the hill, the second continuing south to the sea and forming the western boundary of the site. The delta formed by the two streams was criss-crossed with smaller flood-ways that would subsequently dictate the pattern of streets. However, over time the whole site would require considerable ongoing modification, mainly due to continuous alluviation, although this would not have been initially apparent to the new settlers. Later, the Eretrians would modify the flow of the streams more than once to achieve better control of flooding. These drainage works, so necessary on a site such as Eretria with its frequent inundations and its swamps,[58] were on a scale unknown anywhere else in mainland Greece in this period. On the eastern side of the delta plain lay the noxious marsh that gave the city its reputation for an unhealthy climate. The whole area slopes very gently towards the sea to the south.

From the summit of the defensible *acropolis hill* (see Figures 4.2 and 4.8), levelled in ancient times (Figure 4.3), there are expansive views over the Lelantine and Eretrian Plains and the Euboian Gulf, as far as Khalkis to the west, to the mainland coast opposite and eastward to Cape Aliveri, and in the absence of modern pollution, even beyond (Figures 4.1 and 4.4).[59] It has a height of *c.* 120 m and slopes gently to the east and south but more precipitously to the north and west. The hill both sits astride the easiest land route from Khalkis to Karystos and allows observation of all shipping movements in the south Euboian Gulf. This gave the Eretrians, as early as the mid-sixth century, the means of enforcing the decrees that they promulgated at that time to control and tax shipping in the Euboian Straits, using their considerable naval

Figure 4.2 The ashlar Hellenistic north-west acropolis wall tower.

Figure 4.3 The acropolis from near the West Gate.

Figure 4.4 View over Eretria from the acropolis hill showing the harbour (right), the city delta plain. The green area to the east (left) was part of the ancient (Ptekhai?) swamp. Acropolis fortifications are on the west (right) side.

strength.[60] It is fairly easily defensible. It had provided a refuge for the LN, EH and LH III settlements but lacks a good natural water supply. This defect was rectified by Hellenistic times, if not earlier. The eastern flank of the hill was quarried for building stone.[61]

The *harbour* at Eretria had more potential for development than those at Lefkandi, where the situation was just adequate for the small ships of early antiquity by virtue of the two anchorages east and west of the Xeropolis peninsula, allowing ships to draw up whatever the wind direction. Nevertheless, there was no prospect of enlarging the harbours to accommodate greater numbers of vessels. As is apparent from the maps in Krause's study of the urban evolution of Eretria,[62] the natural harbour at Eretria does not appear much better. But thanks to the engineering works undertaken near the West Gate to divert the western stream eastwards during the eighth and seventh centuries,[63] and then again later in the mid-sixth to redirect it back along its original course,[64] there emerged the opportunity to enlarge and enclose the harbour, as a result of the gradual emergence of an alluvial peninsula extending to the small islet of Pezonisi to the east and then later, when the stream was redirected, the growth of the spit to the west. The Eretrians in the mid- to late sixth century turned their energies to this task, commencing the major harbour works that ultimately resulted in the large and excellent port enjoyed by the city in later times.[65] It was big enough to shelter a fleet of trading vessels, as well as the war fleet, which conferred upon Eretria the status of thassalocrat between 506/5–491/0 according to the *Thalassocracy List*.

Early urbanisation

The EH/LH settlement was on a small promontory[66] near the mouth of the eastern stream.[67] This village became threatened by the action of the stream in flood and its remains were subsequently buried under alluvial deposits.[68] It is entirely likely that alluviation by the streams was accelerated by ruthless denudation of the surrounding hills and valleys, the result of increased population and its demand for ship and building timber.[69] Whether there were any other major Early Helladic settlement foci in the city area remains to be seen. Scattered PG sherds have been found at various locations but not in conjunction with architectural remains.[70] The earliest ceramic finds linked with architecture are from the late ninth/early eighth centuries.[71] During the eighth, the settlement occupied the area between the *temenos* and temple of Apollo, the coast and the necropolis of the later *heroön* by the West Gate.[72] It is presently impossible to say whether the whole of the area was occupied simultaneously or was progressively settled from the coast in a north-westerly direction.[73] It is likely that it was quickly occupied by scattered dwellings surrounded by small family-owned plots.[74] This was apparently especially true of the eastern delta area. The small groups of houses were sufficiently close together for any surge in population growth to unite them together.[75] It is a pattern found in other pre-Archaic and Archaic sites.[76]

Unlike some early colony foundations to which it has been compared, Eretria did not have even a roughly orthogonal *street grid*, undoubtedly due to the fact that there was already habitation on the site preventing any systematic regular allocations of land to the new arrivals as happened, for example, at Megara Hyblaia in Sicily where the archaeological evidence dates back to 750–25.[77] Also militating against orderly development was the fact that the area was broken up irregularly by the numerous sub-branches of the two main torrents.[78] Krause observed 'that any fundamental principle of organisation must be sought for in the specific [topographic] features of the place'[79] and that the irregularity of the plan of the early, as indeed of the later, city was not just due to carelessness. Also the effect of earlier structures on subsequent urban layout is demonstrated by the discovery that the foundations of the LG town wall later formed the curbing of a roadway: 'The Geometric *analemma* [so it was thought to be in 1974] was used during the fourth and third centuries BC as a support for the kerbing of the roadway. Indeed the upper series of stones is clearly an addition, probably of the third century.'[80] The eastward diversion of the western stream[81] resulted in the drying of the various sub-branches of the main streams and people began to use the deep beds ('Hohlwege')[82] as trafficways. This process can be seen by comparing Krause's maps 2 and 3. Later, in the mid-sixth century, when the eastern stream was diverted back into the old western bed, it was channelled within retaining walls to prevent reflooding (see Krause's map 4).[83] This map shows the main east–west road and the principal street leading south from it to the temple of Apollo and the *agora*, which follows the now dry course of the eastern stream. Krause's maps 5 and 6 juxtapose the old stream network and the later (hypothetical) road pattern in the seventh century. The temple and the *agora* thereafter became the main traffic foci of the city. The east–west road led directly from the main western (Khalkis) to a presently hypothetical eastern (Karystos) gate. As part of the main route from Khalkis to the south-east end of the island, this road must have carried much through traffic. Its more ancient eighth-century equivalent ran further to the north, higher up along the foot of the acropolis, outside the Archaic urban area (see Krause's map 2).

After the new basic road plan was established, the impressive *fortifications of the West Gate* were built. The west stream, originally negotiated by a ford here was, in the sixth century, crossed by a *monumental bridge* (Figure 4.5) and

Figure 4.5 The bridge at the West Gate.

Figure 4.6 Fine-fitting archaic polygonal masonry at the West Gate.

channelled under the new West Gate. This was now the main gate in the new, enlarged city walls, which also functioned as a retaining wall for the west stream.[84] The fortifications were (like the drainage works) on a massive scale for so early a period (Figure 4.6).

The open settlement pattern persisted well after the arrival of the newcomers and it was not until much later that most of the enclosed area was covered by buildings. By the LG period, an *enceinte wall* probably surrounded the urban area, though its existence as such remains controversial. Bérard thinks that it enclosed the whole later settlement but Themelis only the northern part. Mazarakis-Ainian, who is inclined to agree with him, dates its construction and the (for him) synchronous destruction of Lefkandi, to *c.* 710.[85] Themelis' excavations in city grid-squares E4/5 revealed what he believes is an early town wall[86] (Map 4, no. 26) with a gateway.[87] Finds from (Euboian) sub-PG II levels indicate that the settlement in this area had already existed unfortified from at least the last quarter of the ninth century.[88] A fairly secure *terminus ante quem* for the enceinte is provided by an amphora that rested upon it, found in an adjacent tomb: '[the amphora] must be dated to the end of the eighth century . . . before the elements of the Orientalising style become dominant and could be perceived here.'[89] Traces also of a (the city?) wall dated *c.* 690 have been uncovered near the West Gate.[90] The defence of the city was certainly secured in the sixth century by a full enceinte. The massive polygonal masonry of its substructure is still in place in several places; its upper levels were probably made of sun-dried brick.[91] The wall thus served a defensive role against both flood and external invasion (Figure 4.7). The West Gate was now elaborately fortified, displaying the results of very early but sophisticated defensive theory and planning, even incorporating a water supply system for the defenders and as a precaution against fire.

> Old Smyrna had a city wall, or so at least it is reported and shown in an often reproduced reconstruction. By the sixth century, some of the western

Figure 4.7 The channel of the western stream and the ashlar masonry of the western section of the enceint wall, which served also as a retaining wall.

> colonies were walled. On the Greek mainland we know of only fortified points of refuge, such as the Acropolis of Athens, down past 500, except for recent evidence of a wall around Eretria where at least its west gate went back to the seventh century.[92]

Thus, the early archaic fortifications under the West Gate are among the earliest known in Greece (Figures 4.4 and 4.5).

During the earliest period, *houses* were built of sun-dried brick, either oval or apsidal in plan.[93] It was only in the late eighth century that rectangular structures began to appear and thereafter coexisted with the earlier forms[94] as at Lefkandi and Pithekoussai,[95] where the apsidal/oval houses paralleled in a quite striking way both in shape and building technique those in Euboia,[96] while the rectangular structures, usually with interior 'benches', are similar to those at Zagora.[97] There were workshops[98] and, we may presume, shops, storerooms and other businesses established within the residential areas.

Mazarakis-Ainian[99] believes that social distinctions are perceptible in housing during the eighth/seventh centuries, with less well-constructed, smaller buildings characteristic of the southern area near the sea and larger, more elaborate ones in the north. He argues that artisans, merchants and sailors would have lived near the shore while the aristocratic landowners gravitated

Figure 4.8 Polygonal masonry of the acropolis wall.

inland. However, the goldsmith's workshop was in fact north of the temple of Apollo and there was a bronze working establishment within the *temenos* itself. Moreover, the site of Eretria is not so very large and there is no reason why merchants would have found it too difficult to walk to the shore from the northern areas if necessary. I have walked from the museum (near the West Gate area where Geometric building remains have been found) to the shore in a leisurely 30 minutes. Those who actually worked on or about the ships would no doubt have preferred to live close to the shore but whether a wealthy trader would so choose is by no means assured. Most of their business in fact would have centred on the *agora*, which was closer to the area of the so-called wealthier habitations. Thus we cannot assume that the inhabitants of the northern area with its 'grander' (can we think of Geometric dwellings in such terms?) freestanding houses were of the Hippobotic class exclusively. We need not disagree with the picture that the archaeologists paint of older, smaller and more frequently repaired houses close to the sea. It was probably the earliest inhabited area of the city.[100] It is true that interments at the site of the *heroön* are rich by comparison with those in the south-western cemetery, as Mazarakis-Ainian points out,[101] but this was a very small burial area and probably the tombs were those of a single important family or clan.[102]

The *agora* was embellished with new roadworks and the eastern *stoa* during the sixth century.[103] This building continued in use until *c.* 400. It is not presently known whether the pre-Archaic *agora* was on the same site as that of the sixth and later centuries, but there would certainly have been a central commercial area almost from the beginning of the city.

There were several *cult and related* places within the Geometric city. The most important was the Sanctuary of Apollo Daphnephoros (Figure 4.9). Since at Eretria no 'royal' building, such as the PG building at Lefkandi has

Figure 4.9 The author at the site of the *temenos* of Apollo Daphnephoros. The foundations of the 'Daphnephoreion' (H) in the foreground.

Figure 4.10 The *temenos* site: (H) the horseshoe-shaped Daphnephoreion (ninth century) touching the walls (E) of the first hekatompedon temple (eighth century), beneath the foundations (N) of the second hekatompedon (seventh century); (A) the foundations of the sixth-century Doric temple.

ever been found, Mazarakis-Ainian[104] suggests that the earliest apsidal building in the sanctuary area (Figure 4.10), resting on virgin soil, the so-called Daphnephoreion,[105] may have been the residence, possibly doubling as a cult house, of a *basileus* or *basileus*-magistrate. If this theory is correct and the 'king' lived on the site of the later temples of Apollo Daphnephoros, something that I doubt, it is possible that the transformation of the site into an exclusively cult-*temenos,* as well as the building of the second temple (the first *hekatompedon*) *c.* 760/750, took place when the kingship was abolished. A very similar structure at Nikhoria in Messenia,[106] interpreted as a chieftain's house, also served as, or became, a cult centre.[107] If Mazarakis-Ainian is right, the other Geometric *temenos* discovered by Themelis, suggested below to be that of Artemis-in-the-city, could have belonged to Apollo before the 'royal' enclosure was transformed into his principal cult site, thus explaining its eclipse.

The Daphnephoreion is however regarded by its excavators as the first temple of Apollo. According to Bérard,[108] who made a particular study of it, the new settlers from Lefkandi brought with them not only their Olympian cult of Apollo Daphnephoros, later the 'official' *polis*-cult, but also the very temple itself, piece by piece. He believes that it was more or less a replica of the original temple at Delphi that Apollo himself built from the laurel branches that he gathered from the Vale of Tempe, after having passed through Euboia[109] and specifically, the Lelantine Plain.[110] His interpretation of the mythology of the temple has influenced later reconstructions of this building, the most authoritative and influential being Auberson's,[111] whose model is figured in most subsequent works dealing with Geometric temple architecture. However, both the theory and reconstruction have been challenged recently, indeed whether it was in fact a Daphnephoreion at all.[112] The very early date originally assigned to it (*c.* 800) has also been seriously doubted. Themelis notes: 'The early dating of the Daphnephoreion to 800 BC is not based on the excavation data.'[113] A more likely date, based on the pottery findings, is 760/750.[114] It remained in use until the end of the eighth century, when it was replaced by the (first) monumental *hekatompedon*, which endured until *c.* 675 and was in its turn replaced by what the excavators describe as 'l'hécatompédon ionique du VIIe siècle', the second *hekatompedon*.[115] This sequence of buildings on the site of the later, and presently visible, sixth century Doric (but incorporating Ionic elements[116]) temple of Apollo therefore suggests that a temple of some kind stood here probably from the very beginning of the 'new' settlement in the late ninth century. Subsequent Swiss excavators still appear confident that the original building was the earliest Daphnephoreion and that the whole site was always a sacred *temenos*.[117] Mazarakis-Ainian's theory that the apsidal building was the residence of the *basileus*, while interesting, is in fact no less conjectural than that it was the earliest Daphnephoreion. Nor should evidence of industrial activity within the *temenos* be seen as weakening the idea that it was always a sacred enclosure for, though rare, it is not a unique conjunction. The site has yielded early indications of its sacred character, and its central position[118] within the area of the city is appropriate enough for the abode of an archegetal god. The temple buildings however did not stand in isolation. At least one other oval (or apsidal) building stood in the *temenos*. Might this rather have been the 'royal' abode? There is also some evidence that a female deity was worshipped on the site. Probably this was Artemis, the second of the great gods of Eretria,[119] whose cult centre at Amarynthos became the main focus of Eretrian popular religious activity.

Another temple on the slopes of the acropolis, probably originally Archaic, was a Thesmophoreion and associated Temple of Artemis Olympia.[120] There is evidence of an Archaic altar on the site, though the present temple remains are of the fifth century (Figure 4.11). Plutarch, however, describes the primitive rites of the Eretrian Thesmophoria, which he relates to the Trojan Expedition, in which women cooked meat by the sun and not with fire, suggesting a prehistoric origin for the cult.[121] There is considerable evidence from the Eretrias of pre-Hellenic cults as we have seen. Themelis has uncovered underground 'chambers' in the city[122] of the Classical period, which he believes were used both for harvest storage places and the worship of chthonian fertility deities (a statue of the Agathos Daimon was found in a deposit next to the room) or Zeus Meilikhios.[123]

Architectural remains, dated by Themelis to the end of the ninth/beginning of the eighth century, seem to have belonged to another *hekatompedon* building, which may have belonged to Artemis Amarysia and which is similar to the first *hekatompedon* of Apollo Daphnephoros.[124] If this earlier sacred enclosure, which is as large as that of Apollo Daphnephoros, belonged to Amarysia, it did not apparently survive as a major cult centre after the town was sacked at the end

Figure 4.11 The small Thesmophoreion on the slopes of the acropolis.

of the eighth century, and Apollo's temple henceforth remained the major *intra muros* cult centre. Perhaps this was due to the reinforcing of the non-indigenous Lefkandiot element by the second wave of immigrants. Apollo it seems was 'the' Lefkandiot god: he had, after all, stopped on the Lelantine Plain on his way to Delphi. But the more ancient religion later reasserted itself for most purposes except those of a political nature, especially those concerned with foreign states and individuals from outside Euboia. The two cults thus probably represent the two elements in the population of the newly emerging *polis*-state: the aboriginal inhabitants and the invaders who, as conquerers, initially assumed the status of a minority ruling class and imposed their own cult within the city proper. Beyond the walls, Amarysia remained supreme.

There was a sanctuary near the West Gate, identified tentatively as that of Aphrodite-Astarte by Kahil from the oriental origin of many finds from its *bothros*.[125] She dates the pottery from *c.* 800 to *c.* 700. An apsidal temple replaced a Geometric building here during the Archaic period.[126] There may also have been a sanctuary of another oriental deity near the harbour.[127] The early Eastern imports, material and cultural, may indicate how quickly the newly revitalised settlement involved itself in overseas commerce. Merchants and their dependents returning from the East perhaps brought in these manifestations of Eastern influence. Nevertheless, we should remember that the strong Euboian/Eretrian presence in the Levantine *emporia* did not continue beyond the eighth century.

The *heroön* by the West Gate[128] was originally a small private cemetery of a noble or royal clan. Within the *temenos* were uncovered sixteen tombs, nine for children, all inhumations, and seven for adults, cremations, dated *c.* 720 to *c.* 690.[129] They are lavish compared with contemporary burials in the cemetery by the sea (see below). Pyres here were lit some distance from the tombs and the remains of the cremated adults were afterwards placed in large and expensive bronze cauldrons and then into carefully constructed pits, a practice unique in Greece (Figure 4.12).[130] The adult males appear to have belonged to a warrior-class and the richest grave (Grave 6) is described as that of a 'prince' or even 'king' of Eretria.[131] About a decade after the last burial (*c.* 680), a triangular enclosure was built over the graves that became the focus of a protective warrior cult, involving sacrifices and votive offerings,[132] guarding the main road to the hereditary enemy, Khalkis. This cult died out finally during the sixth century.[133] The sanctuary was incorporated into the early fortifications that were built about the same time at the West Gate.[134] The date of these defensive works and the establishment of the *heroön* suggest a connection with the final destruction of Lefkandi. It seems reasonable to link literary evidence from Hesiod[135] and Plutarch[136] concerning the death in a sea battle against the Eretrians and the subsequent funeral games of the Khalkidian *basileus* Amphidamas with the events *c.* 700 to *c.* 680, which also perhaps involved the hero of Tomb 6 at Eretria and his peers or descendants. We do not know his

Figure 4.12 Bronze burial cauldrons from the *heroön* site, Eretria Museum.

name but his imposing and lavish burial at the West Gate suggests that his status was comparable.

The main *Geometric cemetery* (Figures 4.13 and 4.14), however, was near the sea to the south-west of the principal settlement. The earliest burials are dated from the sub-PG/MPG II to LG.[137] As at the *heroön* site, children were inhumed and adults cremated.[138] The general practice here was to place the bodies of children in *pithoi* or in amphoras (*enkhytrismos*), though at the *heroön* they were buried in wooden coffins.[139] But, unlike at the West Gate *heroön*, adults were cremated in situ on pyres over the open grave. Similarities of burial customs at Lefkandi, Eretria (particularly between Lefkandiot practice and that at the *heroön* site) and Pithekoussai suggest close cultural and thus perhaps political relationships between these communities and that Lefkandiot emigrés brought them to Eretria, from where they were taken to Pithekoussai. This cemetery continued in use throughout the sixth and fifth centuries.[140]

This completes the survey of the urban area of Eretria from the early ninth to the mid-sixth century.[141]

Figure 4.13 Geometric burial amphora from the south-west cemetery, Eretria Museum.

PART 3: THE EARLY POLITICAL EVOLUTION OF ERETRIA

Monarchy

Homeric Euboia was united, at least in war, under the *hegemon* of the Abantic *ethnos,* which included the men from 'Eiretria' and was governed from Lefkandi. The society Homer describes constitutes an intermediate stage between those of the Bronze Age palace cultures and the true *polis*. War is the leading political occupation of its ruling class; Homer does not tell us what Abantic warrior heroes did in times of peace but there can be little doubt that they were large-scale landowners, the richest of whose estates were on the fertile Lelantine Plain and were maintained by serf labour,[142] with horse-rearing sufficiently prominent to give the class the name it still held at the end of the sixth century, the *Hippobotai* . It is even possible that the serfs continued to exist until much later for we have an indication that there were *perioikoi* in the Eretrias in the fourth century: 'having caused those in the *perioikis* of the Eretrians to revolt, he marched on the *polis* of Dystos.'[143] But whether this hints at an early situation

Figure 4.14 Burial amphoras from the south-west cemetery: (a) and (b) orientalising black-on-red (*c.* 650); (c) 'Herakles-style' black figure amphora (*c.* 550); (d) typically Eretrian loop design. (a) and (c) are from the Eretria Museum, (b) and (d) from the National Archaeological Museum, Athens.

of city-based military rulers surrounded by a serf population, or whether the term was only applied later to new territory conquered by the Eretrian state in the fifth and subsequent centuries, cannot now be determined. This economic and political state of affairs began to change when the *polis*-state began to emerge at about the time 'Old' Eretria was destroyed.

How the Eretrians were ruled before the arrival of the Abantic Lefkandiot refugees is impossible to say with much confidence. The indigenous Dryopians may have had a matriarchal society, reflected in the dominance of the Mother Goddess Amarysia and the inferior role of her divine spouse Amarynthos. If so, it is highly unlikely that this state of affairs still prevailed once the Eretrias had become subject to the Hellenic Abantes, who occupied the land when the refugees from Lefkandi arrived. During the Mycenaean period, the area owed allegiance to the palace at Thebes through the intermediary ruler of Lefkandi. Following the fall of Thebes, the pan-Euboian Homeric *hegemon/wanax* continued to exercise some control over the Eretrian Plain from Lefkandi. Knoepfler however thinks that a prince of Amarynthos was *basileus* of the area: 'Now this important Mycenaean location where there very certainly resided a *qa-si-re-u* (*basileus*) remained – it should be clearly noted – a kind of 'capital' into the historical period.'[144] This chieftain would have been subordinate to the *wanax* at Lefkandi. Certainly Amarynthos was a major settlement before the eighth century and we have noted the evidence of EH circuit walls at Palaioekklisies, the prehistoric settlement site.[145]

Drews says that there is little evidence for monarchy in early Euboia generally.[146] He mentions only Amphidamas of Khalkis and, being concerned only with the Archaic Age, he omits Mycenaean Khalkodon, Elephenor and a few other possibilities;[147] Amphidamas is described as *basileus* in the late and historically very unreliable *Certamen Homeri et Hesiodi,* although Hesiod, who may have competed in his funeral games,[148] does not so refer to him. Since the author uses *basileus* indiscriminately for both Archaic Amphidamas and the Emperor Hadrian, real doubt exists as to his understanding of the significance of the word in the earlier period. Knoepfler believes, along with Mazarakis-Ainian, that there was almost certainly some form of kingship in Eretria before the eighth century and probably even after the arrival of the new settlers from Lefkandi: 'I would willingly believe that the Eretrian *basileus* whose existence we must guess, played, in so far as he was the inheritor of the *qa-si-re-u* of *A-ma-ru-to*, a role in the rites of the ancient Artemis Amarysia.'[149] Moreover, he thinks that there is no inherent difficulty in accepting kings of the 'gift-devouring' kind attacked by Hesiod,[150] in both Eretria and Khalkis up to the Geometric period.[151] We may have a hint of a *basileus* or even a *wanax* at Eretria in a poetic fragment, attributed to Arkhilokhos but which is possibly from a local epic, discussed more fully below, which refers to an *anaktoron* in the context of Homeric-style warfare.[152] Bérard is more cautious:

> We avoid speaking of 'king' in spite of the references to the word *basileus*

> because we do not know what was the role of our prince within the body of the Eretrian nobility and to whom we would doubtless grant too many of its privileges.[153]

Whether the tombs at the *heroön* are of a princely family, as Bérard thinks,[154] or those of an aristocratic *oikos*, or perhaps of a wider group of nobles buried around their prince, as apparently occurred at Lefkandi (although the Eretrian *heroön* is nowhere on the scale of the Toumba cemetery there), it is impossible to decide. As we have seen, Mazarakis-Ainian believes that the Daphnephoreion was the residence of a *basileus* or *basileus*-magistrate.[155] However, if there were ever kings in Eretria they disappeared at an early date.

The rise of the *polis*-state[156]

Snodgrass associates this phenomenon not with fortifications and urbanisation, since these did not, in his opinion, occur so early on the mainland,[157] but rather with the emergence of geographically and politically isolated settlements within their own hinterland, which adhered to a local cult and possessed their own political institutions, specifically including an assembly.[158] He also believes that it was associated with the beginnings of colonisation.[159] But, contrary to his assumptions regarding fortifications and urbanisation, Eretria was, as we have seen, beginning to show these material signs of development during the eighth century (though to be sure, the settlement pattern was of the 'open' type with scattered houses in private gardens over most of the city area). There was a *polis*-cult and indeed, he cites Eretria as an example of a city having a central religious focus, the cult of Apollo Daphnephoros,[160] and specifically for that reason considers it an early *polis*. The earliest cult building, moreover, the original Daphnephoreion, may have also been the political centre.[161] The ninth and eighth centuries, when the change towards the *polis* began to take place, was also the time when Lefkandi was abandoned, and changes in political attitudes later reflected in the emergence of the *polis* may have played some role in these events.[162] Snodgrass suggests that one process by which the *polis*-state emerged was through what Greeks later called *synoikismos*, a term he acknowledges to be ambiguous:

> It covers everything from the notional acceptance of a single political centre by a group of townships and villages whose inhabitants stay firmly put, to the physical migration of a population into a new political centre, which could be either an existing or purpose-built city. The crucial element in all cases is the political unification.[163]

Of the first category, the *synoikismos* of Attica is the best-known early example.[164] Of the second, Snodgrass gives no example, yet he must have known of the movement of population from Lefkandi to Eretria (and perhaps also to Khalkis), since he refers briefly to Lefkandi during its *floruit*.[165] He seems unaware of discoveries at Eretria when he writes: '(If) ninth century Greece lacked sizeable towns . . . there are famous sites – Sparta, Tegea, Mantineia, Eretria [etc.] – where, if anyone was yet living, we have not found material trace of them.'[166] Themelis' earliest report of Geometric architectural remains from the city was published in 1974.[167] However, at the time of his writing, the Swiss excavators' dating of the earliest Daphnephoreion to *c.* 800 had not been challenged.[168] That he was aware of their excavation reports is indicated by his inclusion (as Figure 10) of the Swiss plan of the *temenos* area.[169] Thus, Eretria in fact presents most of the conditions, physical, cultural and spiritual, that scholars have required for the emergence of a *polis*-state.

During the ninth/early eighth centuries, the Abantic *ethnos* evolved into a group of four principal *poleis* scattered throughout Euboia, and this process was completed by the mid-eighth century at the latest, for when the Euboic colonies were established in the West and in the northern Aegean they were remembered, as Aristotle (ap. Strabo) reports,[170] as foundations of individual *poleis*, whereas in the earlier colonisation of Ionia, the Abantic *ethnos* was involved and not individual *poleis*. That *ethne* could later on still be thought of by the Greeks as *metropoleis* in the later colonial movement is demonstrated by the case of the Akhaians who founded Sybaris, Metapontion and Siris,[171] so that the distinction is significant.

Early aristocracy

By the eighth century, political power in the emerging *poleis* was in the hands of narrow aristocratic regimes, sometimes based on one prominent *genos*, such as the Bakkhiadai at Corinth, the Penthilidai in Mytilene and the Basilidai at Erythrai. The Bakkhiadai of Corinth seem to have had royal antecedents (Bakkhis) as did too the aptly named Basilidai.[172] The change from monarchy to aristocracy, I believe, occurred even earlier in Euboia, in the late ninth century, when war and/or early political revolution[173] at Lefkandi, followed by the migration of refugees to Eretria, provided a catalyst for *polis* evolution there. It soon became the first *polis* that modern scholars might recognise on the island. While the destruction of Lefkandi strengthened the old Hippobotic tradition in Khalkis, the refugees at Eretria were less likely to have tolerated the exclusive power of either kings or aristocrats for long, not least because the territorial resources of the Eretrian Plain did not produce the kind of very wealthy landowners that Aristotle at least believed necessary for maintaining aristocratic power.[174]

However tradition, accepted by the philosopher, makes 'Eretria', together with Khalkis and Magnesia and other unidentified *poleis*, paradigmatic of states ruled by horse-rearing aristocracies.[175] However, in the case of 'Eretria' this political regime belongs before the destruction of Old Eretria. *Hippeis* and *Hippobotai* designate a particular economic/political/social class, as Aristotle[176] makes clear. Solon used the term *Hippeis* to designate the second highest census class at Athens[177] whose members had an income equivalent to the value of over 300 but under 500 *medimnoi* of wheat, but what the Eretrian or Khalkidian criteria were at this or any other time is unknown. However, since the Eretrian constitution was later remembered by their name, the *Politeia of the Hippeis*,[178] they must have originally constituted the highest class there. Aristotle notes that in early *poleis* Hippobotic aristocracies generally succeeded monarchies and he attributes this to the fact that at this stage of their evolution, the chief military strength lay in their cavalry.[179] It retained its military importance in most parts of Euboia longer than in most central or southern Greek regions, although by the sixth century this was largely symbolic. We hear nothing of the *Hippobotai* in action in Euboia after Theognis' eye-witness account of the incident at Kerinthos, which I date between 538 and 533,[180] although they remain an important and imposing component in the procession from Eretria to the temple of Amarysia near Amarynthos, the most important of the civic festivals at Eretria, until well after the mid-sixth century.

Commercial oligarchy

While Khalkis long remained controlled by the Hippobotic class, for in 506 and perhaps still in 447/6, the Lelantine Plain was still the 'lands of the *Hippobotai* so-called',[181] its authority at Eretria did not last long, in a political sense at least. Although the *Athenaion politeia*, describing Peisistratos' arrival at Eretria in 546, says that:

> Coming again to Eretria in the eleventh year (of his exile), he undertook for the first time to re-establish his rule by force, being supported in this by many . . . amongst whom were the *Hippeis* who still held power in Eretria,[182]

the regime at Eretria in Peisistratos' time was in fact an oligarchy, and Aristotle in the *Politika* rightly calls it such in his discussion of oligarchies in general,[183] for well before then, its nature had changed radically from its origin as a government by horse-rearing aristocrats with Lelantine landholdings around Lefkandi. In the early eighth century, this oligarchy may in practice have been as exclusive as the aristocratic governments in the early Hippobotic states, although it was probably never made up purely of landowners. Certainly, however, by the sixth century, economic conditions, and as a consequence the nature of the Eretrian *politeia*, had changed considerably. Aristotle's account[184] of the fall of the Eretrian oligarchy clearly reveals that it was by then (after 546 but probably in 538)[185] riven by internal jealousies, suggesting groups with different levels of power and social status and conflicting interests. But we may be permitted to think that, since exclusivity is wont to produce factionalism by its very nature, the Eretrian oligarchy is likely to have experienced the common malaise much earlier than this. If the ruling class at Eretria were in fact originally made up of factions, both commercial (with economic power) and landowning (with traditional social éclat), it would be surprising indeed if tendencies to division had not emerged earlier. But it is unlikely that at Eretria there was ever a politically dominant class of rural 'gift-devouring *basileis*' of whom Hesiod complains in his early cry against injustice and oppression, though no doubt some landowners in the Eretrias similarly tyrannised their local peasant population in the countryside:

> [Justice] sits right beside her father Zeus, son of Kronos, and tells him about men's evil thoughts until the Demos pays for the mad folly of the *Basileis* who, with evil intent, pervert the course of justice and give crooked judgements. Guard yourselves, you *Basileis* who devour gifts, from these things, and put aside crooked judgements from your thoughts altogether.[186]

Read 'bribes' for 'gifts', as is implied.

The upper class in Euboia were as conspicuous consumers of luxury goods as were their Lefkandian antecedents,[187] and excavations at Eretria have revealed the richness of the grave furniture of the wealthy individuals interred at the *heroön* site.[188] Exiled members of the old aristocracy must have quickly seen that the way to renew their fortunes was to join their commercially oriented fellow citizens and engage in trade or possibly mercenary soldiering: we have examples from elsewhere in the Hellenic world. Long before their expulsion from Lefkandi, they would have seen the profits to be made in trade with Levantine *emporia* such as Al Mina and Tell es Sûkâs. We need not suppose that noble *Hippeis* were involved in bargaining in the Levantine souks of Al Mina etc., at least not initially, but Hippobotic resources very probably were. As a result, social distinctions between the old landowning families and the entrepreneurial class began to break down, as men originally non-noble became rich, and some that were anciently wealthy and of noble family sank into relative poverty and obscurity. Over time a new ruling class would emerge, retaining (deliberately adopting?) the old noble class designation and finally, having become very rich through trade, indulging in the ancient aristocratic equestrian pursuits as a status hobby; such behaviour is common at all times and in all societies. Such a class, however, would in practice be very different from the traditional *Hippobotai* of Khalkis, whose main source of wealth was still from pastoralism, not commerce. This could not but affect its attitudes. However, old values and traditions do not always simply vanish with the political eclipse of the class that cherished them. The social and political ambitions of the *Eupatridai* of fifth/fourth century Athens did not disappear with the advent of democracy and many, though by no means all of them, kept their heads down until they judged it expedient to conspire against the hated order. Hippobotic ideals remained significant in Eretrian social and political life to the end of the Archaic period and indeed beyond. We get some idea of the lifestyle of landowning aristocrats in Archaic times from descriptions by Asios and Duris, both of Samos describing the *Geomoroi* there; like the Attic Eupatrids their 'badge' was the gold *tettix* (grasshopper) hairpin, the same as that dedicated by the young Euboian Kharixenos to the nymphs in Roman Amarynthos.[189] Thus, we may believe that from the eighth to the early sixth century, Eretria was ruled by a narrow oligarchy with aristocratic pretensions, whose purpose was to perpetuate its own wealth and power. Although writing of the Khalkidian *Hippobotai*, Strabo's remarks can also be applied even more appositely to the rulers of Eretria:

> The government of the *Hippobotai*, so it was called, was in power; for at the head of it were men chosen according to the value of their property (*timema*) who ruled in an aristocratic way.[190]

For *Hippobotai*, read *Hippeis*.

Subsequent acquisition of land by upwardly mobile members of the commercial oligarchy is likely. Old concepts of landownership as a requirement for full citizenship rights never died out in Greece and wealth based on land was always regarded as being more respectable socially even in Athens, if not necessarily at Corinth, as Aristotle more than once implies.[191] 'Moreover, it is clear that when Aristotle mentions the political privileges of the rich, he is thinking of those whose property has been ascertained by the census, and the same will probably be true of other writers.'[192] The rising merchant class will surely have hastened to acquire land, the essential aristocratic criterion.

The organs of the Eretrian government during the period of oligarchic rule *c.* 825 to *c.* 550 are now explained.

The boule *(council)*

In Greek oligarchies, *to bouleuomenon*, the power of deliberation and, by extension, those that had the money and leisure to deliberate,[193] was the right of a small number of the citizens and normally resided in the hands of members of a *boule* (*bouleutai*), which Aristotle calls 'the special organ of oligarchic government',[194] while 'the executive power in the early aristocracies was generally entrusted to a single magistrate whose powers were as unlimited in scope as those of the king'[195] he replaced. Bengtson however thinks that: 'A concomitant of the change in terminology – *archon* instead of *basileus* – was an essential reduction in authority.'[196] But in Eretria, we are not dealing with a traditional aristocracy, for 'New' Eretria probably never had a purely aristocratic political phase. A single magistracy at Eretria may originally, as Knoepfler argues in spite of the complete silence of the epigraphic and literary record,[197] have had the title *basileus* and later evolved into a college of *basileis*-magistrates, the natural consequence of the increasing complexity of administration of the growing *polis*, but I suspect that the silence is not accidental and certainly by the time the Eretrians were committing records to stone in the sixth century, the name of the *arkhe* (magistracy) had changed.

Early oligarchic councils were invariably small,[198] and the contexts of the few mentions of the Eretrian *Politeia of the Hippeis* in ancient writers make it clear that it was, even at the time of its fall, still very narrow compared with other contemporary oligarchic councils. Such conciliar bodies are characteristically composed of mature-aged members holding office for life.[199] The name often applied to them was *gerousia* (council of elders). Herakleides Lembos reports that: 'The Khalkidians have a law that someone younger than fifty cannot hold office or *presbeusai* (serve on an embassy).'[200] This is the usual translation, but *presbeusai* is better rendered here 'be on council'. Both *presbeutes* and *geron* mean 'old man'. It does not seem very likely that Khalkidians under fifty could never serve as diplomats or on embassies. How the *gerontes* or *bouleutai* were appointed at Eretria is unknown. Nor do we know what were the powers of the *boule* there, but members of oligarchic councils generally held the highest political privileges in the early *poleis*, so we may be sure that they were considerable. The quarrel between Diagoras and the oligarchic regime shows that in the mid-sixth century real power was still in the hands of an elite and was sufficiently great to be jealously guarded by those who enjoyed its privileges. Thus, the early situation at Eretria can in practice not have been so very different from other contemporary *poleis*.

It would be of more interest to know whether the Eretrian *boule* delegated authority, and if so, to whom. In later democratic *poleis*, councils often became too large to function as an executive without further subdivision. They thus normally formed committees, such as the *prytaneis* of the Kleisthenic Council of 500.[201] The earliest *boulai* were much smaller and may not have needed formal working committees. Nevertheless, some division of executive duties among the *bouleutai* is likely and there was a tendency, not universal it is true, for *boulai* over time to get larger rather than smaller. It is thus probable that a small group came to be charged with probouleutic duties such as preparing the agenda for meetings, ensuring that decisions of the full council were carried out, etc. Even small modern bodies such as local councils, seldom larger than twelve to twenty members, form sub-committees: modern aldermen usually have other occupations, and most members of the ancient *boulai* were in the same position, whether they had businesses to manage or large estates to oversee. They would generally not have been full-time politicians. Nevertheless, any probouleutic group would soon come to exercise a considerable, even overriding, influence over the *boule* itself. These even smaller units of power wielders were later seen as even less democratic than the *bouleutai* themselves.[202]

The assembly

Snodgrass thinks that possession of an assembly, however rudimentary, was a distinguishing feature of the emerging *polis*-state of the eighth century.[203] In the earliest times, I doubt that there would have been an assembly with any real authority to check the power of the magistrates or the *boule*:

> But however constituted, the powers of the assembly were inconsiderable beside those of the council, and the oligarchs carried into effect their theory of specialisation of authority, of efficiency, secrecy and despatch by delegation the duties of government to small councils or to the magistrates.[204]

For its existence at Eretria before the late sixth century, we have no evidence. Homer supplies a picture of an early assembly of the 'citizens', where they are called together to listen to and, if necessary, be berated by the *basileis* and allowed to express their approval (but not their disapproval!) by shouts.[205] The role of the lower classes tended to be further reduced as the early monarchies evolved through the stages of aristocracy and oligarchy. Early Sparta provides an example in which additions to the famous *rhetra* indicate the loss of any *kyria* (authority) and *kratos* (sovereignty/real power) that the assembly previously had: 'The *basileis* [Polydoros and Theopompos] inserted this clause into the *rhetra*: "But if the people should adopt a crooked motion, the elders and the kings shall have the power of adjournment" ', that is, should not ratify the vote, but dismiss outright and dissolve the (session of the) assembly.[206]

Possibly the only real power exercised by an assembly would have been some voice in deciding peace or war, as was the case of the Spartan ekklesia (apella). In later Eretrian inscriptions, an assembly is implied in the rubric 'the Demos ': the earliest decree (late sixth/early fifth century) has a democratic preamble: 'It seemed good to the boule and the demos.'207 In a decree of the third century,208 it is called ekklesia, perhaps the result of Athenian influence.

Magistracies

The probouloi

The principal magistracy at Eretria in (almost) all periods of its history, and frequently attested from the fourth century, was the college of the *probouloi*. Holleaux, discussing the aberration in the development of the Eretrian constitution presented by the sudden appearance and brief duration of *polemarkhoi* as chief magistrates between 308 and 304,[209] stresses the special durability and venerability of the *proboulia*. 'At Eretria they appeared, indeed, as heads of the State'[210] and 'presidents'.[211] I believe that the tenacity with which Eretrians in later times clung to the magistracy, whether under democratic or oligarchic governments, indicates a long-established institution. Holleaux postulates an early date for it. The *proboulia* was considered undemocratic by Aristotle[212] but neither was it suitable for aristocracies, and he explicitly contrasts the oligarchic *probouloi* with the aristocratic *nomophylakes*, significantly, quite unattested at Eretria: '*Nomophylakes* are aristocratic; while *probouloi* are oligarchic.'[213] Salmon, writing of Corinth,[214] believes that '*probouloi* are not easily compatible with the aristocratic Bacchiad state: they belong to a more complicated age' Starr thinks that Sparta was the first state to introduce a probouleutic council *c.* 650,[215] but it seems to me likely that *probouloi*, however named, existed in many places well before then.

It may appear rash to deduce the name and existence of the chief magistracy at Eretria during the Archaic period from fourth-century inscriptions, but the *proboulia* was actually a comparatively rare *arkhe*. Apart from Eretria, *probouloi* 'have their one appearance at Athens and appear in scattered instances in Corinth and her north-western colonies. In the Aegean their main home is Euboea, . . . they are characteristically an Eretrian magistracy.'[216] A group of eight magistrates styled *epimenieuontes* (those holding authority for a month),[217] which appear in an inscription of the third century, *IG* XII Suppl. 555, is I think correctly equated with *probouloi* by its editor without reservation.[218] There is, moreover, a much earlier one of the late sixth/early fifth century, *IG* XII Suppl. 549, which reveals a *phyles epimenieuoures* (gen. sing.),[219] surely to be related to the magisterial group: the *epimenieuontes* are thus likely at this time to be the *probouloi* of the 'prytanising' tribe, the Eretrian equivalent of the Athenian *prytaneis,* for a (conciliar) month. We are therefore taken back at least to the early fifth century for *probouloi*. Indeed, writing of Miletos but referring to the Eretrian inscription, Robertson has stated that 'On this evidence it cannot be maintained that the *epimenioi* of Miletus were a late innovation. A term so widely current must come down from an early period – from the seventh century if Miletus was the model for her colonies . . .'[220] But it must be confessed that there is no specific literary or epigraphical evidence for the *proboulia* so named at Eretria earlier than the fourth century. I think Kondoleon is right however to presume that the institution behind *epimenieuontes* in both *IG* XII Suppl. 555 and *epimenieuoures* in 549 is the *proboulia*.[221] But *probouloi* occur epigraphically at Keos and in conjunction with another quite specifically Eretrian constitutional term, as well as at other places which have Eretrian affiliations, and this will be important in my argument for their existence at Eretria before the fourth century. We must thus embark upon an *excursus* into the foreign relations of Eretria during the seventh century.

First, there were *probouloi* at both Corinth and Kerkyra. Plutarch tells us that Corinth 'colonised' Kerkyra (seized is however more appropriate since it was previously an Eretrian colony), during the Kypselid tyranny; the literary date is 734.[222] Whereupon, the Eretrians sailed home only to be confronted and driven away by a barrage of missiles and compelled to set off once more, finally settling at Methone.[223] However, must we necessarily assume that all the Eretrians left, or might a number, perhaps substantial, have acquiesced in the prospect of Corinthian rule and remained? It is highly unlikely that the eighth century Eretrians acquired their *probouloi* from Corinth; rather we may ask whether the Corinthians later acquired them from Eretria via their new acquisition, Kerkyra.[224] Salmon[225] thinks that *probouloi* at Corinth date from Kypselid times at the earliest, and it was then that Kerkyra was won.[226] Eretria, as we shall see, seems everywhere to have given its colonies the nomenclature and probably the forms of its constitution, particularly its chief magistracy. Despite the short duration[227] of the Eretrian colony, the Corinthians would have found a functioning administrative system, no doubt with a *boule* and *proboulia* modelled on that of the *metropolis*. If indeed the Eretrians introduced *probouloi* to Kerkyra, then the magistracy must have already existed at home before 734, when their colonists were expelled.

Second, at some time during the Archaic period according to Strabo: '[the Eretrians] ruled over the Andrians, Tenians, Keians and people of other islands.'[228] But when? If the conclusions of the excavators of Zagora are accepted, Eretria was involved there in the eighth century. The archaeological record says that Zagora on Andros was an Eretrian *emporion* abandoned early in the seventh century, with its apogee rather earlier. Descoeudres thinks that the whole island was an Eretrian dependency.[229] If the empire was flourishing then, as some think,[230] Eretrian influences are likely to have entered Keos about that time. In the Hellenistic period Keos was a federation of four *poleis* and its constitution included *probouloi*.[231] Dunant and Thomopoulos, discussing a treaty of *isopoliteia* (equal citizenship rights) between this federation and Eretria, which also mentions as a Keian territorial division the *khoros*, note that both *probouloi* and *khoroi* are characteristically Eretrian terms and ask whether they are a 'survival in the vocabulary of the Eretrian dominion',[232] for it is striking that not only the typically Eretrian magistrates, but also the territorial term, occur at Keos. These in fact are the only two places where this usage of the latter term occurs.[233] If Eretria ruled Keos at the beginning of the seventh century, it would suggest an early date for the existence of both *probouloi* and *khoroi*. Lewis, however, thinks that these Eretrian influences came to Keos as late as the Euboian revolt of 411 against Athenian rule.[234]

Strabo's reference to Eretria's maritime empire comes directly after his description of the stele, which he or rather his source, probably Ephoros, saw in the temple of Amarysia at Amarynthos, detailing the military resources that Eretria was capable of committing to the festival procession in honour of the goddess: 3000 hoplites, 600 *Hippeis* and 60 (presumably ceremonial) chariots, a not inconsiderable force, as it is not a full wartime muster but one for a religious procession.[235] The juxtaposition of these items may be the result of Strabo's belief that they were related in both a military and a chronological sense.[236] The stele implies that at the time it was inscribed, hoplites were the largest group in the Eretrian military forces.[237] Hoplites, as the principal military arm, would not sit entirely comfortably with a mid-seventh century or earlier date. We are moreover dealing with an inscribed political stele; can we really believe that such a document was inscribed as early as the seventh century? But Jeffery writes, believing in a seventh century date:

> There are no epigraphic records from the protracted struggles of the Lelantine War; the only inscription which is certainly as early as the seventh century is that on a small *aryballos* attributed to Eretria. The literary tradition records, however, that in the precinct of Artemis at Amarynthos near Eretria, there was a stele which preserved a military compact between Chalkis and Eretria during that war, of which an actual phrase is apparently quoted: 'μὴ χρῆσθαι τηλεβόλοις.[238]

I, however, prefer a sixth-century date for the stele and consequently that the empire still endured at that time. The numbers are, moreover, particularly notable (and indicative). Athens, for example, turned out just 8,000 hoplites at Plataia, a later, life-and-death affair, Sparta 5,000, Corinth 5,000, Megara 5,000. Eretria and its dependencies supplied 600, but that was after its destruction in 490. Khalkis, which was not destroyed, sent only 400 men. Salmon says that 3,000 was the likely full levy in Corinth during most of the fifth century. He emphasises the importance of the hoplite class as a factor contributing to the considerable power of this city in the Archaic period and of the farming sector from which they were drawn, which produced the wealth that gave the city the epithet for which it was famous. So, 6,000 hoplites seems too high a number for Eretria in the seventh century or earlier. If Eretrian rule at Keos lasted for a century or more, there was plenty of time for the terminology and practice to take hold.

Strabo mentions 'other islands', besides Keos, Andros and Tenos. Eretrian expansion eastward must have taken it also to Karystos. To postulate that the last too was incorporated for some time into the empire[239] might explain the shadowy presence there of the *proboulia*.[240] Knoepfler has observed well that Karystos has physical features that cause it to resemble an island.[241] If Karystos were incorporated within Eretria's sea empire, this could only have occurred early, and the seventh century would be the latest likely period. There is some evidence that could support such a hypothesis: Geyer wrote that the Petaliai Islands,[242] adjacent to the border between the Eretrias and Karystia 'always' belonged to Karystos but later accepts that they 'might have' belonged to Eretria by the third century.[243] He cites no evidence for Karystian control (and I do not believe that any exists) so he appears to be relying on geographic proximity. However, inscriptions published as an addendum to *IG* XII 9[244] subsequent to Geyer's study reveal that Eretria in some way[245] presumed to exercise naval control over the waters around and so probably also over these islands. Thus, if Geyer's belief that Karystos originally controlled the Petaliai Islands is true, Eretria had seemingly wrested them from the Karystians before 550/525, to which period these inscriptions belong.[246]

There is evidence of early warfare between Karystos and Miletos, Eretria's ancient and enduring ally, while Miletos was still ruled by kings:

> There were two wars between the Karystians and the Milesians . . . Leodamas, having fought very bravely and taken the city by storm and enslaved it, returned to his city, Miletos, and became its *basileus*. He sent, as was customary, a captive Karystian woman, along with many other offerings, being a tithe of the spoils, to Brankhidai [the temple of Apollo].[247]

This incident has been dated to the late eighth/early seventh centuries.[248] However, Drews dismisses this as fable and denies the existence of kings at Miletos in the Geometric period.[249] The later we down-date this incident, the more likely it is that we are dealing with a *basileus*-magistrate, similar to the *arkhon-basileus* at Athens or *rex sacerdotorum* at Rome. If Miletos had captured Karystos at such an early period, it would have been unable to hold such a distant place and may have handed it over to the Euboian city that was ever its loyal ally and which may itself have played some role in events.

Eretrian expansion to the south-east involving Karystos is suggested by a papyrus fragment[250] containing elegiac lines that I believe are from a local epic that deals with events on the border of the Eretrias with Karystos, for as West remarks, elegiacs 'are often chosen for longer poems, especially ones drawing on sub-heroic legend.'[251] We may note the gloss in Suidas: 'Simonides, Karystian or Eretrian epic poet'[252] in the context of this fragmentary poem. Is it a fragment of one of his (unknown) epics? Another epic poet, Leskhes of Mytilene (*fl.* 660–57), referred to Amphidamas and Eretrians in the *Ilias Parva* attributed to him.[253] Another possibility is Kreophylos of Samos (or Chios). Whether the poem is a fragment of such a lost local epic or the work of a later poet such as Arkhilokhos,[254] as Lobel believes, is impossible to say finally, but it does refer to south-eastern Euboia and in a very early period. Examination of the text, and of Lobel's and my own restorations, reveal a lexicon and allusions that are thoroughly 'Homeric': the *tetraphalon*, a four-crested/-horned helmet; *aspidas amphibrotas*, large shields of pre-hoplite style covering the greater part of a man's body (cf. the smaller hoplite *porpax* shield that Arkhilokhos himself jettisoned),[255] and we may here specially note the breast-covers, which also occur in the *Iliad* in a specifically Abantic/Euboian context. *Anaktoron*, as I have already mentioned above, hints at the existence of a *wanax* (at Eretria or Karystos?). The poem may have described an attempt of Karystos to free itself from Eretrian rule or of Eretria to assert control, even perhaps in conjunction with the Milesian attack; or it may merely reflect the traditional hostility between neighbouring Greek states at any period. Nevertheless, as we have seen, it is testified epigraphically and in the literary record that Eretria and Karystos later shared the great festival of the pre-Greek goddess Amarysia.[256] Even in classical times, the Karystia was Dryopian and the inhabitants of the whole area east of Eretria shared a common ancient culture. A perceived common heritage perhaps facilitated Eretrian political aims, but if Eretria seized the Petaliai Islands in the mid-sixth century,[257] then that may be when Eretria and Karystos parted ways.

Revenons à nos probouloi! There is thus a strong possibility that Eretria gave the name and function of her chief magistracy to her dependencies Kerkyra, Keos (and perhaps Karystos: the Karystian inscription *IG* XII 9, 11 of Hadrianic date mentions an *arkheproboulos*) some time between the early seventh and, at the latest, the sixth century. After 490, Eretria controlled no Aegean empire and, with due respect to Lewis, was in no position to influence the constitutional arrangements of anyone else.[258] Therefore, if Eretria took its characteristic magistracy to Keos and Karystos, we are looking at the sixth century at the latest and perhaps the eighth century as the earliest date of its existence there.

If the later functions of the *probouloi* revealed in the epigraphical record provide any clue to their earlier duties, and in the unspecialised governments of the pre-Classical period, these must have been wide ranging, then their powers were great. They had the duty of registering public acts in the city archives and of administering that record; they ordered the proclamation of awards, administered the ceremonies admitting the *epheboi* to citizen status and received the oaths of citizens whenever the city was undertaking some solemn engagement; they presided over the relations of Eretria with the outside world and so exercised great influence over foreign policy; they directed, at least in part, the administration of public finances. So much for their executive role. In the legislative field, they prepared the business of the assembly and presided over the *boule*. In addition, they had the right to present, on their own initiative and authority, drafts of decrees on all matters touching the interests of the state. This right alone conferred great power; other magistrates, e.g. the *strategoi*, could, it seems, present motions only conjointly with them and with their assistance. Thus the *probouloi* in the Classical and Hellenistic periods were indeed, to borrow the phrase the Eretrians themselves used in their decrees, the *tous aei en arkhe ontas* (those in authority duly constituted for the time being). The adverb *aei* is generally translated 'ever' or 'always', but in Eretrian inscriptions it has the force of 'for the time being'.[259] But it inherently implies great antiquity and permanence and so can mean 'forever', suggesting an *arkhe* whose authority, anciently conferred and still active, is taken for granted by anyone perusing the laws;[260] was there ever a time, the 'average citizen' may have wondered, when there was no authority of the *probouloi*?

Any check upon their powers rested with the *boule*. However, they were appointed by and from it, and worked with it, as their name suggests. The archaic *boule* being itself in any case a very exclusive body, there was not likely to have been much conflict between the two groups, especially in early times. The *probouloi* were theoretically supposed to execute the will of the *boule*, which had acquired more or less total control over the political mechanisms of the emerging *polis*. But we may be quite sure that they had great input into the formulation of the opinion of the *bouleutai* on any question at all; it is possible, probable even, that the *probouloi* effectively made the policies emanating from sessions of the *boule*. For, as Aristotle observed, 'whenever both these authorities [exist conjointly] the *probouloi* take precedence over the *bouleutai*'[261] by the inherent natures of the offices. This was doubtless the case in Archaic Eretria.

When the oligarchy was finally overthrown at Eretria in the 530s, the tyrant Diagoras may himself have taken the title *Proboulos* or *Prytanis* (which term is implied later in an unpublished Eretrian inscription)[262] to confer its ancient dignity upon his upstart power. Aristotle notes that: 'Tyrannies moreover occurred in olden times more than now because important offices used to be entrusted to certain men as, for example, at Miletos, a tyranny arose from prytany, for the *prytanis* had control over many important matters.'[263] Much later, the Eretrian philosopher–politician, Menedemos, a respected citizen and member of the ancient aristocratic *genos* of the Theopropidai[264] and friend of the Macedonian king, Antigonos Gonatas, needed nothing more than the title *proboulos* when he assumed responsibility for the direction of the affairs of the *polis*: 'Menedemos drafted a decree in his [Antigonos Gonatas'] honour which was both simple and devoid of flattery, which began as follows: the generals and *probouloi* have moved.'[265] Menedemos himself composed the decree and had it moved by his colleagues. We have noted an *epistates* of the *probouloi* in a third century decree, perhaps the actual title of Menedemos' superior office. Another, Archaic, parallel may be Kypselos, who, Oost has argued, adopted the royal title 'Bakkhis'.[266] Some consider that Diagoras was contemporary with Kleisthenes, the Athenian reformer, and of the same ilk. This is definitely not my view, but he may have kept the existing magisterial titles *probouloi* and *strategoi* after his reforms, as did Kleisthenes the *arkhontes* and *strategoi* at Athens, in this and other ways anticipating the Athenian.

The *arkhe* of the *probouloi* must have chosen one of its number to be something equivalent to *arkheproboulos* and he would have become the eponymous magistrate for a year. The shipping laws, dated *c.* 550/525 mention an *arkhon,*[267] who may have been de facto the *arkheproboulos*. Later, *arkhontes* are inscriptionally attested at Eretria,[268] while Homeric Elephenor is called *arkhos*.

How many *probouloi* were there? Kondoleon discusses at great length the number of *bouleutai* and *probouloi* in the Hellenistic period. His arguments will not hold up. If his arithmetic, which is based on only three tribes, whereas there were at least six, were correct, we would have 108 *bouleutai*.[269] This is far too many for an Archaic *boule*, which was almost certainly smaller and much less structured than his model. However, the traditional four Ionic, expanded later into eight reformed tribes, can be reconciled with groups of eight *epimenieuontes*. Two *epimenieuontes* per Ionian, or later one per 'reformed' tribe in each prytanic group plus an (eponymous) *arkhon* elected or chosen separately, would give, as he wishes, boards of nine *probouloi* (*epimenieuontes*).[270] Knoepfler has argued strongly for six reformed tribes,[271] and I will return to the situation at the end of the sixth century in Chapter 8. I think the earliest *proboulia* would probably have had a multiple of four members, based on the old Ionian tribes, with one being chosen eponymous *arkhon* for the year, decisions being issued 'so-and-so being *arkhon* and the following being fellow-*probouloi*' or some similar formula.[272]

One purpose of Kondoleon's paper was to attempt to prove that the term *aeinautai*[273] was applied to the *probouloi* at Eretria, in other words, that they constituted magistracy, and that 'the institution was very old.'[274] The name occurs in the dedication of a Herm-stele dated *c.* 510–500.[275] His long and complex argument is that a 'new' commercial class, which he also calls *aeinautai*, rose to power in the seventh century, thus at least implying an early supplanting of Hippobotic power, usurping the hitherto exclusive position of the *Hippeis* in the government of Eretria and that later it evolved via becoming a tribe into a de facto *arkhe*,[276] the *probouloi* being also called *aeinautai* during the period(s) when Eretria was ruled in the interests of the merchant class as, he believed, at Miletos, where the *aeinautai* have indeed been alleged to have been an *arkhe* associated with the party of *Ploutis*[277] (wealth), an oligarchic faction. This too is quite unlikely.[278] Though the paper has a number of interesting points, his arguments here fail utterly to convince. I do not believe that there was ever a 'tribe' or 'class' called *aeinautai* at Eretria or that it gave its name to a homonymous magistracy equivalent to the (for him, later) *probouloi*,[279] although I do believe that the mercantile nature of the ruling group at Eretria was established very soon after the first refugees arrived from Lefkandi *c.* 825. However, the *aeinautai* of the Eretrian inscription were possibly a mercantile *koinon* (corporation).[280]

Demarkhoi

Classical Eretria certainly had *demarkhoi* who were deme officials with religious duties;[281] we do not know certainly whether they had other non-religious functions. Whether they existed in any form in archaic times is unknown; they probably did, for the demes existed before the fifth century.

Military officials

At Eretria, we hear of both *strategoi* (generals) and *polemarkhoi* (war leaders), but again the evidence is late. Both are very likely to have had Archaic antecedents; one or more of the *probouloi* may well have been chosen in the early period as *polemarkhos*. The ongoing Lelantine War meant Eretria would seldom have been without the need for war leaders.[282] Aristotle says that the original justification of the *Politeia of the Hippeis* was that cavalry provided the military strength of the state so there may also have been a *hipparkhos* (leader of the cavalry), given the cavalry's early importance. The title existed in the fourth century.[283] Thus, a *polemarkhos* and/or *hipparkhos* appointed from the *probouloi*, together with a board of *strategoi* (generals), one for each of the Ionian tribes, to direct the state-at-war is a possible conjecture. There were certainly *strategoi* in Hellenistic Eretria when they appear in a political context, acting in concert with the *probouloi* moving decrees.[284] It is likely that Eretria would have had a board of *strategoi* earlier than this but of it we know nothing. The decree cited for *hipparkhoi* also mentions *taxiarkhoi* (commanders of tribal levies at Athens). There must have been senior naval magistrates (*nauarkhoi?*) by the mid-sixth century, when Eretria was a significant naval power and the ships provided her principal military force. *Trierarkhoi* are also likely, for Eretria was using triremes as early as 499, as Herodotos tells us, and almost certainly earlier. By the sixth century, there must also have been naval, as well as some kind of military boards, responsible for organising and maintaining the armed forces of the state.

Notes

1 For the history of the urban development of the city: C. Krause, 'Naissance et formation d'une ville', *Dossiers d'archéologie* 94, 1985, 17.

2 Popham *et al.* 1980b, 363–9. Knoepfler (1985b, 50) refers to Lefkandi as 'leur [the Eretrians'] ville primitive.'

3 K. Schefold, 'Die Grabungen in Eretria im Herbst 1964 und 1965', *AK* 9, 1966, 108: 'Eretria ist gleichsam die erste Kolonie von Alt-Eretria.' Schefold was foremost in promoting the hypothesis that Lefkandi/Xeropolis was Old Eretria: however in his first report in *AK* 8, 1965, 104, he locates Old Eretria at the prehistoric site at Kotroni east of the city. It was taken up by Coldstream, 1977, 354, and Bérard, 1970, 68, n. 26, who tries to reconcile contradictary identifications by hypothesising *synoikismos*: 'il est probable que la fondation d'Érétrie est le résultat d'un processus de regroupement de bourgades locales préexistentes comparable avec le synécisme attique; . . . Deux de ces bourgades sont connues: ce pourrait être Lefkandi à l'ouest et Kotroni à l'est, toutes deux pouvant prétendre être considérées comme l'*Ancienne Érétrie*.'

4 Knoepfler 1969, 85 n. 16; Hope-Simpson 1981, 55 (B68); see Boardman (1957, 23), who questions early finds by K. Kourouniotis in 1916: his reports in *AE* 1917 are indeed unenlightening. Those of 1916 and 1917 are summarised 'in a very confused way' (Knoepfler loc. cit.) in *Arch.Anz.* 1922, 316. Much of Kourouniotis's work was lost at Smyrna in the 1922 conflagration but Knoepfler is right to reject Boardman's dismissal of the earlier material even though apparently now lost; Kourouniotis has, in fact, been vindicated by recent investigations at Eretria. On the Mycenaean Period: Jacobsen 1964, 218–9 and n. 29; Themelis 1969, 143–78. Knoepfler 1969, 85, n. 16. For the sub-Protogeometric Period: A. Mazarakis-Ainian, 'Geometric Eretria', *AK* 30, 1987, 3, n. 2 and references. For the Geometric: idem with map Fig. 12; Krause 1982b 139; L. Kahil, 'Érétrie à l'époque géométrique', *ASIAA* 59 1981, 167; A. Altherr-Charon: 'Tombe du 9e siècle avant J.-C.' in Krause *et al.* 'Eretria: Ausgrabungen 1979–80', *AK* 24, 1981, 83.

5 In sector E5 of the grid plan of the city: P. Themelis, ''Ανασκαφὴ στὴν 'Ερετρία', *PAAE* 1974, insert plan A. [Henceforth, Themelis's excavation reports are cited: (Themelis) *PAAE* + year and quotations in English are my translations]. The report is in *PAAE* 1983, 134. See Themelis's chronological framework (*PAAE* 1976, 76): 'Early Geometric period (Attic EG II or MG I) 875–800.' I presume by early Geometric he means Attic EG. See Appendix 1: Chronological tables, with concordance with **Attic** periods. Euboian sub-PG II merges into MG, with which it is sometimes identified as SPG III (corresponding to Attic MG).

6 *PAAE* 1976, 76; 1982, 167.

7 Popham *et al.* 1980b, 368–9.
8 *PAAE* 1983, 132.
9 *PAAE* 1979, 49–50.
10 *PAAE* 1981, 144; 151 for its chronology in relation to other PG/G structures in its immediate vicinity.
11 The early city wall: *PAAE* 1974, 38–9 (Themelis suggests a link with a similarly built wall at the West Gate, citing P. Auberson and K. Schefold, *Führer durch Eretria*, Bern, 1972, 58, Fig. 7; 60, Fig. 8); 1976, 74–5, n. 2, where the wall as a fortification of the early city is first mooted. *PAAE* 1977, 32; 1978, 20: further evidence for the wall as a fortification; 1979, 43–50 has his definitive statement regarding the nature of the wall and its relationship to fortifications at the West Gate; see also 1980, 143–4.; 1983, 137–6.
12 *PAAE* 1980, 86–97; Themelis 1983, 157–65.
13 *PAAE* 1974, 39; 1975, 37; 1979; 50. On the absence of archaeological material at Eretria: Morris 1987, 166.
14 *PAAE* 1979, 50.
15 Reports in *AR*: A. Andreiomenou *et al.*: 1970/71 (late seventh century); 1974/75 (Geom-fifth century); 1976/77 (seventh century); 1982/83; 1983/84 (agora; early stoa, *c.* 550/500.
16 Mazarakis-Ainian 1987, 18 and n. 69.
17 *PAAE* 1983, 137: 'εἶναι γεγονὸς πάντως ὅτι ἀνοικοδομήθηκε καὶ ξανακατοικήθηκε ἀμέσως μετὰ τὴν πρώτη καταστροφη'.
18 Popham *et al.* 1980b, 368.
19 Ibid. 365.
20 *AR* 1976/77, 17.
21 A. Andreiomenou, ''Αρχαικὴ Κεραμεικὴ ἐξ 'Ερετρίας', *AE* 1976 [1977] 6–7, demonstrates the results of accurate provenance and chronology for finds from one such area (Plot OT 112a) near the shore at Eretria.
22 Morris 1987, 166; *AR* 1976/77, 17. Continuity of occupation: ibid.; A. Andreiomenou, 'Γεωμετρικὴ καὶ 'Υπογεωμετρικὴ Κεραμεικὴ ἐξ 'Ερετρίας (I) 1975 [1976] 206–29 and (II)', *AE* 1977 [1979] 126–63.
23 See Boardman 1957, 28.
24 D. Bradeen, 'The Lelantine War and Pheidon of Argos', *TAPA* 78 1947b, 223; n. 1 reviews opinions to that date. See more recently, V. Parker, 'Untersuchungen zum Lelantischen Krieg und verwandten Problemen der frühgriechischen Geschichte', *Historia Einzelschriften* 109, 1997, 59–93.
25 Both Parker and E. Vranopoulos, 'Ιστορία τῆς 'Αρχαίας Εὐβοίας ἀπὸ τοὺς Προϊοτορικοὺς Χρόνους ὡς καὶ τὴ 'Ρωμαιοκρατία, Athens, 1987, 62, adopt a similar position to mine. But on 63 Vranopoulos qualifies it by saying that the war 'έγινε με επίκεντρο τα τέλη περίπου του 8ου αιώνα π. Χ' ('its epicentre occurred about the end of the eighth century.' This statement is based on Bradeen's work: 1947b).
26 *PAAE* 1980, 88; idem 1983, 157–65.
27 *PAAE* 1982, 167. But see Mazarakis-Ainian 1987, 18, n. 69.
28 Camp 1979, 397–411.
29 M. Langdon, 'Sanctuary of Zeus on Mt Hymettos', *Hesperia Suppl.* XVI, 1976, 89–95 and n. 49.
30 'Επίπαγος. *PAAE* 1982, 166. Camp, 1979, was published three years too early for Themelis's Eretrian evidence. A. Snodgrass, 'Two demographic notes (1: The size of Lefkandi; 2: Population in late eighth century Attica)', in R. Hågg *et al.* (eds), *The Greek Renaissance in the Eighth Century: Tradition and Innovation. Proceedings of the Second International Symposium at the Swedish Institute in Athens,* 1–5 June, 1981, Stockholm, 1983, 169–71, attacks Camp's arguments. (However see pp. 210–12 in the same volume for the comments, especially of Camp himself. Themelis has since modified his position somewhat in Camp's favour). Prolonged drought occurred periodically in ancient Greece:

Carpenter 1966 discusses such droughts in earlier (Mycenaean) and later (AD 400–750) periods.

31 A. Cambitoglou, J. Coulton, J. Birmingham and J. Green, *Zagora I: Excavation of a Geometric Settlement on the Island of Andros, Greece. Excavation Season (1967), Study Season (1968/69)*, Sydney, 1971, 11; A. Cambitoglou and J. Coulton, 'Ἀνασκαφαὶ Ζαγορᾶς Ἄνδρου', *AE* 1970, 154–233.

32 Cambitoglou *et al.* 1971, 9.

33 Ibid. 11.

34 R. Nicholls, 'Old Smyrna', *BSA* 53/54, 1958/59, 14.

35 Melaneïs and Arotria: Str. 10, 1, 10 C448.

36 St. Byz. s.v. Ἐρέτρια. The autochthonous inhabitants may have appeared dark to later invaders. Rutter 1975, 17–32.

37 *PAAE* 1982, 164: 'These trenches went down to a depth of 1.86 m., i.e. to the weathered surface of the compacted ancient bedrock (terra rossa) known to us from other trenches, which is the natural, "virgin" subsoil of the area of Eretria, at least in the Geometric, and probably in the PG periods.'

38 W. Heinze, *De rebus Eretriensium*, thesis, University of Göttingen, 1869, 12: 'ad coloniam in regionem aliquam deductam pertinet (nisi fallimur) quae silvosa et opaca erat.'

39 *RE* s.v. Hekate: e.g. Μέλαινα (2773); Μελινόη (2776).

40 Ch. 2, pp. 30–3.

41 *LSJ* 245 s.v. ἀροτρ-; 685–6 s.v. ἐρέσσω (ἐρέττω).

42 Or, if the site were already called Arotria, to have given it a new one more appropriately descriptive of their economic interests.

43 Popham *et al.* 1980b, Appendix B: The ancient name of the site, 423–7.

44 Ibid. 360–1; 366.

45 Demand 1990, 18; see Morris 1987, esp. 202–10. We have archaeological evidence for artisans and, by extension, traders. But that there was a landowning class hardly requires stating. Ch. 3, pp. 80–1, 85–6.

46 Lefkandi: Popham *et al.* 1980b, 93–5; Desborough 1972, 189–99. Eretria: See above, p. 91, n. 12; *PAAE* 1980, 86–97; 1983, 139. A. Altherr-Charon reports an eighth-century bronzeworking establishment in the *temenos* of the temple of Apollo Daphnephoros, *AK* 24 1981, 81–2; *AK* 25 1982c, 154–6, and comments on the existence of a similar (but not in a *temenos*) establishment at the Euboian 'colony' at Pithekoussai. On the Pithekoussan workshop: J. Klein, 'A greek metalworking quarter', *Expedition* 14, 1972, 34–9. See W.-D. Heilmeyer, 'Giessereibetriebe in Olympia', *JdI* 84, 1969, esp. 5; 17. These may have been common in sanctuaries of Magna Graecia in later times: Altherr-Charon 1982c, 156, n. 11.

47 *PAAE* 1980, 95–6; H. Catling, 'Objects of bronze, iron and lead', in Popham *et al.* 1980b, 235ff., pl. 247, nos 12, 15, 16. Lefkandiots trading with the Levant and Cyprus before going to Eretria; Cypriot influence could thus have come via Lefkandi: J. Coldstream, 'The Iron Age', in D. Hunt (ed.), *Footprints in Cyprus. An Illustrated History*, London, 1984, 61–2; 66, presents evidence of early Iron Age trade goods, which he believes were brought by Euboians.

48 Manufacturing: Snodgrass 1980, 40–1; D. Ridgway, *The First Western Greeks*, Cambridge, 1992, 15–20. Fertility: Ch. 5, p. 146 and nn. 44–5; R. Cook, 'Reasons for the foundation of Ischia and Cumae', *Historia* 11, 1962, 113–4.

49 Ch. 5, pp. 142–4.

50 Cambitoglou *et al.* 1971, 60; J.-P. Descoeudres, 'Zagora auf der Insel Andros – eine eretrische Kolonie?', *AK* 16, 1973, 88, n. 15.

51 Ibid. 88: 'Die ganze Insel [Andros] in den Besitz Eretrias übergegangen war.' For its varied trade connections, see his n. 14.

52 Cambitoglou *et al.* 1971, 56.

53 Ibid. 58. Idem *AE* 1970, 228–33.

54 Cambitoglou *et al.* 1971, Fig. 54. Descoeudres 1973, 88, nn. 12–3.
55 Cambitoglou *et al.* 1971, 54; 56, n. 10.
56 Str. 10, 1, 10 C448. Descoeudres 1973, 88, n. 19: a mid-seventh-century empire.
57 Descoeudres 1973, 88, n. 18.
58 Krause 1982b, 137–44: comparison of plans 1 (Eretria third–second millennium) and 2 (Eretria eighth century) indicates the degree of siltation occurring and the likely *natural* evolution of coastline had later engineering operations by the Eretrians not been undertaken.
59 Knoepfler 1969, 85–6.
60 Decrees: *IG* XII 9, 1273–4.
61 P. Friedemann, 'Un établissement hydraulique sur le flanc est de l'acropole d'Érétrie', *AK* 36, 1993, 132: the acropolis 'apparait avoir été dépourvue d'autres points d'eau.' On the quarry: Ch. 1, pp. 19–20 and n. 71 (and figs).
62 See above, n. 58
63 Krause 1982b, 138–9 plans 2–3.
64 Ibid. 141, plan 4. Comparison of plans 2 and 4 shows the evolution of the harbour area and works of the mid-sixth century.
65 Krause, 1982b, 144. A. Georgiadis, 'Εἰς τὴν ἄνω Ἐρετρικὴν ἐπιγραφήν', *AD* 1913, 214–5 (diagram of harbour defence works and mole); C. Starr, *The Economic and Social Growth of Early Greece, 800–500 BC*, New York, 1977, 99.
66 The prehistoric coastline is conjectural: Krause 1983, 65–6; however, that the settlement was on the coast is not in doubt.
67 Krause 1981: report by Tuor, 83–4. It was noted first by Themelis, 1969a, 143–54, and excavated systematically 1979–80. There was also an MH–LH site on the acropolis summit: Krause 1983, 66; 1982a, 138; map 1, nn. 1–2.
68 Krause 1982b, 139.
69 Krause 1983, 66. The remark in Liv. 32, 16, 10 concerning materials to aid in L. Quinctilius Flaminius' siege of Eretria in 198 undoubtedly includes timber but could refer to anywhere in the vicinity, e.g. the foothills of Olympos.
70 Euboian PG: 1050–900. *PAAE* 1976, 76; 1982, 167; Knoepfler 1969, 83–7; Mazarakis-Ainian 1987, 3.
71 Ibid. 3.
72 Krause 1983, 66–7.
73 Ibid. 67, map (Fig. 3).
74 Krause 1982b, 140.
75 Snodgrass 1980, 31.
76 Generally: idem. Athens: ibid. Fig. 5; A. Snodgrass, *Archaeology and the Rise of the Greek State*, Cambridge, 1977, 26–30. Corinth: C. Roebuck, 'Some aspects of urbanization in Corinth', *Hesperia* 41, 1972, 96–105; H. Robinson, *The Urban Development of Ancient Corinth*, Athens, 1965, 4–6; J. Salmon, *Wealthy Corinth. A History of the City to 338 BC*, Oxford, 1986, 79–80 (cautiously).
77 The literary date is 728. On Megara Hyblaia: A. Graham, 'The colonial expansion of Greece', *CAH* III, 3, 1982, Ch. 37, 106–8, with references. The plan was not absolutely orthogonal.
78 Chronologically arranged maps: Krause 1982b, 1, 2; 1979, 1, 2.
79 Krause 1982b, 137: 'deren ursprüngliches Ordnungsprinzip in den spezifischen Merkmalen des Ortes zu suchen ist.'
80 In allotment 740: *PAAE* 1974, 39.
81 Krause 1982b, plans 2–3.
82 Auberson and Schefold 1972.
83 Krause 1979, 46–7; 1982b, 141.
84 C. Krause, 'Das Westtor, Ergebnisse der Ausgrabungen 1964–1968', *Eretria IV; Fouilles et Recherches*, Berne, 1972, 10–29. Idem 1979, 46. Auberson and Schefold 1972, 57.

85 Both Themelis and Bérard believe that a city wall did exist: see esp. excavation reports of the Geometric wall by Themelis (see above, n. 10); C. Bérard, 'Topographie et urbanisme de l' Érétrie archaïque: l' Hérôon', *Eretria; Fouilles et Recherches* VI, 1976, 92–4 and Fig. 3; Mazarakis-Ainian 1987, 16, 18. See Krause 1972 (for West Gate), but see idem. 'Remarques sur la structure et l'évolution de l'espace urbain d'Érétrie', *Architecture et Société* (=*Actes du Colloque de Rome 1980*), Paris/Rome, 1983, 69 (for the seventh century), in which he is more cautious. R. Martin, 'Problèmes de topographie et d' évolution urbaine', in *Contribution à l' étude de la société et de la colonisation eubéennes. Cahiers du Centre Jean Bérard* II, Naples, 1975, 48–52, and C. Rolley, 'Fouilles à Érétrie: archéologie, histoire et religion', *Rev.arch.* 1974, 307–11, deny any seventh-century fortification.

86 Reports by Themelis in *PAAE* (1974–84). Krause 1972, 14–5, Fig. 6, n. 21.

87 *PAAE* 1979, 46–8.

88 *PAAE* 1979, 48–9.

89 Ibid. 52. For other chronological evidence: *PAAE* 1976, 75; wall dated 710–675 in *PAAE* 1981, 144.

90 Krause 1972, plan 2. Mazarakis-Ainian 1987, 18.

91 Ibid. 16.

92 Starr 1977, 99 and P. Fraser, *AR* 1968/69, 8. Early fortifications in general: Nicholls 1958/59, section 3: 'The development of early Greek fortifications', 114–36; Schefold 1966, 116–20. The defence waterworks: C. Krause, 'Brunnenturme in der archaischen Stadtmauer Eretrias', *AK* 25, 1982a, 39–42.

93 Mazarakis-Ainian 1987, 4–10.

94 Ibid. 4.

95 Ibid. 17.

96 Ibid. 17, Fig 11; Popham and Sackett 1968, 14–5; 23–4.

97 Mazarakis-Ainian 1987, 4; Cambitoglou *et al.* 1971, 17–20; 25–6. However A. Johnston, *The Emergence of Greece*, London, 1976, 54–5, is misleading to suggest that there is no similarity between building techniques at Eretria and Zagora in the eighth century.

98 Mazarakis-Ainian 1987, 9.

99 Ibid. 20.

100 Andreiomenou 1977, 126–63; ibid. ''Αψιδοτὰ οἰκοδομήματα καὶ κεραμεικὴ τοῦ 8ου καὶ 7ου αἰ.π.Χ. ἐν 'Ερετρίᾳ', *ASIAA* 59 (n.s. 43), 1981, 187–235; Mazarakis-Ainian 1987, 18–20.

101 Mazarakis-Ainian 1987, 16, 20.

102 See above, pp. 109–10.

103 A. Geiser, 'Un tresor de monnaies d' argent', *Doss.Arch.* 94, 1985, 46–9. For the archaic agora; east stoa (plan); shops: P. Calligas, ''Η 'Αγορᾶ τῆς 'Αρχαίας 'Ερετρίας', *AAA* 15, 1982, 3–9.

104 Mazarakis-Ainian 1987, 21.

105 The letters designating structures in the *temenos* of Apollo Daphnephoros as used in the Swiss plans: *BCH* 96, 1972, 759 (Fig. 398; H = ninth century Daphnephoreion; E = eighth century (first) hekatompedon; N = seventh century (second) hekatompedon; A = foundations of the sixth century Doric temple).

106 Unit IV–1: W. McDonald, W. Coulson and J. Rosser, *Excavations at Nichoria in South West Messenia. (III: Dark Age and Byzantine Habitation)* Minneapolis, MN, 1983, 18–50, including plans and restoration diagrams, esp. plan 3.

107 C. Morgan, *Athletes and Oracles. The Transformation of Olympia and Delphi in the Eighth Century* BC, Cambridge, 1990, 73–9.

108 C. Bérard, 'Architecture érétrienne et mythologie delphique', *AK* 14, 1971, 59–73.

109 Ibid. 71–2.

110 Ibid. 71. It marked a major stopping point of the god himself on the Lelantine Plain on his journey from the Hyperborean lands to Delos: *Hom. Hym. ad PA* 219–20 (quoted Ch. 3, p. 77).

111 P. Auberson, 'La reconstruction du Daphnéphoréion d'Érétrie', *AK* 17, 1974, 60–8. R. Hempe and E. Simon, *The Birth of Greek Art. From the Mycenaean to the Archaic Period*, New York, 1991, Fig. 19.

112 Mazarakis-Ainian 1987, 10–1, nn. 35–6; H. Drerup, 'Das sogenannte Daphnephoreion in Eretria', in *Festschrift Friedrich Hiller*, 1986, 3–21.

113 *PAAE* 1981, 144, n. 5. Bérard 1971, 59–73.

114 *PAAE* 1981, 144.

115 For the early Archaic (seventh-century) and sixth-century temples: P. Auberson 'Le temple d'Apollon Daphnéphoros', *Eretria* I, 1968, 11–24. W. Cummer's review in *AJA* 75, 1971, 341–2, criticises Auberson's interpretation of the seventh-century building: he rejects the reconstruction of a *pteron,* which he says the Swiss maintain on 'uncertain or non-existent' archaeological data. *PAAE* 1981, 144–5, nn. 5 and especially 6, and H. Knell, 'Eretria: zur Grundrissrekonstruktion des alteren und des jüngeren Apollonntempels', *AK* 15, 1972, 40–8, deal with all three temples that succeeded the 'Daphnephoreion'.

116 P. Fraser, *AR* 1966/67; 1968/69. Auberson 1968, 16–23.

117 Altherr-Charon and Amstad, S., 'Eretria. Ausgrabungen, 1981', *AK* 25, 1982, 156.

118 Martin, 1975, 50, thinks that the temple was not the centre of the original urban agglomeration. I do not agree. There were dwellings both near the sea and in the north-west sector from virtually the beginning of the 'new' polis.

119 See above, p. 107 and n. 124: *temenos*. Mazarakis-Ainian 1987, 13–4 (who however does not make this identification); Krause 1981, 82.

120 Themelis 1969a, 177; Auberson and Schefold 1972, 105–7. See the dedication *IG* XII 9, 260 to Artemis Olympia.

121 Auberson and Schefold 1972, 105. Excavation report: I. Metzger, 'Das Thesmophorion von Eretria', *Eretria* VII, 1985. Plut. *Quaest.Graec.* 31.

122 He calls them θάλαμοι.

123 *PAAE* 1980, 97–100.

124 *PAAE* 1978, 20.

125 L. Kahil, 'Contribution à l'étude de l'Érétrie géométrique', in *Στήλη: Τόμος εἰς μνήμην Νικολάου Κοντολέοντος*, Athens, 1980, 526, and reports by J.-P. Michaud: *BCH* 96, 1972, 764; 97, 1973, 365; 98, 1974, 687; Schefold and Auberson 1972, 97; Schefold, *AK* 17, 1974, 70.

126 Mazarakis-Ainian 1987, 14.

127 Loc. cit.; Andreiomenou 1977, 129, n. 1.

128 Bérard 1970; idem, 'Le sceptre du prince', *MH* 29, 1972, 219–27; idem, 'Topographie et urbanisme de l' Érétrie archaïque: l' Hérôon', *Eretria; Fouilles et Recherches* (Eretria) VI, Berne, 1976, 89–95; idem, 'Récoupérer la mort du prince: Héroïsation et formation de la cité', in G. Gnoli and J.- P. Vernant (eds), *La mort, les morts dans les sociétés anciennes,* Cambridge, 1982, 89–105.

129 Bérard 1970, 13–47 (cremations); 48–55 (inhumations).

130 Desborough 1972, 271; R. Vedder, *Ancient Euboea: Studies in the History of a Greek Island from the Earliest Times to 404 BC*, PhD thesis, University of Arizona, Tucson, AZ, 1978, 43, n. 86; Bérard 1970, 27 [bronze cauldrons *c.* 715–685 (photo), 66–7]. Mazarakis-Ainian 1987, 16. For similar practice at Pithekoussai (without the large bronze cauldrons): Ridgeway 1992, esp. 46–52. For Eretria as the Euboian source for the practice: T. Webster, *From Mycenae to Homer*, London, 1958, 140 (but derived originally from Athens). Ridgeway 1992, 20: 'the cultural cargo' carried by the Euboians to the West.

131 Full description of Tomb 6: Bérard 1970, 13–17.

132 Ibid., Chs 2, especially 31–2, 69–70 and 6, esp. 65; idem 1972, 220.

133 For the political ramifications of the *Heröon* cult: see below Ch. 7, pp. 211–12. Berard 1970, 65. For a political explanation for its demise: Ch. 7, loc. cit.

134 Mazarakis-Ainian 1987, 14.

135 Funeral games: Hes. *Op.* 654–62.

136 Plut. *Mor.* fr. 84 *Comm. in Hes.Op.* It is possible that Amphidamas died in some sea-borne raid like that illustrated on an LG vase showing 'Dipylon' warriors fighting to the left of a ship: P. Greenhalgh, *Early Greek Warfare: Horsemen and Chariots in the Homeric and Archaic Ages*, Cambridge, 1973, 67 Fig. 40. On Amphidamas: Ch. 5, pp. 165–6.

137 c. 800–750. Originally excavated by Kourouniotis: reported in *AE* 1903. Coldstream 1977, 197–8. Mazarakis-Ainian 1987, 16, n. 56: 'More than fifty Geometric and Subgeometric child inhumations and eight adult cremations have been investigated up to the present day.'

138 For discussion of the two modes of interment: see above, n. 129.

139 These practices seem to be the rule at Eretria in the Geometric period.

140 A. Andreiomenou, ''Εκ τῆς δυτικῆς νεκροπόλεως 'Ερετρίας' (I), *AAA* 7/1, 1974, 229–48; idem, ''Εκ τῆς δυτικῆς νεκροπόλεως "Ερετρίας' (II), *AAA* 9/2, 1976, 197–212.

141 For more detail of the sixth- and later centuries city: see the various works of Krause and Bérard and, in English, K. Schefold, 'The architecture of Eretria', *Archaeology* 21, 1968, 272–81.

142 For example Thessalian Penestai.

143 St. Byz. Δύστος (citing Theopompos *FGrH* 115F149). But Dystos was not Eretrian until the late fifth century: Gehrke, 1988, 38–9, for the latter view, citing Thessaly as a parallel. But see Knoepfler 1997, 401 and nn. 329–32.

144 D. Knoepfler: review of P. Carlier, *La royauté grecque avant Alexandre*', Strasbourg, 1984, *REG* 99, 1986a, 336. I do not know upon what his 'très certainement' is based.

145 Ch. 2, p. 49 and nn. 190, 196, 222.

146 Drews 1983, 84–5; P. Carlier, *La royauté en Grèce avant Alexandre*, Strasbourg, 1984. See Knoepfler's 1986 review (in which he also attacks Drews), 332–41, which puts kings at Eretria and Amarynthos at an early period.

147 Pyraikhmes: [ps.]-Plut. *Parall. Graec. et Rom.* (*Mor.* 307c); Kryos: Paus. 10, 6, 6. For kings of Euboia: *IG* XII 9, Test. et Not. 146.

148 See above, p. 109; Ch. 5, pp. 165–6.

149 1986, 336.

150 Hes. *Op.* 38–9.

151 1986, 336–7. See above, p. 124, n. 250 (*wanax*?).

152 See above, p. 124 and nn. 250, 255.

153 Bérard 1972, 219–20: 'Nous évitons de parler de 'roi', malgré les références faites au mot βασιλεύς.'

154 Idem. See also ibid. 1982, 89–105; ibid. 1983, especially 47–9; 59. Ibid., 1970, 28, 31, for the status of the dead man whose cremated remains were interred in it.

155 1987, 21.

156 Snodgrass 1980, 28–48. For the nature and period of this phenomenon: W. Runciman, 'The origins of states; the case of Archaic Greece', *CSSH* 24, 1982, 351–77; V. Ehrenberg, 'When did the Polis rise?', *JHS* 57, 1937, 156. [Snodgrass (220) regards Ehrenberg's 1960 study as 'the classic account of Greek state forms' and is his principal reference for his discussion of the early *polis*.] See Ehrenberg 1960, 11: '[evidence and argument] establishes the general conclusion that the formation of the *polis*-town may be dated round 800'; and 'The type of the *Polis* was in existence around about 800 BC.' For a new and rather different discussion of the 'rise' of the *polis*: F. de Polignac, *Cults, Territory and the Origins of the Greek City State*, Chicago, 1995, who has much to say about Eretria and seems to owe much to C. Bérard. Contrary to A. Snodgrass, 'An historical Homeric society?', *JHS* 94, 1974, 114–25, and G. Kirk, 'The Homeric poems as history', *CAH*[3] II, 2a, Ch. 39b, 1980b, 820–50, who think that Homeric society was a poetic fiction and amalgam, I. Morris, 'The use and abuse of Homer', *CA* 5, 1986, 81–138, and K. Raaflaub, 'Homer to Solon: the rise of the early Greek polis', in M. Hansen (ed.), *The Ancient Greek City-State*, Copenhagen, 1993, 41–105, stress the importance of the *polis* in Homer.

157 Snodgrass 1980, 32–3: explains the fortification of non-mainland settlements such as Smyrna and Iasos as the result of the threat posed by inland native tribes of Asia Minor.
158 On cult: ibid. 33–4; de Polignac 1995, especially Chs 1, 2; assembly: Snodgrass 1980, 32; see below, pp. 119–20.
159 Snodgrass 1980, 40–2.
160 Ibid. 33.
161 See above, pp. 106–7. Mazarakis-Ainian 1987, 21: perhaps house of a priest-king.
162 Ch. 3, pp. 84–5.
163 Snodgrass 1980, 34.
164 And, perhaps, Corinth: ibid. 34.
165 Ibid., 18–9; 21, cites no literature in his bibliography and notes.
166 Ibid. 19.
167 *PAAE* 1982, 167.
168 See above, pp. 106–7, cf. n. 112.
169 Snodgrass 1980, 59.
170 Arist. ap. Str. 10, 1, 8 C447.
171 *CAH*[3] III, 165 (table).
172 J. Hasebroek, *Griechische Wirtschafts-und Gesellschaftsgeschichte bis zur Perserzeit*, I Tübingen, 1931, 73–4.
173 Morris 1987, 202–5.
174 Arist. *Pol.* 1289b33–6.
175 Arist. *Pol.* 1289b39. Str. 14, 1, 28 C643; L. Worley, *Hippeis. The Cavalry of Classical Greece*, San Francisco, CA, 1994, 36.
176 Arist. *Pol.* 1289b27–1290a29.
177 Though Aristotle (1274a, 21) makes them the third class.
178 Combining the terminology of [Arist.] *Ath. pol.* 15, 2 (see below, n. 182) and Arist. *Pol.* 1306a36 (Ch. 7, p. 207).
179 Arist. *Pol.* 1289a36–40. Greenhalgh, 1973, 82, equates the Eretrian *Hippeis* and the Athenian *pentekosiomedimnoi* as the highest class in the state.
180 The role of the *Hippeis* as cavalry in the Archaic period is controversial: see Worley 1994, 1–5 for summary of recent positions; Greenhalgh, 1973, *passim*, believes that the *Hippeis* generally rode to war dismounting to fight. Worley makes the cavalry a fighting unit in its own right for our period. See Theognis 885–94.
181 Ael. *VH* 6, 1; Plut. *Per.* 23, 2, uses an almost identical phrase referring to the ruling group in Khalkis at the time of the Euboian uprising 447/6. Geyer, 1903, 63, believes that Ailianos' reference belongs to 447/6, not 506, and regards the outcome of the 'Lelantine War', which he dates to an earlier period, as consolidating control of the *Hippobotai*: 58.
182 [Arist.] *Ath. pol.* 15, 2.
183 Πολιτεία is used in [Arist.] *Ath. pol.* 15, 2 and by many modern historians but see Arist. *Pol.* 1306a36.
184 Arist. *Pol.* 1306a33–7.
185 Ch. 7, pp. 207–11.
186 Hes. *Op.* 259–64.
187 O. Murray, *Early Greece*, London, 1988, 75–6.
188 Lefkandi: Popham *et al.* 1980b; Eretria: Bérard 1970, *passim*.
189 Asios (ap. Ath. *Deipn.* 12, 525e–f) and Duris (*FGrH.* 76F60). Plut. *Quaest. Graec.* 57. See also C. Bowra, 'Asius and the old-fashioned Samians', *On Greek Margins*, Oxford, 1970, 122–33. Ch. 2, pp. 35–6 and nn. 78–9 for Kharixenos.
190 Str. 10, 1, 8 C446. *LSJ* s.v. τίμημα (1794): 'in a political sense the value at which a citizen's property was rated for taxation "ἡ ἀπὸ τιμημάτων πολιτεία": a government of which the magistrates were chosen according to their property, a timocracy.'
191 For example Arist. *Pol.* 1278a25; 1321a29 (at Thebes).

192 L. Whibley, *Greek Oligarchies; their Character and Organization*, London/Chicago, 1896/1975, 129: in n. 12, he cites Strabo. Later (p. 132) he links Eretria and Khalkis as examples of timocratic states.

193 The term, τὸ βουλευόμενον is legislative and administrative: Arist. *Pol.* 1291a28–31; *LSJ* s.v. βουλεύω B. Med. (2) p. 325; Whibley 1975, 140, n. 3.

194 Ibid. 141. Arist. *Pol.* 1298a34. W. Newman *The 'Politics' of Aristotle* IV, Oxford, 1902, 262: 'The name Boulê seems, however, sometimes to be applied to Councils not of a democratic character.'

195 Whibley 1975, 141.

196 H. Bengtson (tr. E. Bloedow), *History of Greece from the Beginnings to the Byzantine Era*, Ottawa, 1969/1988, 60.

197 1986, 334: 'Il me paraît dès lors très probable, en raison des liens étroits de l'Eubée ionienne avec le monde insulaire (notamment avec Paros et Naxos), que des cités comme Chalcis et Érétrie avaient un *basileus*-magistrat – et/ou peut-être un collège de *basileis* -, et cela malgré le silence actuel de l'épigraphie eubéenne.' And, by implication, Mazarakis-Ainian, 1987, 18.

198 Whibley 1975, 157: Sparta 30, Knidos 60, Corinth 80, Elis 90.

199 Areopagites at Athens, *gerontes* at Sparta; also at Knidos, Elis, Crete.

200 Fr. 63.

201 C. Hignett, *A History of the Athenian Constitution to the End of the Fifth Century* BC, Oxford, 1958, 150; Whibley 1975, 163–4. At Corinth there was a committee of eight: Nic. Dam. *FGrH* 90F60 (see below, Ch. 8, n. 84); at Khios, 15: P. Cauer, *Dialectus Inscriptionum Graecarum propter Dialectum Memorabilium*, 2nd edn, Leipzig, 1877, 496. In democratic *poleis*, of course, the assembly was sovereign.

202 Arist. *Pol.* 1299b31–9: they check the power of *bouleutai*.

203 1980, 32.

204 Whibley 1975, 142, n. 8.

205 Hom. *Il.* 2, 188–277; also 3, 205–24; 11, 138–42 (Trojan). On an important role for the assembly in Homer: K. Raaflaub, 'Interstate relations among early Greek *poleis*', paper delivered at the seminar, *Narrating Antiquity. Epic and History in the Graeco-Roman World*, held at the University of New England, Armidale, New South Wales, 2 July 1996; Carlier 1984; contra, see M. Finley, *The World of Odysseus*, 2nd edn, Harmondsworth, 1977, 78–83, 113–6.

206 Plut. *Lyc.* 6, 4 quotes the ῥήτρα as preserved in Tyrtaios.

207 Ἔδοχσεν τε̃ι βολε̃ι καὶ τε̃ι δέμοι: *IG* XII Suppl. 549; *IG* XII 9, 187B, 196, 197, 198, etc.

208 *IG* XII 9, 232, 6.

209 Holleaux 1897, 157–89. Eretria was then a member of the Boiotian Federation and adopted its chief magistracy. Perhaps the Boiotians felt that the institution was so nationally oriented that they abolished it.

210 G. Glotz, *The Greek City and its Institutions*, London, 1929, 88.

211 Loc. cit. Glotz cites C. Michel, *Receuil des inscriptions grecques* (one vol./two supplements) Paris, 1899/1927, no. 345, l. 28–9 (= *IG* XII 9, 211) τὴν ἀρχὴν τὴν ἀεὶ προκα | θημένην, which he interprets as 'presidents'; however, *probouloi* are nowhere mentioned in this particular inscription, and he might better have cited *IG* XII 9, 236, 47, in which a similar phrase is used specifically of *probouloi* (τοὺς προβούλους τοὺς ἀεὶ ἐν ἀρχῇ ὄντας).

212 Arist. *Pol.* 1299b38–9.

213 Arist. *Pol.* 1323a8–9.

214 1986, 205, n. 79; see Schaefer *RE* s.v. πρόβουλος; E. Will, *Korinthiaka. Recherches sur l' Histoire et la Civilisation de Corinthe dès Origines aux Guerres Médiques*, Paris, 1955, 609–15.

215 C. Starr, *The Origins of Greek Civilization*, London, 1962, 346.

216 D. Lewis, 'The Federal Constitution of Keos', *BSA* 57, 1962, 3. Schaefer (*RE*) erroneously attributes *probouloi* to Histiaia, misunderstanding M. Tod (*A Selection of Greek Historical Inscriptions* II: *from 403 to 323 BC*, Oxford, 1968, 124–5, no. 141), whom he believes says that the magistracy existed there; in fact Tod says those responsible for administering the provisions of the treaty at Keos were 'the council(?), the πρόβουλοι (see *IG* XII 5, 647 2; 6), the ἀστυνόμοι (see no. 162, 17) and one other body of magistrates, perhaps the νουοφύλακες, while on 124 he says the responsible magistrates at Histiaia were the στρατηγοί (treaty, ll. 6–11). The same error is made by Glotz, 1929, 88, who says, that *probouloi* at Histiaia 'possessed executive functions' (citing Michel, *RIG* no. 402, ll. 6, 14 etc.; *IG* XII 5, 594, 19). C. Lécrivain, in C. Daremberg and E. Saglio (eds), *Dictionnaire des antiquités grecques et romaines*, Graz, 1963, 660, s.v. Probouloi (following an article by Glotz!) also errs. Both inscriptions are from Keos (the latter being that published as Tod 141; the former a decree of Koressos referring to *probouloi* in a context having no connection with Histiaia).

217 Ch. 8, pp. 243–8, esp. 247–8.

218 *IG* XII Suppl. 555: N. Papadakis, ''Ανασκαφὴ 'Ισείον 'Ερετρίας', *AD* 1915, 174: ''Αλλὰ καὶ διὰ τὴν παρὰ τῷ ἄρχοντι συναναγραφὴν τὸ ἁπλούστατον εἶναι ὡς ἐπιμηνιεύοντας νὰ ἐκλάβωμεν αὐτοὺς τοὺς πασιγνώστους προβόλους τῆς 'Ερετρίας.'

219 *IG* XII Suppl. 549: Μεκισστίδ | ος φυλες: ἐπιμενι | ευούρες.

220 N. Robertson, 'Government and society at Miletus, 525–442 BC', *Phoenix* 41, 1987, 381.

221 Kondoleon 1963/65, 39. B. Petrakos, 'Dédicace des Aeinautai d'Érétrie', *BCH* 87, 1963, 545–7 (re. *aeinautai*: see above, p. 127). Petrakos (545) speaking of the Keian treaty with Eretria (see above, pp. 121–2, nn. 230–5): 'Il est certain que le décret n'appartient pas à l'époque où Kéos était soumise aux Érétriens (Strab. X, 1, 10); mais on ne saurait guère douter que l'institution des magistrats dont nous venons de citer les titres ne remontât jusqu'à ce temps-là.' See also Ch. 8, pp. 240–3.

222 Plut. *Quaest.Graec.* 11. For Eretrians at Kerkyra: Ch. 5, pp. 147–50. Cf. W. Halliday, *The Greek Questions of Plutarch*, Oxford, 1928, 63–4, who doubts whether the passage is good evidence for Eretrians in Kerkyra. *IG* IX 1, 682, 688 have a προστάτας of the *probouloi* at Kerkyra. See *LSJ* s.v. προστάτης (3); *RE* s.v. πρόβουλοι 1229, 35–6 (Schaefer). Str. 10, 1, 15 C449 mentions a Euboia in Kerkyra.

223 Ch. 5, pp. 148, 154.

224 Glotz, 1929, 88, thinks, however, that they, together with the *prostatas* (president), went from Corinth to Kerkyra, though the title *prostates* of the *probouloi* is epigraphically attested at Eretria: *IG* XII 9, 225, 4–5; *epistatai* are chosen from the *probouloi* and they oversee some task set by the *boule* in several other inscriptions..

225 1986 40, n. 265.

226 Ibid. 205, n. 79. Schaefer, *RE* XXIII, (1957) 1222: *probouloi* a Bakkhiad institution, because the office is found on Kerkyra (citing *IG* IX 1, 682).

227 A. Spetsieri-Choremi, *Ancient Kerkyra*, Athens 1991, 6: founded mid-eighth century, ended 734. The Eretrian town was on the shores of the Hyllaian harbour (p. 7; map).

228 Str. 10, 1, 10 C448. J. Myres, 'On the list of "Thalassocracies" in Eusebius', *JHS* 26, 1906, 98: says that Paros was an Eretrian dependency picked up from Naxos. If so, it occurred probably during the late sixth century. Ch. 9, pp. 270–1.

229 See above, p. 96 and nn. 50–1.

230 Descoeudres 1973, 88; C. Dunant and J. Thomopoulos, 'Inscriptions de Céos, I: Traité d' isopolité', *BCH* 78, 1954, 320.

231 Decree of Koresia: *IG* XII 5, 647 (= Boeckh, *CIG* 2360; W. Dittenberger, *Sylloge Inscriptionum Graecarum*[1], Leipzig, 1915/20, no. 348), cited by Holleaux, 1938, 56 n. 1, as referring to πρόβουλοι.

232 Dunant and Thomopoulos 1954, 320: 'survivance dans le vocabulaire de la domination érétrienne.' The relevant sections of the treaty are translated in Ch. 8, p. 243. The political ramifications are discussed on pp. 240–3.

233 But see Lewis, 1962, 2, who argues against *khoroi* as *districts*.

234 Lewis 1962, 3.

235 From the statistics on the stele, M. Sakellariou, *The Archaic Period*, Athens, 1971, 252, estimates the population of Eretria, when the stele was erected, to be *c.* 50,000. Knoepfler, 1985a, 243–59, calculates the total number of hoplites at *c.* 5000 and *c.* 500 *Hippeis*, and of citizens between 5000 and 10,000. In 1997, section II.1, he maintains the numbers at 5000 *hoplitai* and *psiloi* (light-armed troops) combined and 10,000 citizens (n. 162).

236 W. Forrest, 'Colonization and the rise of Delphi', *Historia* 6, 1957, 167, denies its authenticity. I accept it as genuine, even if what Strabo (or his source) saw was a copy, discussed in Appendix 4: The source of Strabo's description of the Amarynthos stele (10, 1, 10 C448). J. Myres, *Herodotus, Father of History*, Oxford, 1953, 387; A. Lloyd, *Marathon*, London, 1975, 176–7. Salmon 1986, 165–9.

237 Early sixth century (Ch. 5, pp. 168–70) cavalry was apparently the mainstay of the Eretrian army against Khalkis. Of course, the number given in the stele may not reflect the actual comparative effectiveness of cavalry as against infantry at any given period. However, the worsting of Hippobotic Khalkis' cavalry by the Eretrians is significant.

238 Jeffery 1961/90, 82.

239 Wallace, 1936a, 95, thought it was.

240 *IG* XII 9, 2, 2.

241 Knoepfler 1997, 353 and n. 14.

242 Str. 10, 1, 1 C444; Plin. *HN* 4, 71; Ath. *Deipn.* 9, 376a–b (quoting the playwright Akhaios of Eretria who says that the name means 'pig island'). W. Wallace, 'The demes and districts of Eretria', *Hesperia* 16, 1947, 131 (map); 133–4 locates the deme Aiglephe(i)ra (ἐξ Αἰγλεφείρας) on the islands. Knoepfler 1997, 366 and nn. 114–6 strongly disputes this location and his arguments are persuasive.

243 Geyer, 1903, 117, wrongly thought they were part of Karystian territory, although later (118) he contradicts this somewhat; similarly 91, n. 1.

244 *IG* XII 9, 1273 and 1274. F. Cairns, 'The "Laws of Eretria" (*IG* XII, 9 1273 and 1274): epigraphic, legal and political aspects', *Phoenix* 45, 1991, 296–313 and E. Vanderpool and W. Wallace, 'The sixth century laws from Eretria', *Hesperia* 33, 1964, 381–91, accept the restoration (originally of Hiller) in l. 11 of Π[ε]ταλάς.

245 Ch. 6, pp. 192–7.

246 Vanderpool and Wallace 1964, 390; Jeffery 1960/90, 84.

247 Konon (*FGrH* 26F1, 44) in Photios, *Bibliotheke*, 140a (cited: *IG* XII 9, Test. et Not. 146.

248 Huxley 1966, 50; C. Thomas, 'From Wanax to Basileus. Kingship in the Dark Age', *Hispania Antiqua* 6, 1978, 187; L. Jeffery, *Archaic Greece*, London, 1976, 210. On the question of the Milesian *basileia*: V. Gorman, *Miletos the Ornament of Ionia. A History of the City to 400* BCE, Ann Arbor, MI, 2001, 88–92. Further on Leodamas: *FGrH.* 90F52 (Nic. Dam.); Gorman 2001, 91.

249 Drews 1983, 17–20.

250 E. Lobel (ed.), *The Oxyrhynchus Papyri*, Pt 30, London, 1964, 2–4: 2508 (?Archilochus). Elegiacs. The text given here is as spaced, accented and supplemented by the ed. with two of my own supplements. Lexical references in the table are from G. Autenreith, *Homeric Dictionary*, London, 1877/1984 (see Table 4.1)

251 M. West, *Introduction to Greek Metre*, Oxford, 1987, 80.

252 Suid. Σιμονίδης· Καρύστιος ἢ Ἐρετριεὺς, ἐποπιός.

253 Plut. *Conv.sept.sap.* (*Mor.* 153F).

254 J. Edmonds, *Greek Elegy and Iambus* II, (Loeb) Cambridge, MA, 1979, 98–9. In his fr. 3 Arkhilokhos described the warlike 'spear-famed lords of Euboia': for the text: Ch. 5, p. 158.

255 Ch. 5, p. 159. Lorimer 1947, 122 [commenting on similar language in Tyrtaios 11 (Loeb) 21–4]: 'At one period, and one only, in the history of Greek warfare was such a shield in use', i.e the sixteenth and fifteenth centuries.

Table 4.1 Text with notes of the papyrus fragment of an early Elegaic poem

Text
]ην τετράφαλον ⟦κυνέην or κόρυθα[a]
σὺν]τοι]σιν ἔβη ταχύ[ς
]εν γὰρ τοῦτ' ἔπος α[ὐδήσας[b][
]ισιν ἕνα πρόμον-[c][
ν τ
]ἀσπίδας ἀμφ[ιβρότας[d]
]τεινησι[e] Καρνσ⟦τίωυ
τ]ὸν χῶρον[f] Ἐρετρι[έων
]ν ἔργον ἐμήσατ⟦ο[g]
ἀντι]πάλων βουσὶν ἐπ[
]ης ἐπ' (vel) ἐς ἀνάκτορ[ον or ίησι[h]
]δνσμενέων ε⟦
]υσαμενειδ[
]ωνδ' εἶπε τάδ[ε
ἐν]οπὴν[i] θωρή[κων[j]
]ν ἄνδρα δμξ[
]ς ἐχέτω δόμο⟦ν[k]
]ανερα τω σφ[

Notes

a τετράφαλον with κυνέην (Il. 12, 384); with κόρυς [acc: κόρυθα] (Il. 11, 351; 13, 131; 22, 315; – 'frequent in Hom. esp. Il.' [LSJ]).

b My suppl.: cf. Il. 19, 407; Od. 5, 334.

c πρόμος: Il. 7, 75.

d ἀμὶβρότης (with ἀσπίς) Il. 2, 389; 11, 32.

e τείνω in Hom. to express spread of combat.

f Hom. = 'spot', 'region' (Il. 13, 473; 21, 262), but note especially the significance of the term in the Eretrian context, i.e. a technical term for a territorial region, see ed. 4, n. 7: 'χῶρον Ἐρετριέων would be a phrase to which I can find no parallel, though Herodotus 9, 15 has τῶν Θηβαίων τοὺς χώρους.'

g Il. 2, 360: to plan shrewdly (cf. Odysseus).

h My suppl. ἀνακτορίησι: Od. 15, 397 'belonging to the wanax'.

i 'Tumult' (with μάχη in Il. 16, 782).

j 'Breastplate', 'chest/thorax'. In Il. 2, 544 in Abantic context: αἰχμηταὶ μεμαῶτες ὀρεκτῇσιν μελίῃσι/θώρηκας ῥήξειν δηΐων ἀμφὶ στήθεσσι.

k δόμον: 'hall' Od. 1, 126; 'temple' Od. 4, 834; 7, 81; 11, 627. Household: A. Ch. 263; S. OC 370; E. Or. 70; one's father's house: A. Pr. 665: ἔξω δόμον τε καὶ πάτρας ὠθεῖν ἐμέ.

256 Ch. 2, pp. 33–4.

257 Geyer 1903, 117.

258 The only one suggesting a later possibility: 1962, 3, n. 27.

259 As it did at Athens, as [Arist.] *Ath. pol.* 30, 2 makes clear.

260 Τοὺς ἀεὶ ἐν ἀρχῇ ὄντας: e.g. *IG* XII 9, 211. *LSJ* s.v (26). For another interpretation: Kondoleon, 1963/65, 6–8, who discusses ἀεὶ in this context.

261 Arist. *Pol.* 1299b36.

262 Kondoleon, 1963/65, 43–4, sees *prytaneis* and *probouloi* as very similar, if not identical (particularly the *prytaneis* of east Greek states, e.g. Miletos). He is probably right. Knoepfler, 1986, 334, draws attention to 'l'apparition à l'Érétrie de la prytanie dans une inscription inéditée du IVe s. avant J.-C.' The relevant line is however given in his 'Décrets érétriens de proxénie et de citoyennité Eretria', *Fouilles et Recherches* XI, Lausanne, 2001a, 88, n. 388: [εἶναι δὲ] καὶ σίτηριν αὐτō[ῖ ἐμ πρυτανείōι ἕως ἂν ζεῖ].

263 Arist. *Pol.* 1305a15–18. The tyranny here referred to is undoubtedly that of Thrasyboulos. But see Gorman 2001, 101. Miletos also had *epimenioi*: R. Meiggs and D. Lewis, *A Selection of Greek Historical Inscriptions to the End of the Fifth Century*, Oxford, 1989, 147, no. 43; Gorman, 91–4.

264 Knoepfler 1986, 391, n. 39; Vial's review of Knoepfler's PhD thesis 'La cité de Ménédème', *Rev.Hist.* 108^{272}, 1984, 242. The Theopropidai appears to have had a religious role at Eretria similar to that of the Attic *gene* of the Eumolpidai, Kerukes and Eteoboutadai.

265 *DL* 2, 141–2.

266 S. Oost, 'Cypselus the Bacchiad', *CP* 67/68, 1972/73, 10–30.

267 *IG* XII 9, 1273/1274 l. 5. M. Grant, *The Rise of the Greeks*, New York, 1987, 118, n. 5: says that the 'shipping law of *c.* 525(?) gives the title of Eretria's principal official as "archos".' The inscription however has the genitive form ἄρχ[ο]ντος for the chief magistrate. The form ἀρχός does also occur but it refers to 'magistrates' (acc. pl. accusative/infinitive construction: 'the magistrates are to act').

268 *IG* XII Suppl. 555, 54–6.

269 1963/65 30–45: 108 *bouleutai* (eleven 'prytanic' groups of nine plus one of eight, which provided the eponymous *arkhon*). According to him the group 'in prytany' were the *probouloi*, holding office for a month; there were thus nine *probouloi* (or eight for the group supplying the eponymous *arkhon*). The other groups awaiting their turn (or who had done duty) were the *epimenioi*. Knoepfler, 1998, 105–8, reveals the name of a second Eretrian tribe, destroying Kondoleon's argument for his hypothetical names of two of his three tribes. See Ch. 8, pp. 243–4 and Cairns 1986, 156, n. 16.

270 Papadakis 1915, 174. I discuss the tribes Ch.8, pp. 240–8.

271 Knoepfler 1997, 390–2.

272 Ἐπὶ τοῦ δεῖνος ἄρχοντος καὶ τῶν δείνων συμπροβουλευόντων.

273 Usually construed 'the ever-sailors'; Kondoleon thinks ἀεί is an early adverbial equivalent of ἐπί and thus ἀειναῦται = those who act 'on behalf of' sailors and compares ἀειμνήμονες (at Knidos) with ἐπίμένιοι.

274 Kondoleon 1963/65, 3, 'Βεβαίως δὲ ὁ θεσμὸς ἦτο παλαιός' For epigraphical evidence for *aeinautai* at Eretria, see Petrakos 1963, 545–7; ibid. Χρονικά: 'Ερέτρια – Εὔβοια', *AD* 17, 1961/2, 144–57; references in *IG* XII 9, 909 and 923 (Khalkis). On the origins of *aeinautai*: M. Arnheim, *Aristocracy in Greek Society*, London, 1977, 53–4.

275 *SEG* 34, 1984, item 898. A. Ritsonis, 'Ein Hermstele aus Eretria', *AAA* 17, 1984 [1985] 147, so dates it on the basis of the herm stele found in 1977 and associated with the inscribed base; see its publisher, Petrakos 1963, 545: late fifth century (Kondoleon 1963/65, 39 agrees).

276 Kondoleon 1963/65, 4–5.

277 On the *aeinautai* at Miletos, see Plut. *Quaest.Graec.* 32. Robertson, 1987, 380–4, identifies the *aeinautai* with *epimenioi*. Miletos was Eretria's ally throughout the Archaic period.

278 For a sceptical recent view: Gorman 2001, 108–10.

279 Kondoleon 1963/65, *passim*. Hsch. s.v. refers to *aeinautai* as an *arkhe,* though this is probably in response to Plut. *Quaest.Graec.* 32.

280 Petrakos 1963, 545; Papadakis 1915, 161, n. 1. Gorman 2001, 108–10.

281 *IG* XII 9, 189, 23–5. They also appear in a religious context in *IG* XII 9, 90 from Tamynai; the *demarkhos* is here threatened with penalty to be levied by *hieropoioi* if he neglects to enforce an oath on unknown defaulters.

282 The Lelantine War: Ch. 5, pp. 156–71. For *polemarkhoi*: Holleaux 1938, *passim*.

283 *Hipparkhoi* at Eretria *c.* 341/40: *IG* II^2, 230b (Athenian treaty with Eretria); Newman 1902, 561.

284 *IG* XII 9, 191 A44; 205/6, 209, 212, 217, 219. For *probouloi* and *strategoi* conjointly at Eretria: *IG* XII 9, 217.

5

ERETRIA

Its history in the wider Greek world during the seventh and early sixth centuries

Trade and colonial expansion

The East

Euboians had been active in the First Colonisation Movement. Abantes sailed from Euboia to Chios and Asia Minor, settling in Erythrai and elsewhere, perhaps Aeolian Kyme.[1] They may also have been among the 'Mycenaean' visitors to Cyprus, for Cypriots were involved in trade with Mycenaean Thebes, and late-Minoan/Mycenaean I copper ingots have been found in the sea off Euboian Kymi, suggesting links with Cyprus or Crete.[2] In the ninth and eighth century Euboians sailed again to the Levant, where they either established trading stations, such as that at Al Mina, or were settled there in originally native towns, such as Tel es Sûkâs on the Syrian coast, in considerable numbers:

> The place [Tel es Sûkâs] never became exclusively Greek; on the contrary, the impression which we get from the finds at Sûkâs taken as a whole is that of a Phoenician town with a strong, at times very strong Greek element. . . . it rather had the character of an ἐνοικισμός, a settling of Greeks *among* Phoenicians.

Boardman asks: 'Who then were the Greeks who established this [Al Mina] trading station?', to which he answers: 'Euboeans'.[3] In this Euboian enterprise in the Levant, the Eretrians were probably leaders from first to last and it indicates that, for them, the riches of the East were at that time a greater priority than the cornlands of the West: 'It seems likely then that it was the Euboeans who led the Greeks to Al Mina, together perhaps with islanders of the Cyclades over some of whom Eretria (in Euboea) apparently enjoyed control in this period', and 'The balance of trade and colonization interest in the two cities probably changed, and it is from Eretria, not (so far) Chalcis, that we find the type of vase still carried to Al Mina.'[4] Riis discusses what the Greeks may have traded with the Levantine merchants in return for largely luxury products: slaves, fish, animal and agricultural produce, and perhaps raw metals.[5] It was probably not ceramic wares. The native people of the region apparently did not like Greek pottery;[6] that was thus probably exported for use by Greeks themselves or as containers for other products such as oil or wheat. However, by the seventh century, Euboian/Eretrian dominance of the market at Al Mina was over and trade was henceforth dominated by Attic ware.[7]

The West

The Eastern trade activities preceded the Second Colonisation Movement to the West and the north Aegean area. Euboians were the frontrunners here also. This later Euboian interest in the West was undoubtedly related to their gradual loss of their Eastern markets during the eighth century.

Pithekoussai (Ischia) and Kyme (Cumae) in Italy

Pithekoussai, the first known Greek colony in the West, is generally dated *c.* 750. However, its offshoot Kyme (Cumae) is also so dated. We must, I think, agree with Bakhuizen, who doubts this chronology and thinks that the foundation of Pithekoussai should be early eighth century.[8] These foundations were associated by Strabo and Dionysios Halikarnasseus with both Eretria and Khalkis. By this time, the political configuration of the island had been transformed from the unitary Abantic *ethnos* into four individual *poleis*. The juxtaposition of words in both writers appears to give primacy to the Eretrians.[9] However, three other texts,[10] which do not mention Eretrians, are, for no good reason, given priority by some modern historians, who therefore only accept Khalkidian involvement, though Euboian Kyme is sometimes grudgingly added as the *metropolis*.[11] Livy says that Cumae was founded by Khalkidians from Pithekoussai who 'later decided to take their chance on the mainland'. Khalkidians from Cumae later founded another settlement at Palaiopolis near Neapolis (Naples), of which it was a precursor: it was originally called Parthenope. Strabo calls Neapolis 'city of the Cumaeans' but says that it was later recolonised by Khalkidians and Athenians and 'some Pithekoussans'. The Roman poet Statius, a native of Neapolis, stresses its Euboian origins. Among the Pithekoussan contingent there may have been some Tanagraians/Oropians, for there was a tribe *Eunostidai* at Neapolis and the legend of Eunostos is associated with Tanagra.[12]

My interpretation of this ensemble of texts is as follows: that originally Pithekoussai was a joint foundation of Eretrians, Khalkidians and (perhaps) Euboian Kymaians, but that *stasis* erupted soon after, perhaps a local problem aggravated by a new episode in the Lelantine saga,[13] prompting the Eretrians to expel the Khalkidians (and perhaps some of the Euboian Kymaians), who then settled at Cumae on the mainland opposite. The fertile plains of Campania in any case would surely have appealed to the more agriculturally oriented Khalkidians. Parthenope was founded later. Was this because dissension persisted? Kymaians, if they were from the northern area of the Eretrias, might not have settled comfortably with Khalkidians.

The original home of the Kymaians who provided one of the *oikistai*[14] of Italian Kyme has been much debated. Were they from the more famous Asiatic Kyme, or from the insignificant Euboian 'town', the exact location of which in ancient times is still not even known for certain? Sampson, writing of his investigations at Kastri Potamias in the Eretrias observes: 'From the few inscriptions and coins, it is not possible to identify this ancient settlement with ancient Kyme as many would wish.' Bakhuizen is categorical: Euboian Kyme did not exist. Sampson doubts its existence as a *polis* in historical times and believes that the name denotes a collection of villages (*komaï*). I agree with him in this. In the so-called 'Old Athenian' dialect of modern Greek, ancient υ has become ου (e.g. Κυμή/Κουμή and 'Αμαρὺσιον/'Αμαρὺσι[ον], the latter also with Euboian connections!). von Willamowitz visited the area in 1895 and came to the conclusion that from the lack 'of inscriptions . . . coins and references in the literary sources, Kyme cannot be located', and, somewhat arbitrarily, that 'Kyme must have been a village of Khalkis and that from this village, Aeolian Kyme took its name in pre-Homeric times.' Geyer also thinks that Kyme 'probably' belonged to Khalkis.

Sapouna-Sakellaraki, on the other hand, believes that remains of the early town will be found in the area of Kastri Potamias and that it belonged within the orbit of Eretria: 'Its geographic position ties it – and this is strengthened epigraphically – rather with Eretria than Khalkis.'[15] Moreover, Skylax[16] indicates that the Eretrias extended to Kyme in his time (for Sapouna-Sakellaraki, the sixth century). The land route to Kyme from Aliverion via Aulonarion in the Eretrias is the easiest from the gulf to the Aegean coast and so it could more easily have been brought under Eretrian than Khalkidian control. Hopper notes that: 'Another [trade route], not so clearly defined, leads from Kyme in Euboea (the Aegean port of Eretria) by way of Lemnos and Imbros to the Hellespont (Dardanelles).'[17] Thus, I believe, with Sapouna-Sakellaraki, that the original home of the settlers was Euboian Kyme, but that: 'It is certain that an independent *polis* with the name Kyme did not exist in Euboia after the sixth century BC.'[18] No coin has ever been certainly attributed to it,[19] and there is only one mention of Euboian Kyme in the surviving literary record.[20] This suggests that Kyme was incorporated early into the Eretrias and that it was not of great significance. The Kymaians were probably the Komaieis of the Eretrian deme lists.[21] Their inclusion in the colonisation accounts would therefore indicate de facto Eretrians. On the other hand, we may note that one of Strabo's sources was Ephoros of Kyme in Asia Minor, a historian who was particularly interested in local matters. He wrote a history of his city, the achievements of which he tended to exaggerate so much that he was ridiculed for it.[22]

The sequel to the passage of Livy cited above continues: 'Thanks to the fleet in which they sailed from their home, they enjoyed much power on the coast of that sea by which they dwell; having first landed on the islands of Ainaria and Pithekoussai, they afterwards ventured to transfer their seat to the mainland.'[23] But whose fleet was it? Livy does not say specifically. Kondoleon's controversial article (not entirely dismissed by Eretrian specialists[24]), which discusses the role of the navies of Eretria and Khalkis, especially in the colonial movement, argues that Khalkis never had a strong navy and sent out all its colonies in Eretrian ships. He certainly marshals telling arguments for its later naval impotence, but it is, I think, far too radical to argue that Khalkis never sent out a colony by itself at any period. Nevertheless, I would agree that, at this early date, it would have been Eretria, the 'rowing city', that provided the ships for the colonisation of Pithekoussai, as is also likely for any venture mounted jointly by both an agriculturally oriented and a mercantile city. Rhotacism and other Eretrian dialect features have been noted at Rhegion,[25] for which archaeological evidence there suggests *c.* 730 as its foundation date, perhaps indicating that Eretrians were either involved in, or pushing into, the early Khalkidian colonies. They may also have had some hand in the foundation of Zankle (*c.* 730–20).[26] Khalkidian colonisation in the West in any case ceases altogether about five years later.[27] If this is the case, then the powerful fleet, which made such an early impression on the native tribes of Campania, was Eretrian.

There has been general scholarly agreement that the principal motivation for colonisation in the eighth/seventh centuries was land hunger.[28] Thucydides[29] put it succinctly: 'Those especially who did not have sufficient land sailed against the islands and conquered them.' Plato anticipates a possible population/land crisis in his ideal state and resorts to 'that ancient device',[30] the sending away of excess population as colonists. Hesiod, living close to the period of colonisation, opined that farmers should restrict themselves to one son: 'May there be only one son to feed in his father's house.'[31] By the ninth/eighth centuries, pastoralism was, in most of Greece, already giving way to agriculture as the principal land-use regime, reflecting a need for more efficient food production to feed an increasing population. Though the overall population was small by modern standards, primitive technology and methods kept production low. The total free population of the Eretrias at the height of its power in the sixth century has been estimated at only *c.* 50,000.[32] With the influx of refugees from Lefkandi, pressure on Eretria's very average-quality land resources would have increased. On the other hand, the Khalkidians who are supposed to have won that phase of the war for the fertile plain should have had a reprieve and their horse/cattle-rearing culture strengthened.

Why then did the Hippobotic government send out colonial expeditions as Strabo explicitly says?[33] I have earlier suggested drought. Camp deals with its effects particularly on Euboia,[34] discussing the implications of Strabo's account of the foundation by the Khalkidians of Rhegion, the earliest of the so-called 'famine colonies': 'Rhegion is a foundation of those men of Khalkis who, in response to the oracle, were dedicated to Apollo – one man in every ten – because of the failure of crops; they say that later they came there as colonists from Delphi taking still others from home',[35] and the comment of Herakleides Lembos: 'Khalkidians who left the Euripos because of drought founded Rhegion.'[36] Years of good rains and their relative abundance of fertile land may have encouraged overproduction and a too-rapid increase in the population so that when drought came, food shortages, resulting in hunger and distress for the less well-off members of the community, caused unrest. The traditional pastoral economy of the *Hippobotai* would scarcely have been easy on parched grazing lands. Even as I write this in mid-2002, on the farmlands of inland eastern Australia the wheat crop has failed and graziers are beginning to sell off or kill stock after only two years of severe drought while businesses in country towns are experiencing economic stress; the climate of Greece, even at the best of times, is scarcely kinder to pastoralists. While the landowning nobles, with their greater resources, may have been shielded for a while against the full effects, traders and artisans would have seen their local markets and profits shrink, when food supplies slowed and, perhaps at times, stopped. This, in turn, would have had an inflationary effect on food costs. Perhaps, therefore, it was common difficulties that caused the commercial oligarchy at Eretria to join the *Hippobotai* of Khalkis in founding the first western colony at Pithekoussai. If so, it was a fairly short-lived arrangement and hints of dissension in the colony itself point to a breakdown in relations at home. Anyway, sending away surplus population would have been only a limited solution involving small numbers. Hard hit by the drought, Khalkis became a frequent 'customer' and so an early favourite at Delphi, the rise of which to mantic primacy was ultimately due to the widespread need for drought relief and the removal of excess population, which led to colonisation, which is likely to have been the only solution to occur to the priests, especially as they probably soon acquired a good fund of knowledge about potential sites as colonial activity increased.

Another motive for the Khalkidian government might have been the need to satisfy the artisan class in the city – for there must surely have been one – by ensuring a regular supply of raw materials, for despite the frequent association of Khalkis with copper,[37] the territory of Khalkis was never endowed liberally with copper ore deposits.[38] This group, together with traders, was a potential source of criticism of Hippobotic rule. Colonial expansion would give such groups another focus for their ambitions. Sparta tried a similar solution, sending what was thought to be a potentially disruptive element of the population to a new colony at Taras.[39]

The motives of the Eretrians were more diverse. For them, with a larger than normal artisan/trading population, land hunger was probably not the only, or perhaps even the main, consideration, although while its agriculture, with its emphasis on olive oil production, would not have been so hard hit, the effects of the shortage of food grain on the poorer classes ought not be underestimated and the productivity of Eretrian lands was generally lower than that of Khalkis. Eretrians and their Lefkandiot ancestors had been trading with the Cyclades and had established themselves in the Levant where their commerce was already threatened. To find alternative markets the Eretrians sailed west and north and established 'colonies' as their forebears had done in the East. I place the word colonies in inverted commas because the earliest Eretrian western settlements resemble more the purely commercial sites of Zagora and the Levantine *emporia* than agriculturally based colonies. Although the distinction between *apoikia* and *emporion* in Greek writers, especially Herodotos, is rather blurred, I use the latter term to indicate a colony that I think is more commercially oriented and *apoikia* for those that were basically agricultural.[40]

Excavations at Pithekoussai have revealed a thriving industrial town with an emphasis on metallurgy.[41] We have already noted strong similarities between burial practices and the ceramic evidence at Eretria and Lefkandi and those of the settlers at Pithekoussai, as well as some literary evidence, and that Eretria was involved here can hardly be doubted. However, why would Khalkidians with their more agricultural biases have come to this particular island? It is often thought of as barren and mountainous, quite unsuitable for farming, thus posing a problem for strict adherents to the theory of land hunger as the sole motive propelling early Euboians overseas. Gwynn completely avoids mentioning Pithekoussai;[42] Graham mentions it twice and then only in passing in an appendix on the western aims of Corinth.[43] Yet Strabo[44] offers two reasons for the great prosperity of the settlement, the first of which is the island's *eukarpia*, its fruitfulness, and scholars who have actually worked on the island remark on its fertile, volcanic soil: 'the fundamental resource of the island in the pre-tourist age has always been agriculture, but in the specialised sense of viticulture, a direct result of the island's hilly terrain, of the climate and of the soil.'[45] Theognis would later describe the Lelantine Plain as having fine vineyards[46] and so farmers from the Lelantine might expect to flourish on Pithekoussai.

But though initially self-sustaining, and perhaps always having a trade in wine and oil, it was never exclusively an agricultural colony.[47] Strabo gives as a second reason for its prosperity its *khryseia*. In the past translated as gold mines, these are geologically impossible on Pithekoussai,[48] so that unless Strabo is simply wrong we need an alternative meaning. This problem has more recently been addressed by scholars with results that at least do not contradict natural and archaeological data.[49] Within the excavated area have been found not only copper and bronze pieces but iron and its by-products (bloom and slag) and lead. Included in the finds was a weight made from a bronze ring filled with lead and weighing almost exactly one Euboic stater, probably used for weighing out precious metals.[50] But considering the many objects of silver from the tombs on Ischia itself,[51] a surprising fact not extrapolated upon is that no gold objects of any kind whatsoever have been reported. This surely is very strange given Strabo's assertion that the settlement's prosperity was based on its *khryseia*. It is very unlikely that if *khryseia* were gold-producing workshops or mines, the total output was exported without a single item being preserved in any tomb or, as far as can be judged from Ridgeway, anywhere else. Poverty among the population of the cemetery cannot be the answer, for there were numerous pieces of silver and bronze jewellery found among the burial offerings. I therefore suggest that in the eighth century settlement there were in fact *no* gold-working establishments or mines. But if Eretria exercised control over the settlement, and as early as the eighth century it seems even to have imposed its own political forms on its dependencies, the commercial oligarchy at home may have decreed that all auriferous raw materials be shipped on for working in the goldsmithies at Eretria, for which we do have archaeological evidence. The small quantities involved with this metal make sea-borne transport simple. Eretrian political and economic dominance within the settlement would also explain the removal of the Khalkidian part of the population to Kyme and beyond. The *khryseia* were merely the offices of merchants who acquired gold from elsewhere, perhaps performed some refining of the ore and then remitted it home. If this is an early case of Eretrian economic imperialism, it would not be the last. On the other hand, less valuable metals, also obtained from outside the island, were refined and/or manufactured before trans-shipment.

Before leaving Pithekoussai, I wish to refer briefly to the vessel found there known as 'Nestor's Cup'. It is inscribed with three lines of hexameter verse in the 'alphabet of Chalcis', according to Ridgeway.[52] This attribution is perplexing. There is much more likelihood that we have here an example of the script used at Eretria at the time. Jeffery notes that 'Punctuation is "as at Eretria."[53] It is written in Phoenician retrograde and an early Eretrian presence in the *emporia* of North Syria is virtually assured.' Jeffery continues: 'Every letter-form has its parallel in the inscriptions of either Kyme or Eretria, except the unique *xi* and *san*. These are not found in actual use in any Euboic inscription.' Moreover, she adds,

> The Eretrian version of the Euboic alphabet was already in use at Pithekoussai and Cumae, and among Cumae's non-Greek neighbours, in the first half of the seventh century, perhaps even before 700; but no surviving inscriptions from Euboia herself are as early . . . the only inscription which is certainly as early as the seventh century is that on a small *aryballos* attributed to Eretria.[54]

There is also, in fact, an inscribed grave amphora from Eretria dated *c.* 625.[55] It seems then that we can make a better case that the alphabet used at Cumae, and ultimately borrowed and modified by the Romans, was that used at Eretria.

Kerkyra

The Eretrians established themselves early in both Kerkyra and around the Gulf of Avlona on the nearby mainland of Albania. Plutarch says that 'Eretrians used to inhabit the island of Kerkyra; but Kharikrates sailed there from Corinth with an army and defeated them in war; whereupon the Eretrians embarked in their ships and sailed home again; when they arrived, they were driven off again with slings', while a scholiast to Apollonios Rhodios notes that 'A peninsula of Kerkyra was called Makridie, perhaps because of the fact that Euboians had established themselves there, for Euboia was formerly called Makris.'[56] The Eretrian *apoikia/emporion* on Kerkyra is now hardly disputed, though it was not always so.[57] Its name was Drepane.[58] Plutarch's note gives no indication of when the Eretrians first established themselves; it was obviously before 734, the year when the Corinthians expelled them. Pithekoussai must have been founded before 750,[59] the date attributed to its offshoot Italian Kyme, so we would expect that Kerkyra and the settlements in Albania en route to Italy[60] were founded at about the same time. I suggest *c.* 785 or slightly later for Kerkyra, roughly a generation before the expulsion of the Khalkidians from Pithekoussai. A date earlier than 750 is certainly required.

Topographical, mythological and historical traces of the original Eretrians are numerous. There was a place called Euboia on the island,[61] and the promontory on which the colony stood was called Makris or Makridie, a Euboian name, derived from the nymph Makris, a daughter of Aristaios/Amarynthos, who was the consort of Eretrian Artemis at Amarynthos. Makris nurtured Dionysos on Euboia. Driven out by Hera, she fled to Kerkyra, land of the Phaiakes. In Plutarch, Makridie is specifically identified with the nymph Euboia. Elsewhere, he makes her the wet-nurse of Hera herself,[62] who was a prominent deity in Kerkyra as indeed she was in Euboia. There was a persistent mythological tradition that identified Kerkyra with Skheria, the land of the Phaiakes, enterprising and skilled sailors in the *Odyssey,* ruled by Alkinoos, and that linked Skheria with Euboia. The Kerkyraians later accepted this ancestral tradition[63] rather than that they were of Corinthian origin.

We have seen that Kerkyra, like Eretria, had *probouloi* as its principal magistrates, as of course did Corinth later.[64] However, after their early and complete rupture with Corinth, would the Kerkyraians have willingly taken or kept institutions from their hostile 'mother-city'? This hostility began almost from the moment of the 'foundation'. The Corinthians later complain: 'But now, as things stood, ever since the island was colonised they have been squabbling among themselves despite their [kinship]',[65] and dissension exploded into open warfare with Corinth as early as 664, in a naval engagement that Thucydides[66] believed to be the earliest known sea battle, only seventy years after the arrival of the Corinthians. Such a state of affairs between any colony and *metropolis* was most unusual, and the Corinthians admit as much in a later speech before the Athenian assembly, for relations did not improve with time: 'Though they are our colonists they have always been hostile to us and now they are at war with us . . . at any rate, the rest of our colonies treat us with honour and indeed we are loved by our colonists.'[67]

It appears, on the other hand, that Eretria's dependencies both in the Aegean and in the West harboured friendly feelings towards their coloniser/ruler, for there is little evidence of attempts to shake off its traditions: Keos retained its characteristically Eretrian institutions, and later Eretria and Andros co-operated in establishing colonies in the north Aegean, and their Aegean empire endured for centuries. It has never been asked whether this atypical attitude of the Kerkyraians among the colonists of Corinth derived from the circumstances of the acquisition of the island. Any Eretrians left on the island when the group that tried to return home departed may have been, or have quickly become, hostile to their new rulers. The introduction of Dorians into other Ionian colonies is known to have provoked dissension, for example at Rhegion[68] and possibly at Gela.[69] On the other hand, evidence that Eretria and Kerkyra were friendly *c.* 500 appears in the dedication by each city of two bronze bulls, side by side, at Olympia.[70] Mother-city and daughter? Wallace thought so.[71] The subsequent history of Kerkyra is noteworthy for the ferocity of its civil strife, as both Diodoros and Thucydides note:

> It happened at about that time in Kerkyra that there occurred serious civil strife and massacre, which are said to have been due to various causes, but mostly due to the ongoing mutual hatred existing between its people. For never in any *polis* have I heard of such killings of citizens nor greater strife and obstinate contentiousness which led to bloodshed.[72]

At Kerkyra, the non-Dorian elements, the remaining Eretrians and the pre-Eretrian (pre-Greek?[73]) natives, may soon have reasserted themselves culturally. The hostility generated would have benefited Eretrian trade with the West.

There are clear similarities between the Eretrian monetary system and that of Kerkyra. The iconographic resemblances suggest shared cults: 'A Euboic tradition in Corcyra is supported by her sixth-century coinage, which alone of those of Corinth's North-West colonies does not bear the Corinthian Pegasus but the Euboic device of the cow suckling her calf.'[74] However, more important historically, and for Eretrian commerce, was its organisational similarity. The numismatist Kraay[75] states that:

> Apart from the issues of the 'pegasi' . . . the most important coinage in northwest Greece was that of the island of Corcyra. The original Euboean settlers were expelled by the Corinthians in the late eighth century, but thereafter the island's relations with its mother-city were chequered, for its size and its strategic position on the route to South Italy enabled it to pursue an independent line. The distinctive coin-type of Corcyra, a cow and calf, which endured unchanged for over three centuries, appears to be derived from the original Euboean settlers; the weight standard of the

> Corcyraean stater is related to the standards of both Corinth and Euboea though identical with neither.

Weighing *c.* 11.6 g, it is equivalent to four Corinthian *drakhmai* (4 × 2.9 g) or two-thirds of a Euboian stater (2/3 × 17.4 g); it could thus be integrated into the coinage of either *polis* and also into that of the colonies of both Corinth and the Euboian cities in the west. Its cow motif appears on coins of Eretria from its earliest issues in the sixth century but only occurs on coins of Federal Euboia from the late fifth century, when Eretria was the seat of the Euboian League and its mint.[76] It was never a motif on Khalkidian coins. 'The cow may be an emblem of the worship of Amarynthian Artemis, or may be connected with the Io myth.'[77]

Finally, there is similarity of cult between the Eretrias and Kerkyra. The pedimental figures of archaic Artemis on her temple in Kerkyra, gorgon-like, with wings outstretched,[78] and flanked by her offspring, Pegasos and Khrysaor by the horse god Poseidon,[79] have strongly oriental characteristics and possibly reflect influences brought by traders from Syria. Similar representations of her have been found on Geometric pottery from Eretria. Hera was also particularly associated with Kerkyra and with Euboia, the latter island being sacred to her; it is where Hera was said to have been wedded to Zeus.[80] Even in Argos, for Homer, her primary home, her greatest temple was on Mt Euboia. In Euboia itself she is associated with Mts Dirphys and Okhe on either side of the Eretrias. Eretria had a Heraia festival, a month Heraion and a deme called Parthenion from her Euboian epithet. Hera and cows were closely associated so it is no accident that the Federal Euboian, Eretrian and Kerkyraian coinage had as an emblem the cow or calf. One of her most common epithets in Homer is 'Ox-eyed Potnia', although the epithet is also applied to Artemis by Bakkhylides. Hera means 'mistress', more or less synonymous with *potnia*.[81]

Syracuse

It is just possible that there may have been an early joint Eretrian/Khalkidian *emporion* on Ortygia.[82] The name of this small offshore island, on which the original settlement of Syracuse was planted, is linked with Artemis: the quail was her and the Kouretes' special bird, [83] and Artemis 'was thus styled [Ortygia] in Euboean worship.'[84] Though there may be something in the idea of an early Euboian presence on Ortygia at Syracuse, it must be admitted that the literary evidence is weak.[85] However, the original site on a small offshore island points to a trading purpose and early Eretrian *emporia* are often so located.[86] Mythologically, Syracusan Ortygia is also associated with Arethousa,[87] the name of fountains both in Euboia, near Khalkis, and in Elis, the latter connected with Eretria mythologically and by dialect. It has been suggested that colonists from Elis itself are symbolised in the myth of Alpheus pursuing the nymph Arethousa, or some say Artemis herself, across the sea to Ortygia island.[88] Perhaps this early association with Elis is to be related to the migration of Eleans to Eretria itself.[89]

Albania

Eretrians settled around the Bay of Avlona (Aulon) in southern Albania. There was also a place called Aulon in the Eretrias, near Tamynai, and another near Arethousa in the territory of Khalkis.[90] Their main town, Orikos,[91] most likely a purpose-built *emporion* as was usual Eretrian practice, was originally established on a small offshore island called Othronos,[92] despite the fertile hinterland in which settlement seems to have been made only later. It was early enough to have been thought a settlement of Abantes returning from Troy, founded by Elephenor: 'Orikos is a Greek city and on the sea, for returning from Ilion, Euboians founded it.'[93] It was well situated for communication with Kerkyra, of which it may have been an offshoot, and while the Eretrians held Kerkyra they would clearly have controlled all shipping between the island and the mainland, an important seaway in all ancient periods. The hinterland of Orikos was called Amantia or Abantia.[94] A major inland city here was at Thronion, also reputedly a foundation of Euboian Abantes. Apart from at Orikos and perhaps on the coastlands immediately opposite Kerkyra, the Euboian presence in Epeiros may be more apparent than real and belong to the age of migrations when ancestors of the various Euboic peoples (Dryopians, Ellopians, Amantes/Abantes, etc.) passed through en route southward. The ruins of the town of Amantia/Abantia are near the present-day town of Pliotsa.[95] That this migratory movement was not forgotten later is shown by the Delian legends of the hyperborean offerings to Apollo, the passage of which passed through both Epeiros and Lelantine Euboia.[96] This journey is thought to reflect later trade routes following the west coast and terminating in Euboia.[97] From there, goods were distributed via a further extension to the Levant.[98] The West was certainly known to Greeks before the eighth century, as Mycenaeans had been trading there in the sixteenth/fifteenth centuries, with the greatest activity in the fourteenth/thirteenth.[99]

Africa

Africa is not usually considered to have been an area of Euboian colonisation. The Italian scholar Mazzarino has however suggested extensive early settlement by Euboians in not only Libya but also Tunisia. His theory was revived by Tedeschi, who cites more recent excavations at Tocra (ancient Taukheira) in Libya, where an Archaic Greek settlement has been discovered by Boardman and Hayes. However, their reports do not indicate Euboian ceramic at this site, unless misattributed, but Boardman had earlier commented on the relationship between seventh/sixth century 'Melian' and 'Cycladic' (both present at Tocra) and Eretrian pottery. Boardman is thus cited in support of Mazzarino by Tedeschi but not, I think, successfully.[100] Mazzarino's argumentation also depends on certain Middle Eastern and biblical texts, the value of which I am not qualified to judge, as well as on obscure references preserved in later Greek and Latin writers: a fragment of Hekataios in Stephanos Byzantios mentioning a 'city of the Ionians' called Kybo (or Kybos) in 'Phoenician Libya' and a place called Hippou Akre, near Bizerta[101] in Tunisia, not far from Carthage and Utica, Phoenician Libya par excellence, and which on some maps is called Acra.[102] The Roman geographer Solinus[103] says that Hippo was founded by 'Greek horsemen' (*Hippeis*). Pseudo-Skylax refers also to 'a large number of islets nearby called the Naxioi; Pithekousai and its harbour. And opposite these [is] an island and the *polis* on the island is [called] Euboia.'[104] Not only have we here the names of Euboia itself, and also Pithekoussai, but also Naxos, that of the earliest Euboian settlement in Sicily. When Homer, in his story of the voyage of the Phaiakian ships from Skheria (i.e. Kerkyra, another Euboian link) to the most distant lands, implies that 'Euboia' was one such remote place,[105] it is unlikely that he is talking of Aegean Euboia. The Aegean was well known to the composer of the *Odyssey*; he certainly knew of many lands more remote than the island of Khalkis and Eretria. Could it be however that he has in mind distant Tunisian Euboia as his paradigm of the place at the end of the world? If so, knowledge of it must have returned to the Aegean area via the stories of the Euboian trader-colonists in the West.

Whether these indications of Euboian penetration in Africa are to be ascribed to Eretria or to Khalkis or to both is impossible to say. Mazzarino thinks that they were Khalkidian.[106] I would however point out that Eretria was dominant in the earliest Euboian colonisation in the West and that Khalkidian colonisation ceases shortly after 730. Mazzarino believes that the Phoenicians, the first colonists in the region, were almost entirely displaced by Greeks by *c.* 650,[107] but that after the revival of Tyre and other cities of the Phoenician coast, following their liberation from the Assyrians after the fall of Nineveh in 612, there was a resurgence of Phoenician activity in Tunisia and the 're-Punicisation' of the Hellenised settlements in the area. The post-650 date rather suggests Eretria. Memory of the Greek period was apparently not lost and the survival of some place names, even in the local indigenous literature,[108] and the occasional disconnected notices allow speculation that there may indeed have been Euboians in north Africa as early as the first half of the seventh century, and certainly Hekataios still retained a memory of Ionians, as opposed to the Dorians of Kyrene, in north Africa *c.* 510.

The northern Aegean

A convenient literary link between the western and northern colonial activity of Eretria is provided by Methone, founded *c.* 733 by the Kerkyraian refugees, who, having arrived back at Eretria, were 'repulsed by slings' by the Eretrians and forced to sail on. This they did and founded Pierian Methone in Macedonia on the shores of the Thermaic Gulf. The epitomator of Strabo[109] places the town 40 *stadia* from Pydna. Thucydides records that it was later occupied by the Athenians to annoy Perdikkas of Macedonia,[110] and as the last remaining possession of Athens on the Macedonian coast, it was attacked by Philip II in 354/53.

Most other Eretrian colonies in the northern Aegean were merely *emporia* rather than *poleis*. Apart from their names, we know virtually nothing of most of them. One or two play a role in the affairs of Greece in the sixth and subsequent centuries. Peisistratos set out from Eretria for the northern Aegean to acquire the wherewithal to finance his final return to power, with the blessing and assistance of the Eretrian regime of the *Hippeis*. He led an expedition from Eretria to Rhaikelos and founded what must have been a joint colony, since it is inconceivable that a privateer would have gone into this area, where Eretrian colonisation was dominant, without Eretrian approval, founding a colony of his own, and still be able to use Eretria itself as a base from which to launch his final bid for power. A strong reason for believing that this establishment was in fact an Eretrian foundation and that Peisistratos was the agent of Eretria is that if Rhaikelos were an Athenian colony, and given its supposed wealth of resources, it would presumably also have made a good base for a future return by his own exiled son Hippias, but he did not go there. It is usually located at or near the site of later Aineia (or Ainos) on the Thermaic Gulf.[111] It was called a *polis* by Lykophron and Stephanos Byzantios[112] but there is no agreement on its precise location. Possibly, as Edson suggests,[113] Rhaikelos was the name of the area while Aineia was the city. It existed to exploit the mineral and timber wealth that made it possible for Peisistratos to finance his return to power.

Bradeen thinks that Euboian colonisation in the northern Aegean was concentrated within the period 775–50,[114] and Kondoleon also believes that it predates that in the West.[115] The foundation dates of most colonies of Eretria (or, for that matter, of Khalkis) are unknown. Euboian activity was mainly between the Axios and Strymon rivers, chiefly on the three-pronged Khalkidike. Eretria alone colonised Pallene (except for Corinthian Potidaia[116]), while Khalkis settled Sithonia. The most easterly peninsula, Akte (Athos), was mainly settled by Eretrians and Andrians,[117] while Thasos was Parian. Both Andros and Paros were both once probable Eretrian dependencies.[118] Thus, with colonies on both sides of the Thermaic Gulf and with a presence in Athos, Eretria was dominant in the region. The name Khalkidike may derive from that of a local tribe, rather than from the Euboian Khalkidians, as some scholars argue.[119] It appears to me for geographic reasons, despite the general belief that Khalkis was first to colonise northward, that the Eretrians were in fact earlier. Not only are the Pierian coast and Pallene, which their colonies dominated, the first likely landfalls, but they are also the most fertile areas in the Khalkidike area. Athos is all mountains, while Sithonia, although it has some small plains, is not much more attractive as a place for self-supporting colonies. Khalkis, it seems, had to be content with second best. Hammond long ago accepted this: 'The choice (of sites) made by the Eretrians, when they were first in the field, shows that Macedonia had much to offer the maritime trader.'[120]

The Eretrian colonies in the north Aegean (certain or possible) were: Methone, Pydna, Dion, Eion, Aloros, Aineia (Ainos), Mende, Sane (on Pallene), Skione, Apollonia (on the Thermaic Gulf), Therambos, Aige and Neapolis (on the Toronian Gulf coast of Pallene), Olophyxos, and Akrothooi (on Athos). Other likely Eretrian foundations were Kharadriai, Palaiorion and Pharbelos.[121] Another, Dikaia Eretrieon, is interesting, not only because it was identified thus in the Athenian Tribute Lists[122] but because its coin types hint at a Karystian presence among its Eretrian colonists.[123] Its location is not certain but was probably close to Lake Bitsonis, not far from Kavala.[124]

Eretria also had one other significant colony, Skábala,[125] which, if it was indeed Neapolis[126] (modern Kavála), opposite Parian Thasos, would have controlled sea access to it and the mines and forests of Mt Pangaion, exploited by Peisistratos during his sojourn in the north. The identification of this place is thus of economic and historical importance. It has also been identified with the proverbially rich Daton,[127] also on the Thracian seaboard opposite Thasos. Such a multiplicity of names acquired over time by places in the Greek world is not uncommon, as Euboia and indeed Eretria itself make clear. Neapolis is generally considered a Thasian settlement. Nevertheless, we do have the close similarity of the names Skábala and modern Kabála (modern Greek Kavála) on more or less the same site. The Turkish name for the town was Kávalo,[128] preserving the ancient accentuation. Stephanos Byzantios is quite explicit that the place was Eretrian and gives a specific source: Theopompos' *Philippika* (Book 24). There is, however, a further argument. Thucydides records that the forebears of the Macedonian Temenid king Alexandros I (*c.* 498–54)[129] had incorporated coastal Pieria into Macedonia and expelled the 'Pieres', who afterwards took up their abode in areas at the foot of Mt Pangaion.[130] When did this expulsion occur? Hammond writes: 'A *terminus post quem* for this event was *c.* 730, for at that time the coast of Pieria was described as "Thrace" and not "Macedonia", presumably because there were Thracians there. This description occurs in the foundation story of a Greek colony [Methone]. For some colonists from Eretria . . . *c.* 730 sailed "for Thrace" (*epi Thrakes*).'[131] He suggests *c.* 650, or shortly after, in the reign of Perdikkas I, the first Temenid king, for the expulsion. Now, if colonists originally from Eretria had been driven to emigrate from Pierian Methone to the foothills of Pangaion about the mid-seventh century and settled at Skábala, this would explain both Theopompos' description of the place as Eretrian[132] in his Macedonian history and the apparent ease with which Peisistratos, with his close Eretrian connections, was able to exploit the mines of the Pangaion. Moreover, the early coinage of Neapolis corresponds exactly with the earliest types of Eretria itself,[133] so that it is not at all impossible that Peisistratos copied its, or Eretria's, *gorgoneion*-type for some of his Athenian issues, following his return from exile in Eretria and its northern colonies.

Before we leave Eretrian colonisation in the north, we may consider the possibility that Eretrians settled, or perhaps had small service depots, on several islands between Eretria and Pallene. Skiathos is said to have been Euboian;[134] Eretria itself is linked to Skyros.[135] However, Khalkis is also said to have colonised some of these islands after they had declined in importance from the days when they were occupied by Minoans from Crete.[136] For either city to have done so would have been very sensible given the difficulties of long distance sailing in the Geometric and early Archaic Periods.

Oropos

It is perhaps appropriate here to at least revisit the relationship of Eretria and Oropos. I have already mentioned this place in the context of possible immigrations from Elis to the Eretrias via eastern Boiotia. However, we possess a text that actually states that 'Oropos is a foundation of the Eretrians; for it is disputed by the Boiotians, the Eretrians, and the Athenians.'[137] Knoepfler accepts this;[138] Wilamowitz thought so even before the text was discovered. But when was it established? Knoepfler places its foundation, the purpose of which he believes was to control the commerce of the Asopos valley, after the establishment of the Lefkandiots at Eretria.[139] He argues that the very 'off-centre' location of (New) Eretria within its territory may be explained by the need to have a short crossing to the mainland at a point where there was a sheltered harbour on both sides of the gulf, and so it was there that the Eretrians established a 'comptoire'. But there were also strategic considerations and Thucydides was well aware of them.[140] Knoepfler observes: 'For since the place is opposite Eretria, it was impossible that if the Athenians held it, that it would not pose a great threat to both Eretria itself and to Euboia in general.'[141] It is no accident that when the Eretrians began actively intriguing against Athens in 411, they quickly betrayed Oropos to the Boiotians and immediately went to Rhodes and invited the Peloponnesians to invade Euboia.

I think, however, that it is more likely that there was a settlement at Oropos since very early times. The name has western Greek connotations and toponyms with the element -οπ- are very early. It may be that the site of Eretria was itself chosen by the retreating Lefkandiots for its position vis-à-vis an already existing mainland town rather than vice versa, as Knoepfler would wish. Later, Eretria had a deme Oropos.[142] Both Wallace and Knoepfler[143] place it [in District IV (not identical for both)] east of the city, but Wallace gives no reason in his brief commentary on the deme. But in a footnote[144] he allows that it may have been west of the city, from the discovery of a grave stele of a demesman, between modern Vasiliko and Eretria, just inland from Lefkandi and opposite mainland Oropos. In the discussions about the location of the deme, no account has been taken of the note in St. Byz., which suggests that Lefkandi and Oropos were not far apart: 'Orope (*sic*); *polis* of Euboia where [there was] a most famous sanctuary of Apollo'.[145] The manuscripts of Thucydides twice call

Oropos *peraia ge*. This, according to Gomme, suggests an Eretrian perspective and that the area was for Eretria the 'land on the further side'.[146] Clearly, however, the two places were closely associated at all periods of their history, and the Eretrians, growing more powerful during the eighth/seventh centuries, took control of its mainland satellite. This could have been quite amicable, for Eretria seems at all times to have enjoyed good will at Oropos and certainly never relinquished hopes of repossessing the town when it was under either Boiotian or Athenian control.[147] It was not until after the destruction of Eretria in 490 that Athens gained control of it. Thenceforth Oropos was a bone of contention between Eretria, Athens and Thebes; Eretria was always hostile towards the foreign occupying power.[148]

Eretria's relations with other independent *poleis*

The Lelantine War

The central factor governing Eretria's relations with states in Euboia itself from the ninth to the end of the sixth centuries was the 'Lelantine War'. Interwoven with this were Eretrian involvements overseas, the result of its control over islands in the Aegean and its wide colonial/trading interests. The very settlement of Eretria itself was almost certainly the outcome of warfare between the Khalkidians and Lefkandiots, and there is evidence that fighting erupted periodically over the following centuries down to 506 between the two *poleis*. The reason scholars give such differing dates for this war is undoubtedly due to the chronic nature of the fighting over a long period. That the 'Lelantine War' was not a single episode or confined within a narrow chronological period but continued, sometimes desultorily, sometimes as a war of pan-Hellenic proportions, from the Heroic Age and even earlier to 506, is a view not shared by most scholars. Geyer, for example, has a bet each way: for him 'the' war was not earlier than 730 (the foundation of Pithekoussai), when Strabo says that the two states were still in harmony, though later they fell out: 'Pithekoussai was founded by the Eretrians and the Khalkidians, who, though prospering there on account of the fertility of the soil and the gold mines, abandoned the island on account of a quarrel.' This co-operation was, in my opinion, only a temporary interval. However, Geyer did accept the ongoing rivalry between Eretria and Khalkis: 'Certainly more wars broke out between the two neighbour-cities.'[149] However Dr Parker, who has made an extensive special study of the war, shares my view.[150]

Because Eretria had overseas interests, fighting on the island inevitably sometimes involved *poleis* outside Euboia. Thucydides, in his brief comment on 'the' Lelantine War, says that this was the first occasion that many Greek states became embroiled in a single conflict: 'And indeed, some time in the past, there occurred a war between the Khalkidians and the Eretrians and the rest of the Hellenic world concluded alliances with one or other side.'[151] Miletos and

Samos were certainly among them. We need not think that a majority of these *poleis* were involved in great battles, actively or passively. Periodically there did occur significant events such as the destruction of Lefkandi, and whichever phase of the war it was that attracted Thucydides' attention, it must have been one of these. But we should not be seduced by Thucydides' note into believing that it usually involved much more than the picture of cross-border raiding in the marches of the Eretrias and the Karystia that emerges from the fragmentary epic referred to in Chapter 4. Such raids were always a feature of Greek life, even under Roman rule. Earlier, the governors of Dareios had to impose order on the Ionian cities after the conquest, because of cross-border raiding.[152] *Hippeis* and *Hippobotai* justified their control of the state by virtue of their martial prowess, and episodes such as these indicate that they had plenty of opportunities to keep in training: 'And this is why in ancient times those states whose strength lay in their cavalry and which used horses in their wars against their neighbours, such as the Eretrians, the Khalkidians and the citizens of Magnesia-on-the-Maiandros [were governed by] oligarchies.'[153]

In whose interest were these local wars? Certainly not the non-Hippobotic classes. The early rural gentry could perhaps carry on their age-old duel with their neighbours in the *eskhatia*, the remote border countryside, where the writ of the *polis* was weakest, in the manner some scholars describe as 'agonistic', in which battles were fought according to well-defined courtly rules. Killing was thereby minimised and hostages were ransomed rapidly after being well treated.[154] The notion of 'chivalric' *agones,* in fact, has as one of its principal foundations Strabo's comments on the conduct of warfare between the two rival Euboian *poleis*:

> Generally these *poleis* agreed with one another and when differences arose concerning the Lelantine [Plain], they did not so completely cease in this as to each wage war with stubborn remorselessness, but developed a convention according to which they would conduct the fighting. This is revealed by a stele in the Amarynthion, which expresses a prohibition against thrown weapons.[155]

It is an extension of Herman's scenario of elaborate friendship links between aristocratic families and individuals from different *poleis*.[156] Often hostages became *xenoi* (guest-friends) of their captors, and networks of relationships between noble houses were built up, some lasting well into the Classical period. But it would be misleading to believe that by the sixth and in later centuries, warfare and associated diplomacy was at all 'chivalric' in any but a few cases such as (perhaps) the Argive/Spartan War for the Thyreatis.[157] Moreover, was even this anything more than a romanticised version of a preliminary skirmish followed by a 'real' battle? I think not. Anyhow, the result was in fact decided by a formal hoplite engagement. It was around Lefkandi on the Lelantine Plain, *c.* 825, that the cosy pattern of war games among aristocratic *oikoi*[158] appears to have ended in a real war, involving annexation by Khalkis of the defeated nobles' territory. Why did Khalkis break the convention?

Severe drought and its consequent economic strains would put paid to the mitigating effects of ancient class-friendship links with neighbouring landowners, along with increased pressure to reform the military efficiency of the state for both attack and defence. However, the emergence of the *polis*-state, associated with both the phenomenon of colonisation and the changes in the methods and conventions of warfare that scholars have called the Hoplite Revolution, will also have played a role. The phase of the Lelantine War leading to the settlement at Eretria was what Kondoleon called 'a manifestation of the struggle between the old order of the *ethnos*-states and the new world of the *polis*-states'.[159] For both Kondoleon and me, Eretria represents the *neos kosmos*, Khalkis the *palaios*. However, the Abantic *ethnos* was already history. Arkhilokhos' 'spear-famed lords of Euboia' were both the heirs of the Homeric warrior Abantes and exemplars of the new hand-to-hand hoplite warfare:

> Not so many bows shall be stretched,
> nor so many slings discharged, when Ares goes forth
> to war on the Plain, but then there will be
> the awful work of the sword, for this
> is the sort of battle in which are masters
> the spear-famed lords of Euboia.[160]

This is not incompatible with a small body of aristocratic warriors riding to battle, then fighting more or less as hoplites with thrusting spears, as the Spartan *Hippeis* still did at the Battle of Mantineia in 419. Nevertheless, the reference to close-up fighting with swords shows that we have moved some way from the older style of waging war. Given the likely very small numbers on both sides, the battle would have been rather removed from the typical hoplite battle of the late-sixth century onwards. The chronology of Arkhilokhos is a topic of dispute, but if we place the poet's *floruit* in the last quarter of the seventh century we would not be far wrong. The dating is important, despite the fact that precision is not to be had, because it reveals fighting in Euboia during his active lifetime and also for dating the introduction there of hoplite armour generally.[161] Homer had already called the Abantes *rhexithorakes* (corslet-cleavers),[162] since their method of using the spear was to stand firm and thrust for the chest. Eustathios, commenting on the Abantic section of the *Iliad* says that: 'The Abantes were spearmen who did not discharge their spears.'[163] The description of the method of fighting by the Abantic contingent in the *Iliad*, quite compatible with that of the hoplite phalanx, has therefore been regarded as a later interpolation.[164]

But were in fact the 'spear-famed lords' of Arkhilokhos still from the old Hippobotic class? And were they the sole custodians of Euboian military ethics anyway? The 'convention' recorded by Strabo [he employs the verb *synethento*, suggesting a *syntheke* (treaty)] against the use of missile weapons, which was preserved in the temple at Amarynthos,[165] is a restated survival from early times. Missiles were an early feature of Eretrian warfare: we see them used against the colonists returning from Kerkyra (734/3).[166] However, the wording favoured users of traditional methods, such as duelling with swords and, especially, those using horses.[167] Valuable and hard to replace, horses were vulnerable to missiles shot from a distance.[168] Thus, the prohibition against *telebola* (long-range missiles)[169] may be seen as an attempt by the Khalkidians to neutralise Eretrian *psiloi* (light-armed troops): the term is later used in the Eretrian military list *IG* XII 9, 241. Lorimer speculates that *telebola* may indicate the presence of mercenary slingers and archers. Perhaps even at this early period the Eretrians had an organised body of slingers.[170] In periods of social tension, attitudes clash and become blurred. The Amarynthos convention appears to be an attempt to re-enforce traditional mores of constraint that were breaking down, while the new all-out approach to winning in war betrays a more opportunistic, hardheaded philosophy. This appears to contrast with the spirit of the *polis*, with its collective rather than individual responsibility in such matters as the defence of the state, reflected militarily in the hoplite phalanx, which required the subordination of individual self-pride in personal glory to the more mundane collective interest of the state and its protection. The military action in Euboia involving Arkhilokhos must have been fought under the terms of the convention imposing a ban on missile weapons,[171] for the similarity between the wording of the stele and his poem is so striking that I am surprised that military historians have not commented on it more.[172] Nevertheless, Eretria still possessed a powerful cavalry that could successfully challenge that of Hippobotic Khalkis for supremacy, as we shall see.

Opportunism, at Eretria and elsewhere, is also manifested by the new dominant class with its more self-centred commercial interests, whose rise to power exhibits features of later class struggles.[173] The hoplite army, whose members were interdependent but at the same time stolid and persistent, was its means of countering the old military dominance of the aristocrats who were much more willing to cut their losses and withdraw to fight another day. Still, it must be confessed that the cynical Arkhilokhos himself did not hesitate to throw away his shield, which was certainly a hoplite *porpax* shield:

> Some Thracian now rejoices in my innocent shield,
> that I chucked away behind a bush.
> But I saved myself. What's that shield to me?
> So what, I say. I'll get me another just as good.[174]

These two fragments of his poetry reveal a quite new attitude to conduct in war and concern (part of) the hoplite panoply, although of course Arkhilokhos' *rhipsaspia* presumably did not occur in Euboia, since a Thracian was beneficiary of his prudence. Elsewhere in Greece at the time, we see the emergence of mercenaries and of tyranny, the appearance of which at Eretria came rather later.[175] 'The old aristocratic republic had been liable to be swayed by sentimental considerations – old guest-friendships with the nobles of other states and the curious and widespread feeling that the national honour demands the vigorous prosecution of ancestral border-feuds – the tyrant cared for none of these things.' 'He was an opportunist.'[176]

The debate concerning the emergence of the hoplite army and the *polis* is not new. Some recent scholarship sees the military reforms as preceding social change: it was the phalanx that produced the tyrants.[177] But in fact: 'We know very little about the introduction of hoplite warfare.'[178] There must however have been some prior socio-economic changes that had already created what Cartledge calls potential revolutionaries, a class of farmers of sufficient substance, or men who had obtained wealth from an expansion of trade opportunities, who were able to afford a hoplite panoply, or part of it. Moreover, any farmers with such resources were likely to have been growing exportable commodities, such as olives, and so were not subsistence peasants. However, we need not imagine a rush to arms by the rising classes. Cartledge for one thinks that they would have been reluctant soldiers: 'The adoption of phalanx tactics did not create a revolutionary situation . . . rather it turned potential revolutionaries . . . into actual revolutionaries.'[179] Morris, however, perceives revolutionary discontent in the classes below the actual rulers.[180] My belief is that as men became more affluent, they were able to acquire, bit by bit, the elements of what would later become the fully fledged hoplite panoply, and that pressure to do so may have been applied by the *polis* government in order to strengthen its military capabilities, even though often that government would still have been in the hands of the old aristocratic class.

Following defeats by Khalkis in the ninth and again in the late-seventh/early-sixth centuries and having undergone economic revolution, Eretria may have been especially willing to adopt the new military tactics and equipment. Few yet seem to have considered that Euboia, with its martial traditions, from the mythical Kouretes and historical Abantes to the lords who fought with/against Arkhilokhos, might have been the original home of the hoplite. One who has is Helbig, who attributes to Khalkis the development of the phalanx to control the numerically superior natives in its areas of colonisation.[181] However, the chronic warfare at home for the Lelantine Plain would have been just as likely an incentive for Khalkis to try new methods. Eretria, which was less encumbered with ancient traditions, would have been an even more likely focus of the experimentation and was just as active in colonisation as was Khalkis. The extent to which Eretrian interest in Al Mina and the metalworking cultures of the Middle East may have encouraged the adoption of new armour and tactics is hard to assess. Did Euboia get its reputation as inventor of bronze weaponry from the trade in arms? We have noted the absence of copper deposits in central Euboia. Both Eretrians and Khalkidians had hoplites at an early date. While discussing the Thessalian hero Kleomakhos of Pharsalos,

Aristotle (of Khalkis?) talks of Eretrian hoplites defeating those of Khalkis but later fleeing the battlefield following his cavalry charge.[182] Of great importance is a LG amphora found at Eretria itself,[183] depicting a file of warriors, each with two spears and blazoned shields, most probably hoplite, bringing to mind Arkhilokhos' description of the 'Euboian lords'. Boardman thinks 'transitional' comes most readily to mind when considering this evidence.[184] The weapons unearthed in the excavation of the West Gate *heroön* (dated *c.* 680) are swords and spears, which might be hoplite equipment, but there are no distinguishing items such as shields or helmets that would settle the matter. The excavators, however, note evidence of Homeric rituals pointing to earlier usage,[185] though there is no necessary correlation between funerary and military practices.

Still, there was a long-standing contempt for non-hoplite methods in Euboia.[186] Euripides in his *Herakles* starkly contrasts the feelings of antagonism between old and new worlds. He wrongly calls Lykos 'king of Thebes' (a recollection of Khalkodontid rule of Thebes from Lefkandi in Mycenaean times?) for he is a Euboian. Amphytryon, Herakles' father, makes it clear that Abantic Dirphys is his homeland, and it is, significantly, mainly in Khalkidian territory:

> What would Abantic Dirphys, your homeland
> have to say about you, if we were to ask?
> It would not praise you, for there is no place
> in your fatherland which could witness
> any noble deed of yours.[187]

Appropriately for a Khalkidian, Lykos espouses the conservative view, echoing the sense of shame and contempt felt by the Euboian Hippobotic aristocrats for men who used missile weapons such as bows and arrows. Arguing against Amphitryon, who speaks for the new way, Lykos makes the traditional, thoroughly Abantic viewpoint forcibly:

> Herakles won his fame fighting animals;
> in other matters, he was no hero – he was nothing!
> His left arm never held a shield, he never faced
> an enemy's spear. He used the bow, the coward's weapon,
> handy for running away. The test of courage is not
> skill with a bow, but in the firm foot, the unflinching eye,
> when the spear drives its hurtling furrow through the ranks.[188]

Herakles is the aggressive outsider and innovator, exploiting the missile arrow. The convention stele thus expresses only the increasingly obsolete Euboian-noble attitudes of the 'spear-famed lords'.[189] Lykos' contempt, together with the angry frustration of the verses of the aristocratic Theognis, dealing with his experiences in Euboia[190] during civil strife there in the mid-sixth century, reveal what must have been a widely felt anger among this class at the total breakdown of the ancient interstate and interfamilial relationships. On behalf of the new way, we have only Amphitryon's frustrated diatribe.

Despite military and political changes, an old notion persisted: whoever fights in defence of the community should have a say in the direction of state policy, especially in relation to war and peace. The revolutionary potential of this idea in the new climate is obvious and it would have a great impact on Eretrian military and civilian life when the fighting class extended downwards into the artisans and labouring sections of the population. The increasing importance of naval warfare[191] would further change, even more radically, the socio-economic composition of the military. There is evidence of late-eighth-century naval battles involving Euboians: Amphidamas of Khalkis died in a naval engagement against Eretrians. Jeffery noted the consequences of these changes for the Euboian *poleis*: 'Thus, when the hoplite element in Chalkis and Eretria realised its potential power, government by the *Hippobotai* became less settled.'[192] By the mid-sixth century, Thersites was no longer to be silenced by a slap from his noble betters and his fellows were not at the scene of battle merely to provide applause for the exploits of heroes.[193] While the sanction of the stele perhaps represents an early setback for the *neos kosmos* in Euboia, change could not be indefinitely postponed, for Euboia was not isolated from the rest of the Greek world. Military defeat had resulted in the breakup of the Lefkandiot community and the relocation of the classes representing the new social forces at Eretria, where they could express the new ideology in the new *polis* through its economic dynamism. The hardheaded driving away of the colonists 'with slings and shots' not long after its foundation displays the new spirit in action early at Eretria.

The 'Lelantine War' and extra-Euboian alliances

The early war involving Karystos and Miletos probably involved an alliance between the latter and Eretria. By *c.* 700, Miletos' ally Paros was also on the Eretrian side and its citizen Arkhilokhos fighting in Euboia. 'Some scholars have even gone so far as to put forward a theory of two "mercantile alliances", mutually hostile, in Archaic Greece.'[194] Kondoleon pushed back the concept of two major groupings of a 'politico-military nature' to the 'end of the Geometric period' and argued that these reflected the characteristics of the component *poleis* so profoundly that they lasted for centuries. Speaking of Thucydides' two 'alliances',[195] he writes: 'towards the end of the Geometric Period, I have hypothesised that these represent not a temporary *separation* [but] were an expression of deep differences between the two sides the members of each of which were united by long standing bonds.'[196] His is the most detailed examination of evidence for this early period, but even he fails to cover all the available data. There is no discussion of the climatic factor and, naturally, the results of the Swiss excavations were not available when Kondoleon wrote in

1963. He is so strongly seduced by his desire to prove his theory that Eretria provided the convoys for all the Khalkidian colonial ventures that he ignores the political implications of non-maritime factors such as the Lelantine land war. His account, though interesting and valuable, is thus unbalanced and incomplete. His firm belief in unchanging alliance groups cannot finally be sustained, as is shown by the alacrity with which Periandros abandoned the long-standing Corinth/Samos alliance for friendship with Thrasyboulos of Miletos, thereby upsetting the balance of power in the Aegean region, a change that had momentous consequences both for Eretria, long-standing ally of Miletos, and for Khalkis, ally of Samos, and indeed for all Greece. His reversal of the old Bakkhiad alliance with the Samian *Geomoroi* (land sharers), whose natural sympathies lay with the Khalkidian *Hippobotai,* shows that Periandros believed that he had more in common with the commercially oriented Eretrians and with the Milesians under a fellow tyrant.[197]

I disagree with those who argue that trade considerations can never ever be used to explain the actions of Archaic Greek *poleis* in general or the Lelantine War in particular.[198] Thus, while concurring with Hasebroek that the idea of predictive commercial planning by Archaic *poleis* is unthinkable, I reject his belief that there were no 'foreign and sea trade and regular trade alliances (resting on a basis of naval strength) with commercial aristocrats.'[199] The examples of the Bakkhiadai and of both Solon and Peisistratos, not to mention the Eretrian oligarchy, should make one pause before asserting this. Trade was important at Corinth, even in the ninth century, and trade considerations were always more important than political ideology in determining policies there.[200] Similarly, we should reject the idea that rulers, and even the people of Archaic *poleis*, did not perceive mutual non-competing interests, commercial, political and racial, and form alliances. It is, for example, unrealistic to believe that Ionians were oblivious to their distinctiveness from, say, Dorians, and vice versa. The variety of colonies established by various states indicates that their *metropoleis* had certain political or economic objectives in mind when sending out colonists. We have already noted that Eretria itself may well have dictated to its Pithekoussan *emporion* over gold trans-shipments. The tyrants Periandros and Thrasyboulos undoubtedly shared similar interests and political goals that were probably, in the last analysis, more important than any personal friendship noted by Herodotos. Of course, before *c.* 550, any ties linking city-states must have been fairly unstructured and personal, not unlike the intra-*poleis* alliance networks among aristocratic families and individuals, which existed from the Heroic Age right down to and beyond the Classical period, as described by Herman.

By the eighth century the middle Aegean and central Greek *poleis* had established alliances based upon perceived common interests, political and commercial, called 'trade leagues' by Burn,[201] which impinged on the series of battles that I call the Lelantine War: 'The great maritime states of Euboia enlisted their trading partners as allies.' And: 'it appears that the political landscape of

Greece (and some enduring alliances between *poleis*) had taken shape.' Hurwit agrees: 'Such as they were, these "leagues" did exist and the wars of the Greek maritime states in the seventh century do seem to be connected in every case, directly or indirectly, with the rivalries of Chalcis and Eretria, Samos and Miletos.'[202] Eretria developed friendships among outward-looking commercial states and may have been the first Euboian *polis* to acquire overseas friends, a natural consequence of its trading interests, while Khalkis later found its allies among conservative states such as Samos with its landowning aristocratic government of the *Geomoroi*. However, such natural alliances were often thwarted by unneighbourly and selfish considerations. Originally, commercial Corinth was an ally of Khalkis, while its neighbour, conservative Megara, was probably in consequence a friend of Eretria. Later, when Corinth allied with Eretria, Khalkis acquired Megarian friendship, which will explain the presence of the archconservative Megarian Theognis at the battle for Kerinthos in Khalkidian territory. A general principle operating from very early in the history of the Greek *poleis* right up to the last phase of their autonomous existence may be expressed as follows: my neighbour is my enemy; my neighbour's neighbour will be his enemy, therefore my neighbour's neighbour can be my friend. Nevertheless, the effect of these alignments on internal politics is hard to estimate. A powerful partner might reinforce an allied regime or perhaps subvert it. The destabilising consequences of Peisistratos' stay in Eretria during the 540s on the stability of the oligarchy are examined in Chapter 6. But later tradition preserved the memory of old alliance groupings involving naturally and predictably friendly pairs. Thessaly, for example, with governments in the hands of horse-rearing aristocracies,[203] belongs within the Khalkidian grouping at this time, as we would expect.[204]

A series of wars involving Eretria and Khalkis and their allies began about the middle of the eighth century. We do not know which side initiated the fighting. The rupture between Eretrians and Khalkidians on Pithekoussai *c.* 750 and the loss in 734 of Kerkyra, and perhaps Syracuse, by Eretria to Corinth as an ally of Khalkis are probably related to the Euboian wars. Was the Miletos/Eretria vs. Karystos war also part of this fighting? Possibly. At about this time the people of Chios helped the Milesians in return for previous help against Erythrai.[205] The fact that, at Khalkis, the *Hippobotai* maintained their control until the troubles there in the second half of the sixth century[206] and the loss by Eretria of some western colonies suggest that the Eretrians were worsted in this mid-eighth century phase of the Lelantine War, which can be linked to other fighting in the Aegean. Kondoleon has written several papers[207] on Arkhilokhos and Paros, in which he discusses the poet's involvement as a mercenary[208] in a series of wars between Paros and Naxos, in which Miletos, Eretria's friend, was allied to Paros. He dates these conflicts to the seventh century. Miletos was indeed still hostile towards Naxos on the eve of the Ionian revolt and the expedition against it by Aristagoras and the Persians. Herodotos did not recognise ancient enmity between the two, but friendly relations between Paros and Miletos were still apparent from the request by the embattled Milesians for a fleet from Paros *c.* 525.[209] The Polykrite incident[210] shows that Milesians and Erythraians jointly attacked Naxos while Paros was also fighting it. Earlier, Miletos and Erythrai joined Paros to found Parion on the Propontis (in 709).[211] Conversely, the already ancient friendship of Khalkis and Naxos was demonstrated by their joint foundation of Naxos in Sicily in 734.[212] Paros and Miletos remained friends of Eretria for centuries, although there was a hiccup in this happy arrangement between 540 and 530, when Paros was briefly hostile to Miletos.[213] Paros may therefore have sent troops to Euboia with, or perhaps even under the command of, its prominent soldier-poet in repayment for some Eretrian help in the Naxos war for which we have no record.

A story, belonging to another episode of the Lelantine War that general opinion dates to *c.* 705, concerns the Khalkidian hero Amphidamas who died fighting against Eretria.[214] Hesiod, who competed in the recitation contest, which was part of the funeral games celebrating the fallen hero, does not call Amphidamas *basileus*. The application of this term to Amphidamas comes only in the late and unreliable *On the Competition between Homer and Hesiod*.[215] However, were the games associated with the funeral of an Amphidamas who was a contemporary of the poet or part of a funeral cult for another Amphidamas long dead? If the latter, was he involved in an earlier outbreak of the war in the late ninth century at Lefkandi? The problem with 705 is that many scholars put Hesiod's *floruit* in the mid-eighth century at the latest.[216] Evelyn-White summarises:

> Critics from Plutarch downwards have almost unanimously rejected the lines 654–662 on the ground that Amphidamas is the hero of the Lelantine War between Chalkis and Eretria whose death may be placed *c.* 705 BC – a date which is obviously too low for the genuine Hesiod. Nevertheless there is much to be said in defence of the passage . . . And there is nothing in the context to show that Hesiod's Amphidamas is to be identified with that Amphidamas whom Plutarch alone connects to the Lelantine War: the name may have been borne by an earlier Chalkidian, an ancestor perhaps of the person to whom Plutarch refers.[217]

But Plutarch ought not to be dismissed too lightly for he shows throughout his works a considerable interest in, and detailed knowledge of, Euboian, and particularly Khalkidian, history. He apparently saw the monument to the later war hero Kleomakhos in the agora of Khalkis; he expressly says that it still stood in his day: 'And the Khalkidians point out his tomb on which stands even today a great column',[218] and, by researching carefully his sources for Eretrian involvement in the Ionian War to correct Herodotos' account, he provides a vital clue nowhere else reported in the surviving literature.[219] Thus, his observation that there was a tradition that Amphidamas died 'in a naval engagement against Eretria over the Lelantine Plain' is particularly interesting, although apparently he himself dismissed it.[220] West thinks that the tradition is 'not likely to have been invented' and that it derives from the Euboian historian Arkhemakhos, who wrote about the Lelantine War according to Aristotle.[221]

There are reasons encouraging us not only to accept, but also to prefer a date *c.* 700 for Amphidamas' exploits. Such a battle seems implied on a LG vase showing 'Dipylon' warriors fighting to the left of a ship.[222] The reader is reminded again of early literary traditions of Euboia 'famed for ships' in the Homeric Hymn, the representations of Euboian ships on vases, including battle scenes,[223] and Euboian trade in the East and the early colonial ventures in the West in the eighth century. That a sea battle occurred so early is not at all impossible, in spite of Thucydides' belief that the earliest did not occur until 644, between Corinth and Kerkyra. There is a convergence of other military data around 705 that also bears examination. We have already seen that there were more or less simultaneous destructions at Lefkandi and New Eretria at the end of the eighth century. Second, Thucydides reports[224] that a Corinthian shipwright built four triremes for Samos 300 years before the end of the Peloponnesian War, i.e. *c.* 704; both Corinth and Samos were then of course friends of Khalkis. Then, archaeological data from Zagora point to *c.* 700 for its abandonment, while Andros colonised in co-operation with Khalkis at Akanthos *c.* 655,[225] suggesting that it had already slipped from Eretrian control. Could these events be associated with anti-Eretrian naval activities by Corinth and/or Samos on behalf of Khalkis? 'We do not possess positive evidence that Khalkis ever had a fleet, contrary to the certainties of contemporary researchers'[226] says Kondoleon, and on this matter I have already expressed my doubts. However, Khalkis could have had help from allies. It may have been the first but it was certainly not the last time that Khalkis triumphed over Eretria, thanks to decisive intervention by foreign powers, and indeed the frequency with which Khalkis would henceforth rely on others for its successes casts doubts about its ability to match Eretria alone in war, either on land or at sea. Already, formal ally of Khalkis or not, Corinth had, some thirty years earlier, stripped Kerkyra from Eretria. The battle in which Amphidamas died thus appears to be just one in a series around 705 involving Khalkis and other states. He was presumably victorious since he received heroic honours. Also around 700, Euboian material ceases at Al Mina while there was a corresponding increase from other sources,[227] indicating that Eretria now had difficulty getting her products overseas. A naval loss and the supremacy of the Corinthian fleet at this time would explain this fact. Nevertheless, Khalkis does not fill the gap; Corinth does that.

> It is clear . . . that most of the Greek pottery arriving at Al Mina in the seventh century is coming from parts of Greece other than those which served the Greeks living there in the eighth century. The Euboean influ-

> ence has virtually disappeared. The years around 700 may have seen the last or most decisive of the struggles between the two main Euboean cities, Eretria and Chalcis (the so-called Lelantine War). The balance of trade and colonization interest in the two cities probably changed, and it is at Eretria, not (so far) Chalcis, that we find the type of vase still carried to Al Mina, but this may mean nothing. Both cities retire from the arena for many years.[228]

Evidence for warfare between the two Euboian cities at this time also comes from the excavators of the Eretrian *heroön* at the West Gate, who date the monument to *c.* 680.[229] Neither archaeological nor early literary dates can be pressed to precision but suffice it to say that about the beginning of the seventh century, the Eretrians also honoured a hero and chose as the site of his memorial rites the Khalkis Gate of the city.[230] The two hero cults complement each other; the anonymous Eretrian provides us with material evidence of heroic burial and rites, while Hesiod's poem tells us about the games. It is thus tempting to see both as victims of the same or related hostilities. In my archaeological survey of the city, I have linked the Eretrian hero cult to the final abandonment of Lefkandi and the destruction of houses and the building *c.* 710/690 of walls at Eretria, certainly on the western side facing Khalkis if not surrounding the entire city.[231] Thus, there is enough evidence of a major eruption of the Lelantine War about the turn of the century to dissuade us from trying to force the literary references back to the mid-eighth century. Most of this evidence suggests that Eretria was defeated, though the hero cult perhaps indicates at least one victory for Eretria. Boardman nevertheless observes that:

> If we are forced to assess the historical value of this [ceramic] evidence, admittedly barely adequate as far as Chalcis is concerned, the most satisfactory explanation would be that Eretria enjoyed continuous prosperity from the eighth to the sixth century with no alarming disasters or change in population; that Chalcis early in the seventh century fell from prosperity, and was perhaps in part abandoned – at any rate suffered some loss of status in comparison with Eretria. One might deduce that Eretria, her close and powerful neighbour, was the cause of this eclipse.

He continues: 'Partial abandonment of the site [of Khalkis] is possible. This might explain the apparent absence of seventh century [pottery].'[232] He regarded Eretria as the ultimate victor in the Lelantine War,[233] and later in his paper, he notes that Eretria was one of the foremost Greek states during the period from the eighth to the sixth century.

At the beginning of the seventh century, 'The War' may have seemed over. Certainly most of the scholars who treat the Lelantine War as a single episode are convinced that it ended then and that Khalkis was victorious. Success once more reinforced the position of the *Hippobotai* and the economic status quo. However, Khalkis was, at the very least, a declining power at sea and her eclipse culminates at the beginning of the fifth century in the debacle of not being able to supply her own ships at Salamis. Moreover, the long drought probably did not end until well into the seventh century and this would have held prosperity in check in a *polis* with apparently little non-rural industry and commerce.

Nevertheless, hostilities were in fact not over, and the Eretrians were shortly able to make yet another challenge for their lost part of the disputed plain. In the meantime, they had to regroup and rebuild their resources and their city which, as we have seen in Chapter 4, had been (partially?) destroyed *c.* 690. Eretria apparently still had her colonial bases in Epeiros, Pithekoussai and the north and, despite the probable loss of Andros, it may have retained most of the Aegean island empire. But the seventh century was necessarily a period of reconstruction and reconsolidation. Despite Boardman's assessment, it must have suffered from its defeat, especially the loss of markets in the East. There were, however, some hopeful signs. Eretria retained friendship and alliance with Miletos, still in the seventh century the greatest commercial, colonising and cultural *polis* in the East. Herodotos[234] has the cities still allies in the mid-sixth century, and the relationship endured into the second/first centuries.[235] In the sixth, Eretria seems to have been Miletos' agent on the Greek mainland, assisting its trade with inland Boiotia via Mykalessos (mod. Rhitsona),[236] and possibly Miletos reciprocated for Eretria through its influence at *emporia* such as Naukratis.[237] Eretria's colonies in Macedonia and Thrace were still intact in the mid-sixth century when Peisistratos left Eretria for the north. These allowed it to exploit abundant mineral and other natural resources, such as timber, furs, and fish. Its ceramic output, as Boardman indicates, was maintained and even increased.[238] This may indicate increased production of olive oil, since as we have noted, though sometimes of competent quality, Eretrian pottery was never likely to have been sought after for itself.[239] I have already noted the expansion of the port and agora at this time.[240] The erection of strong walls, especially on the western boundary, testifies that danger from that quarter was not underestimated. The conditions for continued warfare had, in any case, been laid down long ago in the cycle of attack and counter-attack for possession of the plain.[241] And, by the early sixth century, the changes in Greek warfare, discussed earlier in this chapter, were being implemented.

In the early sixth century, Thessaly, a new and powerful player, entered the Lelantine contest. Plutarch, in the passage of his *Amatorius* cited above, which is one of the very few actually to mention the Lelantine War by name, relates a story about Kleomakhos of Pharsalos.[242] It is not really a description of an episode in the war but rather a paradigm of the ennobling qualities of pederastic love. Kleomakhos, ally of the Khalkidians, sees them getting the worst of an engagement, thanks to Eretria's superiority in cavalry, though apparently the hoplite battle was initially a stalemate, and to set an example to his *eromenos*[243] he leads the Thessalians into what may be the last true cavalry charge in Archaic Greek warfare. In doing so, he lost his life but routed the Eretrians. Thus the war, which was going badly for Khalkis, for they had to depend on their allies for cavalry, was won by the intervention of Kleomakhos. Once more, thanks to foreign aid, the *status quo ante* was restored. Some scholars believe that it was as a result of this defeat that the Eretrians lost both their Boeotian possessions and the western part of the Lelantine Plain. 'Oropos seems to have been an Eretrian possession before it passed into the hands of the Thebans in the Sixth Century and preserved the Eretrian dialect throughout the Boeotian and subsequent Athenian domination.'[244] With Knoepfler, I believe that Oropos was lost in 490. However, Lorimer's interpretation suggests that Khalkis, having won this cavalry battle, dictated the stele from a need to protect its inexperienced phalanx as well as its cavalry from Eretrian missiles.[245] It was, however, to be Khalkis' last victory. Kleomakhos' involvement dates it to the early sixth century, for it was precisely then that the Thessalian League was active in central Greece:

> In the Sixth century, [it] . . . held the majority on the Amphictyony of Thermopylae; she availed herself of it to extend her influence in Central Greece. She took part in the Sacred War to deliver Delphi from the tyranny of Crissa; she intervened in the war between Chalcis and Eretria . . . But the power of the Thessalians was short-lived. Defeated by the Boeotians, . . . they were back in their own country by the Fifth Century.[246]

The Thessalian ruling nobility were *hippotrophoi* (horse rearers) like their Khalkidian allies.[247] As late as 511 they came with cavalry to help Hippias of Athens, though by then they were largely a spent force outside Thessaly.

In the context of this episode, we may also consider a Delphic 'oracle' concerning the status of the Thessalians and Khalkidians. It seems to be an amalgamation of at least two separate oracular utterances:

> Of all the ploughland, that of Pelasgic Argos is better,
> Thessalian cavalry, and Lakedaimonian women,
> and the men who drink the water of lovely Arethousa too; [end 1]
> but even better than these latter are the men who live
> in the land between Tiryns and Arkadia, the land of many sheep,
> the linen-corseleted Argives, the spurs of war. [end 2]
> But you, men of (Aigion; Megara; whoever) are neither third
> nor fourth nor twelfth, nor in the reckoning or listing.[248]

Though not regarded as a genuine response by Fontenrose,[249] it does perhaps outline the political status map of the period. Salmon points out that it represents two separate chronological periods.[250] He argues that the original 'oracle' (lines 1–3) reflects the position of Khalkis 'in the age of cavalry warfare', and the first addition (lines 4–6) became necessary when Argos developed the phalanx in the reign of Pheidon. We should note, first, that the chronology of Pheidon is very vague: the problems are summarised by Tomlinson.[251] Therefore, using Pheidon as a chronological reference point does not tell us when or why the second part was added. Then, though in fact Khalkis is not directly named, its appearance is not for primacy in cavalry fighting. That is, rightly as we have seen, assigned to Thessaly. The text thus does reflect the strategic situation in Euboia *c.* 600: the Khalkidians were not then excellent in cavalry fighting as the Kleomakhos episode makes clear, for it was not its cavalry that did best in the battle but its infantry and it was the intervention of the superior Thessalian cavalry that won a tightly balanced struggle: 'And the infantry of the Khalkidians seemed to be strong, but the cavalry was finding it a big task to stand up to the enemy's [i.e the Eretrians'] cavalry.'[252] The Hippobotic rulers of Khalkis were certainly in no doubt about the crucial role of Kleomakhos and his men; they raised a monument in the agora itself that was still impressive in Plutarch's day, in so doing they conferred on the Thessalian commander the status of second city founder (*oikistes*),[253] so great was their gratitude. It must have been a major and threatening situation.

Over the next decades, new methods of warfare, including the hoplite phalanx on land and the use of the trireme at sea, everywhere replaced the old. The ruling regimes in several important states fell in the first half of the century. Old alignments were modified and powers such as Sparta, which was consolidating and expanding its influence in the Peloponnese and whose League embraced the Isthmus states shortly after the middle of the century, Thebes, which had decisively halted the southward thrust of Thessalian aggression,[254] and naval Corinth began to play a more active role in central Greece. The heavy defeat of the Thessalians may have had something to do with their abandonment of the Khalkidian alliance. Perhaps the Khalkidians were unable or unwilling to come over to the mainland (and not for the last time) to assist their allies. The Thessalians had changed sides by the time of Peisistratos, a friend of Eretria in 556, who named one of his sons Thessalos in honour of his alliance with them.[255] Miletos, debilitated by internal *stasis* for the last half of the sixth century, although still a friend of Eretria, was not of much account internationally. Eretria needed other allies. The Corinthians had long been allies of Khalkis, despite ideological differences after the accession of Kypselos. Now his opportunist son Periandros, having established Corinthian interests in the West at the expense of both Eretria and his ally Khalkis, and seeing no future in maintaining the old Corinth/Samos/Khalkis axis, took his city into the grouping that included Eretria. The tyrant of Miletos became his personal friend. The change in the position of Corinth altered the whole alliance system and encouraged the emergence of new tyrant regimes: at Eretria, Athens and Naxos. At Khalkis, the old order did not go unchallenged. There was a series of coups by aspiring tyrants, followed by reaction.[256] However, by 506 the *ancien régime* had yet again regained power there, to preside over the final humiliation of military defeat and the establishment of an Athenian *kleroukhia* on the Lelantine Plain.

Thus, down to *c.* 570 alliance patterns had remained fairly constant, but in the second quarter of the sixth century the old stability began to collapse. Like the interfamilial relationships that Herman describes, the links between early *poleis* were strongly personal or class based.[257] The very stability of the earliest alliance groups may have been the result of precisely this personal/'class' factor, for the rulers often had more in common with similar groups or individuals in other *poleis* than with other classes in their own. Instability thus emerged when the old, established ruling groups began to lose power. The fact of the short-term tenure of most tyrant dynasties also caused rapid changes of outlook. Sometimes however, traditional loyalties remained very strong and over-rode pure self-interest, and Eretria itself provided an example when, in 499:

> the Eretrians, . . . came to the (Ionian) war to please not the Athenians, but the Milesians themselves, thus repaying their debt, because earlier they had been allies of the Eretrians in their war against Khalkis, when the Samians came to help the Khalkidians against the Eretrians and the Milesians.[258]

Notes

1 Sakellariou 1958, 220–1, 240 (Erythrai); 239 (Teos); 240, 283–90 (Khios); Euboian Abantes who went to Khios were non-Greek Thracians and Hellenised early (287). See Ch. 2, pp. 42–3 and nn. 145–148.

2 E. Sapouna-Sakellaraki, 'Εὐβοϊκὴ Κύμη', *AE* 1984/86, 157: LM I. Sampson 1981a, 50: LH I; evidence of Euboian links with Crete, 52, dated 1600–1500.

3 Al Mina: Boardman 1980, 38–54 (40, 42). Sûkâs: Riis 1970, 126–75, 129; Riis thinks that this is true of Al Mina (159). However the support he cites from Boardman is no longer valid, as the latter has withdrawn his earlier comments, though still allowing that Euboians were not the only inhabitants and that an earlier native population continued to live on the site. Graham, 1982, 93, says that few, if any, Greeks lived in Al Mina or Tell Sûkâs.

4 Boardman 1980, 42; 48.

5 Riis 1970, 164–6.

6 Ibid. 129. See below, n. 239

7 R. Sealey, *A History of the Greek City States 700–338 BC*, Berkeley, CA, 1976, 177.

8 S. Bakhuizen, 'Greek steel', *World Archaeology* 9, 1977, 222.

9 Str. 5, 4, 9 C247: Ἐρετριεῖς ᾤκισαν καὶ Χαλκιδεῖς; D.H. 7, 3, 2: Κύμην τὴν ἐν Ὀπικοῖς Ἑλληνίδα πόλιν, ἣν Ἐρετριεῖς τε καὶ Χαλκιδεῖς ἔκτησαν. There are striking resemblances in burial customs between Kyme (Cumae), Pithekoussai and Lefkandi/Eretria: Ch. 4, p. 110; For Pithekoussai: Ridgway, 1992, Ch. 4; Eretria: Bérard 1970. Comparison of tombs at both sites: C. Albore-Livadie, 'Remarques sur un groupe de tombes à Cumès', *Contribution à l' Étude de la société et de la colonisation eubéennes. Cahiers du Centre Jean Bérard* II, Naples, 1975, esp. 53–7 (53): 'En effet, les tombes érétriennes mises au jour durant les campagnes de 1965 et 1966, près de la Porte Occidentale, présentent d'étroites similitudes avec les sept tombes contemporaines de Cumes (dernier quart du VIIe siècle-début du VIIe siècle av. J.C.). Le rituel funéraire est identique: le corps était incinéré avec une partie des bijoux et du mobilier funéraire loin du lieu de la sépulture, puis déposé dans un lébés de bronze qui était ensuite placé dans un réceptacle de tuf, etc.' (Though the Italian tombs are more richly furnished than their Eretrian counterparts).

The Euboian pottery could as well be of Eretrian origin as of anywhere else on the island. G. Buchner, 'Pithekoussai, oldest Greek colony in the west', *Expedition* 8 (Summer) 1966, 12; Klein 1972, 35; A. Blakeway, ''Demaratus' – a study in some aspects of the earliest Hellenization of Latium and Etruria', *JRS* 25, 1935, 142, n. 52 (mixed population at Kyme; Eretria, and perhaps Euboian Kyme, also involved).

10 Liv. 8, 22, 6; Th. 6, 4, 5; Aristotle ap. Str. 5, 4, 4 C243. This Aristoteles was probably the fourth-century historian of Khalkis (who wrote an Εὐβοϊκά no longer extant), not the philosopher who did indeed write (or supervise) a *Politeia of the Khalkideis*.

11 Bakhuizen (1977, 222) and Mazarakis-Ainian (1987, 21–2) believe that Khalkis alone was involved at Pithekoussai and Kyme. A. Woodhead, *The Greeks in the West*, London, 1962, 34, suggests that Eretria abandoned Pithekoussai/Kyme. Jeffery (1976, 64) doubts any Eretrian presence but that any Eretrians who may have been there were soon submerged: because 'only one author' mentions them!

12 Str. 5, 4, 7 C246; but see 14, 2, 10 C654. Stat. *Silv.* 1, 2, 260–3. Eunostidai: Wallace 1936a, 40. For the story of Eunostos at Tanagra: Ch. 2, p. 56 and nn. 260–1.

13 *Stasis*: T. Dunbabin, *The Western Greeks*, Chicago, 1979, 6.

14 Hippokles of Kyme; Megasthenes of Khalkis; the ἵππος-name may indicate Eretrian connections: F. Bechtel, 'Das Wort ΙΠΠΟΣ in den eretrischen Personennamen', *Hermes* 35, 1900, 326–31, notes its frequency in Eretrian prosopography. Wallace 1947, 128–30. But the distribution of these names is inconclusive for the location of Kyme as a deme in the Eretrias: Knoepfler 1997, 370: 'the 'unhippic' deme of Komaieis'.

15 A. Sampson, ''Αρχαιότητες καὶ Μνημεία Εὐβοίας', *AD* 31, 1976 [1984], B' 1, 155. Bakhuizen 1976, 15, n. 50; 17. Sampson, in 1981b, 60 (English summary), doubts its existence as a *polis* in historical times and believes that the name denotes a collection of villages (κῶμαι); for Koumai and Amarousi(on): Ch. 2, p. 54 and n. 244. See A. Thumb, *Handbook of the Modern Greek Vernacular*, Edinburgh, 1912, 8, §4. U. von Willamowitz (letter to S. Konstantinidis published in the last *Calendar* of the High-School Committee of Kyme, 1898, reprinted by B. Ganosis in *AEM* 1954, 131, cited in Sapouna-Sakellaraki 1984/86, 154; 160. Geyer 1903, 87.

16 Scyl. 58.

17 R. Hopper, *The Early Greeks*, New York, 1976, 3. Str. 10, 1, 15 C449 mentions a Euboia on Lemnos.

18 Sapouna -Sakellaraki 1984/86, 154.

19 Head 1911, 360; C. Kraay, *Archaic and Classical Coins*, New York, 1976, 57, pl. 15. See Head, *A Guide to the Principal Coins of the Greeks from circ. 700 BC to AD 270*, London, 1932, xlix. Wallace 1936a, 99: its coin-types (if correctly attributed) are very close to Eretrian types.

20 St. Byz. (sixth century AD) Κύμη. However, his sources are often much earlier. More significantly, neither Homer nor Strabo mentions Euboian Kyme, though Homer does mention other very small places in Euboia, e.g. Dion and Kerinthos.

21 A. Georgiadis, 'Οἱ ἐν τῇ 'Ερετριακῇ γνωστοὶ δῆμοι οἵδε εἰσιν', *AE* 1916, 50. See Knoepfler 1997, 370, 388; by inference, Bakhuizen 1976, 15, n. 50.

22 *OCD* s.v. 'Επιχώριος λόγος. Str. 13, 3, 6 C622.

23 Liv. 8, 22, 6. Pithekoussai and Aenaria are, in fact, the same.

24 Kondoleon 1963/65, 1–45. Kahil (1980, 527) supports him with reservations. She, Bérard and Knoepfler direct their criticism mainly at those sections dealing with the tribes of Eretria and the number of *probouloi* and *bouleutai*.

25 Arena 1988, 17–9.

26 By Khalkidians from Kyme. But note the name (= reaping hook) is a synonym for Drepane, the name of the Eretrian colony on Kerkyra; see below, n. 58.

27 Archaeological evidence: table in Graham 1982, 160–2.

28 Ch. 4, p. 95. Gwynn 1918, 88–123; J. Bérard, *L'expansion et la colonisation grecques jusqu'aux Guerres médiques*, Paris, 1960, 60–2; A. Graham, *Colony and Mother City in Ancient Greece*, Chicago, 1971, 5; Snodgrass 1980, 35.

29 Th. 1, 15, 1.
30 *Lg.* 740e.
31 *Op.* 376–7. Modern opinion dates Hesiod between the eighth and mid-/late seventh century: e.g. Powell 1997, 3–32 (eighth century); K. Dover (ed.) *Ancient Greek Literature*, Oxford, 1985, 177 (*c.*700); R. Janko, *Homer, Hesiod and the Hymns,* Cambridge, 1982 (mid-seventh); H. Evelyn-White, *Hesiod, the Homeric Hymns and Homerica* (Loeb) Cambridge, MA, 1926, xvi; xxv-xxvi, refers to 'the Hesiodic poems' and implies a plurality of authorship (*c.*830/820 for *Op.*, a century later for *Th.,* though he hesitates to reject the funeral games of Amphidamas of Khalkis which he dates *c.*705).
32 Snodgrass 1980, 36. R. Osborne, *Greece in the Making 1200–479 BC*, London, 1996, 70. Population estimate: Sakellariou 1971, 252; Knoepfler 1997, 372–3 (6,300–8,400 citizens in the fourth century).
33 Str. 10, 1, 8 C447.
34 1979, 406–11.
35 Str. 6, 1, 6 C257.
36 *Politeiai* 55.
37 Χαλκός, and *khalkeiai* χαλκεῖαι 'copper mines'; *khálkeiai* χάλκειαι 'copper work-shops'). Cf. Ch. 1, pp. 14–15.
38 Ch. 1, loc. cit. Bakhiuzen 1976, 48–57 (despite Str. 10, 1, 9 C447).
39 Dates: 706 (literary); 725/700 (archaeological).
40 'Αποικία/ἐμπόριον. Gorman, 2001, 59–64 and nn., offers a succinct overview of Greek colonisation.
41 For fuller information: the reports of Buchner, principal excavator of the settlement, listed in the bibliography in Ridgeway 1992, 159–60, with his own extensive *corpus*: 168–9. His Chapters 3–5 give a full description of the island and the excavations, arranged by site categories. Briefer surveys of the metallurgical settlement: Klein 1966, 34–9; Buchner 1966, 4–12.
42 1918, esp. 96.
43 1971, 219 and 221, n. 2.
44 Str. 5, 4, 9 C247.
45 Ridgeway 1992, 33.
46 Thgn. 392.
47 See Cook 1963, 113–4.
48 Ridgway 1992, 34.
49 Χρυσία is in fact the form found in all except one MS. Ridgway, 1992, 34, suggests that χρυσεῖα be translated as 'goldsmiths' workshops'; χρυσία as 'goldsmiths' products'. P. Mureddu, ΧΡΥΣΕΙΑ a Pithecussai', *PdelP* 27, 1972, 408, holds that χρυσεῖα is not limited just to the mine but includes workshops: 'non se limitivano a designare il luogo da cui veniva estratto il metallo, ma comprendevano tutto l'adiacente complesso di edifici in cui si svolgevano i primi lavori di purificazione del minerale estratto.' He gives the ancient sources in his n. 9; Also C. Gialanella, *Il Museo Archeologico di Pithecusae*, Naples, 1999, 15.
50 Buchner 1966, 12; Klein 1966, 37–9; Gialanella 1999, 15 (photo of ring).
51 See Ridgway 1992, 75, tables of finds.
52 Ridgway 1992, 55 and Fig. 9.
53 Jeffery 1961/90, 236. Early writing at Eretria: *SEG* 12, 1955, items 400a and b (sixth-century vase graffiti), 401; 15, 1958, item 561 (sixth-century graffito); 17, 1960, item 431; 22, 1982, items 858, 859 (seventh-century graffiti); 39, 1989, items 939 (735–25), 940, 941. Graffito: Eretria museum inv. no. V 3348; Kahil 1980, 528.
54 Ibid. 82.
55 Boardman 1952, 21, 26–7; Figs 20; 21e and pl. 5.
56 Plut. *Quaest.Graec.* 11. Also A.R. 4, 1175 and schol. b.

57 For example K. Beloch, *Griechische Geschichte* I², Stuttgart, 1913/26, 247; Halliday 1928, 64.

58 A.R. 4, 990 with schol.; Callim. ap. Plin. *HN* 4, 12, 8f.; the island's shape resembles a reaping hook, cf. Drapanon in Sicily. Hammond 1967, 418, n.1: suggests a pre-Greek origin of the name Kerkyra: Illyrian (mod. Albanian *kjark* = *curved*) but denies that the pre-colonial population was non-Greek.

59 See above, p. 142.

60 Kerkyra's strategic position on the route to Italy: see below, p. 151.

61 Str. 10, 1, 15 C449.

62 Makridie and Makris: schol. Ap. Rh. 4, 540–49a, 982–92g, 1138, 1175b. Plut. *Quaest.conviv.* 3, 9 (*Mor.* 657e); Plut. *peri ton en Plataiais Daidalon* fr. 3; Nonn. *D* 21, 193–4; schol. ad Hom. *Il.* 2, 535. The Argonaut legends about Makris were probably taken to Kerkyra from Euboia by Eretrians (Stoll in *RE:* by the Khalkidians). Hammond 1967, 415–6.

63 Th. 1, 25, 4. The personal name Phaiax occurs four times in the Eretrias; once at Khalkis (*LGPN* s.v.), indicating continuing popularity of legends associated with the Phaiakes. On the strength of the 'Phaiakian' tradition: Calligas 1971, 92.

64 Ch. 4, pp. 121–2. Kerkyra (as also Corinth and Eretria) had eight tribes: P. Calligas, 'An inscribed lead plaque from Kerkyra', *BSA* 66, 1971, 88.

65 Hdt. 3, 49. Lacuna supplemented by A. Godley: *Herodotus,* Books II/III (Loeb II) Cambridge, MA, 1982.

66 1, 13, 3.

67 Th. 1, 38, 1.

68 Messenians vs Khalkidians: Th. 6, 4, 6. Graham 1971, 17–9.

69 Rhodians vs. pre-Dorians from Crete, see Hdt. 7, 170: Minos came to Sicily pursuing Daidalos where he was killed; subsequently Cretans beseiged Akragas. For finds of early Cretan pottery at Gela: Boardman 1980, 178, n. 61; Graham 1971, 19, n. 4. Woodhead 1962, 29–30.

70 Paus. 5, 27, 9. The Eretrian base has been found and dated *c.* 500. Inscription quoted Ch. 8, n. 151; photos Ch. 8, pp. 260–1 and Figs 8.6, 8.7 and 8.8.

71 Wallace 1936a, 26.

72 D.S. 13, 48, 1; Th. 3, 70–85.

73 See above, p. 148 and n. 58.

74 A. Blakeway, 'Prolegomena to the study of Greek commerce with Italy, Sicily and France in the eighth and seventh centuries BC', *BSA* 33 1932/33, 205–6 and n. 4. *Pegasoi* were coins of Corinthian type with the mythical horse Pegasos on the obverse. Since Pegasos was part of Kerkyraian cult symbolism, as we shall see, was this deliberate rejection a political statement? On the other hand, there is an Eretrian coin (Head 1963, 362, Fig. 205; idem 1932, pl. 23, 1) with a cow (Io?) licking her hoof with a bird on her back, probably Zeus, who in this form guided Hermes to where Hera had tied Io to a tree. Io (eponymous heroine of the Ionian sea) gave birth to Paphos on Euboia at Boön Aule. Cf. schol. ad E. *Ph.* 208: 'ἔνιοι δὲ Ἰόνιον πόντον ἀκούουσι τὸ κατ' Εὔβοιαν πέλαγος τὸ περὶ τὴν Ἰόνιαν πόλιν Εὐβοίας, ἥν ἔκτισεν Ἴων ὁ Ξούθου βασιλεύσας ἔτη κζ.' Makris the daughter of Aristaios was, like Io, harried to Kerkyra from Euboia by Hera.

75 1976, 128.

76 W. Wallace, *The Euboian League and its Coinage*, Notes/Monographs 134, New York, 1956, 1.

77 B. Head, *A Catalogue of Coins in the British Museum (Central Greece)*, London, 1884, introd., lviii. Eustath. *ad Hom. Il. pert.* 278, 17–22; Str. 10, 1, 3 C445. On the Io myth: L. Mitchell, 'Euboean Io', paper sent to me by Greg Stanton in March 2001; to be published in *CQ* (22 pp.)

78 Spetsieri-Choremi 1991, 6–7 (map p. 7), 20 and Fig. 13: sculptures from the pediment of the temple of Artemis. Kalligas, 'Κέρκυρα, ἀποικισμὸς καὶ ἔπος', *ASAA* 60 (ns 44),

1982/84, 58: Eretrian colonisation; map/Fig. 1 shows the extent of the Eretrian colony on the harbour of Alkinoös. Idem, 'Τὸ ἐν Κερκύρᾳ ἱερὸν τῆς' Αχραίας Ἥρας', *AD* 24, 1969 A', 56–7. K. Rhomaios in Ἀφιέρωμα εἰς Γ. Χατζιδάχη, 184–92 suggests Κόρκυρα < Γόργυρα < Γοργώ as the derivation; cf. Evangelides 1962, 22, n. 42.

79 In Mycenaean times called *po-ti-ni-ja i-qe-ja* (Potniãi hiqq^{u}eiãi = ἱππείᾳ), appropriate epithet for the wife of Poseidon, mother of Pegasos: M. Ventris and J. Chadwick, *Documents in Mycenaean Greek,* 2nd edn , Cambridge, 1973, 483–4, Py312 = An1281. For Khrysaor: Calligas 1971, 90, n. 67.

80 Schol. ad A.R. 4, 1138.

81 *Il.* 1, 551; 14, 159; Bakkhylides, *Epinikon for Alexidamos of Metapontion*, 98–9.

82 The name means 'quail': schol. ad A.R. 1, 419 (link with Khalkis; cf. also Str. 10, 1, 15 C449). The name is associated with several places with Artemis cults. There was a very Archaic temple to Artemis on the islet. Smith 1856 II, 1063: 'Some remains of this are supposed to be still extant in the north-eastern corner of the modern city, where two columns, with a portion of their architrave, of the Doric order, are built into the walls of a private house. From the style and character of these it is evident that the edifice was one of very remote antiquity.' Cic. *Verr.* 2, 4, 53: 'quarum (sectors of the city) una est ea quam dixi Insula, quae duobus portibus cincta in utriusque portus ostium aditumque proiecta est; in qua domus est quae Hieronis regis fuit, qua praetores uti solent. In ea sunt aedes sacrae complures, sed duae quae longe ceteris antecellant, Dianae.'

83 Str. 14, 1, 20 C639.

84 Farnell *Cults* II 1896, 433 citing S. *Tr.* 212–14. Also *Roscher* s.v. Artemis, 578. See Jebb 1908, 99. The play is not, however, direct evidence of a cult in Euboia (as Farnell thought) but we may note the Euboian context of the play.

85 Str. 449; schol. ad A.R. I, 419; schol. ad *Il.* 9, 557. See Blakeway 1932/33, 205–6: 'I do not believe the modern suggestion that at Syracuse Corinth also supplanted a Euboic settlement.'

86 Pithekoussai, Orikos. Zagora was also very isolated on an arid peninsula (as was the settlement at Lefkandi). The exception might seem to be Kerkyra but the map of the site in Kalligas 1982/84 (Fig. 1) shows that the city was on a peninsula. Schol. ad A.R. 4, 1175b.

87 It is hard to know whether the frequent occurrence of toponyms in -ουσ(σ)α(ι) in Euboian contexts has any significance. Syrakoussai, Arethousa, Pithekoussai and Argous(s)a are associated with Lefkandi by D. Knoepfler: 'Un témoignage épigraphique méconnu sur Argous(s)a, ville de Thessalie', *Rev.phil.* 57 1983, 47–55.

88 Pi. *Nem.* 1, *strophe* 1; Str. 6, 2, 4 C270–1.

89 Chapter 2, p. 55–7.

90 On Eretrian Aulon: Knoepfler 1997, 375–6, n. 193. On Khalkidian Aulon: W. Hazlitt, *The Classical Gazeteer. A Dictionary of Ancient Sites*, London, 1834/1995, s.v. Aulon.

91 Beaumont 1936, 165. But Hammond 1967, 130, 366, 416, n. 2 (he calls Elephenor Elpenor, cf. below, n. 94), 419, 367. n. 2 doubts Euboian penetration of Illyria (Albania); cf. below nn. 95–6, 98. Wilkes, 1992, 110, rejects it.

92 Plin. *HN* 2, 204. Forms in *-os* are earlier than in *-on* (*-um* Plin.). Othronos: schol. Tzetzes ad Lyc. 1042. Identification: Beaumont 1936, 165, n. 4.

93 Scymn. 411–2.

94 Skylax 26–7; Paus. 5, 22, 2: Abantis; St. Byz. s.vv. Ἀβαντίς and Ὀρικός.

95 Evangelides 1962, 10, 24, 34, 75.

96 Callim. *Hymn IV: Delos* 288–90; Hdt. 4, 33; Paus. 1, 31, 2.

97 Beaumont, 1936, Appendix II: Hypothetical overland trade routes, 198–201; ibid. 'Corinth, Ambracia, Apollonia', *JHS 72,* 1952, 68; Grant 1987, 253.

98 On the Mediterranean trade routes from east to west: Ridgway 1992, *passim*, esp. Ch. 2.

99 D. Ridgway, 'Fra Oriente e Occidente: La Pithecusa degli Eubei', *Gli Eubei in Occidente. Atti del diciottesimo Convegno di Studi sulla Magna Grecia. Taranto, 8–12 Ottobre, 1978*, Taranto, 1979; idem 1992, 3–8.

100 S. Mazzarino, *Fra Oriente e Occidente. Richerche di storia greca arcaica*, Milan, 1947/89, especially 116–267 and nn; G. Tedeschi, 'La guerra lelantina e la cronologia eseodia', *Studi triestini di anchità in onore di Luigia Achillea Stella*, Trieste, 1975, especially 155, n. 39; J. Boardman and J. Hayes, *Excavations at Tocra 1963/65: The Archaic Deposits I*, London, 1966. Boardman 1952, 24–9; idem, 'Crete and Libya in the Archaic period', 2[ον] Διεθνὲς Κρητολογικὸν Συνέδριον. Φιλολογικὸς Σύλλογος. «Ὁ Χρσόστοομος» ἐν Χανίοις, I, Athens, 1967, 134–6.

101 St. Byz. s.v. Κύβος [ἢ Κυβώ]·πόλις Ἰώνων ἐν Λιβύῃ Φοινίκων. Ἑκαταῖος περιηγήσει αὐτῆς «καὶ λιμήν που ἄκρη καὶ Κυβώ» = *FGrH* 1F343. This quotation of Hekataios should undoubtedly be emended to «καὶ λιμὴν (Ἵπ)που Ἄκρη καὶ Κυβώ», since there was indeed a place in Tunisia called Hippou Akre (Hippo Diarrhytos): Skylax 110. The name Bizerta is said to preserve the ancient Hippo Diarrhytos: Dessau in *RE* VIII, 1721–2.

102 J. Talbert (ed), *Atlas of Classical History*, London, 1985, 97F4.

103 Gaius Julius Solinus (*c*. AD 200) 27, 7: 'equites Graeci condiderunt': he based his work on Plin. *HN* and Mela (*OCD* s.v.). *RE* s.v. Hippo (9).

104 Skylax 111.

105 Hom. *Od*. 7, 321.

106 Mazzarino 1947/89, 263.

107 Ibid. 117.

108 Ibid. 226.

109 Str. 7, fr. 20.

110 Th. 6, 7, 3.

111 Rhaikelos as an Eretrian colony on Megalo Karavouno: Ch. 6, pp. 188–9 and n. 43. Talbert, 1985, maps 16, 32, identifies Rhaikelos with Aineia. The sources: schol. (Tzetzes) ad Lyc. *Alex*. 1236–7; St. Byz. s.v. Ῥάκελος (*sic*); [Arist.] *Ath. Pol*. 15, 2. The location of Ainia/Rhaikelos: *ATL* fr. 36; S. Dow, 'Studies in the Athenian tribute lists', *TAPA* 72, 1941, 75. T. Figueira, *Athens and Aigina in the Age of Imperial Colonization*, Baltimore, MD, 1991, 134, n. 8: it is possible to construe συνῴκισε ([Ar.] *Ath. Pol*. 15, 2) as 'established a colony in conjunction with others'.

112 Stephanos frequently calls what were probably smaller places χῶρα (χωρίον) Ἐρετριέων, e.g. 'Okolon, *khorion* of the Eretrians'. Larger (?) places, e.g. Methone, are dignified as *poleis*.

113 'Notes on the Thracian 'Phoros'', *CP* 42, 1947, 89–90.

114 *History of Chalkis to 338 BC*, PhD thesis, University of Cincinnati, Cincinnati, OH, 1947a, 28.

115 ''Η Ἀποικιακὴ ἐξάπλωση τῆς Εὐβοίας', *AEM* 13, 1966, 28.

116 Potidaia was founded in the early sixth century (*CAH*[3] 162). Its late date, planted in the midst of Eretrian foundations reflects, as we shall see, changed contemporary pan-Hellenic political alignments.

117 Str. 10, 1, 8 C447.

118 Ch. 4, p. 96 and n. 51; p. 122 and n. 229; Ch. 9, pp. 270–3. Wallace 1936a, 34–5.

119 E. Harrison, 'Chalkidike I', *CQ* 6 1912, 93–103 and 165–78, supported by M. Zahrnt, *Die Herkunft der Chalkidier*, München, 1971, and Bakhuizen, 1976, 14–5. This view is repudiated by D. Bradeen, 'The Chalcidians in Thrace', *AJP* 73, 1952, 356–80. Most scholars, however, seem to have accepted that the name is indeed derived from the Euboian city's name. The arguments can be found in Vranopoulos 1987, 40–1.

120 N. Hammond, *A History of Macedonia* I: *Historical Geography and Prehistory*, Oxford, 1972, 426. Note his comment on the siting of Mende.

121 List based on Herodotos, Thucydides, Strabo, Pliny, etc., coinage types, inscriptions, e.g. *ATL* (Dikaia). Vranopoulos 1987, 38–9.

122 B. Meritt, *The Athenian Tribute Lists*, III, Princeton, NJ, 1950, 318.

123 Kraay 1976, 134, n. 4.

124 Hdt. 7, 109; Skylax 27; Str. 7, frr. 43[44]; 46 [47]; St. Byz. s.v. Δίκαια.

125 St. Byz. s.v. Σκάβαλα. The Σκαβλαῖο[ι] occur in *ATL* 454/3 in conjunction with Olynthos.

126 Neapolis: Str. 7 frr 32; 36; Ptol. 3, 13; Scymn. 685; Plin. *HN* 4, 11. P. Ure, *The Origin of Tyranny*, London, 1922/66, 37, identifies Skábala with Kavala.

127 Str. 7 fr. 36 quotes the proverb; Hdt. 9, 75 recounts the slaying of Leagros, the Athenian general, by the Edonioi fighting for the gold mines; Th. 1, 100; 102.

128 W. Leake, *Travels in Northern Greece*, III, Amsterdam, 1967, 180.

129 E. Borza, *In the Shadow of Olympus. The Emergence of Macedon*, Princeton, NJ, 1992, 2: stemma of Argead dynasty.

130 Th. 2, 99, 3.

131 N. Hammond, *The Macedonian State. The Origins, Institutions and History*, Oxford, 1992, 8.

132 *IG* I² 108+ (*SEG* 10, item 124) ll. 6–7: [ἐπ]αινέσαι τοῖς Νεοπ[ολίταις] ⟨τοῖς⟩ ||παρὰ Θάσον [πρõτον μ]ὲν [ὅτι ἀποικοι ὀντες Θασίον] (rasura) etc. The last phrase, ὅτι ἄποικοι ὄντες Θασίον, (and another in consequence in l. 8) was erased later. Why? B. Meritt and A. Andrewes, 'Athens and Neapolis', *BSA* 46, 1951, 203, say 'at the request of the Neopolitans', confirmed by ll. 58–9. Was this a factual error, because they were not in fact Thasian colonists but originally Eretrian? In the context of events of 411–6, within which the decree belongs, it would not have been diplomatic to claim Eretrian connections, since in 411 Eretria led the revolt of Euboia against Athens and was still allied to the Peloponnesians. Just then, some other loyalty formula was much to be preferred under the circumstances!

133 See the illustration of coin of Neapolis (Smith 1856 II, 411); and Eretrian issues (Head 1963, 360, Fig. 203, description, 361; his dates *c.* 600–511). It is not unlikely that Eretrian Artemid religious symbolism was taken with them to the north: Head 1963, 361.

134 St. Byz. s.v. Σκίαθος.

135 Hekataios ap. Paus. 4, 2, 3; St. Byz. s.v. Σκιάς; Skylax 58. Skyros lies off the northern coast of the Eretrias and is easily reached from Kyme.

136 Scymn. 579–86. A. Sampson, *'Η νῆσος Σκόπελος*, Athens, 1978.

137 Nikokrates, PMich. Inv. 4913. Papyrus fr. now in the University of Michigan. Text: C. Bonner 'A new historical fragment', *TAPA* 72, 1941, 26–35; M. Gigante, 'Frammenti di un'opera periegetica', *Ægyptus* 28, 1948, 3–16. Bonner, 33, suggests that the Nikokrates mentioned, col. 2, ll. 7–9, as the author of *Peri Boiotias* is the same one mentioned by St. Byz. s.v. Βοιωτία. Nikokrates: col. 3, ll. 4–6: [. . . 'Ερε | τριέων κτίσ[μα εἶναι τὸν 'Ω] | ρωπόν· ἀμφίσβητ[ήσιμος] | γὰρ ἐστιν Βοιωτοῖς ['Ερετρι] | εῦσιν 'Αθηναίοις [.

138 Knoepfler 1985b, 50; idem 1997, 358; von Wilamowitz 1886, 91–115; Wallace 1947, 115–46 denies that Oropos was an Eretrian colony on the grounds that rhotacism was not earlier than the fifth century (which is not true). Idem 1936a, 236–47. For rhotacism: Ch. 2, pp. 56–7.

139 1985b, 50.

140 Th. 8, 60, 1–3.; This anti-Athenian activity culminated later the same year in the treachery in the harbour of Eretria against the defeated Athenian ships and their sailors (8, 95).

141 Loc. cit.

142 'Ωρώπιοι. St. Byz. 'Ωρωπός, presumably the deme. But note his comment s.v. Κορόπη, which suggests that Eretrian Oropos might be Lefkandi.

143 Wallace 1947, 144: on readings (two very doubtful; one 'certain') in *IG* XII 9, 241, 84; 89; 90. Knoepfler 1997, 389 and n. 282 (accepts here that Euboian Oropos had prosopographical links with the mainland place).

144 Wallace 1947, n. 91.

145 *IG* XII 9, 744 doubtfully assigned on prosopographical grounds. I presume that Wallace means Vasiliko(n) when he writes Vasilike. There is also a stele for Oropokles (a very rare name) from Magoula (in District III): *IG* XII 9, 772. St. Byz. Κορόπη· Ὀρόπη γὰρ πόλις Εὐβοίας ὅπου Ἀπόλλωνος διασημότατον ἱερόν.

146 Th. 2, 23, 3: γῆν πειραϊκὴν καλουμένην; 3, 91, 3: πέραν γῆς, though both are considered to be corrupt. A. Gomme, *A Historical Commentary on Thucydides* II, Oxford, 1966, ad locc.; 81: πειραϊκὴν, a corruption of Γραϊκὴν. Cf. Eretrian deme περαιόθεν = Περαιεῖς. But Knoepfler, 1997, 388–9 and n. 278, places it on the Aegean coast (District V). On Graia: Fossey 1970, 11.

147 Nikokrates (see above n. 137). Gomme 1966, 81; Knoepfler 1985b, esp. 50; 52–5 for its vicissitudes during historical times. Ch. 6, pp. 191–2, for another theory as to when Eretria lost Oropos.

148 The Eretrian statesman Menedemos was obviously intriguing over it and wrote to Antigonos Gonatas defending himself on the matter: D.L. 2, 141 (= Euphantos *FGrH* III, 19F1).

149 Geyer 1903, 41–2. Str. 10, 1, 12 C448; but 5, 4, 9 C247.

150 Parker 1997 and a note to me.

151 Th. 1, 15, 3. There is disagreement over the interpretation of this passage: S. Lambert, 'A Thucydidean scholion on the Lelantine War', *JHS* 102, 1982, 216–20; *LSJ* s.v. πάλαι; διίστημι.

152 Paus. 7, 14, 7. A. Burn, 'The so-called 'Trade Leagues' in early Greek history and the Lelantine War', *JHS* 49, 1929, 23.

153 Arist. *Pol.* 1289b36–7.

154 *Agon* ('contest'). G. Herman, *Ritualized Friendship in the Greek City*, Cambridge, 1987; Brelich 1961; Mastrocinque 1980, 460–2. P. Gardner, 'A numismatic note on the Lelantine War', *CR* 34, 1920, 91: 'It was a kind of fighting match or ordeal by combat and did not permanently embitter relations between the two cities.'

155 Str. 10, 1, 12 C448.

156 Herman 1987. The best known example is that between Perikles the Alkmaionid and Arkhidamos II the Eurypontid king of Sparta: Th. 2, 13, 1

157 Hdt. 1, 82.

158 Ch. 4 n. 250, for 'house' in the sense of an aristocratic household, specifically in an Eretrian/Karystian conflict scenario.

159 Kondoleon 1963/65, 16: 'ἐκδήλωσιν τοῦ ἀγῶνος μεταξὺ κοῦ παλαιοῦ κόσμου τῶν ἐθνῶν και τοῦ νέου χόσμου τῆς πόλεως'.

160 Arkhilokhos, fr. 3.

161 F. Jacoby, 'The date of Archilochus', *CQ* 35, 1941, 107: *c.* 625 (low chronology), the poet as a young man; A. Blakeway, 'The date of Archilochus', in *Greek Poetry and Life; Essays Presented to Gilbert Murray on his 70th Birthday, 2 January, 1936*, Oxford 1936, 53: his birth 740/30.

162 Θώρακας ῥήξειν: Hom. *Il.* 2, 544.

163 Eust. *ad Hom. Il. pertin.*, 282, 15. Str. 10, 1, 13 C448–9;

164 Lorimer 1974, 114 and especially 121.

165 Συνέθεντο/συνθήκη. Str. 10, 1, 10 C448.

166 Plut. *Quaest.Graec.* 11.

167 *Cui bono?* As far as I know, no commentator on the convention has used this passage in Plutarch. Greenhalgh 1973, 91–2.

168 Th. 6, 22 represents Nikias in 415 saying Athens would have to send many archers and slingers to counter the Syracusan cavalry superiority.

169 Τηλέβολα is not used by Plutarch but rather compounds of σφενδονέω.

170 For example Arkhilokhos and Hybrias (mid-sixth century): D. Page, 'The song of Hybrias the Cretan', *PCPS* 191 (ns 11), 1965, 62–5. Lorimer 1974, 118.

171 Greenhalgh 1973, 90–3.

172 Lorimer, 1974, 118, has only an implicit reference (despite title of the paper); W. Donlan, 'Archilochus, Strabo and the Lelantine War', *TAPA* 101, 1970, 131–42; A. Podlecki, 'Three Greek soldier-poets: Archilochus, Alcaeus, Solon', *CW* 63/64, 1969, 73–81.

173 Kondoleon 1963/65, 16; M. Watson, *Class Struggles in Ancient Greece*, London, 1947, 52–3.

174 Fr. 6. Lorimer 1974, 111.

175 Tyranny at Eretria in the sixth century: Ch. 7.

176 Burn 1929, 23. Herman 1987, *passim*.

177 P. Cartledge, 'Hoplites and heroes; Sparta's contribution to the techniques of ancient warfare', *JHS* 97, 1977, 20–1; J. Salmon, 'Political hoplites?', *JHS* 97, 1977, 95.

178 R. Drews, 'The first tyrants in Greece', *Historia* 21, 1972, 140.

179 Cartledge 1977, 21.

180 Morris 1987: 202–5.

181 *Sitzb.d.Ak.Münch.* 1911, 40 (cited by Kondoleon 1963/65, 1, n. 2).

182 Plut. *Amat.* (*Mor.* 760f–761a). The passage is attributed to Aristotle. He is probably A. of Khalkis and not the philosopher.

183 Boardman 1957, 29.

184 Greenhalgh 1973, 91.

185 Bérard 1970, 28–9, 32, 50. Homeric echoes: 29.

186 Mele 1975, 21–2.

187 Though P. Vellacott's translation, *Euripides: Medea, Hecabe, Electra, Heracles*, Harmondsworth, 1963, 159, does not, since he does not render Δίρφυν . . . 'Αβαντίδα (so I give my own: ll. 185–8).

188 Ll. 157–64. Cf. Pandaros and Paris as contemptible or untrustworthy men who also were archers.

189 E. *Her.* 156–64. The issue of Euboia, Herakles and archery is present in S. *Tr.* 260–8 resulting in the sack of (Eretrian) Oikhalia. Schol. ad Hom. *Il.* 2, 543: ἦν δὲ παρ' αὐτοῖς αἰσχρὸν τὸ τοξεύειν; Eust. δηλοῖμεν ἡ ἱστορία εἰποῦσα αἰσχρὸν εἶναι παρ' αὐτοῖς τὸ τόξεύειν continues this theme, though nowhere does Homer himself say that it was disgraceful for Euboians to use bows and arrows. Both come from the same unknown source (influenced by Euripides, whose play would have been well known). In any case, the aristocracy early regarded Homer's epics as their own and their interpretation will have impressed itself on the public perception of them. However, there were Herakleia in both Eretria: *IG* XII 9, 234, 17–18; 257; 272 (fifth century) and Khalkis: 952 (late second).

190 Thgn. 783–4; 885–94.

191 Th. 1, 13, 4 records 'the earliest naval battle'.

192 Jeffery 1976, 68.

193 Hom. *Il.* 2, 211–82.

194 P. Oliva, *The Birth of Greek Civilization*, London, 1981, 114.

195 In considering alliances in the Lelantine War and Th. 1, 15, 3, we must note (without agreeing) that Schol. thinks that there were no alliances: Lambert 1982, 216–20.

196 Kondoleon, 1963/65, 2: 'κατὰ τὸ τέλος τῆς γεωμετρικῆς ἐποχῆς εἶχον τὴν εὐκαιρίαν . . . νὰ θεωρήσω δὲ ταύτην (separation into alliances) . . . οὐχὶ ὡς μίαν προσκαίρον . . . διάστασιν . . . ἀλλ' ὡς τὴν ἔκφρασιν βαθντέρων διαφορῶν μεταξὺ δὺο παρατάξεων ἑκατέρας τῶν ὁποίων τὰ μέλη ἡνώνοντο διὰ μακροχρονίων δεσμῶν οἵτινες δὲν μᾶς εἶναι πάντοτε ἀμέσως φανερά'; N. Kondoleon, 'Νέαι 'Επιγραφαὶ περὶ 'Αρχιλόχου ἐκ Πάρου', *AE* 1952/54, 83–4; idem ,'Archilochos und Paros', *Entretiens Hardt* X: 'Archiloque', 1963, Genève, 1963.

197 J. Bury and R. Meiggs, *A History of Greece*, London, 1981, 107.
198 Starr 1962, 347.
199 J. Hasebroek, *Trade and Politics in Ancient Greece* (translation of *Staat und Handel im alten Griechenland*), London, 1933, 70–1.
200 Str. 8, 6, 20 C378. L. Siegel, *Corinthian Trade in the Ninth through Sixth Centuries BC*, PhD thesis, Yale University, New Haven, CT, 1978.
201 Though the term is much questioned. Burn 1929, 14.
202 J. Hurwit, *The Art and Culture of Early Greece, 1100–480 BC*, Ithaca, NY, 1985, 81–2.
203 Bradeen 1947b, 223; Bengtson 1988, 30.
204 Forrest 1957, 161. The dominant *polis* in each group was not necessarily either Eretria or Khalkis, but Eretria at times could claim hegemonial status in the central Greek/Aegean area.
205 Hdt. 1, 18.
206 Ch. 7, pp. 218–19; Ch. 8, pp. 260–2: the rise of the tyrant Antileon in Khalkis and its aftermath.
207 See above, n. 196.
208 Description of himself from frr. 1, 2, 6, 14, etc.; cf. Hybrias, the Cretan mercenary, sixth(?) century.
209 Hdt. 5, 28–34.
210 Polyain. 8, 36; Plut. *Mul.virt.* (*Mor.* 254f); Parth. *Myth.* 9.
211 *CAH* III^3, 162 (table).
212 Idem.; Dunbabin 1979, 8.
213 Hdt. 5, 28–34. Decree of Paros, *IG* XI 4, 1065+ *IG* XII 5, i, 128 (ed. pr. E. Hicks, 'The collection of ancient marbles at Leeds', *JHS* 11, 1890, 260–4), honouring Eretrian arbitrators who find in favour of Paros against Naxos (post 194). For later Eretrian/Milesian friendship: *IG* XII 9, Test. et Not. 162–3. For seventh-century trade ties between Paros and Eretria: Kondoleon 1952/54, 59.
214 The Eretrian *heroön*: see above, pp. 161, 167. Texts bearing on this event: Hes.*Op.* 650–62; Plut. *Coviv.septem sap.* (*Mor.* 153f–154a); idem *de Hes. op.* (*Mor.* fr. 84) on *Op.* ll. 651–62; idem *Quaest.conviv.* 6 (*Mor.* 674f–675a); and the anon. (Hadrianic period) *Cert.Hom.Hes.* On the nature of the *agones:* Bérard 1970, 149.
215 Hes. *Op.* 38–9.
216 See above, n. 31.
217 Evelyn-White 1926, intro. xvi: Note his assumptions: (1) Khalkis won the war; (2) the war was early; Plut. fr. 84 and *Mor.* 674f–675a. S. Benton, 'The evolution of the Tripod-Lebes', *BSA* 35, 1934/35, 114, n. 1: 'the ἆθλα then are a local festival (not connected with the Lelantine War).' Burn 1929, 33: Amphidamas a local hero, whose son was killed at Opous (*Il.* 23, 87).
218 *Amat.* (*Mor.* 761a).
219 Plut. *de malign.Hdt.* (*Mor.* 861b) 24.
220 *Mor.* fr. 84 (on Hes. *Op.* 651–3), commenting on an earlier work in turn quoted in Proklos' *Khrestomatheia*, then later preserved in Photios *Bibliotheke*. The tradition thus comes to us second or third or fourth hand.
221 M. West, *Hesiod. Theogony*, Oxford, 1966/97, 43. Arist. *Pol.* 1289b36–9.
222 Greenhalgh 1973, 67 (Fig. 4).
223 Ναυσικλείτης: [Hom.] *ad AP* 219. Battle scenes: Ch. 3, p. 77, nn. 40, 42–3; p. 82, Fig. 3.5.
224 Th. 1, 13, 3.
225 Plut. *Quaest.Graec.* 30.
226 Kondoleon 1963/65, 23 n. 4 and 24 n. 1: 'Θετικὰς μαρτυρίας ὅτι οἱ Χαλκιδεῖς εἶχον ναυτικὸν δὲν ἔχομεν, ἀντιθέτως πρὸς τὰς βεβαιώσεις τῶν σημερινῶν ἐρευνητῶν'.
227 Boardman 1980, 38–9; Popham *et al.* 1980b; M. Popham; H. Hatcher; A. Pollard, 'Al-Mina and Euboea', *BSA* 75, 1980, 151–60; for Rhodes, A. Johnston, 'Rhodian readings', *BSA* 70, 1975, 167.

228 Boardman 1980, 46–7; quotation: 48.
229 War: Ch. 3, pp. 74–6, 82, 84–7. Archaeological evidence: Ch. 4, pp. 91–5. *Heroön*: Ch. 4, pp. 109–100; Bérard 1970, 65.
230 Ibid. 62, 65
231 Walls: Ch. 4, pp. 101–4. Synchronism with destruction of Lefkandi; Ch. 4, pp. 101–4. Popham *et al.* 1980b, 369: 'Then, around 700 BC, Xeropolis was sacked and virtually abandoned thereafter.'; Coldstream 1977, 196, 330.
232 Boardman 1957, 28. But cf. below p. 168.
233 Ibid. 1.
234 Hdt. 5, 99.
235 *IG* XII 9, Test. et Not. 162–3. For Miletos in the sixth century: Ch. 9 *passim*; Gorman 2000, Chs 3–4.
236 R. Burrows and P. Ure, 'Excavations at Rhitsona in Boeotia', *JHS* 29, 1909, 332–4; P. Ure/R. Burrows, 'Excavations at Rhitsona', *BSA* 14, 1907/08, 232–4.
237 H. Prinz, 'Funde aus Naukratis', *Klio Biehefi* 7, 1908, 121.
238 Boardman, 1957, 28.
239 Wine was rarely transported in pottery but in skins (allows for squeezing out of air before sealing). The use of pottery for transport is very speculative, e.g. oil flasks can be, and often were, used for other purposes. Thus, if Khalkis were producing wine from 'vine-rich Lelanton', pottery would not necessarily reveal this. But Eretria, with a much greater area of marginal land, would have tended to produce oil, which was widely transported in pots, and this might explain its greater ceramic output. Recent debate about trade in decorated pottery: J. Boardman, 'Trade in Greek decorated pottery', *OJA* 7, 1988, 27–33 (had a decided intrinsic trading value); reply by D. Gill, 'Trade in Greek decorated pottery: some corrections', *OJA* 8, 1989, 369–70 (largely ballast); Boardman, 'The trade figures', *OJA* 8, 1989, 371–3 (deals with disputed value figures raised by Gill). Gill is preparing a further reply (non vidi): 'Pots and trade: spacefillers or *objets d'art?*' If Boardman is correct, then Eretrian ceramic was probably not good enough to justify the effort to transport it, and its scarcity outside Euboia is probably thereby explained. See D. Gill, 'Positivism, pots and long-distance trade', in Morris, I. (ed.), *Classical Greece. Ancient Histories and Modern Archaeologies*, Cambridge, 1994, 99–107.
240 Port: Ch. 4, p. 100; agora: Ch. 4, p.105.
241 Arkhemakhos ap. Str. 10, 3, 6 C465.
242 *Amat.* (*Mor.* 760e–761b); see above and below nn. 179 and 182, 187 and 218 (quote), 193–4 (quote) and 252–3. For Kleomakhos and Thessalian cavalry intervention: Greenhalgh 1973, 92.
243 Plut. *Amat.* (*Mor.* 760e–761b): the youth was from Thracian Khalkidike: F. Buffière, *L'Éros adolescente; la pédérastie dans la Grèce antique,* Paris, 1980, 103–5. It is chronologically just possible that Khalkis got aid from its colonies in that area.
244 Buck 1928/65, 195.
245 Lorimer 1947, 118.
246 A. Jardé, *The Formation of the Greek People*, London, 1926, 86.
247 Heracl. Pont ap. Ath. *Deipn.* 624c–e.
248 J. Fontenrose, *The Delphic Oracle; its Responses and Operations, with a Catalogue of Responses*, Berkeley, CA, 1981, 276–8.
249 Loc. cit.; he dates it *c.* 700.
250 Salmon 1977, 93.
251 R. Tomlinson, *Argos and the Argolid. From the End of the Bronze Age to the Roman Occupation*, London, 1972, 79–86: the seventh century.
252 Plut. *Amat.* (*Mor.* 760f).
253 Plut. *Amat.* (*Mor.* 761a). For eponymous hero cults generally: L. Farnell, *Greek Hero Cults*, Oxford, 1921 (no mention of Kleomakhos); Bérard 1970, *passim* Bérard 1972, 219–27.

254 Her victory at Kerissos was before 571: Plut. *Cam.* 19: places the battle 'more than 200 years before Leuktra.' (371) Plutarch calls the place Geraistos which is, of course, in Euboia; the error is probably scribal. Cf. Paus. 9, 14, 3–4.

255 Birth-dates for Peisistratos' sons are controversial: see J. Davies, *Athenian Propertied Families*, Oxford, 1971, 446–50. Thessalos was the youngest legitimate brother (γνήσιος ἀδελφός) of Hippias and Hipparkhos: Davies gives 570 as birth year of Hippias, so that Thessalos' must have been rather later (νεώτερος πολύ [Arist.] *Ath. pol.* 18, 2). For the Peisistratid alliance with Thessaly: Hdt. 5, 63; W. How and J. Wells, *A Commentary on Herodotus*, Oxford, 1975, II, 30; 55–6.

256 On the decline of Khalkis: Bérard 1970, 68, n. 31; Boardman, 1957, 28.

257 For example The Samian *Geomoroi* and the *Hippobotai* of Khalkis; the tyrants of Athens, Naxos, Corinth, Miletos and Eretria, or commercial oligarchies at Eretria and Miletos.

258 Hdt. 5, 99. The comment also says something about Eretrian attitudes towards Athens at the time: Ch. 9, p. 275 (for discussion of ἀγόμενοι), pp. 278–9; Ch. 10, pp. 288–9.

6

ERETRIA

Emergent 'great power' of the mid-sixth century

The year 556 is an important year in the history of Eretria, and of Archaic Greece in general: at Sparta, Kheilon was eponymous ephor;[1] at Sikyon, the Orthagorid dynasty of tyrants came to an end;[2] the poet Simonides was born on the island of Keos;[3] and finally, Peisistratos suffered his second exile from Attica and retired to Eretria with his sons and followers,[4] thereby establishing for us the second reasonably 'secure' date in Eretrian history. 'Secure' in this case depends, of course, on the certainty of dating Peisistratos' second exile, which is not secure at all. However, 556 is not likely to be far wrong.[5] All four events impinge on the history of Eretria to a greater or lesser degree, so this date is a convenient point to begin the study of historical Eretria and its place within the wider Hellenic *oikumene* referred to by Thucydides in his vague remark about the Lelantine War, which hints at the great importance of the city, 'some time ago'.[6]

Eretria had been a significant state even in the seventh century. During the sixth it would acquire greater, pan-Hellenic, importance and the choice by Peisistratos to retire there was for good and specific historical, political and strategic reasons rather than simply because of its geographic proximity to his homeland at Brauron in eastern Attica. If the last were all, why not have chosen Khalkis with its 'command' of the Euripos and easy access from the mainland? I shall be arguing that the role of Eretria in Hellenic affairs from the mid-sixth century down to 490 was far more important than is generally credited by modern historians. Indeed, I shall claim for the city hegemonic status, not only over Euboia but over a wider area including the neighbouring coastal areas of Boiotia and Attica, as well as continued rule over its island empire, and that it exercised political influence via its colonial foundations in Macedonia and Thrace and, through its alliance network, in Asia Minor and the East. I shall also show that its power was recognised generally throughout Greece at the time and that it was preserved in later memory in what we may call the alternative tradition[7] and even, often obscurely, in the writings of surviving historians, all of whom were influenced by the fifth century *aura athénienne*. This far-flung influence was established and maintained by means of its naval and commercial strength. Only a faint echo of this early glory has been allowed to come down to the present and it has been largely unheard or, worse, ignored. Peisistratos himself, however, did not under-rate the city's importance, and upon his expulsion from Athens, he hastened forthwith to Eretria where he believed he might expect meaningful support both from its government and through the city's powerful allies and trading network. Eretria, in turn, willingly received him, his family and his followers for its own political reasons. This would not be its last direct involvement in the internal affairs of Athens. The welcome of Peisistratos by the so-called regime of the *Hippeis* nevertheless soon proved costly and subsequent relations between the two cities did not always remain friendly.

Well before 556, economic and social tensions had been increasing in Attica and elsewhere in Greece, including Euboia. Solon was installed as leader at Athens with a mandate to reform the laws. His official title was *arkhon* and he was also described as *dialaktes* (mediator) and *nomothetes* (framer of laws), but the title *aisymnetes* (conciliator), used to describe him by modern historians, was not, apparently, given to him, but it is a designation appropriate for his time and it was the office held by Pittakos of Mitylene.[8] The traditional date for his arkhonship is 594/3, though Miller has advanced arguments bringing his reforms down to 573/2,[9] but even so late a dating is not late enough to accommodate his coinage reforms, which have therefore been attributed by recent numismatists to Peisistratos.[10] Solon's appointment indicates that Athens was beginning to face up to its economic and social problems. The choice of Solon is significant, for his interests crossed the divide between those of the old Hippobotic/Eupatrid families,[11] with their pastoral and agricultural interests, and the new, rising class of traders and artisans, for he, though of Eupatrid background, had also engaged in trade, while his reforms, or those subsumed under his name, show that he clearly perceived that a prosperous future for Athens would in large part be dependent on the development of an expanding artisan and commercial class.[12]

Peisistratos had a close personal association with Solon in his youth. He is said to have been Solon's *eromenos*[13] so that he must have been born *c.* 605/600,[14] making him about twenty years younger. The relationship may have resulted in his adoption of political attitudes quite at variance with his Eupatrid peers. His career exemplified a very different conception of politics from that of both Solon and the aristocrats. He always showed particular interest in the welfare of the productive classes, and this concern may have been at least partly a legacy from the older man.[15] On the other hand, his career shows that he had little patience with Solon's conciliatory approach to socio-economic problems and he certainly did not share the older man's repugnance for tyranny. Peisistratos' family claimed descent from the royal house of Mycenaean Pylos.[16] Thus, although Solon's Eupatrid ancestry might be questioned by some, Peisistratos was a true son of the Attic aristocracy.[17] His rural and aristocratic background would have made it clear to him that Solon's hope for an Attic *concordia ordinum* was in reality futile and that change in the last resort would have to come through the use of force, as had happened at Eretria between *c.* 825 and *c.* 700 as a result of military disasters and the loss of the Lelantine Plain. Whether or not he had long-standing family connections with Eretria, as did several Attic noble families, including the Gephyraioi and the Alkmaionidai,[18] he would certainly have been well aware of Euboian affairs. An astute politician, he would not have retired there in ignorance of the political state of play between and within the *poleis* of the island. Indeed, the progress, if that is the right word, of events in Khalkis during the last half of the sixth century[19] suggests that the political backgrounds in Attica and Khalkis were similar. Perhaps Peisistratos adopted the model of tyranny because, unlike Solon, he could see, thanks to his background and connections, and as events in Khalkis showed, that the land holders would never finally give up control of the *polis* except under duress. Thus, both his background and political interests would have predisposed him towards the commercial oligarchs at Eretria rather than the outdated reactionaries of Khalkis, who had more in common with his political enemies.

Brauron,[20] his home town, was near Prasiai.

> Before the capture of Salamis, some grain was no doubt brought to the Attic plain around Athens by ships willing to run the gauntlet of Megarian patrols. [However] A much safer port of entry than Phaleron was the excellent harbour of Prasiai in east Attica. It may be conjectured that the most important of the trade routes of Attica before the capture of Salamis was that which ran from Thessaly and Macedonia south to Euboea and thence along the friendly Euboean coast to Marathon and the harbours of east Attica.[21]

A glance at a physical map shows that it was the natural port for the produce of the Mesogeia, the grain bowl of Attica. It lies parallel with the Petaliai Islands.[22] The strategic and economic importance of these islands in defining the southern boundary, established by the Eretrians themselves, of the area of the Straits of Euboia, over which they claimed direct control, is discussed later in this chapter.[23] Brauron was, moreover, the site of a very ancient cult of Artemis Iphigeneia, which had a close relationship to that of Artemis Amarysia.[24] Cult centres of Artemis existed, as we have seen, right along the eastern and northern coasts of Attica and Boiotia, suggesting ancient cultural ties between the Eretrias and the mainland coast opposite. Peisistratos thus came from an area that for Athens at the time was both one of the most important commercially, the trade lines of which were directly subject to Eretrian economic control, and one that had age-old religious, racial and linguistic links with Euboia, especially the Eretrias.

Peisistratos' support came from the Attic commercial[25] and thetic classes,[26] who had not really benefited from Solon's reforms:

> To suppose that [Solon] gave to the helpless serfs everything they asked

> for and made no concessions whatever to the all-powerful nobles passes all belief. A compromise that would fit the situation and square with probability was the cancellation of the arrears of debt and the freeing of the serf in return for the recognition by the latter that he had no further claim on his master's estate.

In other words, the land lost by the indebted peasant remained firmly within the landowner's grasp. 'This compromise would meet the worst grievances of the masses – their slavery – without robbing the nobles of anything valuable. A policy of pleasing the poor without robbing the rich usually succeeds in annoying both parties, and so it was with Solon.'[27] No doubt similar socio-economic conditions were being experienced in many other *poleis*, or soon would be, as the experience of Khalkis and Eretria indicates. The delay of crisis conditions at Khalkis can perhaps be explained by the relatively greater fertility of the land there and at Eretria by a more pragmatic ruling class and wider prosperity with a greater basis in commerce. Forrest argues that the Athenian economy between 594 and 560 had undergone 'thirty years of boom' and that this prosperity was the work of a substantial commercial class, but that they were only rewarded politically once Peisistratos was firmly in power: 'Commonsense would suggest some form of link' between the rise of Peisistratos and this economic expansion.[28] Holliday thinks not.[29] He assembles evidence for the economic weakness of Athens at this time and states particularly that it was not a sea power: 'it seems pretty certain that Athenian goods were carried to a large extent in foreign bottoms.'[30] And from Prasiai on the south Euboian Gulf, whose ships would these be? It was in fact not until the early fifth century that Themistokles turned the Athenians decisively towards the sea by further developing the Peiraieus harbour and building a navy. Holliday does, however, note an increase in output from Attic pottery kilns after *c.* 600 as evidence of trading,[31] but pottery output alone does not, I think, provide conclusive evidence of increased interest in matters commercial or naval, despite even the increasing use of the ship motif in vase decoration. Kirk observes, albeit of an earlier period, that the superiority of Attic vase painters in representing ships does not 'necessarily entail . . . the surprising consequence of a greater Athenian interest in naval affairs than Corinthian, for example, or Euboean, for artistic fashion need not march in step with progress in other fields.'[32] It is absolutely crucial for an understanding of the roles of Athens and Eretria in the late sixth century to remember the fact of Athenian naval weakness: 'The Athenian-Khalkidian struggle [of 506] took place on land, and at that period the Athenians did not have a fleet.'[33] Later, Corinth supplied Athens with twenty hulls (at the purely nominal price of five *drakhmai* each) to build up a naval force against their joint enemy, Aigina, in the so-called *akeryktos polemos* (undeclared war) and this took place some time after 506.[34]

Forrest and Holliday agree that Peisistratos had the support of the merchant class, despite having opposing views as to why that support was forthcoming.

Resolution of these differences of opinion are important for Attic history but less so here. However, both Peisistratos and Solon before him, involved as they were with the Attic merchant class, must have had links with the ruling merchant oligarchy at Eretria. The long-established involvement of Eretria in Aegean and Western trade and in the commerce of central Greece makes it certain that many merchants in Athens would have had commercial ties with the group of Eretrians who controlled the government there. Eretria's long-established involvement in shipping and its control over the trade route via the Straits of Euboia to the north, make Eretrian ships the obvious answer to the question in whose vessels Attic exports were carried. Thus, when Peisistratos fled to Eretria in 556, he went with more than good hopes: 'By connections with the Eretrian nobility, the tyrant returned to Athens for a second time.'[35] Holliday is however partly right to say that Peisistratos' support base was fundamentally weak, as is evidenced by his failure for so long to hold his position securely.[36] But permanent success followed his stay in Eretria, where he was able to observe the strengths and weaknesses of the merchant class that had wielded power in government there for so long.[37]

The capture of Salamis by Solon, the defeat of Megara by Peisistratos, and the subsequent expansion of Phaleron to become the main commercial port of Athens led later to a great expansion of Athenian trade, because it freed Athens itself from the threat of blockade by Megara. Nevertheless, Holliday rightly stresses that for a small state such as Megara, even if it had a stronger navy than that of Athens, the enforcement of any lengthy blockade in the sixth century would have been well nigh impossible. Megara and its fleet may therefore have been less of a factor in the changed pattern of Athenian trade routes than that it was a deliberate policy choice by Peisistratos, who seems to have developed into a ruler who saw clearly the 'national interest', placing it above his own local background and ties and any obligations he may have had to foreign supporters such as the Eretrian oligarchs. Any shift of trade from Prasiai to Phaleron is quite sufficient in itself to explain the change in the attitude of the Eretrians towards Athens, from one of extreme cordiality to one that may at best be described as frosty, which we perceive soon after the return of Peisistratos from exile there in 546. This hostility endured until about 508/7, when a radical shift in the political balance brought the two *poleis* together again, for the transfer of the bulk of Athenian trade from the east-coast ports to Phaleron must have had a significantly adverse effect on Eretrian commerce and shipping.

Be that as it may, in 556 Peisistratos both expected and received a warm reception in Eretria, something that scholars seem to have found surprising,[38] although it is clear enough why he would have believed that he would be welcome there. For their part, the Eretrians must have thought that a client ruler at Athens from 'their' east coast would favour their commercial aims and be a useful ally against Khalkis. Scholarly surprise no doubt springs from supposed differences in aims and outlook between the populist tyrant and the traditionalist Eretrian *Politeia of the Hippeis*, so-called, but, as I have already argued at length,[39] this designation masks a very different government from that of Khalkis and rather illustrates the desire of Greek regimes of all sorts, but especially oligarchies, that their constitution reflect the usually imaginary *patrios politeia* (ancestral constitution). In fact, it represented the same merchant class that at Athens was still struggling for political and social recognition. These would no doubt have informed their Eretrian counterparts that Peisistratos was 'their man', and as a result, he got encouragement and active backing from the government of the *Hippeis*. He made good use of it.

Herodotos says that when he heard that the Alkmaionidai were plotting against him: '[Peisistratos] went by himself right away from the country and came to Eretria, and there he took counsel with his sons.' The *Ath. pol.* on the other hand states that:

> first he co-settled (*sunoikise*) a place near the Thermaic Gulf which is called Rhaikelos; from there he went to the area around Pangaion whence he collected money and hired soldiers. Coming again to Eretria in the eleventh year, he began his attempt to recover his rule by force. He was supported in this by a number of people, above all others the Thebans and Lygdamis of Naxos and also the *Hippeis* who held power in Eretria.[40]

Presumably his sons had fled separately, having previously agreed to meet him again at Eretria. Whether Peisistratos remained in Eretria itself for the decade of his second exile or even went straight there upon fleeing from Attic soil are debated questions; I see no reason to disagree with Herodotos.[41] *Ath. pol.* omits any reference to him going first to Eretria and takes him straight to the northern Aegean, but Eretria had long-established connections in the region, as did its ally Miletos, and there were several Eretrian colonies and *emporia* in the precise area to which he eventually went. I believe that Peisistratos would have first visited his contacts within the governing class at Eretria, both as a matter of diplomatic courtesy and to have his way in the north smoothed in advance. To have arrived suddenly with his (presumably armed) retinue in 'Eretrian places', to use a phrase of Stephanos Byzantios to describe Eretrian establishments in the north, [42] within Eretria's patch, would surely have unnecessarily alarmed his Eretrian friends as to his real intentions. It has been argued that when he went north it was in fact a joint Peisistratid–Eretrian colonial expedition that he led to Rhaikelos.[43]

While he was there, Peisistratos used his Eretrian connections to exploit the mineral wealth of the Pangaion region. However, Mt Pangaion is not particularly close to Rhaikelos/Aineia, so the wealth of the mines, if it had to be taken first to Rhaikelos, would have had to make a potentially dangerous journey by sea of at least 300 km around the Khalkidike peninsulas, some with their – probably hostile – Khalkidian colonies, not to mention their frequent storms, or else endure a cumbersome and no less dangerous journey inland,[44] if indeed such a journey were possible at that early period, in a roadless region inhabited by barbarian tribes and Khalkidian settlers. Peisistratos' activities in the north have often been treated rather loosely. It is implied that: (1) he went to Rhaikelos; and (2) he exploited the Pangaion mines, but there is never any attempt to show that the two places are not close together, and so one is generally left with the impression that the mines were somehow within a *sogenannt* northern fiefdom of Peisistratos. This is not so and it is never mentioned that Rhaikelos is not at all suitably located for exploitation of the resources of Pangaion. The *Ath. pol.,* however, states that Peisistratos settled first at Rhaikelos and that he subsequently proceeded to the Pangaion area, where he enriched himself and hired soldiers; he then went (back?) to Eretria. Herodotos alludes to revenues from Peisistratos' properties on the Strymon but makes no mention at all of Rhaikelos, which is not by any means to be located near that river. From Rhaikelos, if he indeed settled there, would have come timber for shipbuilding purposes from the nearby inland forests via the River Axios or from nearby Mt Khortiatis, even today thickly timbered. However, there is no evidence that Peisistratos built ships to create a fleet at this time. But, as I have pointed out, Euboia is deficient in shipbuilding timbers so that the Eretrians themselves may well have been interested. Pangaion itself is also a potential source of timber. But Eretria already had a commercial station at Skabala,[45] which was not very far from the Strymon, for whose identification with modern Kavala I have already argued. Whatever the truth concerning Peisistratos' movements and residences while in the north, considerable logistical problems were involved in his exploitation of the natural wealth of the region. Eretrian participation in, and approval of, his activities would however solve these problems.[46] Why would Peisistratos, if he were in the north for much of his ten-year exile, have risked his precious bullion cargoes on a dangerous route to an intermediate location at Rhaikelos/Aineia, only to have then to organise the onward shipment of an accumulated mass of material, together with his mercenary recruits, to Eretria, his final base, from which all our authorities agree that his final descent on Attica was made? It is extremely unlikely that he, an exile and an Athenian, had any ships of his own, so we must assume that he relied on foreign vessels. The obvious choice, and it is unlikely he would have had a choice, was Eretrian ships. And, if this were indeed so, why would he not have shipped his Pangaion gains directly to Eretria from the nearby Skábala? It is inconceivable that he did not have agents at Eretria organising his affairs. In fact, it is probable that at least one of his sons, Hippias perhaps, remained there acting as marshal of his followers and resources. And the argument might be made that Peisistratos himself stayed in Eretria for the whole or most of the ten years of his exile.[47]

Among the allies involved in the push to restore Peisistratos were significant land powers, whose acquiescence, if not their direct assistance, would be important for his long-term success. Thebes, building up its federal structure in Boiotia,[48] the territory of which lay along the northern border of Attica, and

Thessaly, the horsemen of which would remain faithful allies of the Peisistratidai to the very end of their rule. In the Aegean, Lygdamis of Naxos, a man of great wealth, aspired to tyranny in his homeland. There were also Argos, not yet utterly paralysed as it would be after Sepeia (495) and Corinth, the friendship of which was significant, though at this stage it remained largely passive.[49] Under Periandros, Corinth founded Potidaia between 625–585, a site so important that later, Athens would sacrifice other crucial interests in its struggle to assert control over it. It straddles the isthmus of Pallene, separating the foundation 'of Peisistratos' from the Eretrian colonies on Pallene. Therefore, the agreement of the Corinthians, or at least the absence of hostility, would be important if he were to reap any substantial gain from the establishment of the town. Alliance with Argos, and indirectly perhaps Corinth, was confirmed by Peisistratos' marriage to the Argive Timonassa, daughter of Gorgilos and former wife of Arkhinos of Ambrakia,[50] Kypselid heir and grandson of Periandros.[51] Perhaps this political alliance to Timonassa might have brought with it Kypselid political ideas. For an example of a woman significantly influencing her husband's socio-economic thinking in an Ancient Greek context, one may consider that of Kleomenes III of Sparta (king 235–22), who came under the influence of his wife Agiatis, who imbued him with the political ideas of Agis IV, her previous husband.[52] The marriage was celebrated before Peisistratos' exile in Eretria and it may not have lasted very long, for the vital Eretrian alliance was likewise sealed with another marriage, to an Eretrian of exalted status called Koisyra, whom he may have married while in Eretria. Timonassa must either have died or been divorced, leaving a son, appropriately named Argeios. The tradition confuses and conflates some of Peisistratos' children: Argeios may have been a nickname of Iophon.[53]

Koisyra was undoubtedly from one of the innermost ruling families of the Eretrian oligarchy. A scholiast comments on the term 'Koisyrated', which occurs in Aristophanes' comedy, *Clouds*, as follows: 'Excessively bedecked with jewellery . . . or that the lifestyle of Koisyra was over the top. The name is Eretrian. They [the Eretrians] are slandered as living in luxury. She married Peisistratos while he was aiming at the tyranny.' Labouring the point, he goes on: 'Excessively bejewelled, made up like Koisyra. For she was a woman who used to adorn herself very much both in her dress and in the general manner of her living, so those who saw her were amazed.' Two other Koisyras of the same family were later married to Alkmaionids, one to Alkmaion, grandfather of the reformer Kleisthenes, and the other to Megakles, Kleisthenes' nephew (or perhaps, to his brother Hippokrates according to an ostrakon). Aristophanes' down-to-earth hero Strepsiades gets involved with the family: 'Then I, a peasant, married the niece of Megakles, son of Megakles, she a city girl, a spoilt, stuck-up snob, totally koisyrated' by her mother. All the Koisyras are characterised as 'surpassingly exalted both in family and wealth.' The scholiast sums up: '[the expression] "to play the Koisyra" was to be excessively proud, according to the Eretrians.'[54] We must suppose that the family of Koisyra was already notorious in Eretria for its excess. The marriage was probably a purely political affair and it was ended, perhaps repudiated, a short time later when Peisistratos and the Eretrian government quarrelled,[55] but it seems to have lasted long enough to produce a son, known as Eretrieus.[56] It also shows the importance that the Eretrian oligarchy placed on the alliance with the soon again-to-be, they no doubt hoped, Athenian tyrant. Certainly, if Koisyra were as exalted a figure as our sources suggest, then it must have been a true marriage and any offspring would not later have been counted among Peisistratos' bastards. That her family was later not considered below marriage into the Alkmaionidai (or vice versa!) is an indication of its status. But, if Koisyra were indeed as aristocratically haughty and her lifestyle as profligate as our sources suggest, hers was not an image with which Peisistratos would have cared to identify himself for long once back home, and it may have been a factor in his 'rejection' of her.[57]

For Eretria, there were political benefits to be had from the alliance. In the diplomatic arena, the formation of a coalition to restore Peisistratos would shift the centre of inter-*polis* diplomatic activity there. Herodotos tells us that many *poleis*: 'gave great sums, the Thebans more than any, and after some time . . . all was ready for their return: Argive mercenaries came from the Peloponnese and there also came of his own free will a Naxian called Lygdamis, who was most zealous in their cause and brought them men and money.'[58] Such an inflow of money (to be spent) and men (to spend), not to mention the diplomatic coming and going, must have been a windfall for Eretrian businessmen and made Eretria a major diplomatic focal point.

Nevertheless, there were longer term considerations that should have been on the minds of the Eretrian leadership. Along with men and money for Peisistratos, Lygdamis brought the prospect of enrolling Naxos, an ancient Eretrian enemy, into the Eretrian alliance, allowing Eretrian influence to be pushed further into the central Aegean area. Theban Boiotia, located up against Euboia as well as Attica, was just as important to Eretria as to Athens.[59] Its adhesion to an alliance including Eretria would isolate Khalkis against any help from the mainland, should it ever need it; the importance of mainland Boiotia to the defence of Khalkis and Euboia generally would be made quite apparent by events in 506. However, the greatest hope must have been that a friendly and dependent ruler in Athens would gratefully favour Eretrian political and commercial aims. High among these was the maintenance (or restoration) of Eretria's control over its *peraia ge*, Oropos and its surrounding territory on the mainland opposite the city, which may have at some stage extended as far north as Tanagra in Boiotia. It has long been assumed that Oropos was under Boiotian control in the sixth century,[60] based on two notices in Herodotos,[61] concerning an oracular shrine of Amphiaraos, the context of which indicates that it was in Theban hands. This has naturally enough been identified with his famous shrine at Oropos. However, Knoepfler has argued persuasively that this was still under Eretrian control at the turn of the century and was probably not ceded to Athens until *c.* 470 or later.[62] He observes that the archaeological evidence from the Oropian Amphiaraon does not antedate *c.* 430–410[63] and therefore cannot have been the sanctuary mentioned by Herodotos. Moreover, there appears to have been a family claiming descent from Oropian Amphiaraos at Eretria or perhaps a Koinon of his worshippers, called Amphiastai.[64] But during his exile the Thebans had offered Peisistratos generous financial assistance and so he may have agreed not to interfere in their designs on Oropos. Some time during the sixth century, Eretria tried to seize the coastal area of Boiotia and made a descent by sea upon Tanagra,[65] not far from Oropos, but failed to capture it. The fact that Korinna, the lyric poetess of Tanagra, a contemporary of Pindar, wrote about the incident gives us an approximate *terminus ante quem* (*c.* 520).[66] This means that Eretrian control of the area had already been lost, otherwise the attack is inexplicable.[67] For the time being (*c.* 546), the Eretrians probably tried to extract guarantees from both their Athenian and their Boiotian allies concerning the status of Oropos as an Eretrian dependency. At a time when an alliance was being negotiated between Athens and Thebes, it may have been felt that guaranteeing Eretrian control over the border town might allay fears on both sides of annexation by the other party. Lastly, and certainly by no means least in the eyes of the Eretrians, there must have been an expectation that the man from Brauron near Prasiai would favour a continuation of the dominance by his home region's port of the export of the agricultural produce of the Mesogeia. Despite Peisistratos' possible earlier involvement under the leadership of Solon in the capture of Salamis,[68] the Eretrians must have hoped that Attic regionalist sentiment would prevail over centralism. That these hopes were not fulfilled does not mean that they were unreasonable when Peisistratos set off in 546 to regain his tyranny. However, once securely re-established following his victory at Pallene, Peisistratos proved to be a truly Athenian leader, refusing to be the slave of local Brauronian or of Eretrian commercial interests. For the moment, however, nothing suggested that the role of Prasiai was threatened, or that Attic trade would not continue to move via the south Euboian Gulf, benefiting from the security afforded by Eretrian naval power and ordered according to the regulations established by the Eretrian government covering navigation in the gulf waters (Figures 6.1 and 6.2).

Of these regulations we are fortunate to possess epigraphic evidence, albeit in a fragmentary condition, in inscriptions (*IG* XII 9, 1273/74) dated to the third quarter of the sixth century. I offer the following translation, using Vanderpool and Wallace, but adding, from Schwyzer, τρες to line 3 of the second section. The four-fold division of the text as given below is Vanderpool and Wallace's (although Cairns' suggestion of hῆραι as an Eretrian first aorist infinitive form of ἀείρω: 'let [him] be seized' (for non-payment of fines) has some attraction because of our lack of knowledge of any shrine of Hera into which the fines could have been paid):[69]

Figure 6.1 The Laws of Eretria (*IG* XII 9, 1273/4): *boustrophedon* text beginning at the top, left-hand corner (and reading left to right (downward)). Mansfield 1976, 102 (diag. 14) suggests that another block lay between these two in the space filled by modern mortar. From the Eretria Museum.

I Justice is to be done only after oaths
have been administered. Fines are to
be paid on (or before?) the third day in
khremata dokima[70] (official money). Banishment is the penalty
for non-payment of fines to Hera.

Figure 6.2 The Laws of Eretria (*IG* XII 9, 1273/4): side face (= Vanderpool and Wallace 1964, 1273/74, 4; Mansfield 1976, b1, b2,c1? and c2). Inscription begins at top left-hand corner. From the Eretria Museum.

II In the arkhonship of Golos
----------[15–20 letters]---------- ιν on the next day give
three (τρες) --------------------------------

III -----[*c.* 7 letters]----- ει[. . .]ει he must pay ten staters;
if he does not pay, the *arkhos* (= arkhon ?) is to make
disbursement from the bonded
[covenanted] money;
if he does not do so, he [himself] shall become liable.

IV Those sailing αρ[*c.* 5 letters]θαι payment
whoever αν.π[*c.* 2 letters] the Petaliai Islands or Kenaion

shall be trans-shipped φε[*c*. 4 – 5 letters]εν and everyone who ἐπι[*c*. 6 letters]μος if [*c*. 6 letters]

(V) ------------------------ [too fragmentary] ------------------------
----

These important inscriptions[71] have generated a modest output of scholarly papers, most having as their central interest the dating of the issue of the earliest coinages.[72] I too shall be considering this matter, but for the moment I am interested in them as evidence for the hypothesis that Eretria controlled the waters between Cape Kenaion in the north and the Petaliai Islands in the south, that is the whole of the straits between Euboia and the mainland and which constituted Athens' most important trade route up to the mid-sixth century.[73] The evidence lies in the fourth section of the text. Vanderpool and Wallace's brief notice of it, however, does little other than criticise Hiller von Gaertringen's supplements, but they admit that 'it is easier to show Hiller's ingenious supplements are impossible than to produce acceptable substitutes.'[74] They remark that 'there is no reason to suppose that the inscription deals with "harbour regulations" at all.'[75] However, if the lines do not refer to some kind of harbour-, trade- or navigation-related matters, it is hard to imagine with what they are concerned. Jeffery[76] says: 'The text apparently concerns payments in connexion with shipping and harbourage', and similar views are also expressed by J. and L. Robert,[77] Wallace[78] and Knoepfler, who accepts that *IG* XII 9 1273/1274 does indicate both Eretrian tariff control over the Euripos during the Archaic period and Eretrian thalassocracy.[79] Most numismatists now agree that the primary purpose of early coinage was the payment of state fines and taxes, particularly harbour dues: 'Among receipts may be mentioned harbour dues which are said to have formed the main revenue of the Bacchiads and Cypselids at Corinth, the fines and penalties which are commonly threatened in laws[76] and other taxes.' (Kraay's note 76: 'The so-called Constitution of Chios (cf. *BSA* li (1956) 157) and the Eretrian Laws (*IG* XII 9, 1273–1274) are sixth century examples.').[80]

In any consideration of the possible nature of these inscriptions, the location where the blocks were discovered, built into a later wall raised beside the harbour itself, must be taken into account. The text is certainly fragmentary, but it seems clear enough that it contained regulations, at least some of which concern traffic in Eretrian ships between the Petaliai Islands and Cape Kenaion[81] involving some fixed (rate of) payments. Vanderpool and Wallace suggest that these were infringement fines to be paid 'to Hera'. At Eretria, there was indeed a month Heraion and a festival of Hera but we presently know of no temple to her into which the fines might have been deposited.[82] The known depositories for state fines were the temples of Artemis Amarysia and of Apollo Daphnephoros, the latter in matters involving foreigners, so perhaps that is where the money ended up. It was also located *intra muros* and might therefore have been considered a safer place of deposit than the Amarysion at Amarynthos.

There is a strong similarity between our inscription and a later Athenian decree, which, coincidentally, deals with traffic between Attica and Euboia, in this case between Oropos and Histiaia (beyond Kenaion) and, no doubt, ports in between.[83] Could the earlier Eretrian decree have provided a model? After all, Oropos is directly opposite Eretria itself. 'The traffic between Euboea and the mainland which the Athenians used to conduct in small boats between Eretria and Oropus has in all ages been as important as the sea road through [the Euripos].'[84] A typically Athenocentric remark. Certainly, traffic in all ages was conducted from both sides of the gulf. In the sixth century, it was more likely Eretrians who regulated the traffic as, in later times, did Athenians, as *IG* I³ 41 shows. The community of worship of Artemis on both sides of the south Euboian Gulf meant that the ferrying of her worshippers was always a lucrative source of income, as was the transport of general traffic and goods. We may also compare the Eretrian laws with a Thasian decree regulating the wine trade within a fixed set of geographical boundaries.[85]

The Eretrian decree is thus not unique, though it may have provided a prototype for later laws, especially *IG* I³ 41. It was common enough for Greek *poleis* to proclaim and attempt to enforce monopolistic trade-regulating legislation. The Eretrians adopted the practice early because they were early in a position to enforce their will with some prospect of success, thanks to their naval strength. More important than the fine details of the decree is the fact that they clearly felt able to impose their conditions and fees on all those sailing in Euboian waters at this time and not just within the harbour of Eretria itself. Significantly, given that the Eretrians exercised control over the straits, the port of Khalkis was thus, de facto, subject to Eretrian interference, if not actual control, for no shipping could approach it from either north or south without entering the zone claimed by Eretria as its preserve.[86] Scholarly opinion has long held that Eretria and Khalkis were both strong early naval powers: 'In later times [after the eighth century] . . . the navies of Aegina, Chalcis and Eretria cleared the Aegean of corsairs.'[87] But Kondoleon has shown that there is in fact little evidence that Khalkis possessed a navy of importance and the evidence he offers for this state of affairs in the late sixth and early fifth centuries is particularly strong. He concludes: 'Positive evidence that the Khalkidians had a navy we do not have, contrary to the certainties of recent scholars.'[88] Lastly, as it was very difficult for any Archaic Greek state to effectively enforce any kind of naval blockade or trade sanctions, the modest limits within a narrow waterway, as set out in the regulations, reflect a realistic assessment by the Eretrian legislators of the city's naval capabilities, despite the fact that it exercised suzerainty over several more remote islands.

IG XII 9, 1273/74 are also important for another very important economic question: when did Eretria begin coining? The answer is one for specialist numismatists. The arguments involve comparative dating of the coinages of

Athens, Corinth and the Euboian cities.[89] Recent opinion favours the mid-sixth century for both Euboia and Athens,[90] the dating of Eretria's first issues having been shifted up from *c.* 511. Unless Cairns is right and the inscriptions refer to an earlier pre-coinage situation, with the term *stateres* being a weight of silver and the phrase *khremata dokima* referring to 'objects of fixed value such as spits, tripods and bronze bowls', the dating of the inscriptions confirms the third quarter of the sixth century as a later limit for the introduction of coinage at Eretria.[91] If Eretria did not issue coinage before *c.* 511, we would be forced back to Cairns' hypothesis as to the meaning of *khremata dokima,* but the updating of the earliest Eretrian issues combined with the down-dating of Greek coinage generally is fortunate for my reconstruction of Eretrian economic history in the mid-/late sixth century and meshes well with the generally accepted dating of the inscription. Jeffery, who earlier posed the problem of the non-congruence of the inscriptions and the earliest Eretrian issues, suggested that the 'approved' coinage must have been Attic. [92] But the earlier dating for the introduction of coinage at Eretria now makes it probable that payments (of the fines) would have been mostly, if not entirely, in coins of the Euboian standard, specifically Eretrian staters. 'These are presumably the staters in which the fines for offenders were reckoned in a set of Eretrian inscriptions dated to the third quarter of the century; the same documents refer to δόκιμα χρήματα- "acceptable money".'[93] Unless current views concerning chronology are overturned, we may be reasonably sure that both Athens and Eretria were issuing coins about 550, following Aigina (late seventh/early sixth century) and Corinth (*c.* 575).[94] At least one Eretrian colony in the north was coining at an early period. Dikaia Eretrieon was certainly minting at least as early as *c.* 525,[95] and later at least one Khalkidian colony in the area, Torone, used Eretrian silver staters to make its coins by overstamping them.[96]

It is therefore likely that the bullion Peisistratos collected in the north came down to his Eretrian base in the form of Eretrian *dokima khremata*. Wallace, a specialist in the study of the archaic coinages of Athens and Euboia, believes that the beginning of Athenian coinage is to be dated after Peisistratos' return from Eretria. However he thinks that they should be 'at least as early, one would think', as the first issues of Eretria.[97] Why so? We may just as well, and indeed better, suppose that if the earliest Athenian coinage, the so-called *Wappenmünzen*, was issued after Peisistratos' return in 546, then he got the idea from his experiences in amassing bullion in the north and transporting it and distributing it in Eretria. Indeed, his earliest coins were probably struck in Eretria, judging from their metallic composition:

> The Eretrian coins show a great similarity in composition to the *Wappenmünzen*. Perhaps Eretria, through her colonies, was able to get northern silver . . . our readings (of metallic compositions) do little more than establish a sharp difference between the *Wappenmünzen* and Eretrian coins on one hand, and the (Attic) owls on the other.[98]

There is, in fact, no evidence or reason at all, other than the tendency to automatically give primacy to Athens, to compel us to accept that Eretria was not already coining when Peisistratos arrived, or at least was doing so before he left to return home. It should not be forgotten that the earliest coins of Eretria were for long in fact attributed to Dikaia Eretrieon,[99] although most of these are now attributed to the mother city itself. Both Strabo[100] and Herodotos[101] locate Dikaia Eretrieon in Thrace, on the shores of Lake Bitsonis,[102] not far east of modern Kavala (Skabala) and the Pangaion mines, so it is not at all unlikely that Peisistratos got the idea of using stamped bullion as coinage from the Eretrian dependencies in the north. We need to remember, too, that the early coinages of Athens and Corinth were based on the Euboic standard.[103] Indeed, Kraay observes: 'At the beginning of the sixth century, compared with some of her neighbours in Central Greece, such as Corinth and Sicyon, Athens was still a relatively backward state, dominated by an archaic aristocracy which monopolised political office.'[104] That Athens was issuing coins before Solon, who, according to the *Ath. pol.,* reformed the coinage as well as weights and measures, is untenable.[105] It is unlikely that such a regime would have been very interested in, or capable of, implementing a major economic innovation such as the adoption of coinage. However, the probable relationship between recently adduced reasons for the introduction of coinage and the publication of the Eretrian regulations is one more reason for caution before we deny legislators and their constituency in Archaic Greek *poleis* at least some ability to perceive and formulate economic policy, even if only of a rudimentary kind, in the interests of the state, i.e. their own interests.

In 546 Peisistratos was back in Eretria ready for his final return to Attica, his allies and resources mobilised. The forces of the exiles landed on the Plain of Marathon, a place suitable for a small-scale cavalry engagement, for Peisistratos had with him Thessalians. It is not impossible that there were also some Eretrian cavalrymen, for Eretria in the sixth century still had a considerable cavalry force at its disposal. The expected battle did not eventuate and it was not until the invaders had reached Pallene that there was any engagement, which demonstrates clearly the superiority of the foreign horsemen. The allies also included Lygdamis and his followers, although Naxians were not likely to have been *Hippeis*, and Argive mercenaries, hoplites certainly. Were there any Thebans? We do not hear. Perhaps they only supplied money. However, were they in fact having a bet each way? It would not be atypical of that devious city. For while Herodotos says that 'above all others' they contributed to Peisistratos' war chest, an Alkmeonides (a significant name) of Athens, who won a victory at the Panathenaia that year, was apparently obliged to flee before he could formally dedicate his prize on the Acropolis. He dedicated it instead at the Ptoön in Boiotia, a Theban dependency.[106] The athletic victory thus dates the battle to late August/early September, for the Panathenaia traditionally began on 28 Hekatombaion.[107] Perhaps Peisistratos specifically chose the beginning of the festival because he knew his *kaloi k'agathoi* (beautiful and good, i.e. aristocratic) enemies would be taking part, as indeed Alkmeonides was. The celebration of the festival might also explain why the invaders reached Pallene before meeting their opponents. However, if the Thebans were fully behind Peisistratos, they surely should not have been harbouring, and secretly perhaps, a member of the family that at precisely this, and most other times, was his and his sons' most inveterate enemy.[108]

Once back in power, Peisistratos began to repay some but, significantly, not all of his political debts. In the following year, he is credited with installing Lygdamis as tyrant in Naxos as a kind of vassal.[109] He later used him to guard the sons of exiled opponents who, unlike Alkmeonides, failed to escape before he arrived, though a story in Athenaios implies that Peisistratos merely helped Lygdamis back into power.[110] Aristotle[111] tells us that Lygdamis was himself a member of the Naxian oligarchy. If so, his rise will be paralleled by that of Diagoras at Eretria shortly after.[112] But in 545, Athens, without a credible navy, was not in any position to install Lygdamis on insular Naxos without help. Peisistratos had been dependent on Eretrian ships during his exile and it is likely that he turned again to his ally for ships to invade Naxos. Eretria would have obliged; Naxos had been traditionally a friend of its rival Khalkis.

At this stage, Corinth was not involved, although Corinthian goodwill was almost certainly given to the man who had reduced its ancient enemy, Megara, to impotence. Possibly if Corinth had an active role, it was to check Megara or, more importantly, Aigina in the Saronic Gulf, thus preventing any interference from that quarter in 546/5. We are thus left with Eretria as the only likely source of ships to transport the allies to Naxos. The successful installation of Lygdamis, the candidate of Eretria and Athens (and Corinth?) on Naxos, altered the balance of power in the Aegean still further. From 545 until his fall *c.* 517, Lygdamis kept Naxos within the pro-Eretrian orbit and his adhesion began a 'domino-effect': he later assisted Polykrates to the *tyrannis* of Samos, Khalkis' ancient ally.[113] No record of Eretrian involvement survives, though again its ships may have provided transportation. Samos henceforth could no longer be relied on by the *Hippobotai* of Khalkis.[114] The latter would have been horrified to see their old allies, the *Geomoroi*, dispossessed and exiled by an upstart mercantile tyrant, who was, moreover, indebted to the friend of their most implacable foes. Some time during the sixth century, there was warfare between Eretria's oldest ally, Miletos, and Megara. An epigram[115] records the Milesian dead in a war that Figueira[116] rightly believes could hardly have occurred before rapprochement between Miletos and Corinth. Moreover, I think it unlikely, indeed inconceivable, that any war between these two significant states after 500 would have passed unnoticed in the literature.[117] Since both Miletos and Corinth were in the pro-Eretrian group after *c.* 550, Megara must now be considered pro-Khalkidian. We shall shortly find the Megarian poet Theognis fighting beside Khalkidian *Hippobotai* .[118]

All this military and diplomatic activity thus gave Eretria a central and influential position with respect to the whole western Aegean area. Only

Corinth and perhaps Aigina could challenge it at sea, but since Corinthians and Eretrians had achieved amicable relations, Aigina, thus isolated, posed no real threat to either. Most of Corinth's energies were now directed towards its western interests and to containing both Aigina in the Saronic Gulf and Argos on land. About 544, Corinth and indeed her old enemy Megara were brought into an alliance with Sparta, the rising power in the Peloponnese following her defeat of Argos in the Battle of the Champions in 546. The more or less simultaneous adhesion of both Corinth and Megara to the Spartan alliance would have significant political repercussions for the whole of central Greece, not least for Eretria and Athens. Between 625 and 585, Corinth planted its only colony in the region, Potidaia, athwart the isthmus of Pallene. The foundation would have been viewed favourably by the Eretrians, for it stands between and separates the Eretrian colonies on the peninsula of Pallene from their Khalkidian neighbours. We have seen Eretria assist, in the same area and doubtless partly for like reasons, the establishment of Peisistratos' settlement at Rhaikelos. Later still, Eretria would encourage Athens to perform the same buffer role in Euboia itself by settling *kleroukhoi* on the Lelantine Plain between it and Khalkis, following the latter's decisive defeat in 506. 'The decline of Chalcis was followed by a radical change in the foreign policy of Corinth. This city had formerly cultivated the alliance of Samos. It now deserted this alliance and formed a friendship with her old foe, Miletus.'[119] Bury thus emphasises the crucial role that the perception at Corinth of Khalkidian impotence had in prompting the change that altered the mid-century balance of power in the Aegean. Periandros' shift of Corinth from the old Samos–Khalkis axis in my opinion was, without doubt, the single most important development in Greek interstate affairs to affect the remainder of the sixth century, and though conceived primarily with a view towards his relations with Thrasyboulos' Miletos,[120] the political effects on Eretria were enormous. It soon found practical expression in Euboia with intervention by Periandros, perhaps even with troops, on the side of Eretria against Khalkis. However, all this activity was not without its effects on Eretrian internal affairs, and it is to these that we shall now turn.

Notes

1 P. Poralla (rev. A. S. Bradford), *Prosographie der Lakedaimonier, bis auf die Zeit Alexanders des Grossen*, Chicago, 1985, s.v. Χίλων (Χείλων) 131–2; D.L. 1, 68.

2 The fall of the Orthagorids is linked to Kheilon's ephorate in *Pap.Ryl.* I, 18 (= *FGrH* 105F1).

3 *IG* XII 9, Test. et Not. 147; Bickermann 1980, 169. Suid. s.v. Σιμονίδης (α'); see Eusebios: Ol. 55.3. 56th Olympiad = 556–3; Ol. 55.3 = 558. Simonides and Eretria: Knoepfler 1969, 87.

4 On the chronology of Peisistratos' exiles/returns there is considerable controversy (and literature): for a summary of positions held: J. Hind, 'The "Tyrannis" and Exiles of Pisistratus', *CQ* ns 24, 1974, 1–18. Basic texts: Hdt 1, 61; [Arist.] *Ath. pol.* 15.

5 The first being the expulsion of the Eretrians from Kerkyra in 734. For 556: E. Bickermann, *Chronology of the Ancient World*, London, 1980, 116, 169, etc. (useful synchronisation tables); J. Cadoux, 'The Athenian archons from Kreon to Hypsichides', *JHS* 68, 1948, 108–9.

6 Th. 1, 15, 3.

7 F. Jacoby, *Die Fragmente der griechischen Historiker* IIIb Leiden, 1950/55, F426, 165 and *Kommentar* 250.

8 Αἰσυμνήτης: regulator; judge; umpire. διαλακτὴς καὶ νομοθέτης (mediator and *nomothetes*): Plut. *Sol.* 14, 2. On *aisymnetes*: Arist. *Pol.* 1285a30–b4). On the *aisymnetes* at Miletos: Gorman 2001, 94–9; M. Ostwald, *From Popular Sovreignty to the Sovreignty of Law. Law, Society, and Politics in Fifth-Century Athens*, Los Angeles, 1986, 406, says *nomothetai* are 'not . . . attested in Athens before 403/2 BC.' Presumably he takes the reference in Plutarch as an unofficial title (or is talking about *nomothetai* as a board of magistrates). Perhaps Plutarch did not really know what Solon's real position was; [Arist.] *Ath. pol.* 6, 1 simply says Κύριος δὲ γενόμενος (having become master of affairs), Solon freed the *demos*; ibid. 2, 2: that he became τοῦ δήμου προστάτης (head of the *demos*); the same expression used later at 28, 2 where it is qualified as πρῶτον and compared with the position of Perikles. Both κύριος and προστάτης suggest that he was more than *arkhon*.

9 M. Miller, 'The accepted date for Solon: precise but wrong', *Arethusa* 2, 1969, 62–86.

10 C. Kraay, 'An interpretation of *Ath. Pol.* Ch. 10', in *Essays in Greek Coinage, Presented to Stanley Robinson,* Oxford, 1968, 207. M. Chambers, 'Aristotle on Solon's reform of coinage and weights', *CSCA* 6, 1973, 10.

11 I do not wish to become involved in the debate about whether the *Eupatridai* were a clan, a group of clans, or some other grouping in Attic society, which acquired overtones of noble breeding, as the label itself implies. I use the term to indicate the nobility of Attica, which, though probably never quite so closely identified with horse rearing as that of Euboia and of Khalkis in particular, still had its origins in similar occupations as the social (and later 'Solonian' economic) group, the *Hippeis*, indicates; [Arist.] *Ath. pol.* 7, 4 makes it clear that the Solonian *pentekosiomedimnoi* were horse owners.

12 Plut. *Sol.* 22.

13 Plut. *Sol.* 1; 4–5; Aelian. *VH* 8, 16; [Arist.] *Ath. pol.* 17, 2.

14 Davies 1971, 445.

15 I originally wrote 'must'. I have been asked (by Dr Greg Stanton): 'why not a reaction against Solon's policies and attitude?' As far as we know Peisistratos remained an admirer of his former *erastes*. Although later they 'were at variance about matters of state' and Solon disowned him politically, their political differences did not result in personal enmity (Plut. *Sol.* 1, 2).

16 Hdt. 5, 65, 3. *RE* s.v. Peisistratiden. Davies 1971, 445: the status of the Peisistratidai is 'demonstrably Eupatrid'. Their claimed descent from the Neleids of Pylos evidenced in the names of a sub-branch of the family from Khios (whither they probably went after the fall of the tyranny): W. Forrest, 'A lost Peisistratid name', *JHS* 102, 1982b, 134. He was perhaps also related to the Philaidai. Brauron seems to have been their deme centre: Pl. *Hipparch.* 228b (ἐκ Φιλαιδῶν); D.L. 1, 53. G. Huxley, 'Studies in early Greek poets 1: Neleids in Naxos and Archilochus', *GRBS* 5, 1964, 21–5.

17 Solon's mother was cousin of Peisistratos' mother. The element ἱππ- in Peisistratid names suggests a Hippobotic tradition in the family. 'Hippos-names' were, of course, frequent at Eretria.

18 Ch. 8, pp. 254 (Gephyraioi); 253–4 (Alkmaionidai).

19 Ch. 7, pp. 218–20.

20 On the region: A. French, *The Growth of the Athenian Economy*, London, 1964, Chs 1–3; and with more emphasis on eastern Attica: idem 1959, 46–57.

21 French 1959, 49–50.

22 On the Petalai Islands: Ch. 4, pp. 123, 125.

23 14–5. The northern boundary of the area of control set by the Eretrians was at Cape Kenaion.

24 Ch. 2, pp. 32–3. On Peisistratos and the cult of Artemis Brauronia: Davies 1971, 454.

25 Bengtson 1988, 81; Ure 1962, 37–9; W. Forrest, *The Emergence of Greek Democracy*, London, 1966, 176–81.

26 Plut. *Sol.* 29, 1. [Arist.] *Ath. pol.* 14, 1: he is called δημοτικώτατος, variously translated as 'most democratic'; 'an extreme advocate of the people' etc.

27 A. French, 'The economic background to Solon's reforms', *CQ* ns 6, 1956, 25.

28 Forrest 1966, 176–8.

29 J. Holliday, 'The followers of Peisistratus', *G&R* 24, 1974, 43; 48–53.

30 Ibid. 48.

31 Pottery and trade: Ch. 5, n. 239.

32 'Ships on Geometric vases', *BSA* 44, 1949, 152–3.

33 Kondoleon 1963/65, 24: "Ο ἀγὼν 'Αθηναίων-Χαλκιδέων ἐγένετο κατὰ ξηράν, τὴν ἐποχὴν δ' ἐκείνην οὐδ' οἱ ' Αθηναῖοι εἶχον ναυτικόν.'

34 The ἀκήρυκτος πόλεμος: L. Jeffery, 'The campaign between Athens and Aigina in the years before Salamis (Hdt VI, 87–93)', *AJP* 83, 1962, 44–54.

35 Bengtson 1988, 82. He does not say what these 'connections' were.

36 From 561/60 (first coup) to 546 (final return from Eretria). 1974, 48–56.

37 A later example of a ruler learning while in exile the strengths and weaknesses of his hosts, who later turned the knowledge to his and his state's advantage, was Philip II of Macedonia.

38 For example R. Hopper, 'Plain, shore and hill in early Athens', *BSA* 56, 1961, 198, n. 99.

39 Chs 2 and 4, *passim*.

40 The somewhat contadictory texts are: Hdt. 1, 61 and [Arist.] *Ath. pol.* 15, 2. For *sunoikise*: see below, n. 43; see also n. 47. The passage from Hdt. is continued below, p. 191.

41 J. Cole, 'Peisistratos on the Strymon', *G&R* 22, 1975 42–4. The *Ath. pol.* 15, 2 figures are not reconcilable with Hdt. 1, 61; and Aristotle, if he wrote the *Ath. pol.*, contradicts his own statements in *Pol.* 1315b30–4. A. French, *Sixth Century Athens; the Sources*, Sydney, 1987, 46, n. 1.

42 For terms used by him: D. Whitehead, 'Site-classification and reliability in Stephanus of Byzantium', in D. Whitehead (ed.), *From Political Architecture to Stephanus of Byzantium. Sources for the Ancient Greek Polis*, *Historia Einzelschriften* 87, 1994b, 106; 117–20.

43 Cole 1975, 42–3; D. Viviers, 'Pisistratus' settlement on the Thermaic Gulf; a connection with Eretrian colonization', *JHS* 107, 1987, 193–5; Figueira 1990, 134, n. 8: the Eretrians 'co-settled' (συνῴκισε *Ath. pol.* 15,2) it with Peisistratos.

44 The land journey is about a third of the distance.

45 St. Byz. s.v. Σκάβαλα. *CAH* III Cambridge, 1965, Ch. 25, 650–2. Cf. Bradeen 1952. 374, who despite this thinks it was Khalkidian(!), not Eretrian.

46 Cf. however J. Sandys, *The Constitution of Athens*, London, 1893, 58–9 and n. 2: 'Ραίκελος and τοὺς περὶ Πάγγαιον τόπους.

47 How are we to interpret πάλιν in *Ath. pol.* 15, 2? Could it mean that he returned 'again' or 'afterwards' to Eretria from the north? Such is my opinion and that of e.g. Cole; Sandys. But it may simply 'mark this period as the latest in the *A.p.'s* series of intervals of time' (P. Rhodes, *A Commentary on the Aristotelian 'Athenaion Politeia'*, Oxford, 1981, 208), and thus it was only 'after' ten years that Peisistratos made his next attempt.

48 J. Ducat, 'La Conféderation béotienne et l' expansion thébaine à l' époque archaïque', *BCH* 97, 1973, 72: this process began *c.* 525. R. Buck, 'The formation of the Boeotian League', *CP* 68, 1972, 94–101: 525–520.

49 Cole 1975, 42.

50 Davies 1971, 449–50 dates the marriage *c.* 560.

51 Hind 1974, 11; Forrest 1971, 81. For the family relationships of the Ambrakiot Kypselidai, beginning with Gorgos, son of Periandros: Newman 1902, 329–30.
52 Plut. *Cleom.* 1, 1–2. On politically involved wives: Plut. *Agis* 7, 3.
53 However, ethnic forms are attested in a series of Peisistratid names from Khios: see Forrest 1982b, 134. Likewise there is debate over the identity of Thessalos/Hegesippos. Another nick-name?
54 Schol. ad Ar. *Nu.* 47: ἐγκεκοισυρωμένην· περισσῶς κεκοσμημένην (. . . ἤ τὰ τῆς Κοισύρας φρονοῦσαν) ἔστι δὲ Ἐρετριακὸν τὸ ὄναμα. οὗτοι δὲ εἰς τρυφὴν διαβάλλονται. αὕτη δὲ ἐγαμήθη Πεισιστράτῳ ἐπιχειρήσαντι τυραννεῖν - περισσῶς κεκοσμημένην, κεκαλλωπισμένην, ὁμοίως τῇ Κοισύρᾳ. αὕτη δὲ ἦν γυνή τις πάνυ ἑαυτὴν κοσμοῦσα ἱματίοις καὶ τῇ ἄλλῃ διαίτῃ, ὡς τοὺς ὁρῶντας ἐκπλήττεσθαι. Schol. ad Ar. *Nu.* 46–7: ἔπειτ' ἔγημα Μεγακλέους τοῦ Μεγακλέους ἀδελφιδῆν ἄγροικος ὢν ἐξ ἄστεως σεμνήν, τρυφῶσαν, ἐκεκοισυρωμένην. Schol. ad Ar. *Nu.* 46: 'ἥτις ἦν ὑπερβαίνουσα γένει καὶ πλούτῳ· ἦν δὲ ἐξ Ἐρετρίας. διὸ καὶ κοισυρεῖθαι τὸ μέγα φρονεῖν, παρ' Ἐρετριεῦσιν. Greek scholia from the ed. of F. Dübner, *Scholia Graeca in Aristophanem*, Hildesheim, 1969 ad locc. Ch. 8, pp. 254–5 for the various Koisyras and their marriages. L. Shear, 'Koisyra; three women of Athens', *Phoenix* 17, 1963, 99–112, provides a stemma; Davies, 1971, 380–1, thinks that there were two Koisyras. B. Lavelle, 'Koisyra and Megakles, son of Hippokrates', *GRBS* 30, 1989, 503–13.
55 For the political ramifications of the end of the marriage: Ch. 7, pp. 208, 210. The ostrakon: S. Brenne, 'Ostraka and the process of Ostrakophoria', in W. D. E. Coulson *et al.*, (eds). *The Archaeology of Athens and Attica under the Democracy*, Oxford, 1994, 15–6 and Fig. 10, which has Μέγακλες | Ηιπποκράτους | καὶ Κοισύρας (Megakles, son of Hippokrates and Koisyra).
56 Is Eretrieus another nickname for an as yet otherwise unidentified son?
57 Assuming she did not die or leave him to return home; if either happened, we should probably have some scholastic notice of it.
58 Hdt. 1, 61. Cf. [Arist.] *Ath. pol.* 15. 2. See above, p. 188.
59 Eretria as agent for Miletos in Boiotia in the sixth century: see above, Ch. 5, p. 168; P. Ure and R. Burrows 1907/08, 236–7; R. Burrows and P. Ure 1909, 333. Eretria's ambitions in this area may have given the Tanagraians cause for fear. Tanagra was probably pro-Theban in 506.
60 Following Wilamowitz 1886, 91–115. See e.g. Chandler 1926, 2–3.
61 Hdt. 1, 52; 8, 134.
62 Knoepfler 1985b, 50–5.
63 Ibid. 50. The archaeological data: B. Petrakos, *'Ο Ὠρωπὸς καὶ τὸ ἱερὸν τοῦ' Ἀμφιαράου*, Athens, 1968 and reports in *AD*.
64 P. Ducrey, 'Dédicace inédite d'une association à Érétrie', *Études de lettres* (*Publ. de la faculté des lettres de l'Université de Lausanne*) 4, 1981, 73–8; Charbonnet 1984, 49–53.
65 Paus. 9, 22, 1; schol. ad Lyc. *Alex.* 679; Korinna fr. 5–10. Cf. Roller 1989. Eretria and the coastlands: Geyer 1903 78–9.
66 *OCD* s.vv. Korinna. Pindar: *c.* 518–438.
67 Ch. 8, p. 258. Knoepfler 1985b: Eretria was still struggling to control it in the third century, and had recovered it in 411: Th. 7, 28, 1; 8, 60, 1–2, but by 404, the Thebans had seized it: D.S. 14, 17, 3. Subsequently it was a pawn between Athens and Boiotia, but Eretrian foreign policy was constantly influenced by its current status.
68 Plut. *Sol.* 8, 4.
69 *IG* XII 9 (Addenda et Ultima) 1273/1274 (I, II, III) and plates V, VI. Ed. pr. G. Papavasileiou ''Ερετρικὸς Νόμος', *AD* 1913, iv, 210–5 with memorandum by A. Georgiadis, 1913, 214–5, describing the circumstances of the discovery of the blocks (built into a wall that was part of later harbour works) and including a plan of the area; E. Schwyzer, *Dialectorum Graecarum Exempla Epigraphica Potiora*, Hildesheim, 1960, 376, no. 800. P. Kretchmer, 'Literaturbericht für das Jahr 1913', *Glotta* 7, 1916, 324–5, was

the first to attempt a restoration of the battered text. His work was superseded by E. Vanderpool and W. Wallace 1964, 381–91. F. Cairns, '*IG* XII 9, 244 and the Demes and Districts of Eretria', *ZPE* 54, 1984a, reproduces their text; later, with modifications in idem 1991, 296–313. The most comprehensive study of these inscriptions is that by J. Mansfield, *IG XII 9, 1273/1274: The Eretrian Laws*, unpubl. MA thesis, University of California, Berkeley, CA, 1976. Wallace 1936a, 76, n. 1, has an interesting and rather free translation of 1274. F. Cairns, 'ΧΡΕΜΑΤΑ ΔΟΚΙΜΑ'; *IG* XII 9, 1273 and 1274 and the early coinage of Eretria', *ZPE* 54, 1984b, argues that in ll. 2–3 (Vanderpool and Wallace text): κα[ì φυ]γία ìὰν : μὴ τείσε <ι> [: hέραι], and that φυ]γία must be accusative. Vanderpool and Wallace translate: 'and exile is the penalty for non-payment of the fines', but if we were to take Cairns' point, it would have to be rendered: 'and exile, (and) if he does not pay (the fine) to Hera' [let him suffer exile . . .]. But can we have ἔστω φυγία ìὰν μὴ . . . ? Hence Cairns would wish to see φυ]γία restored to ὑ]γιᾶ, presumably making ὑγιᾶ simply reinforce δόκιμα and so refer to money to be paid to Hera(?). I am not persuaded by Cairns's desire to replace φυγία with hὑγιᾶ.

70 Χρήματα δόκιμα

71 Dated *c.* 550–25 by Jeffery 1961/90, 84. However, Cairns, 1991, 298, says that in a private communication to him, Jeffery indicated that she was prepared to see them down-dated to *c.* 525.

72 See above, nn. 69; 71. Cairns, 1984b, 144–55, concentrates on the significance of the phrase χρήματα δόκιμα (he does not believe that χρήματα denotes coinage) and the question of when Eretria began issuing coins; H. Volkmann, 'Δόκιμα Χρήματα', *Hermes* 74, 1939, 99–102, thinks that the term means money, indeed that it is the first certain use of it for coinage. Also Wallace 1962, 37.

73 French 1959, 49–50 (see above, p. 192).

74 1964, 386.

75 Ibid., n. 8.

76 1961/90, 85.

77 Bull. épigr. 1965, item 322.

78 1936a, 76 n. 1.

79 1969, 85–6. Ch. 7, pp. 219–20; 8, pp. 261–2; Ch. 9, *passim*.

80 C. Kraay, 'Hoards, small change and the origin of coinage', *JHS* 84, 1964, 89–91. See below, n. 90.

81 On these places: see above, nn. 22–3.

82 See above, n. 69, for Cairns's interpretation of Ἥραι.

83 *IG* I^3 41, 67–76:

. . . . ἔ[στο δὲ τοῖ πορθμεύοντι ἐκ Χ]-
[α]λκίδος ἐς 'Οροπὸν πρ[άττεσθαι τρες ὀβολός ·ἐὰν δ]-
[έ] τις ἐχς 'Οροπõ ἐς hεστ[ίαιαν ἒ ἐς Δῖον ἒ ἐκεῖθεν]-ἐ
[ς] 'Οροπὸν πορθμεύει πρ[αττέσθο hεπτ' ὀβολός· ἐὰν δ]-
έ τις ἐκ Χαλκίδος ἐς hε[στίαιαν πορθμεύει, πραττ]-
ἐσθο τέτταρας ὀβõλό[ς . . . . . . 21 . . . . . .]
[.] μὲν hοι πομπεύοντε[ς . . . . . . 18 . . . . . . πομ]-
[π]εύεται, τελέτο τὸ hέ[μισυ. ἐὰν δὲ hο πορθμεύον μὲ]
[ἐ]θέλει ἄγεν τὸν πο[μπεύοντα . . . 7 . . .κατὰ τὰ γεγ]-
[ρα]μμένα, Ε [. . . . . 29 . . . .]

for comparison.

84 Zimmern 1915, 30.

85 *IG* XII 8, 347 II 8–9: μηδὲ πλοῖον Θάσιον ξενικὸν οἶνον ἐσάγετο ἔσω Ἄθω καὶ Παχείης. J. Pouilloux, *Recherches sur l'histoire et les cultes de Thasos*, I, Paris, 1954, 128.

86 Kondoleon 1963/65, 9–10.

87 Quoted in Ure 1922/62, 330, from Mitchell and Caspari (eds), G. Grote's *History of Greece*, intro. 8 (publishing details unknown).

88 Kondoleon, 1963/65, 6, 23–4: 'Θετικὰς μαρτυρίας ὅτι οἱ Χαλκιδεῖς εἶχον ναυτικὸν δὲν ἔχομεν, ἀντιθέτως πρὸς τὰς βεβαιώσεις τῶν σημερινῶν ἐρευνητῶν.' Among the combatants at Artemision, the Khalkidians are singled out (Hdt. 8, 1) as not supplying their own ships: '[The Khalkidians] manned twenty ships, the Athenians providing them, on the other hand, the Eretrians [furnished] seven.' Even Styra (later a deme of Eretria) provided two of its own. This was in a battle of crucial importance for all Greece and which was fought off Euboia itself.

89 Wallace 1962, 23: 'It is, however, clear that the early coinages of Euboia should be considered in connection with those of Athens.'

90 Cairns 1984b, 146: his bibliography contains a useful tabulation of the opinions of four groups of scholars on the dating of the two earliest issues of Eretria. See idem 1991, 298, n. 7: 'The former scholarly view that the first Greek silver was early sixth century BC had been overtaken by a downdating more or less radical.' Starr 1977, 113: the fines at Chios were probably set in terms of bullion which was 'certified' χρήματα δόκιμα). L. Jeffery, 'The courts of justice in Archaic Chios', *BSA* 51, 1956, 157–67: the Chiot inscription is dated 575–550, making it more probable that we are here dealing with a pre-coinage situation (unless Lydian coins were involved). D. Kagan, 'The dates of the earliest coins', *AJA* 86, 1982, 361–80, has a very early date for the introduction of coinage but does not mention Eretria. See J. Kroll and N. Waggoner, 'Dating the earliest coins of Athens, Corinth and Aegina', *AJA* 88, 1984, 328–40.

91 Cairns 1991, 298–9; he sets out his arguments clearly in 1984b. However, I remain convinced by the general opinion (Vanderpool and Wallace; Jeffery; Volkmann; Wallace; Kraay; etc.) that χρήματα δόκιμα is 'acceptable money'. We may compare the use of δόκιμα to describe money in these inscriptions with its use (in its negative form ἀδόκιμον) in Arist. *Oec.* 1347a8 describing Hippias' so-called 'reform' of the currency: 'He declared the existing coinage to be unacceptable (ἀδόκιμον), he fixed a price for it and ordered it to be brought to him.' Cairns does cite this passage but I do not believe that he gives it enough weight, especially as it refers to a sixth-century situation. Kraay's review of P. Radici Colace and M. Caccamo Caltabiano, "Αργυρον δόκιμον . . . τὸ δ' ἐνάντιον παράσημον' (Pollux III, 86)', *ASNP* 13, 1983, 421–47, in *SEG* 33, 1983, item 1621: '"δοκιμασία" of money was meant to guarantee, rather than to establish its authenticity'. Cairns, 1991, 299, n. 9, explicitly allows that the text may refer 'to the abundant Eretrian coinage of the last decade of the sixth century.'

92 1961/90, 84.

93 Kraay 1976, 91.

94 Kroll and Waggoner 1984, 339–40.

95 Kraay 1976, 91; 134. For the coins: C. Seltman, *Greek Coins. A History of Metallic Coins and Currency Down to the Fall of the Hellenistic Kingdoms*, London, 1933, pl. xi, 3, with comparable Eretrian devices, pl. xi, 1, 2.

96 Kraay 1976, 134; N. Hardwick, 'The coinage of Terone from the fifth to the fourth centuries BC', in R. Ashton and S. Hurter (eds, in association with G. Le Rider and R. Bland) *Studies in Greek Numismatics in Memory of Martin Jessop Price*, London, 1998, 119–34 and pl. 29.

97 Wallace 1962, 36.

98 Ibid. 29.

99 G. Jenkins, 'Greek coins recently acquired by the British Museum', *NC* 1955, 136, no. 7.

100 Str. 7, frs 43 (44); 46 (47).

101 Hdt. 7, 109.

102 Talbert 1985, 60 (C1). Ch. 5, p. 154 and nn. 122–4.

103 The '*Wappenmünzen*' *didrakhmon* was of 8.6 g, exactly half the Euboic *stater* of 17.2 g.

104 Kraay 1976, 56.

105 Ibid. One consequence has been the attempt to drastically down-date Solon by Miller 1969, 62–86.

106 Hdt. 8, 135; Paus. 4, 32, 5. Davies 1971, 372–3.

107 Parke 1977, 33.

108 We may note that, later on, some family members (including the 'democrat' Kleisthenes) collaborated with the tyrants: R. Meiggs and D. Lewis 1989, 6C.

109 Hdt. 1, 64. Perhaps the relationship was of *xenia* or *philia*. The latter term, as Greg Stanton has pointed out to me, may indicate unequal status (cf. Roman *amicitia*).

110 Ath. *Deipn.* 8, 348c. Newman 1902, 346: for an alternative reconstruction of events, giving more emphasis to the story in Athenaios.

111 Arist. *Pol.* 1305a40.

112 Ch. 7, pp. 210–11.

113 Polyaen. *Strateg.* 1, 23.

114 For Lygdamis and Samos: Burn 1960, 313, 314; Bengtson 1988, 82, 427–8, n. 35. G. Shipley, *A History of Samos*, Oxford, 1987, 90–1, gives a less significant role to Lygdamis.

115 L. and J. Robert, 'Bull. épigr.', *REG* 80, 1967, item no. 528.

116 'Chronological table: Archaic Megara 800–500 BC', in T. Figueira and G. Nagy (eds), *Theognis of Megara; Poetry and the Polis*, Baltimore, MD, 1985, 296–7.

117 For relations between Megara and Miletos in the seventh/sixth centuries: Burn 1929, 22–5.

118 Ch. 8, pp. 212–17.

119 Bury 1955, 151. Bérard 1970, 68, n. 31.

120 Burn 1929, 24: 'It seems rather to be true to say that both our two despots (i.e. Thrasyboulos and Periandros) abandoned their cities' old alliances.'

7

THE TYRANNY OF DIAGORAS (*c.* 538–509)

There is a natural tendency for firmly established regimes to generate internal elites over time. Oligarchies often contain sub-groups reflecting distinctions between those that actually wield power and those that are in fact only on the fringes of the ruling elite.[1] While the oligarchy at Eretria was at first dynamic and progressive, in so far as it emerged in response to social and economic realities at the time, it seems during its comparatively long life to have slowly stagnated, developing by the mid-sixth century into such mutually exclusive factions, one of which clearly monopolised power. It was a situation reminiscent of the last years of Bakkhiad rule at Corinth, as recorded by Strabo and Herodotos: 'The Bakkhiadai, a rich, numerous and famous *genos* who ruled [*tyrannesantes*] Corinth and held power for about two hundred years and reaped the fruits of commerce unhindered', and 'the *Oligoi* ruled and these, who were called Bakkhiadai, controlled the city, marrying and giving in marriage among themselves.'[2] I am not suggesting that the ruling clique at Eretria was an endogamous *genos* like the Bakkhiadai; its exact nature is unknown. More than likely, it was simply a grouping of very wealthy individuals and families. The exclusivist nature of the ruling group at Eretria is implied by Aristotle who, in a discussion of oligarchies overthrown as a result of one faction being pushed aside by another, or by exclusive marriage suits negotiated to secure political alliances among the ruling group, tells us that this is what happened at Eretria:

> Factions arise also as a result of some members of the oligarchy being pushed aside by others, and being provoked to *stasis* because of marriages or law-suits; examples of this arising from marriage-related causes are the cases already mentioned; also the oligarchy of the *Hippeis* was destroyed by Diagoras after he was wronged in respect to a marriage.[3]

Internal division and jealousy was thus alienating some of its own members.

Meanwhile, what about the workers? Trade required ships and ships required a special class of labourers – rowers. Indeed, Eretria was the 'rowing city'. They were of political significance because they not only laboured but also contributed to the defence of the state as the navy increased in importance. The growing military clout of the rowing class had potential for radical political change. Ships also needed constant servicing and the harbour required men to load and unload the cargoes. Furthermore, developing commercial activity encouraged the expansion of the artisan class. As mentioned earlier, Eretria had a long-established manufacturing tradition going back to Lefkandi and there was metalworking in Eretria itself as early as the eighth century.[4] By the sixth century it was producing derivative pottery of which some was, if not particularly inspiring and certainly not up to the best Corinthian (to *c.* 550) or Attic ware,[5] of export standard, if only on a local regional basis.[6] Most known examples of Eretrian decorated ceramic have been found in local contexts, primarily produced for the home market. The bulk of the output was coarse ware designed to convey other Eretrian products abroad[7] and supply domestic utensils for the poorer classes. In the countryside, where agricultural production turned early to olive and fruit growing because of a relative lack of fertile crop lands and pastures, there was only a seasonal demand for labour for picking, pressing and transporting the produce to the city for consumption and export. Changes in farm production, from traditional livestock rearing or grain growing, were no doubt also accompanied, as in Attica, by a growth in the landless class with peasants squeezed off their small plots by the demands of the new tree crops that took years to reach full production. And, also as in Attica, there was no doubt an increase in rural indebtedness.

All these men constituted the *thetes* in Attica, and for Eretria I employ the term to denote the same group to which it was applied in Athens where the word properly belongs. Under the Solonian reorganisation, they were those belonging to the lowest *telos* (property class), having an annual income below 200 *medimnoi* of natural produce, the minimum in Athens for hoplite status. For Eretria, we know neither the term for this group of people nor the upper property limit. We may however be quite sure that they existed and that their output in labour was an increasing component of the national wealth. Their rising discontent with their political exclusion posed a continuing political threat to the oligarchy. In Athens, they were not full citizens; it was probably Peisistratos who gave them that status.[8] In Eretria, they still awaited their champion. Finley has stressed the continuation of debt bondage outside Attica after Solon's time.[9] The growth of this politically dispossessed class, combined with the increasingly flamboyant wealth and narrow exclusivity of the Eretrian ruling group, exemplified by the women Koisyra,[10] created a potentially volatile social mix.

An increasing reliance by the state upon the navy as its primary military arm in the international arena, into which the ruling oligarchy was increasingly drawn by its interventionist foreign policies, accompanied these socio-economic realities. As later happened at Athens, the Eretrian *thetes* would become ever more conscious (because it was pointed out to them by ambitious or disgruntled individuals from higher socio-economic levels) of their worth to the state and begin to demand political rights, with ultimate results that in fact anticipated, by several years, developments that occurred at Athens after 508/7. Ober has noted the development of this consciousness of the thetic class at Athens as a consequence of Peisistratos' fostering a close association between himself and the citizens as a whole.[11] The drift of unemployed and otherwise unemployable *thetes* into rowing and shipping-related work occurred earlier at Eretria, which, unlike Athens, already had a significant fleet by the mid-sixth century. Thus, discontent was delayed by its absorption of the dispossessed, whereas at Athens the absence of a fleet when Solon had to face the problem meant an ever-increasing pool of unemployed ex-farmworkers. Eretria also possessed both a hoplite army and a significant cavalry during the sixth century. Its 6,000 hoplites[12] made Eretria numerically the military equal of the major powers of central Greece and its hoplite class must have been larger than that of Corinth, even in the fifth century.[13] But, in fact, as the century drew to its close, it is mostly the Eretrian navy that we hear of and not the land forces, though since Eretria was militarily involved at Sardis during the Ionian revolt, it must also have sent hoplites to Asia Minor.

Despite political successes in the arena of inter-*polis* diplomacy, the involvement in the mid-sixth century of at least some members of the ruling oligarchy in Eretria with adventurers such as Peisistratos and Lygdamis and their political models and allies, such as Periandros and Thrasyboulos, soon brought domestic political troubles in its wake. I will not discuss the general arguments concerning the rise of tyrannies in the more commercially developed *poleis* of the isthmus and east Greece here. The literature is large and I have already mentioned related aspects that led to the emergence of the hoplite phalanx.[14] Ultimately, whatever social and economic forces that ambitious men such as Kypselos, and later Peisistratos, were able to exploit, they had also been working within the political fabric at Eretria, albeit at a slower pace. The final catalyst for political upheaval may have been the presence in the city, as guests of the government, of those two exponents of revolutionary change, Peisistratos and Lygdamis, both of whom showed in their subsequent career that they were prepared to actively support the rise to power of like-minded men elsewhere, and they had powerful friends and mentors who had shown the way to do it. Moreover, present with them in Eretria, possibly for up to ten years, was a body of supporters strongly enough committed to their leadership to be prepared to share the risks and pain of exile. Though many of their supporters were clearly mercenaries, it is hard to believe that at least some would not have been ideologically committed to the political aims of their leaders. That men did ponder future political outcomes is demonstrated by the pleas of those wanting Solon to become tyrant in Athens in 594 (or 570): Plutarch and the *Ath. pol.* both imply that there was pressure on him to take the tyranny as indeed does his own poetry.[15] While the Peisistratidai and their principal lieutenants would no doubt have been restrained and diplomatic within the city of their benefactors as they mustered their forces prior to the invasion, there must have been a lot of loose talk around the city of overthrowing aristocrats and of topics such as land/wealth redistribution, whether realistic or not. These lower-order followers would probably have been billeted with precisely the class of Eretrians that we might expect to have shared grievances against the oligarchic regime and thus be susceptible to influence. This need not have involved direct propagandising. Idle conversations, mutual grumbling and gossipy comments would have an effect after a while. The presence in the midst of the Eretrian thetic classes of other men of similar social status who were exercising a role in the rise and fall of governments would have been enough to encourage local dissidents to question the status quo if they were not already doing so.

The combination of relatively deteriorating conditions for the working classes and the presence of outside role models resulted in growing destabilisation following the departure of the foreigners in 546. Questioning of the established regime, the *patrios politeia*,[16] thus gained momentum as a result of its foreign policy gamble, which moreover now failed to pay off as expected, for the expansion of Phaleron made possible by Solon's capture of Salamis, and which now gained momentum under Peisistratos, led to the downgrading of Prasiai as the major trading gateway to Attica. The effects would have been felt in Eretria by the merchants, the natural supporters of the oligarchic government, causing rifts to develop within the ranks of the *Hippeis* themselves as trade and profits dipped. The dependent *thetes* in turn would suffer in any economic downturn. No doubt there had been from the beginning those within the ruling class who thought that dalliance with men such as Peisistratos spelt long-term trouble, and when he ultimately acted against Eretrian political and economic interests, these internal critics would now say, 'I told you so.' However, those who were too compromised by policy, as well as through the marriage alliance and other social, familial and economic ties with the tyrants, could not easily withdraw their support. Our sources say nothing about the fate of Peisistratos' Eretrian wife Koisyra other than that he remarried. But perhaps her family in Eretria had a later political change of heart, for as we have seen, two Koisyras subsequently married into the Alkmaionidai, the political enemies of the Peisistratidai.[17] If Peisistratos rejected his Eretrian wife not long after his return to Athens, it symbolised to the world his refusal to accept a subordinate role for himself and his city. By the 530s, Peisistratos' strong Athenian nationalism was being expressed in the revitalisation of the purely Athenian spectacle of the Panathenaia,[18] the beginning of the grandiose building of the Olympeion[19] and a range of other building and beautification projects.[20] The development of an unrestricted trade outlet at Phaleron in direct competition with the Euboian Gulf port of Prasiai would be natural for a nationalist ruler with an interest in trading.[21]

Increasing destabilisation of the internal political situation seems to have given the disgruntled oligarch Diagoras his chance to seize power. The ostensible cause was his 'wronging' by another faction within the ruling oligarchy in connection with a marriage proposal. Most tyrants in fact emerged from and exploited excluded factions within the oligarchy itself, and fringe groups within the population at large: social (Kypselos), geographical (Peisistratos) or racial (Kleisthenes of Sikyon). The circumstances of Diagoras' rise remind us of those surrounding that of Kypselos, for whom marriage and family marginalisation were key factors. Is it possible that Diagoras believed that his prototype was Kypselos? He later had enduring links with Corinth and is said to have died there in exile.[22] Nevertheless, his inspiration was probably the immediate and present example of Peisistratos, and, possibly even more so, that of Lygdamis, who was a member of an oligarchy and who championed the cause of an oppressed people.[23] Like all aspirants to unconstitutional political power, he needed more than just a sense of outrage at his own personal wrongs. He needed supporters, and plenty of them, men who also felt a sense of grievance and who could be led/manipulated by a dynamic and ambitious personality.[24] Diagoras must have been such a man and most likely his support came not only from the unrepresented and increasingly significant thetic class but also his own faction, as well as those members of the oligarchy disappointed with the policy of support for the new tyrant of Athens. The rejection of Koisyra, symbol of Peisistratos' alliance with the *Hippeis*, was a clear sign to any opposition in Eretria that the ruling elite could expect no help from Athens. Alternatively, Peisistratos may have divorced his wife after Diagoras' coup, for it would then be plain enough that his former personal allies in Eretria would henceforth be of little political value to him.

Diagoras' coup must have occurred after 546 for the *Hippeis* were still in power when Peisistratos left Eretria and they were involved, with their Athenian and Naxian allies, in overseas actions from 546 to *c*. 540, providing a *terminus post quem*. We should allow time for the conspiracy to develop, especially if we believe, as we should, that there was more involved than just the marriage problem. We shall shortly find Periandros, the famous tyrant of Corinth, intervening in Euboia at Kerinthos. It is not impossible that he had a hand in Diagoras' coup, which may have been part of a broader involvement in Euboian affairs. The very latest dating for Periandros' death is *c*. 533.[25] By 530, the Kypselid tyranny had collapsed and Periandros' ephemeral successor Kypselos II (a.k.a. Psammetikhos) was deposed after a strife-troubled reign of less than three years.[26] This makes *c*. 538 the most probable date for Diagoras' accession. After this, relations between Eretria and Athens appear to have become cooler. Having come to power with the support of merchants as well as the thetic class, both of which were suffering the consequences of Peisistratos' trade policies, Diagoras could ill afford to maintain a close relationship with the Athenian tyrant. Moreover, Diagoras probably regarded him as the political and personal friend of his own enemies of the exclusivist old regime.

Diagoras pursued his own 'nationalist' policy abroad during the early period of his rule and fostered the interests of those who helped him to power. He must have been popular with somebody for, sometime after he died (or was killed or commited suicide) at Corinth, following the establishment of the democracy, a statue was raised in his honour.[27] But there is evidence that he harassed the old ruling class, for it is during the sixth century that the ancient aristocratic cult at the West Gate *heroön* ceases: 'continuity of cult is certain through the seventh century and it is during the course of the sixth that all cult traces disappear, a break that he (C. Bérard) explains as being in all likelihood due to the rise of democratic sentiment [at Eretria].'[28] The wealthy were now either unable or unwilling to display traditional status symbols at this time: ostentatious grave stelai are absent at Eretria, but not at this time at Athens: 'it is probable that sumptuary laws linked to the rise of the democratic classes restrained the activities of the old oligarchic groups.'[29] The ladies Koisyra had become proverbial at Eretria for extravagant personal display. Indeed the Koisyras managed to transfer this image on to their city in Athenian minds. However, Eretrian commercial activity continued strongly through the rest of the century and new building works commenced around the agora and the harbour,[30] signs that the new government was not hostile to people in business. Probably it was only the pseudo-aristocrats of the inner circle with their offensive display that were attacked.

Meanwhile Eretria was moving into a closer relationship with Corinth, perhaps one involving military co-operation. Periandros was adept in the art of wooing like-minded rulers. He developed a friendship with Thrasyboulos of Miletos, thereby changing the whole balance of power in the Aegean,[31] and he maintained an alliance with Peisistratos, mediating peace between him and Mytilene, following a war for control of Sigeion, awarding the town to Athens.[32] The Egyptian pharaoh Psamtek was his ally. Clearly, foreign policy interested Periandros greatly. Now that Eretria, ally of his friend Thrasyboulos, was also a *tyrannis*, the old tyrant, who 'was forever making expeditions and was warlike; he built triremes and used both seas',[33] was given a chance to interfere in Euboia, probably at the request of Diagoras, whether originally to aid his coup or, shortly after, to support his first foreign policy adventure. If so, Diagoras' invitation was seconded by other ambitious Euboians. The collaboration was crowned with immediate success, though it was not as permanent as Diagoras, Periandros and their allies might have hoped.

Evidence for this Kypselid involvement in Euboia is to be found in the corpus of poems attributed to Theognis of Megara. His authorship of these particular lines has been disputed. I accept Theognis as author. The writer is both an eye witness and a participant:

> May Peace and Wealth possess the city, that with other men
> I could dance and sing, for I do not love evil War.
> And do not listen too eagerly for the far-sounding herald,
> for we are not doing battle for our ancestral land.
> But for me it would be shameful, being present,
> not to mount the swift-running horses and face woeful War.

Alas for our weakness; Kerinthos is now destroyed,
and the good vinelands of Lelantos are being laid waste;
the *Agathoi* are fleeing and the *Kakoi* controlling the *polis*.
Would that Zeus might destroy the Kypselid race![34]

The putative author was a disgruntled aristocrat of the deepest dye. On a high dating, he was born about 630 and lived on into the sixth century, some time during which his city was governed by an 'unbridled democracy' that he hated, but scholars who adopt a lower chronological framework have his lifetime between *c.* 580 and 500.[35] Exile seems to have been his lot for much of his life and his wanderings took him as far afield as Sicily, as he himself tells us in his poems. Moreover, the same lines tell us that he spent time in Euboia:

For I myself once went to the land of Sicily
and once to the vine-clad plain of Euboia.[36]

Everywhere he went in his exile, he was welcome as *xenos* (guest friend) in the houses of like-minded *kaloi k'agathoi*, aristocrats like himself:

And all men made me very welcome when I came.[37]

At some time in his wanderings, he found himself at Kerinthos, a small town in the north-east of Euboia. But when? And why at Kerinthos of all places? Authorities on Theognis place his *floruit* from 540 to 520,[38] so we should expect that the incidents described occurred within this period. Theognis' Megarian origins would explain the venom directed particularly at the Kypselidai and why he lumped all his opponents at Kerinthos together under the contemptuous 'the Kypselid tribe'.

Interestingly however, not one of the translators available to me actually renders the word *pareonta* in l. 889: [be present, be (someone's) guest[39]], nor do any commentators refer to it. Yet, historically, this is of the utmost importance, for it surely means that Theognis, or whoever wrote the lines, was an actual observer and participant in the events that he describes. Nor do they join ll. 885–90 with 891–4 although they surely demand to be so read.[40] Together, the verses present a coherent picture that is not at all at variance with what we know about the man and times that we are dealing with. The poet is an aristocrat, welcome among aristocratic horse riders. He is hostile to the *demos* and hates the Kypselidai. He is in Euboia. Not many lines previously, the poet lamented the rise of Persian power and the threat it posed for Greece: he appeals to Apollo for protection from the 'wanton outrage of the host of the Medes.' He 'fears, seeing the heedlessness and people-destroying discords of the Greeks'.[41] Sardis had fallen in 546, the very year in which Peisistratos set out from Eretria. But for whom was Theognis, a foreigner far from his 'ancestral land', fighting? He was (of course!) helping the aristocrats, whom he calls the 'Good Men' and who had been at the small town of Kerinthos making a final stand, for Kerinthos has clearly just been destroyed and they are in flight. Their opponents, the *kakoi* ('Bad Men'),[42] also have foreign allies, the Kypselidai. Now victorious in some battle that has already taken place, it is they who are in control of 'the *polis*'. We are definitely no longer in an age in which gentlemen's agonistic contests passed as war, but rather in the midst of social revolution in a *polis*-state, aided and abetted by powerful outside forces,[43] though it may be noted that the aristocrats are mounted as befits Hippobotic lords for 'it would be shameful . . . not to mount swift-footed horses' to go to war. Greenhalgh suggests that by the sixth century soldiers on horseback on vases of the period were in fact mounted hoplites. The Spartan *Hippeis* rode to battle but fought in the hoplite ranks as late as Mantineia in 419. Nevertheless, a cavalry battle cannot be totally ruled out. If so, it would be in fact the last reference to a cavalry battle by the *Hippobotai* in Euboia as a group or class.[44]

Kerinthos lay on a small plain south of the Plain of Histiaia, separated from it by the Xiron highlands. It was linked in the mind of Homer[45] to the latter city and with vines. It may still have been a viticultural area in Theognis' day for he refers to a 'vine-clad plain in Euboia'.[46] It is usually taken for granted that Theognis is talking of the Lelantine Plain, but it could (but not necessarily) be the Plain of Kerinthos/Histiaia that is being described.[47] It is fertile though quite small, which may be why Kerinthos was never a *polis* in its own right.[48] The town is separated by over 40 km of deep mountainous gorges (passes) through the Makistos-Dirphys ranges (1225 and 1743 m respectively) from Khalkis and the Lelantine Plain (Figure 7.1).[49] Eretria is another 25 km distant. But there are two passages of Theognis that mention vine-covered plains and he may be referring to two separate plains. One (l. 892) is specifically named Lelanton and described as the 'good/rich plain of wine' while the other (l. 784) is merely described as 'vine-clad'. But were there two? We know that the poet was at Kerinthos, on the southern limits of Homer's 'many-vined' Histiaian plain, but it may indeed be stretching it to call the flat lands around Kerinthos part of the Histiaian Plain. So did Theognis also visit the Lelantine Plain? He would have heard much mention of it from his Khalkidian host friends and he knew that it was being, or had been, devastated. However, might he have transferred what he would have known of Euboian plains from Homer to both? He could easily, of course, have resided on a noble estate on the Lelantine Plain before he and his friends were forced back on to Kerinthos.

Part of the problem is grammatical: the verb κείρεται is present middle/passive and may be rendered either as 'is now destroyed' (i.e. has been recently destroyed) or 'is being destroyed' (i.e. as I speak). Since the *kakoi* are, Theognis tells us, in control of the *polis*, is this: (1) the result of a prior conflict in which the Lelanton has been destroyed; or (2) because the *kakoi* are in the process of laying waste the estates of the *agathoi* now? Probably the first, but the latter can not be ruled out. Though there is some viticulture on the Lelantine Plain, it was never, apart from this one instance, described in ancient literature by

Figure 7.1 View of mountainous country between Khalkis and Kerinthos.

reference to its vines. Its fame lay rather in its fertile crop-producing soil and its water pastures, on which the *Hippobotai* grazed their horses and cattle. Notwithstanding that the Lelantine Plain does not have strong ancient associations with vines, and that Theognis might have been Homerising, I am of the opinion that Theognis was in fact thinking of the Lelantine Plain in both passages that mention plains in Euboia, but that he refers to incidents at which he was present, in two separate (in time and space) places that are, by Euboian standards, quite far apart. Both theatres of war were geographically, if not always politically, in what was the Khalkidian sphere of influence. Thus, if foreigners, such as Theognis, Periandros and, I suggest, the Eretrians, were involved, we are dealing with an invasion of Khalkidian territory and the government of the *Hippobotai* was well and truly on the defensive.

Who then were fighting at Kerinthos? It is unlikely that either Eretrians or Corinthians were involved there in any numbers, given the isolation of the site by land. It is possible the attack was sea borne. Ancient Kerinthos (Figure 7.2) was on a high promontory at the mouth of the Boudoros River (Homer calls it 'Kerinthos hard-by-sea') and both Eretria and Corinth were sea powers.[50] In such a scenario, the Khalkidians would have had to dash to the aid of the town, probably on horseback, leaving their city vulnerable. Nevertheless, I believe that the Khalkidian aristocrats were already in the town for reasons that will become apparent below. *Stasis* in Khalkis provides the answer. The 'Good Men' were the Khalkidian *Hippobotai,* now defeated in a revolution involving outside

Figure 7.2 Κήρινθόν τ' ἔφαλον (Hom. *Il*. 2, 258). The ancient site was on the plateau above the cliffs on the left of the river.

forces at Khalkis-*polis,* and they had been driven out to this remote town, there to make a last stand. However, Theognis also laments the devastation of the Lelantine Plain. Thus, the *kakoi* must already have won more than one victory for things to have come to this pass. Though neither Eretria nor Khalkis is named in the lines, it is quite inconceivable, given the lurking presence of Kypselid power, that both *poleis* were not involved and that the devastation was solely the result of civil war. The *polis*, already captured and now governed by the *kakoi* and the wasting of the plain, are clearly linked in the poet's mind, both events having happened prior to the situation in which he and his friends now found themselves at Kerinthos. Kerinthos is, moreover, nowhere ever called *polis*. The *polis* is Khalkis.

Who or what initiated these events, and when? Eretria, in revenge for earlier losses? Kypselid (i.e. Periandros') ambition and interference? Possibly both played a part, but the answer lies rather in the internal problems of Khalkis itself, which Eretrians and Kypselids were only too ready to exploit, especially if invited in by one party in a domestic *stasis*. Forrest comments that Theognis 'appears to be talking of *STASIS* in a Euboean city and without further evidence this cannot be expanded into a full-scale war' (his emphasis), 'whereas verses 891–95 [*sic* for 894] appear to bear witness to war in Euboea in the second quarter of the sixth century [and] refer merely to some minor interference by Periander in Euboean affairs.'[51] I agree that we do have *stasis*, and war as a result, but to call it only a 'minor interference' is not acceptable; any interference by Periandros anywhere was important in a seventh/sixth century context. If Corinthians came north as far as Euboia at any point of time, it would not have been a minor event. Forrest, strangely, does not give much credit to this reference to Kypselidai,[52] although he in fact says that Corinth was the directing force in the Lelantine War, for he dates it to the eighth century.[53] If Corinth could intervene then, it certainly could in the sixth century. Given 533 as the probable year of Periandros' death and the involvement of Eretria in overseas adventures continuing until *c.* 540, followed by Diagoras' coup *c.* 538, the Kerinthos affair should be dated between *c.* 536/5 and 533 (530 at the very latest if one were to allow for the unlikely possibility that the Kypselid involved was the ephemeral Psammetikhos/Kypselos II).

According to Aineas Taktikos, Eretrians were invited to intervene by a faction in Khalkis. The story is detailed:[54]

> Khalkis on the Euripos was captured by a fugitive operating from Eretria, aided by one of the inhabitants of the town in the following way. To the most deserted part of the city where the gate was kept closed, he used to bring a saw (fire-pot which he kept going both day and night)*, and so, secretly, one night, he cut (burned)** through the bar of the gate and admitted soldiers through it. When about 2000 men were gathered in the agora, the emergency war alarm was sounded quickly; many of the Khalkidians were killed because from ignorance they ranged themselves

> carrying their arms alongside their enemies, thinking they were friends, each man thinking he was late in arriving. Thus did most of them die in one's and two's, and the city was captured for some time before they realised what had happened.

The Loeb editor believed that 'this incident probably took place during the war over the Lelantine Plain in the latter part of the seventh century.'[55] The city has obviously acquired a strong and, on the whole, reliable set of walls and gates. Eretria had an enceinte wall in the seventh century but we know nothing other than what Aineas reveals about the early defences of Khalkis. Substantial walls did not become the rule in European Greece until the sixth century. However, any dating later than the 350s is excluded by Aineas' *floruit*, which was in the first half of the fourth century. Of two possible fourth-century scenarios, Knoepfler,[56] discussing the war in which Athens went to the aid of Ploutarkhos, tyrant of Eretria, has eliminated 349/8, while Tod long ago ruled out 357/6.[57] During most of the fifth century, all Euboia was under Athenian domination and such an event, unrecorded elsewhere moreover, could hardly have occurred then. The Eretrians, according to this evidence actually take the city, and by treachery, from within. The ruse employed may appear overly elaborate, but there are parallels from Thucydides in the mid-fifth century.[58] This episode would fit perfectly into the scenario described above. When, other than at a time of severe internal *stasis,* might we have expected Khalkis to be betrayed to the old enemy? Aineas also says that casualties arose from the fact that there was confusion as to who were friends and who enemies, which suggests that many locals were part of the revolutionary group so that the city was lost before the loyalists realised what was happening. Two thousand is too many outsiders to have entered *secretly*! Such a number entering via a single gate would have been so obvious that the alarm would have been raised by some loyalist and not, as is apparent, by the rebels themselves to get their enemies out into the streets.

The sequence of events was probably as follows: the Eretrian and Corinthian tyrants combined to invade and devastate the Lelantine Plain causing suffering for the *Hippobotai*. In Khalkis-*polis* meanwhile, and in concert with the invasion, there was a revolution, involving betrayal of the city, that raised a now obscure populist tyrant named Antileon to power.[59] The hard core of the old regime was obliged to flee to Kerinthos, where they regrouped to attempt a comeback. They were followed, attacked and defeated. Thus, the fighting at Kerinthos follows the coup of Antileon at Khalkis. It is entirely possible, and indeed likely, that he and his supporters had been in contact with Periandros and Diagoras. Perhaps Antileon himself, or one of his key supporters, had been the fugitive resident in Eretria and negotiating with the new tyrant there. Soon after the death of his chief patron, Periandros, Antileon was overthrown. He could hardly have continued to rely only on Eretrian support and still maintain popularity in Khalkis, while the prime importance of Periandros is stressed by

Theognis' use of 'Kypselidai' for all his and his Khalkidian supporters' enemies. 'Tyranny . . . can degenerate . . . also into oligarchy, as did that of Antileon at Khalkis.' The *Hippobotai* were restored and he was flayed alive if the tradition is correct: 'Would he not be more deserving than Antileon of flagellation?'[60] The returning aristocrats who had suffered from the devastation of their estates on the plain, as well as political and military humiliation, would no doubt have been vengeful enough to make an example of Antileon. He may have been nicknamed Phoxos in derision by the Homerically literate aristocrats, an allusion to the impudent Thersites, who challenges his betters in the *Iliad* and is slapped down for his trouble by the noble Odysseus.[61] However, this name more likely belongs to a later tyrant of Khalkis for he was, according to Aristotle, followed by a democracy: 'and at Khalkis, the demos, along with the better class, overthrew the tyrant Phoxos and immediately seized control of the government.'[62] It is a sign that the collective 'Thersites' of Khalkis were not so easily to be squashed as was the Homeric buffoon, since he must have followed Antileon and subsequently have lost power, as did the succeeding democracy, some time before 506. For, by then, the estates of the Lelantine Plain were once again back in the hands of the *Hippobotai* : 'The Athenians, having defeated the Khalkidians [in 506] divided up the land into 2,000 lots for *kleroukhoi*, that is, the so-called land of the *Hippobotai* in the area called Lelanton, and offered a portion to Athena.'[63] Thus, the history of Khalkis for the rest of the century appears to have been one of successive upheavals culminating in catastrophic military defeat in 506. We hear of yet another tyrant, Tynondas. His name suggests a Boiotian origin. It may be he who took Khalkis into alliance with Thebes in the later sixth century. However, Plutarch links him with Pittakos (and Sigeion) as an example of a good tyrant.[64] This picture of decline is reinforced by the archaeological evidence, sparse though it is.[65] After that, Khalkis was under Athenian control, with *kleroukhoi* established on the Lelantine Plain. We hear of no more tyrants until the fourth century.

According to this reconstruction, Eretria had intervened decisively in the affairs of her neighbour, and her hegemony within Euboia at this time is clear. Though the rule of their dependent Antileon was short lived, the local impact must have been considerable. Not only was Khalkis defeated but it had fallen temporarily into Eretrian hands. The new Eretrian regime had asserted itself decisively in interstate affairs in concert with powerful Corinth. Diagoras now settled down to what proved to be a long period of rule, and the city to an era of steady growth and generally peaceful foreign relations, based on a continuation of its ancient friendship with Miletos in the east and Corinth and Thebes (down to 519) in central Greece. It is likely that Eretria still maintained its Aegean island empire, which may have once again embraced Andros and Karystos.[66] This would be in keeping with the aggressiveness displayed by Diagoras early in his rule. A sixth-century date for the stele in the temple of Artemis Amarysia listing the military strength of Eretria is more likely than an earlier one and it would be appropriate to this period of military activity.

The festival of Artemis Amarysia was, at least in later times and probably earlier, celebrated by Eretrians and Karystians jointly. The triumphal procession recorded on the celebrated stele may have been held to celebrate victories over Khalkis and perhaps Karystos that possibly lost the Petaliai Islands to Eretria *c.* 525.[67] If so, the Karystians coming to the festival would thus be reminded often of their defeat. No doubt the Eretrians continued to apply the regulations set down in *IG* XII 9, 1273–4 covering navigation and taxes for the whole of the Euboian Straits from Kenaion to the Petaliai Islands, including Khalkidian home waters, for Khalkis would henceforth be unable to do much about such Eretrian activities.

With Athens, however, relations deteriorated further after the death in 527 of Peisistratos. The grave marker of Khairion, an Athenian Eupatrid,[68] discovered at Eretria (Figure 7.3), is dated *c.* 525 by Jeffery: 'This might imply an exile from Peisistratid Athens; but the Eretrians had supported Peisistratos, so the stone may attest only an old family *xenia* (guest-friendship) with no political involvement.'[69] Khairion may indeed have had guest friends in Eretria, and if he were a political refugee, where better to retire than to the house of a guest friend? But Jeffery is assuming in this context that the government that had supported Peisistratos from 556 to 546 was still in power, moreover with its character and policies unchanged, but if my reconstruction of the period is correct, by 525 Diagoras had been in power for a decade. We should, nevertheless, regard Khairion as a political exile from Peisistratid Athens, welcome

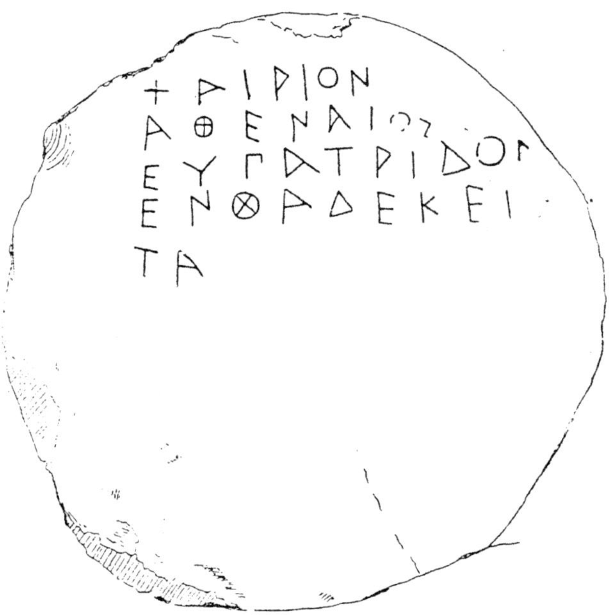

Figure 7.3 The grave-marker of Khairion (*IG* XII 9, 296): (ΧΑΙΡΙŌΝ | ΑΘĒΝΑΙΟΣ | ΕΥ ΠΑΤΡΙΔŌΝ | ΕΝΘΑΔΕ ΚΕΙ | ΤΑ[Ι]). From Kourouniotis 1899, 144, no. 10.

in hostile Eretria. He was an aristocratic *pentekosiomedimnos,* since he is inscriptionally identified as *tamias* of Athene *c.* 550.[70] The flaunting of *eupatridon* in his epitaph, as Davies observes, 'must be the political manifesto of an *ancien régime* family.'[71] His son, Alkimakhos, who was perhaps recalled by the tyrant (cf. Kimon and Kleisthenes) erected a statue to him on the Acropolis *c.* 520.[72] The wording of its inscription, 'son of a noble sire', makes Alkimakhos' own political attitudes as perfectly clear as did the term 'of the *Eupatridai*' on his father's tombstone at Eretria.[73] Khairion's family has been linked by Raubitschek to that of Alkibiades, the Eupatrid Salaminioi.[74] But the presence in Eretria of Alkmaionids, to whom Alkibiades is also said by Isokrates to have been related, strengthens the possibility that Khairion was related somehow to the Alkmaionidai and thus to men who were part of the conspiracy leading to the death of Hipparkhos. By 514 'Eupatrid' was being used as a term of praise for opponents of the Peisistratid government.[75] Khairion was probably not the only noble Athenian political exile in Eretria. We shall shortly see that Alkmaionids, including Megakles and perhaps his son Kleisthenes, were exiled there. However, Kleisthenes at least had been recalled (by Hippias as a goodwill gesture?) by 525 and held the arkhonship in that year, although by 511 the Alkmaionidai were exiled again.[76]

His sons Hippias and Hipparkhos succeeded Peisistratos in 527.[77] 526/5 is generally accepted as the date of Polykrates' death but Dickins has argued persuasively for 517.[78] Periandros, the lynchpin of the diplomatic order from *c.* 570 to *c.* 530 was recently dead.[79] Lygdamis of Naxos survived until 515/4. As the last quarter of the sixth century dawns, Diagoras seems firmly in power at Eretria, but both its ally Miletos and its enemy Khalkis were reduced to impotence by more or less chronic social revolution producing short-lived tyrannies interspersed with ephemeral regimes both oligarchic and democratic. Other figures now begin to impact upon the history of Eretria. By far the most important and interesting would be Kleomenes I of Sparta (king, *c.* 520–487), a descendant of Kheilon, with whose ephorate (556) we began the previous chapter. Sparta had been making headway in the Peloponnese and had supplanted Argos as the natural hegemon of southern Greece. After the fall of the Kypselidai, even powerful Corinth became a member of the Peloponnesian League, though as later events show, a very independently minded one. Sparta had acquired a reputation for suppressing tyrants going back to Kheilon's days, not entirely deserved, for when it served their interests, the Spartans were quite ready to accommodate tyrants.[80] The arrival of Spartan troops in central Greece led by Kleomenes changed the political balance in the region considerably.

Kleomenes played a sophisticated diplomatic game there. His first move, probably within a year of his accession, came in 519.[81] It was a brilliantly mischievous ploy and it impacted significantly on Diagoras and the Eretrians. When the Plataians in Boiotia, threatened by the expansionist activities of Thebes, the ally of Eretria and Athens since at least 546, sought alliance with him, Kleomenes declined the offer and advised them to apply to Hippias at Athens.[82] Hippias accepted the challenge (bait). Naturally, Thebes was enraged and consequently threw over the Athenian alliance, and with it the Eretrians, joining with Khalkis. An alliance with Khalkis was, of course, incompatible with friendship with Eretria. At the time of this affair, Kleomenes was in Megara.[83] By the late sixth century, the radical democracy there had fallen and there was an oligarchy in power, which had a bilateral *symmakhia* with Sparta. It had been fighting Corinth, also oligarchic after the fall of the Kypselidai, and had achieved some success up to this point in time, but Corinth must, ultimately, have prevailed had Kleomenes not presumed to intervene in this dispute between two states allied to Sparta. Corinth, angered by the interference, was long to remain deeply suspicious of Spartan intentions, and her later reactions to Kleomenes' attempts to interfere both in and north of the isthmus must be seen in this context. Corinthian independence of action from Sparta continued to be demonstrated for decades and with Megara in the Khalkidian/Theban camp, she continued to favour the Eretrian/Athenian side with momentous consequences, as we shall soon see.[84]

The new Spartan interest north of the isthmus posed a threat to the tyrants of Eretria and Athens, yet it appears that the danger was at first not fully appreciated in either city. Sparta (in foreign policy in 519, this meant in practice Kleomenes) though technically an ally of Hippias, wanted a less independently minded government to deal with and when the need was present, the old anti-tyrant policies could always be dusted off. The political situation for Hippias was made worse because Argos, which had aided Peisistratos in 546, was, after its defeat in the Battle of the Champions, more and more obsessed with its own weakened position within the Peloponnese, so that in the event of trouble no help could be expected from that quarter. An even more obvious threat was posed by the now hostile Thebes. Thus, for Athens, there remained as allies only Naxos, Thessaly and Corinth, though the continued friendship of the last, a member of the Spartan alliance, could not be predicted with confidence. The Thessalians remained loyal to Hippias to the end,[85] but in 514 Lygdamis, installed by Peisistratos with the support of the then Eretrian government of the *Hippeis*, would be removed by the Spartans with the support of Diagoras.[86] His replacement by an oligarchy of the *Pakheis* (the 'Fat Ones', i.e. the very rich), proved instrumental in the outbreak of the Ionian revolt and the involvement of Eretria in it, for while trying to interest the Persians in an attack on Naxos and Paros, Aristagoras, tyrant of Miletos, pointed out to Artaphernes, the satrap at Sardis, that: 'Starting from these, you will be easily able to attack Euboia.' For Eretria, by then a democracy, was responsible for the overthrow of this regime *c.* 505, causing *Pakheis* exiles to flee to Aristagoras seeking his help towards their restoration.[87] The overthrow of the Naxian oligarchy, together with its later leadership in the attack on Sardis, made Eretria the principal object of the Persian attack in mainland Greece.[88] Hippias' friends were becoming fewer. Therefore, it appears strange that he made no attempt to patch up the friendship with his father's old ally. That he could not do so is due to Eretrian indifference, or rather hostility, for attempts, ultimately successful, were being made from the Eretrian side to undermine the Peisistratidai and there is evidence that Diagoras collaborated with Kleomenes in his intrigues against Hippias.

As early as 525, he was giving asylum to Peisistratid political opponents as we have seen. In 514/3, the year after the fall of Lygdamis, a famous conspiracy was set afoot in Athens, which sheds some light on the attitude of Eretria towards Athens and reveals the real weakness of the Peisistratidai at home and abroad. Hippias' younger brother Hipparkhos was slain during the opening ceremony of the Panathenaia by Harmodios and Aristogeiton, two members of the *genos* of the Gephyraioi, dyed-in-the-wool aristocrats.

> This clan was another offshoot from the stock of Kadmos. Its first home on Greek soil had been Eretria (Euboia). From there it migrated across the straits to Tanagra (Boiotia). Expelled from Tanagra after the Trojan War, it then settled in Athens where it maintained a secret hereditary cult of Demeter Achaia. This we learn from Herodotus (V 57; 61).[89]

Thucydides rightly debunks the idea of them as idealistic tyrant slayers, who gave democracy to their city, a notion assiduously spread around by Eupatrid propaganda that was still widely accepted in his day. The result of their bungled attempt to overthrow the Peisistratid government was, in fact, harsher oppression by the surviving Hippias, although this just increased aristocratic unrest still further, for the Athenians did not rise up against their 'oppressors'. Harmodios was killed on the spot and Aristogeiton arrested and tortured before being executed. Investigations led Hippias to believe that the conspiracy went further than the anger of the two men over a homosexual proposition by Hipparkhos to Harmodios. The origins of the two so-called tyrannicides are however of great interest to us. Their family, the Gephyraioi, claimed Eretria as their ancestral homeland and about their own origins we need not doubt that they knew better than Herodotos and many later historians:

> The Gephyraioi, to whom were related the killers of Hipparkhos, themselves say that they came originally from Eretria; but being unconvinced, I made my own enquiries [and found that] they were Phoenicians who came with Kadmos to the area now called Boiotia, and of that country the region around Tanagra was allotted to them and they settled there.[90]

At some remote period, ancestors of the *genos* had left Eretria and gone first to Tanagra[91] and thence to the Attic deme Aphidna, not far from what may still have been Eretrian Oropos.[92] Perhaps they were constantly driven forth by Eretrian pressure. Perhaps they were inveterate intriguers making themselves unwelcome wherever they tried to settle: if the latter, their sixth and fourth century descendants had not lost the knack. Nor had the latter forgotten their Eretrian origins, for the father of the politician Aristogeiton, condemned to death in 338, fled . . . to Eretria![93]

The semi-abortive coup and the interrogations that followed it may have revealed Eretrian involvement to Hippias.[94] Some conspirators had Eretrian connections. Such definitely were the Gephyraioi and very probably, as we shall see, the Alkmaionidai. Others will have had connections through the institution of *xenia*; such perhaps was Khairion and his son. These links were within the old Eretrian oligarchic families who may have been looking for a way to achieve in Eretria what their Athenian allies and kinsmen were trying to do in Athens, a return to the oligarchic *patrios politeia*. However, why would Diagoras have operated against his neighbour-tyrant using men of this kind? These aristocratic 'front-men' in Athens (for they were nothing more than that) were a group of reactionaries with nothing in common with either ruler. However, all parties appear to have been willing to exploit each other. Diagoras may well have believed that he could control them and limit their meddling to Athens. His objectives, as we shall soon see, appear to have been quite Machiavellian. Indeed Hippias' reaction was sufficiently sharp and widespread to indicate that he was aware that the intrigue extended beyond two jealous lovers and their 'impulsive' act of revenge against his brother. But more importantly, Kleomenes I was also using them and he was by now Diagoras' ally.

Kleomenes was the prime mover behind the push to get rid of the Peisistratid government. To use discontented Eupatrids as his instruments against Hippias inside Athens is an obvious ploy. Now, while Diagoras died at Corinth, he was in fact en route to Sparta.[95] It has never been asked why the tyrant of Eretria was on his way to Sparta. Nevertheless, if he were Kleomenes' ally, it becomes perfectly understandable. Kleomenes seems to have been using Diagoras and the Eretrian families as go-betweens to provide himself with access to the conspirators in Athens. That Diagoras had his own agents within the old oligarchic families of Eretria is quite likely; after all, he was himself originally one of them, even if not of the innermost ruling clique. He would thus have been able to infiltrate the conspiratorial groups and exploit them for his own ends and those of anyone else that he might wish to assist. That his rule lasted so long indicates that he was very much aware of what was going on in his own city. Kleomenes too was a subtle operator, and he would have been well aware of Diagoras' enmity for the Peisistratidai, the presence at Eretria of the exiles, and the Eretrian connections of families of the leading plotters, and, noble as the Gephyraioi were, there were others, still more noble than they, whose current interests converged with those of Kleomenes. There was an Athenian story[96] that the influence of the Alkmaionidai at Delphi, where they had financed the rebuilding of the temple, was responsible for the repeated message to Sparta to liberate Athens. I suspect that it was more the result of a convenient coincidence of interests. The idea that an Athenian family, no matter how wealthy and benevolent to the temple, once more in exile, would have had more influence than the ambitious and interventionist King of Sparta with an army at the isthmus, is hardly to be countenanced. Kleomenes was undoubtedly getting responses that he wanted in order to attempt to neutralise the strong non-interventionist party at home but which would soon act decisively against him. Aristotle, as we have already seen, noted perceptively that Greek oligarchic groups were invariably factionalised, and the conspirators, who on the day of the murder believed that they had been betrayed (and so panicked and bungled the attempt), were no exception, making them easy targets for intelligent and powerful men such as Diagoras and Kleomenes. After 515, Sparta was openly supporting anti-Peisistratid forces within Attica and their kinsmen in exile in various friendly neighbouring states such as Eretria:

> Sparta supports the Athenian malcontents against the tyrants as she had done already in the cases of Samos and Naxos [and] a weak oligarchy in dread of a restoration of tyranny had already proved Sparta's best ally in the Greek towns and we have no reason to believe that Sparta's action in Athens was any exception to her ordinary policy.[97]

Second, other events occurred after 515 that need to be kept well in mind. In 514[98] Lygdamis was removed by an oligarchic coup, aided and abetted by Sparta following its attack on Polykrates of Samos.[99] However, to carry out these operations Sparta needed ships. Myres[100] postulates a Spartan *thalassokratia* between those of Samos (534–517) and Naxos (515–505)[101] of only two (convenient!) years, noting also Dorieus' expedition to Kyrene in 514; Herodotos' attribution of motives for this operation is unsatisfactory.[102] It is better seen as an example of Spartan expansionism at this time: Kleomenes, far from being mad, was an astute politician with a more global view of affairs than most of his contemporaries. His ultimate failure does not change this assessment. But can we really believe that Sparta suddenly rose to thassalocrat status, overthrew two very powerful island tyrants with significant 'thalassocratic' navies in two years, and then fell like a meteor to surrender its status to Naxos, which it had just defeated and upon which it imposed a new government? In fact, Sparta's is the shortest period assigned to any city in the *List*.[103] If Myres is correct that the *Thalassocracy List* is a fifth-century compilation, memory of the separate Spartan naval interventions (Polykrates, Lygdamis, Dorieus' voyage, Ankhimolios) would account for the brief inclusion, for it is quite probable that the political and military initiatives of Kleomenes would be remembered rather than the identity of any agent supplying the ships. I doubt whether the Spartan thalassocracy was based on its own fleet. Sparta has no other known naval tradition earlier than these last years of the sixth century. There is, on the other hand, an indication that Sparta needed outside help for mounting naval operations. The attack on Polykrates, whenever it took place, was 'zealously assisted by the Corinthians',[104] i.e. Sparta (Kleomenes) was unable to undertake such a naval enterprise alone. Of course, the Corinthians must have had reasons to agree to attack Samos and they were certainly not likely to have been those adduced by Herodotos, for the Kypselidai were long gone and a pragmatic, commercially oriented oligarchy now ruled at Corinth. They were, rather, trade related. Corinth would later willingly neutralise Aigina in 506. However, it was a friend of Athens and Eretria, and Athens, but not Eretria, was still friendly with Lygdamis. Corinth, though a member of the Peloponnesian League, shortly demonstrates that it will not obey Spartan orders to attack old friends if it is not in its interests to do so, and it has no apparent motive now. Thus, if I am correct, Kleomenes was in a position rather akin to that of Peisistratos some three decades earlier and we must therefore ask from where else Kleomenes might have obtained the naval support necessary to act against Lygdamis and Phaleron by sea? I suggest that the ships were Eretrian, for Lygdamis would have been seen by both Kleomenes and Diagoras as still too closely attached to the sons of his old benefactor and ally and to the Eretrian oligarchs, Diagoras' political enemies. Evidence for Eretrian naval power, unlike that of Sparta, relies on more than the *List*. And Eretria had in the past been willing to assist others in overseas adventures with ships and money and would later do so in the Ionian revolt and the events leading up to it.

Such then was the diplomatic background in central Greece when, in 514, Hipparkhos was murdered by conspirators with strong Eretrian genealogical connections. The actual degree to which the plot was developed in, or aided from, Eretria cannot now be determined with accuracy. Nevertheless, there was probably considerable involvement, and Diagoras could scarcely have been unaware of all this activity. I believe that he had perceived that Sparta was the rising power and that in central Greece, for the moment, Kleomenes was Sparta and so, around about 519, he had taken positive steps to assure himself of the goodwill of the king. The aggressive intent of Kleomenes was shortly brought home very directly indeed to Hippias and to any other Greek state, the leadership of which was astute enough to read the signs, when about 511, as Herodotos tells us, he sent an expedition under the command of one Ankhimolios against Phaleron by sea (significantly) and sanctioned by Delphi.[105] The attack was, however, foiled on land, thanks to the Thessalian cavalry, and Ankhimolios was killed.

Meanwhile, having apparently at last seen the drift of things, if such is the right phrase to use when we are discussing matters that are being manipulated by men such as Kleomenes and states such as Corinth and Eretria, Hippias took steps to counter the Spartan threat. The Thessalian alliance was maintained and so Thessalian cavalry were on hand to meet the crises of 514 (the murder of Hipparkhos) and 511 (Ankhimolios' incursion). He still cultivated impotent Argos, but this may in fact have been counter-productive, since it would have created the impression at Sparta of Hippias as a dangerous meddler in the affairs of the Peloponnese and so strengthened Kleomenes' hand at home against the anti-interventionists. Overtures were made to Persia and to other foreign tyrants such as Hippoklos of Lampsakos, a client of Persia, again of dubious diplomatic value.[106] But that there was apparently no approach to Eretria to reactivate the old alliance is indicative of continued strained relations between the two *poleis*. Hippias must have known that Diagoras would not respond favourably or, having made an approach, he was rebuffed.

There is some non-literary evidence for a relationship between Sparta and Eretria at this time. We may consider a grave inscription for a Spartan who died at Eretria (Figure 7.4):[107]

> Pleistias,
> Sparta is his fatherland; in wide-landed Athens
> did he earn a living,[108] and he met Death, his fate, here.

The stone belongs to the last quarter of the sixth century. It may appear at first sight that Pleistias was an Athenian *metoikos* of Lakedaimonian origin. But why was he in Eretria? If a metic, he may of course have been there for business reasons. However, in 511, when Ankhimolios launched his attack on the trading centre and port of Phaleron, did Pleistias turn traitor to his adopted city? On the other hand, to betray one's *patris* was the greater crime.[109] Was he perhaps a victim, following the murder of Hipparkhos (514) and the subsequent Spartan raid, of anti-Spartan/anti-Eretrian hysteria, making Attica an unsafe place for Lakedaimonians, who fled (or, wounded, was taken) to pro-Spartan Eretria as a close-by safe haven? The epitaph preserves his own Lakonian Doric dialect and, if it reflects his speech-type, his origins would have been audibly obvious to any Athenian. It also would mean that Pleistias came to Athens reasonably late in life after his speech patterns had formed, and so his primary loyalty was probably still to Sparta. Indeed, the adjective used to describe Athens is one that is more commonly applied to Sparta.[110] Friedländer observes that the phrase 'Sparta is his fatherland' is stronger than simply saying that he was born in Sparta, and I would point out that in this phrase alone is the present tense used.[111] Pleistias clearly set his Spartan origin above that of his metic residence in Athens.

But was he perhaps a Spartiate? Volkmann believes so: 'We can therefore speak in this case only of a Spartiate, not of a Perioikist.'[112] Only those Spartans who fell in battle received a tombstone inscribed with their name.[113] One thinks of the tombs in which, in 403, the Spartiates who fell in the cause of the Athenian oligarchs were interred at Athens, which mention in Archaic Lakedaimonian script simply the names and place of death of the deceased. The Doric of our inscription also suggests that it was Spartans who held Pleistias in such esteem that they had his memory preserved in this distant resting place. It is unlikely that his family would have come all the way to Eretria to commission the stone, rather a Spartan on the spot. Thus I believe that Pleistias was a Lakedaimonian, whether Spartiate (possibly) or *perioikos*, who took part in Ankhimolios' ill-fated attack on Phaleron and received wounds in battle,

Figure 7.4 Grave stele of Pleistias the Lakedaimonian (*IG* XII 9, 286): ΠΛΕΙΣΤΙΑΣ | ΣΠΑΡΤΑ ΜΕΝ ΠΑΤΡΙΣ ΕΣΤΙΝ, ΕΝ ΕΥΡΥΧ | ΟΡΟΙΣ | ΑΘΑΝΑΙΣ ΕΘΡΑΦΘΕ, ΘΑΝΑΤΟ | ΔΕ ΕΝΘΑΔΕ ΜΟΙΡ' ΕΧΙ[Χ]Ε. From the Eretria Museum.

hence his right to a tombstone, and was removed to Eretria where he later died. If Sparta were sending its war casualties to Eretria, it must have had a prior understanding with the Eretrian tyrant. So, did Ankhimolios set out from a friendly Eretria, in Eretrian ships, to launch his attack on Phaleron, which was perhaps for the Eretrians a symbol of the damaging Peisistratid trading policies that had diverted Attic commerce from the Euboian Gulf?

There are two epitaphs from Eretria for Aiginetans, one for Mnesitheos from this very time, something that suggests that citizens from this pro-Spartan/anti-Athenian polis were also welcome at Eretria.[114] He was probably of considerable consequence, for his mother was able to dedicate a grave stele to him bearing a metrical epitaph with literary/heroic allusions.[115] Maybe he too was involved in these shadowy political machinations. Perhaps he too was a battle casualty. It would have been well in character for Aiginetan volunteers to have been involved in an attack on the long-standing enemy, Athens.[116]

The Eretrian ruler must have reached the conclusion, based on his appraisal of recent events in central Greece, that friendship with Kleomenes and Sparta was his best guarantee of future security, for, despite the failure of Ankhimolios' expedition, Diagoras, through his Athenian connections, had probably perceived that Hippias was unsaveable. Kleomenes' determination to achieve his objectives was clear already, and later events show only too well how stubborn he could be in pursuing his goals, and one of his prime aims was the overthrow of the tyranny at Athens and the installation of a pliant oligarchy there. Nevertheless, we should remember that the Spartans in fact had a relationship of *xenia* with the Peisistratidai,[117] and Kleomenes for his own political reasons entirely ignored this. His failures, however, led to the resurgence of the peace party at Sparta and the breach of *xenia* was adduced by them as a reason for Spartan policy failures under Kleomenes' direction.

So Diagoras had not only permitted political enemies of the Peisistratid government to base themselves at Eretria but he had also encouraged them and their Eretrian friends to stir up trouble in Attica. By proving his goodwill in this way, he became the ally (tool?) of the Spartan king. And Kleomenes would surely not forget his Eretrian ally later if circumstances changed for the worse. For the grand plot, conceived by Kleomenes in conjunction with the exiled Athenian dissidents and the willing collaboration of Diagoras, failed in its objective in the immediate term, because the agents, Harmodios and Aristogeiton, botched the attempt to assassinate both brother tyrants simultaneously. But, indirectly, success was ultimately achieved, because the resulting purge of his suspected enemies by the surviving Hippias, and increasing political repression, seriously undermined the popularity of the government, to the extent that in 511/10 Kleomenes was able to directly intervene and expel Hippias from Attica. In Kleomenes' train returned the old oligarchs (the Alkmaionidai *et al.*) from their various places of exile, Eretria a major one among them. With them came also all the ancient factional feuds and jealousies, to which could now be added the split between those who had endured the pains of exile to a greater or lesser extent and those who had temporised and remained at home, some even accepting office and honours from the tyrants. A volatile situation indeed. Making matters worse, Kleomenes took sides, perhaps believing that the Alkmaionidai might follow an independent foreign policy or even attempt to emulate the Peisistratidai. They were rich and had family connections with Eretria, a potentially powerful backer if able to be subverted. So he bypassed their leader, Kleisthenes' son of Megakles and set up the Philaid(?) Isagoras[118] as the leader of the narrow oligarchic regime that he now imposed on Athens. Meanwhile, Hippias, unsurprisingly if our restoration of events is broadly correct (but surprisingly if it is not), did not follow his father's example and flee into exile to Eretria where he himself had spent some ten years, nor to 'Peisistratid' Rhaikelos, but retired to Sigeion and from there finally into Persian-controlled lands. Some members of the family seem to have gone to Khios.[119] At Athens, the oligarchy maintained its position for but a short time until Kleisthenes the Alkmaionid, with his Eretrian family connections, brought in the *Demos* as a political factor and took power. However, at Eretria itself, politics had taken another turn.

Notes

1 Morris 1987, 94–6.
2 Str. 8, 6, 20 C378.
3 Arist. *Pol.* 1306a32–3.
4 Themelis 1983, 157–65. Ch. 4, pp. 95, 105.
5 For Corinthian influence on Eretrian sub-Geometric: Boardman 1952, 17. Boiotian fabric was also very similar to Eretrian. Eretrian pottery of seventh/sixth centuries: idem, 1957, 15–22; Morris 1987; Boardman 1952, 28–39. On ceramic quality: Boardman 1952, 48: 'about 550 BC and soon after . . . large grave amphorae, [were] painted in a competent black figure style at first sight quite Athenian.'
6 Boardman 1952, 48 (to Boiotia; Delos).
7 For the role of pottery in trade: Ch. 5, n. 239.
8 See Hignett, 1952, 118–22, for this argument. While Arist. *Pol.* 1274a and [Ar.] *Ath. pol.* 7, 2–4 attribute some role in the state granted to *thetes* by Solon, they specifically say that he excluded them from all offices, as also does Plut. *Sol.* 18, 2. On the status of *thetes* before Peisistratos: Hignett 1952, 84; 100–1; 122–3; J. Ober, *Mass and Elite in Democratic Athens; Rhetoric, Ideology, and the Power of the People*, Princeton, NJ, 1989, 60–8; Ostwald 1986, 20; 24–5. Even Kleisthenes limited their political rights.
9 M. I. Finley, *Ancient Slavery and Modern Ideology*, Harmondsworth, 1983, 87.
10 Ch. 6, pp. 190–1, n. 54.
11 Ober 1989, 66–7.
12 These figures are for festival/ceremonial troops; they must have been greater in an emergency. Knoepfler, 1997, 371–3 and idem, 1985a, 257–6, calculates from inscriptional evidence probably 5000 hoplites and 500 cavalry respectively with *c.* 6500–8500 citizens in the fourth century.
13 Salmon 1986, 165–9: 3000 the likely 'full levy' during the fifth century.
14 Ch. 5, pp. 184–5.
15 Plut. *Sol.* 13, 2; 14, 3–4; [Arist.] *Ath. pol.* 6, 3; 9, 2; Solon: frr. 32–4; 36.
16 The concept of *patrios politeia,* later adopted by democratic politicians, is essentially aristocratic–oligarchic in nature. Hignett 1952, 2; 93; Ostwald 1986, index: *P. politeia* and *p. nomos*; ibid., *Nomos and the Beginnings of Athenian Democracy*, Oxford, 1969, Ch. 2.
17 Ch. 6, pp. 190–1; Ch. 8, pp. 254–5.
18 Schol. (Sopater?) ad Ael. Arist. *Panath.* 189, 4. H. Parke, *Festivals of the Athenians*, London, 1977, 34; M. McGregor, 'Cleisthenes of Sicyon and the Panhellenic festivals', *TAPA* 72, 1941, 267. Schachermeyr: *RE* s.v. Peisistratos (3).
19 Arist. *Pol.* 1313b24–5.
20 J. Smith, *Athens under the Tyrants*, Bristol, 1989, 53–61.
21 French 1964, 25–6.
22 Heracl. Lemb. *Politeiai* 40; see Ch. 8, p. 237 and n. 14; pp. 238–9.
23 On Lygdamis: Arist. *Pol.* 1305a37–41. W. Forrest, *CAH*[3] III, Ch. 39d: 'Euboea and the islands', 258–9; Athenaios (quoting the lost *Naxion politeia* of Aristotle) 8, 348b (= Rose fr. 558); Hdt. 1, 61; 64; Polyaen. *Strateg.* 1, 23, 2; [Arist.] *Ath. pol.* 15, 2. Lygdamis must have been exceedingly rich for he was able to contribute both money and followers to the Peisistratid cause.

24 Salmon 1986, 188: for this notion in relation to the rise of Kypselos.

25 For the Kypselid (and the low) chronology: Appendix 3. Wallace, 1936a, 65, n. 1, has Periandros' reign entirely within the sixth century. Geyer, 1903, 80, between 539 and 510; H.-J. Gehrke, *Stasis*, Munich, 1985, 63, between 539 and 510; but cf. Knoepfler 1985a, 256, n. 50: 'il semble plus probable de le (Diagoras) placer quelques années après la réforme de Clisthène.'

26 It is generally assumed that the two names applied to the one man: see *FGrH* IIa, 358 supplement to 90F60 (Nic. Dam): Κύψελον· ‹τὸν καὶ Ψαμμήτιχον›.

27 See above, n. 22.

28 P. Bruneau, 'Une nouvelle publication de fouilles; Eretria III', *REG* 83, 1970, 129–30: (my translation), reviewing Bérard 1970. On political uses of hero cult: Snodgrass 1980, 38–40; R. Seaford, *Reciprocity and Ritual. Homer and Tragedy in the Developing City-State*, Oxford, 1994, 110–4, 180–1, 184, 194; Ridgway, 1992, 20, asserts that the hero shrine was used for cult until the early fifth century, citing Bérard, but cf. Bérard himself!

29 Bérard 1970, 65. Morris, 1987, 50–2, discusses the reasons for the introduction of funerary sumptuary laws in sixth century.

30 Ch. 4, p. 100 (harbour); p. 105 (agora).

31 Bury 1955, 151: 'The cause of this change (of Corinthian support from Samos to Miletos) was, at least in great measure, the natural sympathy of tyrannies.'

32 Hdt. 5, 94–5.

33 Nic. Dam. in *FGrH* 90F58, 3; Ar. *Pol.* 1315b29–30: Periandros became both tyrannical and warlike. He allied with Thrasyboulos to attack Sikyon: Frontin. *Strateg.* 3, 9, 7; Hdt. 1, 20. Nic. Dam., in *FGrH* 90F58, 1, notes that he was old when he died, his sons predeceasing him.

34 Thgn 885–94. I take the perfect ἀπόλωλεν (891) followed by the present κείρεται (see below, n. 53), φεύγουσι and διέπουσιν (892–3) to imply that Kerinthos has just now been destroyed resulting in the fact that the Lelantine Plain is (being) destroyed, his friends are now fleeing and his enemies (now) controlling the *polis*. On perfects with a strong future meaning (i.e. that Kerinthos was certainly about to be destroyed): Smyth 1920/59, 1950. We may note (without agreeing) Burn's (1929, 34) interpretation of these lines as 'a phil-Eretrian lament for Chalcidian success.'(!)

35 R. Legon, *Megara: The Political History of a Greek City State to 336 BC*, Ithaca, NY, 1981, Ch. 5, so characterises the democracy, placing it in the seventh century and (111) giving Theognis a birthyear close to 630. Adopting a lower chronological framework, Jeffery, 1976, 157, places the radical democracy in the sixth century, its replacement towards end of the century by a 'moderate' oligarchy and the life of Theognis *c.* 570–490(?). It may have fallen *c.* 544 according to T. Figueira, 'Chronological table: Archaic Megara 800–500 BC' in T. Figueira and G. Nagy (eds) 1985, 299–300 (Chronological table Q). If so, Theognis should have been in Euboia before then; however, Figueira's dates are high (cf. Appendix 3: The Kypselidai, Theognis and the low chronology). On the other hand, Jacobsen 1964, 220, n. 32, dates the destruction of Kerinthos to 506.

36 Thgn. 783–4.

37 Thgn. 786.

38 See above, n. 35. Also: J. Edmonds, *Greek Elegy and Iambus* (Loeb II), Cambridge MA, 1968, intro. 21 (floruit 548); D. Wenden, *Hesiod and Theognis*, Harmondsworth, 1979 162–3 (post 580). J. Carrière, *Théognis de Mégare. Étude sur le recueil élégiaque attribué à ce poète*, Paris(?), *c.* 1948, 10; and idem, *Théognis. Poèmes élégiaques: texte établi et traduit accompagné d'un commentaire*, Paris, 1962 (T. *c.* fifty years old in 544).

39 *LSJ* 1333.

40 As E. Harrison *Studies in Theognis*, Cambridge, 1902, 289 wisely remarked: 'other things being equal, it is desirable that adjacent pieces should be interpreted in the light of one another.'

41 Thgn. 757–86, 773, 775–6, 780–1.

42 On Theognis' use of *agathoi* and *kakoi*, (synonyms: *esthloi* and *deiloi*): P. Greenhalgh, 'Aristocracy and its advocates in Archaic Greece', *G&R* 19, 1972, 197–207. They may sometimes be social class terms, sometimes moral. V. Cobb-Stevens, 'Opposites, reversals and ambiguities: the unsettled world of Theognis', in Figueira and Nagy (eds), 159–75; the intro. to this collection is helpful (7–8 paras 18, 21). Some modern writers use the terms in specially defined ways: Morris 1987, 9, 94–6; Starr 1977, 123–8.

43 Theognis' poetry was written in an age of 'democratic turmoil': T. Hudson-Williams, 'Theognis and his poems', *JHS* 23, 1903, 4–5.

44 Thgn. 889–90. Greenhalgh 1973, 93; Th. 5, 72, 23. A. Snodgrass, *Arms and Armour of the Greeks*, Ithaca, NY, 1967, 85; Gomme (Andrewes and Dover) IV 1970, 121.

45 Hom. *Il.* 2, 537–8.

46 Thgn. 784.

47 In the atlas of Rhodhakis, *c.* 1965, I, 528, it is listed as one of the significant plains (today called the Plain of Mandoudhi) on the island.

48 Geyer 1903, 107–9; Str. 10, 1, 5 C446 calls it merely πολείδιον; St. Byz. s.v. Ἐλλοπία calls it a χωρίον τῆς Εὐβοίας. Kerinthos does not appear in the *Athenian Tribute Lists* and so was probably not autonomous even then (or had been destroyed).

49 Which Theognis mentions in line 892.

50 See above, n. 45. Recent evidence on its location: E. Sapouna-Sakellaraki, 'Mycenaean Kerinthos', in D. Evelly, I. Lemos and S. Sherratt (eds), *Minotaur and Centaur. Studies in the Archaeology of Crete and Euboea Presented to Mervyn Popham*, Oxford, 1996, 106–10.

51 Forrest 1957, 162: he is talking of events that he places in the seventh and not, as I would, in the sixth century.

52 Ibid. Cobb-Stevens, Figueira and Nagy, 1985, intro. 1, para. 2.

53 Forrest 1956, 51.

54 Aen. Tact. 4, 1. D. Whitehead, *Aineias the Tactician. 'How to Survive under Siege'*, Oxford, 1990, 106, suggests ῥινήν (file)* instead of πυργάστρην (brazier, fire-pot) and διαπρίσας (sawing)** instead of διαπρήσας (burning), which I prefer because the bar could have been sawn through with less need for the elaborate ruse that attracted Aineas' interest, but the change would seem to require also the deletion of the consequently superfluous bringing of the fire-pot, kept going day and night, although see Boswell's suggestion (106).

55 W. A. Oldfather: *Aeneas Tacticus, Asclepiodotus, Onasander*, Cambridge, MA, 1928/86, 38, n. 1.

56 Knoepfler 1981, 289–329.

57 Tod 1968, 160. Whitehead mentions events in this year (D.S. 16, 7, 2) but no capture of Khalkis.

58 Bar cutting (if not bar burning): Th. 2, 4, 4 (Plataia, in 431); 4, 111, 2 (Torone, in 424/3).

59 Antileon: Arist. *Pol.* 1316a29–30; Alkaios (see below, n. 63); Ar. *Eq.* 1036–44 is clearly referring to a paradigmatic populist tyrant called Antileon, for he wishes us to compare the Athenian demagogue Kleon with him. Solon fr. 33 (ap. Plut. *Sol.* 14), however (if they are indeed his lines), does not mention any tyrant or city by name. There was a fourth-century politician Antileon from Khalkis-on-the-Euripos (a descendant?) honoured in a decree from Samos (old ally of Khalkis). C. Habicht, 'Samische Volksbeschlüsse der hellenistischen Zeit', *MDAI(A)* 72, 1957, 157–64.

60 Arist. *Pol.* 1316a29–30. Flagellation may have been the standard way of conceiving punishment of defeated tyrants: Alkaios: E. Lobel and D. Page, *Poetarum Lesbiorum Fragmenta*, Oxford, 1955 231 (fr. 296 P2) emended by P. Maas, 'How Antileon's tyranny ended', *CR* ns 6, 1956, 200; accepted by H. Lloyd-Jones, 'More about Antileon, tyrant of Chalcis (Solon, fr. 33 and Aristophanes, *Eq.* 1042–44)', *CP* 70, 1975, 197. Alkaios was born shortly before 600 and died old (he refers to his 'grey breast'); it is therefore not beyond reason he lived on into the 530s.

61 For Phoxos: Hom. *Il.* 2, 218–9. If used as a proper noun the accent alters (Φόξος). φοξός = 'peaked in the head', an indication of impudence: [Arist.] *Phgn.* 812a8. Thersites was φοξός. But φοξοί were thought to possess great physical strength (a working-class quality?): Hippoc. *Epid.* 6, 1, 2. The name occurs at Phokaia, Polyaen. *Strateg.* 8, 37).

62 Arist. *Pol.* 1304a29–30.

63 Ael. *VH* 6, 1. Plut. *Per.* 23, 2 uses a similar phrase: Χαλκιδέων μὲν τοὺς ἱπποβότας λεγομένους, referring to *Hippobotai* as the ruling group when Perikles suppressed the Euboian Revolt in 447/6. Geyer, 1903, 63, believes that the passage from Ailianos belongs to this time and not 506, but regards the outcome of the Lelantine War (which he dates earlier) as consolidating the power of the *Hippobotai* at Khalkis (58).

64 Plut. *Sol.* 14.

65 Boardman 1957, 27–9 n. 163.

66 Ch. 4, pp. 98, 122–5.

67 Ch. 4, p. 123. Liv. 35, 38, 3. E. Sage, *Livy* (Loeb X: Books 35–7), Cambridge, MA, 1934/85, 112–13: though 'the festival may still have existed in Livy's time', the present tense may be preserved from his source. Knoepfler 1972, 282–301; idem, 1988, 382–421. W. Goodwin, *De potentiae veterum gentium maritimarum epochis apud Eusebium*, Göttingen, 1855 (non vidi), 18, believes that it celebrates the victory of 506.

68 *IG* XII 9, 296: Χαιρίōν | 'Αθēναῖōς | Εὐπατριδōν | ἐνθάδε κεῖ - | τα[ι]. K. Kourouniotis, ''Επιθραφαὶ Χαλκίδος καὶ 'Ερετρίας', *AE* 1899, coll. 144, no. 10 (sixth century); A. Raubitschek, *Dedications from the Athenian Akropolis; a Catalogue of the Inscriptions of the Sixth and Fifth Centuries* BC, (with L. Jeffery), Cambridge, MA, 1949, 10, no. 6; 364, no 330 (extends the dating down to 514). For Kharion: Kirchner, *Prosopographia Attica* 1902, 15254; Davies 1971, 9–14.

69 Jeffery 1976, 68.

70 Raubitschek 1949, 364, no. 330; Davies 1971, 13.

71 See above, n. 68: Εὐπατριδῶν. Ibid., 11. Raubitschek 1949, 364, no. 330.

72 Khairion himself had raised an altar on the Acropolis at Athens before his exile: Raubitschek loc. cit.

73 Raubitschek 1949, 11: 'Εσθλō πατρὸς hῦς. On *esthlos*: see above, n. 62 for the references. Davies 1971, 13.

74 Raubitschek 1949, 364–5. Alkibiades and the Salaminioi: Davies 1971, 10–13. On Alkibiades' family and as a Eupatrid, Isocr. 16, 25; Pl. *Alc.* I, 121a; Plut. *Alc.* 1, 1; Didymos (schol. ad Pi. *Nem.* 2, 19). But Davies doubts any connection of Khairion's family with that of Alkibiades.

75 [Arist.] *Ath. pol.* 19, 3 (the Leipsydrion skolion). Davies 1971, 12.

76 [Arist.] *Ath. pol.* 19, 3; Hdt. 5, 62.

77 I accept that Hippias was the elder and succeeded to his father's position. In 526/5 he held the arkhonship, perhaps a formality to stress continuity of the dynasty's rule.

78 G. Dickins, 'The growth of Spartan policy', *JHS* 32, 1912, 28.

79 Sealey 1976, 53–5; 60, n. 5 (Kypselid chronology again! Appendix 3).

80 Hdt. 5, 91.

81 Th. 3, 68, 5: Plataia fell to the Spartans in 427, 93 years after the beginning of its alliance with the Athenians.

82 Hdt. 6, 108.

83 For the sequence: M. Miller, *The Thalassocracies – Studies in Chronography II*, Albany, NY, 1975, 32–39.

84 For these events, with emphasis on Spartan motives: Dickins 1912; for a critique of this paper: G. Grundy, 'The policy of Sparta', *JHS* 32, 1912, 261–9. Dickens' reply: 'The growth of Spartan policy – a reply', *JHS* 33, 1913, 111–2. On Megara: Legon 1981, 136–56. On Corinth: Will 1955, 634–63; Salmon 1986, 240–52.

85 For Thessaly: Ch. 5, pp. 169–70; Forrest 1956, 42.

86 Ch. 8, p. 326. Hdt. 5, 30. J. Myres, 'On the list of 'Thalassocracies' in Eusebius', *JHS* 26, 1906, 97–8, for an interesting reconstruction of events *c.* 515–505.

87 Παχεῖς. Hdt. 5, 31.

88 Myres 1906, 98.

89 Thomson 1965, 123. Hdt. 5, 55–8. For the Gephyraioi as a *genos*: B. Meritt, 'Greek inscriptions' (26: Stele of the Gephyraioi) *Hesperia* 8, 1939, 80–1; idem, 'Greek inscriptions' (17: The Genos of the Gephyraioi) *Hesperia* 9, 1940, 86–96. In the first century the clan was still associated with the north coast of Attica, as these inscriptions show.

90 Hdt. 5, 57.

91 Str. 9, 2, 10 C404 calls Tanagrans γεφυραῖοι. For Gephyra as a name for Tanagra: St. Byz. and *E.M.* s.v. Γέφυρα.

92 Aristoteles of Khalkis identified Tanagra with Oropos: St. Byz. s.v. Τάναγρα. R. Sealey, 'Who was Aristogeiton?', *BICS* 7, 1960a, 38, nn. 62–3.

93 Ibid. 33–43; Kirchner 1902, 1775, 1777, 2232, 8930.

94 Sealey 1976, 145–6.

95 Heracl. Lemb. *Politeiai* 40.

96 Hdt. 5, 63, 1.

97 Dickens 1912, 29.

98 An alternative hypothesis dates his fall to 527/6 as a prelude to that of Polykrates in that year: D. Leahy, 'The Spartan embassy to Lygdamis', *JHS* 77, 1957, 272–5.

99 The attack on Lygdamis is generally so seen: Myres 1906, 98; *RE* s.v. Lygdamis 2 (Kahrstedt); ibid., s.v. Tyrannis, 1831. H. Parke, 'Polycrates and Delos', *CQ* 40, 1946, 105–8 and Sealey 1976, 143 prefer 525/4 [perhaps suggested in Plut. *Lac. apophtheg.* 67 (*Mor.* 236c)].

100 1906, 98–102.

101 Eretria's follows that of Naxos in 505.

102 Hdt. 5, 42.

103 Myres 1906, 88; Miller 1975, 37–9.

104 Hdt. 3, 44–59, esp. 48.

105 Hdt. 5, 63.

106 Hdt. 5, 138; Sealey 1976, 145–6.

107 *IG* XII 9, 286. For a description of this stele in the general formulaic context of Archaic Greek grave markers: C. Sourvinou-Inwood, *'Reading' Greek Death, to the End of the Classical Period*, Oxford, 1995, 168–9 who dates it *c.* 500–475; Jeffery 1961/90, 86: 'first quarter of the fifth century.' Ziebarth in *IG* XII 9: 'saec. VI a.Chr.' H. Volkmann, 'Ein Spartanergrab in Eretria (zu *IG* XII 9, 286)', *Klio* 31, 1938, 248: sixth century.

108 τρέφω (Doric τράφω)= 'I nourish'. *LSJ* cites ἐθράφθη (using this inscription) as the 1 aor. pass. form. P. Friedländer, *Epigrammata. Greek Inscriptions in Verse*, Chicago, 1987, 82 notes (ἐθράφθη as a 'vulgarism'). For other uses of τρέφω in grave markers: Volkmann 1938, 244–9.

109 Volkmann, 1938, 247, discusses a number of similar expressions of patriotism in inscriptional sources. For the Greek attitude to the *patris:* Pl. *Crit.* 51c and *Mx.* 237b–238b.

110 Hom. *Od.* 3, 414; 15, 1; Pi. *Nem.* 10, 52.

111 Σπάρτα μὲν πατρὶς ἐστιν. Friedländer 1987, 82.

112 Volkmann 1938, 249: 'So wie hier kann nur ein Spartiate sprechen, kein Periöke.' Cf. Friedländer.

113 Plut. *Lyc.* 27, 2. Tyrtaios fr. 12 (Loeb 76–7), seventh century implies that only a limited group of the dead would have an ἀρίσημος (notable; visible) tomb, e.g. a fallen soldier and his descendants. An exception was that the kings were buried with named markers following elaborate funerals: Hdt. 6, 58; X. *HG* 3, 3, 3; [X.] *Lac.* 15, 9. Morris 1987, 44–54, esp. 50.

114 *IG* XII 9, 285. Another early epitaph for an Aiginetan and his wife: *IG* XII 9, 300. Sourvinou-Inwood 1995, 211–2.

115 Friedländer 1987, 130–1 notes the incongruities between provincialisms of style and spelling and the generally elevated tone.

116 Hdt. 5, 82.

117 Hdt. 5, 90–1.

118 D. McCargar, 'Isagoras, son of Teisandros and Isagoras, eponymous archon, 508/7 BC' *Phoenix* 28, 1974, 275–81; for doubts concerning the Philaid relationship: Davies 1971, 295–6.

119 Forrest 1982b, 134.

8

THE ERETRIAN DEMOCRACY (*c.* 509–490)

In the midst of this inter-*polis* turmoil and intrigue, and after some thirty years (*c.* 538 to *c.* 509) in power, Diagoras fell and he left Eretria. Although by this time he must have been quite an old man, his exit was not by reason of his death. It is interesting that the end of his political career is so close to that of his enemy Hippias at Athens. So we must ask why it occurred at this particular time, for the two events are probably related. At this distance of time and as a result of the paucity of our sources his disappearance appears to have been sudden, but this is unlikely for there had been both internal and external pressures building against him and his city for some years. But it was ultimately his involvement with Kleomenes that brought him down, though when he decided to become involved with Kleomenes' intrigues in central Greece, and in Attica in particular, it must have seemed to him the safest course of action to follow.

During Diagoras' rule, the entrepreneurial class continued to flourish as it had under the previous regime, while the *thetes* began to acquire more political significance, the result of his own policies of fostering Eretria as a commercial/artisan state, with a navy that had certainly become politically very important in the last decades of the sixth century. The development of industry and trade provided some chance of absorbing the rural dispossessed in the workshops and in shipping. Burn, in his analysis of Eretria's part in the Ionian struggle, was right to observe that: 'Eretria did not rise to this [naval] prominence suddenly from nothing.'[1] It would only be a matter of time before the men who manned the ships would begin to demand some say over matters of war and peace and, by extension, over foreign policy generally. But Diagoras' association with Sparta and Kleomenes, whose policies included placing narrowly based oligarchies into power in states with which Sparta was allied, would not have appealed to the leaders of the emerging thetic group within Eretria, which was being required to help implement some of them, such as the sea-borne intervention against Lygdamis. The political significance of these policies for tyrants such as Diagoras himself should not have escaped him, although there is evidence that he was not in the end abandoned by his ally Kleomenes.

That the thetic class had become important during the last years of Diagoras' tyranny is implied by the fact that his regime was followed directly by a democracy of the 'Kleisthenic' type of which, 'though the public organisation of Eretria owes a lot to the Athenian model, it is not a copy.'[2] There is epigraphic evidence for a democracy at Eretria in the last decade of the sixth century in the form of a proxeny decree, first published and edited by Peek, and later revised, supplemented and dated to the early fifth century by Wallace.[3] However, an earlier date seems preferable, for the closed *heta* used in the inscription 'may be abnormal as late as the early-fifth century.'[4] Wallace believed that 'rhotacism is . . . known not to have occurred earlier than the fifth century'[5] and this undoubtedly influenced his dating of the text. This belief is no longer tenable however, as the more recently discovered sixth-century dedicatory epigram for an athlete clearly demonstrates.[6] Wallace thought that this decree might be 'the earliest proxeny decree to have survived to us on stone by about a quarter of a century'[7] and during discussions in 1989 and subsequently, Professor M. Osborne[8] has confirmed to me that, to his knowledge, no earlier examples had then been discovered.[9] The only possible period of the fifth century to which the decree could be assigned is its first decade. Eretria was destroyed by the Persians in 491/0 and much of its surviving population deported to Asia.[10] Thus, it is unlikely that the decree belongs to the 480s, while the 470s or later may definitely be ruled out on stylistic grounds. Green and Sinclair[11] show that, although Eretria did not disappear altogether as a state after 490, as the presence of the Eretrian ships at Salamis makes clear, 'significant numbers' of Athenians migrated to Eretria over the next two decades. Rhotacism is less likely if Attic speakers were dominant in the city, as is likely in the second quarter of the fifth century. Not only epigraphically but also historically and politically, as we shall see shortly, the decree is better placed in a late-sixth-century context.

The introductory formulae, although incomplete, are characteristic of decrees of a fully democratic state:[12]

> It seemed good to the Boule and the Demos being in regular session, the tribe Mekis(s)tis holding the *epimeneia*,[13] on the fourteenth day of Heraion.

I shall return to its important constitutional implications, but the text also provides interesting details that bear upon events following the fall of Diagoras. The *proxenia* recipient, Aristoteles Kheiloniou, has a most intriguing name in the light of Diagoras' involvement with the Spartan king, and Herakleides Lembos' statement that when he fell, Diagoras set out for Sparta: 'Diagoras having died at Corinth while travelling to Sparta, the Eretrians [later] erected a statue to him.'[14]

Who was the Kheilonios whose son was honoured in a decree of newly democratic Eretria? Kheilon is not a common name in the prosopography of ancient Greece,[15] but Kheilonios is even rarer, a *hapax* in fact.[16] The recent involvement of Kleomenes I, himself a relative of the famous anti-tyrant ephor,[17] in the affairs of Eretria and of Diagoras in particular, makes the award to Aristoteles Kheiloniou unlikely to be fortuitous, especially bearing in mind Diagoras' abortive flight to Sparta. But why would a decree, whose nature implies that the Eretrian democracy awarding it considered the recipient to be a benefactor who had been looking after the interests of the city and its government, have been enacted on behalf of someone apparently related to Kleomenes, the exiled Diagoras' ally? Such decrees were formal political expressions of gratitude to individuals from governments in power in Greek *poleis*. Thus a descendant, familial or political (it is just possible he was the son, perhaps a grandson, but more likely related less directly),[18] of Kheilon himself, has been singled out for special honour and public recognition by the new regime in Eretria in a decree that, as we have noted, is a very early example of its type, one belonging to a period when such honours had not yet become purely routine.

Is the decree related to Diagoras' attempted flight? And, why did he try to go to Sparta? He must surely have gone to ask Kleomenes to reinstate him in power in Eretria, in much the same way as Hippias went to Dareios. After all, since he had been a major instrument in the implementation of Kleomenes' policies in central Greece, he might reasonably have expected a return favour from the Spartan king. If realpolitik required, Sparta would support a tyrant. After the events of 506, the Spartans realised that they had made a mistake in acting against Hippias. They could then speak without embarrassment of 'our good friend Hippias'![19] Diagoras, moreover, unlike Hippias, had never been an enemy, so he need not have gone south without good hopes. He probably intended to ask for a Peloponnesian army to restore him. Khalkis was now a Spartan ally, so passage of the Euripos should have posed no great problem.

However, Kleomenes was himself not without enemies at home. Nor was he the only powerful figure in Sparta claiming descent from the great ephor: Demaratos, his royal colleague and enemy, was also a relation.[20] We may think of each king as representing, within the current state of Spartan foreign policy making, one of two aspects of Kheilon's activities. Kleomenes the interventionist pursued that element of Kheilon's policy, which said go forth, put down tyrants and establish friendly and, above all, dependent oligarchies in their stead. Demaratos seems to have stood for the policy that once the foreign scene was ordered to Sparta's liking, then let sleeping dogs lie. Both kings enjoyed fluctuating support within the Spartan *gerousia* (council), where policy was in practice determined, and this instability within the ranks of the Spartan *gerontes* has been described by modern historians in terms of a struggle for ascendancy between the 'peace' and the 'war' parties. In this context, Kleomenes may be regarded as leader of the 'war' and Demaratos of the 'peace' factions, although these terms are not at all satisfactory and oversimplify the political situation. Probably both sides would have claimed to be the true political heirs of Kheilon. Diagoras, if he had made it to Sparta, would have had to deal with a Spartan government by no means united over how to deal with the political situation in central Greece. And, no doubt, as a former ally and friend of Kleomenes, he would have been aware of these cross-currents within the *gerousia*.[21]

Under such circumstances, the new government at Eretria would be obliged to send a delegation to Sparta to try to forestall Diagoras and counter any arguments for intervention put forward for him by his supporters in the *gerousia*. Such counter-delegations were standard moves in Greek diplomatic practice and Thucydides narrates several such debates at Sparta itself. The democratic delegation would naturally choose a member of the anti-Kleomenid faction to argue its case before the *gerontes*. This man was, I suggest, Aristoteles Kheiloniou, a member of the *gerousia* allied and/or related to the Eurypontid king and so a supporter of the party opposed to Kleomenes. The Eurypontid kings were reputed to be more 'pro-democratic' than their Agiad colleagues, and Demaratos' name seems to symbolise that tradition. The new regime at Eretria would hardly have made its case through a political ally of Kleomenes, friend of their late tyrant. That the Demaratids were already gaining the ascendancy in 509/8 when Diagoras set out seems certain, because in the following year (508/7) they were able to thwart Kleomenes' attempts to restore Isagoras at Athens. But although the Eretrian government envoys probably arrived at Sparta to put their case, Diagoras did not. He reached Corinth, where he died, perhaps in 509.[22] Whether his death was from natural causes or murder, we do not know. Suidas hints at suicide.[23] Although he was old by 509, he was probably assassinated. There would certainly have been people both at Eretria and at Sparta for whom his death would have been welcome. He may have been killed to ensure that Kleomenes would never use him, as he used Isagoras at Athens, as an excuse to intervene in Eretrian affairs. The Eretrian delegation[24] returned home and proposed the decree honouring Aristoteles for his important support.

There remains one problem arising from the passage from Herakleides. He says that after Diagoras' death in Corinth, the Eretrians erected a statue to him. If my reconstruction of events is correct and the remark itself has any truth, this decision is hard to understand unless the statue was set up some time later.[25] Herakleides lived *c.* 170. He, or a source, most likely the writer of an *Eretrieon Politeia,*[26] such as Aristotle the philosopher (not the proxeny recipient), who is said to have died in Euboia, may have seen such a statue, perhaps erected by any one of many later governments at Eretria, which include tyrannies. The city was subject to frequent changes of government from the fourth century onwards and few were democracies. Later Eretrians may have looked back on his *tyrannis* as a golden age of Eretrian achievement, as did Athenians to that of Peisistratos. If such is the case, then they were not far wrong, particularly with respect to the period before he allowed himself to become enmeshed in the schemes of Kleomenes I.

In 507, Kleisthenes Megakleous the Alkmaionid began the reform of the Athenian geo-political structure upon which ultimately the democracy was based. This chapter will offer evidence that his work follows, not only chronologically but substantially as well, the political changes at Eretria, which occurred immediately after the fall of Diagoras. This certainly runs counter to the generally held view that democracy was pioneered at Athens and that it was Athens that influenced and indeed promoted constitutional change at Eretria and elsewhere.

As was post-Kleisthenic Attica, the Eretrias and its citizens were divided for political purposes into districts (*khoroi*), demes (*demoi*) and tribes (*phylai*) but not, apparently, *trittyes*[27]. In 1947 Wallace published his seminal paper, 'The demes of Eretria',[28] upon which all subsequent discussion of Eretrian geo-political arrangements has been based. Recently Gehrke and Knoepfler have very considerably modified Wallace in light of later work on the Eretrian politico-territorial divisions, and Cairns also discusses them in two papers.[29] In the earlier, he devotes a section to the terminology, arguing against the views of Lewis,[30] who thought that *demos* was not used at all at Eretria and that the Eretrian system of territorial division is in fact opposed to the Kleisthenic. However, Lewis is wrong; there were *demoi*, and they were so called at Eretria.

Two terms for territorial divisions of the Eretrias are known from inscriptions: *demos* and *khoros*.[31] The first has become specifically known only since Lewis wrote in 1962, although its existence might have been inferred from the term *demarkhos*, which occurs in inscriptions published in 1915 in the *IG*.[32] Lewis applied *khoros* to the smallest units rather than to those that Wallace called 'districts', using a Keian treaty of *isopoliteia* with Eretria as evidence,[33] restoring it in l. 3. However, the evidence now available certainly seems to require *demos*, as both Knoepfler and Cairns argue,[34] and it could just as well be so restored on the analogy of a similar inscription involving Keos and Histiaia.[35] Presumably Lewis assumed *khoros* from its occurrence at l. 8 but: first, it here refers to a Keian territorial division (cf. the Histiaian treaty); second, the Keian system has the additional division, the *trittys*,[36] absent from both the Eretrian and Histiaian schemes. Even if *khoros* = *demos* at Keos, as Lewis believed,[37] it would not follow that it meant that at Eretria. It seems, in fact, that fourth-century Keos had no demes as such[38] but rather a scheme consisting of *phylai*, *trittyes* and *khoroi* as the inscriptions suggest. Keos by the time of this inscription was made up of four original *poleis*, though Poiessa may not have been part of the federation.[39] Thus the term *khoros* might refer to the territory of the component city-states that made up the Keian Federation; third, one of the two epigraphically attested Eretrian district names, (Mesokhoros)[40] seems to indicate clearly that the *khoroi* were indeed the larger territorial divisions. In another inscription (*IG* XII 9, 189) from Eretria itself, *demarkhoi* are responsible for the organisation of the most important religious festival for all Eretrians, the Artemiria.[41] It also mentions two names, Metaxy and Phylake,[42] that may or may not be district names. Although I have believed for some time that these were toponymic terms, I now allow that Knoepfler may be correct to see them as epithets of Artemis. Phylake is a known by-name of this goddess.[43] Given the period and circumstances of the inscription, Artemis as the city goddess who 'stands between' (Metaxy) factions and is 'protectress' of the *polis* is an attractive suggestion. Cairns believes that *IG* XII 9, 189 describes 'what must have been an administrative feature of this [mid-fourth-century] democratic period at Eretria, religious events organised jointly by two of the Districts and involving the Demes.'[44] But this theory has been criticised in detail by Knoepfler,[45] for it depends upon identifying the certain district name Mesokhoros with the Metaxy of the inscription and this remains at best conjectural. At Tamynai,[46] the *demarkhos* seems to be a quasi-secular official, levying fines on those who violate agreements concerning the leasing of temple lands.

Knoepfler argues convincingly that *demos* was indeed the term applied to the smallest geo-political division as at Athens. These were organised into larger units, the *khoroi* of *IG* XII 9, 241, which Wallace simply called 'districts', and of which he discerned five. He gives the only known name, Mesokhoron (it is more likely Mesokhoros), to his number III. There is a fragmentary second name read by Ziebarth:[47] [. . .]λ[. . .]ασι[. . . . . .] . . ., and tentatively restored, which Wallace[48] tolerates, as Larasiou, for District V; Wallace does not again refer to it; and neither he nor Cairns assigns it to one of the five districts. Knoepfler argues against the name Larasios(-on) suggesting tentatively Karn(ei)asion.[49] In May 1997, I was able to go to Eretria with the specific objective of examining this section of the stone. The results from this autopsy are disappointing. I must assume that considerable deterioration of the surface has occurred since Wallace examined the inscription some time before 1947 (Figures 8.1 and 8.2).[50]

Based on my own observations and what I can see in my photographs, together with a comparison of the restorations of Ziebarth, Peek and Wallace, I offer the comparative table of *IG* XII 9, 241, l. 77 (Ziebarth) or 107 (Wallace) and my own suggestions (Table 8.1).[51]

Paralios(-ion), which echoes territorial names found in Attica and the Corinthia,[52] has not hitherto been proposed and, since Paraliou fits just as well, I would argue for it in preference to Larasion[53] or Karneiasion as the name of District V. But if, despite recent doubts, Metaxy can be equated with Mesokhoros, then Phylake too must be a district name and belong to IV.[54]

Table 8.1 Comparative readings of *IG* XII 9, Suppl. 549

Ziebarth IG XII 9, 241: 77 (107):	ΛΑΡΑΙ[ΟΥ]ΟΠΛΙΤΑΙ
Wallace 1947, 121: 107 (77):	[.]Λ[.]ασι[2/3 letters]όπλῖται
Walker: what I actually saw is: 77 (107): which I would restore as:	 ΑΙ Α \ ΛΙΤΑΙ [Π]ΑΡΑΛΙΟΥΟΠΛΙΤΑΙ

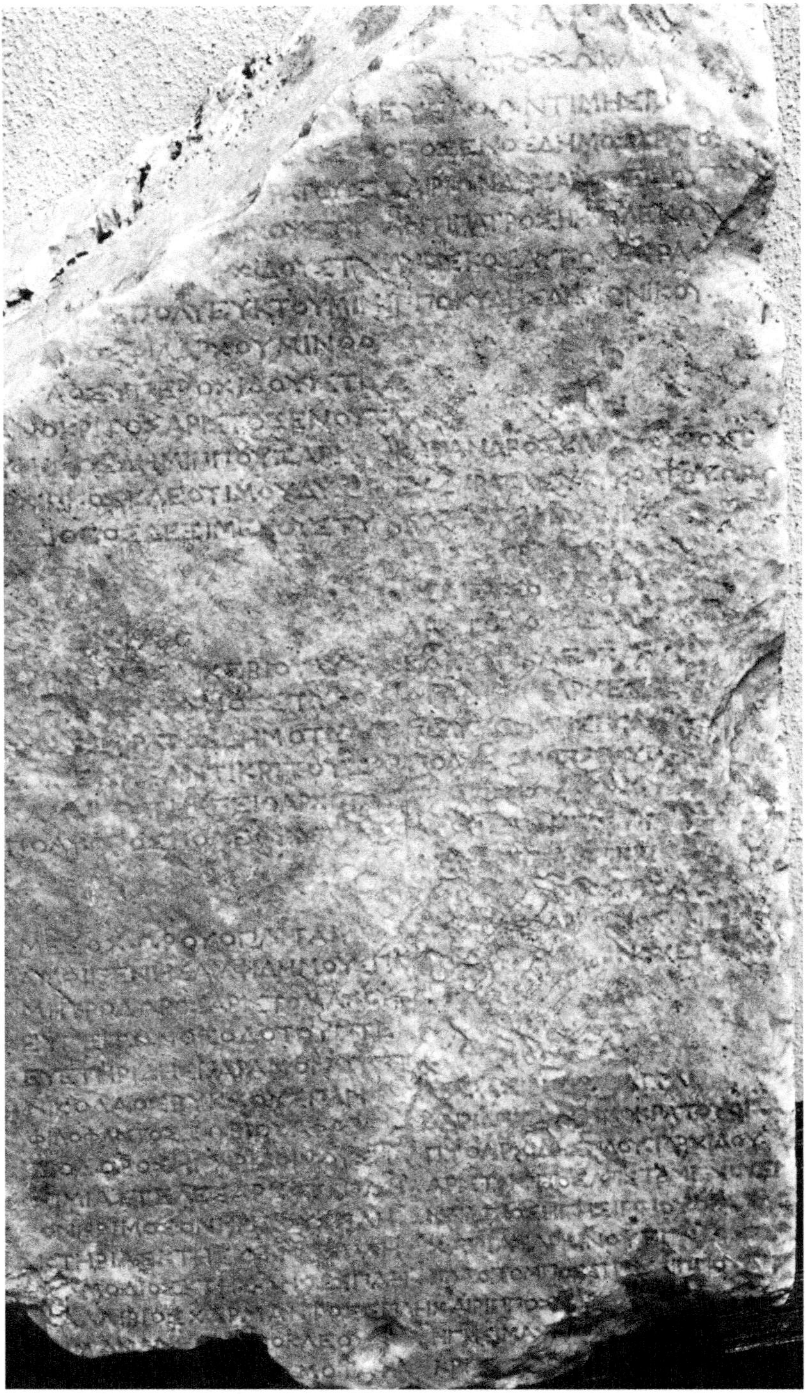

Figure 8.1 *IG* XII 9, 241: inscribed face, Eretria Museum.

In his second paper, while Cairns notes that the demes grouped into *khoroi* do not overlap, he suggests that the *tribes* – of which we now know the names of two, Mekistos and Narkittis[55] – are, like their Attic counterparts, 'artificial entities made up of demes of all five *khoroi* of the Ἐρετρική and so analogous to the Kleisthenic tribes of Athens.'[56] Both Cairns and Knoepfler, who goes well beyond what Cairns established and attempts a reconstruction of the whole Eretrian tribal system, also point out that the artificial names, made up as at Athens from names of local heroes, are quite unlike those of the traditional Ionian tribes, indicating a tribal reform of a 'Kleisthenic' type. Wallace scarcely comments on a possible relationship between the Eretrian and Attic deme systems, remarking only that 'membership in a deme may have been at Eretria, as at Athens, hereditary rather than dependent on where one lived' and '[Eretria] is, on a smaller scale, in this as in other ways, so similar to Athens.'[57] He is talking about territorial states generally rather than specific political structures, but the comment may indicate something of his attitude. However, one fact is the absence of any mention in the corpus of Eretrian inscriptions to *trittyes* or to some equivalent at Eretria. This constitutes a significant difference between the two. Their absence may be due to the accidents of survival in the epigraphic record, but I do not think so, for there is evidence weighing positively against their existence at Eretria in the treaty decree from Keos.[58] The relevant section (ll. 1–8) is as follows:

> If a Keian wishes to participate as a citizen in Eretria, let him register his name and let the generals give to him a *phyle* and a *demos*[59] in which he may be enrolled; and if an Eretrian wishes to participate as a citizen of Keos let him register his name with the *thesmophylakes* [guardians of the law] and let the *thesmophylakes* give him a *phyle*, *trittys* [a local sub-division of a *phyle*] and *khoros*.

Thus, while a citizen of Eretria entering into Keian citizenship required membership of a *trittys* as well as of a tribe and *khoros* (whatever that may have been on Keos), there is no indication that *trittys* membership was required or even possible at Eretria, and if it were we should expect to hear of it here since one would think that the legal procedures would need to be precisely set out, although it must be admitted that there is no mention of units called *khoroi* at Keos in its similar treaty with Histiaia.[60] For Eretria, however, the lack of any reference to *trittyes* in this text is reinforced by a total absence of the term throughout the whole *corpus* of Eretrian inscriptions,[61] so I think that we can reasonably assert that there were indeed no *trittyes* at Eretria. Bradeen[62] believes that the smaller Eretrian probouleutic group would render the *trittyes* superfluous since there was probably only one *proboulos* per tribe. Whereas *trittyes* were already part of the pre-Kleisthenic civic organisation of Attica,[63] they almost certainly were not part of the earlier Eretrian system. This would explain why the two later democratic constitutions differed in this respect;

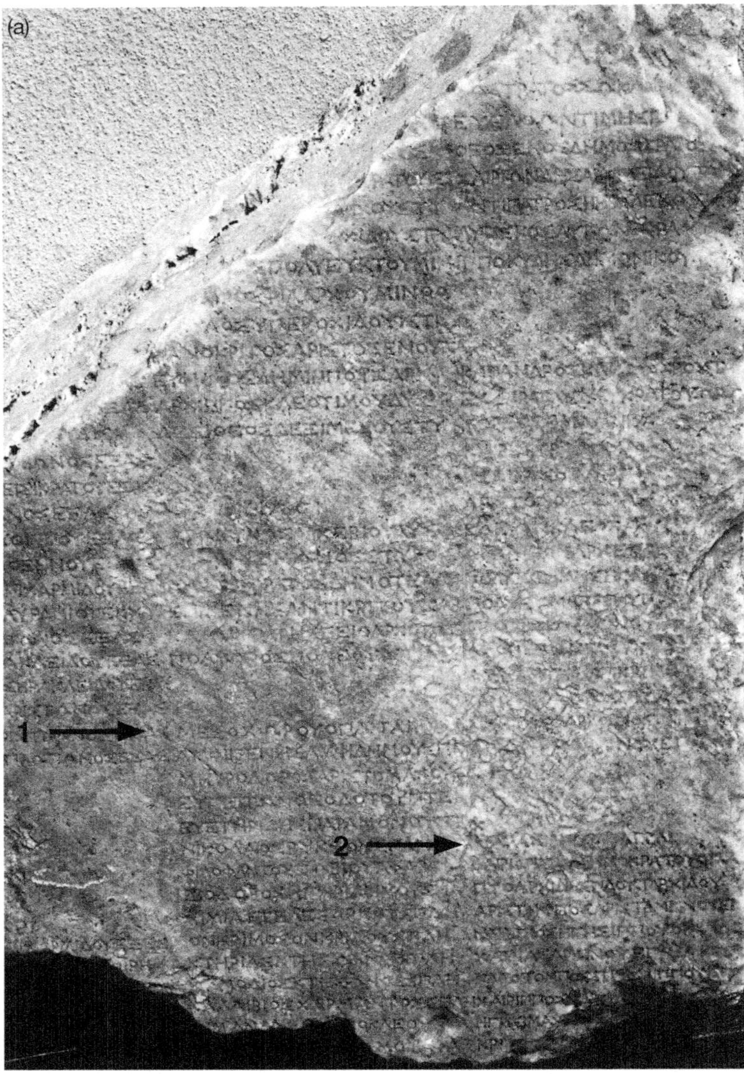

Figure 8.2 *IG* XII 9, 241: (a) line 37 showing the positions of the names (1) ΜΕΣΟΧΩΡΟΥ and (2) ΛΑΡΑΣΙΟΥ (or, I suggest, ΠΑΡΑΛΙΟΥ); (b) close-up photograph of (1); (c) line 77, as it presently appears on the stone, where the second district name (2) [or (3)] occurs (see Table 8.2).

Kleisthenes simply incorporated a pre-existing group and term in his new arrangement of the citizen body.

Knoepfler in 1985 suggested the number of the Eretrian tribes as six in his discussion of the number and composition of the *boule* in the early fourth century, based on a reading of the treaty between Athens and Eretria of 341,[64] and this is still his view in his latest works,[65] though earlier (1981) he had allowed

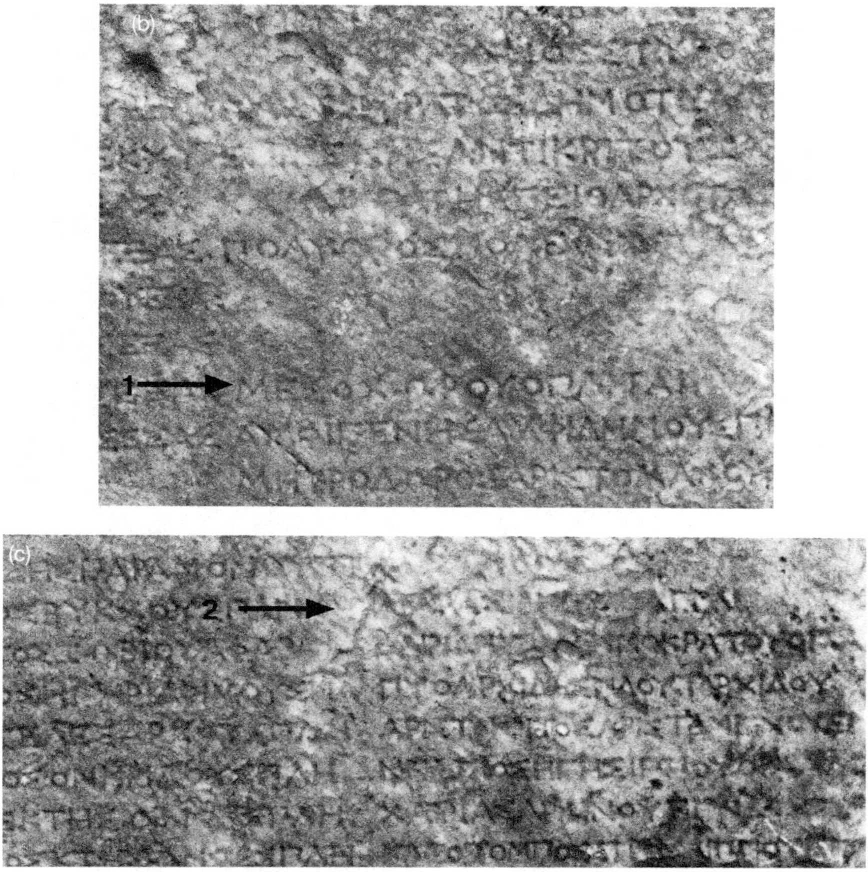

Figure 8.2 (continued).

that there may have been as many as ten.[66] He uses two inscriptions,[67] which also establish the name of a second Eretrian tribe, Narkittis,[68] and concludes that tribes were associated in twos for the choral contests at a local festival similar to the Athenian Thargelia. There could therefore hardly be fewer than four. However, we are again dealing here with late material. There is no reason to suppose that before the 530s there were other than the traditional four Ionic tribes at Eretria or that the number of the *probouloi* would not have been a multiple of that number. Despite Kondoleon's arguments for three and Knoepfler's for six 'reformed' tribes, we can perhaps better accommodate the inscriptionally attested eight *epimenieuontes* of the later texts (that both scholars use), within a framework of eight 'reformed' tribes. I shall return to the number eight below.

There is inscriptional evidence of *phratriai* at Eretria.[69] The text is enigmatic and a satisfactory interpretation is unlikely (Figure 8.3), but it does make it clear that the institution existed in the early fifth century so it is likely that phratries existed earlier and that originally membership of a phratry, as at Athens, may have been a prerequisite for citizenship, but that later, with the establishment of the democracy, deme membership replaced that of the phratry, as the frequent use of demotics in later citizen lists and for proposers of motions etc. seems to imply. By the Classical period, phratry membership may have been a rather exclusive privilege.[70]

It may be argued that the general similarities between the Eretrian and Athenian systems are to be explained in terms of parallel evolutionary patterns of political development from the ninth to the sixth century. Morris[71] has shown, however, that this did not in general occur. This explanation might apply, for example, to the evolution of probouleutic magistracies, *probouloi* (*epimenieuontes*) at Eretria and Corinth, *prytaneis* at Athens or *amnemones* at Knidos, etc., since these would be required by most Greek states. But it is precisely the artificial aspect of the separation of demes into larger geographical units with new and specially created tribes that makes the territorial divisions of Eretria and Athens appear so similar and leads one to wonder whether there may have been a model that served for both. For, though not identical, the similarities are sufficient to propose that they were neither the product of a common natural evolutionary process nor entirely independent creations.

Eretria acquired a democratic system with its associated geo-political structure earlier than Athens, and there had been Athenian political exiles living in Eretria for at least ten years before Kleisthenes carried out his reforms in 507. It is interesting to reflect that practically the only thing that later generations of Athenians remembered as the special contribution of Kleisthenes to their democratic system was his geo-political reorganisation. But, in fact, such an artificial territorial/social rearrangement was not quite unique to Eretria and Athens. Corinth, which had close and friendly relations with both for many decades, also had a system of deme → (*trittys*) → district organisation, with similarities in naming and numbering to those of Athens and, despite the later five districts, Eretria also. Corinth appears to have had artificially created tribes quite distinct from the three ancient Dorian tribes common to its neighbours.[72] Its socio-political and territorial divisions have been the subject of a number of articles in recent years following the publication by Meritt in 1931[73] of an inscription from the city listing names under abbreviated rubrics. Wallace[74] indeed refers to this 'much closer parallel' to the key Eretrian inscription (*IG* XII 9, 241) rather than to Athens. Since the publication of the original Corinthian text, several more inscriptions have been discovered displaying the same abbreviations for what seem to be geo- or socio-political divisions.

Most commentators argue that these abbreviations represent the names of Corinthian tribes together with a third letter, restricted to one of three recurrent letters: E, Ϝ (digamma) and Π. In some of the later inscriptions, this letter is separated from the first two. For some scholars, the third letter represents a territorial division,[75] for others a military grouping.[76] Dow alone regards them as an integral part of the tribal designation,[77] while Stroud thinks that they indicate categories of *trittyes*.[78] Without becoming too involved in controversy

Figure 8.3 The *Horos Phratrikos*, Eretria Museum.

concerning the Corinthian material, I prefer the arguments of the 'territorians' rather than the 'militarists' (though Salmon's assertion[79] that Thucydides[80] informs us that the Corinthians had no cavalry is dubious evidence that military categories are not involved, because Thucydides says no such thing).[81] The Eretrian evidence does not contradict either major interpretation of the Corinthian inscriptions. *IG* XII 9, 241 not only lists men with demotics under districts but also within military categories, specifically, *hoplitai* and *psiloi* (light-armed troops).[82] Wallace was, in fact, first to postulate that the third letter of the Corinthian rubric referred to military groups, no doubt suggested to him by the Eretrian example. A few scholars who have recently discussed the Corinthian material refer to Wallace but do not cite the evidence provided by *IG* XII 9, 241.[83]

The political organisation of the Corinthia shows similarities with both the Eretrias and Attica. First, I believe that Eretria shared with Corinth a system based on eight tribes. As for Corinth, the eight-fold arrangement is attested in the literary record: Nikolaos of Damascus says: '[the People] at once set up a constitution as follows: it created a *Proboulia* of eight, and from the rest they chose a *Boule* of nine' [men from each tribe, i.e seventy-two + eight *probouloi* = eighty]. Indeed it was proverbial that: 'Everything [was] in eights' at Corinth.[84] Although we have the names of only two of the Eretrian tribes, we know that Eretria later had groups of eight probouleutic magistrates, the *epimenieuontes*, who formed a probouleutic committee, possibly akin to the ten *epistates* of the *prytaneis* at Athens who presided over each of the ten groups of fifty *prytaneis* of the ten new tribes, but as at Corinth, based on eight new tribes.[85] The late-fourth-century Eretrian committee of *epimenieuontes* was presided over by the *arkhon* and had a secretary,[86] while the late-sixth century-proxeny decree, *IG* XII Suppl. 549, mentions an *epimenieuoures* (genitive) tribe. Therefore, we should see a direct connection between the later eight *epimenieuontes probouloi* and the tribe(s). The epithet implies that the *probouloi* and a tribally based committee had some monthly or quasi-monthly period of authority. The equivalent Attic term would be the *prytaneuouses* (prytanising) tribe.[87] The early date assigned to this decree mentioning the 'prytanising' tribe is further evidence that the Eretrian democracy had early on begun to develop systems of administration similar to those of Athens.

The three[88] territorial regions of the Corinthia, represented by the letters E, Ϝ and Π, roughly parallel the three-fold division of Attica into 'urban', 'coastal' and 'inland' regions, and they have their equivalents in the Eretrias. However, every scholar who has subsequently discussed the demes and districts of Eretria follows Wallace, certainly with modifications, whose pioneering work was done on the basis of citizen lists of the fourth and third centuries and, for the districts in particular, on *IG* XII 9, 241,[89] which shows the territory divided into five districts.[90]

This was not true of the period before the end of the fifth century at the earliest. Now, we should note that Wallace's Districts I and II (Knoepfler's *khoros* II) in the south-east include the important demes of Dystos, Zarex and Styra, all relatively important places, the locations of which are not in dispute. Knoepfler has shown that Styra (in the extreme south-east.) was not incorporated into the Eretrias until the last decade of the fifth century and this is an earlier date than has generally been accepted.[91] He concludes that the territory between Dystos and Styra was annexed at about the same time.[92] This is important, for it follows that Wallace's Districts I and II were not incorporated into the Eretrias before the last decade of the fifth century. Moreover Athens, which controlled the whole island for much of the century, would not have permitted Eretrian imperialism on such a scale, and indeed Styra is listed separately from Eretria in the *ATL*. Thus, for the late sixth century we are left with the still extensive area covered by Wallace's Districts III, IV and V (Knoepfler's I, III, IV and V), of which we possess the name of District III (in both arrangements), Mesokhoros, together with the fragmentary name of District V, which I restore as Paralios [or Larasion (Wallace) or Karneiasion

(Knoepfler)}. If we hold to Wallace's divisions, we have an originally three-fold arrangement of the territory, bringing the Eretrias into line with the Corinthia and Attica.[93] Knoepfler's would seemingly leave us with four, but we have no precise knowledge of how the territory was originally divided up into its probable tripartite scheme prior to the acquisition of the south-eastern area around Dystos and Styra and perhaps also of the far north-west. We can certainly not assume that it followed the post-fifth-century plan. Indeed on the contrary, it would be unlikely that territorial modifications were not made necessary by the substantial territorial expansion, such as Knoepfler implies were necessary for the tribal organisation.[94] In any case, the city in relation to its overall territory, even without the 'new' south-east district(s) is, as Knoepfler observed, severely 'off-centre'. We can tabulate for each *polis* a tripartite greater regional division, as shown in Table 8.2.

Jones, along with most recent scholars, believes that the eight-fold tribal division with the magistracy of the eight *probouloi* was probably in existence at Corinth before the establishment of the post-Kypselid oligarchy,[96] making the tyranny the most likely period for these changes: 'Both the Corinthian and Kerkyraian reformed tribal organisations . . . were created under the Kypselid tyranny, that is, no earlier than *c.* 658 BC.'[97] Corinth probably underwent a comprehensive civic restructuring under Periandros, for he is said to have tried to keep the population in its home territories,[98] making a reform by him of the territorial divisions of the Corinthia, with population registration and control his primary object, very likely.

We have seen that Periandros was probably Diagoras' first political friend abroad, their alliance manifested in their close co-operation against Khalkis. It is not impossible that Diagoras had been in Corinth before his seizure of power and we have seen that he died there. Periandros was not averse to giving friends political advice; one remembers that given to Thrasyboulos of Miletos concerning 'tall poppies', still proverbial. Who better as a mentor, in matters of political control, than the experienced tyrant of Corinth? If Diagoras wished to reorganise the civic structure of the state for whatever purposes, a Corinthian model was probably already at hand and he may well have had

Table 8.2 The known and hypothetical names of the tripartite territorial divisions of the Corinthia, the Eretrias and Attica

Corinth	*Eretria*	*Athens*
Παράλιος -ία (?) Πέραν τοῦ Ἰσθμοῦ (?) Περαία (St. Byz.)[95]	Λαράσιος -ον (?) Παράλιος -ία (?) Καρνείασιος -ον (?) (V)	Παραλία
Ἔσωθεν (?) Ἐντὸς τοῦ Ἰσθμοῦ (?)	Μεσοχῶρος -ον = Μεταζύ (?) (Wallace and Knoepfler III)	Μεσόγειος
ϝάστυ (?)	(?)	Ἄστυ

similar objectives to those attributed to Periandros. Speaking of Corinth, but his observation is applicable generally, Roebuck says that: 'under the tyranny, particularly at its inception, or in the reign of Periander, there would have been killings, confiscations and presumably redistribution of land . . . As in other Greek states, a reorganisation of the citizen body might well have accompanied such political turmoil.'[99] Thus, if Diagoras had already carried out the basic organisational reforms, the new democracy that followed his fall, like the oligarchy that succeeded the Kypselid tyranny, would have inherited a convenient, depersonalised and geographically random civic structure based on eight new artificial tribes, within which old loyalties had less scope for influence. It was a system that could easily be incorporated into a new democratic constitution. Stanton[100] has already speculated that 'possibly indeed the idea for the Athenian *city, coastal* and *inland* regions was borrowed by Kleisthenes from Korinth, for the regions do not fit the territory of Attike particularly well.'

Figure 8.4 The proxeny decree for Aristoteles Kheiloniou (*IG* XII Suppl. 549), Eretria Museum. Note the angle at the top of the inscribed face, which is not apparent in either Wallace's (1936b) or my own (see Figure 8.5) drawings.

Nor of the Eretrias either! But it was the idea that was important and, while the evidence seems to favour Corinth as the source of the original concept for all three related systems, the Kleisthenic tribal and geo-political divisions also have some similarity to those at Eretria. I therefore think that Kleisthenes got his immediate inspiration not directly from Corinth but rather from Eretria.

What connection then, we might ask, did the Athenian reformer have with that city? Our sources never speak of Corinth as a place to which the political opposition to either the Peisistratidai or the later regime headed by Isagoras went in search of asylum. However, we do know that Eretria had been a place of refuge for anti-tyrant Athenians since at least 525 and, after the fall of Diagoras, anti-oligarchic refugees, too, would be welcome in Eretria. Thus,

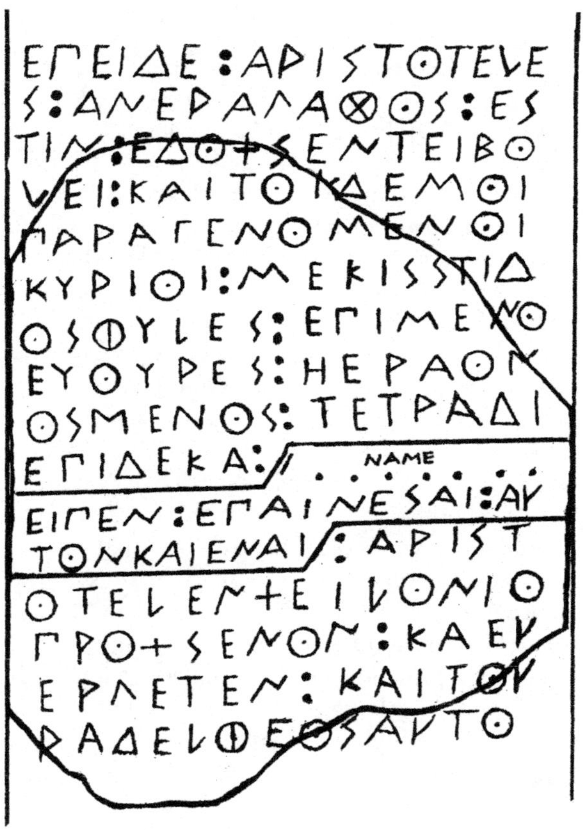

Figure 8.5 *IG* XII Suppl. 549. This restoration is based on the text of Wallace 1936b within the outline of the stone, and Peek 1934 for ΕΙΠΕΝ : ΕΠΑΙΝΕΣΑΙ : within the *rasura*. Cf. Figure 8.4: the angle of the upper left-hand corner, between the front and the horizontal top faces of the block, appears to have been cut later. The vertical height from the first preserved line of script to the top would allow for at least the two additional lines of text that I have suggested. I have based the drawing on Wallace's letter forms. For letters that do not appear on the stone as preserved (⊗, Γ), I have used Jeffery 1961, 79 (chart).

it would have been able to act as a conduit through which the new system of civic organisation might come to Attica. Just how this occurred I shall explain shortly, but first I wish to indicate other similarities between the practices of the Eretrian democracy and that which was introduced by Kleisthenes to Athens and which may have come along with the tribal/territorial reforms.

The preamble of the proxeny decree for Aristoteles Kheiloniou (*IG* XII Suppl. 549) throws some light on the workings of the early Eretrian democracy (Figures 8.4 and 8.5). I use here the text of Wallace, and the restoration of Peek (modified), for the *rasura* in lines 8–10. Wallace ascribes the *rasura* to an error of the mason. No doubt mistakes did occur but such an extensive error over three lines on such an early decree is unlikely.[101] Later Eretrian decrees indicate that high-ranking magistrates were specifically assigned to supervise the inscription of decrees.[102] The restoration of Peek fits and is consistent with formulae of later decrees used over a long period. However, for reasons of letter spacing (see the drawing) I would modify Peek by supplementing AYTON in place of his 'na}|{me', assuming a reference back by the pronoun to 'Aristoteles' in a lost preamble preceding ἐδόξεν such as ἐπειδὴ 'Αριστοτέλης ἀνὴρ ἀγαθός ἐστιν ἐδόξεν τῆι βουλῆι καὶ τῶι δήμωι etc., such as occurs, for example, in the fourth/third century proxeny decree for Glaukippos and his brothers in which, likewise, the names are repeated in the accusative. In any case, there is little evidence left on the stone so any restoration is quite speculative.[103] The erasure of the speaker's name may be ascribed to subsequent political eclipse, an Eretrian Kleisthenes! This decree is particularly interesting because it is one of the earliest preserved examples of democratic legislation of any kind or provenance, yet, despite its early date, it displays features of decrees of a fully developed democracy of the later 'Athenian' kind.[104] To illustrate the similarities, I have tabulated below (Table 8.3) the formulae of this decree alongside a (hypothetical) Attic example.

Behind the similarities was a legislative process that must also have been reasonably close: probouleutic committee → *boule* → assembly. The Eretrian probouleutic committee *c.* 300 BC was made up of eight (or six) *epimenieuontes* demesmen, probably all from different tribes,[105] though we cannot be certain of this, and included a presiding officer[106] and secretary, making it smaller than the later Attic *prytaneia*. This should not surprise us in view of the smaller population of Eretria,[107] though its intention and practice would have been similar. Here we already find a monthly (*epimenieuoura*) *phyle*. The 'monthly' tribal presidency was probably notional, since there were only eight (or six) Eretrian *phylai*. Was there also a conciliar calendar at Eretria, as at Athens?[108] Other features are similar: council, assembly, the latter with both special and regular (*kyria*) sessions, and (later) a *grammateus*. The method of dating is, however, much more specific than in Attic decrees or even in later Eretrian examples, in which a more cumbersome system of expressing dates is used, no doubt under Athenian influence.

But if the Athenians got ideas for their new constitution via Eretria, how

Table 8.3 Comparison of the formulae of Attic proxeny decrees and the Eretrian decree *IG* XII 9, Suppl. 549

Proxeny decree (IG XII Suppl. 549) from Eretria	*Athenian decrees*
1 Formula of enactment: ἔδοχσεν τε̄ι βολε̄ι καὶ το̄ι δέμο̄ι	1 Formula of enactment: ἔδοξεν τῆι βο̄λῆι καὶ το̄ι δέμωι
2ª Type of assembly: παραγενομένο̄ι κυρίο̄ι	
2ᵇ *Epimenieuoura* phyle: Με̄κίσστιδος φυλε̄ς ἐπιμε̄νιευούρες	2 *Prytaneuousa* phyle ἡ δεῖνα ἐπρυτάνευε
3ª Calendar date: Ἡε̄ραόνος με̄νός τετράδι ἐπὶ δέκα	3ª Name of secretary: ὁ δεῖνα ἐγραμμάτευε
3ᵇ Name of chairman (Not found in decrees before the fourth century)	3ᵇ Name of chairman: ὁ δεῖνα ἐπέστατε
4 Name of proposer: ὁ δεῖνα εἶπε (Peek; but this was probably inscribed in the *vacat* of ll. 8–10 [Wallace] 281 and n. 3)	4 Name of proposer: ὁ δεῖνα εἶπε

were they actually transmitted to Attica? If the basic territorial and tribal reforms there had been carried out under Diagoras, and the establishment of democratic structures between his fall in 509 and 507, the full Eretrian reorganisation could have been observed and remembered by any one of several Athenian exiles until Kleisthenes sought to implement his changes. Such a one might have been a later political ally who discussed the Eretrian/Corinthian model with him. Nevertheless, there is a more intriguing possibility. Would it be too daring to suggest that one of the political exiles who resided for a time in Eretria, who observed the functioning of the new democracy there and then later brought the model to Athens, was Kleisthenes himself? I believe that a case can be made, based on both epigraphic and literary evidence, of Alkmaionid connections to the Euboian city, that some of his relatives, and perhaps Kleisthenes too, had been political exiles there before 507.

Kleisthenes had indirect mythological, as well as more immediate family, connections with the aristocracy at Eretria, the former through the eponymous ancestor of the family, Alkmaion, the latter through a marriage of his grandfather, another Alkmaion. Let us first consider the mythological link. Very ancient connections were not unimportant in ancient Greece, nor were they forgotten, as the example of the fourth-century Athenian politician with Eretrian antecedents, Aristogeiton Kydimakhou, indicates.[109]

The Alkmaionid mythological past reveals connections of the family with both Eretria and Oropos and, obliquely, with Argos.[110] The Argive pre-Dorian hero Adrastos,[111] his brother Mekisteus, eponym of the Eretrian tribe, and his sister Eriphyle were the children of Talaos and Lysimakhe, daughter of Abas (eponym of the Euboian Abantes). Eriphyle was husband of Amphiaraos, a descendant of Abas' brother Antiphates. Amphiaraos was later worshipped as a healing hero at Oropos, the former 'colony' of Eretria. Their son was an Alkmaion.[112] One of his sons was Akarnan, eponym of Akarnania, the country of the unshorn neighbours of the Kouretes. He slew Phegeus, eponym of the Eretrian deme Phegous. With its neighbouring territories in north-east Attica and south-eastern Boiotia, Oropos was not only once Eretrian but was also the heartland of the Gephyraioi (formerly from Eretria), the *genos* of the conspirators against Hippias and Hipparkhos. Moreover, Amphiaraos himself is sometimes identified with Amarynthos, eponymous hero of the Eretrian deme Amarynthos and consort of Amarysia its goddess. Adrastos, Alkmaion and Amphiaraos are all closely involved (and confused) in the stories of Herodotos concerning Kroisos.[113] Thus, the Alkmaionidai might, if they chose, trace their ancestry back to Eretria via the same geographical route as did the Gephyraioi, the most visible, although not necessarily the most important, of the anti-Peisistratid conspirators. We may well ask to what extent Alkmaionids too were involved in the original plot. Alkmaionid involvement would provide a plausible explanation as to how the romantic story involving Harmodios and Aristogeiton became the popular 'founding myth' of the Athenian democracy, despite their impeccably non-democratic credentials. It gains some point if both the Alkmaionidai and Gephyraioi were political (and familial?) allies, for then Kleisthenes himself may have promoted the myth. Before Isagoras worsted him in the intra-aristocratic political struggle, there is no suggestion of democratic tendencies on the part of Kleisthenes or his family.[114] Only then may the existing Eretrian model have become relevant to his ambitions. Once Kleisthenes and the *Demos* were joined politically, it may then have become expedient to stress his alternative ancestry leading back to Pylos.

Can mythological links be reinforced by more concrete, more recent connections? Shear's 1963 paper, 'Koisyra; three women of Athens',[115] connects both Peisistratos and the Alkmaionidai through the Eretrian family of the ladies Koisyra.[116] We have already met the eldest Koisyra as the wife of Peisistratos in Chapter 6. Shear argues that Kleisthenes' (paternal) grandmother and her family were Eretrian and that residence in her home town during his exile is therefore not only likely but probable, at a time moreover when Eretria had been, and was still, providing a base for exiled Athenian *Eupatridai* and was actively involved in the intrigues that brought down the tyranny at Athens. This idea has been strengthened by the publication, in 1991, of two *ostraka* linking Megakles Hippokratous (Davies' Megakles III), Kleisthenes' nephew, with both Eretria and one of the Koisyras.[117] Whatever interpretation one may place upon the first fragment, and its meaning is by no means entirely clear, what can not be doubted is that the *ostrakon* provides conclusive ancient and contemporary testimony linking the Alkmaionidai to Eretria. Is ΜΕΡΕΤΡ⟨Ι⟩ΑΖΕ a verb or noun form? I take it as an allative in -ζε(-δε); and the μ as μή elided, i.e. 'do not go to Eretria.' If the residential restrictions on ostracised persons, outlined in *Ath. pol.* 22, 7, were designed to prevent them from going *inter alia* to Eretria, then the phrase of the ostrakon was probably a warning of this prohibition by the writer to one known to have strong Eretrian connections. For Megakles to go to Eretria would leave him open to a charge of *atimia*.[118] It has been suggested, however, that it could be an imperative form of the verb *eretriazein* with pejorative implications.[119] If it is a verb, then the choice must still link Megakles with Eretria since it is certainly not the usual word used for 'mock' or 'ridicule'. Is it an allusion to his dialect? Plato indicates that Eretrians were 'mocked' for their rhotacising dialect. A pun would doubtless be intended based on a perception of Megakles' behaviour. More difficult then would be the 'M' before EPETP<I>AZE; is it an elided pronoun form (μοι)? The second specifically names Megakles as the son of Hippokrates and Koisyra. Shear has constructed a stemma attempting to show where the various ladies named Koisyra fit into this complicated series of marriages. Kleisthenes' Eretrian connections and a period of exile there would provide an obvious explanation as to how the Corinthian/Eretrian model for the tribal and territorial changes reached Attica.

It is not surprising that democracy should have come to Eretria at this time or that it should have preceded its establishment at Athens. In the last three decades of the sixth century, Eretria already had a powerful and expanding navy and consequently, a rowing class, whereas Athens did not. This may explain why democracy had to be conferred there by Kleisthenes, rather than emerge as the result of spontaneous demands from the people itself, for it was in fact the decision of Kleisthenes the Alkmaionid to bring into his party the *demos* that led to its establishment.[120] Nevertheless, once transplanted, the Eretrian plant flourished in Attica.

The two new democracies were not left in peace to develop their new political systems. In the next year, Kleomenes was back in central Greece. He had not at all been reconciled to the failure of his 510/9 settlement of affairs at Athens. By 507, the political pendulum at Sparta had swung back temporarily in favour of interventionism. He had already tried unsuccessfully to intervene and re-establish his nominee Isagoras, using a small force of Spartan troops, but his action had merely succeeded in transforming a squabble between aristocratic clans into the new and threatening democratic political experiment. In 506, he was able to organise a large-scale campaign involving the Peloponnesian League, including Corinth, together with Thebes, Khalkis and Aigina, all now, with the important exception of Corinth, enemies of both Eretria and Athens. If the failed attempt of 507 had not been warning enough to both cities, the sight of a large Peloponnesian army on the march north of the isthmus surely would have. Eretria might expect trouble from Kleomenes. His political, perhaps even personal, friend Diagoras was almost certainly dead by this time. But even if so, there would be plenty of other potential puppets to set up in power in Eretria. Moreover, Eretria in any case had to be punished, not only for Diagoras' sake but also for good political reasons. Kleomenes would have viewed its democracy as the model and inspiration of the new ideological threat to his order in central Greece and even beyond. The new Alkmaionid/democratic leadership at Athens had already sought alliance with Persia to meet his threat, a worrying development for Kleomenes, but 'broke off negotiations when the Persians named as their price the restoration of the old tyrant Hippias.'[121] Horsley believes that Kleisthenes himself was probably not only a member of this embassy but was responsible for urging the delegation to accept the terms, thus explaining his enigmatic disappearance from the political scene and the historical record.[122] The climate was thus propitious for rapprochement between the two old allies of the 550s–540s. They now had politically compatible governments and this was reinforced by the looming threat to the very existence of their political autonomy. One may well imagine how democratic Eretria would fare as a result of a defeat by a coalition led by Kleomenes, and of which Khalkis was a member!

Athens faced the coalition on land, Eretria at sea. Eretria's role was to check neighbouring Khalkis as well as Corinth, Aigina and Megara, all *poleis* that either had a fleet or were subject to control by sea power. These were the only naval powers in the Spartan coalition, and the last two were irreconcilable enemies of Corinth as well as Eretria and Athens. But why would Corinth at this time have desired victory for its two oldest and most bitter enemies, Megara and Aigina, or, for that matter, for its northern neighbour across the Gulf of Corinth, Boiotian Thebes, with whom relations had so recently been strained as a result of the failure of Corinthian mediation in the dispute between Athens and Thebes? (On the role of Corinth at this time, see Appendix 5.) Such a victory would, in fact, be at the expense of old friends, for both Athens and Eretria had continued separately to maintain good relations with the isthmus city. Corinth wavered within the ranks of the coalition. When Kleomenes' army arrived on the borders of Attica, threatening the overthrow of the new regime in Athens, the single most powerful component of that army, with the exception of Sparta itself, was already opposed to the objectives of the expedition, and Corinth found powerful support within the Spartan leadership itself, among the faction led by King Demaratos, who was also with the expedition. This was the group that had de facto approved the overthrow of Diagoras. Dissension erupted in the army when the Corinthians, no doubt with the connivance of Demaratos and his supporters, removed their forces from the coalition. Kleomenes, faced with the disintegration of his army and the hostility of his Spartan enemies, was obliged to return home. Thus, with the tacit support of Corinth, Eretria and Athens were left to face the now isolated Khalkidians and Thebans.

The latter had already begun moving to rendezvous with the main expedition coming up from the Peloponnese, but clearly the Khalkidians had still not crossed to the mainland. Freed from the threat from Kleomenes' army, the Athenians moved towards the Euripos. Herodotos says that Athens defeated Thebes and Khalkis on the same day on both sides of the Euripos, in the so-called 'Double Battle' of 506. General modern opinion, adopting his narrative of this duo of victorious engagements is as follows: the Thebans advanced 'to the Euripos'[123] to aid the Khalkidians, threatened by the force from Athens. The Athenians, meeting them as they came, decided to attack them at once and, following a battle, took away some 700 prisoners in fetters. Then, 'on the same day, they crossed into Euboia, engaged the Khalkidians, defeating them also.'[124] We also have inscriptions from two separate monuments[125] from Athens and a sepulchral epigram, attributed to Simonides,[126] celebrating this victory:

> We were slain in a cleft of Dirphys, and the mound
> of our grave is made beside Euripos at our country's cost.
> And rightly so, for by abiding the onset of the cruel cloud of war,
> we lost our lovely time of youth.

Ure and Burrows,[127] however, believe that this need only mean that the battle was fought in the shadows of Mt Dirphys and not far inland, for the mountain, 'when viewed from the mainland, seems to rise up just behind the Euboean coast', and the second line of the poem says that the grave was in fact near the coast. Nevertheless, there is nothing that makes this imperatively an epitaph to Athenians. It is recorded without scholia. Moreover, Simonides, as von Wilamowitz[128] has shown, wrote sepulchral epigrams for Eretrians before he went to Athens and again after he left there, as Herodotos himself notes.[129]

Is it realistic to believe that the Athenians alone were able to conduct two major engagements, on the same day, in different locations separated by the Euripos, as Herodotos claims? Three questions arise concerning his account:

1. Why did the Khalkidians not go to the aid of their Theban allies? Indeed, why had they not already set out to join the expedition of Kleomenes?
2. How could the Athenians get an army, fresh from a major battle with the Thebans, from one side of the Euripos to the other in less than a single day, much of the day having been already lost, taken up with the first battle and the capturing and securing of 700 prisoners. The Euripos may be narrow but it is swift and notoriously treacherous, making a crossing by boats far from easy, for in 506 there was no bridge. The logistical problems posed here for a sixth century *polis*-army are enormous and novel. Moreover, all these actions took place in the face of the untouched but apparently paralysed Khalkidian land army waiting to defend their city.
3. How is it that both Thebans and Athenians were in eastern Boiotia heading towards Euboia and not towards Athens or, alternatively, towards Thebes?

Those who support the Herodotean account of events have to assume that these feats were achieved without naval support, since Athens itself had as yet no navy capable of both transporting a whole army across the straits and simultaneously providing protection against attack, not only from any weak Khalkidian navy but also from the far more dangerous Aigina, enemy of Athens, Corinth and Eretria. It is moreover unlikely that Athens had the manpower to be able to mount operations more or less simultaneously against a major land power, Thebes, to take and hold 700 prisoners, to man transports and support the fleet, even if it had one, and to provide against a rearguard attack from Boiotian forces. If Athens had the numbers, Thebes had more, so danger from that quarter could not be ignored, despite the victory. The number of troops to be ferried across the Euripos would have to be sufficiently great to have a realistic chance of successfully engaging the whole Khalkidian army defending its own *polis*, fighting for its very existence. How was all this possible for a state that had not up to this time shown much military promise and was seldom, if ever, able to trust its land forces against any reasonably competent military rival?

The answer to the first two questions is, of course, that Athens must have had help, and who better to provide that help, in the political and geographical circumstances, than Eretria, fired by generations of hostility towards Khalkis? Indeed, who else could have, except Corinth, which for all its sympathy, was still a member of the Spartan alliance? Again, with the exception of Corinth, Eretria had the only navy that could match that of Aigina. It was the diadoch thalassocrat of the very next year according to the *Thalassocracy List*. Again, if in respect of an invasion of Khalkis we ask 'cui bono?', the answer must be 'Eretria'. In fact, the result of the action was that Khalkis was 'paralysed for a generation'[130] or more after 506. It has been suggested that Athens sought revenge because Khalkis took part in the Spartan-led coalition against it, but there is no evidence that Khalkis had, in fact, managed to play any active role at all in it. Its army remained on the Euboian side of the Euripos. The fall of Khalkis benefited Eretria, just as the defeat of Thebes did Athens. If Oropos was in Theban hands in 507, Eretria might now even hope to recover its ancient mainland *peraia* and perhaps the attack on Tanagra, described by Pausanias: 'They say that Hermes Promakhos on an occasion when an Eretrian fleet put into the harbour of Tanagra from Euboia, led the youths to battle; he himself, armed with a scraper like a youth, was chiefly responsible for the rout of the Euboians',[131] and alluded to by the poetess Korinna of Tanagra: 'For your sake, Hermes fights Ares with his fists',[132] took place at this time. As to the third question, the answer must be that Eretria was, if not actually setting the agenda itself, certainly having a major input and driving the other players to concentrate on Khalkis. It would already have been under threat from the Eretrian navy as well as from its land army which, as is indicated by the festival stele,[133] was not inconsiderable in the sixth century. Its leading role in Asia Minor during the Ionian Revolt, together with Plato's observation, confirms Eretria as a major military power at this time: 'And he [Datis, the Persian commander] sailed to Eretria, against men who were among the most renowned of the Greeks of that time in war, and who were not few in number.'[134] Therefore, any Athenian troops disembarking on Euboia were not threatened severely by either the Aiginetans at sea or the Khalkidians on land and were, moreover, not fighting alone. As the great Herodotean scholar J. Myres observes, 'What Herodotus relates is surely the Athenian task in a larger battle between Chalcis and Eretria in which Eretria held the strait for her mainland ally.'[135] The Eretrian threat to Khalkis explains its paralysis both now and earlier, when the Peloponnesians were marching on Athens, and the haste of Thebes and Athens to reach the Euripos rather than each other's city. The soldiers who died in the vale of Dirphys were as likely Eretrians as Athenians.

The inscriptions and the epigram commemorate a great victory and the Athenians were proud of their part in it. We can scarcely blame them for not later diluting the praise by reference to the role of others. But had we had the lost *History of Eretria* of Lysanias of Mallos,[136] we might before now have viewed the events of 506 in a very different light, as a victory won partly at least (and probably principally) thanks to the role of the Eretrians by land and, more importantly, by sea, the result of which was Eretrian naval hegemony from 505 to 490.[137] Plato has given us a glimpse of how the Eretrians were perceived even by some Athenians in these their glory years.[138] Eretria was a city whose power was respected and whose aid was sought by 'kinsmen' in Asia Minor five years later.[139] Burrows and Ure[140] observe that 'the omission of Eretria in the Athenian account of the battle would be due to the deportation of its inhabitants in 490 and the inability of the remnant to impress themselves on history.' Perhaps, but the fact is that we have only Athenian sources for these events, and Athenian bias and deliberate disinformation, to use a modern term, has been an issue ever since Plutarch wrote his corrective to Herodotos' *kakoethia* (malice). Unlike many, I do not regard Plutarch's work as a purely rhetorical exercise. He cites his alternative sources and they could have been checked in his day. More will be said about the existence of an alternative historical tradition concerning the Ionian War in the next chapter.[141] Plutarch clearly felt that Herodotos had deliberately suppressed material that might have been detrimental to the image of Athens.[142]

Burrows and Ure[143] also ask a question that illustrates one of the contradictions created by the traditional view of the nature of the Eretrian constitution at the end of the sixth century: 'Can we be sure that its [Eretria's] citizens would give active help to the party [the Alkmaionidai/democrats] that had expelled Hippias when that expulsion was fresh in their minds?' They believe that if Kleomenes had come north to restore Hippias rather than Isagoras, 'Eretria might have been tempted actually to support Sparta in spite of the irritating fact of finding itself on the side of Chalcis.' This view stems from the widely held opinion that the government in power in Eretria in 510–6 was still the old 'government of the *Hippeis*', unchanged since 556, when it nailed its colours to the mast of Peisistratos. However, in 506 Eretria was a democracy so there were no political reasons why Eretria would not have joined Athens.

There were never any reasons at all why it would have allied itself to Khalkis, and, in view of Kleomenes' relationship with the fallen tyrant Diagoras, newly democratic Eretria had nothing to gain by neutrality towards him, particularly since he was now allied to Eretria's enemies, ancient (Khalkis) and recent (Thebes).

The result of the 'Double Battle' was the removal of the danger of Spartan or Theban intervention in the affairs of both Eretria and Athens, and it ensured that the political reforms that had begun in both *poleis* would continue without external interference. In Euboia, it marks the definitive end of Khalkis as a significant power, although it had for a long time been in reality a broken reed. Even in the fifth century, after the Persians had destroyed its rival, Khalkis generally appears weaker than Eretria: it could not supply its own ships at Artemision and on the commemorative Serpent Column, Eretria precedes Khalkis.[144] It is also revealed by its often lower assessments for contributions to the Athenian League: Meritt notes that the change to monetary contributions occurred in 450; in 448/7: 'both names [Khalkis and Eretria] appear in List 7, the former with a tribute of 5 talents, the latter with a tribute which we believe should be restored to 6 talents.' In his n. 96 he says: 'This (Eretria's assessment) is slightly higher than that (5 talents) of Chalkis, but presumably Eretria was a wealthier state.' The assessments of Eretria and Khalkis in List A were 15 and 10 talents respectively.[145]

Before leaving the events of 506, we may note one last – and lasting – result of the 'Double Battle'. After the victory, the Athenians settled *kleroukhoi* on the 'lands of the *Hippobotai* '[146] probably in the area between Khalkis and the River Lelas, long since the boundary between the two hostile *poleis*.[147] This may seem to indicate Athenian dominance over the ordering of affairs in Euboia and indeed it is usually so interpreted. But it need not be so. The Athenians

Figure 8.6 The base with the dedication of the Eretrian bull monument at Olympia.

Figure 8.7 The dedicatory inscription: ΦΙΛΕ̄ΣΙΟΣ ΕΠΟΙΕ | ΕΡΕΤΡΙΕ̄Σ ΤŌΙ ΔΙ.

could have sent the settlers on to Khalkidian lands with full Eretrian approval. The Eretrians may well have seen the settlers as a barrier to further Khalkidian aggression and as hostages to Athenian support. If so, the events of 490 show that it was a misplaced hope. However, in 506 Eretria had no need to be unduly apprehensive concerning Athens, while the long-lost lands east of the Lelas River probably reverted to Eretrian control.

We may see in the 'Double Battle' a final irony, for it was the last battle in the centuries-old Lelantine War, which then closed with victory for Eretria and the loss of a large part of the plain by Khalkis. It is indeed a paradox that a war that raged for generations, from prehistoric times, mainly on land for the control of the horse-rearing plain, should now be decided at sea by the navy of Eretria, and with the thalassocracy of the 'rowing city' as its final result. Myres and Miller, in their studies of the *Thalassocracy List,* agree in placing Eretria's dominance at sea immediately after the defeat of Thebes and Khalkis and the demonstration of Aigina's impotence to influence the outcome. Miller specifically credits Eretria's thalassocrat status to the removal of the rivalry of Khalkis, but Khalkis had never been, at least since the era of colonisation in the eighth century, a great naval power.[148] By the end of the sixth century, it

Figure 8.8 The surviving horn and ear of the bronze bull.

was even weaker than usual. Rather, we should see as a contributing factor the removal of Aigina as a naval threat, following a campaign against it by Eretria's ally, Athens, assisted and subsidised by Corinth.[149] With Athens occupied with Aigina in the Saronic Gulf, Corinth and Eretria were free to pursue their own aims. In the case of Corinth, these took it towards the West. Eretria, however, had loftier aims in the East. And with its navy, what other power would challenge it in the Aegean? Among the monuments to Eretrian triumphs at this time may be the early-fifth-century Eretrian dedication at Olympia of a bronze bull by the Eretrian sculptor Philesios, as noted by Pausanias,[150] the base and a fragment of which have been preserved (Figures 8.6–8.8).

Notes

1 A. Burn, *Persia and the Greeks*, 2nd edn, London, 1984, 190, 199–201.

2 *SEG* 47, 1997, item 1347. Knoepfler, 1998, 105, likewise, believes that a democratic revolution took place at Eretria, but he thinks that: (1) it was against the regime of the *Hippeis* carried through by Diagoras; and (2) it happened shortly after the fall of Hippias. Cf. idem 1997, 352–449.

3 *IG* XII Suppl., 549; ed. pr. W Peek, 'Griechische Inschriften (Euboia)', *AM* 59, 1934, 73–9, re-ed. Wallace 1936b, 275–84.

4 Jeffery 1961/90, 86.

5 1936a, note Appendix 1; idem, 1936b, 279; idem, 1947, 144, n. 90.

6 Dated *c.* 550–30: A. Altherr-Charon and F. Laserre 1981, 25–35 (no. 2 with photos); repr. *SEG* 31, 1981, 806. Additional notes and commentary in *Bull.épigr.* 95, 1982, 271. Luppe, 1982, 22, gives an alternative reading: Τιμοκράτε̄ς ἀνέθε̄κε Δι[ὸς κατ' ἀγο̄να πάλαισμα | ἀνδρο̄(ν) νικε̄ρας το̄ι χάριν ἀν[τιδιδούς] and particularly notes rhotacism in l. 2; the restoration is not in question.

7 Wallace 1936b, 284.

8 Who supervised my earliest work on Eretria, towards an MA Prelim dissertation, at the University of Melbourne.

9 M. Walbank, *Athenian Proxenies of the Fifth Century* BC, Toronto, 1978, who lists no earlier examples. It is sometimes suggested that R. Meiggs and D. Lewis 1989, no. 4 (Kerkyra) is earlier (late seventh century) but it does not award *proxenia*; it is merely the grave marker of a *proxenos*. But it does show that the institution was very early.

10 Plato's two epitaphs for the exiled Eretrians: J. Edmonds, *Greek Elegy and Iambus* II, Cambridge, MA, 1979, nos. 9; 13 (the latter is quoted at the conclusion of Ch. 9). R. Penella, 'Scopelianus and the Eretrians in Cissia', *Athenaeum* 52, 1975, 295–300.

11 J. Green and R. Sinclair, 'Athenians in Eretria', *Historia* 19, 1970, 516; 524.

12 Wallace's (1936b, 277) restoration of ll. 1–8. See below, pp. 000–00.

13 Test. Epict. (*IG* XII 3, 33c) 4, 31; 4, 15, 35, etc.; *LSJ* s.v. ἐπιμηνεία

14 Heraclid. Lemb. 40 = 12 in C. and T. Müller, *FGH* II, 217 (who comment: 'distinguendus procul dubio est a Diagora Melio atheo quem item Corinthi obisse dicunt Hesychius Milesius et Suidas.'); see Suid., in which several Diagorases are conflated, but one died at Corinth: Διαγόρας· κατοικήσας Κόρινθον αὐτόθι τὸν βιον κατέστρεψεν. A fifth-century funerary inscription for a Διαγόρη exists: *IG* XII 9, 299.

15 Kheilon was a Spartan name; Aristoteles was common in Euboia, specifically Eretria: *LGPN* s.v. 'Αριστοτέλης; also Leekly and Efstratiou, 1980, 60, for Aristoteles. The conjunction of names suggests a family at Sparta with links to both the ephor and Euboia; a member of such a family would be a natural recipient of proxeny honours. Poralla 1985 s.vv. Χίλων; 'Αριστοτέλης.

16 W. Pape and G. Benseler, *Wörterbuch der griechischen Eigennamen* II, Graz, 1959, 1683–4, list Χιλώνειος, -ον as an adjective (Chilonisch: like a Khilon; belonging to Khilon). Perhaps it was a personal name of the 'Apollonios' kind, but it could also be applied adjectivally to a group (party) or family, e.g. Χειλωνίου μέρους: *LSJ* s.v. μέρος: 1105, 'class or party', Th. 2, 37, 1; Dem. 18, 292: Χειλωνίου γένους (Sparta had *gene*). If a personal name, it is in any case likely to belong to someone related to, or claiming political descent from, the famous ephor. It is not listed in Bechtel 1964. It is just possible that Kheilonios is the same as Kh(e)ilon, son of Demarmenos, whose daughter was the subject of dispute between Leotykhidas and Demaratos (Hdt. 6, 65).

17 Kheilon's niece was Kleomenes' wife: L. Fitzhardinge, *The Spartans*, London, 1985, 142; W. Forrest, *A History of Sparta, 950 BC to 192 BC*, London, 1971, 86.

18 D.L. 1, 72: Kheilon was an old man in the 52nd Olympiad (572–69) and died at Pisa near Olympia after congratulating his son on his victory in boxing. If the event were in that year and the son in the category of adult men (over 18), he must have been at least 83 in 509. But it is not impossible that the event belonged to the boys class (twelve–eighteen years old): K. Palaeologos, 'Rules of the competition', in N. Yalouris (ed.), *The Olympic Games in Ancient Greece. Ancient Olympia and the Olympic Games*, Athens, 1982. Kheilon was Ephor at Sparta in the 55th (or 56th) Olympiad, i.e. *c.*556: D.L. 1, 68. Dr Greg Stanton in a note to me raises the intriguing possibility that he might have been a son of Kleomenes; if so, he opposed his father's policies.

19 Hdt 5, 91, 2–3.

20 For Demaratos' relationship to Kheilon: Fitzhardinge 1985, 143.

21 Hdt 5, 75–6; 6, 51; 61; 65–6. Factions at Sparta in the reign of Kleomenes I: J. Hooker, *The Ancient Spartans*, London, 1980, 155; Dickins 1912, 28.

22 *IG* XII 9 Test. et Not. 147, 111–17: Heinze suggests 506 and Geyer 1903 ('accuratius') between 539–510. No evidence is offered.

23 See above, n. 14.

24 Was the delegation itself involved in his death?

25 Honorific statues in post-fifth century decrees at Eretria are not uncommon: *IG* XII 9, 196; 198; 236; 237.

26 There is no record of an Aristotelian Eretrian Constitution, though he did produce one of Khalkis. It is however most unlikely that he did not also write one for Eretria, as it was no less important in his day. See V. Rose, *Aristotelis qui ferebantur librorum fragmenta*, Stuttgart, 1886/1967.

27 Χῶροι; δῆμοι; φύλαι; Knoepfler 1997, 400–1.

28 1947, 115–46.

29 Gehrke 1988, 15–42. D. Knoepfler's ideas concerning demes and districts, hitherto scattered in footnotes in various periodical articles have now been gathered together, and sometimes modified, in his very important 1997 publication. See also J. and L. Robert, *Bull. épigr.* 1984, 321. Cairns 1984a, 156–64; idem 1986, 149–58. Gehrke and Knoepfler do not agree with each other on all points but both are critical of Cairns's work. Many, though not all, of Cairns's conclusions have since been questioned or ruled out altogether in Knoepfler's now (surely) standard work on the demes, districts and tribes of Eretria (1997).

30 1962, 1–4; also in P. Rhodes (ed.), *Selected Papers in Greek and Near Eastern History*, Cambridge, 1997, 22–8.

31 *Khoros*: *IG* XII 9, 189, 25 and (probably: see Lewis 1962/97, 25) *IG* XII 9 192, 10–1; *demos*: a rupestral deme boundary marker from Dystos published by S. and H. Apostolidis, '"Ενας ὅρος ἀπὸ Δύστο Εὐβοίας,' *Horos* 1990/1, 131–3.

32 *IG* XII 9, 189, 24–5 and 34 (Eretria); 90, 2 (Tamynai); 139, 3 δημαρχούντων (Amarynthos) with Ziebarth, Test. et Not. p. 163, 102–7.

33 Ed. pr. Dunant and Thomopoulos 1954, 316–22. See Lewis 1962/97, 22. The text and a translation is given below, p. 243.

34 Cairns 1984a 163–4; Knoepfler 1997, 373–5. Cf. Gehrke 1988, 22, n. 34, who tends to agree but allows that Lewis might possibly be right (23, n. 40) and argues against identifying the *khoroi* as districts. H. Bengtson discusses the treaty in *Die Staatsverträge des Altertums*, (II: Die Verträge der griechisch-römischen Welt von 700 bis 338 v.Ch.), München, 1975, 181, also equating *khoros* with *demos*: 'und Choros (= *Demos*) in Eretria.'

35 *IG* XII 5, 594; (= Tod 1968, 141, 123–25).

36 Lewis, 1962/97, 26, attributes the existence of *trittyes* at Keos to needs arising from its federal organisation

37 Ibid. 25.

38 Ibid. 23, 25.

39 Ibid. 23–4.

40 Μεσοχῶρος. *IG* XII 9, 241, 37. See Tables 8.1 and 8.2 for other possible restorations of the second name.

41 One of the perquisites of office was that they kept skins of sacrificial victims. For a parallel of this practice in the deme Skambonidai in Attica: *IG* I^3 244 (*c*. 460): B. Cook, *Greek Inscriptions*, London, 1987, 38, Fig. 31.

42 Μεταξύ and Φυλάκει.

43 Schol. ad Theoc. 2, 12: translated Ch. 2, p. 31 (Greek text: Ch. 2, n. 40).

44 1984a, 162 (Section 5: Two district religious festivals at Eretria). Gehrke, 1988, 21, argues against the two district theory. He regards Μεταξύ and Φυλάκει in *IG* XII 9, 189 as temporal datives, cf. Ziebarth in *IG* XII 9, Test. et Not., p. 163, 130–56. See Knoepfler 1997, 376–7.

45 1997, 376–7 and as he does with regard to Gehrke's belief that the two terms were time determiners.

46 Wallace 1947, 142–3; map, Fig. 1; located in Wallace's District IV.

47 *IG* XII 9, 241, 107.

48 1947, 121; 124.

49 1997, 375–7, 387 [Karn(ei)asion].

50 My warm thanks to Stephan Schmid for assisting me in gaining access to the stone at the Eretria Museum.

51 Letters in bold type differ from what I saw and what I would restore. The letters are placed in relation to each other vertically as they appear in my photographs. For Ziebarth and Wallace I use their font styles.

52 See the table above, p. 241.

53 If Larasion is to be considered, we may note that Λάρισα may have meant 'citadel' in Pelasgic/Dryopian: *LSJ*. s.v.. Λαράσιος (of the citadel or height) was an epithet of Zeus; (the 'Υψιστος' of *IG* XII 9, 58, 59 [Styra]?).

54 Ziebarth also thought so: *IG* XII 9, 103: 'in regione Φυλακῆ prope portum Aliverii.'

55 *IG* XII Suppl., 549: Μεκισστ[ίδ]ος φυλῆς. The name Narkittis is plausibly derived by Knoepfler from Narkissos; Knoepfler 1985b 50–5; 1997, 390. For 'Narkissos the Eretrian': Str. 9, 2, 10 C404. D. Knoepfler/K. Schefold, Forschungen in Eretria 1974 und 1975', *AK* 19, 1976, 57 = (*AD* 30, 1975 [1983] Chron. 169. More recently *REG* 108, 1995, xlix; Cairns 1986, 156 n. 16; Gehrke 1988, 23 n.44. The *editio princeps* is presented by Knoepfler 1998, 105–8.

56 Cairns 1986, 159.

57 Wallace 1947, 136 n. 56; 146.

58 Lewis 1962, 1.

59 As Cairns and Knoepfler would restore it.

60 *IG* I^2 90+ (= Tod 1968, 141).

61 An argument *ex silentio* it is true, but there is now a large *corpus* of inscriptions from Eretria.

62 'The Trittyes in Cleisthenes' Reforms', *TAPA* 86, 1955, 22–30.

63 Hignett 1952, 47; 48; 71–2 et *passim*.
64 *IG* II[2] 230. Knoepfler 1985a, n. 12.
65 1997, 390–3 and 1998, 105–8.
66 *REG* 94, 1981 (*Bull. épigr.*) 221; (*SEG* 30, 1980, 55); Knoepfler 1976, 57: 'De fait, je pense depuis longtemps et je montrerai dans ma thèse qu'il y avait à Érétrie au moins six, et sans doute dix, tribus', although eodem, 1975 [1983], 169, he says 'très probablement six'. This latter figure is his current view (1997 and 1998).
67 Letter to me from Prof. Knoepfler (dated 23 August 1992): one was discovered in 1973 by Dunant, the other by himself on the acropolis (part of choregic monument); these are discussed now in his paper of 1998a.
68 The other: Mekis(s)tis: *IG* XII Suppl. 549 (with double sigma Μηκισστίδι). Knoepfler also speculates on some other possible tribal names at Eretria (e.g. Melaneis; Eurytis; Oreon) in 1997, 393 and 1998a, 107–8.
69 G. Daux, "Note sur "l'horos phratricos" d'Érétrie', *BCH* 74, 1954, 282–4. The stone is a *horos* (boundary marker). *Phratria*: an ancient tribal subdivision, sometimes loosely translated as 'brotherhood'. See generally S. Lambert, *The Phratries of Attica*, Ann Arbor, MI, 1998.
70 Ibid. 3–21.
71 Morris 1987.
72 Salmon 1986, 205–9.
73 *Corinth; Results of Excavations*, VIII, Cambridge, MA, 1931: Pt 1: The Greek inscriptions, no. 11.
74 1947, 119, n. 14.
75 G. Stanton, 'The territorial tribes of Korinth and Phleious', *CA* 5, 1986, 139–53: E = Ἔνδοθεν; *F* = *Fάστυ*; Π = πάραλοι. Salmon 1986: E = Ἐντὸς τοῦ Ἰσθμοῦ; ϝ = ϝάστυ; Π = πέραν τοῦ Ἰσθμοῦ.
76 Wallace: E = Ἐπίλεκτοι; *F* = ?; Π = πελτασταί; Jones: E and Π, ditto; *F* = *Fῖλαι*.
77 S. Dow, 'Corinthiaca', *HSCP* 53, 1942, 97.
78 R. Stroud, 'Tribal boundary markers from Corinth', *CSCA* 1, 1968, 233–42.
79 1986, 418.
80 Th. 2, 9, 3 (beginning of Peloponnesian War) and 4, 44, 1 (Battle of Solygeia, near the Corinthia itself, 425).
81 I am not persuaded that the absence of cavalry at Solygeia is certain evidence that Corinth had no cavalry. Thucydides is referring to the principal contribution made by each state; thus Corinth ναυτικὸν παρείχετο (provided ships), while other states provided infantry, cavalry, etc. That no mention is made of Corinthian πεζόν (infantry), although it is for other states, cannot mean that Corinth therefore had no infantry, which would be absurd, as 4, 44, 1 clearly shows. Thus, the omission of mention of cavalry may simply suggest that the city did not have a particularly noteworthy cavalry arm.
82 ὁπλῖται and ψιλοί. Thus, e.g. l. 37 (Wallace 1947, 120, l. 63 *sic*): Μεσοχώρου (district name) ὁπλῖται (the hoplite contingent of the district).
83 Salmon 1986, 418, n. 21; Stanton 1986, 143, n. 24.
84 Nic. Dam. (*FGrH* 90F60.2 = *FGH* III, 60): records eight *probouloi*. Suid. s.v. πάντα ὀκτώ. Scholars universally experience difficulty with this passage. It only concerns me because it seems to presume that an eight-part system already existed within the Corinthian *boule* at the end of the tyranny. Salmon 1986, 205, 231; Will 1955, 609–15; H. Lutz, 'The Corinthian constitution after the fall of the Cypselides' (*sic*) *CR* 10, 1896, 418–19. Roebuck, 1972, 114, thinks it unlikely that the eight-fold tribal system was introduced after the tyranny; N. Jones, *Public Organization in Ancient Greece. A Documentary Study*, Philadelphia, 1987, 168, concurs.
85 N. Jones 'The civic organization of Corinth', *TAPA* 110, 1980, 170: 'To my knowledge, only one other [i.e. than Corinth] state of the Greek period, Elis, is recorded as having had a civic organization of eight principal divisions.' For Elis: Paus. 5, 9, 6. It is interesting

that it is Elis, for as we have seen in Ch. 1, it had very ancient links with Eretria and it seems to have provided or shared the name of one of its tribes, Mekisstis: St. Byz. Μήκιστον· πόλις . . . ἔστι καὶ ἄλλη τῆς Ἤλιδος: G. Papandreou, *Ἡ Ἠλεία διά Μέσου τῶν Αἰώνων*, Lehaina, 1924/90, 56–66.

86 *IG* XII Suppl. 555, 54–6 (Wallace: *c.* 304–300).

87 Πρυτανευούσης, e.g. Π[ανδιο] | νίδος ἕκτης πρυτανευόσης (*sic*): *IG* II^2 18 (= Tod 1968, 108). A. Henry, *The Prescripts of Athenian Decrees*, Leiden, 1977, 24–32. See below, p. 253 (Table 8.3) for parallels.

88 Jones, 1980, 181, leaves open the possibility that there were four divisions, but he is alone in allowing this.

89 These decrees are: *IG* XII 9, 191 (*c.* 330–310); 241 (320–308); Suppl. 555 (304–300); 245 (*c.* 300); 244 (*c.* 280); 246 (280–275) and 249 (280–275). These are Wallace's dates; Cairns and Knoepfler agree that these need some revision. This does not affect my argument.

90 However Ziebarth thought there were four: Wallace 1947, 122, n. 16.

91 Knoepfler 1971, 242–4, 223, n. 4: bibliography. His arguments are accepted and expanded by M. Moggi, *I sinecismi interstatali greci* (I: Dalle origine al 338 a.C.), Pisa, 1976, 227–36, who argues for a date between 411 and 405. Most other scholars have the annexation at the time of the Lamian War, 323–22. It is possible that these 'new' districts comprised the περιοικίς mentioned by Theopompos (*FGrH* 115F149); Gehrke 1988, 38–42.

92 Knoepfler 1971, 243–4.

93 *IG* XII 9, 267 (third century; from the city) is a dedication to Apollo Trimoridios, who has been compared with Artemis Triklaria at Patrai (Paus. 7, 19, 22), whose temple was common to three cities; does it hark back to a three-fold division of the Eretrias?

94 Knoepfler 1997, 400.

95 For discussion: Stanton 1986, 143. However, no scholar (to my knowledge) considering possible meanings for the abbreviations cites St. Byz. Περαία · ἔστι καί χώρα Κορίνθου Περαία λεγομένη.

96 See above, nn. 84–5.

97 Ibid., 168, n. 6. He uses the 'high' chronology.

98 Heracl. Lemb. 20. Salmon 1986, 203–5.

99 1972, 114–15. See also the 'reform' of tribal names at Sikyon (Hdt. 5, 68) by the tyrant Kleisthenes.

100 1986, 145.

101 On stone-cutting errors: M. Osborne, 'Athenian stone-cutters at work', *ZPE* 19, 1975, 159–77.

102 For example *IG* XII 9, 225, ll. 4–8.

103 Peek 1934, 75. For AYTON: see the Eretrian decree for Glaukippos and his brothers: *IG* XII 9, 210, 11–16 (dated *c.* 302–285) has ἔδοξεν τῷ δήμῳ εἶναι [[α]]αὐτοὺς προξένους καὶ εὐεργέτας τοῦ δήμου τοῦ Ἐρετριέων Γλαύκιππον καὶ Ἱπποδάμαντα καὶ Ἀπολλώνιον Διονυσίου Ἀντιγονεῖς καὶ αὐτοὺς καὶ ἐγγόνους, etc. referring back to Γλαύκιππος καὶ οἱ ἀδελφοὶ in an ἐπειδὴ clause (ll. 2–4). Greg Stanton has also pointed out to me (for Athens): Walbank 1978, 205–6 (no. 56, 2–4: καὶ εν]αι πρόχσ || [ενον καὶ εὐεργέ]τēν ' Αθēναί | [ōν αὐτòν· etc.). The pronoun is repeated in l. 9.

104 Wallace 1936b; Peek 1934, 73–7.The two versions are given for comparison (Table 8.4) For the Athenian type: Henry, 1977, Chs 1, 4, 27, shows the development of a more explicit calendar dating procedure (cf. the Eretrian decree); 37–8 (later examples); ibid., *Honours and Privileges in Athenian Decrees: The Principal Formulae of Athenian Honorary Decrees*, Hildesheim, 1983, Ch. 4 (Proxenia; Euergesia): gives 'early' (mid-fifth century) examples.

105 The eight *epimenieuoures/probouloi*, the *arkhon* and *grammateus* of *IG* XII Suppl., 555 are inscribed without demotics.

Table 8.4 The readings of Peek and Wallace of *IG* XII, Suppl. 549

Peek	*Wallace/IG Suppl.*
[ΝΑΜΕ ΕΤΗΝΙ-]	[ΕΔΟΧΣΕΝ : ΤΕ̄Ι ΒΟ-]
[ΚΟΝ] Ι : ΚΑΙ ΤΟ̄Ι [ΧΣΥΜ-]	ΛΕ̄]Ι : ΚΑΙ ΤΟ̄Ι [ΔΕ̄ΜΟ̄Ι]
[Π]ΑΡΑΓΕΝΟΜΕ[Ν]Ο̄Ι]	[Π]ΑΡΑΓΕΝΟΜΕ[Ν]Ο̄Ι]
ΚΥΡΙΟ̄Ι : ΜΕ̄ΚΙΣΣΤ[ΙΔ-]	ΚΥΡΙΟ̄Ι : ΜΕ̄ΚΙΣΣΤ[ΙΔ-]
ΟΣ ΦΥΛΕ̄Σ : ΕΠΙΜΕ̄Ν[Ι-]	ΟΣ ΦΥΛΕ̄Σ : [Ε]ΠΙΜΕ̄Ν[Ι-]
ΕΥΟΥΡΕ̄Σ : ΗΕ̄ΡΑΟ̄Ν-	ΕΥΟΥΡΕ̄Σ : [Η]Ε̄ΡΑΟ̄Ν-
ΟΣ ΜΕ̄ΝΟΣ : ΤΕΤΡΑΔΙ	ΟΣ ΜΕ̄ΝΟΣ : ΤΕΤΡΑΔΙ
[Ε]ΠΙ ΔΕΚΑ : [[ΝΑΜΕ]	[Ε]ΠΙ ΔΕΚΑ : [[Α[ΡΙΣΤΟΤ-]
[ΕΙΠΕΝ ΕΠΑΙΝΕΣΑΙ ΝΑ-]	[ΕΛΕ̄Ν ΧΕΙΛΟ̄ΝΙΟ] : [Π]
[ΜΕ ΚΑΙ Ε̄ΝΑΙ]] : ΑΡΙΣ[Τ-]	[ΡΟΧΣΕΝΟΝ]]] : ΑΡΙΣ[Τ-]
ΟΤΕΛΕ̄Ν ΤΕΛΛΟ̄Ν[Ι]Ο̄	ΟΤΕΛΕ̄Ν ΧΕΙΛΟ̄Ν[Ι]Ο
ΠΡΟΧΣΕΝΟΝ : ΚΑΙ [ΕΥ-]	ΠΡΟΧΣΕΝΟΝ : ΚΑΙ ⟨ΕΥ-⟩
ΕΡΓΕΤΕ̄Ν : [Κ]ΑΤΤ[ΑΠΕ-]	ΕΡΓΕΤΕ̄Ν : ΚΑΙ Τ[ΟΥ?]
Ρ ΑΔΕΛΦΕ̄ Α[Ι]Τ[ΕΙΤΑΙ]	Ρ ΑΔΕΛΦΕ[ΟΣ ΑΥΤΟ̂]
-----------------------------	*vacat* or EPI?

106 *IG* XII Suppl. 555: he seems to have been called *arkhon,* though the presence of this term in the text does not definitely confirm him as a president of the *epimenieuontes.*

107 Knoepfler 1985a, 246, n. 11; ibid., 1997, 372–3, suggests between 6,300 and 8,400 for the fourth-century civic body. M. Hansen, *Demography and Democracy*, Copenhagen, 1986, 65–9 (conclusions).

108 On the later Euboian conciliar year: D. Knoepfler, 'Le calendrier des Chalkidiens de Thrace: essai de mise au point sur le liste et l' ordre des mois eubeens', *JSavants* 1989, 23–59; idem, 'The calendar of Olynthus and the origins of the Chalcidians in Thrace', in J.-P. Descoeudres (ed.), *Greek Colonists and Native Populations. Proceedings of the First Australian Congress of Classical Archaeology*, Oxford, 1990a, 95–115.

109 Sealey 1960a, 38.

110 Prehistoric Argive/Euboian links: Ch. 2, p. 46 and n. 176.

111 Hdt. 5, 67. It was Kleisthenes' anti-Argive maternal grandfather of the same name, tyrant of Sikyon, who expelled the hero from his cult place in the agora there.

112 Another tradition, which the Alkmaionidai preferred to stress, made the eponym Alkmaion, son of Sillos, grandson of Nestor of Pylos. For the details of all of these figures, see Grimal 1996, s.vv.; Hsych. s.v. Ἀλκμαιονίδαι, which gives as an ancestor a follower of Theseus [he of the short-front/long-back hairstyle (Plut. *Thes.* 5). Hdt. 5, 62 knows nothing of a Pylian ancestor but rather suggests an autochthonous origin]; for him see also Graves 1962, 384–5). If Alkmaion is to be identified with Narkissos, we may note that he, too, was excluded from any place in the great altar in the Amphiaraion at Oropos, probably on account of his matricide, alongside his father Amphiaraos, who in this interpretation must be identified with Amarynthos, and his brother Amphilokhos.

113 Graves 1962, 287–8 (Section 85 [Narcissus] b, n. i); Alkmaion 384–5. Hdt. 1, 41–3; 1, 52; 6, 125.

114 It has been put to me by Dr Greg Stanton that such a promotion would have been at the expense of Alkmaionid claims to have been the most anti-tyrant of families. But no Alkmaionid was ever killed trying to remove the Peisistratids; indeed Kleisthenes must have collaborated for a time since, though in exile in 512, he had been *arkhon* in 527. It may be also that there was an Eretrian family link with the Gephyraioi. Hignett, 1952, 125, citing the *skolion* (*Ath. pol.* 19, 3), links it with Kleisthenes and avers that his and his fellow conspirators' intentions were initially wholly aristocratic.

115 *Phoenix* 17, 1963, 99–112.

116 Davies 1971, 372; 380–1; Table 1. C. Tisdell, *The Political Attitudes of the Alkmeonidai in the VI Century* BC, unpubl. MA thesis, University of New England, Armidale, New South Wales, 1989, 16: a daughter of Megakles, married to Peisistratos, citing Hdt. 1, 61, 1, who however does not mention Koisyra, much less consider that she was the daughter of Megakles. F. Willemsen, 'Ostraka einer Meisterschale', *MDAI(A)* 106, 1991, 144–5 and pl. 26, agrees with Shear, making Koisyra (he sees only one) mother of Megakles (II in Shear's stemma).

117 Willemsen 1991, 144–5 and pl. 24. The text of the ostrakon is:
]ακλες | [. . .] οκρατος | [. . .] λι εχσο | εισελθεις:
MEρετε<ι>αζε
which may be restored as follows:
Μέγακλες | (Η)ιπποκράτους | πάλι ἔξω | μ' Ἐπετρίαζε
εἰσέλθεις.
See Brenne 1994, 15–16 and Fig. 10, which has Μέγακαλες | Ηιπποκράτους | καί Κοισύρας (Megakles, son of Hippokrates and Koisyra).

118 Cf. T. Figueira, 'Residential restrictions on the Athenian ostracized', in *Excursions in Epichoric History. Aiginetan Essays*, Lanham, MD, 1993, 182; Brenne 1994, 22–3; A. Raubitschek, 'Megakles, geh nicht nach Eretria', *ZPE* 100, 1994, 381–2.

119 Hsch. ἐρετριάζει· σκώπτει, παίζει. . Cf. χαλκιδίζειν.

120 See Ober 1989, 66–9. But did Kleisthenes harbour thoughts of tyranny? Hignett, 1952, 125, links Kleisthenes with the *skolion* in *Ath. pol.* 19, 3. As with democracy, the model for tyranny also existed at Eretria.

121 F. Adcock and J. Mosley, *Diplomacy in Ancient Greece*, London, 1975, 23.

122 Hdt. 5, 73. G. Horsley, 'Kleisthenes and the abortive Athenian embassy to Sardis', *Museum Philologicum Londoniense* 7, 1986, 99–105.

123 Hdt. 5, 77, 1

124 Hdt. 5, 77, 2.

125 Text: Meiggs and Lewis 1989, 28–9 (no. 15); translation: C. Fornara, *Translated Documents of Greece and Rome, 1: Archaic Times to the End of the Peloponnesian War*, Cambridge, 1983, 44–5. Raubitschek 1949, 168.

126 D. Campbell, *Greek Lyric* III (Loeb), Cambridge, MA, 520–1 (*Anth.Planud.* 26). On Simonides and Eretria: Harpocr. s.v. Ταμύναι (= *IG* XII 9, Test. et Not. 163 s.v. Λυσίμαχος). He was closely connected with Eretria: Knoepfler 1969, 87 and n. 27.

127 'Excavations at Rhitsona', *BSA* 14, 1907/08, 237.

128 *Aristoteles und Athen* (2 vols), Berlin, 1893, 80.

129 Hdt 5, 102, 3.

130 Myres 1906, 97.

131 Paus. 9, 22, 2.

132 Korinna: D. Campbell, *Greek Lyric* IV, Cambridge, MA, 1992, 44–5 (no. 666).

133 Str. 10, 1, 10 C448.

134 Pl. *Mx.* 10, 240a.

135 1953, 183

136 Lysanias of Mallos wrote a history of Eretria, Περὶ Ἐρετρίας (*FGrH* 426F1 = *FGH* IV, 441–2), cited by Plutarch as an authority in *de Hdt. malign.* 24 (*Mor.* 861b–c) for an important Eretrian naval victory, which Herodotos totally ignores.

137 Myres 1906, 88; 96–7; Miller 1975, Pt 1, 5–22. The variations between these scholars are slight: 508/5 and 490/85.

138 See above, n. 134.

139 The Eretrians are mentioned in two decrees, (*IG* XII 9, Test. et Not., 162–3) from Magnesia-on-the-Maiandros as οἰκεῖοι ὑπάρχοντες ἐκ προγόνων τοῦ δήμου τοῦ Ἐρετριέων (both dated *c*. 206). The feeling of kinship and gratitude for Eretria's sacrifices in Asia Minor lasted long there. The Eretrians and Milesians had a long history of friendship prior to the sixth century. Likewise, we need not doubt the Eretrians' reason

for going to the aid of their Ionian kinsmen: gratitude for past help (from Miletos). We should not overlook Euboian colonisation in Asia Minor in prehistoric times.

140 1907/8, 237.

141 Ch. 9, pp. 275–8.

142 Goodwin 1885, 18; Myres 1906, 96, n. 23. For discussion of this issue, see Ch. 9, pp. 274–5, in which I cite other scholars (Myres; Wallace) who share my views of Herodotos' unsatisfactory treatment of Euboian affairs.

143 1907/8, 238.

144 Cf. Hdt. 8, 1.

145 *ATL* III 1950, 294.

146 Hdt. 5, 77; Ael. *VH* 6, 1.

147 For an Attic inscription mentioning 'Lelanton' in the context of the sale of property belonging to Hermokopidai: W. Prichett, 'Attic stelai' I, *Hesperia* 22, 1953, 252 (l. 178), with *SEG* 13, 1956, item 13. See Popham *et al.* 1980, Appendix B: The ancient name of Lefkandi, 425.

148 Kondoleon 1963/65.

149 Th. 1, 41, 1; Hdt. 6, 87–93.

150 5, 27, 8. W. Dittenberger and K. Purgold 1896, n. 248: Φιλε̄σιος ἐποίε | Ἐρετριε̄ς το̄ι Δί. Interestingly, in view of the relationship suggested in Ch. 5, pp. 148–9, the Eretrian bull is one of a pair, the other of which was dedicated by Kerkyra.

9

ERETRIA IN THE 490s

Following the victory of 506, Eretria entered into fifteen years of *hegemonia* in central Greece, the achievements of which prompted the eulogistic sentiments expressed in Plato's *Menexenos,* which show that the memory of Eretria's years of power and fame was not yet dead in the fourth century.

Eretria now began pursuing imperialist/interventionist political aims, reminiscent of Athens' policies later in the fifth century. Persia was now a political force that Eretria was increasingly obliged to take into account, for it posed a threat to Euboia and Naxos even before 500, as Herodotos makes clear.[1] Miletos was under increasing pressure from Persian expansion into Ionia, which ultimately resulted in the intervention of the Eretrians in the military events of the Ionian Revolt. In Naxos, the oligarchy of the *Pakheis*, installed in 514 by the Spartans with the active support of Diagoras, fell *c.* 505, and it was replaced by a democracy.[2] Myres believes that, thanks to its navy, Eretria was able and willing to assist the Naxians, while at the same time installing a like-minded government in its sphere of interest in the middle Aegean, and that Naxos now became a dependency of Eretria. Naxos was itself the centre of a small 'empire', which included Paros, Eretria's old ally, and its former dependency Andros.[3] In his list of ship contingents at the Battle of Salamis, the Naxian seems to be part of that of the Euboian bloc.[4] Burn points out the vulnerability of Paros and Naxos to any powerful maritime state.[5] Eretrian intervention in favour of the *Demos* at Naxos may have had a price: the return of Andros, and possibly Paros too, to the Eretrian empire. The importance of Andros to Eretria is obvious: in hostile hands, it was the equivalent for Eretria of 'the eyesore of the Peiraieus'. Myres points to 'the significance of Miltiades'' attempt to annex Paros, as soon as Athens is beginning to see her way through her entanglements in Aegina. She is picking up the pieces, as elsewhere, of the Eretrian ἀρχή.'[6]

The fall of the Naxian oligarchy would have momentous consequences, for when the exiles went to Miletos and appealed to Aristagoras to reinstall them with a Persian fleet, that ambitious and unscrupulous ruler took their request along with proposals to attack Euboia as well, which in practice, meant Eretria. The inclusion of Euboia can be explained by the role of Eretria in the overthrow of the Naxian oligarchy and the importance of its fleet in the Aegean. Miletos had experienced a chequered political history during the sixth century. Throughout, it was phil-Eretrian, but had also since the days of Cyrus been consistently loyal to Persia.[7] However, Histiaios, its tyrant, and Aristagoras, his kinsman-deputy who succeeded him, then later 'handed over' power to a 'democracy'. Aristagoras, who 'having first pretended to give up the tyranny, created *isonomie* [equality of rule] in Miletos',[8] may have before then regarded the democracies in Eretria and Naxos as a threat. Perhaps Diagoras, their fellow tyrant at Eretria, had been an ally; if so, they would not have viewed the regime that overthrew him with much favour. The nature of *tyrannis* under Persian control was quite different to that in autonomous Greek *poleis*, being essentially anti-democratic, a de facto oligarchy-of-one.[9] The apprehension of the Milesian tyrants proved to be well founded, for when the Ionian Revolt broke out in 500, there was a general overthrow of these Persian puppets in the subject states and the subsequent establishment of democracies.[10] This would explain the initially favourable reception given to the Naxian *Pakheis* exiles at Miletos and Aristagoras' suggestion for an attack on Euboia. After his 'conversion' to democracy (making a virtue of necessity) and his revolt from Persia, Aristagoras would later plead successfully for help from the three democratic states of Eretria, Naxos and Athens.

Aristagoras' appeal was successful and Artaphernes, satrap of Sardis and brother of Dareios, obtained the king's approval for an expedition with a fleet of no less than 200 triremes, and a very great number of Persian and allied troops under the command of Megabates, a cousin of Dareios.[11] The need for such a huge Persian fleet to restore the exiles can only be explained by another large fleet standing in the way. Since the original plan outlined at Sardis by Aristagoras included an attack on Euboia and not, be it noted, on Athens, we may be confident that had the siege of Naxos succeeded, Eretria would have been the next target. Indeed, Naxos merely stood in the way and was an excuse for the Persians to attempt to destroy the most powerful fleet in the Greek world in 499. The size of the Persian fleet and its large complement of Persian and allied troops was quite excessive if the sole purpose had been the restoration of a few Naxian oligarchs. However, such a force would have been necessary for the conquest of Eretria, its empire and then all Euboia. But the expedition failed at Naxos. Aristagoras and Megabates fell out and Megabates, piqued, forewarned the Naxian democrats and their allies of the impending attack, giving them time to prepare a defence. Although Naxos-*polis* was besieged for four months, the city held out, provisioned, no doubt, by the Eretrian navy. The leadership in disarray, the Persian fleet sailed home. Later, Naxos was the only other state in the western Aegean to send troops along with Eretria and Athens to aid the Ionian cause, so perhaps the Naxian democrats felt that they had good reason to be grateful to Eretria. In these events, we hear of no Athenian involvement, and for a state with a minimal navy we should not have expected it. There is a curious story in Athenaios concerning a first Persian invasion into Euboia:

> It was at the time when the Persians made their first expedition to Euboia, they say, when a man from Eretria, Diomnestos, became master of the commanding officer's money . . . When however the Persian king again sent his army to Eretria, with orders to totally destroy the city, etc.[12]

The details of the story do not concern us. What is interesting is the inference that Dareios sent not one but two expeditions to take Eretria, the first of which, if it ever happened, must have failed to take the city.

The Naxian episode alerted Eretria and Athens to the Persian threat. When the unsuccessful expedition returned, Aristagoras, furious with Megabates' treachery and fearful that his influence at the Persian court would be fatal to his own position as ruler of Miletos, began the intrigues and policy shifts that led to the outbreak of the Ionian Revolt. In this way was Miletos, by another of those ironies of Greek history, established as the agent of the destruction of its ancient kindred city and ally. Because of their very long-standing friendly relationship, it is not surprising that when its 'kinsmen'[13] of Ionia appealed for help in their crisis, the Eretrians should go to their aid with their allies and naval power. Perhaps the Karystians also joined the expedition to Asia Minor. Karystos' later attitude towards Persian demands suggest that it had obligations (treaty? dependency? friendship?) to Eretria. If Cary[14] is correct that 'Carystus was apparently under Eretrian rule as late as 490 BC', it proved loyal when the Persians came to attack Eretria itself and had to be subjected to considerable pressure to co-operate with them: 'When [the Persians] came also to Karystos while sailing round the islands, the Karystians gave no hostages nor would they agree to campaign against neighbour cities, specifying Eretria and Athens, so they laid siege to them and devastated their land.'[15] The other islanders offered no resistance. Sparta was solicited for aid by Aristagoras, who personally appealed to, of all people, Kleomenes! Without success, needless to say. It would not have required his daughter's admonition to dissuade Kleomenes.[16] How was it likely that he would join a relief effort led by precisely those powers that had frustrated his plans and policies in central Greece? When Aristagoras toured Greece seeking support for the Ionians in their rebellion, it was in the guise of a democratic leader of a generally democratic coalition, for his 'selfless' abdication of his autocracy had indeed inspired the majority of the Ionian cities to drive out their pro-Persian tyrants.[17] In his account, however, Herodotos fails to indicate clearly, and we should not overlook it, that whatever the motives of Aristagoras may have been, the Ionians were generally already very ready to revolt.[18] Though successful in Eretria and Athens ('Naturally there is no mention in Herodotos of appeal to Eretria')[19] his democratic veneer contributed to his general failure to win support in most of Greece. Kleomenes had spent much of his life suppressing democracies and tyrannies. Corinth, apart from the westerly direction of its interests, was a steadfastly oligarchic state and averse to any activity that might disrupt its own political and commercial status quo. Aigina and Thebes were Spartan allies and would, in any case, have nothing to do with anything supported by Eretria and Athens. The change in the internal politics of Miletos may not have been a decisive factor, but it undoubtedly made it easier for democratic Eretria, Naxos and Athens to justify publicly the risks in going to the aid of the beleaguered Ionians in 499.

Sealey[20] wonders why Eretria became involved at all: 'the immediate motives of the Eretrians are not known.' I believe that we can now understand these very clearly. He himself refers to the centuries-old alliance between Eretria and Miletos, which ought to suggest at least one motive. This alliance had been effectively in abeyance during the last half of the sixth century as a result of the decline of Miletos, following the death of Thrasyboulos and the resultant political chaos, while the oligarchy at Eretria had fallen, to be replaced by the tyranny of Diagoras, which in turn had been succeeded by the democracy. These political permutations never quite matched, until in 500 Aristagoras transferred his power to a democracy, by which time crisis was upon the Ionians. The decline of Miletos is contrasted by the rise of Eretria. During her evolution from oligarchy via tyranny to democracy, she avoided the political and social excesses of Miletos. Meanwhile, Eretria's main commercial and political interests had moved to the western Aegean and central Greece as well as the northern coastlands of Macedonia and Thrace, especially the mineral and timber-rich region around Pangaion. These shifts in emphasis had made the Milesian alliance less important to the Eretrians. But, though less pivotal, the friendship persisted and obligations were remembered. When revolution and war came to Ionia, Miletos appealed to the old relationship with its now great ally, and Eretria did not fail it:

> when the Athenians came with twenty ships, they were accompanied[21] by five triremes of the Eretrians, who came not as a favour to the Athenians but rather to the Milesians themselves, thereby repaying their debt; for earlier, the Milesians had been allies of the Eretrians in the war against the Khalkidians when the Samians came to the aid of the Khalkidians.[22]

Herodotos omits all reference to the role of Naxos in the Ionian War,[23] and minimises that of Eretria, as he normally does with anything that might diminish the 'glorious role' played by Athens. Was Herodotos' suppression of Eretrian and Euboian affairs the result of his awareness of Eretria's pivotal role before 490 and a deliberate falsification for his Athenian patrons? After all, there were few Eretrians left to object after 490. Moreover, indeed he had much to hush-up with respect to the part played by Athens over the course of the whole Ionian and, later, Persian Wars. Athens' ambiguous role begins as far back as 506, when the Kleisthenic democracy had in fact offered earth and water when their embassy went to Persia to get support against the threat from Kleomenes' great coalition.[24] There was subsequently general censure of the envoys when they returned, so Herodotos says, blame following easily, no doubt, upon failure to secure the help for which they had asked. It long remained a sensitive point at Athens. But Herodotos never suggests that there was ever any public repudiation of the ambassadors' actions and it is hard to imagine that they had not been led to believe that they should offer this gesture in exchange for the desperately needed aid. Eretria never, at any stage, offered earth and water or we would certainly have heard of it from Herodotos. Also reflecting no glory on Athens is the fact that when the going got tough, the Athenians were the first of the western allies to quit Ionia, leaving the Eretrians, and we may presume the Naxians, to carry on without them. The incredible scenes following the production of Phrynikhos' tragedy dealing with the siege and fall of Miletos clearly suggest problems of collective conscience on the part of the *demos* over its poor response to that particular crisis:

> Phrynikhos having written and staged a play entitled *The Fall of Miletos*, the whole audience burst into tears so [the Athenians] fined him 1000 drakhmai for reminding them of a disaster that involved them so closely, and forever afterwards they banned the performance of that play.[25]

A sense of guilt seems also to have inspired Themistokles' tasteless jibe at the Eretrians in 480 about being like cuttlefish (no backbone);[26] the reference is to a symbol used on some Eretrian coins. Eretria had by this time fallen to the Persian attack of 490 and the Athenians had made no real attempt to help the besieged city.

Herodotos succeeds in pushing these failures of duty well into the background, as the now almost universally held laudatory opinion of the role of Athens at this time bears witness. His method is to minimise or omit deeds that might overshadow those of his hero-city. This propensity was noted already in antiquity by Plutarch, who fortunately still had access to the necessary corrective texts, particularly (but not only) for our purposes, Lysanias of Mallos' *History of Eretria*:[27]

> He [Herodotos] mentions the Eretrians quite casually and passes over their great epic achievement in silence . . . Various writers have described these events including Lysanias of Mallos in his *History of Eretria*.[28]

Plutarch's attack on Herodotos has been regarded generally as untrustworthy. But, as far as Euboian affairs are concerned, it is worth remembering that Plutarch was born in central Greece at Khaironeia in Boiotia and that he almost certainly visited Euboia. His comment on the tomb of Kleomakhos in Khalkis[29] sounds like the autopsy report of an interested tourist. He knows that the tomb was surmounted by a column. The inscription, probably in the old Khalkidian epichoric alphabet, may have been difficult to read, resulting in his confusion over the identity of the lover and indeed of the homeland of Kleomakhos himself (Thessaly/Thrace).[30] Cary observes, speaking specifically of Euboia, that he 'had a specialist's acquaintance with the antiquities of Central Greece.'[31] Nor does he, to our knowledge, have any reason to exaggerate Eretria's role, so it is worth noting his descriptive 'great and epic achievement', for he does not simply say 'role' or 'exploit' baldly and he specifically charges Herodotos with suppressing the information by 'passing [it] over in silence.'[32] We shall see shortly what this great success was.

However, Herodotos also uses ambiguously misleading data. For example:

> When the Athenians came with their twenty ships,
> *agomenoi* them five triremes of the Eretrians . . .[33]

This middle participle is usually rendered as 'bringing/leading with' but it may equally mean simply 'accompanied by'.[34] Certainly, the ambiguous verb form is meant to imply that the Athenians were the prime movers in the naval relief effort. Yet, inconsistently, Herodotos notes that the Eretrians did not come at the bidding of the Athenians but spontaneously from motives of gratitude and duty towards their old and faithful ally for their past support. We shall return to the matter of the ships sent by Eretria and Athens, but for the moment we need to consider further the circumstances surrounding the expedition.

Let us return to the Athenian desertion of the Ionian cause. After the (lost) Battle of Ephesos, which followed the burning of Sardis by the Eretrians and Athenians in 498 and the following retreat to the coast, during which the commander, Eualkides of Eretria,[35] was put to the sword by the Persians, the Athenians 'wholly separated themselves from the Ionians and refused to aid them even though Aristagoras sent urgent pleading messages'. But the Ionians, and Eretrians were Ionians and acknowledged kinsmen, 'though deprived of Athenian allies nonetheless continued the war against the king.'[36]

There is no hint of an Eretrian withdrawal, even though their leader had been put to death. Moreover, this general alone is mentioned by name. Why? Herodotos tells us that he was a crowned victor in the games and the recipient of lavish praise in a now lost poem by Simonides of Keos.[37] Fine, but not so rare a feat, and not enough to explain why he, and not an Athenian, was singled out among the notables killed during and after the battle by the Persians.[38] The only sensible explanation is that he was in fact commander-in-chief of the allied forces that had attacked and burnt Sardis. He may earlier have been the Eretrian admiral in the Battle of the Pamphylian Sea.[39] Though the Athenians had abandoned their allies, the Ionians and Eretrians fought on, and Jacoby suggests that an alternative tradition, represented by the now lost writers Dionysios of Miletos, Hellanikos and Kharon, maintained that the Eretrians did not prematurely abandon their allies along with the Athenians.[40] Just before this, the rebels were still winning over other allies, so not everyone considered the Ionian cause to be lost.[41] These new allies included most of Karia and the cities of Cyprus, with the exception of Amathous only. What had happened to induce Karia and Cyprus in the far south to commit themselves at this stage to the Ionian revolt?

The 'great and epic achievement' of the Eretrians, which Herodotos does not even mention but which others fortunately did, occurred at this time of crisis and in that very region, so we must credit to it the adhesion of the new allies who replaced the deserting Athenians. Plutarch (citing Lysanias) tells us that:

> When confusion had already struck in Ionia and the King's fleet was on its way[42] they [the Eretrians] went out to meet it and won a naval victory over the Cypriots in the Pamphylian Sea. They then turned back, left their ships at Ephesos, and attacked Sardis and kept up the siege of the acropolis where Artaphernes had taken refuge; the intention was to raise the siege of Miletos; they succeeded in doing this, causing the enemy troops to withdraw in a remarkable state of alarm; then, attacked by superior force, they retreated. Various writers described these events including Lysanias of Mallos in his *History of Eretria*. If for no other reason, it would have been a fine epitaph on Miletos, after its capture and destruction, to describe this wonderful exploit. However, he says that they were actually defeated by the barbarians and driven back to their ships.[43]

There is no conceivable reason to simply assume that these events are fictitious[44] or that the sources are untrustworthy. The period was famous in antiquity. Scholars would have known of these events and they were eminently verifiable. Jacoby believes that Lysanias was another scholar in the alternative historical tradition.[45] We do not know his date: he probably wrote in the third/second century for, as Jacoby says, this was when revisionist writers were active and Athens was no longer politically dominant. Mallos was on the coast of southern Asia Minor, directly opposite Cyprus and not far from Pamphylia. It was here that Eretria's great victory over the royal fleet, which brought the cities of the region into the war, occurred. We may suppose that Lysanias' city was one of them. Such an epic part of the story of the Ionian insurrection would have lived long in local tradition, and the reputation of Eretria in the region would have been great. We need not therefore be surprised with Miller[46] that a citizen of Mallos would be inspired to write a history of Eretria, whose great victory it had been.

Pearson[47] says that the text, 'if taken literally . . . is somewhat absurd since, according to Herodotus (5, 99), the Eretrians provided only five ships for the expedition sent out to help the Ionians and Plutarch does not complain of this figure', and since such a small number of ships could not by itself have won such a victory, 'we must assume that ships from Miletus and other Ionian cities were present, since not even Lysanias of Mallus, whom Plutarch cites as his authority, can have maintained that five Eretrian ships routed a Persian fleet.' One notes the dismissive tone, though Pearson can have no knowledge of the worth of Lysanias as a historian, other than what is revealed in this, his single preserved passage. But he does add that 'we must not be deterred by the obscurity of Lysanias and the silence of Herodotus from accepting the former's account.'[48]

Let us recapitulate what we know about the naval position in the Aegean in the last decade of the sixth century. The *Thalassocracy List*, whenever and for whatever purpose it was compiled, does make Eretria the current thalassocratic power. The city had long ruled over a group of island *poleis* and had been recently active with its navy in political changes such as that at Naxos. The Persians thought as many as 200 ***triremes*** (the emphasis is necessary, as we shall see) were needed to move against Euboia in 505. The evidence of *IG* XII 9, 1273/1274 suggests that for some decades Euboia had presumed to control shipping in the Euboian Gulf. We have Lysanias as literary evidence for Eretrian naval strength and Herodotos for the likelihood that its general Eualkides was commander-in-chief of operations around Miletos. What, on the other hand, can the tradition offer concerning Athens as a potential leader in 500–498? A state that had to get help from Corinth in order to challenge its direct enemy Aigina,[49] that moreover required the persuasion of Themistokles to bring its naval power up to a point that it might hope merely to defend itself against the Persians ten years later. Athens had no significant naval tradition before the second decade of the fifth century.

Let us return to the ships sent to aid the rebels in Ionia. What are we to make of the statement of Herodotos that Athens sent twenty ships and Eretria five. In fact Herodotos uses different words for the 'ships' of each city: those from Athens are simply *nees*, a general word for any kind of ship, while he specifically uses *triereis* for the Eretrian five.[50] A search in *TLG* produced thirty-seven occasions on which Herodotos uses *trieres* or *trierarkhos*. In twenty cases, the context makes it quite clear that the vessel was a fighting warship; in four, probably a fighting warship; in another, a vessel escorting a treasure ship;[51] in two more they convey embassies including the embassy of Aristagoras to Sparta.[52] In only four cases is it impossible from the context to say what kind of vessel and in only five cases do *trireres* and *naus* seem to be treated as synonyms. Thus, I believe that in Herodotos, it is permissible to assume that when he uses trireme, especially in juxtaposition with *naus*, he means fighting ship while *naus* may mean any kind of ship. Triremes are indeed warships used in naval fighting. Therefore, in Herodotos' description of the ship contributions of Eretria and Athens, the choice of words does indicate a difference in the character and role of the vessels. It has been put to me that the use of alternative words is merely a stylistic device to avoid repetition. I would reply that if this were indeed so, since the Athenian contribution is actually given first (how not in Herodotos?), he might have used triremes to stress the fighting quality of the

Athenian contingent and then *nees* for the vessels of the 'lesser' Eretrian fleet. However, he does not do so; he uses *nees* first and then *triereis* specifically for the Eretrian ships. I therefore suggest that in fact the twenty Athenian ships were troop transports bringing Athenian hoplites that would fight at Sardis and that the Eretrian *triereis* were convoying them while the main Eretrian war fleet was in the south conducting naval operations designed to prevent the movement of the Persian king's ships northward, bringing reinforcements to his land troops. These activities culminated in the great battle that Lysanias has preserved from Herodotean oblivion. This reconstruction certainly gives the Athenians a subordinate role to that of the Eretrians both on land and sea and so we should keep in mind Plato's encomium of the Eretrians at this stage of their history lest it be felt that their status in the Hellenic *oikoumene* is being too much exaggerated. Both Myres[53] and How and Wells[54] believe that, even in Herodotos, one can perceive, running through the narrative of the history of this period, evidence of the political and military primacy of Eretria.

Eretria must have withdrawn when Miletos finally fell in 494. The siege began in 499 but had been raised thanks to the Eretrian efforts on sea and land. But eventually the weight of Persian resources was bound to tell. After its defeat in 498, the royal fleet was re-equipped and came again to Miletos and the city was reinvested. This time the Eretrians could not raise the siege. Miletos fell. No wonder the Athenians publicly wept during the performance of Phrynikhos' play. Their overprompt desertion may merely have hastened what must have been inevitable, but it was disgraceful none the less. Nevertheless, Athens' self-serving desertion would be repeated only four years later.

We are apt to condemn the Spartans for not coming to the aid of Athens in 490 and the Peloponnesians generally for their Peloponnese-first policies as narrowly selfish. Athens was no better when it and its *kleroukhoi* abandoned Eretria without a fight in 490. No wonder that Eretria was frequently in the forefront of attempts to stir up rebellion in Euboia and the Aegean during the fifth century,[55] and that an Eretrian admiral was at Aigospotamoi to help Athens' enemies in the final conflict of the Peloponnesian War. No wonder the Spartans did not hurry to the aid of Athens at Marathon. In the aftermath of the fall of Eretria, Athens must have been viewed widely as pusillanimous. Had the Athenians not subsequently covered themselves with glory, I do not doubt that later ages would have told a very different tale of Athenian participation in the Ionian and Persian Wars. Not that Sparta could boast. It sent no aid to Ionia at all. Sparta was too concerned about Peloponnesian affairs; its leadership of the region was challenged again in 495 by Argos in the Battle of Sepeia. That year saw the destruction of the Ionian fleet by the Persians in the Battle of Lade. We do not hear whether Eretria was involved. Neither Athens nor Corinth sent help.

Having castigated Athens for its actions in the period of the Ionian Revolt, we must now note that its weak responses reflect political divisions in the city. In 496/5 we have the spectacle of the Peisistratid, Hipparkhos son of

Kharmos,[56] being elected eponymous *arkhon*. The family, with its Persian connections, has been seen as the core of the 'peace party'[57] during the Ionian and Persian Wars. This was the man for whom Kleisthenes is said to have specially invented ostracism[58] and who was indeed ostracised in the spring of 487, when appeasement was safely disreputable in Athens. His election had represented the victory of the party supporting the withdrawal. The later Peisistratidai of course had no reasons at all to help Eretria. Also, an *ostrakon* naming an 'Eretrieus' would chronologically tie in with a purge of Peisistratids early in the fifth century, following the fall of Miletos, and which included Hipparkhos, son of Kharmos. Since Peisistratos' son Eretrieus would not have been born before *c.* 546, his age in 494 would have been slightly older than fifty and so he could easily still have been alive and politically active. The fact that only one *ostrakon* has been found probably means that he was not seen as a significant figure.[59] Another, later, Eretrieus, perhaps a grandson, occurs in *IG* I^1 950, 14 (a list of soldiers who fell in a naval engagement in 412/11). Could it be that the battle was associated with the revolt of Euboia, of which Eretria was a prime mover? He may have been there by reason of his descent and some perceived use for his family connections in Eretria. Thucydides describes just such a battle, fought in the very harbour of Eretria itself in 411 (8, 95, 3–7). The name appears to be a personal and not an ethnic one.

The Athenians would later use the excuse of internal dissension at Eretria as their excuse for not helping the city in its dire need in 490. There may indeed have been a minority 'peace party' at Eretria at this time. We will shortly meet with three of its number, all members of the oligarchic faction, who betrayed their city to the Persians and had earlier stirred up the 'divided counsels' that provided the Athenians with their excuse to abandon the city.[60] However, if there had been significant opposition to the war at Eretria, it is most unlikely that Herodotos would have failed to inform us of the fact. It is probable that this faction achieved significance only after the city itself was in immediate peril of invasion, and even then it did not command enough support to make it able to influence decisions without resort to treachery.

Despite the final result in Ionia, Eretria was still seen as 'strong' and 'numerous',[61] even though the city must have suffered considerable losses of men and material in the late war, for Plato's description refers to the eve of Dareios' invasion of 490. Eretria's prominent, if not primary, record in the Ionian struggle was recognised by the non-Herodotean tradition even though he himself minimises it. Plutarch writes:

> Now I shall let it pass that he [Herodotos] calls the Eretrians slaves, though they had shown as much courage and patriotism as any of the Hellenes and suffered a worse fate than their bravery deserved.[62]

This reputation was gained during the Persian Wars and the fact that Plato also knew of it is significant, for it shows that the pro-Eretrian tradition was not confined purely to non-Athenian local historians and that the memory of Eretrian patriotism remained alive throughout the fifth century, the great age of Athenian glory at home and abroad. But then again, Plato did not have a great love for the Athenian democracy.

In 490, when the invasion was imminent, Herodotos provides evidence of dissension in Eretria, as indeed, it should be emphasised, there was in all the Greek *poleis*. Disagreement, however, was not so much over whether to resist or submit, but how resistance was to be mounted. The assembly was divided; some were for defending the walls, while others favoured a guerrilla-type resistance from the mountains, but not surrender, and a few others 'were plotting treason hoping for *kerde* for themselves from the Persians.'[63] *Kerde*, usually translated here as 'gains', can be 'political advantages', which under the circumstances might be a better translation. An almost identical phrase is used of treasonous rewards elsewhere in Herodotos.[64]

The pro-resistance faction that wished to defend the walls won out in the debates in the assembly, its arguments no doubt bolstered by knowledge that the primary involvement of Eretria in the Ionian insurrection made all hope of lenient treatment by Persia out of the question should it be victorious in Greece. But the party of submission was to have the final word. It included in its ranks, according to Herodotos, Aiskhines Nothonos, Euphorbos Alkimakhou and Philagros Kyneou, who were 'leading men' in Eretria.[65] They were certainly members of an oligarchic clique.[66] The last two named actually opened the gates to the Persians. The first, Aiskhines, revealed the 'divisions' in the assembly to the Athenian *kleroukhoi* from the 'lands of the Khalkidian *Hippobotai*',[67] who had been told to assist the Eretrians. Herodotos makes him appear a compassionate and generous man rather than the traitor to his *polis* that he in fact was:

> Aiskhines, son of Nothon, who was one of the foremost men in Eretria, out of his knowledge of both intentions [of the patriots and of the traitors] told those Athenians [from the *kleroukhia*] who had come how things were, and pleaded with them to depart to their own country lest they also be slain with the rest; the Athenians were convinced by the advice given by Aiskhines and followed it. So they saved themselves by crossing over to Oropos.[68]

Nevertheless, had they not fled but remained to help the defence, their presence would have been significant, for they numbered 4000. Aiskhines no doubt embroidered his story of the dissension in the town. The Khalkidians, too, would not have encouraged the Athenians to remain; defeat for Eretria and Athens would have meant the return of the occupied Lelantine Plain. The Athenians jumped at the chance to escape:

> Clearly H is anxious to justify the Athenian people for not sending succour

> from Attica and the Athenian clerouchs for leaving E to its fate by emphasising the divided counsels and positive treachery of the Eretrians. After Marathon it may well have been thought that a bold stand might have been made at Eretria.[69]
>
> Herodotos' whole elaborate and controversial exculpation conveys the impression of after-thought. The calumniators of Athens in later generations can hardly have missed the point that she did eventually profit from the destruction of Eretria and Miletus.[70]

There is altogether too much emphasis placed on the 'dissention' inside Eretria at this time both by Herodotos and those modern historians who follow him. Clearly, the great majority was for holding out, otherwise it would not have rested with but three conspirators to betray the gates to the enemy. No one would deny that there would have been a medising group in the city, as there certainly was in Athens and in other cities too. The Athenian Xenophon goes as far as to say that there was only one(!) Eretrian mediser, Gongylos. However, he belongs to the next round of the Persian Wars. A close friend of Pausanias the Spartan, he acted as his go-between in his treasonous relations with Xerxes.[71] This idea need not be taken as literally true – it clearly was not – but it does show that later Athenian opinion felt that medism had never been particularly strong at Eretria. Gongylos was rewarded with vast estates around Pergamon in Asia Minor, which his descendants were still ruling in the fourth century. We are again reminded of the close relations between the Agid Kleomenes and Eretria in the last part of the sixth century. Gongylos was an aristocrat of the same faction as the other medising traitors who betrayed the city in 490. His name suggests associations with the moon cult of Artemis at Amarynthos, a festival that long had strong aristocratic associations.[72]

In 491/0, the Persians, led by Datis, launched their expected attack on Greece, heading to Eretria as their main objective. Myers says that:

> The raid on Sardis justified reprisals against Eretria and its accomplice, Athens. H(erodotos) lets us see the importance of the contingent from Eretria and of the tie between Eretria and Miletus. He constantly affirms that the expedition of Darius was directed against Eretria as well as against Athens.[73]

Aristeides, in his *Panathenaïkos* also makes this clear: 'But Dareios with this excuse [the burning of Sardis] . . . marshalled his forces, his pretext was that he was defending himself against the Athenians and the Eretrians'; for, significantly, 'he added the Eretrians to make the excuse plausible.'[74] Aristides clearly thinks that many, those who accepted the alternative tradition and perhaps non-Athenians, would not have believed that an attack on Greece could have been plausibly justified if Athens alone were the pretext. Eretria was another matter. It had led the invaders. The Eretrians and their navy were the real and present threat to the Persian hold on the coastal cities of Asia Minor. I have been exhorted to note the freedom with which Aristeides uses history. But why would he have said that the Eretrians were included for plausibility, in an oration extolling the Athenians, if there were no basis for the observation? It detracts from the position of Athens, which he is praising. The later success of Athens and its new navy in detaching the Asia Minor *poleis* from the Persian Empire shows that the assessment by Dareios' strategists was perfectly reasonable. Plutarch (*c.* AD 46–120) was not alone in later antiquity in seeing the primacy of Eretria in the events of 500–494. The tradition I have been calling 'alternative' was strong enough to persist until the period of Aelius Aristides (*c.* AD 117–189).

The fact that there were horse transports in the Persian armament also points to Eretria as the likely first objective. No one expected it to fall easily, least of all the Persians who had experienced at first hand the power of the city and the daring of its citizens at Sardis on land and in the Pamphylian Sea. Tradition long attributed a powerful cavalry to Eretria. Perhaps the Persians were obtaining their intelligence from the aged Hippias who, it will be remembered, had spent a decade in Eretria during his father's exile from 556 to 546. If so, then they may have relied on the outdated, defective memories of an old and embittered man and prepared accordingly. A battle on the plain seemed very likely to them, so:

> the Persians in sailing held a course for Temenos, Khoireai and Aigilea, all places in the Eretrias, and when they had occupied these places, they disembarked their horses immediately and prepared to attack their enemies. But the Eretrians had no intention of coming out and fighting; they put all their effort into guarding the walls if they could.[75]

We have seen that these places are attested epigraphically as *demoi* of Eretria. Wallace[76] comments on this passage locating all three on the coast. He keeps Temenos, although when he wrote in 1947, only one demesman from a deme Tem. was certainly known; there is now a second.[77] Knoepfler[78] places all three close to the sea between Eretria and Amarynthos. We may also observe that the Persians had sailed right past Marathon to the Bay of Aliveri. This strategy strengthens the view that Eretria was indeed the primary target. Wallace thinks that Aigilea [which Knoepfler identifies with the *demos* Aigale (or Aigalea) about 15 km east of Eretria] is where the Persians would have landed their cavalry, far enough from the city for them to have disembarked without too much harassment but near enough to attack it without a long and tiring preliminary march. He notes that this location was 'eminently suitable for their [cavalry] employment',[79] stressing the Eretrian reputation for cavalry power. He rightly attacks Maurice,[80] who thinks that Euboia is totally unsuitable for the deployment of mounted troops. In fact, the intervening area between Aigilea and Eretria is flat coastal plain. The immediate disembarkation of the horses is also significant, for it shows that the Persians believed that they would have to deal quickly with the Eretrian cavalry. Whether it was indeed still as powerful as in the days when the Eretrians helped Peisistratos back to power may be doubted, and this is perhaps why they were so reluctant to confront the Persians immediately. Democratic Eretria relied on other forms of military power though this does not mean that it had no cavalry at all. Perhaps there had been an increase in the relative importance of the 'aristocratic' arm following the Ionian War since losses in hoplites and sailors during those years may have been considerable.

Eretria was alone in 490. En route to Euboia, the Persians had again attacked Naxos,[81] securing it and other islands; Delos was 'propitiated',[82] Karystos was assaulted and forced to submit after resisting.[83] Aigina medised. Corinth was looking to its own defence and the fortress Peloponnese strategy; Athens still could not challenge the Persian fleet. Among the islands secured by the Persians were probably the Eretrian dependencies and Paros. Sparta was not going to help. Eretria had been weakened by the exertions of the Ionian War; perhaps its best hoplites had been lost at Sardis and Ephesos. If it had been present at Lade, the losses of ships would have been greater. Once the Persians had disembarked their troops and horses, they:

> strongly attacked the walls and for six days many fell on both sides, but on the seventh, two Eretrians of repute, Euphorbos, son of Alkimakhos and Philagros, son of Kuneas, betrayed the city to the Persians. They entered and plundered and burnt the temples in revenge for those that were burnt at Sardis; also, they enslaved the people according to Dareios' command.'[84]

After the fall of the city, some citizens escaped to the mountains.[85] The Persians are said to have fanned out and scoured the countryside, 'netting' the fugitives. Such an operation would have required the help of traitors (one recalls the emergence of anti-democratic forces at Athens after the defeat in 404), for the Eretrias is a large and rugged territory. Plato says that: 'Datis . . . sent an alarming account to our city [Athens] of how not a single Eretrian had escaped: the soldiers of Datis had joined hands and swept the whole of the Eretrike clean as with a drawnet.'[86]

A memory of the captured Eretrians, who were exiled to a locality near Babylon called Kissia, is recorded in the late writer Philostratos.[87] He describes their grave markers, significantly, for such a remote inland place, decorated with reliefs of ships commemorating their naval traditions. Plato's epitaphs[88] also emphasise the sea-faring origins of these lonely exiles, far from the 'deep-sounding' Aegean. Descendants of the exiles were later involved on the Persian side in the Battle of Gaugamela: 'After these marched the Gortyae, really an Euboian race who formerly followed the Medes but were now degenerate and ignorant of their native customs.'[89] Strabo likewise notes the presence of Eretrians in Gordyene, the province of Mesopotamia.[90] There can be no doubt that they were descendants of Eretrians exiled by Dareios after the fall of the city.

The destruction of Eretria, so quickly achieved, was both an embarrassment and a blow for Athens and, indeed, it sent shock waves through the rest of Greece. The sequel of Marathon is not really a part of Eretrian history. But we may note with some sadness and irony that among ceramic remains uncovered during excavations of the tumulus at Marathon, raised over the glorious dead, there was found a cinerary urn 'with its row of hooks in the handle zone' which 'may well be from Eretria',[91] perhaps indicating that an Eretrian who escaped the sack of the city and the round-up of fugitives, fought in the ranks of the betrayers of his city. I quote Boardman: 'If it is indeed to be associated with the great burial, one might read into it a tribute to the tragic fate of Eretria immediately before the battle.' A bitter tribute indeed. Athens, having deserted Ionia and betrayed Eretria, its historians henceforth distorted the memory of the achievements of the only state in Hellas proper that fought against the Persians, from the beginning of the war until its own (temporary) elimination as a *polis* for the 'freedom of the Greeks', not offering earth and water as had Athens and Thebes, nor sheltering behind religious forms as had Sparta, but going out to help its old friends and kinsmen from a sense of common heritage and of gratitude for past benefits received. Myres alone of modern historians has recognised the *pietas* of Eretria as the real motive force of the expedition to Ionia.

Perhaps the final word to eulogise Eretria should be left to an Athenian. Plato the Eupatrid, descendant of Solon, whose lover Peisistratos played such an important role in what is left to us of early Eretrian history, seems to have had some special interest in Eretrian affairs. I have already cited his tribute in the *Menexenos*. In the *Laws*[92] he notes that 'not a single Eretrian escaped', when describing the 'combing' of the island by the Persians after the sack. Certainly, not all were killed or captured. However, some were indeed taken and sent into slavery in Asia. Their fate moved Plato deeply, for he wrote not one, but two epitaphs for the city and its people. I can do no better than to quote one of them in conclusion of this study, a fitting tribute to a famous *polis* and its enterprising people, its maritime glory and its bitter fate:

> We who lie here amidst the Plains of Ekbatana
> Once left the deep-sounding Aegean waves.
> Farewell, famous Eretria, our former home;
> Farewell, Athens, neighbour of Euboia.
> Farewell dear sea.[93]

Notes

1 Hdt. 5, 31.
2 Hdt. 5, 30. Myres 1906, 98: 'And in 505, or soon after, one of the first results of the fall of Chalcis was to set Eretria free to support its ancient proteges, the Naxian δῆμος, in a second expulsion of their oligarchy.' Myres gives an interesting and plausible summary of sixth-century Naxian history in terms of pro- or anti-Eretrian regimes.
3 Hdt. 5, 31.
4 Hdt. 8, 46.
5 Burn 1929, 20.
6 Myres 1906, 98, n. 40.
7 Hdt. 1, 141, 143.
8 Hdt. 5, 37.
9 Myres 1906, 98, n. 38.
10 Hdt. 5, 38.
11 Hdt. 5, 31–2.
12 Heracl. Pont. *peri Hedones* ap. Ath. *Deipn.* 12, 536f–537a.
13 Ch. 5, pp. 164–5, 171.
14 M. Cary, 'Northern and central Greece' in *CAH* III, Cambridge, 1965, Ch 24, 621.
15 Hdt. 6, 99.
16 Hdt. 5, 49–51.
17 Hdt. 5, 37.
18 For a succinct survey of the motivation and individual responsibility of Histiaios and Aristagoras for the Ionian Revolt: Emlyn-Jones 1980, 186, n. 132 (with bibliography).
19 Myres 1953, 197.
20 Sealey 1976, 176.
21 I discuss the verb form ἀγόμενοι (ἄγω) above, p. 275 and n. 34.
22 Hdt. 5, 99.
23 Plut. *de Hdt. malign.* 24 (*Mor.* 861b–c). Ephoros (*FGrH* 70F187) says that they sent five, Hellanikos (4F183) six, ships.
24 Ch. 8, p. 256 and nn. 121–2.
25 Hdt. 6, 21:
26 Plut. *Them.* 27. See below, Ch. 10, n. 7.
27 Jacoby *FGrH* IIIb (Kommentar/Noten) 165.
28 Plut. *de Hdt. malign.* 24 (*Mor.* 861b–d). The 'other writers' included Kharon of Lampsakos: *FGrH* 262F10. Perhaps also Dionysios of Miletos and Hellanikos: Jacoby, *FGrH* IIIb (Kommentar/Noten) 250.
29 Plut. *Amat.* 761a.
30 Cf. Bakhuizen 1976, 24–6.
31 Cary 1965, 618.
32 Plut. *de Hdt. malign.* 24 (*Mor.* 861b).
33 Hdt. 5, 99.
34 'Αγόμενοι. *LSJ* s.v. ἄγω I, 2 (17)
35 A rare name, it occurs four times at Eretria; apart from the commander, once on a Styra tablet and twice in citizen lists of the third century as demesmen of Styra (IG *XII* 9, 56, 89; 246B 37; 246A 263.
36 Hdt. 5, 103.
37 Hdt. 5, 102.
38 See Wallace 1936a, 101. It has been suggested to me that Eualkides may have been the only leader captured. But Herodotos singles him out from among the ὀνομαστούς (notables' well-known names) captured: who would still be ὀνομαστοί by Herodotos' day, if not the leaders?
39 Burn, 1962/84, 200, so believes.

40 Jacoby, *FGrH* IIIb (Kommentar/Noten) 250: 'und es gab schon aus dem 5. Jhdt eine Reihe von Darstellungen des ionischen Aufstandes – Dionysios von Milet, Hellanikos, Charon, die von den Eretriern mehr erzahlt haben können: wie es scheint, verliessen sie (the Eretrians) die Sache der Ionier nicht zugleich mit den Athenern.'

41 See Hdt. 5, 103–4.

42 A reference to the siege of Miletos that followed the episodes at Sardis and Ephesos. The year of this battle was probably 498 rather than 499. The Persian fleet was coming to the Aegean from bases in Phoenicia. The Phoenicians at this time contributed a great part of the King's fleet.

43 Plut. *de Hdt. malign.* 24 (*Mor.* 861c). The translation is by L. Pearson, *Plutarch's 'Moralia'* (Loeb XI). Cambridge, MA, 1970, 49–51.

44 See L. Pearson, 'Notes on the text of Plutarch *de malignitate Herodoti*', *AJP* 80, 1959, 261.

45 Jacoby, *FGrH* IIIb (Kommentar/Noten) 250.

46 Miller 1975, 42: 'The date of Lysanias is unknown and so is the reason why a citizen of Mallos in Kilikia should write a book *Περὶ Ἐρετρίας.*'

47 Pearson 1959, 261.

48 G. Gray and M. Cary, 'The reign of Darius' *CAH* IV, Cambridge, 1977, Ch. 7 section 8, 221–2. Also Jacoby, quoted above, n. 40.

49 Th. 1, 41, 1. Jeffery 1962, 44–54.

50 Νῆες; τριήρεις.

51 TLG0016 Herodotus Hist.; Hdt. 3, 136, 2: here used to escort treasure ships.

52 Hdt. 5, 38; 8, 83.

53 Myres 1953, 197–200.

54 W. How and J. Wells, 1975, 58.

55 Evidence (in brief) for troubles: a possible *kleroukhia* at Eretria: *IG* I[2] 396: Hsch. Ἐρετριακὸς κατάλογος; Photios; *Paroem. gr.* II, 168; schol. Ar. *V.* 715. Her tribute was lifted in 425 from three to fifteen talents.

56 Cadoux 1948, 116 (cites the historian Dionysios) in Ol. 71/1; Davies 1971, 451–2.

57 Hurwit 1985, 322; J. Fine, *The Ancient Greeks. A Critical History*, Harvard, MA, 1983, 279.

58 See [Arist.] *Ath. pol.* 22. 4; Cadoux 1948, 116; and D. Kagan, 'The origin and purposes of ostracism', *Hesperia* 30, 1961, 393–401. G. Stanton, 'The introduction of ostracism and Alkmeonid propaganda', *JHS* 90, 1970, 180–3, rejects this (182), arguing that it was aimed at Isagoras (who negated its purpose by retiring from Attica [181], hence the delay before it was finally invoked). See also Cadoux 1948, 116.

59 E. Vanderpool in: H. Thompson, 'Excavation of the Athenian agora, twelfth season, 1947', *Hesperia* 17, 1948, 193–5; R. Thomsen, *The Origin of Ostracism – A Synthesis*, Copenhagen, 1972, 73.

60 Hdt. 6, 100.

61 Pl. *Mx.* X (240c).

62 Plut. *de Hdt. malign.* 24 (*Mor.* 861d).

63 Hdt. 6, 100.

64 *LSJ* s.v. κέρδος p. 942; cf. Hdt. 3, 71.

65 Apart from Aiskhines, these are not common names in the Eretrian prosopography. In *LGPN* I (including these mentions in Heredotus), Aiskhines occurs 24 times; Alkimakhos 4; Euphorbos (cf. *LSJ* s.v. εὐφορβία 'well-fed', 737) is a hapax [as is Kuneas (cf. *LSJ* s.v κύνεος and κύνων). Also possibly κυνεῖν (kiss in a lascivious way): J. Henderson, *The Maculate Muse – Obscene Language in Attic Comedy*, Oxford, 1991, 181–2)]; Nothon (νόθος = bastard) 2; Philagros 2. Some of these names sound suspect: especially Kuneas, Euphorbos and Nothon. Interestingly, translators transliterate Kuneas as Kineas (Cineas). Philagros [fond of the chase (*LSJ* s.v. p. 1931)] and Alkimakhos [brave fighter (*LSJ* s.v. p. 67)] are suitably 'Hippobotic'. The Greek words translated as 'leading men' are

ἄνδρες τῶν ἀστῶν δόκιμοι. *L.S.J.* s.v. δόκιμος (1) 442 suggests 'noble' as one possible translation and hence I think it is likely that these traitorous νόθοι were members of the oligarchic faction.

66 Hdt. 6, 100–1; Plut. *de garr.* (*Mor.* 510b).

67 Hdt. loc. cit.; Ael. *VH* 6, 1.

68 Hdt. loc. cit.

69 How and Wells, 1975, 105.

70 J. Munro and E. Walker, 'Marathon', *CAH* IV, Cambridge, 1977, Ch. 8 section 3: Eretria and Miltiades' decree, 237.

71 Gongylos and family: X. *GH* 3, 1, 6; X. *An.* 7, 8, 8; Th. 1, 128, 6; D.S. 9, 44, 3.

72 Heinze 1869, 17. The name suggests the round face of the moon, associated with Artemis and Hekate.

73 Myres 1955, 201. Also How and Wells, 1975, 105.

74 Ael. Arist. *Panath.* 95.

75 Hdt. 6, 101.

76 Wallace 1947, 130–3; map, Fig. 1.

77 *IG* XII 9 191C 44; 191B 10. Wallace, 1947, 143, has a question mark against Temenos.

78 1997, 379, nn. 219–21 and 402 (map)

79 Wallace 1947, 132 and n. 42.

80 F. Maurice, 'The campaign of Marathon', *JHS* 52, 1932, 17.

81 Hdt. 6, 96.

82 Hdt. 6, 97, 118.

83 Hdt. 6, 99.

84 Hdt. 6, 101.

85 A. Graham, 'Abdera and Teos', *JHS* 122, 1992, 72, defends Herodotos against Philostratos: (1) the majority were enslaved; (2) there were insufficient citizens to refound the *polis*; and (3) possibly (probably) Eretria's relations with her colonies remained good and these were not far distant, so that the city was possibly refounded by an influx of new citizens from these; see Teos from Abdera or Miletos from her colonies.

86 Pl. *Lg.* III, 698d. Plato, shortly before this passage, says that the Persians at Eretria were present μυριάσι συχναῖς (in many thousands). Even so, guides would have been necessary, as well as direct help, in the work of rounding up and removing the captives.

87 Philostr. *VA* 1, 23–4. Penella 1975, 295–300.

88 See below, n. 93.

89 Q. Curtius, 6, 11.

90 Str. 16, 1, 25 C747 derives the name from Gordys, son of Triptolemos, who came to live here. At 16, 2, 5 C750, Triptolemos is sent by the Argives in search of Io. Gordys accompanied him to Asia. Io is said in one tradition to have been transformed into a cow in Euboia (whence 'Eu-boia') after giving birth to Epaphos at a place on the coast of the island known as Βοὸς Αὐλή (the cowyard): Str. 10, 1, 3 C445; Eust. *ad Hom. Il. pert.* 278, 29–34. Smith 1856, s.v. 'Gordyaei Montes' and 'Cordyene/Gordyene'. The Kordyaioi are said to be the ancestors of the present-day Kurds.

91 Boardman 1957, 2; E. Vanderpool, 'Some black figured pottery from the Athenian agora', *Hesperia* 15, 1946, 130.

92 Pl. *Lg.* III (698d).

93 Translation (with minor modifications) from J. Edmonds (ed./tr.), *Greek Elegy and Iambus* II *with Anacreontea*, Cambridge, MA, 1970, no. 13.

10

EPILOGUE

In 487, the leader of the 'peace' faction in Athens, Hipparkhos Kharmou, the pro-Persian arkhon of 496, was ostracised.[1]

By 487 a few Athenians, and perhaps the remnants of the population that had escaped the 'combing' of the Eretrias by the Persians, had come to settle on the site of the ruined city. After the Persian invaders withdrew into Asia Minor, therefore, there were probably enough Eretrian refugees to reconstitute the *polis*. There is some evidence for an Athenian *kleroukhia* at Eretria in the mid-fifth century.[2] The finds of Attic pottery from the period hardly suggest that the majority of the inhabitants came from Attica,[3] although it is likely that 'a few Athenians migrated and settled in Eretria'.[4] The characteristic rhotacising dialect slowly dies out during the fifth and fourth centuries, to be replaced with the Attic.

By 485, Eretria was being rebuilt. Gardner[5] and Head[6] have suggested that this is signalled by the issuing of a new coinage, bearing the traditional cow on one side and the cuttlefish on the other. This emblem of the city became the subject of an Athenian joke in excruciatingly bad taste, given the record of Eretria in the Ionian and Persian Wars, especially if compared with that of Athens, which was uttered by Themistokles during the war conference prior to the Battle of Artemision, to the effect that the creature and the city on whose coins it appeared shared one thing in common, no backbone.[7] Eretria had recovered to be able to send seven ships, and there were also two from Styra, as well as two pentekonters from Keos,[8] to take part in this campaign, whereas Khalkis sent none (the Athenians supplied twenty, which the Khalkidians manned[9]). If the Eretrians were less than enthusiastic about Athenian leadership in the new war, one can understand their attitude very well in the light of recent events.

In 479, Eretrians had fought at Plataia: the name of the city appears on the Serpent Column set up at Delphi to commemorate the victory. Eretria sent 600 men to the common Hellenic army compared with 400 from unscathed Khalkis.[10]

After Plataia, probably about 478, the Eretrian named Gongylos, the only Eretrian to medise according to Xenophon,[11] was involved in the treachery of

Pausanias. He was ultimately rewarded by Xerxes with extensive lands and his descendants still ruled these domains around Pergamon in Asia Minor as late as the fourth century.[12]

The Eretrians were active participants in the Revolt of Euboia (446), suppressed by Perikles.[13]

From the end of the Persian Wars until 411, the history of Eretria is part of that of the Athenian League and Empire. In 411, it led the Euboians in revolt from Athens.[14] Thucydides tells us that not even the Sicilian disaster so distressed the Athenians as what had happened in the harbour of Eretria. The statue of the Eretrian admiral, Autonomos, was on the Spartan dedication at Delphi for the victory at Aigospotamoi,[15] which finally ended the Peloponnesian War with a humiliating naval defeat for Athens.

Notes

1 Ch. 9, pp. 279–80, nn. 56–7.

2 Richardson 1891, 59–69, 240; Farnell 1906, 27–31. *IG* I, 339: τῆς ἀποι[κίας] τῆς ἐς Ἐρ[ετρίαν?]; dated 445 (Ol. 83, 4).

3 Boardman 1952, n. 316.

4 J. Green and R. Sinclair, 'Athenians in Eretria', *Historia*, 19, 1970, 518.

5 P. Gardner, *A History of Greek Coinage*, Oxford, 1918, 127, n. 2.

6 Head 1887, introduction lviii.

7 Plut. *Them.* 11; repeated in *Reg. et imp. apopth.* 14 (*Mor.* 185 e). A small irony given Themistokles' remarks: it was through the Eretrian wife of Artabanes, the Persian *chiliarch,* that Themistokles got his audience with the king when he fled to Persia an exile (Plut. *Them.* 27).

8 Herodotos (8, 46), listing the ship contributions for the Battle of Salamis, gives these two places and Naxos apparently as part of the bloc of Ionian Euboia: Myres, 1953, 262.

9 Hdt. 8, 1. We may also note that Eretria was a ship contributor to the fleet of the Delian League before *c.* 450 BC: *A.T.L.* III 197.

10 Myres 1953, 287.

11 Ch. 9, pp. 281–2 and nn. 71–2.

12 J. Evans, 'The Medism of Pausanias; two versions', *Antichthon* 22, 1988, 1–11.

13 Hsych. and Photios s.v. Ἐρετριακὸς κατάλογος mention that in the arkhonship of Diphilos (442/1) a decree was passed requiring the sons of the richest Eretrians to be transported to Athens as hostages, evidence, as Wilamowitz long ago noted (*Hermes* 20, 1885, 481, n. 1), that Eretria continued to be disaffected for some years after the revolt was suppressed. For the revolt from an Euboian perspective: Vranopoulos 1987, 100–03. The *kleroukhia* may belong to this period (see above, n. 2).

14 Th. 8, 95, 2–7.

15 Meiggs and Lewis 1989, no. 95 (287–90). Along with an Eretrian we find a Milesian, an Ephesian and a Mal(l)iot admiral (for the ethnics of Mallos and Malis: Smith 1856 s.v.), with the rather more expected Megarian, Corinthian, Boiotian, Troizenian and Khalkidian leaders. For the notion that Eretria remained loyal to Athens: Knoepfler 1969, 86. There was, however, never a time when Eretria had any reason to be 'grateful' to Athens: prior to 490 Eretria dealt with Athens as an equal (or rather, as a superior), after that as a betrayer and mistress.

Appendix 1

CHRONOLOGICAL TABLES AND NOTES

Table A1.1 From the Neolithic Age to the sub-Mycenaean period

Neolithic	6200–3000
Early Helladic (EH)	3000–2000
Early Helladic I	3000–2500
Early Helladic II	2500–2200
Early Helladic III	2200–2000
Middle Helladic (MH)	2000–1550
Late Helladic (LH)	1550–1175
Late Helladic I (Mycenaean)	1550–1500
Late Helladic II (Mycenaean)	1500–1400
Late Helladic IIIA (Mycenaean)	1400–1300
Late Helladic IIIB (Mycenaean)	1300–1200
Late Helladic IIIC (Mycenaean)	1200–1100
Sub-Mycenaean	1100–1050

All dates are BC and approximate. The information used to compile this table was obtained from Vermeule 1964, 314–15 and R. Higgins, *The Greek Bronze Age*, London, 1977, 12–13. For greater detail on the Neolithic Age: Sampson 1981. Others, e.g. R. Drews, *The Coming of the Greeks. Indo-European Conquests in the Aegean and the Near East*, Princeton, NJ, 1989, would down-date the periods by *c.* 50–100 years.

Table A1.2 From the sub-Mycenaean period to the sub-Geometric period

Sub-Mycenaean		1100–1050
Protogeometric (PG)		1050–900
Euboian sub-Protogeometric (SPG)	Attic early Geometric (EG) I & II)	900–850
Euboian middle Geometric (MPG)	Attic MG I, II & LG Ia	850–750
Euboian late Geometric (LG)	Attic LG Ib, IIa & b, early proto-Attic (EPA)	750–690
Sub-Geometric (SG)	(Attic EPA, middle PA)	690

Table A1.3 Euboian colonisation in the West

Founding poleis			*Dates*
Khalkis	*Joint*	*Eretria*	
		Kerkyra	Before 734 (prob. *c.*785)
	Pithekoussai		*c.*785 BC
Kyme (Cumae)			*c.*750 BC
	Syracuse (?)[a]		Before 734
		Orikos	*c.*750 or perhaps *c.*734
		Methone	734 BC
Naxos[b]			734 BC
Rhegion			c.730–20
Zankle			c.730–20
Katane			729 BC
Leontinoi			729 BC

Notes:

a The Corinthians ejected the Eretrians, who were probably there before they went to found Pithekoussai, from Kerkyra, in 734. They would then have gone on and expelled the Eretrians (and Khalkidians?) from Ortygia (Syracuse) soon after: Blakeway 1932/33, 205, n. 4: 'The synchronism with Syracuse is supported by schol. A.R. IV, 1212 and Plut. *Amat. Narr.* 772.' The expelled Eretrians then sailed back to Eretria, whence they were driven out by force and went on to found Methone in lower Macedon.

b The exclusively Khalkidian colonies (so-called 'famine colonies') were distinctly later than the Eretrian and Eretrian–Khalkidian commercial *emporia*.

Table A1.4 Some significant dates in Eretrian history (all BC unless otherwise shown)

17th–15th century	Helladic settlement Mythological past; matriarchy(?); Artemis cult
9th century	Destruction of Lefkandi and migration of survivors to Eretria
9th–8th century	Beginnings of the 'new' city of Eretria Evidence of metal-working; foundations of 'public' buildings, e.g, the Daphnephoreion, possibly the oldest monumental temple in all Greece
8th century	Geometric settlement Oligarchic government by exiled landowners from Lefkandi; first colonisation (*emporia*) and trade with both East and West
7th century	The Eretrian 'Empire' Major construction works: stream diversion, harbour, roads, new Daphnephoreion (the first Hekatompedon)
6th century	Peisistratos of Athens at Eretria and in the north (556–46) Decline of the oligarchy; social unrest The tyranny of Diagoras (*c.* 538–509) Ongoing development at Eretria Social revolution at Khalkis; the incident at Kerinthos Kleomenes in central Greece; his alliance with Diagoras Diagoras overthrown(?) in 506; establishment of democracy
506–490	The Eretrian thalassocracy (sea empire/domination) Eretria leads opposition to Persia in Asia Minor

498 (497?)	Eretrian naval victory over Persian fleet off Cyprus
490	Destruction of Eretria by the Persians
446	Conquest of Euboia by the Athenians; Eretria part of Delian League (Athenian Empire)
411	Eretria leads revolt of Euboia against Athens (Battle of Eretria and the Euboian Revolt: Thucydides 8, 7) Eretrian territorial expansion in Euboia
377–57	Eretria in the Second Athenian Confederation Alternation of democratic, oligarchic and tyranical regimes
357–*c.* 200	Eretria, along with the rest of Greece, dependent on Macedon
295–68	Political career of the philosopher Menedemos
267–2	Khremonidian War and the sack of Eretria by the Macedonian king Antigonos Gonatas
198	Sack and occupation of Eretria by the Romans
146	Eretria remains faithful to Rome during the Achaian War
87	Eretria dragged into the Mithridatic Wars

Appendix 2

MINOAN NOTES

There is a tradition that links the Minoans, through Rhadamanthys, son of Minos and judge in Hades, with Euboia. He is said to have come from Crete to 'the islands' where he 'legislated' for the people. Afterwards he fled to Okalia near Haliartos in Boiotia, where he married Alkmene and later died there. However, Okalia may recall the similarly named Oikhalia, which was a deme of the Eretrias and was destroyed by Herakles. Rhadamanthys was one of those credited with teaching Herakles the art of bowmanship; perhaps he came to Oikhalia to help his pupil in his feud with Iphitos its king. St. Byz. preserves the name Okalon, 'town of the Eretrians', citing Theopompos as his authority, and Homer tells us that the Phaiakes from Kerkyra brought Rhadamanthys to Euboia to visit Tityos, son of Gaia, who was later slain by Artemis and Apollo. This seems to reflect the later connection between Eretria and Kerkyra in the eighth century. It is possible that the similarity between Okalia, Oikhalia and Okalon has led to confusion; the Minoans were more likely to have been connected with insular Euboia than mainland Boiotia, especially since Okalia/ Haliartos was inland on Lake Kopaïs.

The references for this reconstruction are: Rhadamanthys to the islands, Apollod. 3, 1, 2; see D.S. 5, 79, 1ff., for his residence at Okalia in Boiotia and marriage to Alkmene; Apollod. 2, 4, 4; 3, 1, 2 and Tzetzes schol. ad Lykoph. 50, his death there; also Plut. *Lys.* 28 and *de gen. Socr.* 5 (= *Mor.* 577E–578A), where the tomb is 'excavated' by the Spartans who found there an ancient tablet with a script no longer intelligible (Linear B?), but see Ant. Lib. 33 and Paus. 9, 16, 7; for Okalon, χώριον Ἐρετριέων: St. Byz. s.v.; for Rhadamanthys as Herakles teacher, Tzetzes schol. ad Lykoph. 50; his voyage from Kerkyra, Hom. *Od.* 7, 321–4 and Str. 9, 3, 14 C423; for Herakles and Oikhalia, S. *Trakh. passim*. The seige was the subject of an epic of the same name (Οἰχαλίας ἅλωσις) by Kreophylos of Samos, though some attribute it to Homer himself: see *RE* s.v. Homeridai. See also Euripides, *Rhadamanthys*(?) fr. 658, in A. Nauck, *Tragicorum Graecorum Fragmenta,* Hildesheim, 1964: οἱ γῆν ἔχουσ' Εὐβοΐδα προσχόρον πόλιν (who held the Euboian land, the neighbour city). Oikhalia was a place of considerable importance in myth and is usually located not far from Kyme, in the Eretrias: see Ch. 2, nn. 116, 126–8, 130 and

253. It is possible that the name Oikhalia is one of the several pre- or early Greek toponyms of that area of the Eretrias; Sapouna-Sakellaraki, 1984/86, 159, thinks it is Mycenaean. The probable location of that very odd deme name, Grynkhai (Minoan?), is not far away, near Cape Okhthonia: see Wallace 1947, 131 (Fig. 1); 135–6. For Minoan contacts in the general area of modern Kimi, see Sampson 1981b, 51–2; also generally Curchin 1979, esp. 273–4 and n. 22. For Rhadamanthys and Euboia and the adjacent Skyros, Skopelos (anc. Peparethos) Halonesos (anc. Ikos), etc.: Hom. *Od.* 7, 320–4; D.S. 5, 79, 1–3. See also N. Platon, "Ο τάφος τοῦ Σταφύλου καὶ ὁ μινωικὸς ἀποικιομὸς τῆς Πεπαρήθου', *Kretika Khronika* 1949, 334–73 and Sampson 1978, 14. I have accepted the island name equivalencies from the *Guide Bleu* (1990).

Appendix 3

THE KYPSELIDAI, THEOGNIS AND THE LOW CHRONOLOGY

The Kypselidai Herodotos implies that Periandros died between 540 and 530. He was still alive when Peisistratos was tyrant of Athens; his arbitration at Sigeion, which was in Peisistratos' favour 5, 94–5 is also mentioned in Arist. *Rh.* 1375b. Such a dating agrees well with Theognis' *floruit*. It allows us to dismiss the notion that the 'Kypselid tribe' involved in Euboia was a cadet branch of the family, such as the Philaidai at Athens or the Ambrakiot branch, descended from Gorgos, an illegitimate son of Kypselos himself: Str. 7, 7, 6 C325; Ps-Skymn. 453–5; see Ant. Lib. 4, 4; Newman 1902, 329–30. Gorgos was sent by Periandros to govern Ambrakia. He had two sons, Psammetikhos (Kypselos II) and Periandros (II). The former succeeded Periandros as tyrant at Corinth, the latter became tyrant of Ambrakia from whom was descended the first husband of Timonassa, the Argive woman who later married Peisistratos. A Kypselos, who was eponymous arkhon of Athens in 597/6 [D. Bradeen, 'The fifth century archon list', *Hesperia* 31, 1963, 187–208; Davies 1971, 8429 V (B), 298] was a member of the Philaid family, father of Miltiades the tyrant of the Khersonesos. (Miltiades III in: Davies 299f.) Forrest, 1982a, 252, n. 6, suggests that some Kypselids seized Kerinthos en route to Potidaia (*c.* 600), attributing the idea to H. T. Wade-Gery.

The problem that arises from the fact that we have an arkhon of Athens of 597/6 with the name Kypselos is not as significant as might appear at first sight; see Bradeen, 1963, 194, n. 31, where he, an adherent of the high chronology, admits that it would not have been impossible for the grandson of the Corinthian tyrant (on Beloch's chronology as modified by Will, coming to power in *c.* 620) to have been arkhon in 597/6. For, in fact, there are indications that point directly to Periandros himself as the Kypselid involved. The reference to 'tribe' need only refer to those associated with Periandros in the poet's mind. Similarly, to reject his involvement solely on the grounds that the Kypselidai 'had no known involvement in Euboea' (Carrière 1962, 45, n. 172.) simply will not do. This is tantamount to saying that we ought not to consider seriously a single reference to ancient events and people in any but a major writer. Moreover, Carrière's hypothesis that it may have been the Philaid 'Kypselid' Miltiades is not based on any solid evidence and to believe that a

Megarian poet would be thinking of the Philaids is ridiculous. T. Hudson-Williams, *The Elegies of Theognis*, New York, repr. 1979, 231, cites a dedication at Olympia by Kypselos himself, which had the dedicatory inscription: εἰ μὴ ἐγὼ χρυσοῦς σφυρήλατος εἰμὶ κολοσσὸς ἐξώλης εἴη Κυψελιδῶν γενεή (Agaklytos, *FGrH* 411F1). On the offering: Plato, *Phd.* 236B; [Arist.] *Oec.* 1346a31–b6); however, Hudson-Williams, 1903, 1–22, regards these lines as of dubious authenticity. For Herodotos' (i.e. the low) chronology: see esp. Will 1955, Ch. 5 and Parker 1993, 386–401.

Only on the 'low' chronology could Periandros have been still alive in the 530s, and then he would have been about seventy-five to eighty years old if he succeeded his father Kypselos *c.* 590 at age twenty: he could then have been alive and even active *c.* 535. That he lived to old age and was unwilling to contemplate loss of power is shown by Nic. Damasc. *FGrH* 90F59, 1. He is not the only elderly and aggressive ruler in antiquity of whom we know; Antigonos Monopthalmos died in battle at age eighty-one (Hieronymos of Kardia, *FGrH* 154F8 = Lucian *Macr.* 11. The *Makrobioi* is a catalogue of men who reached old age ἐν ὑγιαίνουσι τῇ ψυχῇ καὶ ὁλοκλήρῳ τῷ σώματι. It does not however list Periandros.) or eighty-six (Porphyrios, *FGrH* 260F32). Billows, 1990, 185, remarks: 'The ultimately unsuccessful aggressiveness of Antigonos's last years has coloured the judgements of him by both ancient and modern commentators alike.' So too Periandros' aggressiveness.

Sealey 1976, 38–65 gives a brief survey of the growth of tyranny in the seventh and sixth centuries; see also Ure 1922/1966, Andrewes 1956, and, more recently, McGlew 1993. For the Kypselid tyranny at Corinth, I mention here again Édouard Will's monumental 1955 study of archaic Corinth, Chs 5 and 6, 363–571 because it establishes the *low chronology* (see esp. 363–440), which is the basis of my own chronological framework for the history of sixth-century Eretria. This has been attacked, especially by J. Servais, 'Herodote et la chronologie des Cypselides', *L'Ant. class.* 38, 1969, 28–81, and the high chronology is probably still orthodoxy. However, the low position has been stoutly, and I believe successfully, defended by both Raphael Sealey (especially in his papers, 'From Phemios to Ion', *REG* 70, 1957, 342–51; 'Regionalism in Archaic Athens', *Historia* 9, 1960, 155–80; and 'Probouleusis and the sovereign assembly', *CSCA* 2, 1969, 247–69) and, in a major recent paper, Victor Parker, 'Zur griechischen und vorderasiatischen Chronologie des sechsten Jahrhunderts v. Chr. unter besonderer Berücksichtigung der Kypselidenchronologie', *Historia*, 42, 1993, 385–417.

Theognis For an interpretation of lines 885–94 that would place them in a sixth-century context (though earlier than mine): Figueira 1985, 262; 290–3. M. West, *Studies in Greek Elegy and Iambus*, Berlin, 1974, 40, however, suggests that prudence requires that all poems not 'sealed' by the personal name of Kyrnos be regarded as anonymous. For an early survey of the conflict of views on this question, see Geyer 1903, 108–9. More recently, see A. L. Ford, 'The seal of Theognis: the politics of authorship in Archaic Greece', in Figueira and

Nagy 1985, 82–95. The fact that poetry in Archaic Greece circulated, and was recited publicly and privately quite freely, weakens the thesis that the *sphragis* (seal) assures us that Theognis is the sole author of parts that bear this mark. It was in fact applied to the gnomic element of the work; that the geographically descriptive lines do not have the *sphragis* (an address to Kyrnos, always in the vocative is generally considered to constitute Theognis' seal) is not a guarantee that they were not by Theognis. In brief, I accept that the lines are by Theognis because: (1) they are from Book 1, generally accepted by critics as being composed overwhelmingly of poems by Theognis; (2) despite the disputed nature of the late Kypselid dating, it is not precluded by the historical and geographical references in the lines (to the Kypselidai and to Euboia) that the poem is by Theognis; (3) there is another reference in the *corpus* to 'him' going to Euboia (ll. 783–84); and (4) the lines, considered within their immediate context in the *corpus*, present a coherent and convincing psychological and historico-geographic picture of Euboia in the mid-sixth century.

Appendix 4

THE SOURCE OF STRABO'S DESCRIPTION OF THE AMARYNTHOS STELE (10, 1, 10, *c.* 448)

F. W. Walbank[1] links the discussion in Polybios 13, 3, 4 (and that in Str. 8, 33, 3 C375) of conventions limiting warfare with Strabo's description of the stele recording the convention established between Eretria and Khalkis during the Lelantine War, prohibiting the use of 'missile-type' weapons (10, 1, 10 C448). There is no doubt that the wording of the two passages is very similar:

Str. 10, 1, 10: ἀλλὰ συνέθεντο ἐφ οἷς συστήσονται τὸν ἀγῶνα ... μὴ χρήσθαι τηλεβόλοις

Plb: συντήθεντο πρὸς σφᾶς μήτ' ἀδήλοις βέλεσι μήθ' ἐκβόλοις χρήσασθαι κατ' ἀλλήλων.

OR

Str. 8, 33, 3: ἡμὲν ἐκ χειρὸς [χρῆσις] ... καὶ γὰρ συστάδην καὶ κοντοβολούντων.

Plb: μόνη δὲ ἐκ χειρὸς καὶ συστάδην γινομένην μάχην.

We have therefore to ask the question: whence the similarity? Since Polybios (b. *c.* 208) precedes Strabo chronologically (b. 64/3), he clearly did not, as he wrote, have Strabo's text in front of him with its 'reading' of the stele. But did Strabo have a copy of Polybios? It is very unlikely that either scholar had ever visited Eretria. Both wrote at Rome so it seems likely that they both had recourse to a common source.

Strabo (8, 33, 3) deals with another convention of a very similar kind. He takes his information here from the historian Ephoros (Ἔφορος δ' φησιν ... = *FGrH* 70F115), whose dates are *c.* 405–330. J. F. Lockwood in his entry: Apollodorus (6) in *OCD* (69–70) notes among this author's various works:

> a commentary on the Homeric *Catalogue of Ships*, an important work of scholarship based on Eratosthenes and Demetrius of Skepsis, and containing many quotations from poets and historians, and many criticisms of earlier writers; Strabo found it a valuable source for Books VIII to X of his *Geography*.

Walbank thus thinks that Apollodoros is Strabo's source, though he does not seem to extend this observation to Polybios also. Nevertheless, as he himself notes, Ephoros is known to have used inscriptions as a source (*FGrH* 70F199): Polybios observed that 'The genealogical manner attracts the person fond of hearing stories while that which concerns the foundation of cities and kinship ties, as is found in Ephoros for example, attracts the person who is excessively devoted to trivial details of knowledge.[2]

But no one seems to have taken account, in this context, of the fact that Ephoros was from Kyme in Asia Minor and wrote a local history – Ἐπιχώριος λόγος – of his city, and Asian Kyme is usually[3] regarded as a co-founder, with Khalkis and Eretria (*pace* Bakhuizen),[4] of Kyme in Italy. He was, as Strabo himself observed, fanatically interested in the history of his own *polis*, so much so that he attracted ridicule (Str. 13, 3, 6 C623). So, it would not at all be unlikely that, when he came to Athens to study under Isokrates, he visited the other *metropoleis* involved in the joint colonial venture and that while he was there – being a historian and antiquary – inscriptional antiquities would have attracted his attention. It is therefore very likely indeed that Ephoros was the source of both Strabo (8, 33, 3 and 10 1, 10) and Polybios (13, 3, 4) and, since Ephoros' writings were freely accessible at Rome, where both men worked, I see no special reason to postulate an intermediary such as Apollodoros for the information about the stele, though of course it is not impossible. In the case of Polybios, an intermediary is even less likely, given his strictures quoted above.

Both Strabo and Polybios were writing in times of brutal conflicts[5] (in Strabo's time, the civil war preceding the triumph of Octavianus), and so they were both looking back with romantic nostalgia to a more 'civilised' and 'humane' age. At the time Polybios was writing, the Amphiktyonic council was trying to ameliorate the rigours of contemporary warfare. If Polybios had any knowledge of the Lelantine War, he may have known about the involvement in it of Thessaly and its romantic hero Kleomakhos, whose story is told by Plutarch. During his researches in Ephoros, this Euboian convention of war, in which the Amphiktyonic League, through its chief member, Thessaly, was involved, may well have attracted his attention.

The common source of Polybios, Strabo and Plutarch(?) thus seems to have been Ephoros, whether in the original text or in some digest. The importance of Polybios and Strabo is that they show that the convention of Amarynthos was not unique. Gardner (1920) was mistaken to believe so. And there was at least one other similar example, which Livy 42, 47, 5 mentions.[6] Despite his own *caveat* concerning romantic nostalgia, a 'scientific' historian such as Polybios took such conventions seriously. But that there was indeed an inscribed convention between Eretria and Khalkis during some phase of the Lelantine War should not be doubted.

Notes

1 Commentary on Polybius II, Oxford, 1967, 416.

2 9, 1, 4: τὸν μὲν γὰρ φιλήκοον ὁ γενεαλογικὸς τρόπος ἐπισπᾶται, τὸν δὲ πολυπράγμονα καὶ περιττὸν ὁ περὶ τὰς ἀποικίας καὶ κτίσεις καὶ συγγενείας καθά που καὶ παρ' Ἐφόρῳ λέγεται.

3 But see A. Gwynn, 'The character of Greek colonization', *JHS* 38, 1918, 88–123 and Sapouna-Sakellaraki 1984, both of whom argue for a Euboian Kyme.

4 Esp. Kondoleon 1963/65, Klein 1972, and Buchner 1966. See Blakeway 1935; Bakhuizen 1976, 221, who explicitly denies any involvement by states other than Khalkis in the establishment of Pithekoussai and Kyme.

5 For Polybios and Roman brutality: W. Reiter, *Aemilius Paullus, Conqueror of Greece*, London, 1988, Ch. 2: 'Polybius and the Image', 20–68 (hostile to both Polybios and Rome).

6 'Not by ambushes and battles at night, nor by pretended flight and unexpected return to an enemy off his guard, nor in such a way as to boast in cunning rather than real bravery did our ancestors wage war; they were accustomed to declare war before they waged it and even at times to announce a battle and specify the place in which they were going to fight.' E. T. Sage and A. C. Schlesinger (trans.), *Livy XII*, Books XL-XLII, (Loeb) Cambridge, MA, 1979, 433–5.

Appendix 5

CORINTH IN CENTRAL GREECE (519–506)

The chief consideration for Corinth throughout the last two decades of the sixth century was self-preservation rather than ideology. The oligarchy in power there may have considered assisting like-minded governments to power but only if by doing so it would further the city's general political and economic aims. But Corinth did not want to see Sparta or, for that matter, Athens, Eretria or Thebes, or anyone else, all-powerful in central Greece. The post-Kypselid regime at Corinth was notoriously cautious in its approach to foreign affairs. Each new political situation received careful assessment as it arose. As an ally of Sparta, the city could with enthusiasm assist in the overthrow of a commercial rival in the east with whom it had no recent significant ties of friendship. Thus, she provided the ships for Sparta's attack on Polykrates. They could, with great misgivings, be induced to participate in the show of strength against Peisistratid Athens, but Corinth refused to agree to an attack that would have left Athens dependent on its dangerously powerful friend and ally. Nor would it acquiesce in Kleomenes' interference in its own dealings with its neighbour Megara. So, in 519, when Kleomenes advised the Plataians to ally with Athens, after the Thebans had sent an army against Plataia, thereby obliging Athens to respond by sending a force to help her new ally, Corinth decided to intervene. In a passage seldom given its due weight by historians, Herodotos (6, 108) tells us that:

> When the Thebans heard about this (i.e. the advice given to the Plataians by Kleomenes) they marched against the Plataia, and the Athenians came to their aid. But when they were about to join battle, *the Corinthians would not allow it* and as they *chanced to be there* (!) they made a dispensation at the request of both sides and drew a demarcation line, *imposing* [my emphases] the following conditions, namely that the Thebans should not interfere with any Boiotians who did not want to be part of Boiotia (i.e. of the Boiotian League). The Corinthians after having made this settlement left, but the Boiotians set upon the Athenians as they were returning home and they (the Thebans) were defeated in the fight. The Athenians thereupon

made a new frontier beyond that which the Corinthians had made for the Plataians, and set the Asopos itself as the Theban border with Plataia and Hysiai.

This episode provides an interesting insight into the methods of Corinthian diplomacy, and its role was not that of a fomenter of trouble in the region but rather that of a peace keeper. In this instance, Corinth countered Kleomenes' mischief-making and imposed its own settlement, and then withdrew its forces. Surely no one would believe that a Corinthian army, big enough to interpose itself between those of Thebes and Athens, was in the very neighbourhood by chance? (What for? And well away from the Corinthia itself.) In fact, the Corinthian army was already mobilized for action against Megara, and possibly still in the territory of Megara when Kleomenes intervened, stalling any Corinthian counter-offensive against it. So the appearance of the thwarted Corinthians in Boiotia, and obliquely undermining Kleomenes' policy by trying to keep Athens and Thebes (both allies) from coming to blows, should occasion no surprise. Corinth was trying to preserve the balance of power in central Greece even if that were to annoy its Spartan 'friends', friends that had interfered high-handedly against it in Megara and not in Corinth's self-perceived interests. It is noteworthy that, given the hostile attitude towards Athens shown by Kleomenes over the next few years, Corinth's arbitration favoured Athens; the Thebans certainly thought so, for as soon as the Corinthians had withdrawn, they tried to overthrow the decision by force, only to be beaten for their trouble and have a worse demarcation imposed by Athens. Corinth undoubtedly saw Athens as a useful check on Thebes and Aigina, especially since it had as yet no significant navy and posed no military threat.

BIBLIOGRAPHY

Note In general, I have not listed in this bibliography all the separate volumes of the Loeb Classical Library, which have been mentioned in the endnotes to the various chapters. Almost all the classical authors cited are represented in the series and, where possible, it is to the Loeb edition that I have referred. I have done so because this collection is probably the most easily accessible for English-speaking readers who might wish to consult the texts in the original language and it has the bonus of page-by-page translations, although these are often quaintly archaic in style and sometimes misleading. Another, more comprehensive, collection is that published by B. G. Teubner in Germany. This is for readers with Greek and Latin only. Many of the writers I have referred to are translated into English in the Penguin Classics series.

Adcock, F. 'The growth of the Greek city state', *CAH* III, 1965, XXVI, 687–701.

Adcock, F. and Mosley, J. *Diplomacy in Ancient Greece*, Thames & Hudson, London, 1975.

Albore-Livadie, C. 'Remarques sur un groupe de tombes à Cumès', in *Contribution à l' Étude de la société et de la colonisation eubéennes. Cahiers du Centre Jean Bérard* II, Naples, 1975.

Altherr-Charon, A. 'Tombe du 9e siècle avant J.-C.' in Krause, C. *et al.*, 'Eretria: Ausgrabungen 1979–1980', *AK* 24, 1981, 83.

Altherr-Charon, A. and Lasserre, F. 'Heracles à Érétrie, une nouvelle inscription agonistique', *Études de Lettres, (Faculté des Lettres de l'Université de Lausanne)* IV, 4, 1981, 25–35.

Andreiomenou, A. ''Εκ τῆς δυτικῆς νεκροπόλεως 'Ερετρίας' (I), *AAA* 7, 1974, 229–48.

—— 'Γεωμετρικὴ καὶ 'Υπογεωμρτρικὴ Κεραμεικὴ ἐξ 'Ερετρίας' (I), *AE* 1975 [1976], 206–29.

—— ''Εκ τῆς δυτικῆς νεκροπόλεως 'Ερετρίας' (II), *AAA* 9, 1976, 197–212.

—— ''Αρχαικὴ Κεραμεικὴ ἐξ 'Ερετρίας', *AE* 1976 [1977], 1–7.

—— 'Γεωμετρικὴ καὶ 'Υπογεωμετρικὴ Κεραμεικὴ ἐξ 'Ερετρὶας' (II), *AE* 1977 [1979], 126–63.

—— ''Αψιδοτὰ οἰκοδομήματα καὶ καραμεικὴ τοῦ 8ου καὶ 7ου αἰ.π.Χ. ἐν 'Ερετρίᾳ', *ASIAA* 59, ns 43, 1981, 187–235.

Andrewes, A. *The Greek Tyrants*, Hutchinson's University Library, London, 1956.

Apostolidis, S. and H. '''Ενας ὅρος ἀπὸ Δύστο Εὐβοίας', *Horos* 1990/1, 131–3.

Aravantinou, V. 'The Mycenaean inscribed sealings from Thebes. Preliminary notes', *Tractata Mycenaea* 1987, 13–27.

Arena, R. 'Di alcuni tratti dialettali delle colonie euboiche d'occidente', *Acme* 40/1, 1988, 15–19.

Arnheim, M. T. *Aristocracy in Greek Society*, Thames & Hudson, London, 1977.

Aryiriadou, M. *Εὔβοια ὅπως τὴν εἶδα τὴ φωτογράφησα*, Athens, 1981.

Auberson, P. 'Le temple d'Apollon Daphnéphoros', *Eretria, Fouilles et Recherches* I, Francke Verlag, Bern, 1968.

—— 'La reconstruction du Daphnéphoréion d'Érétrie', *AK* 17, 1974, 60–8.

—— 'Chalcis, Lefkandi, Érétrie au 8e siècle', *Contributions à l'étude de la société et de la colonisation eubéennes. Cahiers du Centre Jean Bérard* II, Naples, 1975, 9–14.

—— 'Le temple de Dionysos', *Eretria; Fouilles et Recherches* V, Francke Verlag, Bern 1976, 59–67.

Auberson, P. and Schefold, K. *Führer durch Eretria*, Francke Verlag, Bern, 1972.

Autenreith, G. *Homeric Dictionary*, Duckworth, London, 1984.

Bailey, C., Barber, E. A., Bowra, C. M., Denniston, J. D. and Page, D. L. (eds) *Greek Poetry and Life; Essays Presented to Gilbert Murray on his 70th Birthday, 2 January, 1936*, Clarendon Press, Oxford 1936.

Bakhuizen, S. C. 'The two citadels of Chalcis on Euboea', *AAA* 5, 1, 1972, 134–46.

—— (with R. Kreulin) *Chalcis-in-Euboea: Iron and Chalcidians Abroad*, Chalcidian Studies No. 3, E. J. Brill, Leiden, 1976.

—— 'Greek steel', *World Archaeology* 9, 1977, 220–34.

Bats, M. and d'Agostino, B. *Euboica. L'Eubea e la presenza euboica in Calcida e in Occidente. Atti del Convegno Internazionale di Napoli, 13–16 novembre 1996*, Centre Jean Bérard, Dipartimento di Studi del Mondo Classico, Instituto Universitario Orientale, Naples 1998.

Beattie, A. J. 'Aeschylus "Agamemnon" 281–316', *CR* ns 4, 1954, 77–81.

Beaumont, R. L. 'Greek influences in the Adriatic', *JHS* 56, 1936, 159–204.

—— 'Corinth, Ambracia, Apollonia', *JHS 72,* 1952, 62–73.

Bechtel, F. 'Das Wort ΙΠΠΟΣ in den eretrischen Personennamen', *Hermes* 35, 1900, 326–31.

—— *Die historischen Personennamen des Griechischen bis zur Kaiserzeit*, G. Olms, Hildesheim, 1964.

Beloch, K. J. *Griechische Geschichte*, Tübner, Strassbourg, (Vol. I, 1: 1912; Vol. I, 2: 1913/26).

Bengtson, H. *Die Staatsverträge des Altertums*, (II: Die Verträge der griechisch-römischen Welt von 700 bis 338 v.Ch.), C. H. Beck, Munich, 1975.

—— *History of Greece from the Beginnings to the Byzantine Era*, (trans. E. Bloedow from *Griechische Geschichte*, 2nd edn, 1968), University of Ottawa Press, Ottawa, 1988.

Benton, S. 'The Evolution of the Tripod-Lebes', *BSA* 35, 1934/35, 74–130.

Bérard, C. 'L' Herôon à la Porte de l' Ouest', *Eretria; Fouilles et Recherches* III, Francke Verlag, Bern, 1970.

—— 'Architecture érétrienne et mythologie delphique', *AK* 14, 1971, 59–73.

—— 'Le sceptre du prince', *MH* 29, 1972, 219–27.

—— 'Topographie et urbanisme de l' Érétrie archaïque: l' Hérôon', *Eretria; Fouilles et Recherches* VI, Francke Verlag, Berne, 1976.

—— 'Récoupérer la mort du prince: Héroïsation et formation de la cité', in G. Gnoli and J.-P. Vernant (eds), *La mort, les morts dans les sociétés anciennes,* Cambridge University Press, Cambridge, 1982, 89–105.

—— 'Argoura, fût-elle la «capitale» des futurs Érétriens?', *MH* 41, 1985, 268–75.

Bérard, J. *L'expansion et la colonisation grecques jusqu'aux Guerres médiques*, Aubier, Éditions Montaigne, Paris, 1960.

Bernhardy, G. (ed.) *Suidae Lexicon* (2 vols), B. G. Teubner, Stuttgart, 1968.

Bickermann, E. J. *Chronology of the Ancient World*, Thames & Hudson, London, 1980.

Biers, W. *The Archaeology of Greece: An Introduction*, Cornell University Press, Ithaca, NY, 1980.

Billows, R. A. *Antigonos the One-eyed and the Creation of the Hellenistic State*, University of California Press, Berkeley, CA, 1990.

Blakeway, A. A. 'Prolegomena to the study of Greek commerce with Italy, Sicily and France in the eighth and seventh centuries BC', *BSA* 33 1932/33, 170–208.

—— '"Demaratus" – a study in some aspects of the earliest Hellenization of Latium and Etruria', *JRS* 25, 1935, 129–49.

—— 'The date of Archilochus', in C. Bailey *et al.* (eds), *Greek Poetry and Life; Essays Presented to Gilbert Murray on his 70th Birthday, 2 January, 1936*, Clarendon Press, Oxford 1936, 35–55.

Blegen, C. W. *Troy and the Trojans*, Thames & Hudson, London, 1963.

Boardman, J. 'Pottery from Eretria', *BSA* 47, 1952, 1–48.

—— 'Early Euboean pottery and history', *BSA* 52, 1957, 1–29.

—— 'Crete and Libya in the Archaic Period', *2ου Διεθνὲς Κρητολογικὸν Συνέδριον. Φιλολογικὸς Σύλλογος «Ὁ Χρυσόστομος» ἐν Χανίοις*, I, Athens, 1967, 134–6.

—— *The Greeks Overseas; their Early Colonies and Trade*, Thames & Hudson, London, 1980.

—— 'Trade in Greek decorated pottery', *OJA* 7, 1988, 27–33.

—— 'The trade figures', *OJA* 8, 1989, 371–3.

Boardman, J. and Hayes, J. *Excavations at Tocra 1963/65: The Archaic Deposits I*, British School of Archaeology at Athens, Suppl. Vol. 4, Thames & Hudson, London, 1966.

Boardman, J. and Schweitzer, F. 'Clay analyses of Archaic Greek Pottery', *BSA* 68, 1973, 267–83.

Boardman, J. and Vaphopoulou-Richardson, C. (eds), *Chios: A Conference at the Homereion in Chios, 1984*, Clarendon Press, Oxford, 1986.

Bommelje, S. 'Aeolis in Aetolia: Thuc. III, 102.5 and the origins of the Aetolian "ethnos"', *Historia* 37, 1988, 297–316.

Bonner, C. 'A new historical fragment', *TAPA* 72, 1941, 26–35.

Bornman, F. *Hymnus in Dianam*, La Nuova Italia Publishers, Firenze, 1968.

Borthwick, E. K. 'P.Oxy. 2738: Athena and the pyrrhic dance', *Hermes* 98, 1970, 318–31.

Borza, E. *In the Shadow of Olympus. The Emergence of Macedon*, Princeton University Press, Princeton, NJ, 1992.

Boulanger, R. *Hachette Guide Bleu: Greece*, Paris, 1964.

du Boulay, J. *Portrait of a Greek Mountain Village*, Denise Harvey, Limni Evvias, 1974/79.

Bowra, C. M. 'Signs of storm: Archilochus fr. 56', *CR* 54, 1940, 127–9.

—— 'A Cretan hymn' in M. Kelly (ed.), *For Service to Classical Studies. Essays in Honour of Francis Letters*, F. W. Cheshire, Melbourne, 1966, 31–46.

—— *On Greek Margins*, Clarendon Press, Oxford, 1970a.

—— 'Asius and the old-fashioned Samians' in C. M. Bowra (ed.), *On Greek Margins*, Clarendon Press, Oxford, 1970b, 122–33.

Bradeen, D. W. *History of Chalkis to 338 BC*, unpublished PhD thesis, University of Cincinnati, Cincinnati, OH, 1947a.

—— 'The Lelantine War and Pheidon of Argos', *TAPA* 78 1947b, 223–41.

—— 'The Chalcidians in Thrace', *AJP* 73, 1952, 356–80.

—— 'The trittyes in Cleisthenes' reforms', *TAPA* 86, 1955, 22–30.

—— 'The fifth century Archon List', *Hesperia* 31, 1963 187–208.

Brelich, A. *Guerre, Agone e Culti nella Grecia arcaica*, *Antiquitas*, Reihe I, Abhandlungen zur alten Geschichte, Bd 7, Rudolph Habelt, Bonn, 1961.

Brenne, S. 'Ostraka and the process of ostrakophoria', in W. D. E. Coulson, O. Palagia, T. L. Shear Jr, H. A. Schapiro and F. J. Frost (eds), *The Archaeology of Athens and Attica under the Democracy*, proceedings of an international conference celebrating 2500 years since the birth of democracy in Greece, held at the American School of Classical Studies at Athens, 4–6 December 1992, Oxbow Monograph, 37, 1994, 13–24.

Bruneau, P. 'Une nouvelle publication de fouilles; Eretria III', *REG* 83, 1970, 129–30.

Brunnsåker, S. 'The Pithecusan shipwreck', *Opusc.Romana* 4, 1962, 165–242.

Buchner, G. 'Pithekoussai, oldest Greek colony in the west', *Expedition* 8 (Summer) 1966, 4–12.

Buck, C. D. *The Greek Dialects*, Chicago University Press, Chicago, 1928/1965.

Buck, R. J. 'The middle Helladic Period', *Phoenix* 20, 1966, 193–209.

—— 'The formation of the Boeotian League', *CP* 68, 1972, 94–101.

—— *A History of Boeotia*, University of Alberta Press, Edmonton, 1979.

Buffière, F. *L'Éros adolescente; la pédérastie dans la Grèce antique*, Société d' edition 'Les Belles-Lettres', Paris, 1980.

Burn, A. R. 'The so-called "trade leagues" in early Greek history and the Lelantine War', *JHS* 49, 1929, 14–37.

—— *Persia and the Greeks*, 2nd edn, Duckworth, London, 1984.

Burrows, R. M. and Ure, P. N. 'Excavations at Rhitsona in Boeotia', *JHS* 29, 1909, 308–52.

Bursian, K. *Quæstionum Euboïcarum capita selecta,* Leipzig, 1856.

—— *Geographie von Griechenland* II, (Pt 3: die Inselwelt), Leipzig, 1871.

Bury, J. B., *History of Greece*, 3rd edn, Macmillan, London, 1955 (rev. R. Meiggs, 1981).

Cadoux, J. 'The Athenian archons from Kreon to Hypsichides', *JHS* 68, 1948, 70–123.

Cairns, F. 'A herm from Histiaia with an agonistic epigram of the fifth century BC', *Phoenix* 37, 1983, 16–37.

—— 'IG XII9, 244 and the demes and districts of Eretria', *ZPE* 54, 1984a, 156–64.

—— 'ΧΡΕΜΑΤΑ ΔΟΚΙΜΑ; *IG* XII 9, 1273 and 1274 and the early coinage of Eretria', *ZPE* 54, 1984b, 144–55.

—— 'A "duplicate" copy of *IG* XII 9, 1189 (Histiaia)', *ZPE* 54, 1984c, 133–44.

—— '*IG* XII Suppl. 555, Reinmuth no. 15 and the demes and tribes of Eretria', *ZPE* 64, 1986, 149–68.

—— 'The "laws of Eretria" (*IG* XII, 9 1273 and 1274): epigraphic, legal and political aspects', *Phoenix* 45, 1991, 296–313.

Calder, W. 'The geography of the Beacon Passage in the "Agamemnon" ', *CR* 36, 1922, 155–59.

Calligas, P. G. (see also Kalligas, P. G.) 'An inscribed lead plaque from Kerkyra', *BSA* 66, 1971, 79–93.

—— 'Hero-cult in early Iron Age Greece' in R. Hågg, N. Marinatos and G. Nordquist (eds), *Early Greek Cult Practice, Proceedings of the Fifth International Symposium at the Swedish Institute at Athens, 26–29 June 1986*, Acta Instituti Atheniensis Regni Sueciae, Series in 4o, XXXVIII, Stockholm, 1988, 229–34.

Cambitoglou, A. and Coulton, J. ''Ανασκαφαὶ Ζαγορᾶς ῎Ανδρον', *AE* 1970, 154–233.

Cambitoglou, A., Coulton, J., Birmingham, J. and Green, J. *Zagora I: Excavation of a Geometric Settlement on the Island of Andros, Greece. Excavation Season (1967), Study Season (1968/69)*, The Australian Academy of the Humanities Monograph 2, Sydney University Press, Sydney, 1971.

Camp II, J. McK. 'A drought in the late eighth century BC', *Hesperia* 48, 1979, 397–411.

Carpenter, R. *Discontinuity in Greek Civilization. (The J. H. Grey Lectures 1965)*, Cambridge University Press, Cambridge, 1966.

Carpenter, J. and Boyd, D. 'Dragon houses: Euboia, Attika, Karia', *AJA* 81, 1977, 211–5.

Carrière, J. *Théognis de Mégare. Étude sur le recueil élégiaque attribué à ce poète*, Bordas, Paris(?), n.d., but before 1948.

—— *Théognis. Poèmes élégiaques: texte établi et traduit accompagné d'un commentaire*, Paris, 1962.

Cartledge, P. 'Hoplites and heroes; Sparta's contribution to the techniques of ancient warfare', *JHS* 97, 1977, 1–37.

Cary, M. 'Northern and central Greece' in *CAH* III, 1965, Ch 24, 598–630.

Catling, H. W. 'A Mycenaean puzzle from Lefkandi in Euboea', *AJA* 72, 1968, 41–9.

Cauer, P. *Dialectus Inscriptionum Graecarum propter Dialectum Memorabilium*, 2nd edn, Leipzig, 1877.

Chadwick, J. 'The Greek dialects and Greek pre-history', *G&R*, n.s. 3, 1956, 38–50.

Chambers, M. H. 'Aristotle on Solon's reform of coinage and weights', *CSCA* 6, 1973, 1–16.

Chandler, L. 'The north-west frontier of Attica', *JHS* 46, 1926, 1–21.

Charbonnet, A. 'Amphiaraos à Érétrie', *MH* 41, 1984, 49–53.

Cobb-Stevens, V. 'Opposites, reversals and ambiguities: the unsettled world of Theognis', in T. J. Figueira and G. Nagy (eds), *Theognis of Megara; Poetry and the Polis*, Johns Hopkins University Press, Baltimore, MD, 1985.

Coldstream, J. N. 'Hero cults in the Age of Homer', *JHS* 96, 1976, 8–17.

—— *Geometric Greece*, Methuen, London, 1977.

—— 'The early Iron Age (Cypro Geometric). The rise of the ancient kingdoms *c.* 1100–700 BC' in D. Hunt (ed.), *Footprints in Cyprus. An Illustrated History*, Trigraph, London, 1984, 58–72.

Cole, J. 'Peisistratos on the Strymon', *G&R* 22, 1975 42–4.

Cook, B. F. *Greek Inscriptions*, British Museum Press, London, 1987.

Cook, J. M. 'The Palai-names', *Historia* 4, 1955, 39–45.

—— *The Greeks in Ionia and the East*, Thames & Hudson, London, 1962.

Cook, R. M. 'Reasons for the foundation of Ischia and Cumae', *Historia* 11, 1962, 113–4.

Coulson, W. D. E., Palagia, O., Shear Jr, T. L., Schapiro, H. A. and Frost, F. J. (eds) *The Archaeology of Athens and Attica under the Democracy*, proceedings of an international conference celebrating 2500 years since the birth of democracy in Greece, held at the American School of Classical Studies at Athens, 4–6 December 1992, Oxbow Monograph, 37, 1994.

Coulton, J., 'Euboean Phylla and Greek barracks', in D. Evely, I. Lemos and S. Sherratt (eds), *Minotaur and Centaur. Studies in the Archaeology of Crete and Euboea presented to Mervyn Popham*, Tempus Reparatum, BAR International Series 638, Oxford, 1996, 161–5.

Cramer, J. A. *Anecdota Graeca, e codd. manuscriptis bibliothecarum Oxoniensium*, A. M. Hakkert, Amsterdam, 1963.

Croon, J. H. *The Herdsman of the Dead. Studies of some Cults, Myths and Legends of the Ancient Greek Colonization Area*, S. Budde, Utrecht, 1952.

Curchin, L. 'Minoans at Chalcis?', *Quaderni di Storia* 9, 1979, 271–8.

Daremberg, C. and Saglio, E. *Dictionnaire des antiquités grecques et romaines*, Akademische Druck -u. Verlaganstalt, Graz, 1963.

Daux, G. 'Note sur l' "horos phratricos" d' Érétrie', *BCH* 74, 1954, 282–4.

—— 'La grande Démarchie', *BCH* 87, 1963, 603–34.

Davies, J, K. *Athenian Propertied Families*, Clarendon Press, Oxford, 1971.

Demand, N. H. *Urban Relocation in Archaic and Classical Greece. Flight and Consolidation*, Bristol Classical Press, Bristol, 1990.

Denniston, J. and Page, D. *Agamemnon*, Clarendon Press, Oxford, 1957.

Desborough, V. R. d'A. *Protogeometric Pottery*, Clarendon Press, Oxford, 1952.

—— *The Last Mycenaeans and their Successors*, Oxford, 1964.

—— *The Greek Dark Ages*, Benn, London, 1972.

—— 'The end of Mycenaean civilization and the Dark Ages: The archaeological background', *CAH* II, 2ª, 1980, Ch. XXXVIa, 658–77.

Descoeudres, J.-P. 'Zagora auf der Insel Andros – eine eretrische Kolonie?', *AK* 16, 1973, 87–88.

—— (ed.), *Greek Colonists and Native Populations.Proceedings of the First Australian Congress of Classical Archaeology*, Clarendon Press, Oxford, 1990.

Dickins, G. 'The growth of Spartan policy', *JHS* 32, 1912, 1–42.

—— 'The growth of Spartan policy – a reply', *JHS* 33, 1913, 111–2.

Dickinson, O. 'The shaft graves and Mycenaean origins', *BICS* 19, 1972/73, 146–7.

Dilts, M. R. *Heraclidis Lembi Excerpta Politarum*, GRBS Monographs 5, 1971, Duke University Press, Durham, NC, 1971.

Dittenberger, W. *Sylloge Inscriptionum Graecarum*, Leipzig, 1915/20.

Dittenberger, W. and Purgold, K. *Die Inschriften von Olympia*, Berlin, 1896.

Donlan, W. 'Archilochus, Strabo and the Lelantine War', *TAPA* 101, 1970, 131–42.

—— *The Aristocratic Ideal in Ancient Greece and Other Papers*, Wauconda, IL, 1999a.

—— 'The aristocratic ideal in Ancient Greece', in idem, *The Aristocratic Ideal in Ancient Greece and Other Papers*, Wauconda, IL, 1999b, 1–213.

Dover, K. J. (ed.) *Ancient Greek Literature*, Oxford University Press, Oxford, 1985.

Dow, S. 'Studies in the Athenian tribute lists', *TAPA* 72, 1941, 70–84.

—— 'Corinthiaca', *HSCP* 53, 1942, 89–119.

—— 'The Greater Demarkhia of Erkhia', *BCH* 89, 1965, 180–213.

Drerup, H. 'Das sogenannte Daphnephoreion in Eretria', in *Festschrift Friedrich Hiller*, 1986, 3–21.

Drews, R. 'The first tyrants in Greece', *Historia* 21, 1972, 129–44.

—— *Basileus. The Evidence of Kingship in Geometric Greece*, Yale University Press, New Haven, CT, 1983.

—— *The Coming of the Greeks. Indo-European Conquests in the Aegean and the Near East*, Princeton University Press, Princeton, NJ, 1989.

—— *The End of the Bronze Age. Changes in Warfare and the Catastrophe of* ca. *1200 BC*, Princeton University Press, Princeton, NJ, 1993.

Dübner, F. *Scholia Graeca in Aristophanem, cum Prolegomenis Grammaticorum etc.*, Georg Olms, Hildesheim, 1969.

Ducat, J. 'La Conféderation béotienne et l' expansion thébaine à l' époque archaïque', *BCH* 97, 1973, 59–73.

Ducrey, P. 'Dédicace inédite d'une association à Érétrie', *Études de lettres* (publ. de la faculté des lettres de l'Université de Lausanne) 4, 1981, 73–8.

Dunant, C. and Thomopoulos, J. 'Inscriptions de Céos, I: Traité d' isopolité', *BCH* 78, 1954, 316–22.

Dunbabin, T. J. *The Western Greeks*, Ares Publishers, Chicago, 1979.

Edmonds, J. M. *Fragments of Attic Comedy* (Vol. I), E. J. Brill, Leiden, 1957.

Edson, C. 'Notes on the Thracian "Phoros" ', *CP* 42, 1947, 88–105.

Ehrenberg, V. 'When did the Polis rise?', *JHS* 57, 1937, 147–58.

—— *The Greek State*, Blackwell, Oxford, 1960.

Emlyn-Jones, C. J. *The Ionians and Hellenism. A Study of the Cultural Achievements of Early Greek Inhabitants of Asia Minor*, Faber, London, 1980.

Erbse, H. *Scholia Graeca in Homeri Iliadem. Scholia vetera* (5 vols), W. de Gruyter. Berlin, 1969–1977.

Evangelidis, D. E. *Οἱ Ἀρχαῖοι Κάτοικοι τῆς Ἠπείρου καὶ ἄλλα Μελετήματα*, Etaireia Ipeirotikon Meleton, Ioannina, 1962.

Evely, D., Lemos, I. and Sherratt, S. (eds) *Minotaur and Centaur. Studies in the Archaeology of Crete and Euboea presented to Mervyn Popham*, Tempus Reparatum, BAR International Series 638, Oxford, 1996.

Faraklas, N. 'Περὶ τῆς κατοικήσεως τῶν Λελέγων ἐν Βοιωτίᾳ', *AAA* 2, 1969, 96–7.

Farnell, L. R. *Cults of the Greek States* (5 vols), Clarendon Press, Oxford, 1896–1909.

—— 'An unrecorded Attic colony in Euboea?', *CR* 20, 1906, 27–31.

Figueira, T. J. *Athens and Aigina in the Age of Imperial Colonization*, Johns Hopkins University Press, Baltimore, MD, 1991.

—— 'Residential restrictions on the Athenian ostracized', *GRBS* 28, 1987, 281–305 (repr. with revisions in T. J. Figueira (ed.), *Excursions in Epichoric History. Aiginetan Essays*, Rowman & Littlefield, Lanham, MD, 1993, 173–96.

Figueira, T. J. and Nagy, G. (eds) *Theognis of Megara; Poetry and the Polis*, Johns Hopkins University Press, Baltimore, MD, 1985.

Fine, J. V. A. *The Ancient Greeks. A Critical History*, Belknap, Harvard, MA, 1983.

Finley, M. I. *The World of Odysseus*, 2nd edn, Penguin Books, Harmondsworth, 1977.

—— *Ancient Slavery and Modern Ideology*, Penguin Books, Harmondsworth, 1983.

Fitzhardinge, L. *The Spartans*, Thames & Hudson, London, 1985.

Fontenrose, J. *The Delphic Oracle; its Responses and Operations, with a Catalogue of Responses*, University of California Press, Berkeley, CA, 1981.

Ford, A. L. 'The Seal of Theognis: The politics of authorship in Archaic Greece', in T. J. Figueira and G. Nagy (eds), *Theognis of Megara; Poetry and the Polis*, Johns Hopkins University Press, Baltimore, MD, 1985, 82–95.

Fornara, C. *Translated Documents of Greece and Rome, 1: Archaic Times to the End of the Peloponnesian War*, Cambridge University Press, Cambridge, 1983.

Forrest, W. G. 'The first sacred war', *BCH* 80, 1956, 33–52.

—— 'Colonization and the rise of Delphi'. *Historia* 6, 1957, 161–75.

—— *The Emergence of Greek Democracy*, Weidenfeld & Nicholson, London, 1966.

—— *A History of Sparta, 950 BC to 192 BC*, Hutchinson, London, 1971.

—— 'Euboea and the Islands', *CAH*^{3} III, 3, 1982a, Ch. 39d, 249–60.

—— 'A lost Peisistratid name', *JHS* 102, 1982b, 134.

Fossey, J. 'The identification of Graia', *Euphrosyne* 2, 1970, 3–22.

Fossey, J. M. *The Ancient Topography of Eastern Phokis*, J. C. Gieben, Amsterdam, 1986.

Fossey, J. and Giroux, H. (eds) *Proceedings of the Third International Conference on Boiotian Antiquities, Montreal (31/10–4/11, 1979)*, McGill University Monographs in Classical Archaeology and History 2, J. C. Gieben, Amsterdam, 1985.

Fraser, P. M. and Matthews, E. *A Lexicon of Greek Personal Names* (I: The Aegean Islands, Cyprus, Cyrenaica), Clarendon Press, Oxford, 1987.

French, A. 'The economic background to Solon's reforms', *CQ* ns 6, 1956, 11–25.

—— 'The party of Peisistratos', *G&R* 6 1959, 46–57.

—— *The Growth of the Athenian Economy*, Routledge and Kegan Paul, London, 1964.

—— *Sixth Century Athens; the Sources*, Sydney University Press, Sydney, 1987.

Friedemann, P. 'Un établissement hydraulique sur le flanc est de l'acropole d'Érétrie', *AK* 36, 1993, 132–36.

—— 'De la «carrière» au sanctuaire: investigations archéologiques sur l'acropole d'Érétrie', *AK* 37, 1994, 93–9.

Friedländer, P. *Epigrammata. Greek Inscriptions in Verse*, Ares Publishers, Chicago, 1987.

Gantz, T. *Early Greek Myth. A Guide to Literary and Artistic Sources* (2 vols), Johns Hopkins University Press, Baltimore, MD, 1996.

Gardner, P. 'A numismatic note on the Lelantine War', *CR* 34, 1920, 90–1.

Gehrke, H.-J. *Stasis*, Munich, 1985.

—— 'Eretria und sein Territorium', *Boreas* 11, 1988, 15–42.

—— 'Zur Rekonstruktion antiker Seerouten: Das Beispiel des Golfs von Euboia', *Klio* 74, 1992, 81–102.

Georgiadis, A. 'Εἰς τὴν ἄνω Ἐρετρικὴν ἐπιγραφήν', *AD* 1913, 214–15.

—— 'Οἱ ἐν τῇ Ἐρετριακῇ γνωστοὶ δῆμοι οἶδε εἰσιν', *AE* 1916, 49–61.

Geyer, F. *Topographie und Geschichte der Insel Euboïa im Altertum, I: Bis zum Peloponnischen Kriege*, Weidmannsche Buchhandlung, Berlin, 1903 (translated into modern Greek by A. Zambalos: 'Τοπογραφία καὶ Ἱστορία τῆς Νήσου Εὐβοίας μέχρι τὸν Πελοποννησιακὸν Πόλεμον' in *AEM* 9, 1962, 18–124; page references given in this book are to the Greek edition).

Gialanella, C. *Il Museo Archeologico di Pithecusae*, Soprintendenza Archeologica di Napoli e Caserta Comune di Laco Ameno, Electra, Naples, 1999.

Gigante, M. 'Frammenti di un'opera periegetica', *Ægyptus* 28, 1948, 3–16.

Gill, D. W. G. 'Trade in Greek decorated pottery: some corrections', *OJA* 8, 1989, 369–70.

—— 'Positivism, pots and long-distance trade', in I. Morris (ed.), *Classical Greece. Ancient Histories and Modern Archaeologies*, New Directions in Archaeology Series, Cambridge University Press, Cambridge, 1994, 99–107.

Girard, J. 'Mémoire sur l'île d'Eubée', *Archives des missions scientifiques* II, 1851, Paris, 635–728 (translated into modern Greek by G. Fousaras, 'Ἡ "Ἱστορία τῆς' Ἀρχαίας Εὐβοίας τοῦ Jules Girard', *AEM* 11, 1964, 5–135).

—— 'Inscriptions d'Eubée', *BCH* 1878, 275–9.

Glotz, G. *The Greek City and its Institutions*, Routledge and Kegan Paul, London, 1929.

Gnoli, G. and Vernant, J.- P. (eds), *La mort, les morts dans les sociétés anciennes,* Cambridge University Press, Cambridge, 1982.

Gomme, A. W. *A Historical Commentary on Thucydides* (5 vols), Clarendon Press, Oxford, 1966–81 (vols 4 and 5 with A. Andrewes and K. J. Dover).

Goodwin, W. G. *De potentiae veterum gentium maritimarum epochis apud Eusebium*, thesis, University of Göttingen, Göttingen, 1855.

Gorman, V. B. *Miletos the Ornament of Ionia. A History of the City to 400 BCE*, University of Michigan Press, Ann Arbor, MI, 2001.

Graham, A. J. *Colony and Mother City in Ancient Greece*, Ares Publishers, Chicago, 1971.

—— 'The colonial expansion of Greece', *CAH*[3] III, 3, 1982, Ch. 37, 83–162.

—— 'Abdera and Teos', *JHS* 122, 1992, 44–73.

Grant, M. *The Rise of the Greeks*, Collier-Macmillan, New York, 1987.

Graves, R. *The Greek Myths*, Cassel, London, 1962.

Gray, G. B. and Cary, M. 'The reign of Darius', *CAH* IV, 1977, Ch. 7, 173–228.

Green, J. R. and Sinclair, R. 'Athenians in Eretria', *Historia* 19, 1970, 515–27.

Greenhalgh, P. A. L. 'Aristocracy and its advocates in Archaic Greece', *G&R* 19, 1972, 190–207.

—— *Early Greek Warfare: Horsemen and Chariots in the Homeric and Archaic Ages*, Cambridge University Press, Cambridge, 1973.

Grimal, P. *The Dictionary of Classical Mythology*, Blackwell, Oxford, 1996.

van Groningen, B. A. *Euphorion*, A. M. Hakkert, Amsterdam, 1977.

Grundy, G. 'The policy of Sparta', *JHS* 32, 1912, 261–9.

Gwynn, A. 'The character of Greek colonization', *JHS* 38, 1918, 88–123.

Habicht, C. 'Samische Volksbeschlüsse der hellenistischen Zeit', *MDAI(A)* 72, 1957, 157–64.

Hadzisteliou-Price, T. *Kourotrophos: Cults and Representations of the Greek Nursing Deities*, Studies of the Dutch Archaeological Society VIII, E. J. Brill, Leiden, 1978.

Hågg, R. (ed.) *The Greek Renaissance of the Eighth Century: Tradition and Innovation. Proceedings of the Second International Symposium at the Swedish Institute in Athens, 1–5 June 1981*, Acta Instituti Atheniensis Regni Sueciae, Series in 4o, XXX, Stockholm, 1983.

Hågg, R., Marinatos, N. and Nordquist, G. (eds) *Early Greek Cult Practice, Proceedings of the Fifth International Symposium at the Swedish Institute at Athens, 26–29 June 1986*, Acta Instituti Atheniensis Regni Sueciae, Series in 4o, XXXVIII, Stockholm, 1988.

Halliday, W. *The Greek Questions of Plutarch*, Clarendon Press, Oxford, 1928.

Hamilton, R. *Choes and Anthesteria. Athenian Iconography and Ritual*, University of Michigan Press, Ann Arbor, MI, 1992.

Hammond, N. G. L. 'Prehistoric Epirus and the Dorian invasion', *BSA* 32, 1931/32, 131–79.

—— *A History of Greece to 322* BC, Clarendon Press, Oxford, 1959.

—— *Epirus. The Geography, the Ancient Remains, the History and the Topography of Epirus and Adjacent Areas*, Clarendon Press, Oxford, 1967.

—— *A History of Macedonia* I: *Historical Geography and Prehistory*, Clarendon Press, Oxford, 1972.

—— 'The literary tradition for the migrations', *CAH*[3] II, 2b, 1980, Ch. 36b, 678–712.

—— *The Macedonian State. The Origins, Institutions and History*, Clarendon Press, Oxford, 1992.

Hankey, V. 'Late Helladic tombs at Chalcis', *BSA* 47, 1952, 49–95.

Hansen, M. H. *Demography and Democracy. The Number of Athenian Citizens in the Fourth Century* BC, P. J. Schmidt, Vogens, Gjellerup, 1986.

—— (ed.) *The Polis as an Urban Centre and as a Political Community, Acts of the Copenhagen Polis Centre,* Vol. IV, Copenhagen, 1997.

Hardwick, N. 'The coinage of Terone from the fifth to the fourth centuries BC', in R. Ashton and S. Hurter (eds), in association with G. Le Rider and R. Bland, *Studies in Greek Numismatics in Memory of Martin Jessop Price*, Spink, London, 1998, 119–34 and pl. 29.

Harrison, E. *Studies in Theognis*, Cambridge University Press, Cambridge, 1902.

—— 'Chalkidike I', *CQ* 6 1912, 93–103 and 165–78.

Harrison, J. E. 'The Kouretes and Zeus Kouros: a study in pre-historic sociology', *BSA* 15, 1908/9, 308–38.

—— *Themis. A Study of the Social Origins of Greek Religion*, Merlin Press, London, 1963.

Hasebroek, K. *Griechische Wirtschafts-und Gesellschaftsgeschichte bis zur Perserzeit*, I, Tübingen, 1931.

—— *Trade and Politics in Ancient Greece* (translation of *Staat und Handel im alten Griechenland*, Tubingen, 1928), G. Bell and Sons, London, 1933.

Hazlitt, W. *The Classical Gazeteer. A Dictionary of Ancient Sites*, Senate Books, London, 1995.

Head, B. V. *A Catalogue of Coins in the British Museum (Central Greece)*, British Museum Department of Coins and Medals, London, 1884.

—— *Historia Numorum. A Manual of Greek Numismatics*, Clarendon Press, Oxford, 1887.

—— *A Guide to the Principal Coins of the Greeks from* circ. *700* BC *to* AD *270*, British Museum Department of Coins and Medals, London, 1932.

Heilmeyer, W.-D. 'Giessereibetriebe in Olympia', *JdI* 84, 1969, 1–28.

Heinze, W. *De rebus Eretriensium*, thesis, University of Gottingen, 1869.

Hempe, R. and Simon, E. *The Birth of Greek Art. From the Mycenaean to the Archaic Period*, Oxford University Press, New York, 1991.

Henderson, J. *The Maculate Muse – Obscene Language in Attic Comedy*, Oxford University Press, Oxford, 1991.

Henry, A. S.*The Prescripts of Athenian Decrees*, E. J. Brill, Leiden, 1977.

—— *Honours and Privileges in Athenian Decrees: The Principal Formulae of Athenian Honorary Decrees*, Georg Olms, Hildesheim, 1983.

Herman, G. *Ritualized Friendship in the Greek City*, Cambridge University Press, Cambridge, 1987.

Hicks, E. L. 'The collection of ancient marbles at Leeds',*JHS* 11, 1890, 260–4.

Higgins, R. *The Greek Bronze Age*, British Museum Publications, London, 1977.

Hignett, C. *A History of the Athenian Constitution to the End of the Fifth Century* BC, Clarendon Press, Oxford, 1958.

Hind, J. 'The "tyrannis" and exiles of Pisistratus', *CQ* ns 24, 1974, 1–18.

Holleaux, M. 'Note sur un décret d'Érétrie', *REG* 10, 1897, 157–89.

Holliday, J. 'The followers of Peisistratus', *G&R* 24, 1974, 40–56.

Hood, M. S. F. 'Mycenaeans in Chios', in J. Boardman and C. Vaphopoulou-Richardson (eds), *Chios: A Conference at the Homereion in Chios, 1984*, Clarendon Press, Oxford, 1986, 169–80.

Hooker, J. T. *The Ancient Spartans*, Dent, London, 1980

Hope-Simpson, R. *Mycenaean Greece*, Noyes Press, Park Ridge, NJ, 1981.

Hopper, R. J. 'Plain, shore and hill in early Athens', *BSA* 56, 1961, 189–219.

—— *The Early Greeks*, Barns & Noble, New York, 1976.

Horsley, G. H. R. 'Kleisthenes and the abortive Athenian embassy to Sardis', *Museum Philologicum Londoniense* 7, A. M. Hakkert, Amsterdam, 1986, 99–105.

How, W. and Wells, J. *A Commentary on Herodotus* (2 vols), Clarendon Press, Oxford, 1975.

Hudson-Williams, T. 'Theognis and his poems',*JHS* 23, 1903, 1–22.

—— *The Elegies of Theognis*, New York, repr. 1974.

Hughes, D. D. *Human Sacrifice in Ancient Greece*, Routledge, London, 1991.

Hunt, D. (ed.) *Footprints in Cyprus. An Illustrated History*, Trigraph, London, 1984.

Hurwitt, J. M. *Art and Culture of Early Greece, 1100–480* BC, Cornell University Press, Ithaca, NY, 1985.

Huxley, A. and Taylor, W. *Flowers of Greece and the Aegean*, Chatto & Windus, London, 1977.

Huxley, G. 'Mycenaean decline and the Homeric "Catalogue of Ships" ', *BICS* 3, 1956, 19–31.

—— 'Studies in early Greek poets 1: Neleids in Naxos and Archilochus', *GRBS* 5, 1964, 21–5.

—— *The Early Ionians*, Routledge and Kegan Paul, London, 1966.

Jacobsen, T. W. *Prehistoric Euboea*, unpublished PhD thesis, University of Pennsylvania, Philadelphia,1964.

Jacoby, F. 'The date of Archilochus', *CQ* 35, 1941, 97–109.

James, E. O. *The Cult of the Mother Goddess*, Thames & Hudson, London, 1959.

Jamieson, M. 'Notes on the sacrificial calendar from Erchia', *BCH* 89, 1965, 154–72.

Janko, R. *Homer, Hesiod and the Hymns*, Cambridge University Press, Cambridge, 1982.

Jardé, A. *The Formation of the Greek People*, Routledge and Kegan Paul, London, 1926.

Jeanmaire, H. *Couroi et Courètes: essai sur l'education spartiate et sur les rites d'adolescence dans l'antiquité hellénique*, Arno Press, New York, 1975.

Jebb, R. *Sophocles. 'Trachiniae'*, Cambridge University Press, Cambridge, 1908.

Jeffery, L. H. 'The courts of justice in Archaic Chios', *BSA* 51, 1956, 157–67.

—— *The Local Scripts of Archaic Greece – a Study of the Origin of the Greek Alphabet and its Development from the Eighth to the Fifth Centuries* BC, Clarendon Press, Oxford, 1961 (rev. A. Johnston1990).

—— 'The campaign between Athens and Aigina in the years before Salamis (Hdt VI, 87 – 93)', *AJP* 83, 1962, 44–54.

—— *Archaic Greece*, Methuen, London, 1976.

Jenkins, G. 'Greek coins recently acquired by the British Museum', *NC* 1955.

Johnston, A. 'Rhodian Readings', *BSA* 70, 1975, 145–69.

—— *The Emergence of Greece*, Phaidon, London, 1976.

Jones, N. F. 'The civic organization of Corinth', *TAPA* 110, 1980, 161–93.

—— *Public Organization in Ancient Greece. A Documentary Study*, The American Philosophical Society, Philadelphia, 1987.

Kagan, D. 'The origin and purposes of ostracism', *Hesperia* 30, 1961, 393–401.

—— 'The dates of the earliest coins', *AJA* 86, 1982, 361–80.

Kahil, L. 'Contribution à l'étude de l'Érétrie géométrique', in *Στήλη: Τόμος εἰς μνήμην Νικολάου Κοντολέοντος*, Somateio hoi Philoi Nikolaou Kontoleontos, Athens, 1980, 525–31.

—— 'Érétrie à l'époque géométrique', *ASIAA* 59 1981, 165–72.

Kalemis, A. *Η Αποκάλυψη των Φυσικών και Ιστορικών Θησαυρών της Εύβοιας*, Ekdhoseis Kinitro E. Kalami, Athens, 2000.

Kalligas, P. G. (see also Calligas, P. G.) 'Τὸ ἐν Κερκύρᾳ ἱερὸν τῆς Ἀκραίας Ἥρας', *AD* 24, 1969, 51–8.

—— "Η Ἀγορᾶ τῆς Ἀρχαίας Ἐρετρίας', *AAA* 15, 1982, 3–9.

—— 'Κέρκυρα, ἀποικισμὸς καὶ ἔπος', *ASIAA* 60 (ns 44) 1982/84, 57–67.

Kambouroglou, E. *Ερέτρια· παλαιογεωγραφική και γεωμορφολογική εξέλιξη κατά το Ολόκαινο. Σχέση φυσικού περιβάλλοντος και αρχαίων οικισμών*, Demos Eretrieon, Athens, 1989.

Kearsley, R. 'The pendent semi-circle Skyphos', *BICS Suppl.* 44, 1989.

Keller, O. *Rerum naturalium scriptores Graeci minores*, B. G. Teubner, Leipzig, 1877.

Kelly, M. (ed.), *For Service to Classical Studies. Essays in Honour of Francis Letters*, F. W. Cheshire, Melbourne, 1966.

Kerényi, C. *The Gods of the Greeks*, Grove Press, New York, 1960.

Kirchner, J. *Prosopographia Attica* (2 vols), 2nd edn, G. Reimer, Berlin, 1902–13.

Kirk, G. S. 'Ships on Geometric vases', *BSA* 44, 1949, 93–153.

—— 'The Homeric poems as history', *CAH*[3] II, 2a, Ch. 39b, 1980, 820–50.

—— *The Iliad: A Commentary* (Vol. I: Books 1–4), Cambridge University Press, Cambridge, 1985.

Killen, J., Melena, J. and Olivier, J.-P. (eds) *Studies in Mycenaean and Classical Greek Presented to John Chadwick* (= *Minos* 20–2), Salamanca, 1987.

Klein, J. 'A Greek metalworking quarter: eighth century excavations at Ischia', *Expedition* 14, 1972, 34–9.

Knell, H. 'Eretria: zur Grundrissrekonstruktion des alteren und des jüngeren Apollonntempels', *AK* 15, 1972, 40–8.

Knoepfler, D. 'ΟΦΡΥΟΕΣΣΑ ΠΟΛΙΣ; note sur l' acropole d' Érétrie', *AK* 12, 1969, 83–7.

—— 'La date de l'annexation de Styra par Érétrie', *BCH* 95, 1971, 223–44.

—— 'Karystos et les Artemisia d' Amarynthos', *BCH* 96, 1972, 282–301.

—— 'Argoura: un toponym dans la "Midienne" de Démosthène', *BCH* 105, 1981, 289–329.

—— 'Un témoignage épigraphique méconnu sur Argous[s]a, ville de Thessalie', *Rev.phil.* 57 1983, 47–55.

—— 'Les cinq-cents à Érétrie', *REG* 98, 1985a, 243–59.

—— 'Oropos: colonie d'Érétrie', *Dossiers d'archéologie* 94, 1985b, 50–5.

—— 'Review of P. Carlier, *La royauté grecque avant Alexandre*, Strasbourg, 1984', *REG* 99, 1986, 332–41.

—— 'Sur les traces de l' Artemision d' Amarynthos pres de l' Eretrie', *CRAI* 1988, 382–421.

—— 'Le calendrier des Chalkidiens de Thrace: essai de mise au point sur le liste et l' ordre des mois eubeens', *JSavants* 1989, 23–59.

—— 'The calendar of Olynthus and the origins of the Chalcidians in Thrace', in J.-P. Descoeudres(ed.), *Greek Colonists and Native Populations. Proceedings of the First Australian Congress of Classical Archaeology*, Clarendon Press, Oxford, 1990a, 95–115.

—— 'Dédicaces érétriennes à Ilithyie', *AK* 33, 1990b, 115–27.

—— 'Le territoire d'Érétrie et l'organisation politique de la cité (*démoi*, *chōroi*, *phylai*)', in M. Hansen (ed.), *Acts of the Copenhagen Polis Centre* IV, Copenhagen, 1997, 352–449.

—— 'Le héros Narkittos et le système tribal d'Erétrie', in M. Bats and B. d'Agostino (eds), *Euboica. L'Eubea e la presenza euboica in Calcida e in Occidente*, Naples 1998, 105–8.

—— *Décrets érétriens de proxénie et de citoyennité, Eretria. Fouilles et Recherches* XI, Éditions Payot, Lausanne, 2001a.

—— 'Loi d'Érétrie contre la tyrannie et oligarchie' (Pt 1), *BCH* 125, 2001b, 195–238.

Kock, T. *Comicorum Atticarum Fragmenta* (Vol. I: *Antiquae commodiae fragmenta*), B. G. Teubner, Leipzig, 1880.

Kondoleon, N. M. 'Archilochos und Paros', *Entretiens Hardt* X: 'Archiloque', 26 août – 3 septembre 1963, Genève, 1963.

—— 'Οἱ 'Αειναῦται τῆς 'Ερετρίας' *AE* 1963 [1965], 1–45.

—— ''Η 'Αποικιακὴ ἐξάπλωση τῆς Εὐβοίας', *AEM* 13, 1966, 17–39.

Kourouniotis, K. ''Επιγραφαὶ Χαλκίδος καὶ Ερετρίας', *AE* 1899, coll. 134–47.

—— ''Εκ τοῦ ἱεροῦ τῆς 'Αμαρυσίας 'Αρτέμιδος', *AE* 1900, coll. 5–26.

Kraay, C. M. 'Hoards, small change and the origin of coinage', *JHS* 84, 1964, 76–91.

—— 'An interpretation of *Ath. Pol.* Ch. 10', in C. M. Kraay and G. K. Jenkins (eds), *Essays in Greek Coinage, Presented to Stanley Robinson,* Clarendon Press, Oxford, 1968, 201–09.

—— *Archaic and Classical Coins*, Sandford J. Durst, New York, 1976.

Krause, C. 'Das Westtor, Ergebnisse der Ausgrabungen 1964–1968', *Eretria: Fouilles et Recherches* IV, Francke Verlag, Bern, 1972.

—— 'Structure et developpement urbanistique d'Érétrie archaïque', in *Gli Eubei in Occidente. Atti del diciottesimo Convegno di Studi sulla Magna Grecia, Taranto, 8–12 ottobre 1978*, Instituto per la Storia e l'Archeologia della Magna Grecia, Taranto, 1979, 37–52.

—— 'Brunnenturme in der archaischen Stadtmauer Eretrias', *AK* 25, 1982a, 39–42.

—— 'Zur Städtebaulichen Entwicklung Eretrias', *AK* 25, 1982b, 137–44.

—— 'Remarques sur la structure et l'évolution de l'espace urbain d'Érétrie', *Architecture et Société (=Actes du Colloque de Rome, 1980)*, Paris, 1983, 63–73.

—— 'Naissance et formation d'une ville', *Dossiers d'archéologie* 94, 1985, 17–25.

Kretschmer, P. 'Literaturbericht für das Jahr 1913', *Glotta* 7, 1916, 321–59.

Kroll, J. and Waggoner, N. 'Dating the earliest coins of Athens, Corinth and Aegina', *AJA* 88, 1984, 328–40.

Lambert, S. D. 'A Thucydidean scholion on the Lelantine War', *JHS* 102, 1982, 216–20.

—— *The Phratries of Attica*, University of Michigan Press, Ann Arbor, MI, 1998.

Langdon, M. K. 'Sanctuary of Zeus on Mt Hymettos', *Hesperia Suppl.* XVI, 1976.

Lavelle, B. M. 'Koisyra and Megakles, son of Hippokrates', *GRBS* 30, 1989, 503–13.

Leahy, D. M. 'The Spartan embassy to Lygdamis', *JHS* 77, 1957, 272–5.

Leake, W. M. *Travels in Northern Greece* (4 vols), repr. A. Hakkert, Amsterdam, 1967.

Leekley, D. and Efstratiou, N. *Archaeological Excavations in Central and Northern Greece*, Noyes Press, Park Ridge, NJ, 1980.

Legon, R. *Megara: The Political History of a Greek City State to 336 BC*, Cornell University Press, Ithaca, NY, 1981.

Lewis, D. M. 'The federal constitution of Keos', *BSA* 57, 1962, 1–4.

—— *Selected Papers in Greek and Near Eastern History*, P. M. Rhodes (ed.), Cambridge University Press, Cambridge, 1997.

Lloyd, A. *Marathon*, Souvenir Press, London, 1975.

Lloyd-Jones, H. 'More about Antileon, tyrant of Chalcis (Solon, fr. 33 and Aristophanes, *Eq.* 1042–44)', *CP* 70, 1975, 197.

Lobel, E. (ed.) *The Oxyrhynchus Papyri*, (Part XXX), Egypt Exploration Fund, London, 1964.

Lobel, E. and Page, D. L. *Poetarum Lesbiorum Fragmenta*, Clarendon Press, Oxford, 1955.

Lorimer, H. L. 'The hoplite phalanx with special reference to Archilochus and Tyrtaeus', *BSA* 42, 1947, 76–138.

Luppe, W. 'Zum neuen agonistischen Epigramm aus Eretria', *ZPE* 49, 1982, 22.

Lutz, H. 'The Corinthian constitution after the fall of the Cypselides [*sic*]', *CR* 10, 1896, 418–9

Maas, P. 'How Antileon's tyranny ended', *CR* ns 6, 1956, 200.

McCargar, D. 'Isagoras, son of Teisandros and Isagoras, eponymous archon, 508/7 BC', *Phoenix* 28, 1974, 275–81.

McDonald, W. A., Coulson, W. and Rosser, J. *Excavations at Nichoria in South West Messenia. (III: Dark Age and Byzantine Habitation)*, University of Minnesota Press, Minneapolis, MN, 1983.

McGlew, J. F. *Tyranny and Political Culture in Ancient Greece*, Cornell University Press, Ithaca, NY, 1993.

McGregor, M. F. 'Cleisthenes of Sicyon and the Panhellenic festivals', *TAPA* 72, 1941, 266–87.

Mansfield, J. M. *IG XII 9, 1273/1274: The Eretrian Laws*, unpublished MA thesis, University of California, Berkeley, CA, 1976.

Marinatos, S. 'Kleidung Haar -und Barttracht', *Archaeologia Homerica*, Band I, Vandenhoeck and Ruprecht, Göttingen, 1967.

Marinatos, N. and Hågg, R. (eds) *Greek Sanctuaries. New Approaches*, Routledge, London, 1993.

Martin, R. 'Problèmes de topographie et d' évolution urbaine' in *Contribution à l' étude de la société et de la colonisation eubéennes. Cahiers du Centre Jean Bérard* II, Naples, 1975, 48–52.

Masson, O. 'Noms grecs des femmes formés sur des participes (Type Θάλλουσα)', *Tyche* 2, 1987, 107–12.

Mastrocinque, A. 'La 'Kourá' degli Eubei e la Guerra lelantea', *Athenaeum* 58, 1980, 460–2.

Maurice, F. 'The campaign of Marathon', *JHS* 52, 1932, 13–34.

Mazarakis-Ainian, A. J. 'Geometric Eretria', *AK* 30, 1987, 3–24.

Mazzarino, S. *Fra Oriente e Occidente. Richerche di storia greca arcaica*, Rizzoli, Milan, 1947/89 [with a reply (*Per un 'discorso sul metodo'*) to the methodological criticism of A. Momigliano, see below].

Meiggs, R. and Lewis, D. M. *A Selection of Greek Historical Inscriptions to the End of the Fifth Century*, Clarendon Press, Oxford, 1989.

Meineke, A. *Stephan von Byzanz: Ethnika (Stephani Byzantii Ethnicorum quae supersunt, ex recensione Augusti Meinekii)*, 2nd edn, Akademische Druck-u. Verlagsanstalt, Graz, 1958.

Mele, A. 'I caratteri della società eretriese arcaica', *Contribution à l' Étude de la Société et de la Colonisation eubéennes Cahiers du Centre Jean Bérard* II, Naples, 1975, 15–26.

—— 'I Ciclopi, Calcodonte e la metallurgia calcidese', *Nouvelle contribution à l'Étude de la société et de la colonisation eubéennes*, Cahiers du Centre Jean Bérard, VI, Naples, 1981, 9–33.

Meritt, B. D. *Corinth; Results of Excavations*, VIII (Pt 1: The Greek Inscriptions), Harvard University Press, Cambridge, MA, 1931.

—— 'Greek inscriptions', *Hesperia* 8, 1939, 48–90.

—— 'Greek inscriptions', *Hesperia* 9, 1940, 53–96.

Meritt, B. D. and Andrewes, A. 'Athens and Neapolis', *BSA* 46, 1951, 200–09.

Meritt, B. D., Wade-Gery, H. T. and McGregor, M. F. *The Athenian Tribute Lists*, The American School of Classical Studies at Athens, vols 1 and 2: Harvard University Press, Cambridge, MA, 1939 and 1949; vol 3: B. D. Meritt (only), Princeton University Press, Princeton, NJ, 1950.

Metzger, I. 'Das Thesmophorion von Eretria', *Eretria. Fouilles et Recherches* VII, Francke Verlag, Bern, 1985.

Michel, C. *Receuil des inscriptions grecques* (one vol. and two supplements) Paris, 1899/1927.

Miller, M. 'The accepted Date for Solon: precise but wrong', *Arethusa* 2, 1969, 62–86.

—— *The Thalassocracies – Studies in Chronography II*, State University of New York Press, Albany, NY, 1975.

Mitchell, L. 'Euboean Io', paper to be published in *CQ* (22 pp.).

Moggi, M. *I sinecismi interstatali greci* (I: Dalle origine al 338 a.C.), Edizione Marlin, Pisa, 1976.

Momigliano, A. 'Review of S. Mazzarino, "Fra Oriente e Occidente; Richerche di storia greca arcaica" ', in *Rivista storica Italiana* 60, 1948, 127–32 (reprinted as an appendix in Mazzarino, above, 397–403 together with Mazzarino's reply).

Morgan, C. *Athletes and Oracles. The Transformation of Olympia and Delphi in the Eighth Century* BC, Cambridge University Press, Cambridge, 1990.

Morris, I. 'The use and abuse of Homer', *CA* 5, 1986, 81–138.

—— *Burial and Ancient Society: The rise of the Greek City-state*, Cambridge University Press, Cambridge, 1987.

—— (ed.) *Classical Greece. Ancient Histories and Modern Archaeologies*, New Directions in Archaeology Series, Cambridge University Press, Cambridge, 1994.

Morris, I. and Powell, B. (eds), *A New Companion to Homer*, E. J. Brill, Leiden, 1997.

Muller, K. (ed.) *Geographi Graeci Minores*, Vols I and II, G. Olms, Hildesheim, , 1965.

Müller, S. 'Des Néolithiques aux Mycéniens', *Dossiers d'archéologie*, 94, 1985, 2–16.

Munro, J. A. R. 'Pelasgians and Ionians', *JHS* 54, 1934, 109–28.

Munro, J. A. R. and Walker, E. M. 'Marathon', *CAH* IV, 1977, Ch. 8, 229–67.

Mureddu, P. 'ΧΡΥΣΕΙΑ a Pithecussai', *PdelP* 27, 1972, 407–9.

Murray, O. *Early Greece*, Fontana, London, 1988.

Musgrave, J. and Popham, M. R. 'The late Helladic IIIC intramural burials at Lefkandi, Euboea', *BSA* 86, 1991, 273–96.

Myres, J. L. 'On the List of "Thalassocracies" in Eusebius', *JHS* 26, 1906, 84–130.

—— 'A history of the Pelasgian theory', *JHS* 27, 1907, 170–225.

—— *Herodotus, Father of History*, Clarendon Press, Oxford, 1953.

Nauck, A. *Tragicorum Graecorum Fragmenta*, G. Olms, Hildesheim, 1964.

Newman, W. L. *The 'Politics' of Aristotle* (Vol. IV), Clarendon Press, Oxford, 1902.

Nicholls, R. V. 'Old Smyrna', *BSA* 53/54, 1958/59, 114–36.

Nilsson, M. P. 'Schlagenstele des Zeus Ktesios', *AM* 33, 1908, 279–88.

—— *Griechische Feste von religiöser Bedeutung, mit Außchluss der attischen*, B. G. Teubner, Stuttgart, 1957.

—— *The Mycenaean Origin of Greek Mythology*, University of California Press, Berkeley, CA, 1972.

Ober, J. *Mass and Elite in Democratic Athens; Rhetoric, Ideology, and the Power of the People*, Princeton University Press, Princeton, NJ, 1989.

Oliva, P. *The Birth of Greek Civilization*, Orbis, London, 1981.

Oost, S. I. 'Cypselus the Bacchiad', *CP* 67/68, 1972/73, 10–30.

Osborne, M. J. 'Athenian stone-cutters at work', *ZPE* 19, 1975, 159–77.

Osborne, R. *Greece in the Making 1200–479 BC*, Routledge, London, 1996.

Ostwald, M. *Nomos and the Beginnings of Athenian Democracy*, Clarendon Press, Oxford, 1969.

—— *From Popular Sovreignty to the Sovreignty of Law. Law, Society, and Politics in Fifth-Century Athens*, University of California Press, Berkeley, CA, 1986.

Page, D. L. 'The song of Hybrias the Cretan', *PCPS* 191 (ns 11) 1965, 62–5.

—— (ed./tr.) *Select Papyri III: Literary Papyri; Poetry*, Harvard University Press (Loeb Series), Cambridge, MA, 1970.

Palaeologos, K. 'Rules of the competition', in N. Yalouris (ed.), *The Olympic Games in Ancient Greece. Ancient Olympia and the Olympic Games*, Ekdotike Athenon, Athens, 1982.

Papadakis, N. ''Ανασκαφὴ 'Ισείου 'Ερετρίας', *AD* 1915, 148–90.

Papandreou, G. *'Η 'Ηλεία διὰ Μέσου τῶν Αἰώνων*, NELE of Elis, Lehaina, 1992.

Papavasileiou, G. 'Εὐβοϊκά', *AE* 1905, 1–36.

—— *Περὶ τῶν ἐν Εὐβοίᾳ ἀρχαίων τάφων*, Athens, 1910.

—— ''Ερετρικὸς Νόμος', *AD* 1913, iv, 210–5.

Pape, W. and Benseler, G. *Wörterbuch der griechischen Eigennamen* (2 vols), Akademische – Druck -u. Verlaganstalt, Graz, 1959.

Parke, H. W. 'Polycrates and Delos', *CQ* 40, 1946, 105–8.

—— *Festivals of the Athenians*, Thames & Hudson, London, 1986.

Parker, V. 'Zur griechischen und vorderasiatischen Chronologie des sechsten Jahrhunderts v. Chr. unter besonderer Berücksichtigung der Kypselidenchronologie', *Historia*, 42, 1993, 385–417.

—— 'Untersuchungen zum Lelantischen Krieg und verwandten Problemen der frühgriechischen Geschichte', *Historia Einzelschriften* 109, 1997.

Parlama, A. 'Μικρὴ ἀνασκαφκὴ ἔρευνα στὸν προϊστορικὸ λόφο τῆς 'Αμαρύνθου [Εὔβοια]', *AAA* 12, 1979, 3–14.

Pearson, L. 'Notes on the text of Plutarch *de malignitate Herodoti*', *AJP* 80, 1959, 255–75.

Peek, W. 'Griechische Inschriften (Euboia)', *AM* 59, 1934, 73–9.

—— *Griechische Vers-Inschriften; Grab-Epigramme*, Ares Publishers, Chicago, 1988.

Penella, R. J. 'Scopelianus and the Eretrians in Cissia', *Athenaeum* 52, 1975, 295–300.

Petrakos, B. C. 'Dédicace des Aeinautai d'Érétrie', *BCH* 87, 1963, 545–7.

—— *'Ο 'Ωρωπὸς καὶ τὸ ἱερὸν τοῦ 'Αμφιαράου*, Bibliotheke tes en Athenais Arkhaiologikes Hetaireias, Papadhoyyianis, Athens, 1968.

Philippson, A. *Die Griechischen Landschaften. Ein Landeskunde* (Herausgegeben unter Mitwirkung von H. Lehmann), (Vol. I, 1), V. Klostermann, Frankfurt am Main, 1950/59.

Picard, O. *Chalcis et la Conféderation eubéenne (IV–I siècle). Étude de numismatique et d'histoire*, École française d' Athènes, de Boccard, Paris, 1979.

Pickard, J. 'A topographical survey of Eretria', *Papers of the American School of Classical Studies at Athens* 6, 1890–7, 371–89.

Plassart, A. 'Inscriptiones de Delphes: la liste des théorodoques', *BCH* 45, 1921, 1–85.

Platon, N. ''Ο τάφος τοῦ Σταφύλου καὶ ὁ μινωικὸς ἀποικισμὸς τῆς Πεπαρήθου', *Kretika Khronika* 1949, 334–73.

Podlecki, A. 'Three Greek soldier-poets: Archilochus, Alcaeus, Solon', *CW* 63/64, 1969, 73–81.

de Polignac, F. *Cults, Territory and the Origins of the Greek City State*, University of Chicago Press, Chicago, 1995.

Pollard, A. and Hatcher, H. 'Euboean exports to Al Mina', *BSA* 78, 1983, 281–90 (the archaeological conclusions are by M. R. Popham).

Popham, M. R. 'An early Euboean Ship', *OJA* 6 1987, 353–9.

Popham, M. R. and Milburn, E. 'The late Helladic IIIC pottery of Xeropolis (Lefkandi), a summary', *BSA* 66, 1971, 333–52 and pls 50–7.

Popham, M. R. and Sackett, L. H. *Excavations at Lefkandi, Euboea, 1964–1966*, London, 1968.

Popham, M. R., Hatcher, H. and Pollard, A. 'Al-Mina and Euboea', *BSA* 75, 1980a, 151–60.

Popham, M. R., Sackett, L. H. and Themelis, P. G. *Lefkandi I: The Iron Age*, British School of Archaeology at Athens, London, 1980b.

Popham, M. R., Touloupa, E. and Sackett, L. H. 'The Hero of Lefkandi', *Antiquity* 56, 1982, 169–74.

Popham, M. R., Calligas, P. G., Sackett, L. H. *et al.* *Lefkandi II: The Proto-geometric Building at Toumba*, (Part 1: The Pottery, by R. Catling and I. Lemos), British School at Athens, Thames & Hudson, London, 1990.

Popham, M. R., Calligas, P. G., Sackett, L. H. *et al.* *Lefkandi II: The Proto-geometric Building at Toumba*, (Part 2: The Excavation, Architecture and Finds, by J. Coulton and H. W. Catling), British School at Athens, Thames & Hudson, London, 1993.

Poralla, P. *Prosographie der Lakedaimonier, bis auf die Zeit Alexanders des Grossen* (rev. A. S. Bradford), Ares Publishers, Chicago, 1985.

Porzig, W. 'Sprachgeographische Untersuchungen zu den griechischen Dialekten', *IF* 61, 1954, 147–69

Pouilloux, J. *Recherches sur l'histoire et les cultes de Thasos* I, de Boccard, Paris, 1954.

Powell, B. B. *Homer and the Origin of the Greek Alphabet*, Cambridge University Press, Cambridge, 1991.

—— 'Did Homer sing at Lefkandi? A reply to J. R. Lenz', *Electronic Antiquity* 1, ii, 1993, 8 pp., available by searching database at website: http://scholar.lib.vt.edu/ejournals/ElAnt.

—— 'Homer and writing', in I. Morris and B. Powell (eds), *A New Companion to Homer*, Leiden, 1997, 3–32.

Powell, J. U. and Barber, E. A. (eds) *New Chapters in Greek Literature. Recent Discoveries in Greek Poetry and Prose of the Fourth and Following Centuries*, Biblo & Tannen, New York.

Prichett, W. K. 'Attic stelai' I, *Hesperia* 22, 1953, 225–99.

Psyllas, I. *'Ιστορία τῆς Νήσου Κέας, ἀπὸ τῶν 'Αρχαιοτάτων Χρόνων μέχρι τῶν καθ' ὑμας*, Boukarianis, Athens(?), 1920/92.

Quincey, J. 'The beacon-sites in the *Agamemnon*', *JHS* 83, 1963, 118–32.

Raaflaub, K. A. 'Homer to Solon: the rise of the early Greek polis', in M. H. Hansen (ed.), *The Ancient Greek City-State*, Copenhagen, 1993, 41–105.

—— 'Interstate relations among early Greek *poleis*', paper delivered at the seminar, *Narrating Antiquity. Epic and History in the Graeco-Roman World*, held at the University of New England, Armidale, New South Wales, 2 July 1996.

Radici Colace, P. and Caccamo Caltabiano, M. ''Αργυρον δόκιμον . . .τὸ δ' ἐνάντιον παράσημον' (Pollux III, 86)', *ASNP* 13, 1983, 421–47.

Rangavé, A. 'Mémoire sur la partie méridionale de l'île d'Eubée', *Mémoires presentés à l'Académie des Inscriptions*, Ser. 1, Vol. III, 1853.

Raubitschek, A. 'The Athenian property on Euboia', *Hesperia* 12, 1943, 28–33.

—— *Dedications from the Athenian Akropolis; a Catalogue of the Inscriptions of the Sixth and Fifth Centuries BC*, (with L. H. Jeffery), Harvard University Press, Cambridge, MA, 1949.

—— 'Megakles, geh nicht nach Eretria', *ZPE* 100, 1994, 381–2.

Reiter, W. *Aemilius Paullus, Conqueror of Greece*, Croom Helm, London, 1988.

Rhodhakis, P. *Τα Καβείρια Μυστήρια*, Paraskenio, Athens, 1997.

Rhodhakis, P. and Triandafillidis, K. *Σύγχρονη Γεωγραφία Ἄτλας τῆς Ἑλλάδος* (2 vols), Ekdhoseis Atlas, Athens, (n.d., *c.* 1965).

Rhodes, P. J. *A Commentary on the Aristotelian 'Athenaion Politeia'*, Clarendon Press, Oxford, 1981.

Rhodes, P. J. and Lewis, D. M. *The Decrees of the Greek States*, Clarendon Press, Oxford, 1997.

Richardson, R. 'Eretria; a historical sketch', *AJA* 7, 1891, 236–46; (reprinted in *Papers of the American School of Classical Studies at Athens* 6, 1890–7, 59–69).

—— 'A journey from Athens to Eretria', *Vacation Days in Greece*, Smith, Elder and Co., London, 1903.

Ridgway, D. 'Tra Oriente e Occidente: La Pithecusa degli Eubei', in *Gli Eubei in Occidente. Atti del diciottesimo Convegno di Studi sulla Magna Grecia, Taranto, 8–12 ottobre 1978*, Instituto per la Storia e l'Archeologia della Magna Grecia, Taranto, 1979, 65–81.

—— *The First Western Greeks*, Cambridge University Press, Cambridge, 1992.

Riis, P. *Sûkâs I. The North-East Sanctuary and the First Settling of Greeks in Syria and Palestine*, Publications of the Carlsberg Expedition to Phoenicia 1, Copenhagen, 1970.

Ringwood, I. 'Local festivals of Euboea chiefly from inscriptional evidence', *AJA* 33, 1929, 385–92.

Risch, E. 'Die Gleiderung der griechischen Dialekte in neuer Sichte', *MH* 12, 1955, 61–75.

Ritsonis, A. 'Ein Hermstele aus Eretria', *AAA* 17, 1984 [1985], 141–47.

Robertson, N. 'Government and society at Miletus, 525–442 BC', *Phoenix* 41, 1987, 356–98.

Robinson, H. *The Urban Development of Ancient Corinth*, American School of Classical Studies, Athens, 1965.

Roebuck, C. 'Some aspects of urbanization in Corinth', *Hesperia* 41, 1972, 96–105.

Roller, D. W. 'Graia and Eunostos', in J. Fossey and H. Giroux (eds), *Proceedings of the Third International Conference on Boiotian Antiquities, Montreal (31 October – 4 November 1979)*, J. C. Gieben, Amsterdam, 1985, 155–8.

—— *Tanagran Studies I: Sources and Documents on Tanagra in Boiotia*, J. C. Gieben, Amsterdam, 1989.

Rolley, C. 'Fouilles à Érétrie: archéologie, histoire et religion', *Rev.arch.* 1974, 307–11.

Room, A. *Room's Classical Dictionary. The Origins of the Names of Characters in Classical Mythology*, Routledge and Kegan Paul, London, 1983.

Rose, V. *Aristotelis qui ferebantur librorum fragmenta*, B. G. Teubner, Stuttgart, 1967.

Runciman, W. G. 'The origins of states; the case of Archaic Greece', *CSSH* 24, 1982, 351–77.

Rutherford, W. G. *The New Phrynichus, being a revised text of The 'Ecloga' of the Grammarian Phrynichus*, Macmillan, London, 1881.

Rutter, J. 'Ceramic evidence for northern intruders in southern Greece at the beginning of the late Helladic IIIC period', *AJA* 79, 1975, 17–32.

—— 'A group of distinctive pattern-decorated early Helladic III pottery from Lerna and its implications', *Hesperia* 51, 1982, 459–88.

—— 'Fine Gray-burnished pottery of the early Helladic III period: The ancestry of Gray Minyan', *Hesperia* 52, 1983, 327–55.

Sackett, L. H. and Popham, M. R. 'Lefkandi: a Euboean town of the Bronze Age and early Iron Age, 2100–700 BC', *Archaeology* 25, 1972, 8–19.

Sackett, L. H., Hankey, V., Howell, R. J., Jacobsen, T. W. and Popham, M. R. 'Prehistoric Euboea: contributions towards a survey', *BSA* 61, 1966, 33–112.

Sakellariou, M. B. *La migration grecque en Ionie*, Collection de l'Institute français d'Athènes 17, Athens, 1958.

—— *The Archaic Period*, Ekdotike Athenon and Heinemann, Athens and London, 1971.

Salmon, J. B. 'Political hoplites?', *JHS* 97, 1977, 84–101.

—— *Wealthy Corinth. A History of the City to 338 BC*, Clarendon Press, Oxford, 1986.

Sampson, A. ''Αρχαιότητες καὶ Μνημεία Εὐβοιας', *AD* 31, 1976 [1984], B1, 131–60.

—— *Η νῆσος Σκόπελος*, Athens, 1978.

—— *Εὐβοϊκὴ Κύμη I (Euboean Kyme I)*, Society for Euboian Studies, Khalkis Dept, Athens, 1981a.

—— *'Η Νεολιθικὴ καὶ ἡ Πρωτοελλαδικὴ I στὴν Εὔβοια*, Society for Euboian Studies, Khalkis Dept, Athens, 1981b.

—— *Μάνικα· μιά Πρωτοελλαδική πόλη στη Χαλκίδα* [*Manika; a Protohelladic Town in Chalkis*], Vol. 1: 1985; Vol. 2: 1988, Society for Euboian Studies, Athens, 1985–88.

—— 'Late Neolithic remains at Tharrounia, Euboea: a model for the seasonal use of settlements and caves', *BSA* 87, 1992, 61–101.

—— *Σκοτεινή Θαρρουνίων. Τό σπήλαιο, ο οικισμός καὶ τό νεκροταφείο* [*Skoteini, Tharrounia; The cave, the settlement and the cemetery*], Morfi, Athens, 1993a.

—— *Καλογεροβρύση. Ἕνας οἰκισμὸς τῆς Πρώιμης καὶ Μέσης Χαλκοκρατίας στὰ Φύλλα τῆς Εὐβοίας*, Athens, 1993b.

Sandbach, F. W. 'ΑΚΡΑ ΓΥΡΕΩΝ once more', *CR* 56, 1942, 63–5.

Sandys, J. E. *The Constitution of Athens. A Revised Text with an Introduction, Critical and Explanatory Notes, Testamonia and Indices*, Macmillan, London, 1893.

Sapouna-Sakellaraki, E. 'Εὐβοϊκὴ Κύμη', *AE* 1984 [1986], 151–60.

—— 'Nouvelles figurines cycladiques et petite glyptique du Bronze Ancien d'Eubée', *AK* 34, 1991, 3–12.

—— 'Un dépôt de temple et le sanctuaire d'Artémis en Eubée', *Kernos* 5, 1992, 235–63.

—— 'Mycenaean Kerinthos', in D. Evelly, I. Lemos and S. Sherratt (eds), *Minotaur and Centaur. Studies in the Archaeology of Crete and Euboea Presented to Mervyn Popham*, Tempus Reparatum, BAR International Series 638, Oxford, 1996, 106–10.

Schachermeyr, F. *Die griechische Rückerinnerung im Lichte neuer Forschungen*, Wien, 1983.

Schefold, K. 'The architecture of Eretria', *Archaeology* 21, 1968, 272–81.

Schmid, S. 'Decline or prosperity at Roman Eretria? Industry, purple dye works, public buildings and gravestones', *JRA* 12, 1999, 273–93.

Schumacher, R. 'Three related sanctuaries of Poseidon: Geraistos, Kalaureia and Tainaron', in N. Marinatos and R. Hågg, (eds), *Greek Sanctuaries. New Approaches*, Routledge, London, 1993, 62–87.

Schwyzer, E. *Dialectorum Graecarum Exempla Epigraphica Potiora*, Georg Olms, Hildesheim, 1960.

Seaford, R. *Reciprocity and Ritual. Homer and Tragedy in the Developing City-State*, Clarendon Press, Oxford, 1994.

Sealey, R. 'From Phemios to Ion', *REG* 70, 1957, 342–51.

—— 'Who was Aristogeiton?', *BICS* 7, 1960a, 33–43.

—— 'Regionalism in Archaic Athens', *Historia* 9, 1960b, 155–80.

—— 'Probouleusis and the sovreign assembly', *CSCA* 2, 1969, 247–69.

—— *A History of the Greek City States 700–338 BC*, University of California Press, Berkeley, CA, 1976.

Seltman, C. *Greek Coins. A History of Metallic Coins and Currency down to the Fall of the Hellenistic Kingdoms*, Methuen, London, 1933.

Servais, J. 'Herodote et la chronologie des Cypselides', *L'Ant.class.* 38, 1969, 28–81

Settas, N. ''Η 'Αγροτική 'Ανάπτυξις τῆς Εὐβοίας', *AEM* 10, 1963, 142–217.

Seyffert, O. *A Dictionary of Classical Antiquities; Mythology, Religion, Literature and Art*, Swan Sonnenschein, London, 1891.

Sfikas, G. *Self-propagating Trees and Shrubs of Greece*, Eleftheriades, Athens, 1978.

Shear II, L. 'Koisyra; three women of Athens', *Phoenix* 17, 1963, 99–112.

Shipley, G. *A History of Samos*, Clarendon Press, Oxford, 1987.

Siegel, L. J. *Corinthian Trade in the Ninth through Sixth Centuries BC*, unpublished PhD thesis, Yale University, New Haven, CT, 1978.

Smith, J. *Athens under the Tyrants*, Bristol Classical Press, Bristol, 1989.

Smith, W. *Dictionary of Greek and Roman Geography* (2 vols), Walton and Maberley; John Murray, London, 1856.

Smyth, H. W. *The Greek Dialects: Ionic*, Clarendon Press, Oxford, 1894.

—— *Greek Grammar*, Harvard University Press, Cambridge, MA, 1920/59.

Snodgrass, A. M. *Arms and Armour of the Greeks*, Cornell University Press, Ithaca, NY, 1967.

—— 'An historical Homeric society?', *JHS* 94, 1974, 114–25.

—— *Archaeology and the Rise of the Greek State*, Cambridge University Press, Cambridge, 1977.

—— *Archaic Greece: The Age of Experiment*, University of California Press, Berkeley, CA, 1980.

—— 'Two demographic notes (1: The size of Lefkandi; 2: Population in late eighth century Attica)', in R. Hågg (ed.), *The Greek Renaissance in the Eighth Century: Tradition and Innovation. Proceedings of the Second International Symposium at the Swedish Institute in Athens, 1–5 June 1981*, Stockholm, 1983, 167–71.

Sourvinou-Inwood, C. *'Reading' Greek Death, to the End of the Classical Period*, Clarendon Press, Oxford, 1995.

Spetsieri-Choremi, A. *Ancient Kerkyra*, Ministry of Culture Archaeological Receipts Fund Publications, Athens 1991.

Spyropoulos, T. G. and Chadwick, J. 'The Thebes Tablets II', *Supplementos a Minos* 4, 1975, 85–107.

Spyropoulos, T. G. and Chadwick, J. 'Mycenaean place-names from Thebes: the new evidence', in J. Killen, J. Melena and J.-P. Olivier (eds), *Studies in Mycenaean and Classical Greek presented to John Chadwick* (= *Minos* 20–2), Salamanca, 1987, 33–40.

Stanton, G. R. 'The introduction of ostracism and Alkmeonid propaganda', *JHS* 90, 1970, 180–3.

—— 'The territorial tribes of Korinth and Phleious', *CA* 5, 1986, 139–53.

Starr, C. *The Origins of Greek Civilization*, Jonathan Cape, London, 1962.

—— *The Economic and Social Growth of Early Greece, 800–500 BC*, Oxford University Press, New York, 1977.

Stavropoulos, D. ''Ερετρικὰ Μελετήματα', *AE* 1895, 125–68.

Streep, P. *Sanctuaries of the Goddess. Sacred Landscapes and Objects*, Bulfinch Press, Boston, 1994.

Stroud, R. 'Tribal boundary markers from Corinth', *CSCA* 1, 1968, 233–42.

Stubbings, F. H. 'The recession of Mycenaean civilization', *CAH*[3] II 2a, Ch. 27, 338–58.

Talamo, C. 'Il Mito di Melaneo: Oichalia e la Protostoria eretriese', *Contributions à l' Étude de la Colonisation et la Société eubéennes. Cahiers du Centre Jean Bérard*, No. 2, Naples, 1975, 27–36.

Talbert, J. (ed.) *Atlas of Classical History*, Croom Helm, London, 1985.

Tedeschi, G. 'La guerra lelantina e la cronologia eseodia', *Studi triestini di anchità in onore di Luigia Achillea Stella*, Università di Trieste, Trieste, 1975, 149–67.

Themelis, P. G. ''Ερετριακά', *AE* 1969, 143–78.

—— 'An eighth century goldsmith's workshop at Eretria', in R. Hågg (ed.), *The Greek Renaissance in the Eighth Century: Tradition and Innovation. Proceedings of the Second International Symposium at the Swedish Institute in Athens, 1–5 June 1981*, Stockholm, 1983, 157–65.

Theokhares, D. ''Εκ τῆς προϊστορίας τῆς Εὐβοίας καὶ Σκύρου', *AEM* 6, 1959, 279–328.

Thomas, C. G. 'From wanax to basileus. Kingship in the Dark Age', *Hispania Antiqua* 6, 1978, 187–206.

Thompson, H. A. 'Excavation of the Athenian agora, twelfth season, 1947', *Hesperia* 17, 1948, 149–96 (the section on ostraka is written by E. Vanderpool).

Thomsen, R. *The Origin of Ostracism – A Synthesis*, Gyldendal, Copenhagen, 1972.

Thomson, G. *Studies in Ancient Greek Society I: The Prehistoric Aegean*, Citadel, New York, 1965.

Thumb, A. *Handbook of the Modern Greek Vernacular*, T. & T. Clark, Edinburgh, 1912.

Tisdell, C. *The Political Attitudes of the Alkmeonidai in the VI Century BC*, unpublished MA thesis, University of New England, Armidale, New South Wales, 1989.

Tod, M. N. *A Selection of Greek Historical Inscriptions* (Vol. II): *From 403 to 323 BC*, Clarendon Press, Oxford, 1968.

Toepffer, J. *Attische Genealogie*, [Berlin,1889], Arno Press, New York, 1973.

Tomlinson, R. A. *Argos and the Argolid. From the End of the Bronze Age to the Roman Occupation*, Routledge and Kegan Paul, London, 1972.

Tritle, L. 'Eretria, Argoura and the road to Tamynai. The Athenians in Euboia, 348 BC', *Klio* 74, 1992, 131–65.

Tsigros, N. *Vyriotes in Australia*, The Wednesday Press, Norwood, 1989.

Ure, P. N. *The Origin of Tyranny*, Russell & Russel, London, 1966.

Ure, P. N. and Burrows, R. M. 'Excavations at Rhitsona', *BSA* 14, 1907/08, 226–318.

Vanderpool, E. 'Some black figured pottery from the Athenian agora', *Hesperia* 15, 1946, 120–65.

Vanderpool, E. and Wallace, W. P. 'The sixth century laws from Eretria', *Hesperia* 33, 1964, 381–91.

Vedder, R. *Ancient Euboea: Studies in the History of a Greek Island from the Earliest Times to 404 BC*, unpublished PhD thesis, University of Arizona, Tucson, AZ, 1978.

Vellacott, P. (trans.) *Euripides: Medea, Hecabe, Electra, Heracles*, Penguin Books, Harmondsworth, 1963.

Ventris, M. and Chadwick, J. *Documents in Mycenaean Greek*, 2nd edn, Cambridge University Press, Cambridge, 1973.

Vermeule, E. *Greece in the Bronze Age*, University of Chicago Press, Chicago, 1972.

Vial, C. 'A summary of the presentation of D. Knoepfler's thesis, "La cité de Ménédème" ', *Revue Historique*, 108^{272}, 1984, 241–5.

Viviers, D. 'Pisistratus' settlement on the Thermaic Gulf; a connection with Eretrian colonization',*JHS* 107, 1987, 193–5.

Volkmann, H. 'Ein Spartanergrab in Eretria (zu *IG* XII 9, 286)', *Klio* 31, 1938, 244–9.

—— 'Δόκιμα Χρήματα', *Hermes* 74, 1939, 99–102.

Vranopoulos, E. A. *'Ιστορία τῆς ' Αρχαίας Εὐβοίας, ἀπὸ τοὺς Προϊστορικοὺς Χρόνους ὡς καὶ τὴ 'Ρωμαιοκρατία,* (private printing) Athens, 1987.

Walbank, F. W. *Commentary on Polybius* II, Clarendon Press, Oxford, 1967.

Walbank, M. B. *Athenian Proxenies of the Fifth Century BC*, Samuel Stevens, Toronto, 1978.

Wallace, M. B. 'Early Greek Proxenoi', *Phoenix* 24, 1970, 189–208.

Wallace, W. P. *The History of Eretria to 198 BC*, unpublished PhD thesis, Johns Hopkins University, Baltimore, MD, 1936a.

—— 'An Eretrian proxeny decree of the early fifth century', *Hesperia* 5, 1936b, 275–84.

—— 'The demes of Eretria', *Hesperia* 16, 1947, 115–46.

—— *The Euboian League and its Coinage*, American Numismatic Society, Numismatic Notes and Monographs No. 134, New York, 1956.

Watson, M. O. *Class Struggles in Ancient Greece*, Victor Gollancz, London, 1947.

Webster, T. B. L. *From Mycenae to Homer*, Methuen, London, 1958.

Wenden, D. (trans.) *Hesiod and Theognis*, Penguin Books, Harmondsworth, 1979.

West, M. L. 'The Diktaean Hymn to the Kouros', *JHS* 85, 1965, 149–59.

—— *Studies in Greek Elegy and Iambus*, W. de Gruyter, Berlin, 1974.

—— *Introduction to Greek Metre*, Clarendon Press, Oxford, 1987.

—— *Hesiod. Theogony*, Clarendon Press, Oxford, 1997.

Wheeler, S. *An Island Apart*, Little, Brown & Co., London, 1992.

Whibley, L. *Greek Oligarchies; their Character and Organization*, Ares Publishers, Chicago, 1975.

Whitehead, D. 'From political architecture to Stephanus of Byzantium', in D. Whitehead (ed.), *Sources for the Ancient Greek Polis, Historia Einzelschriften* 87, 1994a, 9–86.

—— 'Site-classification and reliability in Stephanus of Byzantium', in D. Whitehead (ed.), *Sources for the Ancient Greek Polis, Historia Einzelschriften* 87, 1994b, 99–124.

Whitley, J. 'Early states and hero cults; a reappraisal', *JHS* 108, 1988, 73–182.

Wiegand, T. 'Dystos', *MDAI(A)* 24, 1899, 458–67.

von Wilamowitz-Möllendorf, U. 'Oropos und der Graer', *Hermes* 21, 1886, 91–115.

—— *Aristoteles und Athen* (2 vols), Weidmann, Berlin, 1893.

Wilhelm, A. 'Εὐβοϊκά', *AE* 1912, coll. 232–49.

Willemsen, F. 'Ostraka einer Meisterschale', *MDAI(A)* 106, 1991, 137–45.

Wilkes, J. *The Illyrians*, Blackwell, Oxford, 1995.

Will, E. *Korinthiaka. Recherches sur l' Histoire et la Civilisation de Corinthe dès Origines aux Guerres Médiques*, de Boccard, Paris, 1955.

—— 'Histoire grecque', *Rev.hist.* 238, 1967.

Woodhead, A. G. *The Greeks in the West*, Thames & Hudson, London, 1962.

Worley, L. *Hippeis. The Cavalry of Classical Greece*, Westview Press, Boulder, CO, 1994.

Yalouris, N. (ed.) *The Olympic Games in Ancient Greece. Ancient Olympia and the Olympic Games*, Ekdotike Athenon, Athens, 1982.

Yorke, V. 'Excavations at Abae and Hyampolis in Phocis', *JHS* 16, 1896, 291–312.

Zahrnt, M. *Die Herkunft der Chalkidier*, München, 1971.

Zimmern, A. *The Greek Commonwealth. Politics and Economics in Fifth Century Athens*, Clarendon Press, Oxford, 1915.

INDEX LOCORUM

Note Because the details of all ancient texts are given in endnotes, I thought it most convenient to the reader to locate all cited passages by chapter and endnote numbers: 1/49; 55 indicates that the text is referred to in Chapter 1, endnotes 49 and 55.

Literary texts

Aelian: *NA* 2, 8 (1/49); 7, 40 (1/40); 12, 34 (2/50); 17, 8 (1/40); *VH* 6, 1 (4/181; 7/66; 8/146; 9/68); 8, 16 (6/13).

Aelius Aristides: *Panath.* 95 (9/75); schol. (Sopater?) ad 189 (7/18).

Aineias Taktikos: 4, 1 (7/57).

Agathemeros: 5, 25 (1/2; 1/6).

Akhaios: ap. Ath. *Deipn.* 376a–b (4/237).

Akousilaos: emmendation of Probus *ad Verg. Ecl.* 2, 48 (2/89; 2/144).

Alkaios: Lobel/Page fr. 296 P2 (7/63).

Alkman: fr. 66 (2/171).

anonymous: Arkhilokhos? or Simonides Eretrieus/Karystios? (4/245; 247).

anonymous: *Certamen Hom. et Hes.* (2/158; 5/214).

Anthologia Graeca: 6, 156 Theodoridas (2/78).

Antigonos Karystios: *Mirab.* 78 (1/16).

Antonius Liberalis: 4 (2/125); 32 (2/127).

Apollodoros: 1, 7, 3 (2/171); 1, 9, 13 (2/176); 2, 1, 5 (2/176); 2, 2, 1 (2/176); 6, 7–11 (1/20).

Apollonios Rhodios: schol. ad 1, 143 (2/176); schol. ad 1, 419 (5/82; 5/85); schol. ad 1, 1126 (2/26); schol. ad 1, 1165d (2/252); 2, 392 (1/6); schol. ad 2, 527 (2/34); 4, 549–49a; 982–92g (5/62); 4, 990 and schol. ad loc. (5/58); 4, 1131 (2/35); 4, 1138 (5/62); schol. ad 4, 1138 (5/80); schol. ad 4, 1175 (1/6; 5/56; 5/62; 5/86); schol. ad 4, 1175b (5/56).

Aristokrates: ap. St. Byz. s.v. Ἀβαντίς (2/176).

Aristophanes: *Ach.* 878–9 with schol. ad loc. (1/47); schol. *Aves* 873 (2/49; 2/52); *Eq.* 1036–44 (7/62; 7/63); *Nu.* 46–7 with schol. ad locc. (6/54); 212 with schol. ad loc. (1/6); *Pax* 1000–01 with schol. ad loc. (1/47); schol. ad *V.* 715 (9/55).

Aristotle: ap. Str. 10, 1, 8 C447 (4/170); *de Audibilibus* 20, 831c (1/48); fr. 101 Rose (2/46); fr. 558 Rose (7/23); *HA* 4, 6 (1/49); 5, 15 (1/51); 30, 2 (4/254); *Mete.* 2, 8 (1/4); *Oec.* 1347a8 (6/91); *Pol.* 1252b (2/160); 1274a16–22 (4/177; 7/8); 1278a25 (4/191); 1285a–b (2/160; 6/8); 1289b27–1290a29 (4/176); 1289b33–6; 9 (4/174); 1289a36–40 (4/179; 5/153; 5/221);

1291a28–31 (4/193); 1298a34 (4/194); 1299b31–9 (4/202); 1299b36 (4/256); 1299b38–9 (4/206); 1304a29–30 (7/65); 1305a15–18 (4/258); 1305a37–41 (7/23); 1305a40 (6/111); 1306a32–3 (7/3); 1306a33–7 (4/184); 1306a36 (4/178; 4/183); 1313b24–5 (7/19); 1315b30–4 (6/41); 1316a29–30 (7/62); 1321a29 (4/191); 1323a8–9 (4/207).

[Aristotle]: *Ath pol.* 2, 2 (6/8); 6, 1 (6/8); 7, 4 (6/11); 14, 1 (6/26); 15, 2 (4/178; 4/182; 4/183; 5/111; 6/4; 6/40; 6/41; 6/43; 6/47; 6/58; 7/23); 17, 2 (6/13); 18, 2 (5/255); 19, 3 (7/79; 7/80; 8/114; 8/120); 22, 4 (9/59); 28, 2 (6/8).

[Aristotle]: *Phgn.* 812a8 (7/64).

Aristotle (of Khalkis?): ap. Str. 5, 4, 4 C243 (5/10); ap. Plut. *Amat.* (5/243).

Arkhemakhos ap. Str. 10, 3, 6 C465 (2/82; 5/241).

Arkhilokhos: frr. 1; 2; 6; 14 (5/208); fr. 3 (4/249; 5/160; 5/174).

Arrianos: ap. Eust. *ad DP* 520 (2/167).

Asios: ap. Ath. *Deipn.* 12, 5 525e–f (4/189).

Athenaios: *Deipn.* 1, 27–8 (1/47); 1, 30 (1/14); 2, 46c–d (1/33); 2, 54b (1/47; 2/202); 2, 54d (1/47); 3, 75e (1/47); 3, 88f (1/51); 4, 132c (1/50; 1/51); 4, 135e (1/49); 4, 160a–b (1/12; 1/69); 5, 201c (1/39; 1/40); 7, 284b (1/49); 7, 295c (1/49); 7, 302a (1/49); 7, 304d (1/49); 7, 330b (1/49); 8, 348b (7/23); 8, 348c (6/110); 9, 369f (1/42); 9, 376a–b (4/237) 12, 525e–f (4/189); 12, 536f–537a (9/12).

Bakkhylides: *Epinikon for Alexidamos of Metapontion*, 98–9 (5/81).

Cicero: *ND* 2, 33, 83 (2/71); *Verr.* 2, 4, 53 (5/82).

Curtius (Q.): 6, 11 (9/90).

Demosthenes: 18, 292 (8/16).

Didymos: schol. ad Pi. *Nem.* 2, 19 (7/77).

Diodoros Sikeliotes: 4, 37, 1–2 (2/117); 5, 65, 1 (2/23); 9, 44, 3 (9/72); 11, 60, 2 (2/113); 12, 59, 2 (1/4); 13, 48, 1 (5/72); 14, 17, 3 (6/67); 16, 7, 2 (7/60).

Diogenes Laertios: 1, 53 (6/16); 1, 68 (6/1; 8/18); 1, 72 (8/18); 2, 4 (2/131); 2, 133 (1/33); 2, 141 = Euphantos (5/148); 2, 141–2 (4/260).

Diogenianos Paroimiographos: 4, 59 (2/172).

Dion Khrysostomos: 2, 12 (2/18; 2/156); 79, 2 (1/60).

Dionysios Hallikarnaseus: *Ant.Rom.* 1, 61; 2, 70–1 (2/21); 7, 3, 2 (5/9).

Dionysios Kalliphronitis: 30 (2/112).

Dionysios Periegitikos: *Orbis descr.* 520 (1/6).

Duris: *FGrH* 76F60 (4/189).

Epaphroditos ap. St. Byz. s.v. Αἴδηψος (2/5; 2/81).

Ephoros: ap. Str. 5, 2, 4 C221 (2/237); *FGrH* 70F187 (9/24).

Etymologicum Magnum: 77, 42 ᾿Αμάρυνθος (2/89); 389, 2 Μάκρις (1/6).

Euenor: ap. Ath. *Deipn.* 2, 46 (1/33).

Euphantos: ap. D.L. 2, 241 (5/148).

Euphorion: *P. Oxy.* 2528 (1/6; 2/209).

Euphronios ap. schol. Ar. *Aves* 873 (2/49; 2/52).

Euripides: *Helen* 766–7 (1/20); 1126–31 (1/20); *Her.* 156–64 (5/188; 5/189); 185–8 (5/187); *IT* 1448–53; 1458–61 (2/60); schol. ad *Med.* 397 (2/40); schol. ad *Ph.* 208 (5/74).

Eustathios: *ad DP* 517 (1/6); 520 (1/6; 2/167); *ad Hom. 'Il.' pert.* 232 (2/176); 239, 34 (2/268); 278, 29–32 (9/91); 279, 30–32 (2/126; 2/249); 279, 44–5 (2/149); 280, 29–30 (2/134); 281, 40–2 (2/158); 282, 8–10 (2/18); 282, 15 (5/163); 535 (1/6); 536–41 (1/6); 1204 (2/21); *ad Hom. Od. pert.* 24, 465 (2/87).

Frontinus: *Strateg.* 3, 9, 7 (7/33).

Harpokration: Ταμύναι (8/127).

Hekataios: ap. Paus. 4, 2, 3 (1/1; 2/128; 5/135); ap. St. Byz. s.v. Κὺβος [ἢ Κυβώ] (5/101).
Hellanikos: *FGrH* 4F183 (9/24).
Herakleides: ap. Plut. *de mus.* 1122a (2/131).
Herakleides Lembos: *Politeiai*: 20 (8/98); 40 (7/22; 7/99); 55 (5/36); 63 (4/200).
Herakleides Pontikos; ap. Ath. *Deipn.* 536f–537a (9/12); ap. Athen. *Deipn.* 624c–e (5/247).
Hermippos: ap. Ath. *Deipn.* 1, 27–8 (1/47).
Herodotos: 1, 18 (5/205); 1, 20 (7/33); 1, 41–3 (8/113); 1, 52 (6/61; 8/113); 1, 56–7 (2/2); 1, 61 (6/4; 6/40; 6/58; 7/23; 8/116); 1, 64 (6/109; 7/23); 1, 82 (5/157); 1, 141; 143 (9/7); 1, 146 (2/15; 2/122; 2/145; 2/173; 2/238); 1, 171 (2/5); 3, 44–59 (7/108); 3, 49 (5/65); 3, 71 (9/65); 3, 136 (9/52); 4, 33 (5/96); 5, 28–34 (5/209; 5/213); 5, 30 (7/90; 9/2); 5, 31 (1/61; 7/91; 9/1; 9/3); 5, 31–2 (9/11); 5, 37 (9/8; 9/17); 5, 38 (9/10; 9/53); 5, 42 (7/106); 5, 49–51 (9/16); 5, 55–8 (7/93); 5, 57 (7/94); 5, 62 (7/80; 8/112); 5, 63 (6/16; 7/100; 7/110); 5, 67 (8/111); 5, 68 (8/99); 5, 73 (8/122); 5, 75–6 (8/21); 5, 77 (8/124; 8/125; 8/146); 5, 82 (7/121); 5, 90–1 (7/122); 5, 91 (7/84; 8/19); 5, 92 (7/2); 5, 94–5 (7/32); 5, 99 (5/234; 5/258; 9/23; 9/34); 5, 102 (8/130; 9/38); 5, 103 (9/37); 5, 103–4 (9/42); 5, 138 (7/111); 6, 21 (9/26); 6, 51 (8/21); 6, 58 (7/118); 6, 61 (8/21); 6, 65 (8/16); 6, 65–6 (8/21); 6, 87–93 (8/149); 6, 96 (9/82); 6, 97 (9/83); 6, 99 (9/15; 9/84); 6, 100 (9/61; 9/64); 6, 100–101 (9/67; 9/68; 9/69); 6, 101 (2/209; 2/211; 9/76); 6, 107 (2/209); 6, 108 (7/86); 6, 118 (9/83); 6, 125 (8/113); 7, 109 (5/124; 6/101); 7, 170 (5/69); 8, 1 (6/88; 8/144; 10/9); 8, 31 (2/112); 8, 46 (2/15; 2/238; 9/4; 10/8); 8, 73 (2/117); 8, 83 (9/53); 8, 134 (6/61); 8, 135 (6/106); 9, 75 (5/127).
Hesiod: *Aspis* 141 (2/228); *Op.* 38–9 (4/150; 5/215); 259–64 (4/186); 376–7 (5/31); 650–62 (5/214); 654–62 (4/135); frr. 3 (1/6); 47 (2/6).
Hesykhios: s.v. Ἀειναῦται (4/274); Ἐλιεύς (2/164) ἐρετριάζειν (8/119); Ἐρετριακὸς κατάλογος (9/56; 10/13); Κουρεῶτις (2/80); Τιτανίδα (1/6); χαλκιδίζειν (8/119).
Hippokrates: *Epid.* 6, 1, 2 (7/64).
Homer: *Il.* 1, 551 (5/81); *Il.* 2, 188–277 (4/282); *Il.* 2, 211–82 (5/193); *Il.* 218–9 (7/64); *Il.* 2, 505 (2/216); schol. ad *Il.* 2, 535 (1/6; 5/62); *Il.* 2. 536–49 (1/14; 1/19; 2/19; 2/156; 2/236; 3/39; 5/162; 7/46); schol. ad *Il.* 2, 536 (2/176); schol. ad *Il.* 2, 543 (5/189); *Il.* 3, 205–24 (4/282); schol. ad *Il.* 9, 557 (5/85); *Il.* 11, 138–42 (4/282); *Il.* 14, 159 (5/81); *Il.* 15, 355–6; 677 (3/41); *Il.* 16, 233 (2/104); *Il.* 23, 87 (5/217); *Il.* 23, 127 ad fin. (3/61); *Il.* 23, 678–80 (2/232); *Od.* 3, 414 (7/115); *Od.* 7, 321 (5/105).
[Homer]: *Hymn. ad Apoll. Pyth.* 219–21 (3/39; 4/110; 5/223).
Hyginus: 116 (1/20); 157 (2/176).
Ion: ap. Str. 1, 3, 19–20 C60 (1/4); ap. Paus. 7, 4, 9 (2/145).
Isokrates: 16, 25 (7/77); *Paneg.* 108 (1/62).
Kallimachos: fr. 200b Pfeiffer (2/53); ap. Plin. *HN* 4, 12, 8–9 (5/58); *Dieg. Iamb.* 10 (2/53); *Hymn.* 3, 188 (1/6); schol. ad *Hymn.* 4, 20 (1/6); *Hymn.* 4, 288–90 (5/96); *Hymn.* 4, 289 (1/12).
Kharon of Lampsakos: *FGrH* 262F10 (9/29).
Konon: *FGrH* 26F1, 44 (1/31; 4/242).
Korinna: frr. 5–10 (6/65); 666 (8/133).
Livy: 8, 22, 6 (5/10; 5/23); 32, 16, 10 (4/68); 32, 37, 4 (1/22); 35, 38, 3 (2/63; 7/70).
Lucan: schol. ad 3, 179–80 (2/112).
Lykophron: schol./Tzetzes ad *Alex.* 386 (1/20); schol./Tzetzes ad *Alex.* 679 (6/65); *Alex.* 1042 and schol./Tzetzes ad loc. (5/88); schol. ad *Alex.* 1093 (1/20); *Alex.* 1236–7 and schol./Tzetzes ad loc. (5/111).

Lysanias of Mallos: *On Eretria* ap. Plut. *de Her. malign.* 24 = *Mor.* 861b–c = *FGrH* 426F1 (8/137; 9/47).

Makarios: 4, 5 (1/40).

Menaikhmos: ap. Plin. *HN* 4, 64 (1/6).

Metagenes: Kock *CAF* I, 705 (2/52).

Nikephoros: (1/6).

Nikokrates: PMich. Inv. 4913 (5/137; 5/147).

Nikolaos Damaskenos: *FGrH* 90F52 (4/243); F58, 1–3 (7/33); F60 (4/201; 7/26; 8/84).

Nonnos: *D* 13, 166 (2/18); 21, 193–4 (5/62).

Orphika: 38, 14 (2/20).

Parthenios: *Myth.* 9 (5/210).

Pausanias: 1, 17, 6 (2/19); 1, 31, 2 (5/96); 1, 31, 5 (2/51); 2, 16, 2 (2/176); 2, 21, 2 (2/176); 4, 2, 3 (1/1; 2/128); 4, 8, 3; 4, 18, 3 (2/114); 4, 32, 5 (6/106); 4, 32, 9 (2/30); 4, 34, 9–11 (2/116; 2/122; 2/137); 5, 9, 6 (8/85); 5, 13, 3 (1/49); 5, 22, 2 (5/94); 5, 22, 4 (2/174); 5, 22, 14 (1/6); 5, 27, 9 (5/70); 7, 2, 3 (2/173); 7, 4, 9 (2/145; 2/173); 7, 14, 7 (5/152); 7, 19, 22 (8/93); 8, 1, 5 (1/40); 8, 5, 1 (2/202); 9, 14, 3–4 (5/254); 9, 19, 3 (2/231); 9, 19, 7 (2/48); 9, 22, 1 (6/65); 9, 22, 2 (8/132); 10, 6, 6 (4/147); 10, 35, 1 (2/176).

Philostratos: *VA* 1, 23–4 (9/88); 1, 24 (1/49).

Photios: s.v. *Ἐρετριακὸς κατάλογος* (9/56; 10/13).

Phrynikhos: 88 (2/161).

Pindar: *Nem.* 1, str. 1 (5/88); schol. (Didymos) ad *Nem.* 2, 19 (7/77); schol ad *Nem.* 5, 37 (2/209); *Nem.* 10, 52 (7/115); schol. ad *Ol.* 1, 11 (2/68); schol. ad *Ol.* 6, 149 (1/18); schol. ad *Pyth.* 8, 73 (2/176).

Plato: *Alc.* 1, 121a (7/77); *Cra.* 434c (2/257); *Cri.* 51c (7/114); *Epigr.* 9 (8/10); 13 (8/10; 9/94); *Hipparch.* 228b (6/16); *Lg.* 698d (9/87); 740e (5/30); *Mx.* 237b–238b (7/114); 240a (8/135); 240c (9/62).

Pliny: *HN* 2, 204 (5/92); 4, 2 (2/6; 2/112); 4, 8 (5/58); 4, 11 (5/126); 4, 18 (5/124); 4, 53 (2/6); 4, 63 (1/2); 4, 64 (1/4); 4, 71 (4/237); 10, 48 (1/40); 11, 42 (1/48); 14, 76 (1/14); 16, 197 (1/35); 25, 94 (1/36); 32, 18 (1/49); 36, 48 (1/60); 36, 49 (1/60).

Plutarch: *Agis* 7, 3 (6/52); *Alc.* 1, 1 (7/77); *Amat.* = *Mor.* 760f–761a (5/182; 5/218; 5/242; 5/253); *Amat. narr.* = *Mor.* 774c (2/158; 2/230; Appendix 1/3, n. 1); *Cam.* 19 (5/254); *Cleom.* 1, 1–2 (6/52); *Comm. in Hes. op.* = *Mor.* fr. 84 (4/136; 5/214; 5/217; 5/220); *Conv. sept. sap.* = *Mor.* 153f (4/248; 5/214); *de def. or.* 43 = *Mor.* 434a (1/60); *de garr.* = *Mor.* 510b (9/67); *de Hdt. malign.* 24 = *Mor.* 861b–d (5/219; 9/24; 9/29; 9/33; 9/44; 9/63); *de mus.* = *Mor.* 1132a (2/132); *Lac. apophtheg.* 67 = Mor. 236c (7/103); *Lyc.* 6, 4 (4/283); 27, 2 (7/118); *mul. virt.* = *Mor.*254f (5/210); *Per.* 23, 2 (4/181; 7/66); *peri ton en Plataiais Daidalon* = *Mor.* fr. 3 (5/62); *Phoc.* 13, 4 (2/140); *Quaest. conviv.* 3, 9 = *Mor.* 657e (5/62); 5 = *Mor.* 674f–675a (5/217); 6 = *Mor.* 674f–675a (5/214); *Quaest. Graec.* 11 = *Mor.* 293b (4/217; 5/56; 5/166); 22 = *Mor.* 296d–e (2/170; 2/171; 2/241); 30 = *Mor.* 298a–b (5/n. 225); 31 = *Mor.* 298b–c (4/n. 121); 32 = *Mor.* 298c–d (4/n. 272; 274); 40 = *Mor.* 300d–301a (2/260); *Reg. et imp. apopth.* 14 = *Mor.* 185 e (10/7); *Sol.* 1 (6/13); 2 (6/15); 4–5 (6/13); 8, 4 (6/68); 13, 2 (7/15); 14, 2 (6/8); 14, 3–4 (7/15; 7/67); 18, 2 (7/8); 22 (6/12); 29, 1 (6/26); *Sull.* 26 (1/4); *Them.* 11 (10/7); 27 (9/27; 10/7); *Thes.* 5, 35 (2/19).

[Plut.] *Parall. Graec. et Rom.* = *Mor.* 307c (4/147).

Pollux: 5, 37; 5, 40 (1/40); 8, 91 (2/70).

Polyainos: *Strateg.* 1, 9 (2/209); 1, 23 (6/113; 7/23); 8, 36 (5/210); 8, 37 (7/64).

Polybius: 18, 11, 5 (1/22).

Porphyrios: ap. Eust. *ad Hom. 'Il.' pert.* (2/158); *de Abst.* 3, 17; 4, 16 (2/55).

Priscianus: *Perieg.* 514 (1/6); 544 (1/6).
Probus: *ad Verg. Ecl.* 2, 48 (2/87); emended by Akousilaos (2/89).
Ptolemy: *Geogr.* 3, 15, 25 (1/25); 3, 13 (5/126).
Seneca: *QN* 4, 17, 25 (1/4).
Servius: *in Verg. Aen.* 3, 131 (2/31); 8, 285 (2/21); 9, 260 (1/20).
Simonides: *Anth. Plan.* 26 (8/127).
Skylax: *Peripl.* 26–7 (5/94; 5/124); 58 (1/2; 5/16; 5/135); 110 (5/101); 111 (5/104).
Skymnos: 411–2 (5/93); 567–9 (1/6); 575 (2/171); 579–86 (5/136); 685 (5/126).
Solinus: 27, 7 (5/103).
Solon: frr. 32–4; 36 (7/15); 33 ap. Plut. *Sol.* 14 (7/62).
Sophokles: *OC* 128–33 (2/87); *Skyrioi* Loeb fr. 5b (2/60); *Tr. passim* (3/76); *Tr.* 212–14 (5/84); 260–8 (5/189); schol. ad *Tr.* 345 (2/131).
Statius: schol. ad *Achill.* 1, 93 (1/20); *Silv.* 1, 2, 260–3 (5/12)
Stephanos Byzantios: s.v. 'Αβαντίς (1/6; 2/176; 5/94); Αἰγιαλός (2/209) Αἴδηψος (1/59); Βοιωτία (5/137); Βολισσός (2/145); Γέφυρα (7/95); Δίκαια (5/124); Δύστος (4/143); 'Ελευθερίς (2/171; 2/240) 'Ελλοπία (7/49); 'Ερέτρια (2/126; 2/152; 4/36); 'Εστίαια (2/135); 'Ιστίαια (2/135); Κορόπη (4/110; 5/142); Κύβος [ἢ Κυβῶ] (5/101); Κύμη (5/20); Μεθώνη (5/112); Μήκιστον (8/85); Νέμεα (2/14); Οἰχαλία (2/128); ῎Οκωλον (5/112); 'Ορικός (5/94); Περαία (8/95); 'Ράκελος (5/111); Σκάβαλα (5/125; 6/45); Σκίαθος (5/134); Σκιάς (2/128; 5/135); Ταμύνα (7/96); Τελέθριον (1/8); 'Ωρωπός (5/142).
Strabo: 1, 3, 16 C58 (1/4); 5, 2, 4 C221 (2/103; 2/112; 2/237); 5, 4, 4 C243 (5/10); 5, 4, 7 C246 (5/12); 5, 4, 9 C247 (5/9; 5/44; 5/149); 6, 1, 6 C257 (5/35); 6, 2, 4 C270–1 (5/88); 7, 7, 1–2 C321 (2/105; 2/114; 2/171; 2/172); 7 fr. 20 (5/109); 7 fr. 32 (5/126); fr. 36 (5/126; 5/127); 7, frr. 43[44]; 46 [47] (5/124; 6/100); 7 fr. 50 [51] (2/22); 8, 3, 6 (2/128); 8, 3, 21 C348 (2/11); 8, 3, 25 (2/128); 8, 6, 8 C 371 (1/18); 8, 6, 13 C373 (2/114); 8, 6, 20 C378 (5/200; 7/2); 9, 2, 10 C404 (2/87; 7/95; 8/55); 9, 5, 10 C434 (2/112); 9, 5, 16 C437 (1/60); 10, 1, 1 C444 (4/237); 10, 1, 2 C444 (1/2; 1/6); 10, 1, 3 C445 (1/6; 2/166; 2/171; 2/242; 5/77; 9/91); 10, I, 4 C445–6 (1/34); 10, 1, 5 C446 (1/25; 7/49); 10, 1, 6 C446 (1/60); 10, 1, 8 C446 (2/171; 2/242; 4/170; 4/190; 5/33; 5/117); 10, 1, 9 C447 (1/4; 1/58; 2/68; 5/38); 10, 1, 10 C448 (2/42; 2/64; 2/126; 2/128; 2/177; 2/242; 2/243; 2/249; 2/257; 2/269; 4/35; 4/56; 4/216; 4/223; 5/165; 8/134); 10, 1, 12 C448 (5/149; 5/155); 10, 1, 13 C448–9 (5/163); 10, 1, 14 C449 (1/16); 10, 1, 15 C449 (4/217; 5/17; 5/61; 5/82; 5/85); 10, 3, 1 C462 (2/3); 10, 3, 3 C464 (2/3); 10, 3, 6 C465 (2/3; 2/4; 2/82); 10, 3, 19 C472 (2/3; 2/5; 2/17; 2/82); 13, 3, 6 C622 (5/22); 14, 1, 4 C634 (2/145); 14, 1, 20 C639 (5/83); 14, 1, 28 C643 (4/175); 14, 2, 10 C654 (5/12); 16, 1, 25 C747 (9/91).
Suidas: s.v. 'Αβαντίς (1/6); Διαγόρας (8/14); Κρεώφυλος (2/128); πάντα ὀκτώ (8/84); Σιμονίδης, Καρύστιος ἢ 'Ερετριεύς (4/247); χαλκιδίζειν (2/172; 2/174).
Theodoridas: *Anth. gr.* 6, 156 (2/78).
Theognis: 392 (5/46); 757–86; 773; 775–6 (7/42); 783–4 (5/190; 7/47); 885–94 (7/35; 7/45; 7/50).
Theokritos: schol ad 2, 12 (2/40; 8/43).
Theophrastos: *HP* 4, 5, 2 (1/16); 5, 1, 5–8 (1/35); 8, 8, 5 (1/12); 9, 15, 4 (1/16); 9, 9, 15, 8 (1/16); 9, 20, 5 (1/34).
Theopompos: *FGrH* 115F149 (4/143; 8/91).
Thucydides: 1, 13, 3 (5/66; 5/224); 1, 13, 4 (5/191); 1, 15, 1 (5/29); 1, 15, 3 (5/151; 5/195; 6/6); 1, 25, 4 (5/63); 1, 38, 1 (5/67); 1, 41, 1 (8/149; 9/50); 1, 98, 2 (2/113); 1, 100; 1, 102 (5/127); 1, 128, 6 (9/72); 2, 4, 4 (7/61); 2, 9, 3 (8/80); 2, 13, 1 (5/156); 2, 23, 3 (5/146); 2, 37, 1 (8/16); 2, 99, 3 (5/130); 3, 68, 5 (7/65); 3, 70–85 (5/72); 3, 89, 2 (1/4); 3, 91, 3

(5/146); 4, 44, 1 (8/80; 8/81); 4, 61, 2 (2/122); 4, 111, 2 (7/61); 5, 72, 23 (7/45); 6, 4, 5 (5/10); 6, 4, 6 (5/68); 6, 7, 3 (5/110); 6, 22 (5/168); 7, 28, 1 (6/67); 7, 57, 4 (2/15; 2/122; 2/238); 8, 60, 1–3 (5/140; 6/67); 8, 95 (5/140; 5/141; 10/14).

Tyrtaios: fr. 12 Loeb (7/118).

Tzetzes: ad Lyc. *Alex.* 386 (1/20); ad Lyc. *Alex.* 651 (2/11); ad Lyc. *Alex.* 1093 (1/20); ad Lyc. *Alex.* 1236–7 (5/111).

Varro: *RR* 8, 2, 4 (1/40).

Velleius Paterculus: 1, 4 (2/171).

Xenophon: *An.* 7, 8, 8 (9/72); *HG* 3, 1, 6 (9/72); 3, 3, 3 (7/118).

[Xenophon]: *Lac.* 15, 9 (7/118).

Inscriptions

Altherr-Charon, A. and Lasserre, F. 'Heracles à Érétrie, une nouvelle inscription agonistique', *Études de Lettres,* Lausanne, IV 4, 1981, 25–35 (2/68).

Apostolidis, S. & H. '"Ενας ὅρος ἀπὸ Δύστο Εὐβοίας', *Horos* 1990/1, 131–3 (8/31).

ATL III 1950, 294 (8/145).

Brenne, S. 'Ostraka and the process of ostrakophoria', in W. Coulson *et al.* (eds), *The Archaeology of Athens and Attica under the Democracy*, Oxford, 1994, 15–6 and Fig. 10 (8/117).

Cairns, F. 'A herm from Histiaia with an agonistic epigram of the fifth century BC', *Phoenix* 37, 1983, 16–37 (2/68).

Corpus Inscriptionum Atticarum (*CIA*): II, 467 (2/70).

Daux, G. 'Note sur l' "horos phratricos" d' Érétrie', *BCH* 74, 1954, 282–4 (8/69).

Dittenberger, W. and Purgold, K. *Die Inschriften von Olympia*, Berlin, 1896, 248 (8/150).

Dunant, C. and Thomopoulos, J. 'Inscriptions de Céos, I: Traité d' isopolité', *BCH* 78, 1954, 316–22 (8/33); modified by D. Lewis, 'The Federal Constitution of Keos', *BSA* 57, 1962, 1–4 (8/58).

Inscriptiones Graecae (*IG*): I: 339 (10/1); I²: 90+ (8/60); 108+ (*SEG* 10, no. 124) ll. 6–7 (5/132); 376 (2/209); I³: 41 (6/83); 244 (8/41); II²: 18 (8/87); 230 (4/278; 8/64); IX 1: 682 (4/217; 4/221); 688 (4/217); 4, 1065 + XII 5, I, 128 (5/213); XII 3: 33c (8/13); XII 5: 594 (4/210; 8/35); 647 (4/210; 4/226); XII 8: 347 (6/85); XII 9: 2 (4/235); 53 (2/12); 54 (2/12); 56 (2/161; 2/171; 9/36); 58 (2/12; 8/53); 59 (2/12; 8/53); 75 (2/170); 89 (9/36); 90 (2/171; 4/276; 8/32); 90–95a (2/12); 139 (8/32); 187 (4/284); 189 (2/173; 2/257; 4/276; 8/31; 8/32; 8/44); 191 (2/68; 2/111; 4/279; 8/89; 9/78); 192 (8/31); 196 (4/284; 8/25); 197 (4/284); 198 (4/284; 8/25); 205/6 (4/279); 209 (4/279); 210 (8/103); 211 (4/205; 4/255); 212 (4/279); 213 (2, p. 29; 2/112; 2/267); 217 (4/279); 219 (4/279); 225 (4/217; 8/102); 232 (4/285); 234 (5/189); 236 (2/68; 4/205; 8/25); 237 (2/68; 8/25); 241 (2/139; 5/143; 8/40; 8/47; 8/74; 8/82; 8/89); 244 (8/89); 245 (2/252; 8/89); 246 (2/209; 8/89; 9/36); 249 (8/89); 257 (5/189); 258 (2/41); 259 (2/24); 260 (2/54; 4/120); 263 (2/10); 267 (8/93); 269 (2/17); 272 (5/189); 285 (7/119); 286 (7/112; 7/116); 296 (7/71; 7/74); 299 (8/14); 300 (7/119); 681 (2/174); 744 (5/145); 772 (5/145); 900; 945 (2/79); 952 (5/189); 954 (2/65); 1050 (2/174); 1105 (2/174); 1189 (2/252); 1190 (2/68); XII 9 Addenda et Ultima: 1273/1274 (4/239; 6/69; 6/71; 6/72); XII Suppl.: 184 (2/24); 549 (2/11; 2/254; 2/256; 2/257; 2/264; 4/214; 4/284; 8/3; 8/55; 8/68; 8/103; 8/104); 555 (4/213; 4/263; 8/86; 8/89; 8/105; 8/106); 572+560; 559 (2/41); XII 9 Testamonia et Notae: Inscrr. 5 = *Inschr. Magn.* 48; 6 = Rhem *Milet* I, 3, n. 154 (8/140).

Knoepfler, D. 'Le héros Narkittos et le système tribal d'Erétrie', in M. Bats and B. d'Agostino (eds), *Euboica. L'Eubea e la presenza euboica in Calcida e in Occidente*, Naples, 1998, 105–8 (8/55).

Meiggs, R. and Lewis, D. M. *Inscriptions* 4 (8/9).

Meritt, B. D. *Corinth; Results of Excavations*, VIII, Pt 1: The Greek Inscriptions, No. 11 (8/73).

Meritt, B. D. 'Greek Inscriptions "26: Stele of the Gephyraioi"', *Hesperia* 8, 1939, 80–81 (7/93).

Meritt, B. D. 'Greek Inscriptions "17: The Genos of the Gephyraioi"', *Hesperia* 9, 1940, 86–96 (7/93).

Papyrus Rylands 1, 18 = *FGrH* 105F1 (6/2).

Raubitschek, A. *Dedications* 6 (7/76); 330 (7/73).

REG 1932, 217; re-ed. by D. Knoepfler in: 'Karystos et les Artemisia d' Amarynthos', *BCH* 96, 1972, 282–301, with commentary (2/63).

Supplementum Epigraphicum Graecum (*SEG*): 10, 1949, item 304 (2/209); 12, 1955, items 400a,b; 401 (5/53); 13, 1956, item 13 = Pritchett, W. 'Attic stelai' I, *Hesperia* 22, 1953, 252 (8/148); 15, 1958, item 561 (5/53); 17, 1960, item 431 (5/53); 22, 1982, items 858; 859 (5/53); 30, 1980, item 55 (8/66); 31, 1981, item 184 (1/1); 806 (8/6); 32, 1982, item 855 (2/171); 33, 1983, item 716 (2/68); 1621 (6/91); 34, 1984, item 898 (4/270); 37, 1987 item 737 (2/266); 39, 1989, items 939; 940; 941 (5/53); 47, 1997, item 1347 (8/2).

Willemsen, F. 'Ostraka einer Meisterschale', *MDAI(A)* 106, 1991, 144–5 and pl. 26 (8/116; 8/117).

GENERAL INDEX

Note Any terms in Greek script are transliterated in the index into the forms used throughout the text of the book.

Abai, 45–6, 56, 58, 67
Abantes, 3, 27–30, 36, 38, 41–7, 51, 53–4, 58–9, 64–7, 70, 76–7, 81, 111, 113, 141, 151, 158, 160, 171, 253
Abantia/Amantia (in Epeiros), 48, 46, 67, 151, 175
Abantis (*phyle* name at Khalkis), 55, 67
Abantis/Abantias (alternative name for Euboia q.v.)
Abas (eponym of the Abantes), 46, 53, 58, 67, 254
Abas (son of Lynkeus), 46, 67
Adrastos, 58, 254
aei (as an early adverbial equivalent of *epi*), 139–40
aeinautai (*arkhe* at Miletos), 127
aeinautai (*koinon* at Eretria), 23, 127, 137
Aeolic speech, 43, 45–6, 55
aeimnemones (suggested as an amendment for *amnemones* q.v.), 140
Africa, 59, 151–2
Agathoi see Kaloi k'agathoi
Agathos Daimon, 109
Agiad kings, 239, 281
Agis IV, 190, 203
agomenoi (middle participle of *agō* – to lead/accompany), 182, 275, 285
agonistic warfare, 59, 157, 178, 214
agon (pl. *-es*), 178, 180
Aidepsos, 15, 21, 24, 58
Aigale (deme of the Eretrias), 30–1, 50–1, 68–9, 282
Aigihaliān-de see Aigale
Aigilea *see* Aigale
Aigina, 176, 186, 197, 199–200, 202, 205, 226, 229, 255–6, 258, 261–2, 273, 277, 283, 302
Aiglephe(i)ra (deme of the Eretrias), 138
Aiklos and Kothos, 45, 54–5, 67, 77
Ainaria, 144, 172
Aineia *see* Rhaikelos
Aiolos, 45
Aiskhines Nothonos, Euphorbos Alkimakhou and Philagros Kyneou (Eretrian traitors in 490), 280, 286
aisymnetes/dialaktes, 184, 201
Aitolia, 27, 29–30, 38, 44, 57
Akarnanes, 27
Akarnania, 27, 254
akeryktos polemos (undeclared war between Athens and Aigina), 186
Akhaians, 115
Akheron (deme of the Eretrias?), 58
a-ki-a$_2$-ri-ja (also spelt *a$_3$-ki-a$_2$-ri-ja-de*) *see* Aigale
Akte (Athos), 153

Al Mina, 77, 85, 88–9, 98, 117, 141–2, 160, 166, 167, 171
Albania, 22, 148, 151, 174–5
Aliverion (mod. Aliveri), 16, 143, 264
Alkibiades, 221, 233
Alkimakhos, son of Khairion, 221
Alkmaion [eponymous ancestor(s) of the Alkmaionidai], 253–4
Alkmaion (grandfather of Kleisthenes), 190
Alkmaion (identified with Narkissos q.v.), 267
Alkmaionidai, 178, 185, 188, 190–1, 201, 210, 221, 224, 229–30, 239, 253–6, 259, 267
Alkmeonides, 198–9
Alkon (Attic hero), 67
alliances, 156, 162–4, 168, 170–1, 183, 200, 207
Almiropotamos, 42
alphabet, 72, 86, 89, 147, 173, 275
'alternative' historical tradition, 276
Amarousi(on) *see* Athmonon
a-ma-ru-to-de (Amarunthon-de 'to Amarynthos'), 49
Amarynthia *see* Amarysia
Amarynthian Artemis *see* Amarysia
Amarynthis *see* Amarysia
Amarynthos: festival of Artemis at *see* Artemiria; *Kouros*-god at, 31, 33, 37, 42, 59, 62, 148, 254; *see also* Zeus; sanctuary of Artemis *see* Amarysion; town and deme of the Eretrias, 6, 8, 14, 16, 24, 26, 31–3, 36–7, 42, 45–6, 48–9, 51–2, 55, 58, 60, 74, 83, 85, 108, 113, 118, 123, 281–2
Amarynthos 'convention', 157–9, 161, 298–9
Amarysia (Artemis at Eretria), 28, 30–5, 42, 51, 54, 58–9, 64, 83, 108–9, 113, 116, 122, 124, 148, 150, 185, 195, 219–20, 254
Amarysia (at Athmonon in Attica), 32, 54–5
Amarysion, 31–6, 60, 69, 116, 122, 159, 195–6
Amathous, 276
Ambrakia, 190, 295
amicitia see philia, xenia
amnemones (at Knidos), 140, 245. *See also probouloi*
Amphiaraos, 37, 62, 67, 191–2, 253–4, 267
Amphiastai, 192
Amphictyony of Thermopylae, 169, 299
Amphidamas, 66, 83, 109, 113, 124, 134, 162, 165–6, 173, 180
Amphiktyon, 44, 53
Amphytrion, 161–2 *see also* Amphiktyon
Anatolia, 36, 47
Andros, 10, 93, 96, 98, 122–3, 130, 149, 153, 166, 168, 219, 270 *see also* Zagora
'animal style', (Lefkandiot pottery style) 75
Ankhimolios, 225–9
Antigonos Gonatas, 126, 178
Antigonos Monopthalmos, 296
Antileon, 180, 218–19, 232
Apatouria, 36
apella, 120
Aphidna (Attic deme), 223
apoikia see colonisation
Apollo, 29–30, 45, 58–9, 62, 65, 77, 90–1, 100–1, 105–09, 114, 124, 144, 151, 155, 213, 293; Daphnephoros 29, 31, 105–9, 114–15, 130, 132, 195; Tamynaios 58; Trimoridios 266
Ares, 43, 61, 158, 258
Arethousa, 67, 150–1, 169, 175
Argeios [son of Peisistratos (Iophon?)], 190
Argolis, 37–8, 40, 44, 48–9, 55, 58
Argos, 46, 129, 150, 157, 169, 181, 190–1, 198, 200, 221–2, 226, 253, 278, 295
Argous(s)a, 175
Aristagoras, 164, 222, 270–7, 285
Aristaios *see Kouros*-god at Amarynthos
Aristogeiton *see* Harmodios and Aristogeiton, tyrannicides
Aristogeiton Kydimakhou, 224, 234, 253
Aristoteles Kheiloniou, 237–9, 251–2, 262

arkhe, 119, 121, 125–7, 140
arkheproboulos (at Karystos), 125
arkheproboulos (at Eretria?), 126
Arkhidamos II, 178
Arkhilokhos, 83, 113, 124, 158–65
Arkhinos of Ambrakia, 190
arkhon, 124, 126–7, 140, 184, 194, 201, 221, 233, 248, 266–7, 279, 288–9, 295
arkhon-basileus (at Athens) *see basileus*-magistrate
arkhos, 44, 126, 140, 194
Arotria (early name for Eretria), 94, 130
arotreuō (to plough) *see* Arotria
Artabanes, 289
Artaphernes, 222, 271, 276
Artemiria, 28–9, 31–6, 41, 60–1, 220, 240
Artemis, 23, 28, 36, 51, 94, 107–9, 113, 123, 174–5, 196, 266, 293 *see also* Amarysia; and human sacrifice to, 33, 81; and Kolainis, 32, 60–1; as Hekate, 30–3, 60, 287; as Eileithyia, 59–60; as Iphigeneia, 33, 185; as kourotrophos, 60; as Selene, 60; at Athmonon in Attica, 54; at Kerkyra, 150; Brauronia, 202; 'in-the-city', 107; Olympia, 33, 61, 108, 133; Ortygia, 150; Parthenos Agrotera (virgin huntress), 35, 62; Phylake Metaxy (Guardian, Who stands between), 41, 59, 64, 240; Proseoa at Histiaia, 34, 61–2; Tauropolos, 33; Triklaria, 266
Artemision, 4, 8, 28, 49, 61, 205, 260, 288
artisans, 39, 79, 80, 85–6, 89, 95, 104, 130, 145, 162, 184, 207
Asia Minor, 10, 28–9, 36, 39, 40, 43, 65, 93, 135, 141, 143, 183, 209, 258–59, 268, 272, 276, 281–82, 288–9, 299
Asine *see* ex As
Asopis (alternative name of Euboia q.v.), 21
Asopos, 30, 55–6, 71, 155, 302
Asty (*wasty*), 249
astynomoi (at Keos), 137
Athene, 33, 221
Athenian League, 260, 289
Athenian Tribute Lists, 154, 176–7, 232, 248, 289
Athens, 26–9, 33, 35–6, 45, 47, 49, 54–5, 57, 59, 63, 65, 68, 70, 76, 87, 103, 116–18, 121, 123–4, 126, 128, 131, 133, 136, 139, 153, 155–6, 169–70, 177–8, 182, 184–8, 190–2, 195, 197–200, 205, 208–12, 218, 220–30, 233, 236, 239–41, 243, 245–6, 248–9, 252–63, 266, 270–84, 288–9, 295–6, 299, 301–02
Athmonon, {deme of Attica [mod. (A)Marousi(on)]}, 32, 54–5, 70, 172
Athos, 153–4
atimia, 255
Attica, 1, 10, 15, 22, 32–3, 35, 54–6, 61. 65, 67, 75–7, 84, 93, 114, 129, 142, 183–5, 189, 191–2, 196, 198, 201, 203, 208, 210, 223, 225, 227–9, 233–4, 236–7, 240–1, 243, 247–49, 252–6, 264–5, 281, 286, 288
Aulis, 9, 32–3
Aulon(arion) [in the Eretrias (mod. Avlonari)], 33, 64, 143, 175
Aulon (Khalkidian), 175
autochthonous inhabitants, 27, 39, 42, 130
Autonomos, 289
Axios River, 153, 189

Bakkhiadai, 115, 137, 163, 207
basileus (pl. *-eis*), 44, 52–3, 66, 83, 86, 106–7, 109, 113–14, 117–18, 120, 124, 136, 138, 165
basileus-magistrate, 106, 114, 124
Basilidai, 115
Battle of Lade, 278, 283
Battle of Mantineia (419), 158, 214
Battle of Salamis, (480), 168, 237, 270, 289
Battle of Sepeia (495), 190, 278
Battle of Solygeia (425), 265
Battle of the Champions (546), 200, 222
Battle of the Pamphylian Sea, 275–6, 282
Bay of Aliveri, 7, 282

Bay of Avlona (in Albania), 148, 151
boar-tusks helmet, 53
Boiotia, 1, 29, 37, 39, 45–6, 48–50, 54–6, 59, 62, 65, 67, 70–1, 77, 136, 155, 168, 177, 183, 185, 189, 191, 198, 203, 221, 223, 230, 254, 256–8, 274, 289, 293, 301–2
Boudion (deme of the Eretrias), 30, 66
Boudoros River, 7, 216
boule, 118–22, 125–6, 136–40, 172, 237, 244–5, 248, 252, 265
bouleutai see boule.
bouleuomenon, to, (the power to deliberate; those who had that power), 118–19
Brauron, 33, 183, 185, 192, 201
Bronze Age, 26, 35, 36, 38, 48, 57, 67, 69–70, 74, 77, 111, 181
Bronze bull dedicated by the Eretrians at Olympia, 149, 262, 269
burial practices, 38, 46, 52, 54, 67, 74–7, 81–7, 89, 90–2, 105, 109–10, 114, 117, 133, 146–7, 155, 167, 171, 173, 212, 220, 227–8, 230–1, 234–5, 257, 262, 283–4

capital (financial), 44, 46, 51–2, 78, 116–18
cavalry, 34, 116, 127, 135, 138, 157, 159, 161, 168–70, 178, 181, 198, 209, 214, 226, 230, 247, 265, 282–3
Centaur of Lefkandi, 79, 84, 88
chariots, 34–5, 38, 82–3, 89, 122
Chios, 43, 45–6, 65, 136, 141, 164, 171, 195, 201, 203, 205, 230
chronology, 129, 142, 158, 169, 178, 197, 200–1, 231, 233, 266, 295–6 *see also* low chronology
chthonian deities, 30–1, 33, 60, 94, 108
class attitudes and social distinctions, 20, 34–6, 39, 52–4, 62, 71, 78, 80–6, 95–6, 104–5, 109, 111, 115–18, 120, 123, 127, 130, 135, 145, 157–62, 164, 171, 179, 184–91, 199, 207–12, 214, 219, 220–1, 232–3, 236, 255, 263
coinage and money, 12–13, 23, 143, 149–50, 154, 172, 174, 177, 184, 193–8, 201, 204–5, 226, 272, 274, 288–9; Euboian coinage standard, 149–50, 197
colonisation, 9, 11, 22, 25, 36, 43, 45, 54–7, 59, 63–4, 67–8, 71, 83, 85–6, 90, 94, 96, 100, 103, 114–15, 121–2, 130–2, 138, 141–56, 158–60, 162–4, 168, 171–7, 181, 183, 188, 190, 197, 200, 202, 254, 261, 267–8, 287, 299
Comae Abanticae, 27, 29–30, 43–4, 53–4, 59, 267
'coming of the Greeks, the', 37
conciliar calendar, 121, 252, 267
confiscation and redistribution of land, 250
conspiracy against the Peisistratidai, 211, 221, 223–6, 229, 254
Constitution of Chios, 195, 205
copper, 14–15, 24, 27, 49, 89, 95, 141, 145–6, 160, 173 *see also* mining and minerals.
Corinth, 14–15, 22, 45, 50, 115, 118, 121–3, 131, 135–7, 146, 148–50, 153, 163–4, 166, 170, 174–5, 180, 182, 186, 190, 195, 197–200, 205, 207–9, 211–12, 216–19, 221–2, 224–6, 230–1, 233, 237, 239, 241, 246–51, 253, 255–6, 258, 262, 265, 273, 277–8, 283, 289, 295–6, 301–02
Corinthia, 241, 246–9, 302 *see also* Corinth
Crete, 21, 27–30, 35, 39, 49, 58–9, 77, 84, 89, 136, 141, 155, 171, 174, 176, 179–80, 232, 293
culture-myths, 30, 59
Cumae *see* Kyme in Italy
Cyclades, 39, 70, 141, 146, 151
Cyprus, 21, 29, 49, 59, 77, 84–5, 95, 130, 141, 276

Dareios I, 157, 238, 271–2, 279, 281–4, 286
'Dark Ages', 70, 73, 76, 83–4, 87
Datis, 258, 281, 283
Daton, 154
deiloi (synonym for *Kakoi* q.v), 232

Delphi, 29, 31, 43, 107, 109, 132, 138, 145, 169, 224, 226, 288–9
Demaratos, 238–9, 256, 263
demarkhos (pl. *-oi*), 127, 140, 240–1, 263
demes and demesmen, 5, 16, 27–8, 30–1, 40–2, 45, 49–51, 54–6, 58, 61–2, 65–6, 68–70, 127, 138, 143, 150, 155, 172, 177–8, 201, 204–5, 223, 240–1, 243, 246–8, 252, 263–4, 282, 285, 293–4
Demeter, 30–1; Achaia, 223
democracy, 72, 117, 136, 202, 212–13, 219–23, 230–2, 236–73, 280
demos (pl. *-oi*) *see* demes
Demos (the assembly; the People), 23, 117, 120, 213, 219, 230, 237, 254–5, 264, 270, 274
depas ware, 52, 70
Dexitelos, 36
Diagoras (tyrant of Eretria *c.* 538 to *c.* 509), 119, 126, 199, 207–40, 249–53, 255–6, 260, 262, 270–1, 273
dialaktes, 184, 201
Dikaia Eretrieon, 154, 177, 197–8
Dion (town in Euboia), 43, 172
Dion (Eretrian colony in Macedonia), 154
Dionysios of Miletos, 275
Dionysos, 24, 148
Dioskouroi (Zeus-boys), 14, 28, 58
Dirphys, 5–6, 16, 22, 150, 161, 214, 257, 259
Dismaros (deme of the Eretrias), 28, 70
'districts', 15, 40–2, 46, 64–5, 69, 71, 138, 178, 204, 240–1, 244–50, 263–6
Dodona, 28, 39, 58
dokimasia (of coinage), 205
Dolopes, 40, 62
Dorians, 40, 45, 58, 94, 149, 152, 163, 174, 246, 253
Doric dialect, 55, 67, 69–70, 107, 227, 234
Dorieus, 225
Doros, 45
Double Battle (506), 256–61
'Dragon Houses', 64
Drepane (Eretrian colony on Kerkyra), 148, 172
drought, 81, 88, 93, 96, 129, 144–5, 158, 168
Dryopā (Dryopē, place in Thessaly), 39
Dryope (daughter of Eurytos of Oikhalia), 41
Dryopes, 27–8, 31, 37–43, 58–9, 62–4, 71, 94, 113, 124, 151, 264
Dystos (town and deme of the Eretrias), 15, 17–18, 23, 25, 28, 37, 41–2, 45, 58, 65, 111, 134, 248–9, 263

early Geometric, 76, 90, 95, 128
early Geometric amphoriskos, 90
early Helladic, 36, 37–9, 43, 47–8, 52, 63, 74, 90, 94, 100–1, 113
Egypt, 12, 23, 49, 77, 84, 212
ekklesia, 114, 119–20, 125, 135–6, 148, 252, 280
Eleian dialect, 55–6, 72
Eleion, 71
Elephenor, 29, 41–4, 52–3, 66, 83, 113, 126, 151, 175
Eleusis, 31
Eleutherai, 54–5, 67, 70
Eleutheris *see* Eleutherai
Elis, 27, 37–8, 44, 55–6, 58, 70–3, 136, 150–1, 155, 265–6
Ellopia, 2, 21, 41, 58–9, 62, 64–5, 69, 232
Ellopians, 37, 39, 41–3, 58, 59, 64, 69
Ellops, 37, 42, 45, 62, 64, 67
Emborio, 43, 65
emporion, 20, 93, 96, 109, 117, 122, 146–8, 150–1, 153, 163, 168, 173, 188 *see also* colonisation
enoikismos, 141
Eniautos Kouros see Zeus
Enienes, 58
Enyalios (war god), 35, 61
Enyo (consort of Ares), 61
Epeiros, 22, 27, 39–40, 45–6, 58, 62–3, 65, 151, 168
ephebeia, 28, 34–5, 125
ephebic lists, 34
Ephesos, 275–6, 283, 286
ephor, 183, 200, 238, 262–3
Ephoros, 54, 122, 138, 143, 298–99
epikhorios logos (local history), 172
epimeneia, 237, 262 *see proboulia*, *prytaneia*

epimenieuontes, 121, 126, 245–6, 248, 252–3, 266 *see probouloi*, *prytaneis*
epimenioi (at Miletos), 121, 140
epistates, 126, 248
Epops, 37, 42, 62
Erasinos River, 8, 22, 69
Eretria, *passim;* absence of early archaeological data, 91–2, 129; acropolis, 19, 28, 40, 46, 90, 97–9, 100, 105–6, 108, 131, 135; *agora*, 34, 102, 105, 129, 132, 165, 168, 170, 181, 212, 231; American excavations at, 10–11; commercial premises, 104; communications, 8, 98; *Daphnephoreion* (as 'royal' residence), 106–7, 114; *Daphnephoreion* (earliest temple of Apollo Daphnephoros), 97, 106–7, 114–15, 132–3; destruction *c.* 690, 91–2, 103, 167; drainage works, 10, 97–8, 101–2; dyeing industry, 14, 20, 24, 80; earliest fortifications, 91, 97, 103–4, 109, 114, 129, 167–8; early environmental degradation, 101; early Geometric settlement, 14, 95, 97; early Helladic/late Helladic settlement, 63, 101; eastern stoa, 97, 105, 129, 132; eastern stream, 98, 100–1, fishing, 14; first and second hekatompedons, 107–8; flood plain / alluviation, 98, 100–1, 131; Greek excavations at, 26, 128; gold and silver working at, 20, 25, 91, 95, 105, 147; harbour, 9, 11, 85, 100, 109, 131, 177, 203, 208, 212, 231, 279, 289; *Herakleia*, 61, 179; herm-*stele* from, 127, 140; hegemony in central Greece, 183; *heroön* at the West Gate, 61, 89, 97, 109–10, 114, 117, 132–3, 161, 167, 180–1, 212; *hekatompedon* temple of Artemis?, 32, 47, 97, 108; *Hippos*-names at, 172, 201; houses, 101, 104–05, 114, 132, 167; island-empire, 98, 122–3, 125, 130, 137, 149, 168, 183, 219, 270–1; *kalos*-inscription on acropolis, 19–20; late Geometric settlement, 90, 92; later fortifications, 97, 102–5, 129, 132, 167–68, 280–3; Macedonian tomb, 98; member of the Boiotian Federation, 136; metalworking at, 105, 208 *see also* gold and silver working at; monarchy at, 106–7, 111, 113–14, 133; name derived from *eretto* (I row), 94; *necropoleis*, 100, 105, 109–10, 112, 133–4; Neolithic finds from, 26, 30, 90, 94, 100; 'Old' Eretria, 15, 46, 64, 90–1, 98, 113, 115, 128 *see also* Lefkandi, Xeropolis; physical geography, 10, 23, 98–110; *polis*-cult, 107, 114; pottery industry, 20, 25, 85, 96, 168, 181, 208; rise of the *polis*-state at, 109, 114–15, 156–62; secondary industries at, 20; serfs and *perioikoi*, 111, 113; settlement from Lefkandi, 92; site, 10–11, 23, 90–110; street pattern, 101–3; swamp (Ptekhai), 10–11, 35, 98–9; Swiss excavations at, 26, 106–7, 115, 128, 132–3, 162; *temenos* of Aphrodite-Astarte, 109; *temenos* of Apollo Daphnephoros, 29–30, 91, 97, 101, 105–7, 133; temple of Dionysos, 14, 24, 97; *Thesmophoreion* and Temple of Artemis Olympia, 97, 108, 133; urban development of, 45, 90, 98–110, 114–15, 128, 133; unhealthy atmosphere at, 10; water supply, 23, 98, 100, 103, 132; West Gate and bridge, 97, 100–5, 109, 129, 132; western stream, 97–8, 100, 102–4
Eretria (a location in Attica?), 70
Eretriakos Katalogos, 286, 289
Eretrian alphabet at Pithekoussai, 147
Eretrian *Hymn to the Daktyloi*, 29–30
Eretrian Plain, 6, 8, 14, 16, 18–19, 94–5, 98, 113, 115
Eretrians, *passim*
Eretrias, 5–7, 14–20, 26–8, 30–1, 33, 38, 40–3, 45–6, 48–53, 55–6, 108, 111, 113, 117, 123–4, 143–4, 150–1, 155, 157, 172, 174, 177, 185, 201–2, 205, 240, 247–9, 251, 262, 266, 268, 282–3, 288–9, 293–4; *perioikis*/*perioikoi*, 111; territorial

divisions of, 122, 240–1, 243, 246, 248–9, 252–3, 255
Eretrias (used by the Eretrians to refer to their territory), 20
eretriazō (mock; ridicule), 255, 268
erettō/eressō (row), 94, 130
Eretrieon Politeia, 239, 263
Eretrieus (Athenian soldier named in *IG* I[1], 950), 14, 279
Eretrieus (eponymous hero of Eretria), 41, 55, 64
Eretrieus (son [or grandson?] of Peisistratos), 191, 203, 279
Erinyes, 62
Erythrai, 115, 141, 164–5, 171
esthlos (synonym for *Agathoi* q.v.), 232–3
ethnos, 44, 83, 111, 115, 142, 158
Eualkides, 275, 277, 285
Euboia, *passim*
Euboia: agriculture, 6–7, 12–14, 22–4, 16–17, 20, 43, 45, 80, 83–4, 94–5, 141–2, 144–6, 181, 208, 214–15; climate, 10–11; derivation of name, 12, 23, 287; flora, 11–13, 23; fishing, 14; harbours, 8–9, 11, 45, 85, 100; mining and minerals, 14–15, 19–20, 24–5; modern life in, 21; Mycenaean overlordship of, 51–4, 74–6; Neolithic and proto-Helladic, 26, 30, 36–40, 43, 47, 52, 57, 63, 90, 94, 100; nymphs (eponymous), Makris and Euboia, 21, 40; pastoralism, 7, 12–14, 20, 23, 45, 51, 80, 144, 208, 215; physical geography, 1–25 *passim*; protogeometric, 23, 76–7, 80, 83, 90, 100, 103, 105, 110, 129–31; secondary industries, 15, 20, 24, 80, 83, 86; seismic activity, 2–3, 21, 93; toponyms as evidence of population movements, 27, 36–7
Euboia (island off Tunisia), 152
Euboia (mountain in the Argolis), 150
Euboia (in Kerkyra), 137, 148
Euboia (in Lemnos), 172
Euboian Gulf, 1, 8–9, 16, 22, 32–3, 50, 51, 98, 185–6, 192, 196, 210, 228, 277
Euboic monetary standard, 146, 149–50, 198
Euergesia, 266
Eunostidai [at Neapolis (Naples)], 71, 142, 172
Eunostos, 56, 71, 142, 172
Eupatridai, 36, 117–18, 184, 201, 220–1, 223–4, 233, 254, 284
Eurypontid kings, 178, 239
Euripos, 1, 8–9, 21, 45, 49, 52, 145, 183, 195–6, 217, 232, 238, 256–9
Eurytheos (Eretrian culture-hero), 30
Eurytis (possible tribal name at Eretria), 265
Eurytos, 41, 64, 83, 94
'everything in eights' at Corinth, 248, 265
ex As(ine), [ex As(typalaia), deme of the Eretrias], 40, 63
ex Eni. (deme of the Eretrias), 58

factionalism (in oligarchies), 116
Fall of Miletos (tragedy by Phrynikhos), 274
famine colonies, 144
fines and taxes, 34, 80, 98, 192–3, 195, 197, 204–5, 220, 241
First Colonisation Movement, 115, 141
First Sacred War, 58, 169
Flaminius (L. Quinctilius), 131

Gela, 149, 174
genos, 71, 115, 126, 140, 207, 223, 234, 254, 263
Geometric period, 14, 46, 59, 66–7, 76, 83, 88, 90, 92, 95, 101, 103, 105, 107, 109, 113, 115, 124, 128, 130, 132, 134, 150, 155, 162, 202
Geomoroi, 118, 163–4, 182, 199
Gephyra (as a name for Tanagra), 234
Gephyraioi, 185, 201, 223–4, 234, 254, 267
Geraistos, 28, 58, 182
gerontes (or *bouleutai*), 119, 136, 138–9
gerousia, 119, 238–9
Gongylos, 281, 287, 289
Gorgos (illegitimate son of Kypselos), 203, 295
Gortyae (people in Mesopotamia), 283
Graia, 37, 71, 178
grammateus, 252, 266

Gray-burnished ware, 37–8, 48, 63
Gray Minyan, 37–8, 48, 63
Grynkhai (deme of the Eretrias), 28, 37, 294
Gulf of Avlona (Albania), 148
Gulf of Corinth, 256

Halai, 33
Halonesos (anc. Ikos), 294
Harmodios and Aristogeiton (tyrannicides), 223, 229, 254
hegemon (pl. *-es*), 29, 36, 44, 52–3, 62, 83, 111, 113, 180, 270
Hekate, 30–1, 33, 59–60, 94, 287; Melaina, 130; Melinoe, 130
Hellanikos, 275
Hellen, 45
Hellespont, 143
Hellopes (Epeirote tribe), 58
Hera, 148, 150, 174, 192–3, 195, 204
Herakles, 21, 40–1, 51, 55, 58–9, 61, 84, 94, 161, 179, 293
Heraion (month of the Eretrian calendar), 150, 195, 237
Hermes Promakhos, 258
Hero Tomb *see* protogeometric building at Toumba
hero-cult, 70, 87, 167, 181, 231
heroön (of Narkissos Sigelos, the Eretrian), 37, 62 *see also* Narkissos
Hestiaia *see* Histiaia
hieron of the *kourotrophoi* at Eretria, 59
hieropoioi (officials at Tamynai), 140
hipparkhos, 127
Hipparkhos, 182, 221, 223, 226–7, 254, 279, 288
Hipparkhos son of Kharmos, 278
Hippeis, 12, 34–5, 83, 96, 115–19, 122, 127, 135, 138, 152–3, 157–8, 184, 188, 198, 201, 207, 210–11, 214, 222, 259, 262
Hippias, 153, 169, 182, 189, 205, 221–7, 229, 233, 236, 238, 254, 256, 259, 262, 282
Hippobotai, 7, 12, 36, 71, 80–1, 82–3, 85–6, 105, 111, 115–18, 127, 135, 138, 144–5, 157–9, 161–4, 167, 170, 182, 184, 199, 201, 214–16, 218–19, 233, 260, 280, 286
Hippokles of Kyme [*oikistes* of Italian Kyme (Cumae)], 172
hippos-names *see* Eretria
Hippotrophoi, 169
Hippou Akre (Hippo Diarrhytos/mod. Bizerta), 152, 176
Histiaia, 4, 7, 12, 22, 34, 41, 43–4, 52, 54, 61, 65, 70, 137, 196, 214, 240, 243
Histiaieis (Attic deme), 54
Histiaieis (deme of the Eretrias), 41–2
Histiaios, 271, 285
Histiaiotis *see* Histiaia
Hollows of Euboia, 9, 23
Homeric *Catalogue of Ships*, 52, 65–6, 298
Homeric *Hymn to Apollo*, 77, 88, 166, 180
Homeric *Hymn to Artemis*, 62
Homeridai, 293
hoplite, 34–5, 66, 122–4, 138, 157–62, 168–70,179, 198, 208–9, 214, 230, 247, 265, 278, 283
hoplite panoply, 158–62
horoi, 29, 67, 263, 265
horos phratrikos from Eretria, 265
Hybrias the Cretan, 179–80
hymnos kletikos (Cretan Hymn to the *Kouros*), 28–9, 35, 58
Hyperborean offerings, 132, 151
Hypothebai, 69

Idaioi Daktyloi, 29–30, 41, 58–9
IG I[1] 950, 279
IG I[3] 41, 196
IG XII 9, 189, 32, 34, 41, 240–1
IG XII 9, 241, 159, 241, 246–8
IG XII 9, 1273/4 (Eretrian sixth century naval regulations), 98, 131, 138, 140, 192, 195–6, 204, 220, 277
IG XII Suppl. 549, 58, 70–2, 121, 236–7, 248, 252–3, 262, 264–5
IG XII Suppl. 555, 61, 121, 137, 140, 266
Iliad, 29, 43, 52–3, 58–9, 63–7, 69–70, 72, 77, 88–9, 124, 136, 139, 158, 174–5, 178–80, 219, 232–3, 287
Ilias Parva, 124
Illyria, 67, 174–5

Imbrasos (Parthenios) River, 8, 22
Io, 150
Iolkos, 52, 73
Ion, 45, 54, 67, 296
Ionia, 43, 65, 115, 138, 270, 272–4, 276–9, 284
Ionian dialect, 55
Ionian revolt, 164, 209, 222, 226, 258, 270–5, 278–81, 283, 285, 288
Ionians, 28, 36, 41, 42–3, 45–6, 54–5, 63, 65, 73, 77, 81, 82, 149, 152, 157, 163, 271–3, 275–6
Ionic tribes, 126–7, 243–5
Iphigeneia, 33, 185
Iphitos, 293
Iron Age, 23, 45, 47, 67, 73, 81, 87, 130
Isagoras, 229, 235, 239, 251, 254–5, 259, 286
Ischia, 130, 142, 146
isonomie (*isonomia*), 271
isopoliteia, 122, 240
Isthmus of Corinth, 170, 209, 222, 225, 255–6
Italy, 20, 83, 85, 142, 148–9, 174, 299

Kabeiroi, 29, 59
Kakoi (the 'Bad', the lower classes), 213–14, 217, 232
kaloi k'agathoi (the 'Beautiful and Good', the upper classes), 36, 115–18, 198, 213–14, 216, 232
Kaloyerovrisi Bronze Age settlement, 57
Kalydon, 30
Kaphareus, 8–9
Kares, 39, 43
Karia, 64, 276
Karkinousioi (deme of the Eretrias), 30
Karn(ei)asion, 241, 248, 264 *see also* Larasios, Paralios
ka-ru-to (Karystos), 49
Karystia, 6, 15, 28, 31, 33, 40–1, 48, 51–2, 54–5, 64, 124, 157 *see also* Karystos
Karystos, 4, 7, 10, 12, 14–15, 22, 24, 28, 31, 33–4, 40, 42–4, 48–9, 51–2, 58, 61–3, 80, 98, 102, 123–5, 162, 164, 219–20, 272, 283
Kastri Potamias *see* Kyme in Euboia
keiretai (pres. pass. of *keirō*), 214, 231
Kenaion, 4, 40–1, 77, 194–6, 202, 220
Keos, 31, 42, 59, 98, 121–3, 125, 137, 149, 183, 240, 243, 264, 288
kerde, 280, 286
Kereus River, 7, 22
Kerinthos, 4, 7–8, 14, 41–3, 52, 62, 64, 69, 116, 164, 172, 211, 213–14, 216–18, 231–2, 295
Kerkyra, 121–2, 125, 137, 147–52, 159, 164, 166, 174–5, 201, 262, 269, 293
Kerkyra (Eretrian colony on), 121–2, 137, 175
Khairephanes, 23, 35
Khairion, 220–1, 224, 233
Khalkidike, 39, 153, 181, 188
khalkidizō (= *paiderastō*), 57, 72, 268
Khalkis, 4–9, 12–16, 21–2, 24, 27, 36, 38, 41–3, 45–9, 51–9, 61, 66–7, 69, 72, 80, 83, 85–7, 89, 92–3, 98, 102, 109, 113, 115–17, 123, 135–6, 138, 140, 142–6, 150–3, 155–6, 158–75, 179–83, 185–8, 191, 196, 199–201, 214, 216–22, 232–4, 238, 249, 255–6, 258–61, 263, 274, 288, 298–9
Khalkodon, 44, 46, 53, 66, 113
Khalkodontiades *see* Elephenor
Khalkodontis (alternative name for Euboia q.v.)
Khalkon *see* Khalkodon
khalkos see copper
Kharixenos, 35, 118, 135
Kheilon, 183, 200, 221, 237–8, 262–3
Kh(e)ilon, son of Demarmenos, 263
Kheilonios, 237, 263 *see also* proxeny decree for Aristoteles Kheiloniou
Khoireai (deme of the Eretrias), 30, 49–51, 68–9, 282
khoroi (districts of the Eretrias and Keos), 34, 41, 64, 122, 138, 240–4, 248–51, 263–4
khremata dokima, 193, 197, 204–5
Khrysaor, 150, 175
khryseia, 146–7, 173
Khytrai (Festival of the Pots at Athens), 60

Khytroi (deme of the Eretrias), 21, 30
Kimi *see* Kyme
Kissia, 24, 283
Kleisthenes, 126, 190, 206, 211, 221, 229–30, 239, 244, 246, 250–6, 267–8, 279
Kleisthenes of Sikyon, 211, 266
Kleisthenic Council of 500, 119
Kleisthenic tribes of Athens, 240, 243, 251
Kleomakhos of Pharsalos, 160, 165, 168–70, 181, 274–5, 299
Kleomenes I, 190, 221–9, 236–9, 255–7, 259–60, 263, 272, 274, 281, 301–2
Kleomenes III, 190
kleroukhia, 170, 280–1, 288–9
kleroukhia (at Eretria?), 286, 289
kleroukhoi (on the Lelantine Plain after 506), 200, 219, 260, 278, 280
koinon, 127, 192
Koisyra, 190–1, 208, 210–12, 254–5
'koisyrated' (term of abuse in Aristophanes), 190, 203
Kolainis (Kolainia) *see* Artemis
kome (pl. *-ai*), 44–5, 74, 83, 143
Komaieis (deme of the Eretrias), 45, 143, 172
konis Elephenoris ('sod/dust of Elephenor': district, or alternative name of Khalkis), 66
Korybantes, 29, 59
Koumai (Kyme in Euboia q.v.), 172
Kotylaion range, 6, 8, 16, 51
koura (hair-cropping) see Kouretes, *Comae Abanticae*
Koureotis *see* Apatouria
Kouretes, 27–31, 35–6, 38–41, 44–5, 57–9, 66, 71, 150, 160, 254
Kouretic/Abantic hairstyle *see Comae Abanticae*
kouros, 28–9, 31, 36, 42
Kouros see Zeus, Amarynthos, Aristaios
kourotrophoi, 28–9, 59
Kreophylos, 41, 64–5, 124, 293
Kretes, 36
Kronos, 28, 117
Kybo/Kybos, 152, 176
Kybo (suggested amendment – *Hippou akre kai Kybo*), 176
Kyme, 7–8, 16, 22, 25, 43, 49, 57, 65, 142–3, 172, 177, 294
Kyme (in Asia Minor), 65, 68, 141, 143, 299
Kyme (in Euboia), 7–8, 16, 22, 25, 43, 57, 65, 96, 142–3, 147, 172, 177
Kyme in Italy (Cumae), 77, 96, 130, 142–3, 147–8, 171–2, 299
Kypselidai, 94, 121–2, 190, 203, 211–14, 217, 219, 221–2, 226, 231, 233, 249–50, 295–7, 301
Kypselos (I), 126, 170, 209, 211, 231, 295–6
Kypselos (II: Psammetikhos), 211, 217, 295
Kypselos (eponymous arkhon at Athens), 295
Kyrene, 59, 152, 225
kyria ekklesia, 253

Lamian War, 25, 266
landowners, 57, 74, 78, 80–1, 83, 85–6, 95–6, 104, 111, 115–18, 158, 186
Larasios (Larasion), 241, 249, 264
Larisa ('citadel' in Pelasgic/Dryopian?), 264
late Geometric, 90, 92, 101, 103, 110, 134, 161, 166
late Helladic II/III (Mycenaean), 23, 35, 37–8, 41, 43, 46, 48–9, 51–2, 55, 57, 60, 62–3, 66–70, 73, 75–7, 87, 100–1, 128, 130, 133, 175, 232
late protogeometric, 90
Lefkandi, 6, 9, 14–15, 20, 23, 33, 35, 37–8, 43–56, 61–2, 67, 70, 73–89, 90–8, 100, 103–05, 107, 109–17, 127–30, 135, 144, 146, 155–7, 161, 165–7, 171, 175, 177, 181, 208, 269
Leipsydrion *skolion*, 233
Lelantine Plain, 6–8, 13, 15, 19–20, 27, 31, 36, 45–6, 49, 51, 53, 57, 67, 77, 80, 84, 92–6, 107, 109, 111, 116, 132, 146, 157, 160, 165, 169–70, 185, 200, 214, 217–19, 231, 280
Lelantine War, 6, 87, 92–3, 123, 127, 129, 135, 140, 142, 156, 158, 162–

8, 176, 178–9, 180, 183, 217, 233, 261, 298–9
Lelanton, 14, 181, 214, 219, 269
Lelas River, 8, 15, 19, 91, 96, 260–1
Leleges, 27, 39
Lemnos, 143
Leodamas of Miletos, 124, 138
Lerna, 37
Leskhes of Mytilene, 124
Leukalphitos (rich in pearl barley – epithet bestowed on Eretria), 16, 25
Leuke Akte, 8
Levant, 49, 77, 85, 88, 98, 109, 117, 130, 141, 146, 151
Libya, 59, 151–2, 176
Linear B, 42, 48–9, 51, 293
low chronology, 295–6
Lygdamis, 188, 190–1, 198–9, 206, 209, 211, 221–3, 225–6, 230, 234, 236
Lykos, 161
Lysanias of Mallos, 259, 268, 274, 276–8
Lysimakhos of Eretria, 268

Macedonia, 11, 22, 44, 84, 98, 126, 152–4, 168, 176–7, 183, 185, 202
Magnesia-on-the-Maiandros, 115, 157, 268
Magoula, 23, 51, 178
Makisteus (-stos) *see* Mekisteus
Makistos (town and mountain in Triphylia), 55, 266
Makistos (mountain in Euboia), 4, 6, 28, 56, 214
Makris (alternative name for Euboia q.v.), 21
Makris (nymph), 31, 148, 174
Makris (or Makridie, promontory on Kerkyra), 148, 174
Mallos, 259, 274, 276, 286, 289
Manika, 33, 38–9, 57, 63
Mantoudhi *see* Kerinthos
Marathon, 61, 138, 185, 198, 278, 281–2, 284, 287
Marousi *see* Athmonon
Mars Gravidus, 35
matriarchy, 30, 33, 36, 113
Megabates, 271–2
Megakles Hippokratous, 203, 254, 268
Megakles Megakleous, 190, 268
Megara, 123, 131, 164, 169, 185, 187, 199–200, 206, 212–13, 222, 231, 233, 256, 296, 301–02
Megara Hyblaia, 101, 131
Megasthenes of Khalkis, 172
Mekisteus, 53, 55, 58, 71, 253
Mekis(s)tis (tribal name at Eretria), 22, 28, 53, 55–6, 71, 264, 266
Mekistos, 22, 243
Makis(s)tis *see* Mekis(s)tis
Melaneïs (early name of Eretria), 40, 64, 94
Melaneus, 40, 64, 94
Mende (Eretrian colony), 154, 176
Menedemos, 31, 69, 126, 178
mercantile alliances, 162–3, 178
mercenary troops, 117, 159–60, 164, 180, 189, 191, 198, 209
Mesogeia (in Attica), 185, 192
Mesokhoros (Mesokhoron), 240–1, 244, 248–9, 264–5
Messenia, 30, 40, 55, 64, 107, 132
Metagenes, 32
metallurgy *see* also mining and minerals
Metaxy, 41, 64, 240–1, 264 *see also* Artemis
Methone, 121, 152, 154, 176
metoikos, 227
metropolis, 11, 115, 122, 142, 148, 163, 299
middle Geometric, 88, 128
middle Helladic, 37–8, 47–8, 67, 73
migration, 27, 39–40, 43, 45, 47, 55, 85, 95, 114–15, 151, 155
Miletos, 10, 64, 121, 124, 126–7, 138–40, 156, 162–5, 168, 170–1, 181–2, 188, 199–200, 201, 203, 206, 212, 219, 221–2, 231, 249, 268, 270–9, 281, 285–7
Miltiades (tyrant of the Khersonesos), 295
mining, minerals and metalworking, 14–15, 20, 24, 27, 49, 77, 80–1, 84, 95, 130, 141, 145–7, 153–4, 156, 160, 168, 174, 188–9, 198, 273

Minoans, 36, 49, 62, 141, 155, 293, 294
Minos, 39, 68, 174, 293
Minthountothen (deme of the Eretrias), 30, 37, 70
Mnesitheos, 228
Molossoi, 44, 58
Mycenae, 38, 44, 47, 75, 133
Mycenaean *see* late Helladic
Mycenaean collapse, 73
Mycenaean *koine*-style, 75
Mycenaeans, 48, 51–3, 75, 151
Mykalessos (mod. Rhitsona), 168, 181, 268
Mytilene, 115, 124, 212
mythology, 21, 26, 28–31, 36, 38, 42, 44, 55, 64, 84, 107, 148, 150, 253–4

Narkissos, 30, 37, 42, 59, 62, 264, 267
'Narkissos the Eretrian' see Sigelos, *heroön* of S.
Narkittis (phyle-name at Eretria), 59, 243, 264
nauarkhoi, 128
Naukratis, 168, 181
Nauplios, 8, 67
Nausikleite ('famed for ships' – epithet applied to Euboia), 180
naval power, 9–11, 28, 39, 43, 77, 96, 98, 100–1, 123, 128, 143–4, 148, 152, 162–3, 165–6, 168, 170, 177, 179, 183, 185–7, 189, 192, 195–6, 199, 205, 207–09, 225–6, 228, 236–7, 255–62, 265, 268, 270–2, 275–9, 282–3, 285–6, 289, 302
Naxos, 136–7, 152, 164–5, 170, 180, 182, 188, 190–1, 198–9, 201, 211, 221–2, 225, 234, 270–89
Neapolis (in Macedonia), 142, 154, 177
Nedon (deme of the Eretrias), 64
nees and *triereis* in Herodotos, 277–8, 286
Neleids, 201
Neleus River, 7, 22
Neolithic, 26, 30, 36–40, 43, 47, 52, 57, 63, 90, 94, 100
Nestor of Pylos, 267
'netting' of the Eretrias by the Persians, 283

Nikhoria, 107, 132
nomophylakes, 121, 137
nomothetes, 184, 201
northern Aegean, 49, 115, 142, 149, 152–3, 188

Oikhalia (deme of the Eretrias), 22, 40–1, 46, 51, 55, 64–5, 69, 83–4, 94, 179, 293–4
oikistes (pl. *-ai*), 67, 143, 170
oikos, 88, 114, 157
Oinopion, 43
Okalia, 293
Okalon (town of the Eretrians?), 176, 293
Okhe (mountain in the Karystia), 6, 15, 150
Okhe (alternative name of Euboia q.v.), 21
Okhthonia, 1–2, 6, 9, 294
'Old Athenian' dialect, 70, 143, 172
Old Eretria *see* Eretria
oligarchy, 96, 116, 118–21, 126–7, 147, 163–4, 185, 187–8, 190–1, 199, 207–12, 219, 221–2, 224–6, 229–31, 236, 238, 249–51, 270–1, 273, 279–80, 285, 287, 301
oligarchy of the *Hippeis see Politeia* of the *Hippeis*
Olympia, 28, 38, 130, 149, 262–3, 296
Olympian gods, 30–3, 42, 66, 107
Olympos (mountain near Eretria), 6, 16, 22–3, 131
oracles, 31, 43, 60, 94, 144, 169, 181, 191, 224–5
Oreon (possible Eretrian tribal name), 265
Orikos, 151, 175
Orope (in Euboia?), 155
Oropos, 30, 37, 56, 62, 71, 73, 155–6, 169, 177–8, 191–2, 196, 223, 234, 253–4, 258, 267, 280
Oropos (deme of the Eretrias), 30, 155
Orthagorids, 183, 200
Ortygia, 150
ostracism, 254, 268, 279, 286, 288
ostraka, 190, 254–5, 279
ostrakon (against Megakles Hippokratous), 203, 254

ostrakon (against Megakles Megakleous), 268
Othronos, 151

Pakheis (oligarchic party on Naxos), 222, 234, 270–1
Palaeolithic, 38
Palaiokastritsa, 64 *see* Kyme in Euboia
Palaioekklisies Amarynthou *see* Amarynthos (town)
Palamedes, 8, 67
Pallene (in Attica), 192, 198
Pallene (peninsula of the Khalkidike), 153–5, 190, 200
Panathenaia, 198, 210, 223
Pangaion, 154, 188–9, 198, 202, 273
Paralios (Paralion), 241, 249
pareonta ('being present' in Theognis), 213
Paros, 136–7, 153–4, 162, 164–5, 179–80, 222, 270, 283
Parthenion (deme of the Eretrias?), 66, 150
Parthenope (Naples), 142
patriarchy, 30, 42, 66, 88
patrios politeia, 188, 210, 224, 230
Pausanias (of Sparta), 281, 289
Pegasos, 150, 174–5
Peisistratidai, 182, 188, 190, 201, 203, 209–10, 220–1, 223–5, 228–30, 251, 254, 267, 278–9, 301
Peisistratos, 22, 116, 153–4, 163–4, 168, 170, 182–92, 197–202, 208–13, 220–2, 226, 230, 239, 254, 259, 268, 279, 283–4, 295
Pelasgic Argos, 169
Pelasgoi, 27, 39, 42, 54, 63–4, 169, 264
Peloponnese, 28, 37–8, 44, 55, 58, 166, 170, 191, 200, 221–2, 226, 255–6, 278, 283
Peloponnesian League, 221, 226, 255
Peloponnesian War, 12, 166, 265, 268, 278, 289
pendent semi-circle *skyphos*, 43, 79, 81–3, 88–9
pentekosiomedimnoi, 35, 135, 201, 221
Penthilidai, 115
peraia ge, 156, 178, 191, 258
Peraieis (deme of the Eretrias), 178
Periandros (I), 163, 170, 190, 200, 203, 206, 209, 211–12, 215, 217–18, 221, 231, 249–50, 295–6
Periandros (II), 295
Perikles, 54, 178, 201, 233, 289
Perikles' conquest of Euboia (446), 54, 289
perioikis/perioikoi, 111, 227, 234
Persia, 226–7, 256, 261–2, 270–1, 274, 280, 286, 289
Persians, 24, 50, 92, 164, 213, 222, 226–7, 230, 237, 256, 258, 260, 270–84, 287–9
Petaliai islands, 9, 22, 123, 125, 185, 194–5, 220
Perrhaiboi, 39, 41–3, 58
Phaiakes, 148, 152, 174, 293
Phaethon (Titan and father of Eretrieus), 64
phalanx, 66, 158–60, 169–70, 209
Phaleron, 185, 187, 210, 226–8
Phegous (deme of the Eretrias), 254
Pheidon, 94, 129, 169–70
Philaidai, 201, 229, 235, 295–6
Philesios, 260–1, 269
philia see amicitia, xenia
Philip V of Macedonia, 22
Phoenicia, 84, 89, 141, 147, 152, 286
Phokion, 42, 65
Phokis, 45, 56, 58, 67
Phoxos (possibly Antileon q.v.), 219, 233
phratriai, 245–7, 265
Phrynikhos (Athenian playwright), 274, 278
Phylake, 31, 41, 59, 240–1, 264, see also Artemis
Phylakos, 41
phyle (pl. *-ai*), 21–2, 28, 30, 40, 45, 53, 55–6, 58, 65, 67, 71, 121, 126–8, 135, 140, 142, 172, 174, 237, 240, 243, 245–50, 252–3 263, 265–6
phylēs epimēnieuourēs (gen.), 121, 248, 252–3
Pieria, 152–4
pietas of Eretria, 284
Pithekoussai, 77, 85–6, 88, 96, 104, 110, 130, 133, 142, 144–8, 152, 156, 163–4, 168, 171–2, 175
Pittakos of Mitylene, 184, 219

Plataia, 123, 221, 232–3, 288–9, 301–02
Pleistias, 227–8
Ploutarkhos (tyrant of Eretria), 218
polemarkhoi, 35, 120, 127, 140
Politeia of the Hippeis, 116, 119, 127, 188, 262
Politeia of the Khalkidians, 172
Politeia of the Naxians, 230
Polykrates, 199, 221, 225, 234, 301
porpax shield, 124, 159
Poseidon, 58, 63, 67, 150, 175
Potidaia, 153, 176, 190, 200, 295
Potnia, 30–1, 150, 175
Potnia Theron kai Phyton, 30
pottery, 20, 25–6, 29, 35, 37–8, 43, 47–8, 51–2, 71, 74–7, 79, 81, 83–5, 87–90, 92–3, 96, 98, 101, 103, 107, 109, 141–2, 146, 150–1, 166–8, 172, 174, 181, 186, 208, 230, 284, 288
Prasiai, 22, 185–7, 192, 210
pre-Hellenes, 27–31, 36–43, 45, 94, 108
pre-Hellenic languages, 24, 27–8, 36–7, 39, 40, 42, 174
presbeutes see gerontes, *bouleutai*
proboulia, 119–23, 125–8, 136–7, 139–40, 148, 172, 243, 245–6, 248–9, 252, 265–6
proboulos (pl. *-oi*) *see proboulia*
procession at the Amarysia, 34–5, 116, 122, 220
Prometheus *see* Eurytheos
prostates (Dor. *prostatas*), 137, 201
protogeometric, 23, 65, 76–7, 80, 83, 90, 101, 103, 105, 110, 128–31
protogeometric building at Toumba, 80–2, 85, 88
proto-Greek dialect, 55
proto-Helladic, 57, 90
proxenia, 237, 239, 252, 267
proxeny decree for Aristoteles Kheiloniou, 237–9, 248, 252, 262–3
prytaneia, 119, 121, 126, 246, 248, 252–3, 266
Psamtek, 212
psiloi (peltasts/light-armed troops), 159, 138, 247
Ptekhai (deme and swamp near Eretria), 10, 23, 35, 37
Ptolemy II Philadelphus, 12, 23
Ptoön, 198
Pydna, 153–4
Pylos, 44, 184, 201, 254, 267
Pyrrhic dance in arms at Artemiria, 29, 34–6, 60–1
pyrrhikistai (*Epheboi* at Eretria in the last year of the *ephebeia* q.v.), 35

qa-si-re-u of *A-ma-ru-to* (*basileus* of Amarynthos), 113

revenue *see* fines and taxes
Revolt of Euboia (447/6), 135, 233, 289
Revolt of Euboia (411/10), 25, 122, 177, 279, 289
revolution, 80, 84, 88, 96, 115, 160, 162, 209, 211–12, 214, 216–18, 221, 223–6, 229, 254, 262, 273, 281
rex sacerdotorum see basileus-magistrate
Rhadamanthys, son of Minos, 293–4
Rhaikelos (Aineia), 153, 176, 188–9, 200, 202, 229
Rhea, 27–8, 30
Rhegion, 57, 144–5, 149
rhetra, 120, 136
rhexithorakes (Homer – *thorakas rhexein*), 158, 178
Rho of the Eretrians, 72 *see also* rhotacism
rhotacism, 56–7, 71–2, 144, 177, 237, 255, 262, 288
rhotacism (at Khalkis?), 72
rise of the *polis*-state, 81, 88, 109, 114–15, 119, 134, 156–62
Rome (and Romans), 21, 23–4, 33, 35–6, 38, 59, 64, 66, 118, 124, 142, 147, 152, 157, 206, 298–9
rowing city *see* Eretria, *erettō*/*eressō*

Salaminioi, 233
Sarandapotamos *see* Erasinos River
Salii see *Selloi*
Samos, 118, 124, 157, 163–4, 166, 170–1, 199–200, 206, 225–6, 231–2, 273, 293
Sardis, 209, 213, 222, 268, 270–1, 275–6, 278, 281–3, 286

Saronic Gulf, 199–200, 262
Selloi, 35, 39, 58
Serpent Column, 260, 288
Sicily, 21, 83, 85, 101, 152, 165, 174, 213
Sigeion, 212, 219, 229, 295
Sigelos, 37, 264 *see hieron* of Narkissos the Eretrian, Narkissos
Sikyon, 15, 183, 198, 211, 231, 266–7
Sikyonia *see* Sikyon
Sithonia, 153
sixth-century shipping regulations *see* IG XII 9, 1273/1274.
Skábala, 154, 177, 189, 198, 202
Skheria, 148, 152
Skiathos, 155, 177
Skopelos (anc. Peparethos), 177, 294
Skoteini cave, 26, 38, 43, 57
Skyros, 40, 45, 59, 63–4, 155, 177, 294
Smyrna, 93, 103, 128, 130, 135
socio-economic forces, 80, 94, 160, 162, 184, 186, 190, 208
Solon, 96, 116, 163, 179, 184–7, 192, 198, 201–2, 206, 208–10, 230, 232, 284
Sparta, 15, 26, 44–5, 115, 120–1, 123, 136, 145, 157–8, 169–70, 178–9, 183, 190, 200, 214, 221–2, 224–9, 233–4, 236–9, 255–6, 258–60, 262–3, 270, 272–3, 277–8, 281, 283–4, 289, 293, 301–02
sphendonetai (slingers), 159
sphendonaō (use a sling), 179
sphragis ('seal' in Theognis' poetry), 297
stasis, 142, 170, 207, 216–18, 231
stele at Amarynthos, 34–5, 83, 122–3, 127, 138, 157, 159, 161–2, 169, 219–20, 258, 298–9
strategoi, 125–8, 137, 140
Strymon River, 153, 189, 202
Styra, (town and deme of the Eretrias), 5, 14–15, 24–5, 28, 40–3, 45, 56, 58, 64–5, 71–2, 205, 248–9, 264, 285, 288
sub-Mycenaean (LH IIIC), 29, 44, 47, 67, 73–4, 76–7, 87
sub-protogeometric, 128
sumptuary laws, 212, 231
synoikismos, 114, 128
synoikise ('established a colony in conjunction with others'), 176
syntheke (treaty), 159, 178
Syracuse, 150, 164, 175
Syria, 85, 89, 98, 141, 147, 150

Talaos (father of Mekisteus), 53, 58, 253
Tamynai (town and deme of the Eretrias), 21, 28, 37, 56, 58, 72, 140, 151, 241, 263, 268
Tanagra, 56, 71, 142, 172, 191–2, 203, 223, 234, 258
taxiarkhoi, 128
telebola (missile weapons), 159, 179
Telkhines, 29
Tell es Sûkâs, 85, 89, 117, 141, 171
Tem. *see* Temenos
Temenos (deme of the Eretrias?), 50–1, 68–9, 282, 287
Tenos, 98, 122–3
tettix hairpin, 118
thalassocracy, 49, 137, 195, 225, 233–4, 258, 261, 277
Thalassocracy List, 101, 137, 225, 258, 261, 277
Thargelia, 35, 245
Tharrounia, 26, 38, 57, 63
Thasos, 153–4, 177, 196, 204
Thebes, 12, 42, 44, 48–54, 58, 66, 68–9, 71, 73–4, 80, 113, 135, 141, 156, 161, 169–70, 188–9, 191–2, 198–9, 203, 219, 221–2, 255–61, 273, 284, 301–02
Themistokles, 186, 274, 277, 288–9
Theopropidai, 31, 126, 140
Thermaic Gulf, 153–4, 188, 202
Thersites, 162, 219, 233
Theseus, 29, 59, 267
Thesmophoria, 108, 133
thesmophylakes, 243
Thessalos (son of Peisistratos), 170, 182, 203
Thessaly, 39–40, 44–5, 49, 55, 63–5, 71, 84, 134, 160, 164, 168–70, 181–2, 185, 190, 198, 222, 226, 234, 275, 299

thetes, 185, 208–11, 230, 236
Thrace, 11, 39, 154, 159, 168, 176, 183, 198, 267, 273, 275
Thrasyboulos, 140, 163, 200, 206, 209, 212, 231, 249, 273
Thyreatis, 157
timber, 11, 80, 101, 153, 168, 189, 273
Timonassa, 190, 295
timocracy, 135–6
Tocra (Taukheira), 151, 176
toponyms, 27, 36–7, 40, 42, 50–2, 58, 64, 155, 175, 294
Torone, 197, 205, 232
Toumba see Lefkandi
tous probolous tous aei en arkhe ontas, 125, 136
trade, 9, 12, 20, 23–5, 48–52, 55, 67, 70, 75, 77–81, 83–5, 88, 95–6, 98, 100, 104–5, 109, 117–18, 127, 130, 141–51, 155–56, 159–60, 163–8, 174–5, 178, 180–1, 184–9, 191–2, 195–6, 202, 207–8, 210–12, 226–8, 230, 236, 273, 301
trade routes, 9, 151, 185, 187
trephō (raise, nourish, earn a living), 234
trierarkhoi, 128
Triphylia, 55, 56, 64
trireme, 128, 166, 170, 212, 271, 273, 275, 277
triereis see triremes
trittys (pl. *-yes*), 240, 243, 246, 264
Trojan expedition, 51, 53, 69, 108, 151, 223
Troy, 8–9, 29, 32, 40, 52, 61, 70, 77, 83
Tunisia, 151–2, 176
'two dialects' theory of dialect spread, 55, 70
Tynondas, 219
tyrants and tyranny, 20, 94, 121, 126, 140, 160, 163, 170–1, 177, 179–80, 182–5, 187, 190–2, 199, 201, 207–39 *passim*, 249–51, 254, 256, 260, 265–8, 271–3, 295–6

wanax, 44, 49, 52–3, 113, 124, 134, 139
Wappenmünzen, 197, 205
'wave' theory of dialect spread, 55
warfare, 9–10, 15, 44, 85–5, 87, 92–3, 109, 111, 113, 115, 123–4, 129, 135, 138, 144, 148, 156–60, 162–71, 178, 180, 186, 199, 212, 214–15, 217–18, 228, 257, 261, 273, 275–6, 278–9, 298–9, 305
weapons, 14–15, 29, 33, 43, 77, 81–2, 157–9, 161, 298

xenia (guest-friendship; political links amongst aristocrats), 157, 206, 213, 220, 224, 229
xenos see xenia
Xeropolis *see* Lefkandi, Old Eretria
Xouthos, 45, 67

Zagora, 93, 98, 104, 122, 130, 132, 146, 166, 175
Zankle, 144
Zarex (town and deme of the Eretrias), 5, 28, 31, 41–2, 45, 56, 58–61, 65, 71, 129, 174, 248
Zeus, 27–31, 35, 39, 58, 93–4, 108, 117, 150, 213; Amarios, 59; Basileios at Khalkis, 61; Dodonaios, 39, 58; as Eniautos Kouros, 28–9, 58; Epopetes, 62; Hypsistos, 264; as *Kouros,* 28, 30–1, 35, 58–9; Ktesios, 31, 60; as Megistos Kouros, 28; Meilikhios, 108; Nemean, 58; Olbios (at Dismaros), 28; Ombrios (in Attica), 93; and oracles of the dead, 31, 44; Pelasgian (see Z. Dodonaios); Soter (at Karystos), 28, 58; Tamynaios, 28, 58

INDEX OF AUTHORS

For citations in the notes, see the index locorum.

[Aristotle] *Athenaion politeia*, 116, 188–9, 198, 209, 254
Aelian, 32–3
Aineas Taktikos, 217–18
Akousilaos, 37
Alkaios, 97
Antoninus Liberalis, 41, 293, 295
Apollonios Rhodios, 148
Aristides, 281–2
Aristophanes, 32, 190
Aristotle, 44–5, 83, 115–16, 118, 121, 126–7, 161, 166, 199, 207, 219, 225, 239
Arkhemakhos, 27, 36, 166
Arrian, 45
Asios, 118
Athenaios, 14, 199, 272
Bakkhylides, 31, 150
Callimachus, 32
Diodoros, 149
Dionysios Halikarnasseus, 142
Duris, 118
Epaphroditos (M. Mettius), 27, 36
Euphronios, 32
Euripides, 33, 161, 293
Hekataios, 152
Herakleides Lembos, 119, 145, 237
Herakleides Pontikos, 239
Herodotos, 15, 28, 39–40, 42, 50, 54, 128, 146, 163–5, 168, 188–9, 191–2, 198, 207, 223, 225–6, 254, 256–7, 259, 270, 272, 273–81, 295–6, 301
Hesiod, 45, 62, 66, 83, 88, 109, 113, 117, 133, 144, 165, 167, 173, 180, 231
Hesykhios, 36
Homer, 2, 3, 14, 29, 39, 41–5, 51–3, 58, 62, 65–6, 69–70, 77, 81, 83, 88–9, 94, 111, 113, 120, 124, 126, 133–4, 136, 138, 143, 150, 152, 158, 161, 165–6, 172–3, 179, 214, 219, 231, 293, 298; anti-Euboian bias in, 66
Kharon, 275, 285
Korinna, 192, 203, 258, 268
Livy, 142–4, 299, 306
Lucian, 296
Lykophron, 153, 293
Nikolaos of Damascus, 248, 296
Orphic Hymn, 29, 59
Pausanias, 12, 29–30, 32–3, 40, 42, 49, 53, 258, 262
Pindar, 192
Plato, 56, 144, 255, 258–9, 270, 278–80, 283–4, 296
Plutarch, 29, 44–5, 51, 53–4, 56, 108–9, 121, 148, 165, 168, 170, 209, 219, 259, 274, 276, 279, 282, 299

Polybios, 298–9, 305
Pomponius Sabinus, 37
Porphyrios, 296
Servius Maurus Honoratus, 30
Simonides (of Keos), 124, 183, 257, 275
Simonides (of Eretria or Karystos), 124
Skylax, 143, 152
Solinus, 152
Sophokles, 293
Statius, 142
Stephanos Byzantios, 27, 152–5, 188, 249, 293
Strabo, 4, 11, 15, 27, 32, 34, 36–7, 45–6, 51, 54–6, 83, 98, 115, 118, 122–3, 142, 143–4, 146, 153, 156–8, 198, 207, 284, 293, 295, 298–9
Suidas, 57, 124, 239
Theodoridas, 35
Theognis, 14, 83, 116, 146, 161, 164, 199, 212–15, 217, 219, 295–7
Theophrastos, 6, 11
Theopompos, 120, 154, 293
Thucydides, 28, 40–1, 54, 144, 148–9, 153–7, 162, 166, 183, 218, 223, 239, 247, 279, 289
Tzetzes, 293

eBooks

eBooks – at www.eBookstore.tandf.co.uk

A library at your fingertips!

eBooks are electronic versions of printed books. You can store them on your PC/laptop or browse them online.

They have advantages for anyone needing rapid access to a wide variety of published, copyright information.

eBooks can help your research by enabling you to bookmark chapters, annotate text and use instant searches to find specific words or phrases. Several eBook files would fit on even a small laptop or PDA.

NEW: Save money by eSubscribing: cheap, online access to any eBook for as long as you need it.

Annual subscription packages

We now offer special low-cost bulk subscriptions to packages of eBooks in certain subject areas. These are available to libraries or to individuals.

For more information please contact webmaster.ebooks@tandf.co.uk

We're continually developing the eBook concept, so keep up to date by visiting the website.

www.eBookstore.tandf.co.uk

Printed in Dunstable, United Kingdom

83750490R00208